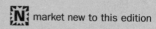

2008 GUIDE TO LITERARY AGENTS KEY TO SYMBOLS

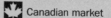

N market new to this edition

✱ Canadian market

🌐 international market

◐ agency actively seeking clients

◑ agency seeking both new and established writers

◓ agency seeking mostly established writers through referrals

◎ agency specializing in certain types of work

⊘ agency not currently seeking new clients

● comment from the editor of *Writer's Market*

O—ℼ agency's specializations

ms, mss manuscript(s)

SASE self-addressed, stamped envelope

IRC International Reply Coupon

For definitions of words and expressions used throughout the book, see the Glossary.

TEAR ALONG PERFORATION

2008 GUIDE TO LITERARY AGENTS
KEY TO SYMBOLS

 market new to this edition

 Canadian market

 international market

 agency actively seeking clients

 agency seeks both new and established writers

 agency seeking mostly established writers through referrals

 agency specializing in certain types of work

 agency not currently seeking new clients

● comment from the editor of *Writer's Market*

○━ agency's specializations

ms, mss manuscript(s)

SASE self-addressed, stamped envelope

IRC International Reply Coupon

For definitions of words and expressions used throughout the book, see the Glossary.

WritersMarket.com
WHERE & HOW TO SELL WHAT YOU WRITE

Here's what you'll find at WritersMarket.com:

✴ **More than 6,000 listings** — At WritersMarket.com, you'll find thousands of listings that couldn't fit in the book! It's the most comprehensive database of verified markets available.

✴ **Easy-to-use searchable database** — Looking for a specific magazine or book publisher? Just type in the title or keyword for broad category results.

✴ **Listings updated daily** — It doesn't look good to address your query letter to the wrong editor or agent...and with WritersMarket.com, that will never happen. You'll be on top of all the industry developments...as soon as they happen!

✴ **Personalized for you** — Customized **Favorites Folders** keep your best-bet markets, manuscript submissions and more just a click away; and your personalized **Dashboard** provides updated market listings, query reminders and recommended resources at-a-glance, every time you log in.

✴ **And so much more!**

Exclusive 30-day free trial.
Visit WritersMarket.com to sign up today!

Tear out your handy bookmark
for fast reference to symbols and abbreviations used in this book

GLA08

2008
Guide to Literary Agents®

Chuck Sambuchino, Editor

WRITER'S DIGEST BOOKS
CINCINNATI, OH

Editorial Director, Writer's Digest Books: Jane Friedman
Managing Editor, Writer's Digest Market Books: Alice Pope

Guide to Literary Agents Web site: www.guidetoliteraryagents.com
Writer's Market Web site: www.writersmarket.com
Writer's Digest Web site: www.writersdigest.com
F+W Publications Bookstore: http://fwbookstore.com

Distributed in Canada by Fraser Direct
100 Armstrong Ave.
Georgetown, ON, Canada L7G 5S4
Tel: (905) 877-4411

Distributed in the U.K. and Europe by David & Charles
Brunel House, Newton Abbot, Devon, TQ12 4PU, England
Tel: (+44) 1626 323200, Fax: (+44) 1626 323319
E-mail: postmaster@davidandcharles.co.uk

Distributed in Australia by Capricorn Link
P.O. Box 704, Windsor, NSW 2756, Australia
Tel: (02) 4577-3555

Distributed in New Zealand by David Bateman Ltd.
P.O. Box 100-242, N.S.M.C., Auckland 1330, New Zealand
Tel: (09) 415-7664, Fax: (09) 415-8892

Distributed in South Africa by Real Books
P.O. Box 1040, Auckland Park 2006, Johannesburg, South Africa
Tel: (011) 837-0643, Fax: (011) 837-0645
E-mail: realbook@global.co.za

ISSN: 1078-6945
ISBN-13: 978-1-58297-503-0
ISBN-10: 1-58297-503-5

Cover design and illustration by Josh Roflow
Interior design by Clare Finney
Production coordinated by Kristen Heller and Greg Nock
Illustrations © Dominique Bruneton/PaintoAlto

Attention Booksellers: This is an annual directory of F+W Publications.
Return deadline for this edition is December 31, 2008.

Contents

INDEXES

From the Editor

Flip through the pages of this year's *Guide to Literary Agents* edition and the first thing you may notice is the large number of new literary agents added. As it's becoming increasingly important for aspiring authors to secure an agent who can sell their work to publishing houses, more new agents keep popping up in the literary world—each with her own specialties and areas of interest. That's why we beefed up this year's listings, especially with newer agents—this way, writers can query more representatives who are actively building their client lists.

At a recent writing conference, a writer told me my book is obsolete in this electronic age of information. My response to her: Not so. I've perused almost all online lists of agents, and each one is either outdated, incomplete, or contains incorrect information. There's only one true definitive, reputable source for information about agents and what they're looking for—and that's the book you hold in your hands. Agents or Writer's Digest Books editors verify every agency listing contained in this book each year.

Inside the 2008 edition, you'll find plenty of new articles—including a host of fresh topics discussed by agents, editors and writers alike. The publishing world is ever changing, and the advice included herein discusses how you can stay on top of these changes; check out "The Evolution of Agenting" by Stephany Evans of Imprint Agency on page 68; also don't miss "Almost Famous" (page 25), Christina Katz's great advice on building your platform.

And since acquiring an agent takes hard work, good writing and determination, you'll find motivation in "Success Stories" on page 83.

While *Guide to Literary Agents* provides articles and listings each year, the book also educates writers on protecting themselves. Besides things such as safeguarding your work with a copyright, there's also a little matter of unscrupulous agents lurking on the Internet who try to cajole you out of some capital—otherwise known as scammers. Almost every article here touches on agent warning signs to beware, as to better protect yourself, your money and your manuscript.

As always, please continue to stay in contact with me at www.guidetoliteraryagents.com, passing along success stories, improvement ideas and news from the ever-changing agent world.

Chuck Sambuchino
literaryagent@fwpubs.com
www.guidetoliteraryagents.com

How to Use
This Book

Searching for a literary agent can be overwhelming, whether you've just finished your first book or you have several publishing credits on your résumé. More than likely, you're eager to start pursuing agents and anxious to see your name on the spine of a book. But before you go directly to the listings of agencies in this book, take time to familiarize yourself with the way agents work and how you should approach them. By doing so, you will be more prepared for your search and ultimately save yourself effort and unnecessary grief.

Read the articles

This book begins with feature articles that explain how to prepare for representation, offer strategies for contacting agents, and provide perspectives on the author/agent relationship. The articles are organized into three sections appropriate for each stage of the search process: **Getting Started**, **Contacting Agents** and **Sealing the Deal**. You may want to start by reading through each article, and then refer back to relevant articles during each stage of your search.

Since there are many ways to make that initial contact with an agent, we've also provided a section called **Perspectives**. These personal accounts from agents and published authors offer information and inspiration for any writer hoping to find representation.

Decide what you're looking for

A literary or script agent will present your work directly to editors or producers. It's the agent's job to get her client's work published or sold and to negotiate a fair contract. In the **Literary Agents** and **Script Agents** sections, we list each agent's contact information and explain what type of work the agency represents as well as how to submit your work for consideration.

For face-to-face contact, many writers prefer to meet agents at **Conferences**. By doing so, writers can assess an agent's personality, attend workshops and have the chance to get more feedback on their work than they get by mailing submissions and waiting for a response. The conferences section is divided into regions, and lists only those conferences agents and/or editors attend. In many cases, private consultations are available, and agents attend with the hope of finding new clients to represent.

Utilize the extras

Aside from the articles and listings, the book offers a section of **Resources**. If you come across a term with which you aren't familiar, check out the Resources section for a quick explanation. Also, note the gray tabs along the edge of each page. The tabs block off each section so they are easier to flip to as you conduct your search.

Frequently Asked Questions

1 **Why do you include agents who are not seeking new clients?** Some agents ask that their listings indicate they are currently closed to new clients. We include them so writers know the agents exist and know not to contact them at this time.

2 **Why do you exclude fee-charging agents?** We have received a number of complaints in the past regarding fees, and therefore have chosen to list only those agents who do not charge fees.

3 **Why are some agents not listed in *Guide to Literary Agents?*** Some agents may not have responded to our requests for information. We have taken others out of the book after receiving very serious complaints about them. Refer to the General Index in the back of the book to see why a previously listed agency isn't listed in this edition.

4 **Do I need more than one agent if I write in different genres?** More than likely, no. If you have written in one genre and want to switch to a new style of writing, ask your agent if she is willing to represent you in your new endeavor. Most agents will continue to represent clients no matter what genre they choose to write. Occasionally, an agent may feel she has no knowledge of a certain genre and will recommend an appropriate agent to her client. Regardless, you should always talk to your agent about any potential career move.

5 **Why don't you list more foreign agents?** Most American agents have relationships with foreign co-agents in other countries. It is more common for an American agent to work with a co-agent to sell a client's book abroad than for a writer to work directly with a foreign agent. We do, however, list agents in the United Kingdom, Australia, Canada and other countries who sell to publishers both internationally and in the United States.

6 **Do agents ever contact a self-published writer?** If a self-published author attracts the attention of the media or if his book sells extremely well, an agent might approach the author in hopes of representing him.

7 **Why won't the agent I queried return my material?** An agent may not answer your query or return your manuscript for several reasons. Perhaps you did not include a self-addressed, stamped envelope (SASE). Many agents will discard a submission without a SASE. Or, the agent may have moved. To avoid using expired addresses, use the most current edition of *Guide to Literary Agents* or access the information online at www.WritersMarket.com. Another possibility is that the agent is swamped with submissions. Agents can be overwhelmed with queries, especially if the agent has recently spoken at a conference or has been featured in an article or book. Also, some agents specify in their listing that they never return materials of any kind.

Finally—and perhaps most importantly—are the **Indexes** in the back of the book. These can serve as an incredibly helpful way to start your search because they categorize the listings according to different criteria. For example, you can look for literary agents by name or according to their specialties (fiction/nonfiction genres). Similarly, you can search for script agents by name or according to format (e.g., plays/sitcoms). Plus, there is a General Index that lists every agent and conference in the book.

Listing Policy and Complaint Procedure

Listings in *Guide to Literary Agents* are compiled from detailed questionnaires, phone interviews and information provided by agents. The industry is volatile, and agencies change frequently. We rely on our readers for information on their dealings with agents and changes in policies or fees that differ from what has been reported to the editor of this book. Write to us (*Guide to Literary Agents*, 4700 E. Galbraith Road, Cincinnati, OH 45236) or e-mail us (literaryagent@fwpubs.com) if you have new information, questions or problems dealing with the agencies listed.

Listings are published free of charge and are not advertisements. Although the information is as accurate as possible, the listings are not endorsed or guaranteed by the editor or publisher of *Guide to Literary Agents*. If you feel you have not been treated fairly by an agent or representative listed in *Guide to Literary Agents*, we advise you to take the following steps:

- First try to contact the agency. Sometimes one phone call, letter or e-mail can clear up the matter. Politely relate your concern.

- Document all your correspondence with the agency. When you write to us with a complaint, provide the name of your manuscript, the date of your first contact with the agency and the nature of your subsequent correspondence.

We will keep your letter on file and attempt to contact the agency. The number, frequency and severity of complaints will be considered when deciding whether or not to delete an agency's listing from the next edition.

Guide to Literary Agents reserves the right to exclude any agency for any reason.

Do I Need an Agent?

Preparing for Representation

A writer's job is to write. A literary agent's job is to find publishers for her clients' books. Because publishing houses receive more unsolicited manuscripts each year, securing an agent is becoming increasingly necessary. Finding an eager and reputable agent can be a difficult task. Even the most patient writer can become frustrated or disillusioned. As a writer seeking agent representation, you should prepare yourself before starting your search. Learn when to approach agents, as well as what to expect from an author/agent relationship. Beyond selling manuscripts, an agent must keep track of the ever-changing industry, writers' royalty statements, fluctuating reading habits—and the list goes on.

So, once again, you face the question: Do I need an agent? The answer, much more often than not, is yes.

WHAT CAN AN AGENT DO FOR YOU?

For starters, today's competitive marketplace can be difficult to break into, especially for unpublished writers. Many larger publishing houses will only look at manuscripts from agents—and rightfully so, as they would be inundated with unsatisfactory writing if they did not. In fact, approximately 80 percent of books published by the major houses are acquired through agents.

But an agent's job isn't just getting your book through a publisher's door. The following describes the various jobs agents do for their clients, many of which would be difficult for a writer to do without outside help.

Agents know editors' tastes and needs

An agent possesses information on a complex web of publishing houses and a multitude of editors to ensure her clients' manuscripts are placed in the right hands. This knowledge is gathered through relationships she cultivates with acquisition editors—the people who decide which books to present to their publisher for possible publication. Through her industry connections, an agent becomes aware of the specializations of publishing houses and their imprints, knowing that one publisher only wants contemporary romances while another is interested solely in nonfiction books about the military. By networking with editors, an agent also learns more specialized information—which editor is looking for a crafty Agatha-Christie-style mystery for the fall catalog, for example.

Agents track changes in publishing

Being attentive to constant market changes and shifting trends is another major requirement of an agent. An agent understands what it may mean for clients when publisher A merges

To-Do List for Fiction Writers

1 **Finish your novel** or short story collection. An agent can do nothing for fiction without a finished product.

2 **Revise your novel.** Have other writers offer criticism to ensure your manuscript is as polished as you believe possible.

3 **Proofread.** Don't ruin a potential relationship with an agent by submitting work that contains typos or poor grammar.

4 **Publish** short stories or novel excerpts in literary journals, proving to potential agents that editors see quality in your writing.

5 **Research** to find the agents of writers whose works you admire or are similar to yours.

6 **Use the indexes in the back of this book** to construct a list of agents who are open to new writers and looking for your type of fiction (e.g., literary, romance, mystery).

7 **Rank your list.** Use the listings in this book to determine the agents most suitable for you and your work and to eliminate inappropriate agencies.

8 **Write your synopsis.** Completing this step will help you write your query letter and be prepared for when agents contact you.

9 **Write your query letter.** As an agent's first impression of you, this brief letter should be polished and to the point.

10 **Read about the business** of agents so you are knowledgeable and prepared to act on any offer. Start by reading this book's articles section completely.

with publisher B and when an editor from house C moves to house D. Or what it means when readers—and therefore editors—are no longer interested in Westerns, but instead can't get their hands on enough suspense novels.

Agents get your manuscript read faster

Although it may seem like an extra step to send your manuscript to an agent instead of directly to a publishing house, the truth is an agent can prevent writers from wasting months sending manuscripts that end up in the wrong place or buried in someone's slush pile. Editors rely on agents to save them time as well. With little time to sift through the hundreds of unsolicited submissions arriving weekly in the mail, an editor is naturally going to prefer a work that has already been approved by a qualified reader (i.e., the agent) that knows the editor's preferences. For this reason, many of the larger publishers accept agented submissions only.

Agents understand contracts

When publishers write contracts, they are primarily interested in their own bottom line rather than the best interests of the author. Writers unfamiliar with contractual language may find

To-Do List for Nonfiction Writers

(1) **Formulate a concrete idea** for your book. Sketch a brief outline making sure you have enough material for an entire book-length manuscript.

(2) **Research** works on similar topics to understand the competition and determine how your book is unique.

(3) **Write sample chapters.** This step should indicate how much time you will need to finish and if your writing needs editorial help.

(4) **Publish** completed chapters in journals and/or magazines. This validates your work to agents and provides writing samples for later in the process.

(5) **Polish your outline** so you can refer to it while drafting a query letter and you're prepared when agents contact you.

(6) **Brainstorm** three to four subject categories that best describe your material.

(7) **Use the indexes in this book** to find agents interested in at least two of your subject areas and who are looking for new clients.

(8) **Rank your list.** Narrow your list further by reading the listings of agencies you found in the indexes, and organize the list according to your preferences. Research agent Web sites to be even more selective.

(9) **Write your query.** Give an agent an excellent first impression by professionally and succinctly describing your premise and your experience.

(10) **Read about the business** of agents so you're knowledgeable and prepared to act on any offer. Start by reading this book's articles section completely.

themselves bound to a publisher with whom they no longer want to work. Or, they may find themselves tied to a publisher who prevents them from getting royalties on their first book until subsequent books are written. Agents use their experiences and knowledge to negotiate a contract that benefits the writer while still respecting the publisher's needs. After all, more money for the author will almost always mean more money for the agent—another reason they're on your side.

Agents negotiate—and exploit—subsidiary rights

Beyond publication, a savvy agent keeps in mind other opportunities for your manuscript. If your agent believes your book will also be successful as an audio book, a Book-of-the-Month Club selection or even a blockbuster movie, she will take these options into consideration when shopping your manuscript. These additional opportunities for writers are called subsidiary rights. Part of an agent's job is to keep track of the strengths and weaknesses of different publishers' subsidiary rights offices to determine the deposition of these rights regarding your work. After the contract is negotiated, the agent will seek additional moneymaking opportunities for the rights she kept for her client.

Agents get escalators

An escalator is a bonus that an agent can negotiate as part of the book contract. It is commonly given when a book appears on a bestseller list or if a client appears on a popular television show. For example, a publisher might give a writer a $50,000 bonus if he is picked for a book club. Both the agent and the editor know such media attention will sell more books, and the agent negotiates an escalator to ensure the writer benefits from this increase in sales.

Agents track payments

Since an agent only receives payment when the publisher pays the writer, it's in the agent's best interest to make sure the writer is paid on schedule. Some publishing houses are notorious for late payments. Having an agent distances you from any conflict regarding payment and allows you to spend your time writing instead of making phone calls.

Agents are strong advocates

Besides standing up for your right to be paid on time, agents can ensure your book gets a better cover design, more attention from the publisher's marketing department or other benefits you may not know to ask for during the publishing process. An agent can also provide advice during each step of the process, as well as guidance about your long-term writing career.

ARE YOU READY FOR AN AGENT?

Now that you know what an agent is capable of, ask yourself if you and your work are at a stage where you need an agent. Look at the To-Do Lists for fiction and nonfiction writers on pages 6 and 7, and judge how prepared you are for contacting an agent. Have you spent enough time researching or polishing your manuscript? Does your nonfiction book proposal include everything it should? Is your novel completely finished and thoroughly revised? Sending an agent an incomplete project not only wastes your time, but also may turn off the agent in the process. Literary and script agents are not magicians, and they can't solve your personal problems. An agent will not be your banker, CPA, social secretary or therapist. Instead, agents will endeavor to sell your book because that's how they earn their living.

Moreover, your material may not be appropriate for an agent. Most agents do not represent poetry, magazine articles, short stories, or material suitable for academic or small presses; the agents' commission does not justify spending time submitting these types of works. Those agents who do take on such material generally represent authors on larger projects first, and then adopt the smaller items as a favor to the client.

If you strongly believe your work is ready to be placed with an agent, make sure you're personally ready to be represented. In other words, consider the direction in which your writing career is headed. Besides skillful writers, agencies want clients with the ability to produce more than one book or script. Most agents will say they represent careers, not books. So as you compose your query letter—your initial contact with an agent—briefly mention your potential. Let an agent know if you've already started drafting your second novel and that your writing is more than a half-hearted hobby.

WHEN DON'T YOU NEED AN AGENT?

Although there are many reasons to work with an agent, an author can benefit from submitting his own work directly to a book publisher. For example, if your writing focuses on a very specific area, you may want to work with a small or specialized press. These houses are usually open to receiving material directly from writers. Small presses can often give more attention to a writer than a large house can, providing editorial help, marketing expertise and other advice directly to the writer.

Academic books or specialized nonfiction books (such as a book about the history of Rhode Island) are good bets if you're not with an agent. Beware, though, as you will now be responsible for negotiating all parts of your contract and payment. If you choose this path, it's wise to use a lawyer or entertainment attorney to review all contracts. If a lawyer specializes in intellectual property, he can help a writer with contract negotiations. Instead of giving the lawyer a commission, the lawyer is paid for his time only.

And, of course, some people prefer working independently instead of relying on others to do their work. If you're one of these people, it's probably better to shop your own work instead of constantly butting heads with an agent. Let's say you manage to sign with one of the few literary agents who represent short story collections. If the collection gets shopped around to publishers for several months and no one bites, your agent may suggest retooling the work into a novel or novella(s). Agents suggest changes—some bigger than others—and not all writers think their work is malleable. It's all a matter of what you're writing and how you feel about it.

Author FAQs

Expert Answers to Common Questions

There are some questions writers ask time and time again. A handful of the most common ones are answered below by several professional literary agents. You can find these, and other frequently asked questions, on WritersMarket.com.

I simultaneously queried six agents to represent my literary novel and received three favorable responses requesting sample chapters. Is it acceptable for me to reply to them all at once, or should I send material only to one and wait for a decision before sending to others?

As a courtesy, I would let agents know that other agents have also requested the material. Some agencies prefer exclusive submissions, though they realize you may have been querying a variety of agents prior to that request. If an agent asks for an exclusive read, it's reasonable for the author to ask that it be time-limited.

I admit to being a bit dismayed when I spend many hours reading something only to find the author has signed with someone else. Requesting sample chapters should allow faster answers than having sent the agent the whole manuscript. I see no problem sending all the agents sample chapters as long as you extend the courtesy to let them know

Michael Mancilla

others are interested, especially if and when they ask for the whole manuscript.

—**Michael Mancilla** *handles nonfiction, self-help, psychology and illustrated books at Greystone Literary Agency in Washington, D.C.*

If I submit a novel to a publisher who agrees to publish it, would it be in bad taste to write to an agent who had rejected me earlier and ask for representation again? I don't know anything about publishing contracts and would like someone to help walk me through it should the time come.

It's fine to approach an agent at any point in the process. We've taken on new clients in cases where we're the first person to see the work and also in cases where there's already an offer on the table. In fact, sometimes, the editor who has made the offer will recommend the author contact us.

As your question implies, agents do more than just secure an offer. They also negotiate contracts, act as the author's advocate and champion, and help the author navigate the path after publication.

It's an agent's job to deal with issues and (sometimes) the problems that can arise after a publishing contract is secured. That way, the author can have a productive and creative relationship with her editor. A good agent will also think not just about fostering the success of a single book but also the big picture of a client's career.

—**Laura Rennert** *is a senior agent with the Andrea Brown Literary Agency in Palo Alto, Calif. She specializes in all categories of children's books.*

I'm talking with an agent who politely refused to share a list of clients he represents and titles he's recently sold. Is this normal?

I understand agencies that don't list clients in directories and public access places. That's a personal choice. Hartline lists authors and books sold right on their Web site. To get down to the point of considering representation, however, not knowing anything about whom they have represented and what success they've had would, to me, be like agreeing to surgery without knowing for sure that my doctor has a medical degree. If someone applies for a job, they have to provide a résumé and show their experience and qualifications. An agent is not going to take on a client without knowing the critical details about them, and I believe the client is entitled to the same consideration. Before you sign with an agent, know who they are and what they've sold.

Terry W. Burns

—**Terry W. Burns** *recently joined Hartline Literary Agency as a member agent.*

Is it wise to follow trends? I've heard that politics is a hot topic and YA is a hot genre right now. Should I strike while the iron's hot?

It's always tempting to write something that seems trendy. Much of this business is about the selling aspect, so writers often think that if they write what publishers seem to be publishing, or what seems to be appearing on bestseller lists, then they have a greater chance of getting a contract—but I honestly don't think it's the wisest way to go. Sure, a writer needs to be aware of what's out there, both so you're not reinventing the wheel (i.e., writing a book that's essentially already been published), as well as so you know how to position your book—but you really need to write what you write best. This means if you've never written for the YA market

Felicia Eth

and have little sense of that audience, then starting now probably doesn't make sense, nor for that matter does reinventing yourself as a political writer if you don't already have a column or blog that's well known in that arena. You're not likely to "fool" publishers simply by trying to do what's hot.

Beyond this, though, there's the issue of timing. This is a business where things move slowly, so whatever it is you'd be selling today most likely won't come out for a year to two-and-a-half years. Who knows where the market will be at that point? Being conscious of the market is key—but above all, your book needs to be the best it can be. Who knows—maybe if it's terrific, you'll start the next trend.

—**Felicia Eth** *has her own literary agency based in Palo Alto, Calif. She represents a variety of nonfiction subjects as well as novels.*

What is the difference between a literary agent and a literary manager?

Whether working with writers of scripts or books, a literary manager will help clients develop and research story ideas, edit and polish the writer's work, guide the course of the writer's career, and introduce their work. Agents' expertise in literary sales, coupled with the role filled by a literary manager, makes it advantageous for writers to be represented by both.

Both agents and managers serve an important role, not only for the writer, but to each other as well. Typically, literary managers will have fewer clients than agents due to the vast amount of time they spend nurturing the writer's career.

Reputable agents and managers will not accept or charge fees for their services. Their payment is received upon the sale of a property with the following commission rates usually applying: 10% to agents, 15% to managers, and 5% to lawyers. The expertise and connections that these professionals possess equates to money well spent and, hopefully, the launch of a successful career.

—**Margery Walshaw** *is the principal of Evatopia, Inc., a literary management firm. She represents 15 screenwriters as a literary manager.*

I'm querying agents right now and wondered if it's worth mentioning the awards I've won. Some I consider rather minor, and other more notable accolades have to do with poetry and nothing to do with the book I'm trying to sell. Should I include these on my cover letter or does that make me look amateurish?

A prospective agent's first question to you is simple: Can you write? A mention of your awards, even out of the genre of the proposal, is going to be helpful. The agent may or may not advise you to include this information in the final proposal that goes to the publisher. At the end of the day, your agent is like your doctor. Withholding any information about your qualifications as a writer isn't a good idea. Use whatever you can to sell yourself to an agency, then together decide on the best approach to sell your proposal to a publisher.

Dr. Robert D. Wolgemuth

—**Dr. Robert D. Wolgemuth** *of Wolgemuth & Associates, Inc. specializes in nonfiction.*

A week from now, my self-published novel will come rolling off the presses—all 500 copies. I made the very expensive investment in those 500 for two reasons: I got the rare joy of designing a book from cover to cover; and I wish to use the finished product as bait upon which a reputable agent might nibble. Was my second reason the foolish dream of a wishful angler?

Frankly, my sense is that providing an agent or editor with an already produced book only reduces its attractiveness as a potential property. First, the extra effort and expense smacks of trying too hard. And second, it conveys the sense that the material may already have made the rounds before—else why the desperation to self-publish?

Agents, in particular, want the sense that they are discovering something precious and unknown. And to that end, less really is more, in terms of presentation. A simple and straightforward cover letter without any cheesy come-ons, complete with an appropriately modest listing of awards or other writing credentials, is all that should accompany a manuscript. The rest is up to the work itself.

—**Rob McQuilkin** *specializes in fiction, memoir, history, sociology, psychology and graphic works at Lippincott Massie McQuilkin in New York City.*

I've heard that you shouldn't (can't?) have two different agents represent your work, but what if your varying genres demand it?

Most agents handle genres of fiction and nonfiction, so in many cases, there won't be a problem with an agent handling whatever work, categorically, his or her client turns to. However, if one's agent, obviously wanting to serve each and every book optimally, says honestly that he or she truly wouldn't do the job for whatever reason, then the client should certainly feel free to seek appropriate representation for the book in the "new" genre. What's more, if the situation is succinctly explained to the new agent(s) being approached, they will certainly be understanding (in my view, anyway), and evaluate the submission on merit. And if the writer plans to continue in the new genre, so that the submission in question is not a one-shot, the new agent is even more likely to be open to acting as the writer's "second" agent—even if he or she won't be doing the usual, representing all of that writer's work.

John Ware

—**John Ware** *represents nonfiction books and novels at his New-York-City-based agency.*

I've read some articles that say "Agents agent," meaning that their job is to sell your work, rather than do other tasks such as assisting to edit a manuscript. But other articles say agents are now responsible for lots of editing throughout the process. Which is correct?

It's been a long time since any good agent I know has *just* sold books. Agenting is a full-service business and, in this day and age, when editors sometimes seem to be playing musical chairs and projects are orphaned almost as soon as they're bought, providing editorial feedback for our clients is increasingly important. Here at Dystel & Goderich, we edit an author's work before it goes out on submission in order to optimize its chances in the marketplace. Occasionally, we also offer editorial support once the book is sold and the acquiring editor is unable or unwilling to edit. We like to think that our role is to "cause" books to be published, and for that to happen, we need to be involved at every step of the way.

—**Miriam Goderich** *is a founding agent of Dystel & Goderich Literary Management in New York City.*

Do agents usually hold out for a good deal on a book or do they take the first acceptable offer that comes along?

Well, an offer in your pocket is always better than none. Certainly, if an agent feels she can demand more for a book, she should hold out; however, usually the editor who makes the first offer is the most enthusiastic and thoroughly understands the book, and may turn out to be the best editor and in-house advocate for that book. The most money is not necessarily the best deal for an author. That enthusiasm, commitment and support from all divisions within a publishing house often means more than those dollars in your bank account.

Laura Langlie

We do *see* editors on a regular basis. Again, working from experience, an agent helps her client make the best possible decision. We all want our authors to be published successfully and accomplish their goals.

—**Laura Langlie** *is a Brooklyn-based literary agent. She represents nonfiction books, novels, short story collections, novellas and juvenile books.*

Assessing Credibility

The Scoop on Researching Agents

Many people wouldn't buy a used car without at least checking the odometer, and savvy shoppers would consult the blue books, take a test drive and even ask for a mechanic's opinion. Much like the savvy car shopper, you want to obtain the best possible agent for your writing, so you should do some research on the business of agents before sending out query letters. Understanding how agents operate will help you find an agent appropriate for your work, as well as alert you about the types of agents to avoid.

Many writers take for granted that any agent who expresses interest in their work is trustworthy. They'll sign a contract before asking any questions and simply hope everything will turn out all right. We often receive complaints from writers regarding agents *after* they have lost money or have work bound by contract to an ineffective agent. If writers put the same amount of effort into researching agents as they did writing their manuscripts, they would save themselves unnecessary grief.

The best way to educate yourself is to read all you can about agents and other authors. Organizations such as the Association of Authors' Representatives (AAR; www.aar-online.org), the National Writers Union (NWU; www.nwu.org), American Society of Journalists and Authors (ASJA; www.asja.org) and Poets & Writers, Inc. (www.pw.org), all have informational material on finding and working with an agent.

Publishers Weekly (www.publishersweekly.com) covers publishing news affecting agents and others in the publishing industry, discusses specific events in the "Hot Deals" and "Behind the Bestsellers" columns, and occasionally lists individual author's agents in the "Forecasts" section. The Publishers Lunch newsletter (www.publishersmarketplace.com) comes free via e-mail every workday and offers news on agents and editors, job postings, recent book sales and more.

Even the Internet has a wide range of sites where you can learn basic information about preparing for your initial contact, as well as specific details on individual agents. You can also find online forums and listservs, which keep authors connected and allow them to share experiences they've had with different editors and agents. Keep in mind, however, that not everything printed on the Web is solid fact; you may come across the site of a writer who is bitter because an agent rejected his manuscript. Your best bet is to use the Internet to supplement your other research.

Once you've established what your resources are, it's time to see which agents meet your criteria. Below are some of the key items to pay attention to when researching agents.

LEVEL OF EXPERIENCE

Through your research, you will discover the need to be wary of some agents. Anybody can go to the neighborhood copy center and order business cards that say "literary agent," but that title doesn't mean she can sell your book. She may lack the proper connections with others in the publishing industry, and an agent's reputation with editors can be a major strength or weakness.

Agents who have been in the business awhile have a large number of contacts and carry the most clout with editors. They know the ins and the outs of the industry and are often able to take more calculated risks. However, veteran agents can be too busy to take on new clients or might not have the time to help develop the author. Newer agents, on the other hand, may be hungrier, as well as more open to unpublished writers. They probably have a smaller client list and are able to invest the extra effort to make your book a success.

If it's a new agent without a track record, be aware that you're taking more of a risk signing with her than with a more established agent. However, even a new agent should not be new to publishing. Many agents were editors before they were agents, or they worked at an agency as an assistant. This experience is crucial for making contacts in the publishing industry and learning about rights and contracts. The majority of listings in this book explain how long the agent has been in business, as well as what she did before becoming an agent. You could also ask the agent to name a few editors off the top of her head who she thinks may be interested in your work and why they sprang to mind. Has she sold to them before? Do they publish books in your genre?

If an agent has no contacts in the business, she has no more clout than you do. Without publishing prowess, she's just an expensive mailing service. Anyone can make photocopies, slide them into an envelope and address them to "Editor." Unfortunately, without a contact name and a familiar return address on the envelope, or a phone call from a trusted colleague letting an editor know a wonderful submission is on its way, your work will land in the slush pile with all the other submissions that don't have representation. You can do your own mailings with higher priority than such an agent could.

PAST SALES

Agents should be willing to discuss their recent sales with you: how many, what type of books and to what publishers. Keep in mind, though, that some agents consider this information confidential. If an agent does give you a list of recent sales, you can call the publishers' contracts department to ensure the sale was actually made by that agent. While it's true that even top agents are not able to sell every book they represent, an inexperienced agent who proposes too many inappropriate submissions will quickly lose her standing with editors.

You can also find out details of recent sales on your own. Nearly all of the listings in this book offer the titles and authors of books with which the agent has worked. Some of them also note to which publishing house the book was sold. Again, you can call the publisher and affirm the sale. If you don't have the publisher's information, simply go to your local library or bookstore to see if they carry the book. Consider checking to see if it's available on Web sites like Amazon.com, too. You may want to be wary of the agent if her books are nowhere to be found or are only available through the publisher's Web site. Distribution is a crucial component to getting published, and you want to make sure the agent has worked with competent publishers.

TYPES OF FEES

Becoming knowledgeable about the different types of fees agents may charge is vital to conducting effective research. Most agents make their living from the commissions they receive after selling their clients' books, and these are the agents we've listed. Be sure to ask about any expenses you don't understand so you have a clear grasp of what you're paying for. Described below are some types of fees you may encounter in your research.

Office fees

Occasionally, an agent will charge for the cost of photocopies, postage and long-distance phone calls made on your behalf. This is acceptable, so long as she keeps an itemized account of the expenses and you've agreed on a ceiling cost. The agent should only ask for office expenses after agreeing to represent the writer. These expenses should be discussed up front, and the writer should receive a statement accounting for them. This money is sometimes returned to the author upon sale of the manuscript. Be wary if there is an up-front fee amounting to hundreds of dollars, which is excessive.

Reading fees

Agencies that charge reading fees often do so to cover the cost of additional readers or the time spent reading that could have been spent selling. Agents also claim that charging reading fees cuts down on the number of submissions they receive. This practice can save the agent time and may allow her to consider each manuscript more extensively. Whether such promises are kept depends upon the honesty of the agency. You may pay a fee and never receive a response from the agent, or you may pay someone who never submits your manuscript to publishers.

Officially, the Association of Authors' Representatives' (AAR) Canon of Ethics prohibits members from directly or indirectly charging a reading fee, and the Writers Guild of America (WGA) does not allow WGA signatory agencies to charge a reading fee to WGA members,

Warning Signs! Beware of . . .

Important

- Excessive typos or poor grammar in an agent's correspondence.

- A form letter accepting you as a client and praising generic things about your book that could apply to any book. A good agent doesn't take on a new client very often, so when she does, it's a special occasion that warrants a personal note or phone call.

- Unprofessional contracts that ask you for money up front, contain clauses you haven't discussed or are covered with amateur clip-art or silly borders.

- Rudeness when you inquire about any points you're unsure of. Don't employ any business partner who doesn't treat you with respect.

- Pressure, by way of threats, bullying or bribes. A good agent is not desperate to represent more clients. She invites worthy authors but leaves the final decision up to them.

- Promises of publication. No agent can guarantee you a sale. Not even the top agents sell everything they choose to represent. They can only send your work to the most appropriate places, have it read with priority and negotiate you a better contract if a sale does happen.

- A print-on-demand book contract or any contract offering you no advance. You can sell your own book to an e-publisher any time you wish without an agent's help. An agent should pursue traditional publishing routes with respectable advances.

as stated in the WGA's Artists' Manager Basic Agreement. A signatory may charge you a fee if you are not a member, but most signatory agencies do not charge a reading fee as an across-the-board policy.

Reading fees vary from $25 to $500 or more. The fee is usually nonrefundable, but sometimes agents agree to refund the money if they take on a writer as a client, or if they sell the writer's manuscript. Keep in mind, however, that payment of a reading fee does not ensure representation.

No literary agents who charge reading fees are listed in this book. It's too risky of an option for writers, plus nonfee-charging agents have a stronger incentive to sell your work. After all, they don't make a dime until they make a sale. If you find that a literary agent listed in this book charges a reading fee, please contact the editor at literaryagent@fwpubs.com.

Critique fees

Sometimes a manuscript will interest an agent, but the agent will point out areas requiring further development and offer to critique it for an additional fee. Like reading fees, payment of a critique fee does not ensure representation. When deciding if you will benefit from having someone critique your manuscript, keep in mind that the quality and quantity of comments varies from agent to agent. The critique's usefulness will depend on the agent's knowledge of the market. Also be aware that agents who spend a significant portion of their time commenting on manuscripts will have less time to actively market work they already represent.

In other cases, the agent may suggest an editor who understands your subject matter or genre and has some experience getting manuscripts into shape. Occasionally, if your story is exceptional or your ideas and credentials are marketable but your writing needs help, you will work with a ghostwriter or co-author who will share a percentage of your commission, or work with you at an agreed upon cost per hour.

An agent may refer you to editors she knows, or you may choose an editor in your area. Many editors do freelance work and would be happy to help you with your writing project. Of course, before entering into an agreement, make sure you know what you'll be getting for your money. Ask the editor for writing samples, references or critiques he's done in the past. Make sure you feel comfortable working with him before you give him your business.

An honest agent will not make any money for referring you to an editor. We strongly advise writers not to use critiquing services offered through an agency. Instead, try hiring a freelance editor or joining a writer's group until your work is ready to be submitted to agents who don't charge fees.

Getting Started

With an Agent's Eye

Edit Your Work Like a Pro

by Candy Davis

Your well-crafted query letter, brilliant synopsis and three stunning chapters have brought you an invitation from your favorite agent to send the entire manuscript. Now you're quaking in your boots. How can you make sure your book will keep her reading to the last page?

Agents really do want to fall in love with your book. They demand intangible qualities like passion, emotional power and good storytelling. But what does that look like on the page? Does your book have that certain *je ne sais quoi* an agent expects? To answer that question, take a few weeks away from your story and come back ready to scrutinize and edit it as ruthlessly as though you were a stranger—one who's paid to notice every sweet turn of plot as well as every misplaced modifier. You can do this by answering the questions that an agent asks—questions that will help you view your manuscript with an agent's eye.

Make them love it

An agent wants your novel to reveal itself as a heartfelt work that induces a physical sensation of deep attentiveness and breathless anticipation from the very first line. She immediately wants to feel the love between you and the still-bleeding story you have ripped out of the very depths of your own soul.

- *Do you still love this story with all your heart?*
- *Do you still experience a physical response to key scenes?*

Make them feel it

Nothing hooks an agent like emotional truth. She prays for a writer who deftly and simply handles complex emotions without melodrama or extravagant prose. Give your main character room to explore their deepest reactions to an opening predicament that by its very nature demands the reader's empathy.

- *Is the main character emotionally accessible to the reader?*
- *Does the book open in a way that reflects that character's emotional need?*

Keep them awake

Agents want authors who can offer them something "fresh," meaning that the story frames common human experiences in a way that other writers have not tried. So how can you perk

CANDY DAVIS (www.inkdance.biz) is a screenwriter whose credits include *Monsoon Wife* and the in-production *Warrior Without a Gun*. She is the president of Ink Dance Literary Services, an active Web-based editing business.

up a timeworn tale? Do what agents do: Make yourself part of the publishing community. Read online trade publications and surf major Web sites to understand the range of stories already on the market.

Scour the online Amazon bookstore (www.amazon.com) for quick synopses of books that seem similar to yours. Buy or borrow those books for a closer look. Canvass the subject-searchable Internet Movie Database Web site (www.imdb.com) to gauge whether your story is already a cliché. If so, find a new twist.

- *Does the story offer the reader something unique?*
- *Are the names and plot twists new and surprising?*

Convince them you know your readers

Unless you write phone books, don't expect to stake out a universal readership. Agents need a book that corners one segment of the market—a recognized genre. An author may dream of selling her historical romantic mystery comedic suspense thriller, but it isn't going to happen.

If you want your book on the shelves, find the most comfortable genre for you, and then concentrate on learning its characteristics. Revise your work to those guidelines.

- *Do you have a specific audience in mind?*
- *Does the story match the chosen genre profile?*

Show where the story's going

An agent looks at your first few paragraphs for hints of a strong spine and definite direction. If the opening artfully reveals an engaging main character, exposes his innermost need for change and suggests a path to achieving resolution, the agent reads on. A character burdened with interchangeable themes tangles your storylines and leaves the reader confused. Worse, a character with no theme at all is a lone wolf without a story.

- *What single internal element does the main character seek?*
- *If he could achieve only one worthy goal, what would that be?*

Review your cast list

Agents expect to encounter interesting, fully developed central characters with complex, thematically driven motivations. The main character should be strong enough to shoulder noble aspirations but flawed enough to make achieving his goals difficult. The antagonist, an especially important character, must offer a formidable challenge without hijacking the story.

An over-abundance of supporting characters won't make up for a weak main character, and can take up valuable space that should be devoted to deeper development. Cut all loiterers. Leave only the characters necessary to move the story ahead.

- *Does the main character hold the reader's attention without being overshadowed by any other character?*
- *Is the antagonist powerful enough to be a credible threat?*
- *Is every character vital and effective?*

Compose fully realized characters

Although the mechanics of good technique should be invisible to the average reader, an agent immediately recognizes and appreciates good characterization. Show that you have mastered a broad selection of techniques to create a lifelike protagonist.

An agent looks for effortlessly introduced setting and description that does double duty to deepen your character and his emotions. How the character processes his surroundings reveals more depth and subtle shading in his story than any amount of authorial explanation. Use body language and facial expression to expose raw conflict and emotion.

- *Does your writing suggest emotion, rather than explain it, through a good balance of the full range of characterization tools such as action, internal voice, reflection, sensory cues and body language?*
- *Have you alternated between all available techniques in a skillful fashion?*

Let them know who's driving

Controlling point of view is one acid test an agent will certainly apply to your manuscript. Choosing which character will take over the storytelling in each scene gives you a powerful and subtle tool with which to manipulate the reader's experience. A writer who allows the viewpoint to wobble from character to character or even to inanimate objects during a scene reveals himself as a neophyte.

- *Does the main character carry the major portion of the viewpoint?*
- *Have you chosen just a few key characters to present other viewpoints?*
- *Have you been careful to maintain a single character's point of view in each scene?*

Create deep structure

An agent wants to see a layered plot packed with surprises and steadily increasing tension. Good plot development builds on the theme(s) as well as on previously introduced circumstances. Demonstrate that you can take charge of the story like an expert by including only the most important and connected plot events. Move the story ahead with solid pacing and a clear trajectory.

The agent is likely to check the first and last chapters to determine whether he wants to spend more than a few minutes with your manuscript. Pay special attention to opening with the central character and his thematic issue. The final chapter should resolve the same issue.

An agent will probably spot-check the middle of the manuscript to see if the quality of the narrative voice remains consistent throughout the second act. He has seen many stories that fracture at this point when the writer ran out of ideas to spice up the plot. New characters may appear and take over the story or the main character might abandon his original mission and choose a new, unrelated theme. Don't let this happen to you.

- *Is the story strongly paced and does it move unswervingly toward the conclusion?*
- *Does the writing maintain a consistently high quality from first to last chapters?*
- *Does the ending answer the main question posed at the beginning?*

Let them feel the pulse

Your book's unique proportion of scenes and sequels should produce a characteristic rhythm your agent can easily recognize as the perfect pulse for the work: staccato for quick-paced action genre, more legato for a genre that focuses on internal process. Running too many scenes together allows no space for the character to evaluate his progress.

Each scene should begin and end with a hook, and should capture a complete and meaningful "story event." Keep scene length appropriate to your genre, and never longer than necessary to cover the episode. Cut mundane interactions, placeholder dialogue and extraneous background information. A sequel generally follows a major plot point, steps up the stakes and turns the story in a new direction. Allow the character a moment to evaluate past mistakes, realize a previously overlooked or rejected option, and take the first step toward executing a new and more desperate plan.

- *Is every scene well structured and thriftily written?*
- *Does the work have a vital pulse, with fewer sequels than scenes?*

Win them over with appearance

Format is the one element that shouldn't make your manuscript unique. White paper, succinct headers, a standard font such as Courier New, perfect spelling and punctuation, and double-spacing are just a few qualities of a manuscript that make the agent's job easier.

- *Have you checked the entire manuscript thoroughly for spelling, punctuation and pagination errors?*
- *Is the formatting consistent with professional industry standards?*

What's next?

If you can't answer yes to these questions without your nose growing longer, or you honestly can't tell if you've covered every base, go back to work on the manuscript. Share it with a writing group, give it another objective read or possibly seek help from a professional editor. In the end, it's crucial that you be able to realize when your manuscript is not yet ready for an agent. Don't worry—he's happy to wait until it reads with that certain *je ne sais quoi*.

Use all the wisdom and professional advice at hand to conquer the revision process, and you can make this story a success. It's time to revise your work with an agent's eye.

Querying Hollywood

Know Your Target and Pitch That Script

by Candy Davis

Ideas are cheap on the streets of Hollywood. Every car mechanic, housewife and self-proclaimed guru is also a wannabe produced screenwriter with killer-bee selling instincts. Sunshine and 24/7 access to the film industry attract these people to the beehive called Hollywood—and that makes it tough for writers living outside the magic buzz to get any traction.

Getting the attention of an agent means making a positive and indelible impression. You can do this by writing a great script query. Concise, business-like communications combined with characteristic Hollywood snap will get your pitch heard.

QUERY THE RIGHT PERSON

The first thing you need to know is that an "agent," per se, is not necessarily the best target for a newbie writer unless you happen to be in his immediate family. An "agent" is a wheeler-dealer who tends his own hive of already famous worker bees. He creates placements for the proven moneymakers he knows he can count on. As a general rule, he's not interested in new writers, and the words *pro bono* are not in his dictionary.

If you're indeed a newbie, try targeting people who bill themselves as "managers." A manager is someone who makes herself available to new talent and helps develop and polish a script. She's just as picky as any agent, and yes, she gets a bigger percentage of your take—somewhere around 15 percent. To the writer living outside Tinseltown, she's worth it. Managers nurture new talent with deft coaching, high expectations and a kick in the pants when needed.

Once you've done your research, completed your script and found several managers who look like a good fit to represent your work, it's time to compose the best query possible.

Paragraph one: the irresistible hook

Like bees in a hive, everyone in the film industry is related in some way. To become part of this close-knit tribe, take full advantage of the six degrees of separation when you introduce yourself briefly in the first crucial paragraph. A wise motto: *Be bold.* Maybe you went to high school with the daughter of what's-his-name who worked at the gas station down the street from the manager's office. Don't be afraid to do what it takes to connect yourself to the inner sanctum of the hive. It's worked for other writers. It can work for you.

CANDY DAVIS (www.inkdance.biz) is a screenwriter whose credits include *Monsoon Wife* and the in-production *Warrior Without a Gun*. She is the president of Ink Dance Literary Services, an active Web-based editing business.

Hollywood is about entertainment, so sneak in the information about your script while you entertain your elusive quarry. Make your letter sparkle with personality and a fresh voice. Neither grovel nor brag, but do show off your willingness to play her game, her way.

Every manager wants to determine within a few short sentences if you're a prospect she can market. Each has specific wants based on personal contacts and openings they need to fill. Effortlessly mention the title of your screenplay and be specific about genre. Get to the point fast, but don't forget to mention what you want: representation for your script.

Notice how the elements of voice and tone work in this winning first paragraph by screenwriter Jo Jo Jensen:

> "I heard from Candy Davis that you gave a whopper of a workshop at the recent Surrey B.C. Writing Conference about the concept behind concept films—I'm sorry I missed it. Candy has great things to say about you, thinks we'd make a good match and suggested that I talk with you regarding representation. She spoke with you about my comedy feature script, *Well Rounded*, and you expressed interest in taking a look. I'd love to send it to you."

Crucial items in the first paragraph:

- Personal connection
- Appropriate story genre and length
- Script title
- A request for representation
- Your interesting, flexible personality
- Brevity and bouncy trade-speak

Paragraph two: the fascinating pitch

In Hollywood, the trailer is often the main event. Whole careers are founded or broken on these mile-a-minute, highly visual cuts that market films not only to viewers but also to those who make the financial decisions. A few films have even entered the production phase with nothing more to stand on than a trailer. Write your second paragraph to serve as your trailer: Open your story summary with the basic premise in a few sparkling words. Then hit three or four major plot points in stunning, visual language and close it up fast.

Hollywood admires a certain type of ending twist expressed as a punch line, also known as a "button." Your story summary, like your screenplay, must come back around to answer the major story question proposed in the first sentence.

Here is the exemplary story summary from Jensen's query:

> "Socialite, gold digger Kirby Vance is willing to put up with almost anything, including starvation, to obtain a wedding ring. But instead of getting her dream life, she's kicked out of her million-dollar life and must learn to fend for herself. She faces homelessness, junk food benders and a community service stint raking up bird poop. In the end, Kirby learns to succeed or fail on her own. Only then can she decide if life is better on a man's arm or in his heart."

Crucial items in the second paragraph:

- Name and thumbnail of crucial character(s)
- Story premise
- Three major plot points
- Hollywood ending
- Brevity

Paragraph three: wonderful, qualified you

Believe it or not, a manager wants to admire you as a credentialed, highly productive and interesting personality. Speak to her in an honest, forthright tone about your accomplishments. Don't diminish or flaunt. Just be you. She also wants to know she can trust you, so mention past kudos she can check, such as film credits, published books and college degrees.

Hollywood keeps no secrets. Start your own buzz by letting this manager know that other industry professionals already consider you a hot item. Say it simply and with confidence. Make it mean as much to her as it does to you. Any film credits are the most relevant and should go up front. Drop names in a manner that hints at business associates rather than beer buddies. Link yourself to the business as a professional.

No matter what you've written, be specific about which genre is your specialty. Hollywood typically caters to three genres—comedy, horror and action—because these genres sell to its biggest paying audience: guys under the age of 25 who are preferably mad about videogames. Note: You won't convince a manager or agent that you're a whiz at more than one genre. Pick your best and run with it. A claim that you're versatile enough to write in every genre hints at mushy crossovers and weak structure.

Notice the self-assured tone of Jo Jo Jensen's credential paragraph:

> "I'm a published author and an editor of both books and screenplays. Comedy is definitely my strength. *Well Rounded* has received great reviews from Max Thayer at Mindbender Films, and from producer Sandra Smart (*Time on My Side*) as well as other industry professionals in Hollywood and is just looking for the right home. I've worked with Fearopolis Entertainment on their feature *The Evelyn Experiment*, which is under consideration by MTV Films. My other current projects include screwball comedy *Inkspot* and *The Gatekeeper*, a comedy with a dark twist."

Crucial items in the third paragraph:

- Confident tone
- Past industry credits, film or otherwise
- Associates in the industry
- Upcoming projects

Paragraph four: the last dance

Screenwriters have a major rule of thumb: When the scene action is over, get out fast. You've impressed this manager with a tantalizing story, unsinkable confidence and a voice that hints at your screenwriting talent. Now it's time to wrap it up. Fast. Invite her to ask for a bigger bite of your work with a closing that says you move at the light speed of Hollywood.

Jensen's final sentence is a simple, clear reminder about what she wants this manager to do next:

> "I'm excited to talk with you further about representation."

MOVING UP OR MOVING ON

Don't be discouraged by rejection. Hollywood is about trends. Last spring's fabulous idea is now utterly dead, and every film executive is buzzing back and forth on the scent of this fall's clover patch. Maybe you're simply ahead of the curve. If a manager decides she isn't for you, thank her for her time and ask for a recommendation to a colleague—or better yet, two colleagues.

Get a firm grip on your nerves and take a chance on your talent. Remember your motto: *Be bold*—and you, too, can write a query that will get you an invitation to the hive.

Almost Famous

*Start Building a Platform to Garner
More Attention and Respect*

by Christina Katz

Don't turn on me when I tell you that it's not enough to simply write these days. Chances are, you've heard this pronouncement recently at a writers' conference, in a professional journal, in a forum discussion or at your writing group. Certainly, if you spend any amount of time with authors, agents or editors, they'll confirm the buzz: It's time to get to work on your platform.

There's good news: The word "platform" simply describes all the ways you're visible and appealing to your potential, future or actual readership. To build a platform, an author must create and maintain a Web presence without sacrificing too much regular writing time or paying a fortune in fees. Platform development is not only important for existing authors, it's also crucial for wannabe authors or soon-to-be authors. And not only is platform development a refreshing switch from the daily grind, it promptly offers satisfaction and possible additional income streams for your writing career.

PLATFORM DEVELOPMENT 101: NEWSLETTERS AND YOUR NICHE

Some say the e-mail newsletter is dead. I say not true. As long as there is e-mail, there will be newsletters zipping through the ethers. Besides, if you're an unpublished writer, starting a newsletter is a terrific way to bring organization to your expertise—so you can deliver material and information to a specific audience. Most writers have way more raw material and ideas than they actually use in their published books and articles, so why not put more of your usable content to use? Whether you're just starting to formulate your first book pitch or you're already published, a newsletter is the perfect way to zoom in on your topic and your audience.

Don't wait; do it now

I bet you could sit down right now, open a new e-mail document and draft up a newsletter in one sitting. Before you begin, quickly study some newsletters sitting in your inbox.

Here's a very basic format to help you get started. In your newsletter or zine, include:

- a banner at the top including the name of the newsletter, the mission statement, the volume, issue number and date

---

CHRISTINA KATZ is an Oregon-based freelancer, the author of *Writer Mama* (Writer's Digest Books) and the editor of the "Writers on the Rise" newsletter. Visit www.christinakatz.com and www.thewritermama.com for more information.

- a letter from the editor
- a few short newsy blurbs relevant to your audience and subject matter
- a feature article or two with helpful advice
- a mention of the products and services that you offer
- contributions from friends, colleagues or "the competition"

Why would you invite the competition into your newsletter? Because they'll help spread the word! Don't forget to include easy-to-find instructions for subscribing or unsubscribing. Consider launching your newsletter or zine by inviting whoever is in your address book to subscribe. If you include only those who give you permission on your subscriber list, you won't have to worry about spamming, which is annoying at best, and alienating at worst.

Penny pinch

Mary Hunt began working her family out of more than $100,000 of unsecured debt 13 years ago, and as a result started a newsletter called "The Cheapskate Monthly." I picked up the print version at my local library years ago and admired how Hunt had turned the lemons of her life into helpful lessons for others. Today, that little newsletter has evolved into a debt reduction mini-empire with numerous books (traditionally published, self-published and e-published), online tools and tips intended to convert spendthrifts into "cheapskates," just like her.

Take a lesson from Hunt and don't feel like you have to aim sky high from the get-go or spend a lot of money connecting with your audience, because you don't. At the outset, a straightforward, text-only e-mail newsletter will serve you and your readers just fine. I started my newsletter, "Writers on the Rise," this way four years ago, in order to keep in touch with my former students. Though I began with a mere 100 subscribers, today my newsletter is online with color photos, 15 contributors and two more editors—and is read by thousands monthly.

PLATFORM DEVELOPMENT 102: A BRANDED WEB SITE

A Web site is like the proverbial "shingle" you hang up so all the world can become familiar with who you are what you have to offer. But before you jump into Web site development, you need to clarify what the world needs to know about you. The key to a successful Web site isn't just what you do, since others could possibly do the same thing; the key is how you do it—because that's what people will remember. What good is your excellent reputation and expertise if no one knows about you or it?

Shy author, impressive brand

You must brand yourself before you build. Branding involves making an indelible mark or impression on someone—exactly what you want your Web site to do for you. Just because you can't touch a Web page doesn't mean its impact is ephemeral—especially when you infuse your site with weight and substance by branding it. Hope Clark is the queen of online branding. In fact, she purposely hides behind her brand, "FundsforWriters," because she's shy by nature. Clark says branding is her number one recommendation for those who want to avoid the pressure writers sometimes feel "to put on a dog and pony show." Instead of making herself do all the leg work, her site offers resources (books, e-books and newsletters) that help writers "find funds." With a subject matter like grants, contests and markets that only pay in cold, hard cash, what writer wouldn't be interested?

Brand yourself, here and now

If you haven't already branded yourself, now's the time. Don't panic. To start, answer the following questions:

1. How are your products or services distinguishable from the competition? (A book is a product, by the way.)
2. How are they better than the competition? (Emphasize this.)
3. How are they worse than the competition? (De-emphasize and address this.)
4. What emotional need(s) do your products or services satisfy? (Do not skip this one.)
5. What colors, images and font style might make sense for your identity? (These will aid with your logo design.)

Don't forget to stand out

Clark is not the only person in this line of business, by any means, but she sets herself apart by being accessible, down-to-earth and sympathetic to the challenges writers face. An agent recently commented on her ability to incorporate her knowledge into everything she does, which is shrewd advice for the rest of us. The cumulative results are the clarity of her brand, genuine helpfulness, and a lasting impression that stays with visitors long after they've traveled on down the e-road.

Tsssst. Hear that sound? That's your Web site making an impression on someone out in cyberspace while you're sleeping. Good, bad or indifferent impression—that's the measure of your brand.

PLATFORM DEVELOPMENT 103: BLOGGING

If you have gobs of free time on your hands, blogging is great. If you're a social butterfly who likes to update your blog and then go visit every blog online on the same topic on a regular basis while leaving a trail of comments for people to follow back to your blog, then even better. But blogs can be tricky to sustain if you're already a busy working writer with multiple deadlines and other priorities (including those small, frequently hungry people called children).

I suggest instead, you try what Seth Godin does—especially since he's the bestselling author of eight books on interactive marketing: Brand your blog with the identity of your book before, during and just after your book's release. Then, after the publicity period is over, move on to your next book project. When your next book comes out, start a new blog and repeat. Write book. Blog. Move on. You'll leave a trail of blogs behind for every new reader who stumbles upon your book in the future. They'll find all the supplemental information folks got when the book came out and, if you link your branded blogs to your branded mother-ship Web site, eventually your site will become the nucleus of your platform. Your blogs and newsletters will float around it like protons and electrons. When you get to this level, you can be pretty sure your platform is buzzing and not just online.

PLATFORM DEVELOPMENT 104: (CLASSES NEXT SEMESTER)

If you're already on a first-name basis with Oprah, Diane and Dave, then congratulations, you don't need to worry about Platform Development 101-103. But for the rest of us aspiring or professional writers, today is the day to get busy building a platform that will bring visibility, credibility and professional satisfaction to our literary career in the long run. If you want readers someday, begin developing your platform today.

Avenues to an Agent

Getting Your Foot in the Door

O nce your work is prepared and you have a solid understanding of how literary agents operate, the time is right to contact an agent. Your initial contact determines the agent's first impression of you, so you want to be professional and brief.

Again, research plays an important role in getting an agent's attention. You want to show the agent you've done your homework. Read the listings in this book to learn agents' areas of interest, check out agents' Web sites to learn more details on how they do business, and find out the names of some of their clients. If there is an author whose book is similar to yours, call the author's publisher. Someone in the contracts department can tell you the name of the agent who sold the title, provided an agent was used. Contact that agent, and impress her with your knowledge of the agency.

Finding an agent can often be as difficult as finding a publisher. Nevertheless, there are four ways to maximize your chances of finding the right agent: submit a query letter or proposal; obtain a referral from someone who knows the agent; meet the agent in person at a writers' conference; or attract the agent's attention with your own published writing.

SUBMISSIONS

The most common way to contact an agent is through a query letter or a proposal package. Most agents will accept unsolicited queries. Some will also look at outlines and sample chapters. Almost none want unsolicited complete manuscripts. Check the "How to Contact" subhead in each listing to learn exactly how an agent prefers to be solicited.

Agents agree to be listed in directories such as *Guide to Literary Agents* to indicate what they want to see and how they wish to receive submissions from writers. As you start to query agents, make sure you follow their individual submission directions. This, too, shows an agent you've done your research.

Like publishers, agencies have specialties. Some are only interested in novel-length works. Others are open to a variety of subjects and may actually have member agents within the company who specialize in only a handful of the topics covered by the entire agency.

Before querying any agent, first consult the Agent Specialties Indexes in the back of this book for your manuscript's subject, and identify those agents who handle what you write. Then, read the agents' listings to see which are appropriate for you and your work.

REFERRALS

The best way to get your foot in an agent's door is through a referral from one of her clients, an editor or another agent she has worked with in the past. Since agents trust their clients, they'll usually read referred work before over-the-transom submissions. If you are friends

Communication Etiquette

Via Mail
- Address the agent formally and make sure her name is spelled correctly.
- Double-check the agency's address.
- Include a SASE.
- Use a clear font and standard paragraph formatting.
- A short handwritten thank-you note can be appropriate if the agent helped you at a conference or if she provided editorial feedback along with your rejection.
- Don't include any extraneous materials.
- Don't try to set yourself apart by using fancy stationary. Standard paper and envelopes are preferable.

Via E-mail
- Address the agent as you would in a paper letter—be formal.
- If it's not listed on the Web site, call the company to get the appropriate agent's e-mail address.
- Include a meaningful subject line.
- Keep your emotions in check: Resist the temptation to send an angry response after being rejected, or to send a long, mushy note after being accepted. Keep your e-mails businesslike.
- Don't type in all caps or all lower case. Use proper punctuation and pay attention to grammar and spelling.
- Don't overuse humor—it can be easily misinterpreted.
- Don't e-mail about trivial things.

On the Phone
- Be polite: Ask if she has time to talk, or set up a time to call in advance.
- Get over your "phone phobia." Practice your conversation beforehand if necessary.
- Resist the urge to follow up with an agent too quickly. Give her time to review your material.
- Never make your first contact over the phone unless the agent calls you first or requests you do so in her submission guidelines.
- Don't demand information from her immediately. Your phone call is interrupting her busy day and she should be given time to respond to your needs.
- Don't call to get information you could otherwise obtain from the Internet or other resources.
- Don't have your spouse, secretary, best friend or parent call for you.

In Person
- Be clear and concise.
- Shake the agent's hand and greet her with your name.
- Be yourself, but be professional.
- Maintain eye contact.
- Don't monopolize her time. Either ask a brief question or ask if you can contact her later (via phone/mail/e-mail) with a more in-depth question.
- Don't get too nervous—agents are human!

Contacting Agents

with anyone in the publishing business who has connections with agents, ask politely for a referral. However, don't be offended if another writer will not share the name of his agent.

CONFERENCES

Going to a conference is your best bet for meeting an agent in person. Many conferences invite agents to give a speech or simply be available for meetings with authors, and agents view conferences as a way to find writers. Often agents set aside time for one-on-one discussions with writers, and occasionally they may even look at material writers bring to the conference. These critiques may cost an extra fee, but if an agent is impressed with you and your work, she'll ask to see writing samples after the conference. When you send your query, be sure to mention the specific conference where you met and that she asked to see your work.

When you're face to face with an agent, it's an important time to be friendly, prepared and professional. Always wait for the agent to invite you to send work to them. Saying "I'll send it to your office tomorrow" before they've offered to read it comes off wrong. Don't bring sample chapters or a copy of your manuscript unless you've got a professional critique arranged beforehand. Agents will almost never take writers' work home (they don't have the suitcase space), and writers nervously asking agents to take a look at their work and provide some advice could be considered gauche.

Remember, at these conferences, agents' time is very valuable—as is yours. If you discover that agent who's high on your list recently stopped handling your genre, don't hunt her down and try to convince her to take it on again. Thank the agent for her time and move on to your next target.

If you plan to pitch agents, practice your speech—and make sure you have a pitch that clocks in at less than one minute. Also have versions of your pitch for 2-minute pitches and 3-minute pitches, depending on the conference. Keep your in-person pitch simple and exciting—letting the agent become interested and ask the follow-up questions.

Because this is an effective way to connect with agents, we've asked agents to indicate in their listings which conferences they regularly attend. We've also included a section of Conferences, starting on page 253, where you can find more information about a particular event.

PUBLISHING CREDITS

Some agents read magazines or journals to find writers to represent. If you have had an outstanding piece published in a periodical, an agent wanting to represent you may make contact. In such cases, make sure the agent has read your work. Some agents send form letters to writers, and such representatives often make their living entirely from charging reading fees and not from commissions on sales.

However, many reputable and respected agents do contact potential clients in this way. For them, you already possess attributes of a good client: You have publishing credits and an editor has validated your work. To receive a letter from a reputable agent who has read your material and wants to represent you is an honor.

Occasionally, writers who have self-published or who have had their work published electronically may attract an agent's attention, especially if the self-published book has sold well or received a lot of positive reviews.

Recently, writers have been posting their work on the Internet with the hope of attracting an agent's eye. With all the submissions most agents receive, they probably have little time to peruse writers' Web sites. Nevertheless, there are agents who do consider the Internet a resource for finding fresh voices.

A Perfect Pitch

Selling Your Story with a Carefully Composed Query

by Daniel Lazar

You've written your novel, and it's brilliant. It's a magnum opus. It's going to change the world. Congratulations! Writing your novel for the past 47 years was the easy part. Get ready to start pitching to literary agents.

There are many ways to get your manuscript into the hands of an agent. But only one method works every time. (Well, two. The first method is: be a celebrity. If you're not, shucks. Don't worry.) The surefire way of tempting a literary agent into reading your work is by sending them a fabulous query letter. Note how this method doesn't involve calling an agent. It also doesn't involve a referral. True—look through the listings in this guide, and you'll see that most agents take on the majority of their work by referral. For most agents, the referral percentage is more than 90%. That's because good writers travel in packs. So the more time an agent spends in business, the more his talented clients refer their talented friends. But here's the key: A referral will get your work read faster, but it *won't* get it signed. My uncle recently asked me to look at his accountant's manuscript—a collection of accounting tales. Hmm. Did that writer's work get requested and read quickly? You bet. I like my uncle. Did that writer's work get signed by this agent? No.

A great query letter trumps all, every time. But how, you're wondering, can you possibly encapsulate your amazing manuscript—your sweat and tears, your next Great American (if you're Canadian, then your next Great North American) novel—into one letter? Just remember, at the end of the day, it all comes down to the writing. If you're a great writer who's written a great novel, you can write a great query letter. Period.

Before you even start the letter, it's important to research. Many agents are based in New York, but successful and reputable agents are located all over the world. (All an agent needs to operate is a phone, computer and the ability to calculate 15% in his sleep.) There's no license or official accreditation for literary agents, though many belong to the AAR (www.aar-online.org)—or if they're starting out, belong to an agency that's accredited by the AAR. The guide you're holding is a good start to finding a reputable representative; Web sites such as PublishersMarketplace.com are good too. Be wary of any random Web site that isn't updated regularly. Also, legitimate agents do *not* charge up front fees. If you submit your work to agent who requires a nebulous processing or reading fee, you're being scammed. Run, don't walk, the other way.

A pitch letter is like a business letter in some ways: It must look clean and professional,

DANIEL LAZAR is an agent at Writers House. His specialties include commercial and literary fiction, pop culture, narrative nonfiction, women's interest, memoirs, Judaica and humor.

with standard font and margins. (It doesn't matter if you use Times New Roman or Courier New, 1.5-inch margins or 1-inch—just make it look neat.) No pink paper. No flowery graphics. You don't need an inkwell cartoon—the agent knows you're a writer, don't worry.

But unlike a business letter, the best query letters have a voice and personality that pops off the page, especially for fiction. Here's yet another little secret: Even if a writer can't immediately nail down the plot, a voice will save the day. (By the way, a voice doesn't mean you should write the letter in your character's voice: "Hi! I'm Sally, the star of my writer's novel . . ." That's a gimmick; it doesn't work.)

So you've done your research and you're ready to write the letter. The basic rules are these:

The salutation: Dear [Agent's Name]

Make sure you have the correct spelling of the name and the agency. (For example, Writers House is not spelled Writer's. I would never reject a letter because of that, but such a mistake does register.) "Dear Sir/Madam" or "Dear Agent" is an automatic rejection.

First paragraph

Compose a familiar opening that explains why you're contacting the specific agent, then introduce the title of your project. "Familiar" can mean several things:

- "I met you at a XYZ Writers' Conference."
- "Our mutual friend, John Smith, suggested I contact you."
- Or best of all: "I read your author's book, and I love it. I'm hoping you'll love mine too." Try a variation on that.
- If the agent represents a big name bestseller, but also some smaller literary writers, go for the gold by acknowledging their work for [big blockbuster author] but "especially for your work on [smaller literary author]." Chances are, that smaller author required more passion and persistence, and the agent will love to hear that. And if you haven't actually read the books, go to the bookstore, read the first 10 pages, and lie. (If that agent signs you, though, be sure to go buy the books and read them *fast*.)

It's also helpful to include genre or category here. Memoir? Mystery? Romance? If you're writing in a specific genre, it should be fairly obvious already. But if you can't pin down your exact genre, *don't worry*. Some authors sweat so badly to pigeonhole their book and only end up with: "My novel is women's fiction/suspense/multicultural/ . . ." The agent is already asleep. Just call it "a novel." Onward!

Second paragraph

Here's where you include the pitch, summarizing the novel. Start by introducing your main character(s) with a sentence or two about the details that sum them up and make them unique. Then, launch into the story itself. The big trap here to avoid is being generic. Be specific. Details, details, details. That doesn't mean you should turn your pitch into a synopsis—a play-by-play of the entire story. What you should do is pick a small detail—something specific and visceral—and use it. Instead of saying "Jane Smith is tall, blonde and pretty," try something less cliché, such as: "Jane Smith turned heads wherever she went; she hadn't paid for a drink since high school."

It's also important here to nail down some kind of central conflict. Again, try to avoid generic descriptions. A main character "finding himself" is too generic. Generic = boring. Every character goes through internal changes in a novel; that goes without saying. Saying "my novel is exciting" or "is full of passion and suspense" is also too generic. You're telling, not showing. The central conflict is usually some kind of external conflict, goal or mission that your main character(s) have to work though. There's usually an interpersonal relationship at stake as well, (that you should mention), which in itself will imply a character changes. In short, show why your future reader will *care* about your character.

Third paragraph

On to your favorite subject! You. First, tell the agent about your writing history. Have you published stories or essays? Do you write a column? A notable blog? Don't be shy. If you speak regularly in front of large audiences, host your local news or are related to Oprah, now's the time to spill. If you don't have any writing credits, it's not the end of the world. Remember, you're such a good writer that the agent would love to read even your grocery list. So use this space to tell the agent something interesting and eloquent about yourself. Skip "I've always dreamed of being a writer." Congratulations—who hasn't? Try something more unique about yourself—whether it's a personal connection to your novel or a funny visual about your spouse cooking dinner while you wrote all last year. Anything.

This is just a basic framework. If your pitch needs two paragraphs, don't worry. No one will get arrested. As a rule of thumb, just try to keep the query to one page. Again, here are some tips of mistakes to avoid:

• **Be specific,** but don't vomit information. Saying "My novel is about a mom going through some life challenges" is vague. And remember: Vague = boring. However, be careful not to stuff your letter with so many plot details that it's confusing to decipher what's going on. Reading your pitch letter out loud can often help you identify these flaws.

• **Avoid the "duh" trap.** Don't bog down your writing by overstating the obvious. For example: "I'm writing this letter to tell you about my fictional novel, which I'd like to send

Contacting Agents

The In-Person Pitch

Besides pitching an agent with a query letter, you may also have an opportunity to speak with an agent face-to-face at a writers' conference. Although not surefire, some authors find agents like this, and you should take advantage of the chance if it comes your way. If you decide to pitch your project at a conference, prepare. Check out some of the books the agent you're meeting with represents (or their company represents). If you can't find any sales by that agent, perhaps you should reconsider the meeting.

Once you're sitting across, introduce yourself by saying "I loved your book, [title]" and watch that agent's eyes light up. When you talk about your own book, don't try to cram every plot point into two minutes. A great pitch introduces a character first—with some specific, visceral image—and then briefly touches on the main conflict. "Brief" is the key word here; instead of mowing down the agent with a long description until their eyes glaze over, let them become intrigued; let them ask questions. Ultimately, remember that it's impossible to transmit the magic of your writing in a conversation. It all comes down to what's on the page. All you can do is rehearse your speech, practice answering questions and not get too nervous during the meeting.

For an agent, a conference is a numbers game. She can meet 100 writers at a conference, sign one or 10 or none; or sit in her office, read 100 query letters, and sign one or 10 or none.

you, and it is called [title]." That's an awkward sentence. A simple "I'd love to send you my novel, [title]" is short and sweet. If this is confusing, read both out loud. Seriously. Try it. Reading your own words out loud can sometimes reveal the awkward or run-on sentences.

• **Another "duh" trap would be:** "My novel will make you laugh," or "My writing is lush and literary." You're begging the agent to disagree. Many writers say "My novel will be a bestseller," or "My book could easily be made into film," in an effort to excite an agent. But truthfully, this is borderline offensive—it's presumptuous and naïve to assume your work can easily bypass all the guardians and hard work it takes to make book into a bestseller or a movie.

• **Don't call your manuscript a "fiction novel."** There's no other kind. If you don't know that, it's a problem.

• **Don't say other readers loved the book,** unless those other readers are published authors of note. If you're writing a children's book, saying your students loved the book is equally unhelpful.

Many agents now accept e-mail queries, so here are several tips:

• **Make sure the agent accepts them.** Just because his e-mail is listed somewhere, doesn't mean that agent wants e-queries. Most agents now have Web sites; check their submission guidelines. If you're not sure, send your query by snail mail.

• **E-mail must also look neat.** Colorful border, graphics or emoticons are not only unprofessional, they're often caught by spam blockers. And if the agent requests your work by e-mail, send it in one or two attachments. Not 20.

A thousand other questions may be running through your head now—but what we've gone over are the important and necessary basics. For all else, use your common sense. Courier New versus Times New Roman? One-inch margin versus 1.25? Doesn't matter, trust me. Just write a great letter—you'll hear back. Now, get to it!

Crafting a Query

Writing the Best Possible Letter

The query letter is the catalyst in the chemical reaction of publishing. Overall, writing a query letter is a fairly simple process that serves one purpose—getting an agent or editor to read your manuscript. A query letter is the tool that sells you and your book using brief, attention-getting words. Fiction and nonfiction query letters share the same basic elements, but there are differences you should consider for each category.

FICTION QUERIES

Here's a general rule of thumb when querying an agent for a fiction manuscript: Do not contact the agent regarding your novel until the entire manuscript is written and ready to be sent. A query letter for a work of fiction generally contains the following elements.

- **The hook.** Your first paragraph should be written to hook the agent and get her to request a few chapters or the whole manuscript. The hook is usually a special plot detail or a unique element that's going to grab the agent's attention.
- **About the book.** It is important to provide the agent with the technical statistics of your book: title, genre and word count. An easy way to estimate your manuscript's word count is to multiply the number of manuscript pages by 250 and then round that number to the nearest ten thousand.
- **The story.** This is the part of your letter where you provide a summary of your plot, introduce your main characters and hint at the main conflict that drives the story. Be careful not to go overboard here, either in content or in length. Only provide the agent with the basic elements she needs to make a decision about your manuscript.
- **The audience.** You must be able to tell the agent who the intended audience is for your novel. Many writers find it helpful to tell the agent the theme of their novel, which then signifies the intended audience and to whom the novel will appeal.
- **About you.** Tell the agent who you are and how you came to write your novel. In this paragraph, you should only provide those qualifications that are relevant to your novel. List any special qualities you have for writing a novel in your genre. Also, list any writing groups to which you belong, publishing credentials, awards won, etc. Remember, though, if you don't have any of the above, don't stress your inexperience or dwell on what you haven't accomplished.
- **The closing.** Make sure you end your query on a positive note. You should thank the agent for her time and offer to send more information (a synopsis, sample chapters or the complete manuscript), upon request. Be sure to also mention that you've enclosed a self-addressed, stamped envelope (SASE) for the agent's convenience.

NONFICTION QUERIES

Unlike fiction manuscripts, it is acceptable to query an agent about a nonfiction book before the manuscript is complete. The following seven elements should be included in a nonfiction query.

● **The hook.** The hook is usually a special detail or a unique element that's going to grab the agent's attention and pull her in. Oftentimes, nonfiction writers use statistics or survey results, especially if the results are astounding or unique, to reel in the agent.

● **The referral.** Why are you contacting this particular agent? A recommendation from an author she currently represents, an acknowledgment in a book they have represented, or because the agent has a strong track record of selling books on the subject about which you're writing? No matter the answer, knowing what type of work the agent represents shows her that you're a professional.

● **About the book.** It is important to provide the agent with the technical statistics of your book, including the title and sales handle—a short, one-line statement explaining the primary goal of your book. In his book *How to Write a Book Proposal,* 3rd Edition (Writer's Digest Books), agent Michael Larsen says that a book's handle "may be its thematic or stylistic resemblance to one or two successful books or authors." One example Larsen uses to further explain a sales handle is "*Fast Food Nation* meets fashion." Essentially, the handle helps the agent decide whether your book is a project she can sell.

● **Markets.** Tell the agent who will buy your book (i.e., the audience) and where people will buy it. Research potential markets according to various demographics (including age, gender, income, profession, etc.), and then use the information to find solid figures that verify your book's audience is significant enough to warrant publication. The more you know about the potential markets for your book (usually the top three or four markets), the more professional you appear to the agent.

● **About you.** Tell the agent who you are and why you are the best person to write this book. In this paragraph, you should only provide qualifications that are relevant to your book, including career and academic background and publication credentials (as they relate to the subject of your book).

Mistakes to Avoid

- Don't use any cute attention-getting devices like colored stationery or odd fonts.

- Don't send any unnecessary enclosures, such as a picture of you or your family pet.

- Don't waste time telling the agent you're writing to her in the hopes that she will represent your book. Get immediately to the heart of the matter—your book.

- Don't try to "sell" the agent by telling her how great your book is or comparing it to those written by best-selling authors.

- Don't mention that your family, friends or "readers" love it.

- Don't send sample chapters that are not consecutive chapters.

• **The closing.** Make sure you end your query on a positive note. Thank the agent for her time and tell her what items you have ready to submit (proposal, sample chapters, complete manuscript, etc.) upon request. Also mention that you've enclosed a self-addressed, stamped envelope (SASE) for the agent's convenience.

FORMATTING YOUR QUERY

There are no hard-and-fast rules when it comes to formatting your query letter, but there are some widely accepted guidelines like those listed below, adapted from *Formatting & Submitting Your Manuscript*, by Jack and Glenda Neff, and Don Prues (Writer's Digest Books).

- Use a standard font or typeface (avoid bold, script or italics, except for publication titles), like 12-point Times New Roman.
- Your name, address and phone number (plus e-mail and fax, if possible) should appear in the top right corner or on your letterhead. If you would like, you can create your own letterhead so you appear professional. Simply type the same information mentioned above, center it at the top of the page and photocopy it on quality paper.
- Use a 1-inch margin on all sides.
- Address the query to a specific agent, preferably the one who handles the type of work you're writing.
- Keep it to one page.
- Include a SASE or postcard for reply, and state in the letter you have done so (preferably in your closing paragraph).
- Use block format (no indentations or extra space between paragraphs).
- Single-space the body of the letter and double-space between paragraphs.
- Thank the agent for considering your query letter.

Bad Fiction Query

The author's phone number and e-mail address are missing—include all pertinent contact information.

Always address your query to a specific agent.

Do not query an agent if your fiction manuscript is not finished and fully revised.

Don't ask an agent for advice or criticism—that's not the agent's job nor the purpose of the query.

Never mention that this is the first book you've written—it singles you out as an amateur. While it's good to have publishing credits or professional expertise, they're only worth mentioning if they are relevant to the book being proposed.

This is vague and has no "hook" to capture the agent's attention. What will make it different from other romance novels?

Vincent Barnes
1302 Amateur Road
Sheboygan, WI 53081

May 1, 2007

General Agents, Inc.
10 Anywhere Drive
Detroit, MI 48215

Dear Sir/Madam,

I'm about to finish my novel and wanted to give you a heads up because I know I'll need an agent to help sell it. Please take a look at the enclosed sample chapters and let me know if you think publishers will like my book.

This is my first time writing a romance novel, but I've had a couple science articles published in online magazines. I worked in a hospital laboratory for 15 years and thought it would be fun to trade in all those cold hard facts for a good old-fashioned love story.

My novel—titled *Many Miles of Love*—is about a shy midwestern girl named Lauren who falls in love with Ray, a boisterous salesman from Baltimore. The couple goes through many highs and lows together, including being separated from one another several times due to circumstances beyond their control. In the end, of course, they are able to come together and make a happy life for themselves.

The book will probably end up around 70,000 words and will be read mostly by women. I've already had a variety of family members look over the beginning chapters, and all of them are curious to know what happens next.

I put in an application with the U.S. Copyright Office last week. I've also been doing some research on how much authors get paid for novels these days. When you respond, please include any information on possible advances and royalties for my book.

Many thanks,

Vincent Barnes

You should describe your potential audience more specifically than just men or women. Also, mentioning that your family likes the book will get you nowhere. You would be better served to point out if it has been read/critiqued by a few local writing groups.

Don't mention copyright information or payment expectations. This is simply a query to assess an agent's interest in your novel.

Good Fiction Query

Brent Thompson
62 Fiction Drive
Naples, FL 34104
(630)555-6009
brent.thompson@email.com

February 27, 2007

Mr. Alexander Diaz
The Best Literary Agency
546 Representative Blvd.
New York, NY 10001

Address your query to a specific agent.

Dear Mr. Diaz,

Say why you have chosen to query this particular agent.

I heard you speak at the Southwestern Florida Writer's Conference last month, where you mentioned an interest in seeing more young adult fiction submissions filled with both adventure and heart. I have just the story for you—a 60,000-word novel geared toward preteen and teenage boys entitled *The Mysterious Map*.

Always state your novel's genre, title and word count.

The book opens in the North Carolina countryside, where 15-year-old Rowan Hampton has discovered a secret map. He's certain it will lead to treasure, but he and his best friend Karl soon realize the clues are of a more personal nature. As they move from town to town, Rowan begins to question details of his childhood that now seem unclear. What really happened to his younger sister? Can he trust everything his parents say? Who left him this map, and where will it lead?

Briefly tell what the novel is about.

Provide relevant background information about yourself, including professional experience, publishing credentials, etc.

I'm a native of the Carolinas, where I taught middle-school English for 35 years. While I was teaching, a few chapters of Rowan's journey were published in the *Lowland's Literary Journal*. After retiring last year, I dedicated myself to completing the novel.

My manuscript is ready to be sent at your request.

I look forward to hearing from you.

Sincerely,

Brent Thompson

Bad Nonfiction Query

The author's address and phone number are missing—include all pertinent contact information.

Always address your query to the agent's full name, even if you've seen it shortened elsewhere. It's professional to make a formal first impression.

Questions can prove to be an interesting way to "hook" an agent, but don't be too vague. Ask a question nobody is asking—one that shows why your book is unique.

Only send these materials if requested in the agent's submission guidelines. Also, don't bother telling an agent what your friends think; show the agent why the book must be published and must be written by you.

Try to include a few main points that differentiate your book from others on the market. Also, make sure you are enough of an expert to provide this information to potentially thousands of readers.

Juanita Nielson
Kansas City, MO
badwriter@email.com

March 30, 2007

Charles Mortenson
Agent & Agent Representatives
39 W. Main St.
Boston, MA 02209

Dear Chuck,

Did you know there are actually six branches—or types—of yoga that people can practice? Did you know that chanting the word "Om" stems from the scientific theory that the universe is constantly in motion?

For more enlightening information on yoga, please look over my outline and sample chapters and let me know if you think this book will interest publishers. I have already shared my idea with a few friends and they all agree I would be great at writing this book.

I've been taking yoga classes on and off for several years now, and they have really helped me get through some tough times. I want to write a book about yoga so other people can see the benefits of it. I have never attempted to write a book before, but I've been taking some local college courses and even attended a writer's conference last year.

Yoga has been such a big trend lately that there are probably lots of interested readers out there. I know other books about yoga have already been published, but mine will be more personal and geared toward people who don't know much about the physical and spiritual practice.

I've been a stay-at-home mom for the past 8 years, and think this book can signify a new direction for my life. Hopefully with your help selling and an editor's help revising, this book can land on the bestseller list.

Thanks for your time,

Juanita Nielson

Don't pitch an idea based on a trend because trends eventually fade. Make sure you have a deep grasp on who your target readers will be, and make sure you will actually be able to reach them if they aren't already reading books on your topic.

Don't point out your (or the book's) shortcomings. If it needs editorial help, get some before you send it to an agent.

Good Nonfiction Query

Contacting Agents

Gayle Matthews
1999 Published Way
Durham, CA 95938
(773)555-6868
gmatthews@email.com

July 30, 2006

Lynn Kobayashi
Kobayashi & Brown, Inc.
55 Acceptance St. NW
Seattle, WA 98101

Always address a specific agent.

Dear Ms. Kobayashi,

The hook: Provide concrete information and indisputable reasoning for why your book fills a void in the market. Explain how your target audience fits into the proposal.

California, Washington and Oregon have long been the wine centers of the United States, but they are far from being the only places people can learn about and enjoy the vineyard culture. Nearly every state in the country—including Alaska—has a winery, and many of them are producing quality, affordable products. Recent research shows that wine is the favored alcoholic drink among Americans, and that almost all who drink it regularly are purchasing American wines. However, many do not have the time or money to travel all the way to the West Coast to do tours and tastings.

Explain a few details about the book, as well as why you are querying this particular agent.

Your Web site states you specialize in travel writing, so I'd like to propose a series of guidebooks that take people on tours of local vineyards. The books would be categorized by region (Northeast, Mid-Atlantic, Southeast, Midwestern, etc.) and would focus on the best wineries to visit in each neighboring state. Not only would each entry provide specific travel details, but information on the vineyard's history, specialties and overall atmosphere would also be included. There would also be a tremendous opportunity for beautiful photography and detailed maps.

If possible, talk about your book from a sales perspective.

Since no other travel books about wine have been broken down in this manner, there are multiple sales opportunities. Aside from national bookstores, the guidebooks could be marketed in vineyards, wine shops, tourism bureaus and local specialty stores in each region.

Provide professional background information relevant to the writing of this book.

I have been a professor of Viticulture and Enology for the past 12 years and help organize an annual conference with other wine professionals to discuss industry trends. I have a deep love for both wine and travel, and have already visited more than 100 wineries across the country. I also write a syndicated newspaper column about wine and have contributed to both consumer and trade magazines on the topics of travel and vineyards.

Show you've followed the agent's submission guidelines and make a polite offer.

Enclosed are a detailed outline, professional bio and three sample chapters. I would be glad to go over more specifics of my proposal at your convenience.

Sincerely,

Gayle Matthews

Synopsis Workshop

Summing Up Your Novel

by Ian Bessler

A punchy, carefully composed query letter is only the first step to getting an agent's attention. Once you receive word back from that agent expressing interest, she will likely request more materials to gauge your writing prowess. These materials I speak of involve a portion of the work—sample chapters or a specific number of pages—as well as a synopsis. (Some agents will request these additional materials right off the bat whereas others will want to see a query before anything else; read agents' preferences before submitting.)

Whereas nonfiction writers will craft an outline at this stage as part of a proposal, fiction writers need to compose a stellar synopsis, summing up their work. Your goal when selling a novel manuscript is to show the characters, the flow of events and how these events are propelled forward by the conflict. A novel synopsis, therefore, is a condensed narrative version of your story from beginning to end that, ideally, reads like your novel, conveys a similar style of writing and sells your work by grabbing the reader's attention much like a full-scale manuscript.

The synopsis is a useful means for both the writer and the agent to ''step back'' from the finished manuscript and look at the larger outlines of structure and plot.

THE SYNOPSIS

A well-written synopsis is an important tool when marketing your novel, and many agents and editors will use it to judge your ability to tell a story. The synopsis is a condensed narrative version of the novel that should hook the editor or agent by showcasing the central conflict of the book and the interlocking chain of events set off by that conflict. It should incorporate every chapter of your book, and distill every main event, character and plot twist. A synopsis must highlight the element of human drama and emotion that explains *why* your characters took their particular path. When crafting your synopsis, these pointers form a set of guidelines to lead you through the process of condensing your manuscript:

• **Format:** Type a heading in the upper left-hand corner of the first page, featuring the title of your novel, the genre, an estimated word count for the full manuscript and your name. At the end of the synopsis, type out ''THE END'' to signify the conclusion of the story.

• **Stay present:** Write the synopsis in the present tense and third-person point of view. Even if your novel is written in first person, use third person for the synopsis. This allows for consistency and ease in summarizing. Such a summary will also help when an agent pitches the work to an editor.

• **Don't hold back:** Tell the entire story, including the ending. Do not tease—tell who

---

IAN BESSLER is the editor of *Songwriter's Market*.

lives, who dies, who did it and so on. At this stage of the query process, the agent or editor has already been hooked by your brilliant query letter with the clever teaser, and now they want an overview of the entire project, so don't leave anything out.

• **Hook:** Start with a hook detailing your primary character and the main conflict of the novel. Give any pertinent information about the lead character, such as age, career, marital status, etc., and describe how that character manifests or is drawn into the primary conflict.

• **Spotlight:** The first time you introduce a character, spotlight that character by capitalizing his name. If possible, weave the character's initial description into the flow of the text, but don't stray from the narrative with a lengthy or overly-detailed character sketch.

• **Condense:** Don't defeat the purpose of the synopsis by letting it run too long. A workable rule of thumb for calculating the length of the synopsis is to condense every 25 pages of your novel synopsis down to 1 page. If you follow this formula for a 200-page novel manuscript, you should wind up with 8 pages or fewer. This formula is not set in stone, however, since some agents like to see even more compression and will frequently ask for a two-page synopsis to represent an entire novel. If in doubt, ask the agent what length she prefers, and tailor your synopsis to her requirement.

• **Cut out the fat:** Be concise. Include only details of the action essential to the story, and excise excessive adjectives and adverbs. Dialogue is rarely used, but at the same time don't be afraid to feature pivotal quotes, descriptive gems or a crucial scene when you know it will enhance the impact of your synopsis at critical points.

• **Retell:** Work from your manuscript chapter by chapter, and briefly retell the events of each chapter. You should tell one complete account of your book, although you may use paragraphs to represent chapters or sections. Whenever possible, use a style reflecting the tone of the actual novel—if the novel is dark and moody in tone, then a dark and moody tone is called for in the synopsis.

• **Be seamless:** Do not intrude in the narrative flow with authorial commentary, and do not let the underlying story framework show in your synopsis. Don't use headings such as "Setting" or phrases like "At the climax of the conflict . . ." or "The next chapter begins with . . ." In short, do not let it read like a nonfiction outline. Your goal is to entrance the agent or editor with the story itself and not to break the spell by allowing the supporting scaffolding to show. These elements should already be self-evident and woven into the narrative. You should also avoid reviewing your own story; the agent or the editor will make her own judgment. Your work should speak for itself.

The example synopsis on page 44 condenses an entire novel in one page. This is an extreme example of compression as noted above but a demonstration of the principles involved.

A FEW LAST BITS

Other tips to consider:

- Include two SASEs with your submission: a #10 business-size SASE for reply and a larger SASE big enough to hold your manuscript, along with enough postage for its return
- Be sure your crucial materials are either laser-printed or neatly typed on clean paper sufficiently strong to stand up to handling (do not use erasable bond or onionskin). Also, put a blank piece of paper at the end of the manuscript to protect the last page.
- Be sure to use proper manuscript format (one-inch margins on all four sides of the page, double-spaced, one-sided and left-justified only).

Not all agents or editors have boiled down an explicit set of nuts-and-bolts guidelines, but the methods outlined in this article will provide you with a repeatable set of steps for framing your ideas with clarity and precision.

Formatting Your Synopsis

Type your real name
(not a pseudonym if
you are using one).

Your novel's genre.

Double space twice.

Type your name (or
pseudonym if you
are using one).

Indent first
paragraph and
start text of
synopsis.

Use headers
as shown.

Your name   Science Fiction
Street address
City, State ZIP code
Phone numbers
E-mail address
Web site

OBELISK

by

Maxwell Parker

    ARCAS KANE, newly minted agent for the Imperial
Galactic Security Apparatus, is eager for promotion within the
ranks. Security Apparatus Director DELSIN HISTER, leader of
an Imperial faction hostile to the current ruler, sees Kane's
ambitions and picks the young man for a mission on the fringe
of the galaxy, where archaeologists make a startling discovery.

    Buried in the sands of a sparsely populated desert world they
find artifacts from times beyond the reckoning of even the oldest
histories of the Imperium. The artifacts include obsidian obelisks,

Parker/OBELISK/Synopsis2

perfectly preserved and carved with glyphs and signs. Using bits
of lore preserved by the desert planet's nonhuman natives, the scientists decipher part of the message and send news of their discovery.

    Kane arrives with the crew of a supply ship and finds the
archaeologists murdered, the artifacts destroyed. He searches
through bits of surviving scientific data. The obelisks describe a
planet, the mythical home system of the human race. The obelisks
tell of the abandonment of the home world and the wamdering of
the human race. They also refer to an ancient doomsday weapon,
the source of the destruction.

Professional Proposals

Launching a Winning Nonfiction Proposal

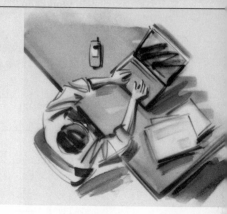

by Elizabeth Lyon

First-time authors write most published books, and 75 percent of all new books each year are nonfiction. Put those facts together and you get this: Writing a nonfiction book is one of the best ways to break into publishing. If this isn't enough good news, consider the fact that you won't have to write the whole book until you have a contract. Instead of writing a complete manuscript, you'll need to create a compelling book proposal that answers the seven questions agents and editors consider as they decide whether or not to request your proposal.

Below is an explanation of the sections of a standard proposal (check specific agent and publisher Web sites for variations), followed by the seven critical questions. Study them well.

PARTS OF A PROPOSAL

A complete proposal may have as many as a dozen sections plus a title page and table of contents. These sections are as follows:

Concept Statement: The concept statement is your hook—a sizzling summary of your book in 250 words or fewer that stirs excitement. It describes your subject, including how it's unique and timely. It states the primary way your book will benefit the reader, briefly gives your name and qualifications, and describes your potential audience. The concept statement may allude to your competition, indicate your promotional prowess and/or list some of the features particular to your book. It ends on a note that makes literary agents and editors sit up and salivate over a book they feel compelled to shepherd into print.

About the Book: While the concept statement starts your sales presentation, this section elaborates on your book's subject, purpose, timeliness, uniqueness and benefit to the reader—supporting your statements with facts, figures and quotes by authorities.

About the Author: Not a résumé, this section touts your authority to write on your proposed subject and toots that horn about your prior accomplishments—including any awards or honors in your field or related to your book. Publication of books or magazine articles help, as does prior experience as a public speaker or workshop leader. If your proposed book is a memoir, develop how you came to write this book and emphasize any published essays on the subject/theme of your text.

ELIZABETH LYON has worked as an independent book editor, writing teacher, speaker, and workshop presenter for more than 20 years. Her bestselling books for writers include *Nonfiction Book Proposals Anybody Can Write*, *The Sell Your Novel Tool Kit*, *A Writer's Guide to Nonfiction*, *A Writer's Guide to Fiction*, *National Directory of Editors & Writers* and *Revise, Polish, Sell Your Fiction*. A book on editing and revising nonfiction is forthcoming. Her articles and essays have appeared in magazines, anthologies, and Web resources. She can be reached at www.elizabethlyon.com.

Preparing Your Proposal

DO type on one side of 8 1/2 x 11, 20-pound bond paper.

DO number pages consecutively, not by section or chapter.

DO use a standard 12-point typeface (printers like Times New Roman).

DO type 25, 10-word, 60-character lines—about 250 words on a page.

DO double-space your proposal (including quotes and anecdotes).

DON'T add extra spaces between paragraphs.

DON'T justify the right margin.

DON'T leave "widows"— a subhead at the bottom of a page, or the last line of a chapter at the top.

3

ABOUT THE BOOK

On the day she learned that she had cancer, Carolyn Scott Kortge put on her walking shoes and headed to a nearby park. She climbed the slopes of a rural hillside fighting back despair and fear with a cadence of words and steps. "One-step-for-ward at a time, one step for-ward as I climb." She chanted the words mentally. One step per syllable. One foot at a time. Over and over, fear broke through her focus, pushing questions and doubts into her mind. "Why me? Why now? What did I do wrong?" Over and over, she blocked the barrage and returned to the reassuring cadence of a chant that blocked the questions for a moment.

For thirty minutes she sustained the mental struggle, rebuffing terror with a mantra that moved with her up the hill. "One-step-for-ward-at-a-time, one-step-for-ward-as-I-climb." In the clarity of a silent moment between a breath and a waiting thought, she realized a path through the months ahead. In a miraculous moment, she was able to shift from guilt to action—a transition from looking back to looking forward.

The *real* miracle, Kortge reveals in *Healing Walks for Hard Times: An 8-Week Program*, lies in the healing elixir of breath and circulation. Walking releases the restorative power of movement and oxygen, enhancing resourcefulness, balance, and clarity when disaster knocks us to our knees. Tens of thousands of people encounter the jolt of such life-changing moments.

AUTHOR PLATFORM

Planned Sequels (optional): If you envision a sequel, it can add interest to what you propose by telling prospective publishers what future books they can expect. More books = a more recognized author = more sales.

About the Market: Your market is your readers. What sociological particulars—age, income, gender, race, interests—describe your primary and secondary audiences? Can you find statistics to substantiate the size of your readership or prove how that audience is growing? List any special venues or outlets where your book might be sold. Possible special venues include college course adoptions, book clubs (name them), foreign countries for translation publication, museums, church bookstores and so forth.

About the Competition: Look for books similar to yours by using every conceivable synonym while searching at www.amazon.com. Scour local bookstores as well. In this section, provide bibliographic information for these competitive books: title, author, publisher, edition, date, number of pages, hardback or softback, and retail price. Omit books published more than five years ago, unless they have been reprinted or are known classics in your subject area. In one paragraph, describe the contents, breadth, slant or style of each book in turn. In a second paragraph, specifically describe the similarities and differences between your book and the one you profiled. Repeat this pattern for all comparable books.

Production Details: This section lists your book's organization, including the following details:

- estimated length
- how soon you can deliver the finished manuscript (e.g., six months after contract signing)
- front matter (foreword, preface, introduction, maps, etc.)
- back matter (resource directory, annotated bibliography, glossary index, etc.)
- authorities or recognized people from whom you'll seek cover testimonials, endorsements or a foreword
- a list and description of your book's necessary artwork and/or photography
- a list of how many sidebars you envision
- any other considerations that would affect your book's production

About Promotion: Agents and editors want to know how you can promote your book using your own resources and time. Develop three to six pages of a marketing plan that includes what you can accomplish. Indicate what magazines, journals, newspapers and e-zines you contribute or can contribute to, as each article is another chance to slip your name and bio to readers. List past and upcoming media interviews regarding you and your subject. (Here's a good place to list any inside contacts you have in the media.) Mention possible book announcements, public appearances and talks—at bookstores, clubs and organizations (name them). Will you be presenting or speaking at any conferences or conventions in the future? If so, list them. Lastly, show how you'll use the Internet, blogs and development of your Web site to further the book's potential.

Table of Contents (book): Before you can compose a table of contents, you'll need to think through your book's outline, content and special approach (slant). Then you can create chapter titles, making sure they're parallel in grammatical construction—all nouns or gerunds or prepositional phrases, one part or two parts, etc. Make sure your titles stimulate reader interest.

Chapter Outlines: Write summaries, not a Roman numeral outline—ideally about half a page per chapter, directed to the agent and editor rather than the reader. Emphasize the core material of each chapter and add specific examples or topics you expect to cover. Avoid bulleted lists, although you may use sentence fragments that begin with active verbs (e.g., "explores," "outlines," "defines," "explains," "covers," "summarizes").

Contacting Agents

A Professional Presentation

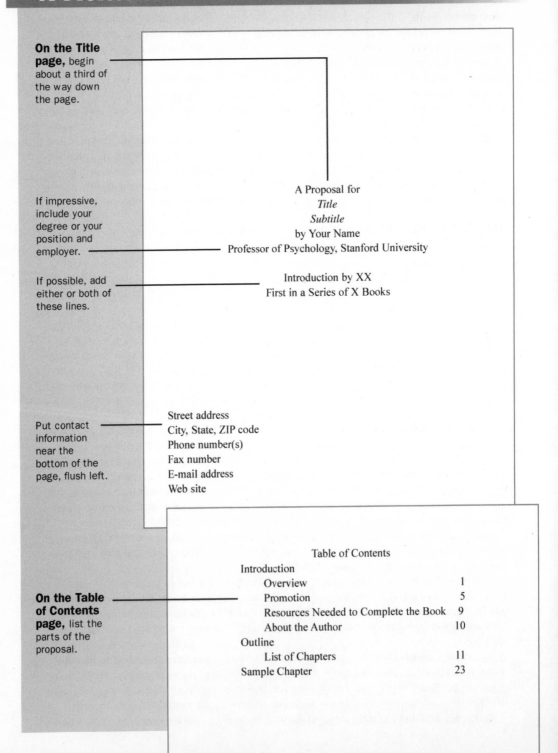

On the Title page, begin about a third of the way down the page.

If impressive, include your degree or your position and employer.

If possible, add either or both of these lines.

Put contact information near the bottom of the page, flush left.

A Proposal for
Title
Subtitle
by Your Name
Professor of Psychology, Stanford University

Introduction by XX
First in a Series of X Books

Street address
City, State, ZIP code
Phone number(s)
Fax number
E-mail address
Web site

On the Table of Contents page, list the parts of the proposal.

Table of Contents

Sample Chapters: The prior sections of your proposal are full of promises; now you must deliver on them. In fact, some literary agents and editors read little of the proposal before they flip to the sample chapters to see if you can write and how you engage your reader. Most proposals include approximately 60 pages of the proposed book. While chapter one (not usually a preface or author introduction) is almost always included, you can choose what other chapters to include. Try to submit chapters that represent your book's uniqueness or contribution to the field. In contrast, memoirists need to submit half or even the entire book, because memoirs require outstanding writing that demonstrates art and style as much as a compelling story. Upon request by an agent or editor, submit your proposal with the first, consecutive 60 pages of your memoir—but while waiting for a response, keep writing and be prepared to submit more chapters.

Appendix: This part of the proposal showcases copies of published articles or other materials written about or by the author or the subject of the book. Typical materials include flyers or printed materials about a business or presentations related to the subject, reviews of former published books, testimonials, lists of venues of former speaking engagements/workshops or anything else you may see as supportive material that fills out your sales package.

THE SEVEN QUESTIONS

1. Why you? Many creative people come up with terrific ideas for books. Are you an authority on the subject, or could you become one? Do you have the enthusiasm to commit several years to your idea—developing the book and promoting it, perhaps following it up with another book on the same or a similar subject? Your answers belong in the *Concept Statement*, *About the Author* and in your query letter.

2. Why now? Timing of an idea is as important as any other factor in book publication. Two common reasons for a book's rejection: It's already been done, and it's never been done! Is your book idea a rehash of existing books on the subject? If your book seeks a place in a flooded market, you could have a good idea too late. If you're ahead of the pack with a new idea, publishers may not want to risk an untested market. Your answers for why your book should be published "now" belong in two sections of the proposal: *Concept Statement* and *About the Book*, as well as in the query letter.

3. Who is Your Audience? Remember the publishing adage: "A book written for everyone is a book written for no one." Define your audience with the precision of a pollster. Test your idea on book retailers; ask them who would purchase your book and where it would be shelved. The broader your subject, the larger your audience. A narrower or specialized idea may be more suitable for a small, regional or university press. Answers about your readers—who they are and how large a market they represent—belong in the query letter and in three sections of the proposal: *Concept Statement*, *About the Book* and *About the Market*.

4. What books already exist on your subject? Finding similar books to yours doesn't quash your chances of getting published. They actually help you refine your idea and define how it's unique. Agents and editors may also check with www.amazon.com, as they must be convinced that your book will not only interest new readers but also people who may have read one of the competitive titles. A comparison of your book with others belongs in *About the Competition*. A briefer mention belongs in *About the Book*, and in the query letter

5. How well can you write? Success in gaining a book contract is based not only on how well you write your proposal but, of course, on how well you write your book. A book's style, diction, vocabulary, density of detail, and organization vary according to its subject and intended audience. To enhance your chances, take courses in writing, study books on the craft and build success by selling essays or short memoirs. Your skill in writing will show throughout your proposal, especially in *Chapter Outlines* and *Sample Chapters*.

6. Do you have an established platform? Landing a large publisher means, in most cases, that the author already has a recognized name or can reach a wide audience. This is called a national platform. The writer may be a well-known speaker or teacher, have regularly published articles or features written about them, or be a host of a TV/radio show. If you don't come close to having this kind of dossier, you can extend your platform enough to convince a large publisher that you can rake in the sales. Without a national platform, you can still succeed, but your book will probably find a home with a smaller or specialized press. All publishers expect their authors to promote their books. They look closely at the proposal section, *About Promotion*. Status as a nationally known person should also be mentioned in the *Concept Statement*, *About the Author*, *About the Book*, and in the query letter.

7. What kind of book organization have you planned? Crafting a proposal leads you to make decisions about your proposed book. Your book's uniqueness defines your slant, which is your perspective and approach to the subject, and allows you to create a title and subtitle that reflect it. Next, you can plan the *Table of Contents*. If you multiply your number of chapters by the average length of your sample chapters, you'll be able to estimate the length of your book. The organization of each chapter must be appropriate to your type of book and your special approach to your topic. Reflect this organization in your *Chapter Summaries*.

How long will it take you to write a fully developed proposal? To research, write, and revise your proposal, including the sample chapters, budget for 100 hours. That's not too much time for the goal of becoming a published author. Marketing your completed proposal begins with sending a query letter, or directly pitching your book idea, to an agent or editor. Then, upon request, you mail your proposal and wait for good news!

Start now!

Tips for Proofreading and Submitting

- **Read aloud** and follow along with your index finger under each word.

- **Proofread back to front** so you can concentrate on the words and not be seduced into reading the proposal.

- **Submit without staples** or any other form of binding. Paper clips are acceptable, but they leave indentations.

- **Use paper portfolios.** Insert your proposal in the right side of a double-pocket folder. You can use the left pocket for writing samples, illustrations, supporting documents and your business card if the left flap is scored. Put a self-adhesive label on the front of the folder with your book's title and your name.

- **Make everything 8½ × 11.** This makes it easy to reproduce and submit via mail or e-mail.

Sign on the Dotted Line

Research Your Options and Beware of Scams

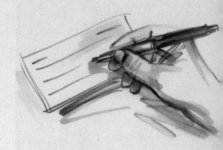

O nce you've received an offer of representation, you must determine if the agent is right for you. As flattering as any offer may be, you need to be confident that you are going to work well with the agent and that she is going to work hard to sell your manuscript.

EVALUATE THE OFFER

You need to know what to expect once you enter into a business relationship. You should know how much editorial input to expect from your agent, how often she gives updates about where your manuscript has been and who has seen it, and what subsidiary rights the agent represents.

More importantly, you should know when you will be paid. The publisher will send your advance and any subsequent royalty checks directly to the agent. After deducting her commission—usually 10 to 15 percent—your agent will send you the remaining balance. Most agents charge a higher commission of 20 to 25 percent when using a co-agent for foreign, dramatic or other specialized rights. As you enter into a relationship with an agent, have her explain her specific commission rates and payment policy.

Some agents offer written contracts and some do not. If your prospective agent does not, at least ask for a "memorandum of understanding" that details the basic relationship of expenses and commissions. If your agent does offer a contract, be sure to read it carefully, and keep a copy for yourself. Since contracts can be confusing, you may want to have a lawyer or knowledgeable writer friend check it out before signing anything.

The National Writers Union (NWU) has drafted a Preferred Literary Agent Agreement and a pamphlet, *Understand the Author-Agent Relationship*, which is available to members. The union suggests clauses that delineate such issues as:

- the scope of representation (One work? One work with the right of refusal on the next? All work completed in the coming year? All work completed until the agreement is terminated?)
- the extension of authority to the agent to negotiate on behalf of the author
- compensation for the agent and any co-agent, if used
- manner and time frame for forwarding monies received by the agent on behalf of the client
- termination clause, allowing client to give about 30 days to terminate the agreement
- the effect of termination on concluded agreements as well as ongoing negotiations
- arbitration in the event of a dispute between agent and client.

If you have any concerns about the agency's practices, ask the agent about them before you sign. Once an agent is interested in representing you, she should be willing to address any questions or concerns that you have. If the agent is rude or unresponsive, or tries to tell

What Should I Ask?

The following is a list of topics the Association of Authors' Representatives suggests authors discuss with literary agents who have offered to represent them. Please bear in mind that most agents are not going to be willing to spend time answering these questions unless they have already read your material and wish to represent you.

1. Are you a member of the Association of Authors' Representatives or do you adhere to their basic canon of ethics?

2. How long have you been in business as an agent?

3. Do you have specialists at your agency who handle movie and television rights? Foreign rights?

4. Do you have subagents or corresponding agents in Hollywood and overseas?

5. Who in your agency will actually be handling my work? Will the other staff members be familiar with my work and the status of my business at your agency?

6. Will you oversee or at least keep me apprised of the work that your agency is doing on my behalf?

7. Do you issue an agent/author agreement? May I review the language of the agency clause that appears in contracts you negotiate for your clients?

8. How do you keep your clients informed of your activities on their behalf?

9. Do you consult with your clients on any and all offers?

10. What are your commission rates? What are your procedures and time frames for processing and disbursing client funds? Do you keep different bank accounts separating author funds from agency revenue? What are your policies about charging clients for expenses incurred by your agency?

11. When you issue 1099 tax forms at the end of each year, do you also furnish clients—upon request—with a detailed account of their financial activity, such as gross income, commissions and other deductions and net income for the past year?

12. In the event of your death or disability, what provisions exist for my continued represenatation?

13. If we should part company, what is your policy about handling any unsold subsidiary rights to my work?

Reprinted with the permission of the Association of Authors' Representatives (www.aar-online.org).

you that the information is confidential or classified, the agent is uncommunicative at best and, at worst, is already trying to hide something from you.

AVOID GETTING SCAMMED

The number of literary agents in the country, as well as the world, is increasing. This is because each year, aspiring authors compose an increasing number of manuscripts, while publishing houses continue to merge and become more selective as well as less open to working directly with writers. With literary agents providing the crucial link between writers and publishers, it's no wonder dozens of new agencies sprout up each year in the United States alone.

While more agencies may seem like a good thing, writers who seek to pair up with a successful agent must beware when navigating the murky waters of the Internet. Because agents are such a valuable part of the process, many unethical persons are floating around the online publishing world, ready to take advantage of uninformed writers who desperately want to see their work in print.

To protect yourself, you must familiarize yourself with common agent red flags and keep your radar up for any other warning signs. First of all, it can't be stressed enough that you should never pay agents any fees just so they consider your work. Only small fees (such as postage and copying) are acceptable—and those miniscule costs are administered *after* the agent has contacted you and signed you as a client.

A typical scam goes something like this: You send your work to an agency and they reply with what seems like a form letter or e-mail, telling you they love your story. At some point, they ask for money, saying it has to do with distribution, production, submissions, analysis or promotion. By that point, you're so happy with the prospect of finding an agent (you probably already told family and friends) that you nervously hand over the money. Game over. You've just been scammed. Your work may indeed end up in print, but you're likely getting very little if any money. To be a successful author, publishers must pay you to write; you must never pay them.

When a deal seems too good to be true, it likely is. If you want to learn more about a particular agent, look at her Web site. If she doesn't have a Web site (some small agents do not), look in this book to see if she has legitimate sales in the industry. Google her name: You'll likely find a dozen writers just like you discussing this agent on an Internet forum asking questions such as "Does anyone know anything about agent so-and-so?" These writer-oriented Web sites exist so writers like you can meet similar persons and discuss their good/bad experiences with publications, agents and publishing houses.

Protect yourself from scams by getting questions answered before you make any deals. When an abundance of research material is not available, you must be cautious. Ask around, ask questions and never pay upfront fees.

If you've been scammed

If you have trouble with your agent and you've already tried to resolve it to no avail, it may be time to call for help. Please alert the writing community to protect others. If you find agents online, in directories or in this book who aren't living up to their promises or are charging you money when they're listed as non-fee-charging agents, please let the Web master or editor of the publication know. Sometimes they can intervene for an author, and if no solution can be found, they can at the very least remove a listing from their directory so that no other authors will be scammed in the future. All efforts are made to keep scam artists out, but in a world where agencies are frequently bought and sold, a reputation can change overnight.

If you have complaints about any business, consider contacting The Federal Trade Commission, The Council of Better Business Bureaus or your state's attorney general. (For full details, see Reporting a Complaint below). Legal action may seem like a drastic step, but sometimes people do it. You can file a suit with the attorney general and try to find other writers who want to sue for fraud with you. The Science Fiction & Fantasy Writers of America's Web site offers sound advice on recourse you can take in these situations. For more details, visit www.sfwa.org/beware/overview.html.

If you live in the same state as your agent, it may be possible to settle the case in small claims court. This is a viable option for collecting smaller damages and a way to avoid lawyer fees. The jurisdiction of the small claims court includes cases in which the claim is $5,000 or less. (This varies from state to state, but should still cover the amount for which you're suing.) Keep in mind that suing takes a lot of effort and time. You'll have to research all the necessary legal steps. If you have lawyers in the family, that could be a huge benefit if they agree to help you organize the case, but legal assistance is not necessary.

Above all, if you've been scammed, don't waste time blaming yourself. It's not your fault if someone lies to you. Respect in the literary world is built on reputation, and word gets around about agents who scam, cheat, lie and steal. Editors ignore their submissions and writers avoid them. Without clients or buyers, a swindling agent will find her business collapsing.

Meanwhile, you'll keep writing and believing in yourself. One day, you'll see your work in print, and you'll tell everyone what a rough road it was to get there, but how you wouldn't trade it for anything in the world.

Reporting a Complaint

If you feel you've been cheated or misrepresented, or you're trying to prevent a scam, the following resources should be of help.

- The Federal Trade Commission, Bureau of Consumer Protection. While the FTC won't resolve individual consumer problems, it does depend on your complaints to help them investigate fraud, and your speaking up may even lead to law enforcement action. Visit www.ftc.gov.

- Volunteer Lawyers for the Arts is a group of volunteers from the legal profession who assist with questions of law pertaining to the arts. Visit www.vlany.org.

- The Council of Better Business Bureau is the organization to contact if you have a complaint or if you want to investigate a publisher, literary agent or other business related to writing and writers. Contact your local BBB or visit www.bbb.org.

- Your state's attorney general. Don't know your attorney general's name? Go to www.attorneygeneral.gov. This site provides a wealth of contact information, including a complete list of links to each state's attorney general Web site.

Copyrights and Wrongs

Knowing the Lingo of Legalese

by Chuck Sambuchino and Brian A. Klems

Imagine you're at a writers' conference. You're getting ready to pitch that great novel idea to a bunch of powerful agents. As you walk up to the microphone, you start to notice all the other writers in the room staring, pens and pads in their hands. That's when the questions start flooding your head. Should you have secured a copyright before spilling your idea like this? Will other writers steal your concept? Can they do that? Will the agents ignore your pitch because the book title comes from a Billy Joel song?

Don't panic—a little paranoia is almost expected. It's natural for you to want to protect your work from others. Along with protecting your work from pilferers, you also have to protect yourself from being sued for legal infringement. As you compose your work and enter into the publishing world, it's vital to know how to navigate the murky waters of copyrights, libel and other contractual small print. Here's the scoop on some commonly asked questions about copyrights and other rights.

What is a copyright?

A copyright is a proprietary right designed to give the creator of a work the power to control that work's reproduction, distribution and public display or performance, as well as its adaptation into other forms. If another artist copies your work, the copyright will help you sue for proper compensation.

How long does a copyright last?

Usually, a copyright is valid until 70 years after the creator's death, but rare circumstances can cause this to fluctuate. Works written before 1978 do not adhere to current copyright laws. It's best to ask the U.S. Copyright Office about pre-1978 works and your specific circumstances. (You may have to pay to have the records checked for you.) The office's online site—www.copyright.gov—lists all copyright records dating back to 1978.

Do I need to register my work with the U.S. Copyright Office to hold a copyright on the work?

No. Your work is copyrighted the moment it hits a tangible medium—everything from your scribbles on a piece of paper to your musings on your Internet blog are protected. Putting

CHUCK SAMBUCHINO is the editor of *Guide to Literary Agents* and an assistant editor of *Writer's Market*. He is a former staffer on *Writer's Digest*. To contact him or learn more, visit www.guidetoliteraryagents.com.
BRIAN A. KLEMS is the online managing editor of *Writer's Digest* (www.writersdigest.com).

the word "Copyright" or the symbol © at the front of your text is also advisable, as it will prevent those who steal your work from pleading innocence down the road. Using the Copyright symbol on your manuscript is a topic of contention, though, as agents and editors tend to see it as the sign of an amateur—because they obviously know your work is protected. Try to avoid inserting the symbol © or the word "Copyright" when querying agents and editors, but remember to use it when passing your work around—such as to peers, other writers or on public forums (e.g. the Internet).

Though it's not mandatory, formally registering your work will certainly help your cause in court should that scenario occur. If someone steals your work and you take the thief to court, the possible compensation and damages awarded to you are greater if your work is registered.

"Poor man's copyright" is a questionably effective tactic where you mail yourself a manuscript and never open the envelope, thereby "proving" that you had written your work by a specific date. This is what the U.S. Copyright Office said about the idea: "The practice of sending a copy of your own work to yourself is sometimes called a 'poor man's copyright.' There is no provision in the copyright law regarding any such type of protection, and it is not a substitute for registration."

Does a copyright protect ideas?

No. Let's say you write a sci-fi story about a soldier who battles aliens on the moons of Neptune. Your idea—or concept—cannot be copyrighted, and therefore, can be used by anyone. If someone wants to try their hand at the same basic premise (soldier, aliens, our solar system), they may, but they can't use your characters, dialogue or passages from your text. If specific things from your story are stolen or copied, you can sue—but just because someone ripped off your basic concept doesn't make them culpable.

What are the legal ramifications of reproducing song lyrics in a manuscript? Also, can I use a song title as the title of my book?

Song lyrics are copyrighted, which means you need permission to use them. Although there isn't any specific law about how much you can take under fair use, it's common for the music industry to say you need permission for even one line of a song. One way you can check to see if the song is still under copyright protection is to visit www.copyright.gov. Publishers will usually assist in securing necessary permissions for you during the publishing process.

Differently, song and book titles of any kind generally aren't copyrightable—the only exception being those rare titles subject to trademark or unfair competition laws. Titles that fall in this small category are closely tied to a specific artist. (Think "Yellow Submarine" or "Stairway to Heaven.")

Can I use a minor character from a famous work as the protagonist of my novel?

Original characters—from Atticus Finch to Hermione Granger—are protected by copyright as long as the characters are both original and well defined. You can't use them without permission from the copyright holder. Now, just because you can't use someone else's work doesn't mean you can't be inspired by it. If the character has a rather common name and isn't particularly fleshed out, she's up for grabs (e.g., a perky young college student named Jennifer who used to baby-sit the main character and doesn't play much of a role in the book).

According to *Writer's Digest* legal expert Amy Cook, character names can even warrant trademark protection, depending on how distinctive the name is and to what extent the public associates the name with the original author. It's in your best interest to avoid names like Buzz Lightyear or James Bond.

Know Your Rights

Now imagine this: You've sold your book to a small publishing house. You're at home, reading a magazine, sipping some rare tea that cool writers like to drink while sitting at home and reading—when you see that characters from your book are being manufactured as toys. It's all part of merchandising done for the movie created as a result of your story. How come no one contacted you about the toys or the film? Simple. You signed away all the necessary rights for them to deny you royalties in contracts with your publisher.

To prevent signing away important (and often lucrative) rights, always study and negotiate your contract. The first and best step to do this is to secure a good agent. If a book deal befalls you and you proceed sans agent, help yourself by perusing the list of terms below and understanding some of the basic rights that come up in contracts. To see more on rights, see an article from the 2006 edition of *Guide to Literary Agents* at www.guidetoliteraryagents.com.

Audio rights—rights to produce the book in audio form—whether through cassette tape, compact disc or uploading onto an iPod.

Book club rights—rights to include the book in book clubs.

British rights—rights sold to sell the book to publishers in England.

Electronic rights—rights regarding hand-held electronic, Internet and print-on-demand versions of the book.

Foreign language rights—subsidiary rights to publish a work outside its country of origin. These rights include translation rights, the right to publish a work in a particular country, or worldwide rights exclusive of the country of origin.

Merchandising rights (commercial rights)—rights to create products—such as calendars, cards, action figures, stickers and dolls—that are based on characters or other elements of your book.

Performance rights—rights sold to someone in the entertainment industry. This includes if your work is adapted into a film, television production or theatrical performance.

Reprint rights—rights in publishing regarding a reprint fee when the book is printed in paperback form.

Serial rights—rights regarding excerpts of the book that appear in a magazine or other publications. These excerpts will provide you with additional money as well as publicity. There are two types: first serial rights and second serial rights. First serial rights refers to excerpts before the book is published and available; second serial rights refers to excerpts after the book is published and available. Nonfiction is more commonly excerpted than fiction.

Sealing the Deal

What's the difference between slander and libel?

Simple: Slander is spoken; libel is written. Note that to be considered either, the words must inflict defamation of character—thereby falsely and negatively reflecting on a living person's reputation. Whenever concerned that your work may contain libelous material (such as in a memoir), always consult an attorney. Better safe than sued.

This is as good a place as ever to note that, although publishers should help purge libelous material in pre-production, they still will likely want you to an agreement that indemnifies them against all claims, suits and judgments.

In a work of fiction, what restrictions exist on using the names of professional sports teams, TV networks or real people

If your character is a Dodgers fan who watches CNN and walks past Rupert Murdoch on the street, you generally won't have lawyers calling for your head. You can use these well-known proper names in your text as long as you don't intentionally try to harm the reputation of that person or product.

Normally you won't catch much grief for writing neutral or positive words about real people, places and things. It's the negative press you provide that could be considered trade libel or commercial disparagement—both ugly phrases that could cost you plenty of cash in a court of law.

Once an agent wants to take me on as a client and sends me a contract, do I need to have the agreement looked at by a contract lawyer before I sign to protect my rights?

It would probably be wise to have a lawyer who knows a thing or two about publishing look over the contract. Most contracts vary from agent to agent, and it's important to know exactly what agreements you make by signing. If you don't read the fine print or understand the legal language, months down the road you could find out that you gave up the right to profits from international sales.

About 20 years ago, I sold a short story to a magazine. One line in my contract stated the payment was for "full rights." Does this mean I can't sell the story ever again?

Selling full rights, or "all rights", to your work is like selling your car—once the contract is signed, you have no rights to the piece and can't sell it again. The new owner has that copyright protection, even if the original publication went defunct. The best option is to find the former publisher and buy back the copyright.

Who holds the copyright in a work-for-hire?

With a work-for-hire, the buyer is usually obtaining the copyright. (Read your contract thoroughly to know for sure.) Also note: When a writer works for an organization as an employee and produces creative works as part of his job, the copyright to those works belongs to the employer.

Improve Your Book Contract

Nine Negotiating Tips

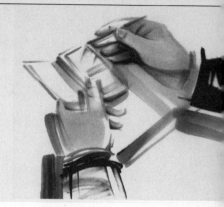

by The Authors Guild

Even if you're working with an agent, it's crucial to understand the legal provisions associated with book contracts. After all, you're the one ultimately responsible for signing off on the terms set forth by the deal. Below are nine clauses found in typical book contracts. Reading the explanation of each clause, along with the negotiating tips, will help clarify what you are agreeing to as the book's author.

1. Grant of Rights

The Grant of Rights clause transfers ownership rights in, and therefore control over, certain parts of the work from the author to the publisher. Although it's necessary and appropriate to grant some exclusive rights (e.g., the right to print, publish and sell print-book editions), don't assign or transfer your copyright and use discretion when granting rights in languages other than English and territories other than the United States, its territories and Canada. Also, limit the publication formats granted to those that your publisher is capable of exploiting adequately.

- Never transfer or assign your copyright or "all rights" in the work to your publisher.
- Limit the languages, territories and formats in which your publisher is granted rights.

2. Subsidiary Rights

Subsidiary rights are uses that your publisher may make of your manuscript other than issuing its own hardcover or paperback print book editions. Print-related subsidiary rights include book club and paperback reprint editions, publication of selections, condensations or abridgments in anthologies and textbooks and first and second serial rights (i.e., publication in newspapers or magazines either before or after publication of the hardcover book). Subsidiary rights not related to print include motion picture, television, stage, audio, animation, merchandising and electronic rights.

Subsidiary rights may be directly exploited by your publisher or licensed to third parties. Your publisher will share licensing fees with you in proportion to the ratios set forth in your contract. You should receive at least 50 percent of the licensing proceeds.

- Consider reserving rights outside the traditional grant of primary print book publishing rights, especially if you have an agent.

- Beware of any overly inclusive language, such as "in any format now known or hereafter developed," used to describe the scope of the subsidiary rights granted.
- Make sure you are fairly compensated for any subsidiary rights granted. Reputable publishers will pay you at least 50 percent of the proceeds earned from licensing certain categories of rights, much higher for others.

3. Delivery and Acceptance

Most contracts stipulate that the publisher is only obligated to accept, pay for and publish a manuscript that is "satisfactory to the publisher in form and content." It may be difficult to negotiate a more favorable, objective provision, but you should try. Otherwise, the decision as to whether your manuscript is satisfactory, and therefore publishable, will be left to the subjective discretion of your publisher.

- If you cannot do better, indicate that an acceptable manuscript is one which your publisher deems editorially satisfactory.
- Obligate your publisher to assist you in editing a second corrected draft before ultimately rejecting your manuscript.
- Negotiate a nonrefundable advance or insert a clause that would allow you to repay the advance on a rejected book from re-sale proceeds paid by a second publisher.

4. Publication

Including a publication deadline in your contract will obligate your publisher to actually publish your book in a timely fashion. Be sure that the amount of time between the delivery of the manuscript and the publication of the book isn't longer than industry standard.

- Make sure you're entitled to terminate the contract, regain all rights granted and keep the advance if your publisher fails to publish on or before the deadline.
- Carefully limit the conditions under which your publisher is allowed to delay publication.

5. Copyright

Current copyright law doesn't require authors to formally register their copyright in order to secure copyright protection. Copyright automatically arises in written works created in or after 1978. However, registration with the Copyright Office is a prerequisite to infringement lawsuits and important benefits accrue when a work is registered within three months of initial publication.

- Require your publisher to register your book's copyright within three months of initial publication.
- As previously discussed in Grant of Rights, don't allow your publisher to register copyright in its own name.

6. Advance

An advance against royalties is money that your publisher will pay you prior to publication and subsequently deduct from your share of royalty earnings. Most publishers will pay, but might not initially offer, an advance based on a formula which projects the first year's income.

- Bargain for as large an advance as possible. A larger advance gives your publisher greater incentive to publicize and promote your work.
- Research past advances paid by your publisher in industry publications such as *Publishers Weekly*.

7. Royalties

You should earn royalties for sales of your book that are in line with industry standards. For example, many authors are paid 10 percent of the retail price of the book on the first 5,000 copies sold, 12.5 percent of the retail price on the next 5,000 copies sold, and 15 percent of the retail price on all copies sold thereafter.

- Base your royalties on the suggested retail list price of the book, not on net sales income earned by your publisher. Net-based royalties are lower than list-based royalties of the same percentage, and they allow your publisher room to offer special deals or write off bad debt without paying you money on the books sold.
- Limit your publisher's ability to sell copies of your book at deep discounts—quantity discount sales of more than 50 percent—or as remainders.
- Limit your publisher's ability to reduce the percentage of royalties paid for export, book club, mail order and other special sales.

8. Accounting and Payments

Your accounting clause should establish the frequency with which you should expect to receive statements accounting for your royalty earnings and subsidiary rights licensing proceeds. If you are owed money in any given accounting period, the statement should be accompanied by a check.

- Insist on at least a bi-annual accounting.
- Limit your publisher's ability to withhold a reserve against returns of your book from earnings that are otherwise owed to you.
- Include an audit clause in your contract which gives you or your representative the right to examine the sales records kept by the publisher in connection with your work.

9. Out of Print

Your publisher should only have the exclusive rights to your work while it is actively marketing and selling your book (i.e., while your book is "in print"). An out-of-print clause will allow you to terminate the contract and regain all rights granted to your publisher after the book stops earning money.

It is crucial to actually define the print status of your book in the contract. Stipulate that your work is in print only when copies are available for sale in the United States in an English language hardcover or paperback edition issued by the publisher and listed in its catalog. Otherwise, your book should be considered out of print and all rights should revert to you.

- Don't allow the existence of electronic and print-on-demand editions to render your book in print. Alternatively, establish a floor above which a certain amount of royalties must be earned or copies must be sold during each accounting period for your book to be considered in print. Once sales or earnings fall below this floor, your book should be deemed out of print and rights should revert to you.
- Stipulate that as soon as your book is out of print, all rights will automatically revert to you regardless of whether or not your book has earned out the advance.

The Next Steps

So You Have an Agent—Now What?

by Chuck Sambuchino

In this book, we've told you all about contacting and securing agents. Details on everything from writing to pitching to getting the most out of your subsidiary rights are included in these pages. But should your hard work and passion pay off in a signed deal with a big-shot agent, the journey isn't over. Now it's time to learn what lies in store after the papers are signed.

LET YOUR AGENT WORK

In the time leading up to signing a contract, you may have bantered around plenty with your agent—realizing you both love the New York Yankees and Kung Pao Chicken. But don't let this camaraderie allow you to forget that the relationship is a business one first and foremost. Does this mean you can't small talk occasionally and then ask your agent how her children are doing? No. But don't call every day complaining about the traffic and your neighbor's habit of mowing his lawn before the sun comes up.

Your agent is going to read your work again (and again . . .) and likely suggest possible changes to the manuscript. "When you sign with an agent, you should go over next steps, and talk about what the agent expects from you," says Sorche Fairbank, principal of the Fairbank Literary Agency. "This can vary with each author-agent relationship, and on the type of book project. We (at the Fairbank agency) are fairly hands-on with shaping and polishing a proposal or manuscript, and there often is quite a bit of work to be done before we and the author feel it's ready to send out.

"If you have a nonfiction project, there is certain to be some final tweaking of the proposal and sample chapter(s)," Fairbank says. "If you have a novel, then I hope you would be . . . taking any agent advice on tightening and polishing it. Go through it one more time and weed out extraneous words, overused pet words and phrases, and stock descriptions."

KEEP WRITING

If you're not working with your agent on rewrites and revisions, it's your responsibility to continue creating. One challenge is over—another begins. As your agent is trying hard to sell your work and bring home a nice paycheck, you're expected to keep churning out material for her to sell. Keep her informed of what you're working on and when it'll be ready.

Stay passionate. Once you've convinced yourself that your first book was not a fluke,

CHUCK SAMBUCHINO is the editor of *Guide to Literary Agents* and an assistant editor of *Writer's Market*. He is a former staffer on *Writer's Digest*. To contact him or learn more, visit www.guidetoliteraryagents.com.

you've convinced yourself that you're a capable writer—and a capable writer needs to keep writing and always have material to sell. Always be considering new projects and working on new things, but give preference to the first work that got you a contract. Rewrites and revisions—wanted by agents and editors alike—will likely take months and become somewhat tedious, but all that frustration will melt away when you have that first hardcover book in your hands.

SELLING THE BOOK

When the book is as perfect as can be, it's time for your agent to start shopping it to her publishing contacts. During this process, she'll likely keep you abreast of all rejections. Don't take these to heart—instead, learn from each one, especially those with editors who have kindly given a specific reason as to why they don't want the book. "When the project is being shopped around, discuss rejections with your agent. There may be patterns that point to a fixable weak spot," Fairbank says.

Your book may be bought in a pre-empt. That's when a publishing house tries to beat other potential buyers to your work and offers a solid price in the hopes of securing your book early and avoiding a bidding war. An actual bidding war—or "auction"—happens when a work is so stunningly marvelous that every house in town wants it bad enough to compete against each other, offering different perks such as a large advance and guaranteed ad dollars. Traditionally, the best deal (read: most money and enthusiasm) wins and signs. After the auction was finished for Elizabeth Kostova's *The Historian*, her advance was a cool $2 million. (Note: First-time novelists will likely get an advance of $50,000 to $75,000, but hey, anything can happen!)

Your agent will submit the work to publishers (either exclusively or simultaneously, depending on her opinion) and hold a private auction if need be to secure the best deal possible. Fairbank says it's important for writers to relax during the auction process and not call every 30 minutes for an update. "In an auction, everything should go through the agent, but writers may be called upon to do a few things," she says. "I have had some cases where it made sense to bring the author around to meet with the various interested houses, usually to drive home the author's expertise and promotability. In every instance, it increased the size of the offers. There have also been times where a particular house asked for more specifics on something, and I needed my author ready to respond ASAP."

PROMOTE YOURSELF

Besides continuing to write and revise, the most important thing a writer needs to focus on is promotion. It's likely your work will not have the benefit of countless publicists setting up interviews for you. How you want to promote your work is up to you. (For more on specific ways to publicize your work, see W.E. Reinka's article on publicity, "Great Expectations," on page 75.)

According to Regina Brooks, president of Serendipity Literary Agency, "It's always a great time to research who you might want on your team once the book is published (e.g., publicists, Web developers, graphic artists, etc.). Often times, authors wait until the last minute to start researching these options. The more lead time a publicist has to think about your project, the better. This is also an ideal time to attend conferences to network and workshops to tighten your writing skills."

GO WITH THE FLOW

An agent's job is to agent. That means knowing which people are buying what, and where they're headed if a move is in the works. Throughout the editing process, you'll work hand-in-hand with your agent and editor to revise and polish the manuscript. But let's say the

Sealing the Deal

editor makes the not-so-uncommon decision to switch jobs or switch houses. Ideally, an agent will shepherd you through the change.

"It happens more often than we'd like," says Brooks. "When it does, you hope that someone in-house will be as excited about the project as the acquiring editor initially was, but there's no guarantee." Fairbank agrees: "The most important thing the author and agent can do in that case is take a deep breath, pick up the phone, and wholeheartedly welcome the new editor to the book team. Once they have their feet under them and have reviewed your work, ask them what they think, and listen to any questions or comments they may have."

In addition to switching editors at publishing houses, a writer must concern himself with the possibility of his agent hitting the lottery and quitting (or just quitting without hitting the lottery, which is more probable). To protect yourself, make sure that this scenario is clearly addressed in your contract with the agent. "It really depends on the initial written agreement between the agent and the author," says Brooks. "It's important that the agreement cover such situations in their termination language. This assures that all parties including the publishing company know how to proceed with royalty statements, notices, etc."

AND WHAT IF . . . ?

A difficult question that may come up is this: What should you do if you think your agent has given up on you, or isn't fulfilling her end of the bargain? (In other words, how do you get out? *Can* you get out?) First, consider that if an agent is trying and failing to sell your manuscript, then at least the *trying* part is there. It could just be an unfortunate instance where you and an agent both love a work but can't find anyone else who feels the same. This is no one's fault. As far as simply quitting an agent is concerned, you can't opt out of a contract until the contract says so. Many agencies have termination clauses, with notices of 30 days up to two years.

A similar dilemma involves authors who have a satisfactory agent but want out in favor of one perceived to be better. If you already have an agent, but others are calling in hopes to work with you, the new agents likely don't know you already possess representation. Obviously, you need to tell them you are currently represented. That said, you most likely can't just switch agents because you're under contract. When the time comes when you can legally opt out of a contract (and you think your agent has had ample time to make a sale), consider your options then. Miss Snark, an anonymous literary agent who hosts a popular blog (misssnark.blogspot.com), puts it this way on her blog: "If you squirm out a deal with Agent No. 1 in favor of super big and powerful Agent No. 2, how will Agent No. 2 know that you're really with them and not going to squirm away should Agent No. 3 come along?"

GET READY FOR YOUR RIDE

Hopefully, you'll never need to experience the difficulty and confusion of switching agents and/or editors. Hopefully, your work will smoothly find a house and then a large audience once it's published. Just remember that the smoother things go, the less excuses exist for you not to keep writing then promote the heck out of your work. Simply do what you do best (write) and continue to learn what you can about the publishing world. As Fairbank puts it so simply, "Be available, willing, and ready to help your agent."

Agents' Pet Peeves

Getting Your Manuscript Read

by Chuck Sambuchino

Here's a secret many writers don't know about agents. When agents go looking for new clients (much like when editors accept entries in a writing contest), they are flooded with hundreds, sometimes thousands, of submissions. With such an overwhelming volume of potential clients to consider, agents are looking for reasons *not* to choose a particular writer. They're looking for any sign of weakness in your writing or professionalism that will justify rejecting your work and making their huge stack of queries decrease by one. All it takes is one misspelling in your query, one hint of arrogance in your bio, or one phone call when the agent requests ''no phone calls''—and your chance with that agent is done. It's because of this that your work must be as perfect as it can be. And before an agent even reads your work, you've got to do something more important: Avoid agent pet peeves.

There's a scene in the television show *Arrested Development*, where the character Tobias Fünke, an aspiring actor, starts packaging his headshot to send out to different casting directors in Hollywood. Each headshot is placed in a decorative bag filled with glitter, candy and a note saying, ''I know where you live, ha ha.'' We then see a casting director struggling to open one of these glittery bags, then looking at the headshot and telling herself aloud never to hire Tobias Fünke. This is a quintessential example of an amateur implementing gimmicks to get his work noticed—and remember gimmicks and ''cute'' don't work. In fact, they're huge agent pet peeves.

If you've read the articles to this point, you know that good writing and a strong query/proposal are the most important things in nabbing an agent and publishing deal. But even superb writing isn't the end-all-be-all answer. You have to be a professional and manageable client—meaning you don't test agents' pet peeves. Glitter and unfunny notes aren't the only dislikes in the agent world—there are plenty more. Keep your work concise and professional to help avoid annoying possible representatives for your work.

Below you'll find a series of tips and need-to-know facts that will help your work get a fair read by the people in power. Study them well.

REGARDING SUBMISSIONS

- **Any type of misspelling of gross formatting error** will make an agent grimace and reject your query immediately.
- **No matter how much you want to woo a specific agent, never submit a work to**

CHUCK SAMBUCHINO is the editor of *Guide to Literary Agents* and an assistant editor of *Writer's Market*. He is a former staffer on *Writer's Digest*. To contact him or learn more, visit www.guidetoliteraryagents.com.

an agent who doesn't represent that genre—you're just showing you can't follow directions (and wasting postage).

• **Don't embellish your accomplishments;** that just leads to a very awkward moment later when you have to explain yourself. If you get caught in a lie, it's likely the agent will start to wonder what else you were untruthful about.

• **Tell an agent about your promotional ideas, but never include anything that's too idealistic.** In other words, don't mention getting a book blurb from Stephen King, if you have absolutely no means to do so.

• **Don't mention ideas for your book's cover design or inside art.** If you have suggestions, let that conversation happen naturally down the road. Likely, such decisions will be out of your hands, and offering your input too soon makes you look amateurish. This brings up another point: Know when to work your tail off, and when to step away and let other people operate.

• **Single-space query letters. Double-space your manuscript.**

• **Never pitch a fiction work before it's complete.** If the agent likes your idea, she'll immediately ask to see part or all of it, which will lead you to either hastily finish the manuscript or sheepishly admit it's not done—both bad options.

• **Agents may assist with editing, but they're not there to act as the world's editors.** If your query or pitch has a sentence such as "Chapter 3 needs a little tweaking," then you should never have submitted it in the first place.

• **Submit one work at a time—always.** If you have other writings in your arsenal, it's best to let the first work hook an agent, then politely mention to them that you have more manuscripts ready to go.

REGARDING APPEARANCE

• **Avoid fluffy letterhead or large logos.** Remember: Always avoid "cute."

• **Keep things short** (e.g., query letters should be one page). You may go long because you feel that your plot can't properly be condensed into just one or two paragraphs. This leads to a larger problem: If you can't summarize your work with a short explanation, then the agent won't be able to summarize the work when talking to publishing house editors who may consider the book. You put her at a disadvantage in selling your work.

• **Format your materials and always use a standard font.** When in doubt, Times New Roman is always the default.

ON ETIQUETTE

• **Act with humility always,** whether when writing your query or speaking with an agent in person. If you can show that agent that you deeply respect her time, you've shown you're a professional and courteous writer, which ups your value as a potential client.

• **Don't write an agent and tell her she's an idiot for not signing you.** Let's say Agent X sends you a form rejection letter and you've got an inkling that she gave your manuscript a quick read let alone any true consideration at all. You're frustrated. Sending an angry letter giving your candid thoughts is not the answer. The letter isn't likely to make an agent change her submission review procedures, and a worse scenario is that agent contacting fellow agents and warning them against taking you on as a client.

• **Mentioning Oprah's Book Club is a big no-no.** Writers, many of which are very proud of their work, will often compare their book to a current blockbuster, or mention how they "think the book will be great on Oprah." Because agents are so turned off by such statements, it's best to not even joke about these clichés.

• **Don't say your family members or writing group liked your work.** Their opinion, though kind, means nothing to agents. And because agents think that writers should know these opinions are of little true value, they'll look down on writers who make such statements.

ON CONTACTING

• **Though it's been said before, it bears repeating: Personalize your queries.** "A little pet peeve of mine is a mass e-query that starts out as 'Dear Agent' and lists in the cc: section the e-mail addresses of 20 or more agents," says Michael Mancilla of the Greystone Literary Agency. "To me, this is like spamming and will usually be deleted without being read. I prefer the personal touch, and it often shows that the author did not take the time to learn what we as agents like as individuals."

• **If you receive a rejection letter from an agent,** you likely won't get any personal feedback on your work (though some nicer agents may provide a little on occasion). If this happens, don't contact that agent after a rejection and ask her for feedback, or a specific reason as to why you received only a generic rejection letter. I know you're thinking that you're entitled to a reason as to why your work was rejected (and perhaps you are), but agents are too busy to give personal feedback to everyone. Instead of contacting the agent, get feedback from where it would logically come—peers in a writing group. Use their criticism to retool your work, then think about resending that work back to an agent. Politely mention that you've retooled the work after much feedback from writing peers.

• **Never ask an agent if she charges fees.** Use Internet forums and blogs to weed out inappropriate agencies before pitching, then you'll know you'll dealing with someone legitimate.

ON FOLLOWING UP

• **Absolutely do not call any agents without a request.** I know this is tempting because you may actually get a live person on the end of the phone, but it provides for a massively awkward situation with agents as they're requested to explain why they haven't gotten back to you yet. The last thing an agent wants is to have that awkward moment on the phone.

• **If the agent takes you on, make sure you don't clamor** for an unrealistic advance. If you've done your homework, you should know what a logical advance will be.

Signing with an agent requires a careful balance of what to do and what not to do, but the basic will always be the same: Be professional, write well and always follow directions. Avoid the pet peeves of agents and ensure that your work ends up in the hands of a big-time editor, not a trash bin.

The Evolution of Agenting

An Agent Talks of Change

by Stephany Evans

When I began agenting at Sandra Martin/Paraview in 1990, a frequent mantra was: "It's not the '80s any more!" Usually intoned when an agent griped about a paltry advance, the deeper message was that the entire landscape of mainstream publishing was changing.

These changes have continued up to today. From how writers submit their work, to their credentials as an author, to the duties of agents today, publishing and bookselling has changed dramatically throughout the past 20 years—and agents have changed right along with it.

AGENTS AS EDITORS

Since the 1980s, the world of publishing—especially at the top—has become increasingly corporate. Independent houses of yesteryear were bought and absorbed into larger houses; operations were streamlined, and the bottom line (read: sales) became ever more the focus. Editors were asked to wear as many hats as Bartholomew Cubbins, and were frequently expected to deal with numbers as much as words. With so many other responsibilities, editors had less time to actually edit their books—and so placed increasing value on signing up projects they could rely upon to be delivered "clean," with reasonably little editing required.

Additionally, the corporate view of a book as a "product" gave rise to new acquisitions procedures—the use of focus groups (the editorial board), and seeking out input from the publisher's sales and marketing departments, and sometimes even the top book chains before making a commitment to publish. Needless to say, these shifts necessitated new procedures for agents, in response. As publishing houses at the top consolidated, in effect squeezing out mid-list authors, new independent presses spring up across the country to accommodate the market that still exists for their books—and agents try to stay current with these new opportunities for their clients.

Literary agent Paige Wheeler of Folio Literary Management observes how her role has changed: "To give an author her best shot, I've become more hands-on with my projects. I'm tinkering with, and fine tuning manuscripts before they hit an editor's desk." Already accustomed to helping their authors shape an idea or tweak a title, most agents have taken on this added role of first editor for their authors. Wheeler expressed concern with the power

STEPHANY EVANS (www.imprintagency.com) is the president of Imprint Agency Inc. in New York City. She is a member of the Association of Author's Representatives, the Author's Guild, the Romance Writers of America, and a member and former co-chair of New York Women in Publishing. Gary Heidt, of Imprint Agency, contributed to this article.

that sales and marketing have over editorial considerations. "From a business perspective, I understand the need to be sure that there's an audience and that the project is salable," Wheeler says. "But from a creative perspective, it's a shame that a lot of good, important books don't get picked up because they're not an 'easy sell'—so the agent has to be super resourceful in finding the right home for these books."

Although an agent's duty will likely include some editing and tweaking on a manuscript, don't think we're enthusiastic to help rewrite mediocre work so it's up to snuff. The same rules apply now as 20 years ago: Only send your work out when it's in top form and when you have a platform. (See Christina Katz's article on platform, "Almost Famous," on page 25.)

TECHNOLOGICAL ADVANCES AND A GLUTTED INBOX

Computers, the Web and e-mail have changed everything in publishing—from how writers write to how the books are sold—and agents are always in the thick of things. Until the late 1980s, computers were not even in general use. I recall that at Simon & Schuster Audio, where I worked in 1987 as assistant to the editorial director, there was one computer that everyone in the department was instructed to become familiar with. On each of our desks, however, sat a sturdy IBM Selectric typewriter. It was state of the art, and nearly all of us who remember that machine think of it fondly. I was slow to get onto the tech train. I didn't bother with e-mail until I relocated briefly to California in 1997. Suddenly, it made sense to me: With e-mail, though I was living in the Mojave Desert, I was still knitted in with New York City, a.k.a. publishing central.

E-mail, however, is a double-edged sword. It's great to be able to respond to crises, request and send information, review and give notes on revisions, reply to queries and take care of a host of other tasks so quickly and easily. Most editors will now accept submissions of proposals and manuscripts from agents via e-mail, which saves time, and the expense of copying, packaging and postage. Yet for many agents, the boon is also a bludgeon.

Writing, in the first place, is almost too simple now. The ease of the physical process—means that a would-be writer need not be particularly staunch, or steadfast to their craft. It seems anyone now can write a book—or at least type one. It's also incredibly easy now to submit query letters. (Even if an agent doesn't accept e-mailed queries, the computer makes it a snap to print multiple letters to be sent by regular mail.) Inboxes and slush piles have swelled accordingly, and agents—in spite of the fact that there are more of us now (many of us editorial refugees from corporate publishing)—are ever more swamped with submissions. Unfortunately, the percentage of truly talented authors has not risen proportionately to the increased number of queries and submissions, which means that agents and their assistants and interns are spending more time winnowing and less time working with authors.

Susan Ann Protter, an independent literary agent for more than 30 years, misses the intimacy of earlier days. "I feel that things were more personal before mail merges, and that an author came to an agent on a different footing," she says. "The agent was happy to consider a project and spend time with an author when the author was not sending the material to a dozen or more agents at once. In the past, it was more about the author and the book. Now (for authors and agents alike), it's about platform and media savvy. Everyone has to have a profile and market themselves."

As Protter acknowledges, technology has an immediate upside. The prevalence of agency Web sites allows authors to get to know an agent and her interests with just a few keystrokes and clicks. Agents also post upcoming conference appearances so any interested author can make plans to meet them in person before deciding to query. In some ways, agents have never been more reachable and knowable. This, of course, makes it all the more puzzling when we receive countless queries a day that seem to have no connection with who we are and what we do!

It's never been simpler to learn an agent's likes and interests before querying. But just as you have more access to agent information, publishers and agents have more access to information about you—especially if you've already had a book published. Introduced in 2001, Neilsen's BookScan collects data from major book retailers, Amazon and a growing list of independent bookstores. While not completely accurate, the site allows editors a chance to "run the numbers" on books in the "competing titles" sections of their proposals. If too many show lackluster volume, an editor may conclude that the potential market for your book is not worth pursuing. They will also use BookScan to see how your own previous titles have done. If you have published before, be sure to provide your agent with solid sales figures and be prepared to detail how and where the books were sold, whether you sold them out of the trunk of your station wagon, or at pet stores, or via your Web site. And if editors are paying attention to things such as BookScan, rest assured agents are too. An agent needs to know about a project's vulnerabilities from the get-go.

When you research agents' Web sites to learn about their submission guidelines, pay attention as to how they like to receive materials. Some have mastered the paperless office; some want to read real pages on the train or curled in a comfortable chair.

THE CHANGING E-WORLD

Peter Rubie of the Peter Rubie Literary Agency teaches the course "The Role of the Literary Agent" through New York University's Center for Publishing. It is the only university level course of its type in the country. Looking forward as often as he looks behind, Rubie identifies another change—one that affects mainly writers of genre fiction: the decline, over the last 20 years, in the profitability of the mass market paperback, which has long been the vehicle by which commercial fiction authors' careers have been built.

Today, at eight dollars, mass-market books are too expensive for a format that *feels* disposable. There's too much competition "from TV, movies, video games, the Internet and so forth," Rubie says. "I think the major impact of these alternative forms of entertainment has been on the mass market." The solution, Rubie believes, will not be "the current $300 reader from Sony, but the upcoming electronic text version of the iPod," he says. "I firmly believe it will revolutionize publishing in many ways and reinvigorate it at the same time." What will this mean to authors' advances and royalties? As always, agents will grapple with publishers to determine what is equitable.

Individually and collectively through the AAR, agents negotiate what is fair exchange regarding the plethora of new electronic rights, from complete downloadable books to online anthologies or reference works compiled from the books of numerous authors, and wrestle with whether POD (print on demand) capability constitutes that a book is "in print," or whether selling the U.S. edition of the book in cyberspace (Amazon, bn.com, etc.) will erode the value of foreign editions to be published later. Yeah. We're keeping busy!

THE BASICS DON'T CHANGE

We're busier, and we're adapting to technological advances, but we're still looking for good work. Compose a personal submission with a top-notch manuscript and agents will contact you. Keep polishing your prose and building your platform, and you will be an agent's dream come true.

Ken Sherman

*A Script and Book Agent Talks About
Searching for That Killer Writing Sample*

by Chuck Sambuchino

I t was in Paris, observing French director Claude Sautet shoot a film, that script agent Ken Sherman officially fell in love with writing and movies.

"I observed the making of a Sautet film standing behind the director the entire shooting," says Sherman, whose company, Ken Sherman & Associates, works out of Beverly Hills. "I also went to movies every day and came back (to Los Angeles) after two years living in Paris—half of that time was spent extensively traveling."

Sherman, a Los Angeles native and University of California-Berkeley psychology graduate, returned from his adventures in Europe and started his career in film and television as a reader for Columbia Pictures. After less than a year reading screenplays, he interviewed at the William Morris Agency and was accepted into a training program the next day. Thus began his foray into the world of agenting.

It wasn't until a few years later, in the early 1980s, however, that Sherman would open his own agency. "I found space and opened my first literary agency where I am today. After two years, The (Robby) Lantz Office in New York bought my company. I worked in their L.A. office for four years. I kept my space here—the first office space—and reopened my agency in 1989. I decided it was time to be on my own again and that's what I've been doing ever since. I really like it. I find the independence and the ability to choose clients and projects much more satisfying than servicing a list of existing clients for other people."

Nowadays, Sherman's agency handles approximately 35 clients; he makes contact with most of his new writers through referrals, and he handles just about every topic you can think of in nonfiction, fiction and scripts. But no matter where a new writer comes from, what Sherman's looking for hasn't changed throughout his years as an agent: "It's about passion. If writers don't feel obsessed about what they're writing, it won't come through on the paper. It's the basic adage to write what you know—better yet, right *about* what you know."

When a writer is composing his first screenplay, should he aim to write something perceived as trendy, marketable or salable? Or should he just write the best he can, even if the script will likely be unproducable?

What I'm looking for, and what every producer, studio, network and agent I know is looking for, is a killer writing sample—meaning something that we can send out in one day to 30

---

producers and have them say, "This may not be exactly the story I'm looking for, but I need to know this writer." And hopefully, each one of them will call me back and say, "We want the story. We want to option the material or purchase it outright." But most important is that they want to know the writer and meet with the writer and talk about other projects because the writer has a unique voice.

You just finished reading a book that'll make a great television series or movie. How does a work like that get optioned?

One of my internationally known book authors recently had his book on the *New York Times* bestseller list for a couple of months. There was a real flurry of interest in it. Finally, someone who really, really felt passionate about the story and was a proven producer called an executive at one of the movie studios and said, "I want to do this." The head of the studio called me to check if the rights were available because he wanted to make an offer—and he did. The offer of an option is for two things. First, the option guarantees the exclusive rights to the producer for a certain amount of time—in this case, 18 months. Nobody else can have the rights to that story during those 18 months. In that time, the producer can have a screenplay or teleplay developed. Second, the producer can then decide if they want to pay the purchase price and fully own the rights to the book.

Does some work get optioned more than once?

Yes. I have a client whose first book became an Oprah's Book Club book after it was published. We then had it under contract to Dreamworks, attached to a specific writer-director. The one-year option expired and we've just set it up with one of last year's Oscar-nominated producers. Sometimes a project will have many, many homes before it's actually produced. And there's no guarantee that anything will be produced even if the rights have been purchased.

In addition to working with television writers, screenwriters and book writers, you also deal with buying and selling life rights. How does that work?

Here's an example: I was sitting in my office one day and a TV/movie producer I know called me. He said, "I've spoken to a lady and the fireman who saved her life during the Oklahoma City bombing. Would you mind handling the life rights—the option and purchase price and contract for them?" I then negotiated for both (individuals). Their life rights were optioned and then the purchase price for the exclusive use of their stories for the TV movie *Oklahoma City: A Survivor's Story* was exercised.

If a writer wishes to see his idea on the big screen, is it more practical to write a good book and get it optioned into a film, rather than try to sell an original screenplay?

It depends in which form the author writes best. If the writer is a great screenwriter, I would hope they'd attack the story and characters as a screenplay, because, traditionally, screenplays take less time to write. I want to preface this by saying that there are no rules or answers to any of these questions. What I'm suggesting today are just a few ideas of a few ways things can happen for individuals—but everybody needs to find their own way in their own time. One prominent client wrote eight screenplays before things finally clicked.

Does an author get the first crack at writing an adapted screenplay of his own novel?

If the author is seriously interested in adapting his or her own book into a screenplay, I highly suggest they write a spec screenplay (or one based on their book) while they're waiting for

Writers' Advice on Scriptwriting

What's the most common thing you see new screenwriters doing wrong?
They don't give an honest appraisal of their own work. It's so important for writers to read good screenplays, and the really good work of other people. I shudder to think of all the people in writing classes at college who kind of just compare their work to the other people around them and go, "Well, my stuff is better than his." You need to aim higher. That's why I spent a lot of time reading Woody Allen and Aaron Sorkin. That's how you teach yourself. See how the good stuff looks on the page.
 —Marc Cherry, executive producer and writer of *Desperate Housewives*

What's the most common thing you see new screenwriters doing wrong?
I think they overexplain. Unless your script is a parable or something that's not realistic, you shouldn't try to make it too profound or affecting or sentimental. A lot of new screenwriters don't write the way people talk. And often, what's not said is just as important as what is said.
 —Diana Ossana, screenwriter of *Brokeback Mountain* and *Pretty Boy Floyd*

What's your advice for dealing with rejection?
I don't take it to heart when material gets turned down because it always happens the same way. Most of the producers and studio executives have all gone and taken these writing courses to learn what to look for in a script, and they're getting all the wrong criteria. Any time you write something really good, you're going to get turned down. If it's good, it's got to be original—and if it's original, it'll probably be turned down.
 —Larry Cohen, screenwriter of *Phone Booth* and *Cellular*

What makes a script salable in Hollywood?
For the vast majority of people, it's not just about selling a script but actually making a career out of screenwriting—that's the goal. Scripts that can't sell on the open market can open doors and get you writing assignments immediately and serve as a sample for your writing career. That's a lesson worth taking to heart. If you write a fantastic thriller or sword-and-sorcery epic, when they need a writer for one of those things, you're going to be the guy they call.
 —Zak Penn, screenwriter of *X2* and *X-Men: The Last Stand*

What's your advice for writers starting out in the business?
Write, write, write! And then write some more! If your first script doesn't sell, write another one—and then another one. The cream really does rise to the top.
 —Andrea Berloff, screenwriter of *World Trade Center* and *Harry and Caresse*

the book to be published. That way, they can show the studio or the network or whomever is optioning the material that they can deliver the goods.

Do you pay any attention to what studios are buying?

I don't worry too much about that. I prefer to try and find really first-rate material that stands on it own. And even though it may be a genre that's a bit out of favor at the moment—maybe something that was hot three or five years ago for some reason—we can reignite interest with a solid screenplay or book. One thing I've noticed is that many executives in this business are very happy not to take a risk on anything. They're very happy to go along with what other people say, which is why sometimes you can get an auction going with multiple bids on the same project. You say, "Well so-and-so just made an offer on it," or "Such-and-such studio wants it." And they think that if another studio wants it, it must be something good. Of course it is...

Kind of like the business phrase "Don't sell the steak. Sell the sizzle"?

Sometimes you can sell the sizzle, but more importantly, the material really has to stand on its own. Because don't forget that even with a TV movie, a producer or writer is with the project for a good six months to a year, if not more. A producer needs the passion to stay with the project and to be able to sell it, because they're constantly selling and reselling the material to new people who join the project.

Let's say someone writes a great script. You read it and love it. Before you sign a contract, is it important that the writer has other screenplays waiting in the wings?

That's ideal. Again, as I've said before, I'm looking for that killer writing sample: a screenplay I can send to anybody anywhere anytime and have them sit up and say, "Wow, this is a serious and professional writer." And more often than not, I won't take on clients without knowing that there are three or four or five good pitches behind them if they're to go into a meeting, and ideally another one or two screenplays that are polished and ready to be sent out.

What else should writers know about dealing with Hollywood agents?

I think (writers) should keep in mind that it's a collaborative effort between the writer and the agent. We work as a team. I've found that my reputation is only as good as the quality of writing I send from my office. Therefore the author should do everything they can to help themselves and help me get the material into perfect form so that people will sit up and say, "Yes, we want to be in business with this writer."

Perspectives

Great Expectations

Working with a Book Publicist

by W.E. Reinka

When Naomi Epel's book, *The Observation Deck: A Toolkit for Writers*, was published, her knowledge of the publishing industry gave her a leg up over most authors. Not only did she have the experience of a previous book, she had also served as media escort for many touring writers who visited San Francisco. In that business, she had worked with scores of publicists and learned every promotional trick in the trade.

But after her book came out, instead of experiencing the joy of putting her professional speaking skills to work on national shows, Epel felt frustrated to appear on media spots she thought obscure. Her publicist became an easy target for her frustration. Now, upon reflection, Epel says her publicist did a great job. "I was caught up in the emotion of having a new book," she says. "We're all blinded by the hopes and dreams for our baby. Now I realize that mine was a niche book—aimed at the writing community—not a book with a widespread national audience. My expectations were totally unrealistic."

Great expectations: the bane of writers and publicists alike. But isn't it the writer's job to write the book and the publisher (and its publicists) to sell it? That sounds right—but the reality is that new and mid-list writers must take an active role in book promotion and sales. "A writer's number one job is to sell books for his publisher," declares mystery writer and book promotion expert J.A. Konrath.

Whether you're teamed with an assigned in-house publicist or working with a hired independent professional, you've got to know how to communicate, work together and distribute duties.

IN-HOUSE PUBLICISTS

Forget the perfect world. Most in-house publicists are already scrambling just to promote the front-list authors upon whom the house relies to meet is expenses (including paying advances to newcomers). Though new writers may feel somewhat ignored, rarely is anyone actually working against them. The potential for publicity is still there.

"Everybody at the publisher is very proud of their first novels. We all have that kind of lottery feeling that we're going to have the book of the year," says Sally Anne McCartin of Lakeport, Conn., whose career as a publicist has ranged from promoting unknown authors to conquering the logistical challenges of Mitch Albom's exhaustive book tour.

Almost every publicist will emphasize that the surest way for writers to get the most from their publicists is to nurture them as allies and look for ways to make their jobs easier. Start

---

W.E. REINKA is a veteran freelancer who often writes about books and authors.

by putting yourself in your publicist's shoes. Save the phone calls for urgent matters. Rely on e-mail instead; however, expect the courtesy to be returned. Kathy Daneman, publicity director for Farrar, Straus & Giroux, says that writers have a right to expect e-mail replies within 24 to 48 hours.

In many ways, writers with assigned or hired publicists should follow the same initial path as writers handling their own promotion—starting with the author's Web site. Publicists are not responsible for building author Web sites. Instead, writers must contact a local consultant or go to construct-your-own sites such as Geocities.yahoo.com, Self-edit.com or TalkSpot .com. Web sites and other major aspects of the promotion process cannot be started too early. Creating a site after publication (and thus missing the chance to list the site on the book cover) is a major missed opportunity.

THINKING AHEAD

Advanced timing is so important in promotion that Kim Dower, a long-time independent publicist who worked under the business name "Kim from L.A.," says her first question when a writer approaches her is "When does the book come out?" (She hopes that the answer is months hence.)

Likewise, writers, with or without publicists, should compile mailing lists of almost everyone they ever knew to receive a promotional postcard announcing their books. While your publicist will get to work on media spots, she can't know the e-mail addresses of your old high school chums or the parishioners at your church—but these friends and acquaintances are a great market for your book. In putting together your mailing lists, you may discover that a reading back in your hometown might draw 300 people.

Every crime fiction writer wants to get noticed by Sarah Weinman, influential proprietor of the crime and mystery fiction blog, "Confessions of an Idiosyncratic Mind." She says that she sorts through 50 books each week. (*The New York Times* winds up with about 500 more books per week than it can cover.) Daneman suggests that, instead of writers simply demanding that their publicist secure a Weinman review, they should scour their backgrounds for ammunition to give their publicist's presentation a bang that makes it stand out from the crowd. "What makes you, beyond your obvious gift with words, worthy of the world's attention?" asks Daneman. "Were you in a street gang, but now rescue puppies? Is your book set in Umbria and you make amazing tomato sauce?"

Look for news hooks that tie your book to current events and therefore make you an easier sell to broadcast media, or the all-important non-book pages in the newspaper. Remember that you, not your publicist, are the expert in your field. You must make the connection between your biography of a 19th-century educator and modern school reform issues, rather than presuming the publicist will see it. On the other hand, don't waste her time with stretches that would tax Mr. Fantastic—your book on military deforestation agents won't land you a guest slot on the local gardening show.

Everyone wants to go on Oprah. When clients tell Dower they want to go on Oprah, Dower doesn't blow them off. "First I always ask 'Why?'" Dower says. "If the answer is 'Because Oprah sells a lot of books,' that isn't good enough. If the answer is more along the lines of, 'Because my book focuses on child abuse prevention and that's a cause that Oprah champions,' then we've got something to work with."

POLISHING AND PROMOTION

Every publicist has war stories about cookbook authors who lobby to go on political talk shows. A universal complaint among publicists stems from writers who question their publicists' knowledge of media or who mistake the publicist's assessment that certain media gigs are unrealistic as "uncooperative." According to Dower, "Many writers don't have a clue what they're asking for. They don't watch TV. They don't listen to the radio. The publicist's job is not just to go after media but to get the *right* media."

It's vital that authors repay their publicists' efforts in getting them on-air exposure with interesting and entertaining interviews. Dower augments her publicity business with media training. While training helps a client articulately control an interview, that's not its only purpose. Media training offers writers new perspectives on how others see them. "No one has a true picture of himself," she maintains.

Even good writers sometimes need media training. James Meader, publicity manager at Picador, observes, "The conventional wisdom remains that the person tuning in to NPR is very likely to buy the book of the author being interviewed. So getting the author on the radio is a primary goal. Unless, of course, the author is not particularly good on the air because that does everyone a disservice: Listeners may connect poor public speaking with poor writing when that's not the case, and the show's producer and host, whose jobs it is to present a smooth and engaging listening experience for their audience, will feel burned by the publicist who arranged the interview, and then they probably won't trust that publicist the next time around."

Promotional budgets increase with bookstore events, book tours, advertising and so forth. (By the way, many publicists concede that advertising doesn't sell books but serves more effectively to announce new offerings from name-brand authors.) Not surprisingly, the higher the expectations (and publisher's advance to the writer), the higher the promotional budget. One fantasy novelist with a modest advance who felt ignored by her in-house publicist proactively set up her own bookstore events and then felt perplexed when the publicist who had ignored her became upset that she was left out of the loop. The writer didn't realize that bookstores, especially the large chains, charge back "co-op advertising" money to the publisher on in-house events. They're not free to the publisher. No one likes a budget-busting surprise.

That's not to say that writers should keep their hands tied—but they should always keep their publicist in the loop on their own promotional efforts. If they've established a solid relationship with the publicist, they're more likely to find the publicist receptive to suggestions such as offers to stay with friends instead of hotels that might make a mini-tour feasible.

A healthy dose of self-deprecatory humor about where you fit into the universe helps win publicists over. But if the in-house publicist remains a negative life force, McCartin advises to then "bring in your agent. Never do the heavy-lifting ugly stuff yourself. Never argue with your publisher. You want wonderful relationships with all the in-house people. Everyone expects agents to be jerks. Your agent has to protect you, and any agent who takes a fee and disappears after the book is sold is not a proper agent."

SEEKING OUTSIDE HELP

Writers who remain unhappy with in-house promotional support can turn to independent publicists. John Kremer, author of *1001 Ways to Market Your Books*, lists publicity contacts at www.bookmarket.com/101pr.html. Quality publicists aren't cheap. Fees may range from $1,000 to $6,000/month, depending upon the scope of the contracted services. A review campaign alone can run up to $10,000.

Is it worth the money?

McCartin says that first-time novelists and most first-time nonfiction authors are best advised to stay in-house. "Writers should use their first book to learn the ropes of the publishing. A first book is easier to promote than a second or third because the publicist can capitalize on the writer's personal story, for instance. That story may grow stale by the time the second or third book rolls around. No matter what anyone says, we all know the same reviewers. There's no sense in paying an independent publicist for information that's available in-house."

As for how to select an independent publicist, Dower encourages writers to begin by trusting their vibes. Are you getting a good feeling from this person or is she perhaps promising anything just to get your business? Dower suggests approaching potential publicists like a doctor's visit. "You take a list of what's wrong and what you want to see fixed to the doctor. Likewise, when a writer sits down with a publicist, he or she should have a list of wants. The process won't work unless each side clearly understands and accepts what the other party wants from the experience."

By establishing a mutual promotional plan of attack, both writer and publicist have a yardstick to measure success and realistic, albeit still great, expectations.

Leaping Into the Fray

My First Year with an Agent and Editor

by Katharine Noel

I n 2003, six years into writing my novel *Halfway House*, I made a list of agents I might want to work with. I wrote each of the people on my list a letter in which I talked about how my work overlapped with that of authors they represented. Just as I was finishing these letters, but before I'd sent any of them out, I got a call from Kim Witherspoon, an agent at Inkwell Management. A friend had mentioned my name to Kim, along with the fact that I'd just won a Rona Jaffe award; Kim was calling to see if I'd send her my novel.

Amazingly, Kim happened to be one of the agents on my list. On a Thursday, I overnighted her the first 100 pages of the book. Monday, she called to request the rest of the manuscript, and four days after that, she was my agent.

It was the only easy part of the process.

Working together to whittle

It took eight and a half years to write *Halfway House*. When I mention this timeframe, people invariably offer, soothingly, "But you were writing other things too, right?"

No, I say. Just the novel.

Katharine Noel

I was, of course, *doing* other things. I had a full-time job with mothers and children at a large homeless shelter in Oakland. It took me three years—writing every morning before work and all weekend—to finish a first draft. Then I won a writing fellowship that allowed me to scale back my hours at the shelter, and in the next three years, I wrote second, third and fourth drafts. Because I'm an inefficient writer—in order to find the story, I write lots and lots of scenes—I'd written somewhere around 1,400 pages. Before I started looking for an agent, I managed to winnow the book down to about 600.

When Kim took me on as a client, she was excited about the novel, but she had ideas for making it tighter. The book's second section slowed down too much, she felt; some secondary characters were taking up more than their share of oxygen. Also, at 600 pages, it was too long.

I spent six months rewriting the book, trying, in general, to make each chapter responsive

KATHARINE NOEL's novel *Halfway House* was a *New York Times* Editor's Choice and the winner of the 2006 Kate Chopin Award for fiction. Chapters have been anthologized in *Best New American Voices* and *Outside Rules*. Katharine teaches at Stanford University, where she held Wallace Stegner and Truman Capote fellowships from 2000-2002.

"A stunning novel."—Ann Packer

Halfway House

KATHARINE NOEL

A NOVEL

Courtesy of Grove/Atlantic

to the one before. *Halfway House* is about the dissolution of a family after one of its members—a high school honors student—has a psychotic break. The book shifts among five characters' points of view, and the constant movement from one plot or subplot to another meant that I had to be careful not to let the energy sag. When I sent the book back to Kim in April 2004, she liked the changes. I still had to shorten the book, though.

But I *had* shortened the book, I assured her. In this rewrite, I'd cut it down to a lean 550 pages.

Kim wanted me to shorten the book by another 100 pages. If I missed the material, she reminded me, I could always put it back in later—but when editors hefted a five-pound debut novel, their hearts were going to sink. She didn't suggest specific scenes or plot lines to take out; the book was just too long.

In the original telling of "Cinderella," the stepsisters don't try to squeeze their feet into the glass slipper. Instead, their mother hands them a knife and instructs them to cut off their heels and toes. Was this what it meant to work with an agent—that I'd have to hack away at the book in order to fit someone else's idea of its size?

At first, I was sure nothing could be jettisoned, and I spent several sullen days in front of my computer, arguing with Kim in my head about how she didn't understand true art. I wondered if I'd made a terrible mistake by choosing her to represent me. But then I began to discover whole chapters that, like toes, could be lived without. As hard as I'd worked on them, some of the scenes just weren't necessary.

Two months later, I was down to 470 pages. I changed the bottom margin of the document, making it a fifth of an inch longer, which cut 18 pages. I sent the book off to Kim.

From agent to editor

It was now early June of 2004. August is a notoriously difficult time to sell a book, so Kim wanted to get *Halfway House* to editors before then. My boyfriend, Eric, and I were also getting married at the end of the month, and I had the idea that having the book out of the house would allow me to turn my attention to other matters.

Kim told me she'd work around my "blackout dates" and I said yes, great, we'll have blackout dates. I wasn't thinking that the process would require much of me—Kim, after all, was taking over now. I'd been so focused for the past seven years on writing the thing that selling it seemed abstract and out of my hands.

The novel went out to eight editors—people Kim had chosen because they seemed particularly good at editing novels similar to mine. More than I'd realized, agents act like marriage brokers: They aren't just trying to sell a book, but also thinking about what choice will best help a writer's long-term career. Often, securing the biggest possible advance is less important than making the right match. It's essential to find an editor who will do a great job with the book, at a publishing house that will promote it. If a book isn't well managed by an editor

Perspectives

or house, and fails to sell well, it can hurt a writer's chances to publish a next book.

In her marriage broker role, Kim didn't just set me up with people; she actually arranged our dates. Interested editors called her; she called me, talked a little bit about the editor, and then fixed a time for us to talk. Like suitors, the editors sent gifts—big Fed-Ex'ed boxes of books. I was now days away from my wedding. What had I meant when I'd accepted the idea of "blackout dates"? Was I really going to stop the whole process, with whatever momentum it might have built?

The day after the wedding, Eric and I drove up the northern California coast. We'd decided to forgo a more traditional honeymoon and just spend the week outdoors, relaxing, being together; the plan was to hike, sleep late and talk to no one.

Instead, more than once, I left Eric alone in the middle of the woods so that I could hike back to a trailhead and take calls from editors in New York. I get migraines when I'm stressed out—the kind of migraine that makes you puke. So that was my honeymoon: leaving Eric alone in the middles of trails, talking to editors, taking more Imitrex than is medically prudent, puking.

Elisabeth Schmitz at Grove/Atlantic was the only editor who replied and thought the book needed major work—an opinion that impressed me. She could see beyond the words on the page to a different, stronger novel. Her offer was less than we'd hoped for, but Kim urged me to take it: We could get more money elsewhere, but she thought Elisabeth was an editor I shouldn't pass up.

You would think that finally selling a book would be liberating, but I found the process taxing and overwhelming. When I accepted the Grove/Atlantic offer, I did it without any celebration or relief. It felt like an anticlimax. I equated the size of the advance with the worthiness of the book, and I worried that, by not taking a bigger offer, I was dooming the novel to obscurity.

Cut, revise, cut, revise...

Most of my worries soon disappeared when I saw why Kim had thought I should work with Elisabeth. She was an amazing, careful, insightful editor—able both to pinpoint sentence-level changes and also see ways of making the whole novel stronger. She suggested a handful of changes: Most radically, a secondary character, Wendy—the girlfriend of one of the central characters—didn't really need to have her own chapters.

Elisabeth was right, absolutely, that Wendy's chapters made the book's structure messier—but I liked that messiness. I struggled with the question of whether to cut sections of the novel that are from Wendy's point of view. Finally, I wrote Elisabeth a long letter, telling her I was too attached to Wendy to cut her chapters ("I tried taking her out, but I really missed her"). Luckily, I sent the letter to my agent first. I was expecting Kim's approval, but instead she called me immediately and said, "If you don't want to make the changes, don't make the changes, but don't be passive-aggressive about it by offloading your anxiety onto Elisabeth in advance. And being attached to Wendy is not a sufficient reason to keep her."

It was difficult to hear it put so bluntly, but Kim was right. Characters need to justify their existence on the *page*, rather than through pleading or rationalizations. I went back to the rewrite focused on the role Wendy serves and cut chapters that digressed. I sent Elisabeth the draft, number seven, in the winter of 2004. I also sent a letter saying that I trusted her judgment, and that if she still didn't think the novel worked, I'd cut the chapters from Wendy's point of view. Elisabeth liked the changes I'd made, though, and the book went to a copy editor.

When the book came back to me for final changes in the summer of 2005, I did my last revision and sent the final draft—399 pages long—to Elisabeth and Kim. It had been almost exactly a year since I'd sold the book; now it finally was out of my hands, for readers to make of it what they would.

Moving on

During the time she was selling my book, Kim's focus was on me absolutely, but our contact these days is minimal: There's just not much I need from her. She's available to me, but I'm in the early stages of a new novel (once again a messy and totally inefficient process), and I want to concentrate entirely on its writing, not on when it might sell.

In hindsight, I think a good advance from a great house was the best thing that could have happened to me—and I'm incredibly grateful that Kim urged me to accept Elisabeth's proposal.

One day, I checked out feedback on barnesandnoble.com. One customer had written that after all the reviews and the hype, she expected the book to be really good, but instead it just felt really long. The comment was weirdly thrilling: I'd been afraid that the book would disappear into obscurity, and here someone was complaining about "hype."

As to the length: The reviewer has no idea what she's missing.

Success Stories

Real Writers with Real Praise for
Guide to Literary Agents

"Last summer, I embarked on writing a story that turned into a young adult novel. After many drafts and critiques, I began submitting to a few well-chosen agents listed in *Guide to Literary Agents*. Your guide led me to the Larsen Pomada Agency, which led me to a match with Laurie McLean, an agent interested in new clients writing for young adults. I e-mailed her a query letter; one week later, she offered me representation. After a synergetic phone conversation, I knew we were a great match. Within 10 days of initial submission, I found an energetic and amazing agent—and it's all thanks to your publication! Many thanks."

—Jennifer Cervantes
Las Cruces, N.M.

"As a first-time author, I found the book, *Guide to Literary Agents*, and the Web site, www.WritersMarket.com, invaluable—particularly with the Web site's ability to screen for agents and publishers by area of specialty. Simply put, www.WritersMarket.com is what brought Whimsy Literary Agency and me together. And for the money, it is undoubtedly the best option out there."

—Buddy Howard
Raleigh, N.C.

"I was looking for an agent for my supplemental textbook and had tried for seven years to find a publisher. I had enough rejection letters to wallpaper my office. Finally, in March 2006, I researched both www.WritersMarket.com and *Guide to Literary Agents*. I sent out query letters and proposals to five agencies that I thought would represent my book. One responded and asked for the manuscript. Three months later, I had a contract with an agent and a publisher. Thank you for the access to agencies that will work with writers who specialize."

—Guinevere Durham
Perry, Ga.

"I would like to thank you and your book, *Guide to Literary Agents*. My eyes were opened to scams because of the information contained in it. It's a great resource for new and experienced writers alike. Thank you for all your help."

—Lucy Raia
Sparta, N.J.

Literary Agents

Agents listed in this section generate 98-100 percent of their income from commission on sales. They do not charge for reading, critiquing or editing your manuscript or book proposal. It's the goal of an agent to find salable manuscripts: Her income depends on finding the best publisher for your manuscript.

Since an agent's time is better spent meeting with editors, she will have little or no time to critique your writing. Agents who don't charge fees must be selective and often prefer to work with established authors, celebrities or those with professional credentials in a particular field.

Some agents in this section may charge clients for office expenses such as photocopying, foreign postage, long-distance phone calls or express mail services. Make sure you have a clear understanding of what these expenses are before signing any agency agreement.

SUBHEADS

Each agency listing is broken down into subheads to make locating specific information easier. In the first section, you'll find contact information for each agency. You'll also learn if the agents within the agency belong to any professional organizations; membership in these organizations can tell you a lot about an agency. For example, members of the Association of Authors' Representatives (AAR) are prohibited from charging reading or evaluating fees. Additional information in this section includes the size of each agency, its willingness to work with new or unpublished writers, and its general areas of interest.

Member Agents: Agencies comprised of more than one agent list member agents and their individual specialties. This information will help you determine the appropriate person to whom you should send your query letter.

Represents: This section allows agencies to specify what nonfiction and fiction subjects they represent. Make sure you query only those agents who represent the type of material you write.

⚬ᷓ Look for the key icon to quickly learn an agent's areas of specialization. In this portion of the listing, agents mention the specific subject areas they're currently seeking, as well as those subject areas they do not consider.

How to Contact: Most agents open to submissions prefer an initial query letter that briefly describes your work. While some agents may ask for an outline and a specific number of sample chapters, most don't. You should send these items only if the agent requests them. In this section, agents also mention if they accept queries by fax or e-mail, if they consider simultaneous submissions, and how they prefer to obtain new clients.

Recent Sales: To give you a sense of the types of material they represent, the agents list specific titles they've sold, as well as a sampling of clients' names. Note that some agents consider their client list confidential and may only share client names once they agree to represent you.

Terms: Provided here are details of an agent's commission, whether a contract is offered and for how long, and what additional office expenses you might have to pay if the agent agrees to represent you. Standard commissions range from 10-15 percent for domestic sales and 15-20 percent for foreign or dramatic sales (with the difference going to the co-agent who places the work).

Writers' Conferences: A great way to meet an agent is at a writers' conference. Here agents list the conferences they usually attend. For more information about a specific conference, check the Conferences section starting on page 253.

Tips: In this section, agents offer advice and additional instructions for writers.

SPECIAL INDEXES

Literary Agents Specialties Index: This index (page 284) organizes agencies according to the subjects they are interested in receiving. This index should help you compose a list of agents specializing in your areas. Cross-referencing categories and concentrating on agents interested in two or more aspects of your manuscript might increase your chances of success.

Agents Index: This index (page 344) provides a list of agents' names in alphabetical order, along with the name of the agency for which they work. Find the name of the person you would like to contact, and then check the agency listing.

General Index: This index (page 356) lists all agencies and conferences appearing in the book.

Quick Reference Icons

At the beginning of some listings, you will find one or more of the following symbols:

N Agency new to this edition

Canadian agency

International agency

Agency actively seeking clients

Agency seeking both new and established writers

Agency seeking mostly established writers through referrals

Agency specializing in certain types of work

Agency not currently seeking new clients

Find a pull-out bookmark with a key to symbols on the inside cover of this book.

[N] [◎] A + B WORKS

E-mail: amy@aplusbworks.com. **Contact:** Amy Jameson. Estab. 2004.
- Prior to her current position, Ms. Jameson worked at Janklow & Nesbit Associates.

Represents Nonfiction books, novels. **Considers these fiction areas:** Young adult; women's
- ⚬ This agency specializes in middle grade and YA fiction, women's fiction and some adult nonfiction. "We are only interested in established writers at this time." Does not want to receive thrillers or science fiction.

How to Contact Query with SASE. Query via e-mail only. Send queries to query@aplusbworks.com. No fax queries.

Recent Sales *Sun and Moon, Ice and Snow*, by Jessica Day George (Bloomsbury); *River Secrets*, by Shannon Hale (Bloomsbury); *Tall Tales*, by Karen Day (Wendy Lamb Books).

[◎] DOMINICK ABEL LITERARY AGENCY, INC.

146 W. 82nd St., #1B, New York NY 10024. (212)877-0710. Fax: (212)595-3133. E-mail: agency@dalainc.com. Estab. 1975. Member of AAR. Represents 100 clients. Currently handles: adult nonfiction books; adult novels.

How to Contact Query with SASE.

Terms Agent receives 15% commission on domestic sales; 20% commission on foreign sales.

[◎] CAROLE ABEL LITERARY AGENT

160 W. 87th St., #7D, New York NY 10024. Fax: (212)724-1384. E-mail: caroleabel@aol.com. 50% of clients are new/unpublished writers. Currently handles: nonfiction books.

How to Contact Query with SASE or via e-mail or fax.

Recent Sales *Living With Fibromyalgia*, by David Trock and Frances Chamberlain (Wiley); *What's Toxic, What's Not*, by Gary Ginsberg and Brian Toal (Berkley).

[⛊] [◎] ACACIA HOUSE PUBLISHING SERVICES, LTD.

62 Chestnut Ave., Brantford ON N3T 4C2 Canada. Phone/Fax: (416)484-8356. **Contact:** (Ms.) Frances Hanna. Estab. 1985. Represents 100 clients. Currently handles: 30% nonfiction books; 70% novels.
- Ms. Hanna has been in the publishing business for 30 years, first in London as a fiction editor with Barrie & Jenkins and Pan Books, and as a senior editor with a packager of mainly illustrated books. She was condensed books editor for 6 years for *Reader's Digest* in Montreal and senior editor and foreign rights manager for William Collins & Sons (now HarperCollins) in Toronto. Mr. Hanna has more than 40 years of experience in the publishing business.

Member Agents Frances Hanna; Bill Hanna, vice president (self-help, modern history, military history).

Represents Nonfiction books, novels. **Considers these nonfiction areas:** Animals; biography/autobiography; language/literature/criticism; memoirs; military/war; music/dance; nature/environment; theater/film; travel. **Considers these fiction areas:** Action/adventure; detective/police/crime; literary; mainstream/contemporary; mystery/suspense; thriller
- ⚬ This agency specializes in contemporary fiction—literary or commercial. Actively seeking outstanding first novels with literary merit. Does not want to receive horror, occult or science fiction.

How to Contact Query with outline, SASE. *No unsolicited mss.* No e-mail or fax queries. Responds in 6 weeks to queries. Returns materials only with SASE.

Recent Sales This agency prefers not to share information on specific sales.

Terms Agent receives 15% commission on English language sales; 20% commission on dramatic sales; 25% commission on foreign sales. Charges clients for photocopying, postage, courier.

Tips "We prefer that writers be previously published, with at least a few short stories or articles to their credit. Strongest consideration will be given to those with three or more published books. However, we would take on an unpublished writer of outstanding talent."

[◎] ADAMS LITERARY

7845 Colony Road C4, #215, Charlotte NC 28226. (212)786-9140. Fax: (212)786-9170. E-mail: info@adamsliterary.com. Web site: www.adamsliterary.com. **Contact:** Tracey Adams. Estab. 2004. Member of AAR.
- Prior to becoming an agent, Ms. Adams worked in the marketing and editorial departments of Greenwillow Books and Margaret K. McElderry Books.

Member Agents Tracey Adams; Josh Adams
- ⚬ Adams Literary is a full-service literary agency exclusively representing children's book authors and artists. "Although we remain absolutely dedicated to finding new talent, we must announce that, until further notice, we can no longer accept unsolicited manuscripts. We also cannot accept queries or submissions via e-mail."

How to Contact Please visit this agency's Web site for updates regarding submissions policy, as it is in flux. No e-mail or fax queries.
Recent Sales Two novels, by Cynthia Lord (Scholastic).

ⓝ ⓜ THE AGENCY GROUP, LLC

1880 Century Park E., Suite 711, Los Angeles CA, 90068. (310)385-2800. E-mail: marcgerald@theagencygroup.com. Web site: www.theagencygroup.com. **Contact:** Marc Gerald, Caroline Greeven. Estab. 2002. Represents 50 clients. 10% of clients are new/unpublished writers. Currently handles: 60% nonfiction books; 30% novels; 10% multimedia.
- Prior to becoming an agent, Mr. Gerald owned and ran an independent publishing and entertainment agency.

Represents Nonfiction books, novels. **Considers these nonfiction areas:** Anthropology/archaeology; art/architecture/design; biography/autobiography; business/economics; child guidance/parenting; cooking/foods/nutrition; ethnic/cultural interests; government/politics/law; health/medicine; history; how-to; humor/satire; memoirs; money/finance; music/dance; nature/environment; popular culture; psychology; self-help/personal improvement; sports; true crime/investigative; interior design/decorating. **Considers these fiction areas:** All subjects except science fiction/fantasy.
- ⚷ "While we admire beautiful writing, we largely represent recording artists, celebrities, authors, and pop culture and style brands with established platforms. When we represent fiction, we work almost exclusively in genre and in areas of expertise. We tend to take a non-linear approach to content—many of our projects ultimately have a TV/film or digital component." Actively seeking books with epic, world-changing ideas. Does not want to receive science fiction, fantasy, and books billed as the "next Harry Potter."

How to Contact Submit query letter, bio, sample chapters, proposal, SASE. Considers simultaneous queries. Responds in 1 month to queries; 3 months to mss. Obtains most new clients through recommendations from others.
Recent Sales Sold 40 titles in the last year. *50 by 50*, by 50 Cent (Pocket); *Sew U*, by Wendy Mullin (Bullfinch); *Little Things*, by Jeffrey Brown (Fireside); *The Hustler's Wife #2*, by Nikki Turner (Random House); *One Red Paperclip*, by Kyle MacDonald (Three Rivers Press). Other clients include Tim McGraw, Eminem, Project Alabama, Wahida Clark, Steve Rinella, Meta Smith, Joy King, Merlin Bronques, Jim Limburgh, Chris Jericho.
Terms Agent receives 15% commission on domestic sales; 20% commission on foreign sales. Offers written contract. Charges clients for office fees (only for mss that have been sold).

ⓜ AGENTS INK!

P.O. Box 4956, Fresno CA 93744. (559)438-8289. **Contact:** Sydney H. Harriet, director. Estab. 1987. Member of APA. Represents 20 clients. 70% of clients are new/unpublished writers. Currently handles: 80% nonfiction books; 20% novels.
- Prior to opening his agency, Dr. Harriet was a psychologist, radio and television reporter, and professor of English. Ms. McNichols has a BA in classical Greek and an MA in classics. She has more than 20 years of experience as an editor for daily and alternative newspapers, major syndicates, and independent authors.

Member Agents Sydney Harriet; Dinah McNichols.
Represents Nonfiction books, novels. **Considers these nonfiction areas:** Animals; cooking/foods/nutrition; government/politics/law; health/medicine (mind/body healing); history; language/literature/criticism; psychology; science/technology; self-help/personal improvement; sociology; sports (medicine, psychology); foreign affairs; international topics
- ⚷ This agency specializes in writers who have education experience in the business, legal and health professions. It is helpful if the writer is licensed, but not necessary. Prior nonfiction book publication is not necessary. For fiction, previously published fiction is a prerequisite for representation. Does not want to receive memoirs, autobiographies, stories about overcoming an illness, science fiction, fantasy, religious materials or children's books.

How to Contact Query with SASE. Considers simultaneous submissions. Responds in 1 month.
Terms Agent receives 15% commission on domestic sales; 20% commission on foreign sales. Offers written contract, binding for 6-12 months (negotiable).

ⓜ THE AHEARN AGENCY, INC.

2021 Pine St., New Orleans LA 70118. E-mail: pahearn@aol.com. **Contact:** Pamela G. Ahearn. Estab. 1992. Member of MWA, RWA, ITW. Represents 35 clients. 20% of clients are new/unpublished writers. Currently handles: 10% nonfiction books; 90% novels.
- Prior to opening her agency, Ms. Ahearn was an agent for 8 years and an editor with Bantam Books.

Considers these nonfiction areas: Animals; child guidance/parenting; current affairs; ethnic/cultural interests; gay/lesbian issues; health/medicine; history; popular culture; self-help/personal improvement; theater/film; true crime/investigative; women's issues/studies. **Considers these fiction areas:** Action/adventure; contemporary issues; detective/police/crime; ethnic; family saga; feminist; glitz; historical; humor/satire; literary; mainstream/contemporary; mystery/suspense; psychic/supernatural; regional; romance; thriller

    o⚬ This agency specializes in historical romance and is also very interested in mysteries and suspense fiction. Does not want to receive category romance, science fiction or fantasy.

How to Contact Query with SASE. Accepts e-mail queries (no attachments). Considers simultaneous queries. Responds in 8 weeks to queries; 10 weeks to mss. Obtains most new clients through recommendations from others, solicitations, conferences.

Recent Sales *Red Chrysanthemum*, by Laura Joh Rowland; *Only a Duke Will Do*, by Sabrina Jeffries; *The Alexandria Link*, by Steve Berry.

Terms Agent receives 15% commission on domestic sales; 20% commission on foreign sales. Offers written contract, binding for 1 year; renewable by mutual consent.

Writers' Conferences Moonlight & Magnolias; RWA National Conference; Thriller Fest; Florida Romance Writers; Bouchercon; Malice Domestic.

Tips "Be professional! Always send in exactly what an agent/editor asks for—no more, no less. Keep query letters brief and to the point, giving your writing credentials and a very brief summary of your book. If one agent rejects you, keep trying—there are a lot of us out there!"

◪ ALIVE COMMUNICATIONS, INC.

7680 Goddard St., Suite 200, Colorado Springs CO 80920. (719)260-7080. Fax: (719)260-8223. Web site: www.alivecom.com. Estab. 1989. Member of AAR, Authors Guild. Represents 100+ clients. 5% of clients are new/unpublished writers. Currently handles: 50% nonfiction books; 35% novels; 5% novellas; 10% juvenile books.

Member Agents Rick Christian, president (blockbusters, bestsellers); Lee Hough (popular/commercial nonfiction and fiction, thoughtful spirituality, children's); Beth Jusino (thoughtful/inspirational nonfiction, women's fiction/nonfiction, Christian living).

Represents Nonfiction books, novels, short story collections, novellas. **Considers these nonfiction areas:** Biography/autobiography; business/economics; child guidance/parenting; how-to; memoirs; religious/inspirational; self-help/personal improvement; women's issues/studies. **Considers these fiction areas:** Action/adventure; contemporary issues; detective/police/crime; family saga; historical; humor/satire; literary; mainstream/contemporary; mystery/suspense; religious/inspirational; thriller

    o⚬ This agency specializes in fiction, Christian living, how-to and commercial nonfiction. Actively seeking inspirational, literary and mainstream fiction, and work from authors with established track records and platforms. Does not want to receive poetry, young adult paperbacks, scripts or dark themes.

How to Contact Query with SASE. Be advised that this agency works primarily with well-established, bestselling, and career authors. Returns materials only with SASE. Obtains most new clients through recommendations from others.

Recent Sales Sold 300+ titles in the last year. A spiritual memoir, by Eugene Peterson (Viking); A biography of Rwandan president Paul Kagame, by Stephen Kinzer; *Ever After*, by Karen Klingsbury (Zondervan).

Terms Agent receives 15% commission on domestic sales; 15% commission on foreign sales. Offers written contract; 2-month notice must be given to terminate contract.

Tips "Rewrite and polish until the words on the page shine. Endorsements and great connections may help, provided you can write with power and passion. Network with publishing professionals by making contacts, joining critique groups, and attending writers' conferences in order to make personal connections and to get feedback. Alive Communications, Inc., has established itself as a premiere literary agency. We serve an elite group of authors who are critically acclaimed and commercially successful in both Christian and general markets."

Ⓝ ◪ ALLEN O'SHEA LITERARY AGENCY

615 Westover Road, Stamford CT 06902. (203)359-9965. Fax: (203)357-9909. E-mail: ma615@aol.com. **Contact:** Marilyn Allen. Estab. 2007. Represents 100 clients. 20% of clients are new/unpublished writers. Currently handles: 100% nonfiction books.

    ● Prior to becoming agents, both Ms. Allen and Ms. O'Shea held senior positions in publishing.

Member Agents Marilyn Allen; Coleen O'Shea.

Represents Nonfiction books. **Considers these nonfiction areas:** Animals (pet books); biography/autobiography; business/economics; cooking/foods/nutrition; current affairs; health/medicine; history; how-to; humor/satire; military/war; money/finance; popular culture; psychology; self-help/personal improvement; sports; interior design/decorating

    o⚬ This agency specializes in practical nonfiction including health, cooking, sports, business, pop culture, etc. "We look for clients with strong marketing platforms and new ideas coupled with strong writing."

Actively seeking narrative nonfiction, craft, health and history writers. Does not want to receive fiction, poetry, textbooks or children's.

How to Contact Query with SASE, submit outline, author bio, marketing page. No phone or fax queries. Considers simultaneous queries. Responds in 1 week to queries; 1-2 months to mss. Returns materials only with SASE. Obtains most new clients through recommendations from others, conferences.

Recent Sales Sold 45 titles in the last year. This agency prefers not to share information about specific sales.

Terms Agent receives 15% commission on domestic sales. Offers written contract, binding for 2 years; 1-month notice must be given to terminate contract. Charges for photocopying large mss, and overseas postage—"typically minimal costs."

Writers' Conferences ASJA, Publicity Submit for Writers, Connecticut Authors and Publishers, Willamette Writers' Conference.

Tips "Prepare a strong overview, with competition, marketing and bio."

☑ ALTAIR LITERARY AGENCY, LLC

P.O. Box 11656, Washington DC 20008. Web site: www.altairliteraryagency.com. Estab. 1996. Member of AAR. Represents 50 clients.

Member Agents Andrea Pedolsky, partner; Nicholas Smith, partner.

Represents Nonfiction books

   O—⚡ This agency specializes in nonfiction with an emphasis on authors who have credentials and professional recognition for their topic, and a high level of public exposure.

How to Contact This agency is not taking queries at this time.

Recent Sales *Performance Nutrition for Runners*, by Matt Fitzgerald (Rodale); *Online Roots*, by Pamela Porter, CGRS, CGL and Amy Johnson Crow (Rutledge Hill Press).

Terms Agent receives 15% commission on domestic sales; 20% commission on foreign sales. Offers written contract, binding for 1 year; 2-month notice must be given to terminate contract.

☑ MIRIAM ALTSHULER LITERARY AGENCY

53 Old Post Road N., Red Hook NY 12571. (845)758-9408. **Contact:** Miriam Altshuler. Estab. 1994. Member of AAR. Represents 40 clients. Currently handles: 45% nonfiction books; 45% novels; 5% story collections; 5% juvenile books.

   ● Ms. Altshuler has been an agent since 1982.

Represents Nonfiction books, novels, short story collections, juvenile books. **Considers these nonfiction areas:** Biography/autobiography; ethnic/cultural interests; history; language/literature/criticism; memoirs; multicultural; music/dance; nature/environment; popular culture; psychology; sociology; theater/film; women's issues/studies. **Considers these fiction areas:** Literary; mainstream/contemporary; multicultural

   O—⚡ Does not want self-help, mystery, how-to, romance, horror, spiritual, fantasy, poetry, screenplays, science fiction or techno-thriller.

How to Contact Query with SASE. Prefers to read materials exclusively. If no SASE is included, no response will be sent. No unsolicited mss. No e-mail or fax queries. Considers simultaneous queries. Responds in 3 weeks to mss. Returns materials only with SASE. Obtains most new clients through recommendations from others.

Terms Agent receives 15% commission on domestic sales; 20% commission on foreign sales. Charges clients for overseas mailing, photocopies, overnight mail when requested by author.

Writers' Conferences Bread Loaf Writers' Conference; Washington Independent Writers Conference; North Carolina Writers' Network Conference.

Ⓝ ☑ ☑ AMB LITERARY MANAGEMENT

104 Fulton Ave., Toronto Ontario M4K 1X8, Canada. (416)467-1695. Fax: (416)467-7924. E-mail: contact@ambliterarymanagement.com. Web site: www.ambliterarymanagement.com. **Contact:** Amy Moore-Benson. Estab. 2006.

   ● Prior to her current position, Ms. Moore-Benson was an editor at MIRA Books/Harlequin.

Represents Nonfiction books, novels.

How to Contact Query with SASE, submit synopsis, publishing history, author bio. Send no mss until requested. No attachments. Send a one-page query letter, by e-mail or snail mail. Please indicate if the submission is a simultaneous submission. No fax queries.

Recent Sales Three romance books, by Marcia King-Gamble (Kimani); *A Necessary Evil*, by Alex Kava (Mira); *Blue Murder*, by Linda Richards (Thomas Dunne Books). Other clients include Beth Ciotta, Michelle Monkou.

𝔑 ◑ AMBASSADOR LITERARY AGENCY

P.O. Box 50358, Nashville TN 37205. (615)370-4700. E-mail: Wes@AmbassadorAgency.com. Web site: www.A mbassadorAgency.com. **Contact:** Wes Yoder. Estab. 1997. Represents 25-30 clients. 25% of clients are new/unpublished writers. Currently handles: 95% nonfiction books; 5% novels.

- Prior to becoming an agent, Mr. Yoder founded a music artist agency in 1973; he established a speakers bureau division of the company in 1984.

Represents Nonfiction books, novels. **Considers these nonfiction areas:** Biography/autobiography; business/economics; child guidance/parenting; current affairs; education; ethnic/cultural interests; government/politics/law; health/medicine; history; how-to; memoirs; money/finance; popular culture; religious/inspirational; self-help/personal improvement; translation; women's issues/studies. **Considers these fiction areas:** Action/adventure; ethnic; family saga; literary; mainstream/contemporary; mystery/suspense; religious/inspirational; thriller; westerns/frontier

- ⊶ This agency specializes in religious market publishing and has excellent national media relationships, dealing primarily with A-level publishers. Actively seeking popular nonfiction themes, including the following: practical living; Christian spirituality; literary fiction. Does not want to receive short stories, children's books, screenplays or poetry.

How to Contact Query with SASE, submit proposal package, outline, synopsis, 6 sample chapter(s), author bio. Accepts e-mail queries. No fax queries. Considers simultaneous queries. Responds in 2-4 weeks to queries. Obtains most new clients through recommendations from others.

Recent Sales Sold 20 titles in the last year. *The Unusual Suspect*, by Stephen Baldwin (Hachette); *Amazing Grace: William Wilberforce and the Heroic Campaign to End Slavery*, by Eric Mataxas (Harper San Francisco); *Life@The Next Level*, by Courtney McBath (Simon & Schuster); *Women, Take Charge of Your Money*, by Carolyn Castleberry (Random House/Multnomah).

Terms Agent receives 15% commission on domestic sales; 20% commission on foreign sales. Offers written contract.

🌐 ◑ THE AMPERSAND AGENCY

Ryman's Cottages, Little Tew, Oxfordshire OX7 4JJ United Kingdom. (44)(16)868-3677. Fax: (44)(16)868-3449. E-mail: peter@theampersandagency.co.uk. Web site: www.theampersandagency.co.uk. **Contact:** Peter Buckman. Estab. 2003. Member of AAR. Represents 35 clients. 75% of clients are new/unpublished writers.

- Prior to opening his agency, Mr. Buckman was a writer and publisher in England and America.

Member Agents Peter Buckman (literary fiction and nonfiction); Peter Janson-Smith (crime, thrillers, biography); Anne-Marie Doulton (historical and women's fiction).

Represents Nonfiction books, novels, juvenile books, scholarly books. **Considers these nonfiction areas:** Animals; biography/autobiography; cooking/foods/nutrition; current affairs; education; ethnic/cultural interests; government/politics/law; health/medicine; history; humor/satire; language/literature/criticism; memoirs; military/war; music/dance; popular culture; psychology; theater/film; translation; true crime/investigative. **Considers these fiction areas:** Action/adventure; comic books/cartoon; confession; detective/police/crime; ethnic; family saga; fantasy; historical; juvenile; literary; mainstream/contemporary; mystery/suspense; romance; thriller; young adult; glitz

- ⊶ "Being a new agency, we specialize in new writers, although we also represent well-established names. We are small, experienced, and professional. We know what we like, respond quickly, and enjoy working with the writers we take on to present their work in the best possible way. We also offer a foreign rights service and have well-established contacts on both sides of the Atlantic in film, TV, broadcasting, and publishing." Actively seeking commercial and literary fiction and nonfiction. Does not want science fiction or works with only regional appeal.

How to Contact Submit outline, 1-2 sample chapters. Accepts queries via e-mail. Considers simultaneous queries. Responds in 1 week to queries; 1 month to mss. Returns materials only with SASE. Obtains most new clients through recommendations, writers' handbooks, word of mouth.

Recent Sales Sold 14 titles in the last year. *Q&A*, by Vikas Swarup (Scribner/Doubleday); *My Side of the Story*, by Will Davis (Bloomsbury); *Digging Up the Dead*, by Dr. Druin Burch (Chatoo & Windus); *Neptune's Daughter*, by Beryl Kingston (Transita). Other clients include Geoff Baker, Max Barron, Rob Buckman, Anna Crosbie, Andrew Cullen, Tom Darke, Francis Ellen, Justin Elliott, Cora Harrison, Georgette Heyer, Michael Hutchinson, Jim McKenna, Euan Macpherson, Bolaji Odofin, Rosie Orr, Philip Purser, Penny Rumble, Nick van Bloss, Mike Walters, Norman Welch, Kirby Wright.

Terms Agent receives 10-15% commission on domestic sales; 20% commission on foreign sales. Offers written contract. "By agreement with the author, we charge for extra photocopying in the case of multiple submissions and for any lawyers or other profesional fees required by a negotiation."

Literary Agents

☑ BETSY AMSTER LITERARY ENTERPRISES

P.O. Box 27788, Los Angeles CA 90027-0788. **Contact:** Betsy Amster. Estab. 1992. Member of AAR. Represents more than 65 clients. 35% of clients are new/unpublished writers. Currently handles: 65% nonfiction books; 35% novels.

• Prior to opening her agency, Ms. Amster was an editor at Pantheon and Vintage for 10 years, and served as editorial director for the Globe Pequot Press for 2 years.

Represents Nonfiction books, novels. **Considers these nonfiction areas:** Biography/autobiography; child guidance/parenting; ethnic/cultural interests; gardening; health/medicine; history; money/finance; psychology; sociology; women's issues/studies. **Considers these fiction areas:** Ethnic; literary; mystery/suspense (quirky); thriller (quirky); women's (high quality)

☛ Actively seeking strong narrative nonfiction, particularly by journalists; outstanding literary fiction (the next Richard Ford or Jhumpa Lahiri); witty, intelligent commerical women's fiction (the next Elinor Lipman or Jennifer Weiner); mysteries that open new worlds to us; and high-profile self-help and psychology, preferably research based. Does not want to receive poetry, children's books, romances, Western, science fiction or action/adventure.

How to Contact For fiction, send query, first 3 pages, SASE. For nonfiction, send query or proposal with SASE. No e-mail or fax queries. Considers simultaneous queries. Responds in 1 month to queries; 2 months to mss. Obtains most new clients through recommendations from others, solicitations, conferences.

Recent Sales *The Blessing of a B Minus*, by Dr. Wendy Mogel (Scribner); *Winners and Lovers: Balancing Love and Power in All Your Relationships*, by Dr. Elaine N. Aron (Little, Brown); *Wild Indigo and Wild Inferno*, by Sandi Ault (Berkley Prime Crime); *Mona Lisa in Camelot: Jacqueline Kennedy and the True Story of the Painting's High-Stakes Journey to America*, by Margaret Leslie Davis (DaCapo); *The Girl I Left Behind: A Narrative History of the Sixties*, by Judith Nies (HarperCollins); *The Battle for Wine and Love (Or How I Saved the World from Parkerization)*, by Alice Feiring (Harcourt); *Mutts*, by Sharon Montrose (Stewart, Tabori & Chang); *A Vicky Hill Exclusive!*, by Hannah Dennison (Berkley Prime Crime); *100 Trees and How They Got Their Names*, by Diana Wells (Algonquin). Other clients include Dr. Linda Acredolo and Dr. Susan Goodwyn, Dwight Allen, Barbara DeMarco-Barrett, Robin Chotzinoff, Rob Cohen & David Wollock, Phil Doran, Ruth Andrew Ellenson, Maria Amparo Escandon, Paul Mandelbaum, Joy Nicholson, Christopher Noxon, Edward Schneider and R.J. Smith.

Terms Agent receives 15% commission on domestic sales; 20% commission on foreign sales. Offers written contract, binding for 1 year; 3-month notice must be given to terminate contract. Charges for photocopying, postage, long distance phone calls, messengers, galleys/books used in submissions to foreign and film agents and to magazines for first serial rights.

Writers' Conferences Squaw Valley Writers' Workshop; San Diego State University Writers' Conference; UCLA Extension Writers' Program; The Loft Literary Center.

☑ MARCIA AMSTERDAM AGENCY

41 W. 82nd St., Suite 9A, New York NY 10024-5613. (212)873-4945. **Contact:** Marcia Amsterdam. Estab. 1970. Signatory of WGA. Currently handles: 15% nonfiction books; 70% novels; 5% movie scripts; 10% TV scripts.

• Prior to opening her agency, Ms. Amsterdam was an editor.

Represents Novels, feature film, TV movie of the week, sitcom. **Considers these fiction areas:** Action/adventure; detective/police/crime; horror; mainstream/contemporary; mystery/suspense; romance (contemporary, historical); science fiction; thriller; young adult. **Considers these script subject areas:** Comedy; mainstream; mystery/suspense; romantic comedy; romantic drama.

How to Contact Query with SASE. No e-mail or fax queries. Responds in 1 month to queries.

Recent Sales *Rosey in the Present Tense*, by Louise Hawes (Walker); *Flash Factor*, by William H. Lovejoy (Kensington).

Terms Agent receives 15% commission on domestic sales; 20% commission on foreign sales; 10% commission on dramatic rights sales. Offers written contract, binding for 1 year. Charges clients for extra office expenses, foreign postage, copying, legal fees (when agreed upon).

Tips "We are always looking for interesting literary voices."

ℕ ☑ ANDERSON LITERARY MANAGEMENT, LLC

12 W. 19th St., New York NY 10011. (212)645-6045. Fax: (212)741-1936. E-mail: info@andersonliterary.com. Web site: www.andersonliterary.com.

• Prior to her current position, Ms. Anderson was with Grinberg Literary.

Member Agents Kathleen Anderson, agent, kathleen@andersonliterary.com (serious nonfiction and literary journalism, such as narrative nonfiction, psychology, history, science, anthropology, memoir, cultural studies, biography, and women's studies; also, literary fiction, general women's fiction, and very well-written commercial fiction, such as psychological suspense, historical fiction, lady-lit, chick-lit); Liz Gately, associate agent, liz@andersonliterary.com (literary fiction, commercial fiction, women's fiction, young adult, children's, multi-

cultural, middle-grade history, biography, science, memoirs, travel, current affairs, health/fitness, journalism).
Represents Nonfiction books, novels, juvenile books.
How to Contact Query with SASE, submit proposal (for nonfiction); proposal, synopsis and up to 50 pages (for creative nonfiction and fiction). Send all e-queries to clarissa@andersonliterary.com. No fax queries. Obtains most new clients through recommendations from others, solicitations.
Recent Sales *The Assassins' Gate*, by George Packer; *17 Huntley Gardens*, by Richard Mason (Knopf); *The Reindeer People*, by Piers Vitebsky (Houghton Mifflin); *Maps for Lost Lovers*, by Nadeem Aslam (Knopf). Other clients include Emma Donoghue, Charles Bowden, Rafi Zabor, Marcia Willett, Jane Shaw, Molly Peacock, Anna Oliver, Conn Iggulden, Bella Bathurst, Kerry Hardie, Anna Beer, Janet Todd, Glen Hirshberg, Deanne Stillman, Chuck Wachtel, Barry Lyga, Craig Childs, Sarah Bilston.

🌐 ◎ ANUBIS LITERARY AGENCY

7 Birdhaven Close Lighthorne Heath, Banbury Road, Warwick Warwickshire CV35 0BE, United Kingdom. Phone/Fax: (44)(192)664-2588. E-mail: anubis.agency2@btopenworld.com. **Contact:** Steve Calcutt. Estab. 1994. Represents 15 clients. 50% of clients are new/unpublished writers. Currently handles: 100% novels.
• In addition to being an agent, Mr. Calcutt teaches creative writing and American history (U.S. Civil War) at Warwick University.
Represents Novels. **Considers these fiction areas:** Horror; science fiction; dark fantasy
○→ Actively seeking horror fiction. Does not want to receive children's books, nonfiction, journalism or TV/film scripts.
How to Contact Query with proposal package, outline, SASE/IRCs. Returns materials only with SASE/IRCs. No e-mail or fax queries. Responds in 6 weeks to queries; 3 months to mss. Obtains most new clients through personal recommendation.
Recent Sales *Berserk* and *Dusk*, by Tim Lebbon (Dorchester); *The Beloved*, by J.F. Gonzalez; *Breeding Ground*, by Sarah Pinborough (Dorchester); *Gradisil*, by Adam Roberts (Orion). Other clients include Steve Savile, Lesley Asquith, Anthea Ingham, Brett A. Savory.
Terms Agent receives 15% commission on domestic sales; 20% commission on foreign sales.

◙ APPLESEEDS MANAGEMENT

200 E. 30th St., Suite 302, San Bernardino CA 92404. (909)882-1667. **Contact:** S. James Foiles. Estab. 1988. 40% of clients are new/unpublished writers. Currently handles: 15% nonfiction books; 85% novels.
Represents Nonfiction books, novels. **Considers these nonfiction areas:** True crime/investigative. **Considers these fiction areas:** Detective/police/crime; mystery/suspense.
How to Contact Query with SASE. Responds in 2 weeks to queries; 2 months to mss.
Recent Sales This agency prefers not to share information on specific sales.
Terms Agent receives 10-15% commission on domestic sales; 20% commission on foreign sales. Offers written contract, binding for 1-7 years.
Tips "Because readership of mysteries is expanding, Appleseeds specializes in mysteries with a detective who could be in a continuing series."

◙ ARCADIA

31 Lake Place N., Danbury CT 06810. E-mail: pryor@arcadialit.com. **Contact:** Victoria Gould Pryor. Member of AAR.
Represents Nonfiction books, literary and commercial fiction. **Considers these nonfiction areas:** Biography/autobiography; business/economics; current affairs; health/medicine; history; memoirs; psychology; science/technology; true crime/investigative; women's issues/studies; investigative journalism; culture; classical music; life transforming self-help.
○→ "I'm a very hands-on agent, which is necessary in this competitive marketplace. I work with authors on revisions until whatever we present to publishers is as perfect as it can be. I represent talented, dedicated, intelligent and ambitious writers who are looking for a long-term relationship based on professional success and mutual respect." Does not want to receive science fiction/fantasy, horror, humor or children's/YA. "We are only able to read fiction submissions from previously published authors."
How to Contact Query with SASE. This agency accepts e-queries (no attachments).
Recent Sales This agency prefers not to share information on specific sales.

🅝 ◯ EDWARD ARMSTRONG LITERARY AGENCY

19 Bronte Way, Suite 31M, Marlborough MA 01752. (401)569-7099. E-mail: edward.armstrong@earthlink.net. **Contact:** Edward Armstrong. Estab. 2006. Currently handles: 100% fiction.

- Prior to becoming an agent, Mr. Armstrong was a business professional specializing in quality and regulatory compliance.

Represents Novels, short story collections, novellas. **Considers these fiction areas:** Mainstream/contemporary; romance; science fiction; thriller; suspense.

○━ Does not want to receive nonfiction or textbooks.

How to Contact Query with SASE, submit synopsis, 3 sample chapter(s), author bio. Accepts e-mail queries. No fax queries. Considers simultaneous queries. Responds in 2-4 weeks to queries; 3 months to mss. Returns materials only with SASE. Obtains most new clients through solicitations.

Terms Agent receives 5% commission on domestic sales; 5% commission on foreign sales. This agency charges for photocopying and postage.

☑ ARTISTS AND ARTISANS INC.

104 W. 29th St., 11th Floor, New York NY 10001. Fax: (212)931-8377. E-mail: adam@artistsandartisans.com. Web site: www.artistsandartisans.com. **Contact:** Adam Chromy. Estab. 2002. Represents 40 clients. 80% of clients are new/unpublished writers. Currently handles: 63% nonfiction books; 35% novels; 2% scholarly books.

- Prior to becoming an agent, Mr. Chromy was an entrepreneur in the technology field for nearly a decade.

Represents Nonfiction books, novels. **Considers these nonfiction areas:** Biography/autobiography; business/economics; child guidance/parenting; cooking/foods/nutrition; current affairs; ethnic/cultural interests; health/medicine; how-to; humor/satire; language/literature/criticism; memoirs; money/finance; music/dance; popular culture; religious/inspirational; science/technology; self-help/personal improvement; sports; theater/film; true crime/investigative; women's issues/studies; fashion/style. **Considers these fiction areas:** Confession; family saga; humor/satire; literary; mainstream/contemporary.

○━ "My education and experience in the business world ensure that my clients' enterprise as authors gets as much attention and care as their writing." Working journalists for nonfiction books. No scripts.

How to Contact Query with SASE. Considers simultaneous queries. Responds in 2 weeks to queries; 2 weeks to mss. Returns materials only with SASE. Obtains most new clients through recommendations from others, solicitations, conferences.

Recent Sales Sold 12 titles in the last year. *Dr. Z on Scoring*, by Victoria Zdrok (Touchstone Fireside); *Winning Points with Your Woman*, by Jaci Rae (Touchstone); *From Binge to Blackout*, by Chris Volkmann and Toren Volkmann (NAL Penguin Group); *Modest Mouse*, by Alan Goldsher (Thomas Dunne Books); *Jewtopia*, by Brian Fogel and Sam Wolfson (Warner Books).

Terms Agent receives 15% commission on domestic sales; 25% commission on foreign sales. Offers written contract; 1-month notice must be given to terminate contract. "We only charge for extraordinary expenses (e.g., client requests check via FedEx instead of regular mail)."

Writers' Conferences ASJA Writers Conference.

Tips "Please make sure you are ready before approaching us or any other agent. If you write fiction, make sure it is the best work you can do and get objective criticism from a writing group. If you write nonfiction, make sure the proposal exhibits your best work and a comprehensive understanding of the market."

Ⓝ ☑ ROBERT ASTLE AND ASSOCIATES LITERARY MANAGEMENT, INC.

820 West End Ave., Suite 15F, New York 10025, NY. (646)682-7864. E-mail: robert@astleliterary.com. Web site: www.astleliterary.com. **Contact:** Robert Astle.

- Prior to becoming an agent, Mr. Astle spent 25 years in theater.

Represents Nonfiction books, novels.

○━ "We are especially interested in receiving nonfiction projects with a wide range of topics, including narrative nonfiction, popular culture, arts and culture, theater and performance, sports, travel, celebrity, biography, politics, memoir, history, new media and multi-ethnic. We are actively seeking writers of literary fiction and commercial fiction—mysteries and suspense, thrillers, mainstream literary fiction, historical fiction, women's fiction, humor/satire and graphic novels. We will also seek writers in the genre of young audiences: middle grade and teen."

How to Contact Use the online form to query. Specifications for nonfiction and fiction submissions are online. No e-mail or fax queries. Returns materials only with SASE. Obtains most new clients through recommendations from others, solicitations.

Tips "Please read the submission guidelines carefully, and make sure your query letter is the best it can be."

☑ THE AUGUST AGENCY, LLC

E-mail: submissions@augustagency.com. Web site: www.augustagency.com. **Contact:** Cricket Pechstein, Jeffery McGraw. Estab. 2004. Represents 25-40 clients. 50% of clients are new/unpublished writers. Currently handles: 75% nonfiction books; 20% novels; 5% other.

• Before opening The August Agency, Ms. Pechstein was a freelance writer, magazine editor and independent literary agent; Mr. McGraw worked as an editor for HarperCollins and publicity manager for Abrams.

Member Agents Jeffery McGraw (politics/current affairs, entertainment, business, psychology, self-help, narrative nonfiction, contemporary women's fiction, literary fiction); Cricket Pechstein (mystery/crime fiction, chick lit, thrillers).

Represents Nonfiction books, novels. **Considers these nonfiction areas:** Biography/autobiography; business/economics; child guidance/parenting; cooking/foods/nutrition; current affairs; ethnic/cultural interests; gay/lesbian issues; government/politics/law; health/medicine; history; how-to; humor/satire; interior design/decorating; memoirs; military/war; money/finance; music/dance; popular culture; psychology; self-help/personal improvement; sociology; sports; theater/film; true crime/investigative; women's issues/studies; inspirational.

Considers these fiction areas: Action/adventure; detective/police/crime; ethnic; family saga; gay/lesbian; historical; humor/satire; literary; mainstream/contemporary; mystery/suspense; psychic/supernatural; thriller; smart chick lit (non-genre romance).

O→ "We actively pursue an array of fiction and nonfiction writers to represent, with an emphasis in media (seasoned journalists receive special favor here), popular culture/entertainment, political science, diet/fitness, health, cookbooks, psychology, business, memoir, highly creative nonfiction, accessible literary fiction, women's fiction, and high-concept mysteries and thrillers. When it comes to nonfiction, we favor persuasive and prescriptive works with a full-bodied narrative command and an undeniable contemporary relevance. Our favorite novelists are as eclectic as our minds are broad, yet they all share one common denominator that might explain a peculiar predisposition for what we prefer to call 'emotional fiction'—a brand of storytelling defined not so much by a novel's category as by its extraordinary power to resonate universally on a deeply emotional level." Does not want to receive academic textbooks, children's books, cozy mysteries, horror, poetry, science fiction/fantasy, short story collections, Western's, screenplays, genre romance or previously self-published works.

How to Contact Submit book summary (1-2 paragraphs), chapter outline (nonfiction only), first 1,000 words or first chapter, total page/word count, brief paragraph on why you have chosen to write the book. Send via e-mail only (no attachments). Responds in 2-3 weeks to queries; 3 months to mss. Obtains most new clients through recommendations from others, solicitations, conferences.

Terms Agent receives 15% commission on domestic sales; 20% commission on foreign sales. Offers written contract; 1-month notice must be given to terminate contract.

Writers' Conferences Surrey International Writers' Conference; Southern California Writers' Conference; Naples Writers' Conference, et al.

✇ AUTHENTIC CREATIONS LITERARY AGENCY

911 Duluth Hwy., Suite D3-144, Lawrenceville GA 30043. (770)339-3774. Fax: (770)339-7126. E-mail: ron@authenticcreations.com. Web site: www.authenticcreations.com. **Contact:** Mary Lee Laitsch. Estab. 1993. Member of AAR, Authors Guild. Represents 70 clients. 30% of clients are new/unpublished writers. Currently handles: 60% nonfiction books; 40% novels.

Member Agents Mary Lee Laitsch; Ronald Laitsch; Jason Laitsch.

Represents Nonfiction books, novels, scholarly books. **Considers these nonfiction areas:** Anthropology/archaeology; biography/autobiography; child guidance/parenting; crafts/hobbies; current affairs; history; how-to; science/technology; self-help/personal improvement; sports; true crime/investigative; women's issues/studies. **Considers these fiction areas:** Action/adventure; detective/police/crime; family saga; literary; mainstream/contemporary; mystery/suspense; romance; sports; thriller.

How to Contact Query with SASE. No e-mail or fax queries. Considers simultaneous queries. Responds in 2 weeks to queries; 2 months to mss.

Recent Sales Sold 20 titles in the last year. *Secret Agent*, by Robyn Spizman and Mark Johnston (Simon & Schuster); *Beauchamp Beseiged*, by Elaine Knighton (Harlequin); *Visible Differences*, by Dominic Pulera (Continuum).

Terms Agent receives 15% commission on domestic sales; 15% commission on foreign sales. This agency charges clients for photocopying.

🅽 ⬭ AVENUE A LITERARY

419 Lafayette St., Third Floor, New York NY 10003. (212)624-5859. Fax: (212)228-6149. E-mail: info@avenuealiterary.com. Web site: www.avenuealiterary.com. **Contact:** Jennifer Cayea. Estab. 2006. Represents 20 clients. 75% of clients are new/unpublished writers. Currently handles: 40% nonfiction books; 45% novels; 5% story collections; 10% juvenile books.

• Prior to opening her agency, Ms. Cayea was an agent and director of foreign rights for Nicholas Ellison, Inc., a division of Sanford J. Greenburger Associates. She was also an editor in the audio and large print divisions of Random House.

Represents Nonfiction books, novels, short story collections, juvenile books. **Considers these nonfiction areas:** Cooking/foods/nutrition; current affairs; ethnic/cultural interests; health/medicine; history; memoirs; music/ dance; popular culture; self-help/personal improvement; sports; theater/film. **Considers these fiction areas:** Family saga; feminist; historical; literary; mainstream/contemporary; thriller; young adult; women's/chick lit.

    O→ "Our authors are dynamic and diverse. We seek strong new voices in fiction and nonfiction, and are fiercely dedicated to our authors." Actively seeking upmarket commercial fiction, literary fiction, narrative nonfiction, young adult and memoir. Does not want to receive romance or mysteries.

How to Contact Query with SASE. Accepts e-mail queries. No fax queries. Considers simultaneous queries. Responds in 6-8 weeks to queries. Returns materials only with SASE. Obtains most new clients through recommendations from others, solicitations, conferences.

Recent Sales Two young adult novels, by Sofia Quintero (Knopf). Other clients include K.L. Cook, Dr. Raeleen D'Agostino, Elisha Miranda, Mario Bosquez, Jennifer Calderon, Daniel Serrano, Yasmin Davidds.

Terms Agent receives 15% commission on domestic sales; 15% commission on foreign sales. Offers written contract; 30-day notice must be given to terminate contract.

Tips "Build a résumé by publishing short stories if you are a fiction writer."

⬛ THE AXELROD AGENCY

55 Main St., P.O. Box 357, Chatham NY 12037. (518)392-2100. Fax: (518)392-2944. E-mail: steve@axelrodagenc y.com. **Contact:** Steven Axelrod. Estab. 1983. Member of AAR. Represents 20-30 clients. 1% of clients are new/ unpublished writers. Currently handles: 5% nonfiction books; 95% novels.

    • Prior to becoming an agent, Mr. Axelrod was a book club editor.

Represents Nonfiction books, novels. **Considers these fiction areas:** Mystery/suspense; romance; women's.

How to Contact Query with SASE. Considers simultaneous queries. Responds in 3 weeks to queries; 6 weeks to mss. Returns materials only with SASE. Obtains most new clients through recommendations from others.

Recent Sales This agency prefers not to share information on specific sales.

Terms Agent receives 15% commission on domestic sales; 20% commission on foreign sales. No written contract.

Writers' Conferences RWA National Conference.

Ⓝ ⬛ BAKER'S MARK LITERARY AGENCY

P.O. Box 8382, Portland OR 97207. (503)432-8170. E-mail: info@bakersmark.com. Web site: www.Bakersmark. com. **Contact:** Bernadette Baker or Gretchen Stelter. Estab. 2005. Currently handles: 35% nonfiction books; 25% novels; 40% graphic novels.

    • Prior to becoming an agent, Ms. Baker received an M.S. in professional writing and publishing from Portland State University. She was the marketing director for Beyond Words Publishing—where she headed up marketing campaigns for two *New York Times* bestsellers. Ms. Stelter has worked as a freelance editor and writer for several Australian newspapers and Bond University; she also worked for Ooligan Press.

Represents Nonfiction books, novels, novellas, scholarly books, animation, anthologies, graphic novels (preferably with art). **Considers these nonfiction areas:** Anthropology/archaeology; art/architecture/design; biography/autobiography; business/economics; child guidance/parenting; ethnic/cultural interests; gay/lesbian issues; government/politics/law; how-to; humor/satire; interior design/decorating; popular culture; true crime/ investigative; women's issues/studies. **Considers these fiction areas:** Comic books/cartoon; detective/police/ crime; erotica; ethnic; experimental; fantasy; feminist; gay/lesbian; glitz; historical; horror; humor/satire; literary; mainstream/contemporary; mystery/suspense; psychic/supernatural; regional (Pacific Northwest); thriller; women's; chick lit.

    O→ "Baker's Mark specializes in graphic novels and popular nonfiction with an extremely selective taste in commercial fiction." Actively seeking graphic novels, nonfiction, fiction. Does not want to receive Western, poetry, sci-fi or children's.

How to Contact Query with SASE, submit proposal package, synopsis, 5 sample chapter(s), author bio, sample art and script for graphic novels. Accepts e-mail queries. No fax queries. Considers simultaneous queries. Returns materials only with SASE. Obtains most new clients through recommendations from others, solicitations.

Recent Sales *City of Readers: A Book Lover's Guide to Portland, Oregon*, by Gabriel Boehmer (Tall Grass Press); *Unaffordable Nation: Searching for a Decent Life in America*, by Jeffrey D. Jones (Prometheus Books); *German Town*, a graphic novel, by Laurence Klavan and Susan Kim (:01 First Second Books). Other clients include David Quinn, Susan DiPlacido, Farel Dalrymple, Shay Youngblood on behalf of Victoria Sanders, Adam Mansbach on behalf of Victoria Sanders, Chris Ryall and Scott Tipton.

Terms Agent receives 15% commission on domestic sales; 20% commission on foreign sales. Offers written contract, binding for 18 months; 30-day notice must be given to terminate contract.

Writers' Conferences New York Comic Convention, BookExpo of America, Comic Con, Stumptown Comics Fest, Emerald City Comic Con.

☑ BALKIN AGENCY, INC.

P.O. Box 222, Amherst MA 01004. (413)548-9835. Fax: (413)548-9836. E-mail: rick62838@crocker.com. **Contact:** Rick Balkin, president. Estab. 1972. Member of AAR. Represents 50 clients. 10% of clients are new/unpublished writers. Currently handles: 85% nonfiction books; 5% scholarly books; 5% textbooks; 5% reference books.

- Prior to opening his agency, Mr. Balkin served as executive editor with Bobbs-Merrill Company.

Represents Nonfiction books, scholarly books, textbooks. **Considers these nonfiction areas:** Animals; anthropology/archaeology; current affairs; health/medicine; history; how-to; language/literature/criticism; nature/environment; popular culture; science/technology; sociology; translation; biography.

    ◐⇥ This agency specializes in adult nonfiction. Does not want to receive fiction, poetry, screenplays or computer books.

How to Contact Query with SASE, submit proposal package, outline. Accepts e-mail queries. No fax queries. Responds in 1 week to queries; 2 weeks to mss. Returns materials only with SASE. Obtains most new clients through recommendations from others.

Recent Sales Sold 30 titles in the last year. *The Many Faces of God*, by (W.W. Norton Co.); *A Perfect Mess*, by Eric Abrahamson and David H. Freedman (Little Brown); *1491*, by Charles Mann (Knopf).

Terms Agent receives 15% commission on domestic sales; 20% commission on foreign sales. Offers written contract, binding for 1 year. This agency charges clients for photocopying and express or foreign mail.

Tips "I do not take on books described as bestsellers or potential bestsellers. Any nonfiction work that is either unique, paradigmatic, a contribution, truly witty, or a labor of love is grist for my mill."

Ⓝ ☑ THE PAULA BALZER AGENCY

55 Eastern Parkway, #5H, Brooklyn NY 11238. (347)787-4131. E-mail: info@pbliterary.com. Web site: www.pbliterary.com. **Contact:** Paula Balzer. Member of AAR. Represents 35 clients. 50% of clients are new/unpublished writers. Currently handles: 50% nonfiction books; 50% novels.

- Prior to her current position, Ms. Balzer was with Carlisle & Company, as well as Sarah Lazin Books.

Represents Nonfiction books, novels. **Considers these nonfiction areas:** Biography/autobiography; child guidance/parenting; cooking/foods/nutrition; current affairs; education; gay/lesbian issues; government/politics/law; history; how-to; humor/satire; memoirs; popular culture; psychology; science/technology; self-help/personal improvement; women's issues/studies. **Considers these fiction areas:** Erotica; family saga; gay/lesbian; glitz; historical; horror; humor/satire; literary; mainstream/contemporary; mystery/suspense; thriller; women's.

    ◐⇥ Humor and popular culture.

How to Contact Query with SASE, submit proposal package, author bio, 50 sample pages. Accepts e-mail queries. No fax queries. Responds in 3 weeks to queries; 4-6 weeks to mss. Returns materials only with SASE. Obtains most new clients through recommendations from others.

Recent Sales *Separated*, by Sheldon Rusch (Berkley); *Pledged: The Secret Life of Sororities*, by Alexandra Robbins (Hyperion); *Quarterlife Crisis: The Unique Challenges of Life in Your Twenties*, by Alexandra Robbins (Penguin Putnam); *Dear Mrs. Lindbergh: A Novel*, by Kathleen Hughes (W.W. Norton & Company).

Terms Agent receives 15% commission on domestic sales; 20% commission on foreign sales. Offers written contract.

☑ LORETTA BARRETT BOOKS, INC.

101 Fifth Ave., New York NY 10003. (212)242-3420. Fax: (212)807-9579. E-mail: query@lorettabarrettbooks.com. Web site: www.lorettabarrettbooks.com. **Contact:** Loretta A. Barrett, Nick Mullendore. Estab. 1990. Member of AAR. Currently handles: 50% nonfiction books; 50% novels.

- Prior to opening her agency, Ms. Barrett was vice president and executive editor at Doubleday and editor-in-chief of Anchor Books.

Represents Nonfiction books, novels. **Considers these nonfiction areas:** Biography/autobiography; child guidance/parenting; current affairs; ethnic/cultural interests; government/politics/law; health/medicine; history; memoirs; money/finance; multicultural; nature/environment; popular culture; psychology; religious/inspirational; science/technology; self-help/personal improvement; sociology; spirituality; sports; women's issues/studies; nutrition; creative nonfiction. **Considers these fiction areas:** Action/adventure; contemporary issues; detective/police/crime; ethnic; family saga; historical; literary; mainstream/contemporary; mystery/suspense; psychic/supernatural; thriller.

    ◐⇥ This agency specializes in general interest books. No children's, juvenile, science fiction, or fantasy.

How to Contact Query with SASE. Accepts e-mail queries. No fax queries. Considers simultaneous queries. Responds in 2-3 weeks to queries. Returns materials only with SASE.

Recent Sales *Spiritual Progress*, by Thomas D. Williams (Hachette); *The Hazards of Space Travel*, by Neil Comins (Ballantine); *Mother Angelica's Little Book of Life Lessons*, by Raymond Arroyo (Doubleday) and more.
Terms Agent receives 15% commission on domestic sales; 20% commission on foreign sales. Offers written contract. Charges clients for shipping and photocopying.

[N] ◙ BARRON'S LITERARY MANAGEMENT

4615 Rockland Drive, Arlington TX 76016. E-mail: barronsliterary@sbcglobal.net. **Contact:** Adele Barron-Brooks, president.
Represents Nonfiction books, novels. **Considers these nonfiction areas:** Business/economics; cooking/foods/nutrition; ethnic/cultural interests; health/medicine; history; multicultural; science/technology; sports; travel.
Considers these fiction areas: Fantasy; juvenile; mystery/suspense; romance; science fiction.

    O→ "We are a small Dallas/Fort Worth-based agency with good contacts in New York and London. I'm seeking talented writers in a broad range of categories."
How to Contact Contact by e-mail initially. Send only a brief synopsis or overview/proposal of your project. Include a brief bio with any published work, writing training/degrees. Accepts e-mail queries. No fax queries. Obtains most new clients through recommendations from others, solicitations.
Tips "I strongly favor an initial e-mail query. Send only a brief synopsis or overview of your project. Please include a brief bio on all submissions. I respond quickly and if interested may request an electronic or hard copy mailing."

[N] ◙ VIVIAN BECK AGENCY

124 Zandra Ave., Lyons GA 30436-4006. Fax: (912)526-6112. E-mail: query@vivianbeck.com. Web site: www.vivianbeck.com. **Contact:** Vivian Beck. Estab. 2005. Member of RWA; adheres to AAR canon of ethics. Currently handles: 100% novels.

    ● Prior to her current position, Ms. Beck took an apprenticeship with the Ferguson Literary Agency. She has more than 21 years combined professional experience as a literary agent, editor, writer and bookseller.
Represents Novels. **Considers these fiction areas:** Romance; science fiction; thriller; women's.

    O→ Does not want to receive short stories, novellas, poetry, autobiographies, nonfiction, self-help or erotica.
How to Contact E-queries only. Include a brief summary of your story, and all pertinent information concerning the author. Responds in 1 month to queries. Obtains most new clients through recommendations from others, solicitations.
Recent Sales *Tempted by Innocence*, by Linda Raper (Harlequin Mills & Boon); *Warrior or Wife*, by Linda Raper (Mills & Boon); *Maidensong*, by Diana Groe (Leisure).
Writers' Conferences First Coast Romance Writers' 2006 Southern Lights Conference; RT Booklovers Convention 2006; Writers' Institute Conference; RWA National Conference; Book Island Festival; Fantasies by the Sea Conference.
Tips "Don't ramble; get right to the point. What is your story about? What genre? What is the word count of your book? You would be amazed at the number of queries I receive that do not include the genre and length of the story. All unsolicited materials will be deleted or shredded and recycled. Under no circumstances will we read an unsolicited manuscript."

[N] ⊕ ◙ LORELLA BELLI LITERARY AGENCY

54 Hartford House, 35 Tavistock Crescent, Notting Hill, London England W11 1AY, United Kingdom. (44)(207)727-8547. Fax: (44)(870)787-4194. E-mail: info@lorellabelliagency.com. Web site: www.lorellabelliagency.com. **Contact:** Lorella Belli. Estab. 2002. Member of AAA.
Represents Nonfiction books, novels. **Considers these nonfiction areas:** Business/economics; current affairs; history; science/technology; self-help/personal improvement; travel; women's issues/studies; politics; food/wine; popular music; lifestyle. **Considers these fiction areas:** Historical; literary; genre fiction; women's; crime.

    O→ "We are interested in first-time novelists, journalists, multicultural and international writing, and books about Italy." Does not want children's books, fantasy, science fiction, screenplays, short stories, or poetry.
How to Contact For fiction, send query letter, first 3 chapters, synopsis, brief CV, SASE. For nonfiction, send query letter, full proposal, chapter outline, 2 sample chapters, SASE. Accepts initial query letters via e-mail. Send all submissions via postal mail.
Terms Agent receives 15% commission on domestic sales; 20% commission on foreign sales.

◙ FAYE BENDER LITERARY AGENCY

337 W. 76th St., #E1, New York NY 10023. E-mail: info@fbliterary.com. Web site: www.fbliterary.com. **Contact:** Faye Bender. Estab. 2004. Member of AAR.
Represents Nonfiction books, novels, juvenile books. **Considers these nonfiction areas:** Memoirs; popular

culture; women's issues/studies; young adult; narrative; health; biography; popular science. **Considers these fiction areas:** Literary; young adult (middle-grade); women's; commercial.

> O➤ "I choose books based on the narrative voice and strength of writing. I work with previously published and first-time authors." Does not want receive genre fiction (Western, romance, horror, fantasy, science fiction).

How to Contact Query with SASE and 10 sample pages via mail or e-mail. No fax queries.

Recent Sales *Science Experiments*, by Karen Romano Young (National Geographic Society); *The Last Beach Bungalow*, by Jennie Nash (Berkley).

Tips "Please keep your letters to the point, include all relevant information, and have a bit of patience."

N ⬤ BENNETT & WEST LITERARY AGENCY

1004 San Felipe Lane, The Villages FL 32159. (352)751-2314. Fax: (352)748-6108. E-mail: joanpwest@comcast.n et. Web site: www.bennettwestlit.com. **Contact:** Joan West or Lois Bennett. Estab. 2005; adheres to AAR canon of ethics. Represents 80 clients. 60% of clients are new/unpublished writers. Currently handles: 25% nonfiction books; 65% novels; 10% juvenile books.

> • Prior to becoming an agent, Ms. West was a college professor and editor; Ms. Bennett was a psychologist and writer.

Member Agents Joan West (fiction, nonfiction); Lois Bennett (YA and fiction).

Represents Nonfiction books, novels, juvenile books. **Considers these nonfiction areas:** Biography/autobiography; current affairs; government/politics/law; health/medicine; history; how-to; memoirs; military/war; nature/environment; New Age/metaphysics; psychology; self-help/personal improvement; sociology; sports; true crime/investigative; women's issues/studies. **Considers these fiction areas:** Action/adventure; detective/police/crime; family saga; fantasy; historical; juvenile; literary; mainstream/contemporary; mystery/suspense; psychic/supernatural; regional; romance; science fiction; sports; thriller; young adult.

> O➤ "We are sensitive to the writer's needs and friendly to new writers." Does not want to receive erotica, horror, screenplays, picture books or academic.

How to Contact Query with SASE, submit proposal package, outline/proposal, synopsis, 3 sample chapter(s), author bio. Query only, if contacting by e-mail. Accepts e-mail queries. No fax queries. Considers simultaneous queries. Responds in 2-4 weeks to queries. Returns materials only with SASE. Obtains most new clients through recommendations from others, solicitations.

Recent Sales A full list of sales is available online.

Terms Agent receives 15% commission on domestic sales; 20% commission on foreign sales. Offers written contract, binding for 1 year; 30-day notice must be given to terminate contract. Charges for postage and copying fees (five cents per page) for material sent to publishers.

Writers' Conferences Literary Festival (in The Villages).

Tips "Proofread and edit your material. Be sure you have your submission in the proper format. Read a book about it if you are not sure. Nonfiction writers must have appropriate credentials."

N ⬤ BENREY LITERARY

P.O. Box 812, Columbia MD 21044. (443)545-5620. Fax: (886)297-9483. E-mail: info@benrey.com; query@benr eyliterary.com. Web site: www.benreyliterary.com. **Contact:** Janet Benrey. Estab. 2006. Represents 25 clients. 30% of clients are new/unpublished writers. Currently handles: 40% nonfiction books; 60% novels.

> • Prior to her current position, Ms. Benrey was with the Hartline Literary Agency.

Represents Nonfiction books, novels, scholarly books (narrow focus). **Considers these nonfiction areas:** Howto; religious/inspirational; self-help/personal improvement; true crime/investigative; women's issues/studies. **Considers these fiction areas:** Action/adventure; detective/police/crime; family saga; literary; mainstream/contemporary; mystery/suspense; religious/inspirational; romance; thriller; women's.

> O➤ This agency's specialties include romance, women's fiction, mystery, true crime, thriller (secular and Christian), as well as Christian living, church resources, inspirational. Actively seeking women's fiction, romance, mystery, suspense, Christian living, church resources. Does not want to receive fantasy, science fiction, Christian speculative fiction, erotica or paranormal.

How to Contact Query with SASE, submit proposal package, synopsis, 3 sample chapter(s), author bio. More submission details available online. Accepts e-mail queries. No fax queries. Considers simultaneous queries. Responds in 6 weeks to queries; 3 months to mss. Returns materials only with SASE. Obtains most new clients through recommendations from others, solicitations, conferences.

Recent Sales Sold 30 titles in the last year. *Hunt Club*, by Lisa Landolt (Avon); *Soldier on the Porch*, by Sharon Wildwind (Five Star); *In the Dead of Winter*, by Nancy Mehl (Barbour); *A Bird in the Hand*, by Nancy Mehl (Barbour). Agent receives 15% commission on domestic sales; 20% commission on foreign sales. Offers written contract; 30-day notice must be given to terminate contract. "We pass on the out-of-pocket costs of copying and shipping manuscripts for new clients until we have made their first sales."

Tips "Understand the market as best you can. Attend conferences and network. Don't create a new genre."

◱ MEREDITH BERNSTEIN LITERARY AGENCY

2095 Broadway, Suite 505, New York NY 10023. (212)799-1007. Fax: (212)799-1145. Estab. 1981. Member of AAR. Represents 85 clients. 20% of clients are new/unpublished writers. Currently handles: 50% nonfiction books; 50% fiction.

• Prior to opening her agency, Ms. Bernstein served at another agency for 5 years.

Represents Nonfiction books, novels. **Considers these nonfiction areas:** Any area of nonfiction in which the author has an established platform. **Considers these fiction areas:** Literary; mystery/suspense; romance; thriller; women's.

O→ This agency does not specialize. It is very eclectic.

How to Contact Query with SASE. No e-mail or fax queries. Considers simultaneous queries. Obtains most new clients through recommendations from others, conferences, developing/packaging ideas.

Recent Sales Three untitled novels of suspense, by Nancy Pickard (Ballantine); *Why Women Lie*, by Susan Baresh; *Bride's Diplomacy Guide*, by Sharon Naylor (Adams); *Mortgage Brokering*, by Darrin Seppinni (McGraw, Hill).

Terms Agent receives 15% commission on domestic sales; 20% commission on foreign sales. Charges clients $75 disbursement fee/year.

Writers' Conferences Southwest Writers' Conference; Rocky Mountain Fiction Writers' Colorado Gold; Pacific Northwest Writers' Conference; Willamette Writers' Conference; Surrey International Writers' Conference; San Diego State University Writers' Conference.

◱ DANIEL BIAL AGENCY

41 W. 83rd St., Suite 5-C, New York NY 10024-5246. (212)721-1786. Fax: (309)405-0525. E-mail: dbialagency@j uno.com. **Contact:** Daniel Bial. Estab. 1992. Represents under 50 clients. 15% of clients are new/unpublished writers. Currently handles: 95% nonfiction books; 5% novels.

• Prior to opening his agency, Mr. Bial was an editor for 15 years.

Represents Nonfiction books, novels. **Considers these nonfiction areas:** Animals; anthropology/archaeology; biography/autobiography; business/economics; child guidance/parenting; cooking/foods/nutrition; current affairs; ethnic/cultural interests; government/politics/law; history; how-to; humor/satire; language/literature/criticism; memoirs; military/war; money/finance; music/dance; nature/environment; New Age/metaphysics; popular culture; psychology; religious/inspirational; science/technology; self-help/personal improvement; sociology; spirituality; sports; theater/film; travel; true crime/investigative; women's issues/studies. **Considers these fiction areas:** Action/adventure; contemporary issues; detective/police/crime; erotica; ethnic; humor/satire; literary.

How to Contact Submit proposal package, outline. Responds in 2 weeks to queries. Returns materials only with SASE. Obtains most new clients through recommendations from others, solicitations, "good rolodex."

Recent Sales *The Unknown Terrorist War*, by Yossef Bodansky; *The Worst Call Ever*, by Kyle Garlett and Patrick O'Neal; *Everything By Design*, by Alan Lapidus and Robert Pack; *The Theatre of the Face*, by Max Kozloff.

Terms Agent receives 15% commission on domestic sales; 25% commission on foreign sales. Offers written contract, binding for 1 year with cancellation clause. Charges clients for overseas calls, overnight mailing, photocopying, messenger expenses.

Tips "Publishers want their authors to have platforms. In other words, they want authors to have the ability to sell their work or get themselves in the media even before the book comes out. And successful agents get publishers what they want."

◱ BIGSCORE PRODUCTIONS, INC.

(717)293-0247. E-mail: bigscore@bigscoreproductions.com. Web site: www.bigscoreproductions.com. **Contact:** David A. Robie. Estab. 1995. Represents 50-75 clients. 25% of clients are new/unpublished writers.

Represents Nonfiction and fiction (see Web site for categories of interest).

O→ Mr. Robie specializes in inspirational and self-help nonfiction and fiction, and has been in the publishing and agenting business for over 20 years.

How to Contact See for submission guidelines. Query by e-mail only. Do not fax or mail queries. Considers simultaneous queries. Only responds if interested.

Terms Agent receives 15% commission on domestic sales. Offers written contract, binding for 6 months.

Tips "We are very open to taking on new nonfiction clients. We only consider established fiction writers. Submit a well-prepared proposal that will take minimal fine-tuning for presentation to publishers. Nonfiction writers must be highly marketable and media savvy—the more established in speaking or in your profession, the better. Bigscore Productions works with all major general and Christian publishers."

◐ DAVID BLACK LITERARY AGENCY

156 Fifth Ave., Suite 608, New York NY 10010-7002. (212)242-5080. Fax: (212)924-6609. **Contact:** David Black, owner. Estab. 1990. Member of AAR. Represents 150 clients. Currently handles: 90% nonfiction books; 10% novels.

Member Agents David Black; Susan Raihofer (general nonfiction, literary fiction); Gary Morris (commercial fiction, psychology); Joy E. Tutela (general nonfiction, literary fiction); Leigh Ann Eliseo; Linda Loewenthal (general nonfiction, health, science, psychology, narrative).

Represents Nonfiction books, novels. **Considers these nonfiction areas:** Biography/autobiography; business/economics; government/politics/law; health/medicine; history; memoirs; military/war; money/finance; multicultural; psychology; religious/inspirational; sports; women's issues/studies. **Considers these fiction areas:** Literary; mainstream/contemporary; commercial.

   O⇥ This agency specializes in business, sports, politics, and novels.

How to Contact Query with SASE, outline. No e-mail or fax queries. Considers simultaneous queries. Responds in 2 months to queries. Returns materials only with SASE.

Recent Sales *Body for Life*, by Bill Phillips with Mike D'Orso (HarperCollins); *Devil in the White City*, by Erik Larson; The Don't Know Much About series by Ken Davis; *Tuesdays with Morrie*, by Mitch Albom.

Terms Agent receives 15% commission on domestic sales. Charges clients for photocopying and books purchased for sale of foreign rights.

◑ BLEECKER STREET ASSOCIATES, INC.

532 LaGuardia Place, #617, New York NY 10012. (212)677-4492. Fax: (212)388-0001. **Contact:** Agnes Birnbaum. Estab. 1984. Member of AAR, RWA, MWA. Represents 60 clients. 20% of clients are new/unpublished writers. Currently handles: 75% nonfiction books; 25% novels.

   ● Prior to becoming an agent, Ms. Birnbaum was a senior editor at Simon & Schuster, Dutton/Signet, and other publishing houses.

Represents Nonfiction books, novels. **Considers these nonfiction areas:** Animals; biography/autobiography; business/economics; child guidance/parenting; computers/electronic; cooking/foods/nutrition; current affairs; ethnic/cultural interests; government/politics/law; health/medicine; history; how-to; memoirs; military/war; money/finance; nature/environment; New Age/metaphysics; popular culture; psychology; religious/inspirational; science/technology; self-help/personal improvement; sociology; sports; true crime/investigative; women's issues/studies. **Considers these fiction areas:** Ethnic; historical; literary; mystery/suspense; romance; thriller; women's.

   O⇥ "We're very hands-on and accessible. We try to be truly creative in our submission approaches. We've had especially good luck with first-time authors." Does not want to receive science fiction, westerns, poetry, children's books, academic/scholarly/professional books, plays, scripts, or short stories.

How to Contact Query with SASE. No email, phone, or fax queries. Considers simultaneous queries. Responds in 2 weeks to queries; 1 month to mss. Returns materials only with SASE. Obtains most new clients through recommendations from others, solicitations, conferences, "plus, I will approach someone with a letter if his/her work impresses me."

Recent Sales Sold 20 titles in the last year. *Following Sarah*, by Daniel Brown (Morrow); *Biology of the Brain*, by Paul Swingle (Rutgers University Press); *Tripoli*, by David Smethurst (Ballantine); *Phantom Warrior*, by Bryant Johnson (Berkley).

Terms Agent receives 15% commission on domestic sales; 25% commission on foreign sales. Offers written contract; 1-month notice must be given to terminate contract. Charges for postage, long distance, fax, messengers, photocopies (not to exceed $200).

Tips "Keep query letters short and to the point; include only information pertaining to the book or background as a writer. Try to avoid superlatives in description. Work needs to stand on its own, so how much editing it may have received has no place in a query letter."

◑ THE BLUMER LITERARY AGENCY, INC.

350 Seventh Ave., Suite 2003, New York NY 10001-5013. (212)947-3040. **Contact:** Olivia B. Blumer. Estab. 2002. Member of AAR. Represents 34 clients. 60% of clients are new/unpublished writers. Currently handles: 67% nonfiction books; 33% novels.

   ● Prior to becoming an agent, Ms. Blumer spent 25 years in publishing (subsidiary rights, publicity, editorial).

Represents Nonfiction books, novels. **Considers these nonfiction areas:** Agriculture/horticulture; animals; anthropology/archaeology; art/architecture/design; biography/autobiography; business/economics; cooking/foods/nutrition; ethnic/cultural interests; health/medicine; how-to; humor/satire; language/literature/criticism; memoirs; money/finance; nature/environment; photography; popular culture; psychology; religious/inspirational; self-help/personal improvement; true crime/investigative; women's issues/studies; New Age/metaphysics; crafts/hobbies; interior design/decorating. **Considers these fiction areas:** Detective/police/crime; ethnic; family saga; feminist; historical; humor/satire; literary; mainstream/contemporary; mystery/suspense; regional; thriller.

   O→ Actively seeking quality fiction, practical nonfiction, and memoir with a larger purpose.

How to Contact Query with SASE. No e-mail or fax queries. Responds in 3 weeks to queries; 4-6 weeks to mss. Returns materials only with SASE. Obtains most new clients through recommendations from others, but significant exceptions have come from the slush pile.

Recent Sales *The Color of Law*, by Mark Gimenez; *Still Life with Chickens*, by Catherine Goldhammer; *Demolition Desserts*, by Elizabeth Falkner; *Fat* by Jennifer McLagan; *Carpool Diem*, by Nancy Star. Other clients include Joan Anderson, Marialisa Calta, Ellen Rolfes, Laura Karr, Liz McGregor, Lauri Ward, Susann Cokal, Dennis L. Smith, Sharon Pywell, Sarah Turnbull, Naomi Duguid, Jeffrey Alford.

Terms Agent receives 15% commission on domestic sales; 20% commission on foreign sales. Charges for photocopying, overseas shipping, FedEx/UPS.

Ⓝ ◲ THE BLYTHE AGENCY

25 Washington St., Ste 614, Brooklyn NY 11201. (718)781-6489. Web site: www.blythe-agency.com. **Contact:** Rolph Blythe. Estab. 2006. Member of AAR.

   • Prior to his current position, Mr. Blythe was an agent with Dunow, Carlson & Lerner Literary Agency.

Represents Nonfiction books, novels. **Considers these nonfiction areas:** Biography/autobiography; history; memoirs; narrative nonfiction. **Considers these fiction areas:** Detective/police/crime; literary; mystery/suspense; thriller.

   O→ Actively seeking unique, voice-driven fiction, biography, history, science, lifestyle, and mystery and crime books. Does not want to receive screenplays, poetry, children's or Christian/inspirational.

How to Contact Query with SASE, submit synopsis, 1-2 (50-75 pp.) sample chapter(s), author bio. Writers can query through the Web site form. This agency only responds if interested. No e-mail or fax queries. Responds in 4-6 weeks to queries. Obtains most new clients through recommendations from others, solicitations.

Recent Sales *Four-Letter Words and Other Secrets of Crossword Puzzle Champions*, by Michelle Arnot (Perigee); *Madly*, by William Benton.

Terms Agent receives 15% commission on domestic sales; 20% commission on foreign sales.

◲ BOOKENDS, LLC

Web site: www.bookends-inc.com; bookendslitagency.blogspot.com. **Contact:** Jessica Faust, Jacky Sach, Kim Lionetti. Estab. 1999. Member of AAR. Represents 50+ clients. 10% of clients are new/unpublished writers. Currently handles: 50% nonfiction books; 50% novels.

Member Agents Jessica Faust (Fiction: romance, erotica, chick lit, women's fiction, mysterious and suspense. Nonfiction: business, finance, career, parenting, psychology, women's issues, self-help, health, sex); Jacky Sach (mysteries, women's fiction, suspense, self-help, spirituality, alternative and mainstream health, business and career, addiction, chick-lit nonfiction).

Represents Nonfiction books, novels. **Considers these nonfiction areas:** Business/economics; child guidance/parenting; ethnic/cultural interests; gay/lesbian issues; health/medicine; how-to; money/finance; New Age/metaphysics; psychology; religious/inspirational; self-help/personal improvement; sex; spirituality; true crime/investigative; women's issues/studies. **Considers these fiction areas:** Detective/police/crime (cozies); mainstream/contemporary; mystery/suspense; romance; thriller; women's; chick lit.

   O→ BookEnds does not want to receive children's books, screenplays, science fiction, poetry, or technical/military thrillers.

How to Contact Review Web site for guidelines.

Recent Sales *1,000 Wine Secrets*, by Carolyn Hammond (Sourcebooks); *Wolf Tales III*, by Kate Douglas (Kensington Aphrodisia); *Women at Ground Zero*, by Mary Carouba and Susan Hagen (Alpha Books).

◲ BOOKS & SUCH LITERARY AGENCY

52 Mission Circle, Suite 122, PMB 170, Santa Rosa CA 95409. E-mail: representative@booksandsuch.biz. Web site: www.booksandsuch.biz. **Contact:** Janet Kobobel Grant, Wendy Lawton. Estab. 1996. Member of CBA (associate), American Christian Fiction Writers. Represents 80 clients. 5% of clients are new/unpublished writers. Currently handles: 50% nonfiction books; 50% novels.

   • Prior to becoming an agent, Ms. Grant was an editor for Zondervan and managing editor for *Focus on the Family*; Ms. Lawton was an author, sculptor and designer of porcelein dolls.

Represents Nonfiction books, novels. **Considers these nonfiction areas:** Child guidance/parenting; humor/satire; religious/inspirational; self-help/personal improvement; women's issues/studies. **Considers these fiction areas:** Contemporary issues; family saga; historical; mainstream/contemporary; religious/inspirational; romance; African American adult.

o→ This agency specializes in general and inspirational fiction, romance, and in the Christian booksellers market. Actively seeking well-crafted material that presents Judeo-Christian values, if only subtly.

How to Contact Query with SASE. Considers simultaneous queries. Responds in 1 month to queries; 2 months to mss. Returns materials only with SASE. Obtains most new clients through recommendations from others, conferences.

Recent Sales Sold 112 titles in the last year. *Awaken My Heart*, by Diann Mills (Avon Inspire); *My Life As a Doormat (In Three Acts)*, by Rene Gutterridge; *Having a Mary Spirit*, by Joanna Weaver; *Finding Father Christmas*, by Robin Jones Gunn; *No More Mr. Christian Nice Guy*, by Paul Coughlin. Other clients include Janet McHenry, Jane Orcutt, Gayle Roper, Stephanie Grace Whitson, Dale Cramer, Patti Hill, Gayle Roper, Sara Horn.

Terms Agent receives 15% commission on domestic sales; 15% commission on foreign sales. Offers written contract; 2-month notice must be given to terminate contract. Charges clients for postage, photocopying, telephone calls, fax, express mail.

Writers' Conferences Mount Hermon Christian Writers' Conference; Wrangling With Writing; Glorieta Christian Writers' Conference; Writing for the Soul; Blue Ridge Mountains Christian Writers' Conference; American Christian Fiction Writers' Conference; Sandy Cove Christian Writers' Conference; San Francisco Writers' Conference.

Tips "The heart of our agency's motivation is to develop relationships with the authors we serve, to do what we can to shine the light of success on them, and to help be a caretaker of their gifts and time."

◓ THE BARBARA BOVA LITERARY AGENCY

P.O. Box 770365, Naples FL 34107. (941)649-7237. Fax: (239)649-7263. E-mail: barbarabova@barbarabovaliteraryagency.com. Web site: www.barbarabovaliteraryagency.com. **Contact:** Barbara Bova. Estab. 1974. Represents 30 clients. Currently handles: 20% nonfiction books; 80% novels.

Represents Nonfiction books, novels. **Considers these nonfiction areas:** Biography/autobiography; science/technology; self-help/personal improvement; true crime/investigative; women's issues/studies; social sciences. **Considers these fiction areas:** Action/adventure; detective/police/crime; mystery/suspense; science fiction; thriller; young adult; women's; teen lit.

o→ This agency specializes in fiction and nonfiction, hard and soft science.

How to Contact Query through Web site. Obtains most new clients through recommendations from others.

Recent Sales Sold 13 titles in the last year. *Powersat* and *Titan*, by Ben Bova; *So Lyrical* and *Overnight Sensation*, by Patricia Cook; *Springheel Jack*, by Virginia Baker; *Written on the Wind* and *To the Edge of the Stars*, by Joyce Henderson; *Shell Game*, by Jeff Buick.

Terms Agent receives 15% commission on domestic sales; 20% commission on foreign sales.

Tips "We also handle foreign, movie, television, and audio rights."

Ⓝ ◓ BRADFORD LITERARY AGENCY

10353 San Diego Mission Road, Suite 333, San Diego CA 92108. (615)521-1201. E-mail: laura@bradfordlit.com. Web site: www.bradfordlit.com. **Contact:** Laura Bradford. Estab. 2001. Represents 14 clients. 20% of clients are new/unpublished writers. Currently handles: 10% nonfiction books; 90% novels.

• Ms. Bradford has been a literary agent straight out of college and has 12 years of experience as a bookseller in parallel.

Represents Nonfiction books, novels, novellas (within a single author's collection), anthology. **Considers these nonfiction areas:** Business/economics; child guidance/parenting; current affairs; government/politics/law; health/medicine; history; how-to; memoirs; money/finance; popular culture; psychology; religious/inspirational; self-help/personal improvement; women's issues/studies. **Considers these fiction areas:** Action/adventure; detective/police/crime; erotica; ethnic; family saga; historical; humor/satire; mainstream/contemporary; mystery/suspense; religious/inspirational; romance; thriller; young adult; women's (and chick lit); psychic/supernatural.

o→ Actively seeking romance (including category), romantica, women's fiction, mystery, thrillers and young adult. Does not want to receive poetry, short stories or screenplays.

How to Contact Query with SASE, submit first 30 pages of completed ms. Accepts e-mail queries. No fax queries. Considers simultaneous queries. Responds in 1-4 weeks to queries; 6-8 weeks to mss. Returns materials only with SASE. Obtains most new clients through recommendations from others, solicitations.

Recent Sales Sold 8 titles in the last year. *Witch Fire*, by Anya Bast (Berkley Sensation); *Body Moves*, by Jodi Lynn Copeland (Kensington Aphrodisia); *Night Fire*, by Vonna Harper (Kensington Aphrodisia); *What Happens in Vegas...*, by Anya Bast, Lauren Dare, Jodi Lynn Copeland and Kit Tunstall (Harlequin Spice).

Terms Agent receives 15% commission on domestic sales; 25% commission on foreign sales. Offers written contract, binding for 2 years; 45-day notice must be given to terminate contract. Charges for photocopies, postage, extra copies of books for submissions.

Writers' Conferences RWA National Conference; Romantic Times Booklovers Convention.

BRANDS-TO-BOOKS, INC.

419 Lafayette St., New York NY 10003. E-mail: agents@brandstobooks.com. Web site: www.brandstobooks.com. **Contact:** Kathleen Spinelli, Robert Allen. Estab. 2004. 70% of clients are new/unpublished writers. Currently handles: 100% nonfiction books.

- Prior to co-founding Brands-to-Books, Mr. Allen was president and publisher of the Random House Audio Division; Ms. Spinelli was vice president/director of marketing for Ballantine Books.

Member Agents Kathleen Spinelli (lifestyle, design, business, personal finance, health, pop culture, sports, travel, cooking, crafts, how-to, reference); Robert Allen (business, motivation, psychology, how-to, pop culture, self-help/personal improvement, narrative nonfiction).

Represents Nonfiction books, ghostwriters. **Considers these nonfiction areas:** Anthropology/archaeology; art/architecture/design; biography/autobiography; business/economics; child guidance/parenting; computers/electronic; cooking/foods/nutrition; crafts/hobbies; current affairs; ethnic/cultural interests; gay/lesbian issues; government/politics/law; health/medicine; history; how-to; humor/satire; interior design/decorating; language/literature/criticism; memoirs; money/finance; music/dance; photography; popular culture; psychology; self-help/personal improvement; sports; theater/film; books based from brands.

- ⟳ "We concentrate on brand-name businesses, products, and personalities whose platform, passion, and appeal translate into successful publishing ventures. We offer more than literary representation—we provide clients a true marketing partner, pursuing and maximizing every opportunity for promotion and sales within the publishing process." Actively seeking nonfiction proposals supported by strong media platforms and experienced ghostwriters—especially those who have worked with brands/personalities. Does not want fiction or poetry.

How to Contact E-Query with book overview, résumé/platform. Accepts e-mail queries. No fax queries. Considers simultaneous queries. Responds in 3 weeks to queries. Obtains most new clients through recommendations from others, outreach to brand managers and the licensing industry.

Recent Sales *The Travel Mom's Ultimate Book of Family Travel*, by Emily Kaufman (Broadway Books); *TV Guide: TV on DVD 2006*, by the editors of *TV Guide* (St. Martin's Press); *Signature Weddings: Creating a Day Uniquely Your Own*, by Michelle Rago (Gotham Books); *A Passion for Jewelry*, by Temple St. Clair (Regan Books).

Terms Agent receives 15% commission on domestic sales; 20% commission on foreign sales. Offers written contract; 3-month written notice must be given to terminate contract. Charges for office expenses (copying, messengers, express mail).

Tips "In your query, clearly show your passion for the subject and why you are the best person to write this book. Establish your media experience and platform. Indicate you have done your market research and demonstrate how this book is different from what is already on the shelves."

BRANDT & HOCHMAN LITERARY AGENTS, INC.

1501 Broadway, Suite 2310, New York NY 10036. (212)840-5760. Fax: (212)840-5776. **Contact:** Gail Hochman. Estab. 1913. Member of AAR. Represents 200 clients.

Member Agents Carl Brandt; Gail Hochman; Marianne Merola; Charles Schlessiger; Bill Contardi.

Represents Nonfiction books, novels, short story collections, juvenile books, journalism. **Considers these nonfiction areas:** Biography/autobiography; current affairs; ethnic/cultural interests; government/politics/law; history; women's issues/studies. **Considers these fiction areas:** Contemporary issues; ethnic; historical; literary; mainstream/contemporary; mystery/suspense; romance; thriller; young adult.

How to Contact Query with SASE. No e-mail or fax queries. Considers simultaneous queries. Responds in 1 month to queries. Returns materials only with SASE. Obtains most new clients through recommendations from others.

Recent Sales *Season of Betrayal*, by Margaret Lowrie Robertson (Harcourt); *The Misremembered Man*, by Christina McKenna (Toby Press). Other clients include Scott Turow, Carlos Fuentes, Ursula Hegi, Michael Cunningham, Mary Pope Osborne, Julia Glass.

Terms Agent receives 15% commission on domestic sales; 20% commission on foreign sales. Charges clients for ms duplication or other special expenses agreed to in advance.

Tips "Write a letter which will give the agent a sense of you as a professional writer—your long-term interests as well as a short description of the work at hand."

THE JOAN BRANDT AGENCY

788 Wesley Drive, Atlanta GA 30305-3933. (404)351-8877. **Contact:** Joan Brandt. Estab. 1980.

Member Agents Joan Brandt; Alan Schwartz.

Represents Nonfiction books, novels, short story collections.

How to Contact Query with SASE. No e-mail or fax queries. Considers simultaneous queries. Returns materials only with SASE.

Recent Sales This agency prefers not to share information on specific sales.

Terms Agent receives 15% commission on domestic sales; 20% commission on foreign sales. No written contract.

☙ BARBARA BRAUN ASSOCIATES, INC.

104 Fifth Ave., 7th Floor, New York NY 10011. Fax: (212)604-9041. E-mail: bba230@earthlink.net. Web site: www.barbarabraunagency.com. **Contact:** Barbara Braun. Member of AAR.

Member Agents Barbara Braun; John F. Baker.

Represents Nonfiction books, novels.

> ⊶ "Our fiction is strong on women's stories, historical and multicultural stories, as well as mysteries and thrillers. We're interested in narrative nonfiction and books by journalists. We do not represent poetry, science fiction, fantasy, horror, or screenplays." Look online for more details.

How to Contact Query with SASE. Accepts e-mail queries (no full mss).

Recent Sales *Luncheon of the Boating Party*, by Susan Vreeland (Viking/Penguin); *Looking for Salvation at the Dairy Queen* and a second novel, by Susan Gregg Gilmore (Shaye Areheart/Crown); *Vivaldi's Girls*, by Laurel Corona (Hyperion); *Heartbreak Town* and a sequel, by Marsha Moyer (Three Rivers/Crown); *The Lost Van Gogh*, by A.J. Zerries (Tor/Forge); *Terror in Michigan*, by Arnie Bernstein (Univ. of Michigan Press); *A Strand of Corpses* and *A Friend of Need*, by J.R. Benn (Soho Press).

Terms Agent receives 15% commission on domestic sales; 20% commission on foreign sales.

ℕ ☙ PAUL BRESNICK LITERARY AGENCY, LLC

115 W. 29th St., 10th Floor, New York NY 10001. (212)239-3166. Fax: (212)239-3165. E-mail: paul@bresnickage ncy.com. **Contact:** Paul Bresnick.

> ● Prior to becoming an agent, Mr. Bresnick spent 25 years as a trade book editor.

Represents Nonfiction books, novels. **Considers these nonfiction areas:** Biography/autobiography; health/medicine; history; humor/satire; memoirs; multicultural; popular culture; sports; travel; true crime/investigative; celebrity-branded books, narrative nonfiction, pop psychology, relationship issues. **Considers these fiction areas:** Mystery/suspense; thriller.

How to Contact For fiction, submit query/SASE and 2 chapters. For nonfiction, submit query/SASE with proposal. Accepts e-mail queries. No fax queries.

Recent Sales *I, Goldstein: My Screwed Life*, by Al Goldstein with Josh Alan Friedman (Thunder's Mouth Press); *Time Traveler: A Physicist's Search for the Ultimate Breakthrough*, by Ron Mallett with Bruce Henderson (Thunder's Mouth Press); *West of Jesus*, by Steven Kotler (Bloomsbury); *Jeans: A Cultural History of an American Icon*, by James Sullivan (Gotham); *Sons of Providence: The Brown Brothers, the Slave Trade and the American Revolution*, by Charles Rappleye (Simon & Schuster).

☑ BRICK HOUSE LITERARY AGENTS

80 Fifth Ave., Suite 1101, New York NY 10011. Web site: www.brickhouselit.com. **Contact:** Sally Wofford-Girand. Member of AAR.

Member Agents Sally Wofford-Girand; Judy Heiblum; Melissa Sarver, assistant.

Represents Nonfiction books, novels. **Considers these nonfiction areas:** Ethnic/cultural interests; history; memoirs; women's issues/studies; biography; science; natural history. **Considers these fiction areas:** Literary.

How to Contact Query via mail or e-mail.

☙ M. COURTNEY BRIGGS

Derrick & Briggs, 100 N. Broadway Ave., 28th Floor, Oklahoma City OK 73102-8806. (405)235-1900. Fax: (405)235-1995. Web site: www.derrickandbriggs.com. Estab. 1994.

> ● Prior to becoming an agent, Ms. Briggs was in subsidiary rights at Random House for 3 years; an associate agent and film rights associate with Curtis Brown, Ltd; and an attorney for 16 years.

Represents Nonfiction books, novels, juvenile books. **Considers these nonfiction areas:** Young adult.

> ⊶ "I work primarily, but not exclusively, with children's book authors and illustrators. I will also consult or review a contract on an hourly basis." Actively seeking children's fiction, children's picture books (illustrations and text), young adult novels, fiction, nonfiction.

How to Contact Query with SASE. Only published authors should submit queries. No e-mail or fax queries. Returns materials only with SASE. Obtains most new clients through recommendations from others.

Recent Sales This agency prefers not to share information on specific sales.

Terms Agent receives 15% commission on domestic sales; 25% commission on foreign sales. Offers written contract; 60-day notice must be given to terminate contract.

Writers' Conferences SCBWI Annual Winter Conference.

🖎 ⬗ RICK BROADHEAD & ASSOCIATES LITERARY AGENCY

501-47 St. Clair Ave. W., Toronto ON M4V 3A5 Canada. (416)929-0516. Fax: (416)927-8732. E-mail: rba@rbalite rary.com. Web site: www.rbaliterary.com. **Contact:** Rick Broadhead, president. Estab. 2002. Member of Authors Guild. Represents 50 clients. 50% of clients are new/unpublished writers. Currently handles: 100% nonfiction books.

- Prior to becoming an agent in 2002, Mr. Broadhead discovered his passion for books at a young age and co-authored his first bestseller at the age of 23. In addition to being one of the few literary agents with a business background, he has the rare distinction of having authored and co-authored more than 34 books.

Represents Nonfiction books. **Considers these nonfiction areas:** Animals; anthropology/archaeology; biography/autobiography; business/economics; child guidance/parenting; cooking/foods/nutrition; crafts/hobbies; current affairs; government/politics/law; health/medicine; history; how-to; humor/satire; memoirs; military/war; money/finance; music/dance; nature/environment; popular culture; psychology; science/technology; self-help/personal improvement; sports; true crime/investigative; women's issues/studies.

- ⟳ "Rick Broadhead & Associates is an established literary agency that represents primarily nonfiction projects in a wide variety of genres. Priority is given to original, compelling proposals as well as proposals from experts in their fields who have a strong marketing platform. The agency represents American authors to American and foreign publishers in a wide variety of nonfiction genres, including narrative nonfiction, business, self-help, environment/conservation, history/politics, humor, sports, science, current affairs, health/medicine and pop culture. The agency is deliberately small, which allows clients to receive personalized service to maximize the success of their book projects and brands." Actively seeking compelling nonfiction proposals, especially narrative nonfiction (history, current affairs, business) from authors with relevant credentials and an established media platform (TV, radio, print exposure). Does not want to receive novels, television scripts, movie scripts, children's or poetry.

How to Contact Query with SASE, submit publishing history, author bio. E-mail queries preferred. Agency will reply only to projects of interest and request a full ms. Accepts e-mail queries. No fax queries. Considers simultaneous queries. Obtains most new clients through recommendations from others, solicitations.

Recent Sales Sold more than 30 titles in the last year. *The Secret Life of Meat*, by Susan Bourette (Putnam/Penguin); *The Subway Chronicles*, by Jacquelin Cangro (Plume/Penguin); *The Trouble with Africa: Why Foreign Aid Isn't Working*, by Robert Calderisi (Palgrave/St. Martin's Press); *101 Foods That Could Save Your Life*, by Dave Grotto (Bantam/Random House); *The Elements of Great Public Speaking: How to Be Calm, Confident and Compelling*, by Lyman MacInnis (Ten Speed Press); *Bad Bridesmaid: Bachelorette Brawls and Taffeta Tantrums—Tales from the Front Lines*, by Siri Agrell (Henry Holt); *The Quantum Ten and the Birth of a Troubled Science*, by Sheilla Jones (Thomas Allen).

Terms Agent receives 15% commission on domestic sales; 20% commission on foreign sales. Offers written contract. Charges for postage and photocopying expenses.

Tips "The agency has excellent relationships with New York publishers and editors and many of the agency's clients are American authors. The agency has negotiated many six-figure deals for its clients and has sold numerous unsolicited submissions to large publishers. We're good at what we do! E-mail queries are welcome."

🅽 ◎ BROCKMAN, INC.

5 East 59th St., New York NY 10022. Web site: www.brockman.com. **Contact:** Katinka Matson. Currently handles: 100% nonfiction books.

- Prior to her current position, Ms. Matson did many things, including writing *The Psychology Today Omnibook of Personal Development*, *Short Lives: Artists in Pursuit of Self-Destruction* and *The Working Actor: A Guide to the Profession*.

Member Agents John Brockman, agent; Katinka Matson, president and agent.

Represents Nonfiction books. **Considers these nonfiction areas:** Science/technology.

- ⟳ This agency specializes in representing leading scientists.

Recent Sales *Corporatism*, by Douglas Rushkoff (Random House); *Generation Debt: Why Now is a Terrible Time to Be Young*, by Anya Kamenetz; *Science Friction*, by Michael Shermer (Times Books). Other clients include David Gelernter, Brian Greene, Alan Guth, Jordan Pollack, Jaron Lanier, Lee Smolin.

🅽 🅱 ⬗ CURTIS BROWN (AUST) PTY LTD

P.O. Box 19, Paddington NSW 2021, Australia. (61)(2)9361-6161. Fax: (61)(2)9360-3935. E-mail: info@curtisbrown.com.au. Web site: www.curtisbrown.com.au. **Contact:** Submissions Department. Estab. 1967. Represents 350 clients. 10% of clients are new/unpublished writers. Currently handles: 30% nonfiction books; 30% novels; 25% juvenile books; 5% scholarly books; 5% textbooks; 5% other.

- "Prior to joining Curtis Brown, most of our agents worked in publishing or the film/theatre industries in Australia and the United Kingdom."

Member Agents Fiona Inglis, managing director; Fran Moore, agent/deputy managing director; Tara Wynne, agent; Pippa Masson, agent.

Represents Nonfiction books, novels, novellas, juvenile books.

    O➤ "We are the oldest and largest literary agency in Australia and we look after a wide variety of clients." No poetry, short stories, film scripts, picture books or translations.

How to Contact Submit 3 sample chapters, cover letter with biographical information, synopsis (2-3 pages), SASE. No fax queries.

Recent Sales *The Messenger*, by Marcus Zusak (Pan Macmillan); *Holly, Jess and C*, by Jane Burke (Random House); *Dark Space*, by Marianne De Pierres (Orbit UK).

✪ MARIE BROWN ASSOCIATES, INC.

412 W. 154th St., New York NY 10032. (212)939-9725. Fax: (212)939-9728. E-mail: mbrownlit@aol.com. **Contact:** Marie Brown. Estab. 1984. Represents 60 clients. Currently handles: 75% nonfiction books; 10% juvenile books; 15% other.

Member Agents Janell Walden Agyeman (Miami).

Represents Nonfiction books, juvenile books. **Considers these nonfiction areas:** Biography/autobiography; business/economics; ethnic/cultural interests; history; juvenile nonfiction; music/dance; religious/inspirational; women's issues/studies. **Considers these fiction areas:** Ethnic; juvenile; literary; mainstream/contemporary.

    O➤ This agency specializes in multicultural and African-American writers.

How to Contact Query with SASE. Prefers to read materials exclusively. Reports in 6-10 weeks on queries. Obtains most new clients through recommendations from others.

Recent Sales *Kwanzaa*, by Maetefa Angana; *Kinky Gazpacho*, by Lori Tharps; *Lovers Rock*, by Colin Channer; *Succulent Tales*, by Valinda Brown.

Terms Agent receives 15% commission on domestic sales; 20% commission on foreign sales. Offers written contract.

✪ ANDREA BROWN LITERARY AGENCY, INC.

1076 Eagle Drive, Salinas CA 93905. E-mail: andrea@andreabrownlit.com. Web site: www.andreabrownlit.com. **Contact:** Andrea Brown, president. Estab. 1981. 10% of clients are new/unpublished writers.

    • Prior to opening her agency, Ms. Brown served as an editorial assistant at Random House and Dell Publishing and as an editor with Knopf.

Member Agents Andrea Brown; Laura Rennert (laura@andreabrownlit.com); Michelle Andelman; Caryn Wiseman; Jennifer Jaeger; Robert Welsh.

Represents Nonfiction books, novels. **Considers these nonfiction areas:** Juvenile nonfiction; memoirs; young adult; narrative. **Considers these fiction areas:** Juvenile; literary; picture books; thriller; young adult; women's.

How to Contact For picture books, submit complete ms, SASE. For fiction, submit short synopsis, SASE, first 3 chapters. For nonfiction, submit proposal, 1-2 sample chapters. For illustrations, submit 4-5 color samples (no originals). Accepts e-mail queries. No fax queries. Considers simultaneous queries. Obtains most new clients through referrals from editors, clients and agents.

Recent Sales *Chloe*, by Catherine Ryan Hyde (Knopf); Sasha Cohen Autobiography (HarperCollins); *The Five Ancestors*, by Jeff Stone (Random House).

Terms Agent receives 15% commission on domestic sales; 20% commission on foreign sales. Offers written contract. Charges clients for shipping costs.

Writers' Conferences SCBWI; Asilomar; Maui Writers' Conference; Southwest Writers' Conference; San Diego State University Writers' Conference; Big Sur Children's Writing Workshop; William Saroyan Writers' Conference; Columbus Writers' Conference; Willamette Writers' Conference; La Jolla Writers' Conference; San Francisco Writers' Conference; Hilton Head Writers' Conference.

✪ CURTIS BROWN, LTD.

10 Astor Place, New York NY 10003-6935. (212)473-5400. Web site: www.curtisbrown.com. Alternate address: Peter Ginsberg, president at CBSF, 1750 Montgomery St., San Francisco CA 94111. (415)954-8566. Member of AAR; signatory of WGA.

Member Agents Laura Blake Peterson; Emilie Jacobson, senior vice president; Maureen Walters, senior vice president; Ginger Knowlton, vice president; Mitchell Waters; Elizabeth Harding; Holly Frederick; Timothy Knowlton, CEO; Ginger Clark; Katherine Fausset.

Represents Nonfiction books, novels, short story collections, juvenile books. **Considers these nonfiction areas:** Agriculture/horticulture; americana; animals; anthropology/archaeology; art/architecture/design; biography/autobiography; business/economics; child guidance/parenting; computers/electronic; cooking/foods/nutrition; crafts/hobbies; current affairs; education; ethnic/cultural interests; gardening; gay/lesbian issues; government/politics/law; health/medicine; history; how-to; humor/satire; interior design/decorating; juvenile nonfiction; language/literature/criticism; memoirs; military/war; money/finance; multicultural; music/dance; nature/environment; New Age/metaphysics; philosophy; photography; popular culture; psychology; recreation;

regional; religious/inspirational; science/technology; self-help/personal improvement; sex; sociology; software; spirituality; sports; theater/film; translation; travel; true crime/investigative; women's issues/studies; young adult; creative nonfiction. **Considers these fiction areas:** Action/adventure; comic books/cartoon; confession; contemporary issues; detective/police/crime; erotica; ethnic; experimental; family saga; fantasy; feminist; gay/lesbian; glitz; gothic; hi-lo; historical; horror; humor/satire; juvenile; literary; mainstream/contemporary; military/war; multicultural; multimedia; mystery/suspense; New Age; occult; picture books; plays; poetry; psychic/supernatural; regional; religious/inspirational; romance; science fiction; short story collections; spiritual; sports; thriller; translation; westerns/frontier; young adult; women's.

How to Contact Query individual agent with SASE. Prefers to read materials exclusively. *No unsolicited mss.* No e-mail or fax queries. Responds in 3 weeks to queries; 5 weeks to mss. Obtains most new clients through recommendations from others, solicitations, conferences.

Recent Sales This agency prefers not to share information on specific sales.

Terms Offers written contract. Charges for photocopying and some postage.

BROWNE & MILLER LITERARY ASSOCIATES

410 S. Michigan Ave., Suite 460, Chicago IL 60605-1465. (312)922-3063. E-mail: mail@browneandmiller.com. **Contact:** Danielle Egan-Miller. Estab. 1971. Member of AAR, RWA, MWA, Author's Guild. Represents 150 clients. 2% of clients are new/unpublished writers. Currently handles: 40% nonfiction books; 60% novels.

Represents Nonfiction books, novels. **Considers these nonfiction areas:** Agriculture/horticulture; animals; anthropology/archaeology; biography/autobiography; business/economics; child guidance/parenting; cooking/foods/nutrition; crafts/hobbies; current affairs; ethnic/cultural interests; health/medicine; how-to; humor/satire; memoirs; money/finance; nature/environment; popular culture; psychology; religious/inspirational; science/technology; self-help/personal improvement; sociology; sports; true crime/investigative; women's issues/studies. **Considers these fiction areas:** Detective/police/crime; ethnic; family saga; glitz; historical; literary; mainstream/contemporary; mystery/suspense; religious/inspirational; romance (contemporary, gothic, historical, regency); sports; thriller.

"We are generalists looking for professional writers with finely honed skills in writing. We are partial to authors with promotion savvy. We work closely with our authors through the whole publishing process, from proposal to after publication." Actively seeking highly commercial mainstream fiction and nonfiction. Does not represent poetry, short stories, plays, screenplays, articles, or children's books.

How to Contact Query with SASE. *No unsolicited mss.* Prefers to read material exclusively. Responds in 6 weeks to queries. Returns materials only with SASE. Obtains most new clients through referrals, queries by professional/marketable authors.

Terms Agent receives 15% commission on domestic sales; 20% commission on foreign sales. Offers written contract, binding for 2 years. Charges clients for photocopying, overseas postage, faxes, phone calls.

Writers' Conferences BookExpo America; Frankfurt Book Fair; RWA National Conference; CBA National Conference; London Book Fair; Bouchercon.

Tips "If interested in agency representation, be well informed."

PEMA BROWNE, LTD.

11 Tena Place, Valley Cottage NY 10989. Web site: www.pemabrowneltd.com. **Contact:** Pema Browne. Estab. 1966. Member of SCBWI, RWA; signatory of WGA. Represents 30 clients. Currently handles: 25% nonfiction books; 50% novels/romance novels; 25% juvenile books.

• Prior to opening her agency, Ms. Browne was an artist and art buyer.

Represents Nonfiction books, novels, juvenile books, reference books. **Considers these nonfiction areas:** Business/economics; child guidance/parenting; cooking/foods/nutrition; ethnic/cultural interests; gay/lesbian issues; health/medicine; how-to; juvenile nonfiction; money/finance; New Age/metaphysics; popular culture; psychology; religious/inspirational; self-help/personal improvement; spirituality; women's issues/studies; reference. **Considers these fiction areas:** Action/adventure; contemporary issues; feminist; gay/lesbian; glitz; historical; juvenile; literary; mainstream/contemporary (commercial); mystery/suspense; picture books; religious/inspirational; romance (contemporary, gothic, historical, regency); young adult.

"We are not accepting any new projects or authors until further notice."

How to Contact Query with SASE.

Recent Sales *The Champion*, by Heather Grothaus (Kensington/Zebra); *The Highlander's Bride*, by Michele Peach (Kensington/Zebra); *Whispers*, by Samatha Garver (Kensington/Zebra); *Yellowstone Park*, by Linda Cargill (Cora Verlag); *The Daring Harriet Quimby*, by Suzane Whitaker (Holiday House); *One Night to Be Sinful*, by Samantha Garver (Kensington); *Point Eyes of the Dragon*, by Linda Cargill (Cora Verlag).

Terms Agent receives 20% commission on domestic sales; 20% commission on foreign sales.

Tips "We do not review manuscripts that have been sent out to publishers. If writing romance, be sure to receive guidelines from various romance publishers. In nonfiction, one must have credentials to lend credence to a proposal. Make sure of margins, double-space, and use clean, dark type."

⊞ ⊘ BRYSON AGENCY AUSTRALIA

(61)(3)9329-2517. Fax: (61)(3)9600-9131. E-mail: fran@bryson.com.au. Web site: www.bryson.com.au. **Contact:** Fran Bryson.

Represents Nonfiction books, novels, movie scripts, TV scripts, stage plays.

   ○━ "We are not accepting submissions at this time."

Recent Sales *Notes from the Teenage Underground*, by Simmone Howell; Trudi Canavan's The Traitor Spy trilogy; *The Lost Thoughts of Soldiers*, by Delia Falconer (Picador); *After the Party*, by Jesse Blackadder (Hardie Grant Books); *Judy Cassab: A Portrait*, by Brenda Niall (Allen & Unwin).

ℕ ⚑ ◎ THE BUKOWSKI AGENCY

14 Prince Author Ave., Suite 202, Toronto Ontario M5R 1A9, Canada. (416)928-6728. Fax: (416)963-9978. E-mail: info@thebukowskiagency.com. Web site: www.thebukowskiagency.com. **Contact:** Denise Bukowski. Estab. 1986. Represents 70 clients.

   • Prior to becoming an agent, Ms. Bukowski was a book editor.

Represents Nonfiction books, novels.

   ○━ "The Bukowski Agency specializes in international literary fiction and up-market nonfiction for adults. Bukowski looks for Canadian writers whose work can be marketed in many media and territories, and who have the potential to make a living from their work." Actively seeking nonfiction and fiction works from Canadian writers. Does not want submissions from American authors, as well as genre fiction, poetry, children's literature, picture books, film scripts or television scripts.

How to Contact Query with SASE, submit proposal package, outline/proposal, synopsis, publishing history, author bio. Send submissions by snail mail only. See online guidelines for nonfiction and fiction specifics. Responds in 6 weeks to queries.

Recent Sales *The Girls*, by Lori Lansens (Little, Brown); *Holding My Breath*, by Sidura Ludwig (Shaye Areheart Books); *The Rules of Engagement*, by Catherine Bush (Farrar, Straus & Giroux); *Night Watch*, stories by Kevin Armstrong (Harcourt Brace). Other clients include A full list of this agency's clients is online.

◖ SHEREE BYKOFSKY ASSOCIATES, INC.

16 W. 36th St., 13th Floor, New York NY 10018. E-mail: submitbee@aol.com. Web site: www.shereebee.com. **Contact:** Sheree Bykofsky. Estab. 1984, incorporated 1991. Member of AAR, ASJA, WNBA. Currently handles: 80% nonfiction books; 20% novels.

   • Prior to opening her agency, Ms. Bykofsky served as executive editor of The Stonesong Press and managing editor of Chiron Press. She is also the author or co-author of more than 20 books, including *The Complete Idiot's Guide to Getting Published*. Ms. Bykofsky teaches publishing at NYU and SEAK, Inc.

Member Agents Janet Rosen, associate; Caroline Woods, associate.

Represents Nonfiction books, novels. **Considers these nonfiction areas:** Americana; animals; art/architecture/design; biography/autobiography; business/economics; child guidance/parenting; cooking/foods/nutrition; crafts/hobbies; current affairs; education; ethnic/cultural interests; gardening; gay/lesbian issues; government/politics/law; health/medicine; history; how-to; humor/satire; interior design/decorating; language/literature/criticism; memoirs; military/war; money/finance (personal finance); multicultural; music/dance; nature/environment; New Age/metaphysics; philosophy; photography; popular culture; psychology; recreation; regional; religious/inspirational; science/technology; self-help/personal improvement; sex; sociology; spirituality; sports; theater/film; translation; travel; true crime/investigative; women's issues/studies; anthropolgy; creative nonfiction. **Considers these fiction areas:** Literary; mainstream/contemporary; mystery/suspense.

   ○━ This agency specializes in popular reference nonfiction, commercial fiction with a literary quality, and mysteries. "I have wide-ranging interests, but it really depends on quality of writing, originality, and how a particular project appeals to me (or not). I take on fiction when I completely love it—it doesn't matter what area or genre." Does not want to receive poetry, material for children, screenplays, westerns, horror, science fiction, or fantasy.

How to Contact Query with SASE. No unsolicited mss, e-mail queries, or phone calls. Considers simultaneous queries. Responds in 3 weeks to queries with SASE. Responds in 1 month to requested mss. Returns materials only with SASE. Obtains most new clients through recommendations from others.

Recent Sales Sold 100 titles in the last year. *Self-Esteem Sickness*, by Albert Ellis (Prometheus); *When the Ghost Screams*, by Leslie Rule (Andrews McMeel); *225 Squares*, by Matt Gaffney (Avalon).

Terms Agent receives 15% commission on domestic sales; 20% commission on foreign sales. Offers written contract, binding for 1 year. Charges for postage, photocopying, fax.

Writers' Conferences ASJA Writers Conference; Asilomar; Florida Suncoast Writers' Conference; Whidbey

Island Writers' Conference; Florida First Coast Writers' Festibal; Agents and Editors Conference; Columbus Writers Conference; Southwest Writers Conference; Willamette Writers Conferece; Dorothy Canfield Fisher Conference; Maui Writers Conference; Pacific Northwest Writers Conference; IWWG.

Tips "Read the agent listing carefully and comply with guidelines."

◢ CANTON SMITH AGENCY

E-mail: bookhold2@yahoo.com; bookhold1@yahoo.com. Web site: www.cantonsmithagency.com. **Contact:** Eric Smith, senior partner (esmith@cantonsmithagency.com); Chamein Canton, partner (chamein@cantonsmithagency.com); Netta Beckford, associate (nettab@cantonsmithagency.com). Estab. 2001. Represents 28 clients. 100% of clients are new/unpublished writers.

- Prior to becoming agents, Mr. Smith was in advertising and bookstore retail; Ms. Canton was a writer and a paralegal; Ms. Beckford attended Johnson and Wales University.

Member Agents Eric Smith (science fiction, sports, literature); Chamein Canton (how-to, reference, literary, women's, multicultural, ethnic, crafts, cooking, health); Melissa Falcone (childrens, juvenile, young adult, teen, fantasy); Netta Beckford (cookbooks, health, new age, metaphysical, holistic healing, astrology, numerology, Eastern medicine).

Represents Nonfiction books, novels, juvenile books, scholarly books, textbooks, movie scripts. **Considers these nonfiction areas:** Art/architecture/design; business/economics; child guidance/parenting; cooking/ foods/nutrition; education; ethnic/cultural interests; health/medicine; history; how-to; humor/satire; language/ literature/criticism; memoirs; military/war; music/dance; photography; psychology; sports; translation; women's issues/studies. **Considers these fiction areas:** Fantasy; humor/satire; juvenile; multicultural; romance; young adult; Latina fiction; chick lit; African-American fiction; entertainment. **Considers these script subject areas:** Action/adventure; comedy; romantic comedy; romantic drama; science fiction.

- ○┐ "We specialize in helping new and established writers expand their marketing potential for prospective publishers. We are currently focusing on women's fiction (chick lit), Latina fiction, African American fiction, multicultural, romance, memoirs, humor and entertainment, in addition to more nonfiction titles (cooking, how to, fashion, home improvement, etc)."

How to Contact Only accepts e-queries. Send a query, not sample chapters and/or proposals, unless specifically requested. Considers simultaneous queries. Responds in 5 months to queries; 5 months to mss. Obtains most new clients through recommendations from others.

Recent Sales Sold 7 titles in the last year. Clients include Robert Koger, Olivia, Jennifer DeWit, Sheila Smestad, James Weil, Jaime Nava, JC Miller, Diana Smith, Robert Beers, Marcy Gannon, Keith Maxwell, Dawn Jackson, Jeannine Carney, Mark Barlow, Robert Marsocci, Anita Ballard Jones, Deb Mohr, Seth Ahonen, Melissa Graf, Robert Zavala, Cliff Webb, John and Carolyn Osborne.

Terms Agent receives 15% commission on domestic sales; 20% commission on foreign sales. Offers written contract; 2-month notice must be given to terminate contract.

Tips "Know your market. Agents, as well as publishers, are keenly interested in writers with their finger on the pulse of their market."

◢ CARNICELLI LITERARY MANAGEMENT

30 Bond St., New York NY 10012. (212)979-0101. E-mail: matthew@carnicellilit.com. **Contact:** Matthew Carnicelli. Estab. 2004. Represents 40 clients. 25% of clients are new/unpublished writers. Currently handles: 90% nonfiction books; 5% novels; 5% scholarly books.

- Prior to opening his agency, Mr. Carnicelli held senior editorial positions at the Penguin Group, Contemporary Books and McGraw-Hill.

Represents Nonfiction books, novels. **Considers these nonfiction areas:** Anthropology/archaeology; biography/autobiography; business/economics; child guidance/parenting; current affairs; education; ethnic/cultural interests; gay/lesbian issues; government/politics/law; health/medicine; history; memoirs; money/finance; popular culture; psychology; religious/inspirational; science/technology; sociology; sports. **Considers these fiction areas:** Literary.

- ○┐ "Our main areas of interest are popular and serious nonfiction, including current events, history, biography/memoir, science, business, sports, health, spirituality, and psychology. We only consider fiction from authors who have had their work published in established literary journals or magazines. Our goal is to discover important new voices that have something unique and important to contribute to the world, be they experts in their fields or simply great storytellers. We are inolved with the author's work every step of the way, from refining an idea and developing a strong book proposal, to selling the project to the right publisher and monitoring the book's progress after publication."

How to Contact Query with SASE or via e-mail (no attachments). Considers simultaneous queries. Returns materials only with SASE. Obtains most new clients through referrals from other writers.

Recent Sales Sold 15 titles in the last year. *Move Into Life: The Nine Essentials For Lifelong Vitality*, by Anat

Baniel with Hal Zina Bennett (Harmony); *Never Been a Time: The Race Riot That Ignited the Civil Rights Movement*, By Harper Barnes (Walker); *Fair And Balanced, My Ass: The Bizarre Reality Of Fox News*, by Joseph Minton Amann & Tom Breuer (Nation Books); *Move The World: Persuade Your Audience, Change Minds, And Achieve Your Goals*, By Dean Brenner (Wiley); *Women's Rits Of Passage: How To Embrace Change And Celebrate Life, by Abigail Brenner (Rowman & Littlefield); The Comfort of Our Kind*, by Tom Stoner (Thomas Dunne/St. Martin's). Other clients include Chuck Todd, Steve Weinstein, Emerson Baker, Dara Colwell, Paul Donahue, Jim Gorant, Pam Grout, Fran Harris, Brigitte Humbert, Brad Karsh, Roland Lazenby, Michele Simon, Jim Taylor, Donna Vinson.

Terms Agent receives 15% commission on domestic sales; 20% commission on foreign sales. Offers written contract; 30-day notice must be given to terminate contract. Charges for photocopying/messenger and express mail services.

Tips "It's very important that authors present themselves to agents in a formal, professional, and specific way. I simply ignore mass e-mails and most queries, though I will pay more attention if it's clear the author has actually researched the types of books I represent. It's also very important for authors to be as focused and as specific as possible about their writing. Ask yourself: Why am I the only one who can write this book? What are my unique credentials? How will my book be different from the many other books already published on this subject? What is my big idea, why is it relevant, and why will people want to read about it?"

◪ MARIA CARVAINIS AGENCY, INC.

1350 Avenue of the Americas, Suite 2905, New York NY 10019. (212)245-6365. Fax: (212)245-7196. E-mail: mca@mariacarvainisagency.com. **Contact:** Maria Carvainis, Donna Bagdasarian. Estab. 1977. Member of AAR, Authors Guild, Women's Media Group, ABA, MWA, RWA; signatory of WGA. Represents 75 clients. 10% of clients are new/unpublished writers. Currently handles: 35% nonfiction books; 65% novels.

● Prior to opening her agency, Ms. Carvainis spent more than 10 years in the publishing industry as a senior editor with Macmillan Publishing, Basic Books, Avon Books, and Crown Publishers. Ms. Carvainis has served as a member of the AAR Board of Directors and AAR Treasurer, as well as serving as chair of the AAR Contracts Committee. She presently serves on the AAR Royalty Committee. Ms. Bagdasarian began her career as an academic at Boston University, then spent 5 years with Addison Wesley Longman as an acquisitions editor before joining the William Morris Agency in 1998. She has represented a breadth of projects, ranging from literary fiction to celebrity memoir.

Member Agents Maria Carvainis, president/literary agent; Donna Bagdasarian, literary agent; Moira Sullivan, literary associate/subsidiary rights manager; Christopher Jaskot, literary assistant.

Represents Nonfiction books, novels. **Considers these nonfiction areas:** Biography/autobiography; business/ economics; history; memoirs; science/technology (pop science); women's issues/studies. **Considers these fiction areas:** Historical; literary; mainstream/contemporary; mystery/suspense; thriller; young adult; women's; middle grade.

○ァ Does not want to receive science fiction or children's picture books.

How to Contact Query with SASE. Responds in up to 3 to mss. Obtains most new clients through recommendations from others, conferences, query letters.

Recent Sales *Simply Magic*, by Mary Balogh (Bantam Dell); *Save Your Own*, by Elizabeth Brink (Houghton Mifflin); *Ricochet*, by Sandra Brown (Simon & Schuster); *The Marriage Wager*, by Candace Camp (Mira); *Jeb: America's Next Bush*, by S.V. Date (Penguin Group/Tarcher Imprint); *A Widow's Curse*, by Phillip DePoy (St. Martin's Press); *A Falconer's Voice*, by Tim Gallagher (Houghton Mifflin); *Into the Dark*, by Cindy Gerard (St. Martin's Press); *Picture Perfect*, by D. Anne Love (Simon & Schuster Children's Publishing). Other clients include Sue Erikson Bloland, David Bottoms, Pam Conrad, John Faunce, Samantha James, Lucy Lehrer, Dushan Zaric and Jason Kosmas.

Terms Agent receives 15% commission on domestic sales; 20% commission on foreign sales. Offers written contract. Charges clients for foreign postage and bulk copying.

Writers' Conferences BookExpo America; Frankfurt Book Fair; London Book Fair; Mystery Writers of America; Thrillerfest; Romance Writers of America.

◪ CASTIGLIA LITERARY AGENCY

1155 Camino Del Mar, Suite 510, Del Mar CA 92014. (858)755-8761. Fax: (858)755-7063. Estab. 1993. Member of AAR, PEN. Represents 50 clients. Currently handles: 55% nonfiction books; 45% novels.

Member Agents Julie Castiglia; Winifred Golden; Sally Van Haitsma.

Represents Nonfiction books, novels. **Considers these nonfiction areas:** Animals; anthropology/archaeology; biography/autobiography; business/economics; child guidance/parenting; cooking/foods/nutrition; current affairs; ethnic/cultural interests; health/medicine; history; language/literature/criticism; money/finance; nature/ environment; psychology; religious/inspirational; science/technology; self-help/personal improvement; women's issues/studies. **Considers these fiction areas:** Ethnic; literary; mainstream/contemporary; mystery/suspense; women's.

   ○➔ Does not want to receive horror, screenplays, poetry or academic nonfiction.

How to Contact Query with SASE. No fax queries. Returns materials only with SASE. Obtains most new clients through recommendations from others, solicitations, conferences.

Recent Sales Sold 26 titles in the last year. *Big Brown*, by Greg Neimann (Wiley); *From Baghdad With Love*, by Jay Kopelman with Melinda Roth (Lyons Press); *Illuminations*, by Mark Tompkins (Ten Speed/Celestial Arts); *Midnight Brunch*, by Marta Acosta (S&S); *Teardrops*, by Doug Keister (Gibbs Smith); *Orphan's Journey*, by Robert Buettner (Little, Brown/Orbit).

Terms Agent receives 15% commission on domestic sales; 25% commission on foreign sales. Offers written contract; 6-week notice must be given to terminate contract.

Writers' Conferences Santa Barbara Writers' Conference; Southern California Writers' Conference; Surrey International Writers' Conference; San Diego State University Writers' Conference; Willamette Writers' Conference.

Tips "Be professional with submissions. Attend workshops and conferences before you approach an agent."

☑ JANE CHELIUS LITERARY AGENCY

548 Second St., Brooklyn NY 11215. (718)499-0236. Fax: (718)832-7335. E-mail: queries@janechelius.com. Web site: www.janechelius.com. Member of AAR.

Represents Nonfiction books, novels. **Considers these nonfiction areas:** Humor/satire; women's issues/studies; popular science; parenting; medicine; biography; natural history; narrative. **Considers these fiction areas:** Literary; mystery/suspense; women's; men's adventure.

   ○➔ Does not want to receive children's books, stage plays, screenplays, or poetry.

How to Contact Query with synopsis, cover letter, SASE. Accepts e-mail queries. *No unsolicited chapters or mss.* Responds in 3-4 weeks to queries.

N ☑ ◎ ELYSE CHENEY LITERARY ASSOCIATES, LLC

156 Fifth Ave., Suite 1134, New York NY 10010. (212)277-8007. Fax: (212)691-3540. E-mail: elyse@cheneyliterary.com. Web site: www.cheneyliterary.com. **Contact:** Elyse Cheney.

   ● Prior to her current position, Ms. Cheney was an agent with Sanford J. Greenburger Associates.

Represents Nonfiction books, novels. **Considers these nonfiction areas:** Biography/autobiography; history; multicultural; sports; women's issues/studies; narrative. **Considers these fiction areas:** Historical; horror; literary; romance; thriller.

How to Contact Query this agency with a referral. Snail mail queries only. No e-mail or fax queries.

Recent Sales *Moonwalking With Einstein: A Journey into Memory and the Mind*, by Joshua Foer; *The Coldest Winter Ever*, by Sister Souljah (Atria); *A Heartbreaking Work of Staggering Genius*, by Dave Eggers (Simon & Schuster).

N ☑ THE CHOATE AGENCY, LLC

1320 Bolton Road, Pelham NY 10803. E-mail: choateagency@optonline.net. **Contact:** Mickey Choate. Member of AAR.

Represents Nonfiction books, novels. **Considers these nonfiction areas:** History; memoirs (by journalists, military or political figures); biography; cookery/food; journalism; military science; narrative; politics; general science; wine/spirits. **Considers these fiction areas:** Historical; mystery/suspense; thriller; select literary fiction.

   ○➔ Does not want to receive chick lit, cozies or romance.

How to Contact Query with brief synopsis and bio. This agency prefers e-queries, but accepts snail mail queries with SASE. Accepts e-mail queries. No fax queries.

Recent Sales *The King of Lies*, by John Hart (St. Martin's Minotaur); *Heart-Shaped Box*, by Joe Hill (William Morrow); *Simply Michael Mina*, by Michael Mina (Bulfinch/Little, Brown).

N ◻ ◎ THE CHUDNEY AGENCY

E-mail: steven@thechudneyagency.com. Web site: www.thechudneyagency.com. **Contact:** Steven Chudney. Estab. 2002. Member of SCBWI. 90% of clients are new/unpublished writers. Currently handles: 100% juvenile books.

   ● Prior to becoming an agent, Mr. Chudney held various sales positions with major publishers.

Represents Juvenile books. **Considers these nonfiction areas:** Juvenile nonfiction. **Considers these fiction areas:** Juvenile; young adult.

   ○➔ This agency specializes in children's books, but is leaning more toward literary now. Actively seeking children's books. Does not want to receive fantasy, sci-fi, poetry, nonfiction or novelty items.

How to Contact Query with SASE, submit proposal package, 4-6 sample chapter(s). Accepts e-mail and fax queries. Considers simultaneous queries. Responds in 2-3 weeks to queries; 3-4 weeks to mss.

Recent Sales Sold 25 + titles in the last year. The Youngest Templar trilogy, by Michael Spradlin (Putnam); Do the Math series, by Wendy Lichtman (Greenwillow/HarperCollins); *Sir Ryan's Quest*, by Jason Deeble (Roaring Books Press); *Braless in Wonderland*, by Debbie Reed Fischer (Dutton Books/Penguin). Other clients include Barry Varela, Linda Johns, Dorian Cirrone, Leda Scubert, Deborah Lynn Jacobs, Shirley Harazin, Julie Sitegemeyer, Carol Baicker-McKee.

Terms Agent receives 15% commission on domestic sales; 20% commission on foreign sales. Offers written contract, binding for 1 year; 30-day notice must be given to terminate contract.

Tips "If an agent has a Web site, review it carefully to make sure your material is appropriate for that agent. Read lots of books within the genre you are writing; work hard on your writing; don't follow trends—most likely, you'll be too late."

☑ CINE/LIT REPRESENTATION

P.O. Box 802918, Santa Clarita CA 91380-2918. (661)513-0268. Fax: (661)513-0915. E-mail: cinelit@msn.com. **Contact:** Mary Alice Kier. Member of AAR.

Member Agents Mary Alice Kier; Anna Cottle.

Represents Nonfiction books, novels.

    ○— Actively seeking mainstream, thrillers, mysteries, supernatural, horror, narrative nonfiction, environmental, adventure, biography, travel and pop culture. Does not want to receive Western's, sci-fi or romance.

How to Contact Query with SASE. Accepts e-mail queries. No fax queries.

Recent Sales *Solos and Souvenir of Cold Springs*, by Kitty Burns Florey; *Snow In July*, by Heather Barbieri; *The Sound of Her Name*, by Mary Morgan; *Bait and Switch*, by Larry Brooks; *The Last Giant of Beringia*, by Dan O'Neill.

Ⓝ ☑ EDWARD B. CLAFLIN LITERARY AGENCY, LLC

128 High Ave., Suite #4, Nyack NY 10960. (845)358-1084. E-mail: edclaflin@aol.com. **Contact:** Edward Claflin. Estab. 2004. Represents 30 clients. 10% of clients are new/unpublished writers.

    ● Prior to opening his agency, Mr. Claflin worked at Banbury Books, Rodale and Prentice Hall Press. He is the co-author of 13 books.

Represents Nonfiction books. **Considers these nonfiction areas:** Business/economics; cooking/foods/nutrition; current affairs; health/medicine; history; how-to; military/war; money/finance; psychology; sports; theater/film.

    ○— This agency specializes in consumer health, narrative history, psychology/self-help and business. Actively seeking compelling and authoritative nonfiction for specific readers. Does not want to receive fiction.

How to Contact Query with synopsis, bio, SASE or e-mail attachment in Word. Responds in 1 month to queries. Obtains most new clients through recommendations from others.

Recent Sales Sold 40 titles in the last year. *The Real History of the American Revolution*, by Alan Axelrod (Sterling); *Being Human*, by Daniel Gottlieb (Sterling); *Fails to Meet Expectations*, by Corey Sandler and Janice Keefe (Adams); *Sister Dorothy Stang*, by Binka Lebreton (Doubleday); *Too Young to Feel Old*, by Richard Blau and E.A. Tremblay (Da Capo). Other clients include Ellen Brown, Mark Bricklin, Carlo Devito, Matthew Hoffman, Charles Phillips, Sara Purcell, Jonathan Rand.

Terms Agent receives 15% commission on domestic sales.

☑ WM CLARK ASSOCIATES

154 Christopher St., Suite 3C, New York NY 10014. (212)675-2784. Fax: (646)349-1658. E-mail: query@wmclark.com. Web site: www.wmclark.com. Estab. 1997. Member of AAR. 50% of clients are new/unpublished writers. Currently handles: 50% nonfiction books; 50% novels.

    ● Prior to opening WCA, Mr. Clark was an agent at the William Morris Agency.

Represents Nonfiction books, novels. **Considers these nonfiction areas:** Art/architecture/design; biography/autobiography; current affairs; ethnic/cultural interests; history; memoirs; music/dance; popular culture; religious/inspirational (Eastern philosophy only); science/technology; sociology; theater/film; translation. **Considers these fiction areas:** Contemporary issues; ethnic; historical; literary; mainstream/contemporary; Southern fiction.

    ○— "Building on a reputation for moving quickly and strategically on behalf of his clients, and offering individual focus and a global presence, William Clark practices an aggressive, innovative, and broadranged approach to the representation of content and the talent that creates it. His clients range from authors of first fiction and award-winning bestselling narrative nonfiction, to international authors in translation, musicians, and artists."

How to Contact E-mail queries only. Prefers to read requested materials exclusively. Responds in 1-2 months to queries.

Recent Sales Sold 25 titles in the last year. *Fallingwater Rising: E.J. Kaufman and Frank Lloyd Wright Create the Most Exciting House in the World*, by Franklin Toker (Alfred A. Knopf); *The Balthazar Cookbook*, by Riad Nasr, Lee Hanson, and Keith McNally (Clarkson Potter); *The Book of 'Exodus': The Making and Meaning of Bob Marley's Album of the Century*, by Vivien Goldman (Crown/Three Rivers Press); *Hungry Ghost*, by Keith Kachtick (HarperCollins). Other clients include Russell Martin, Daye Haddon, Bjork, Mian Mian, Jonathan Stone, Jocko Weyland, Peter Hessler, Rev. Billy (a.k.a. Billy Talen).

Terms Agent receives 15% commission on domestic sales; 20% commission on foreign sales. Offers written contract.

Tips "WCA works on a reciprocal basis with Ed Victor Ltd. (UK) in representing select properties to the US market and vice versa. Translation rights are sold directly in the German, Italian, Spanish, Portuguese, Latin American, French, Dutch, and Scandinavian territories in association with Andrew Nurnberg Associates Ltd. (UK); through offices in China, Bulgaria, Czech Republic, Latvia, Poland, Hungary, and Russia; and through corresponding agents in Japan, Greece, Israel, Turkey, Korea, Taiwan, and Thailand."

FRANCES COLLIN, LITERARY AGENT

P.O. Box 33, Wayne PA 19087-0033. Web site: www.francescollin.com. **Contact:** Frances Collin. Estab. 1948. Member of AAR. Represents 90 clients. 1% of clients are new/unpublished writers. Currently handles: 50% nonfiction books; 48% novels; 1% textbooks; 1% poetry.

Represents Nonfiction books, fiction.

O→ "We are accepting almost no new clients unless recommended by publishing professionals or current clients." Does not want cookbooks, crafts, children's books, software, or original screenplays.

How to Contact Query with SASE, brief proposal. No phone, fax, or e-mail inquiries. Enclose sufficient IRCs if outside the US. Considers simultaneous queries.

Terms Agent receives 15% commission on domestic sales; 20% commission on foreign sales. Offers written contract. Charges clients for overseas postage for books mailed to foreign agents; photocopying of mss, books, proposals; copyright registration fees; registered mail fees; passes along cost of any books purchased.

COLLINS LITERARY AGENCY

30 Bond St., New York NY 10012. (212)529-4909. Fax: (212)358-1055. Web site: www.collinsliterary.com. **Contact:** Nina Collins. Estab. 2005. Represents 30 clients. 40% of clients are new/unpublished writers.

- Prior to opening her agency, Ms. Collins was a literary scout for foreign publishers and American film companies.

Member Agents Nina Collins (memoir, literary fiction, lifestyle, young adult, travel, psychology, and women and/or mother/daughter issues); Matthew Elblonk (literary fiction, narrative nonfiction, pop culture, music, young adult and anything that is slightly quirky or absurd).

Represents Nonfiction books, novels.

O→ No genre fiction.

How to Contact Query with SASE. Send queries via snail mail. No e-mail or fax queries. Considers simultaneous queries. Responds in 2 weeks to queries; 1 month to mss. Returns materials only with SASE. Obtains most new clients through recommendations from others.

Recent Sales *Why the Devil Chose New England to Do His Work*, by Jason Brown (Open City Books); *The Mother Daughter Project*, by Hamkins & Schulz (Hudson St. Press); *Over the Hill and Between the Sheets*, by Gail Belsky (Warner); *Evo-lution*, by Stephanie Staal (Bloomsbury); *Gonzo Gardening*, by Katherine Whiteside (Clarkson Potter).

Terms Agent receives 15% commission on domestic sales; 20% commission on foreign sales. Offers written contract; 1-month notice must be given to terminate contract.

DON CONGDON ASSOCIATES INC.

156 Fifth Ave., Suite 625, New York NY 10010-7002. (212)645-1229. Fax: (212)727-2688. E-mail: dca@doncongdon.com. **Contact:** Don Congdon, Michael Congdon, Susan Ramer, Cristina Concepcion. Estab. 1983. Member of AAR. Represents 100 clients. Currently handles: 60% nonfiction books; 40% fiction.

Represents Nonfiction books, fiction. **Considers these nonfiction areas:** Anthropology/archaeology; biography/autobiography; child guidance/parenting; cooking/foods/nutrition; current affairs; government/politics/law; health/medicine; history; humor/satire; language/literature/criticism; memoirs; military/war; music/dance; nature/environment; popular culture; psychology; science/technology; theater/film; travel; true crime/investigative; women's issues/studies; creative nonfiction. **Considers these fiction areas:** Action/adventure; detective/police/crime; literary; mainstream/contemporary; mystery/suspense; short story collections; thriller; women's.

○━ Especially interested in narrative nonfiction and literary fiction.

How to Contact Query with SASE or via e-mail (no attachments). Responds in 3 weeks to queries; 1 month to mss. Obtains most new clients through recommendations from other authors.

Terms Agent receives 15% commission on domestic sales; 19% commission on foreign sales. Charges client for extra shipping costs, photocopying, copyright fees, book purchases.

Tips "Writing a query letter with a self-addressed stamped envelope is a must. We cannot guarantee replies to foreign queries via e-mail. No phone calls. We never download attachments to e-mail queries for security reasons, so please copy and paste material into your e-mail."

Ⓒ CONNOR LITERARY AGENCY

2911 W. 71st St., Minneapolis MN 55423. (612)866-1486. E-mail: connoragency@aol.com. **Contact:** Marlene Connor Lynch. Estab. 1985. Represents 50 clients. 30% of clients are new/unpublished writers. Currently handles: 50% nonfiction books; 50% novels.

● Prior to opening her agency, Ms. Connor served at the Literary Guild of America, Simon & Schuster and Random House. She is author of *Welcome to the Family: Memories of the Past for a Bright Future* (Broadway Books) and *What is Cool: Understanding Black Manhood in America* (Crown).

Member Agents Marlene Connor Lynch (all categories with an emphasis on these nonfiction areas: Child guidance/parenting; cooking/foods/nutrition; crafts/hobbies; current affairs; ethnic/cultural interests; government/politics/law; health/medicine; how-to; humor/satire; interior design/decorating; language/literature/criticism; money/finance; photography; popular culture; self-help/personal improvement; women's issues/studies; relationships. Considers these fiction areas: historical; horror; literary; mainstream/contemporary; multicultural; thriller; women's; suspense); Deborah Coker (mainstream and literary fiction, multicultural fiction, children's books, humor, politics, memoirs, narrative nonfiction, true crime/investigative); Nichole L. Shields/Chicago (multicultural fiction and nonfiction with an emphasis on African-American literature, poetry and children's content); Brenda Lee Mann (mainstream, historical, and women's fiction, general nonfiction including cooking, self improvement, spiritual/religious popular psychology, child guidance, etc.).

Represents Nonfiction books, novels.

○━ Actively seeking mysteries.

How to Contact Query with SASE. All unsolicited mss returned unopened. Obtains most new clients through recommendations from others, conferences, grapevine.

Recent Sales *Beautiful Hair at Any Age*, by Lisa Akbari; *12 Months of Knitting*, by Joanne Yordanou; *The Warrior Path: Confessions of a Young Lord*, by Felipe Luciano.

Terms Agent receives 15% commission on domestic sales; 25% commission on foreign sales. Offers written contract, binding for 1 year.

Writers' Conferences National Writers Union, Midwest Chapter; Agents, Agents, Agents; Texas Writers' Conference; Detroit Writers' Conference; Annual Gwendolyn Brooks Writers' Conference for Literature and Creative Writing.

Tips "Previously published writers are preferred; new writers with national exposure or potential to have national exposure from their own efforts preferred."

Ⓒ THE DOE COOVER AGENCY

P.O. Box 668, Winchester MA 01890. (781)721-6000. Fax: (781)721-6727. Web site: doecooveragency.com. Estab. 1985. Represents more than 100 clients. Currently handles: 80% nonfiction books; 20% novels.

Member Agents Doe Coover (general nonfiction, cooking); Colleen Mohyde (literary and commercial fiction, general and narrative nonfiction); Amanda Lewis (children's books); Frances Kennedy, associate. **Considers these nonfiction areas:** Biography/autobiography; business/economics; cooking/foods/nutrition; gardening; history; science/technology; social issues, narrative nonfiction. **Considers these fiction areas:** Literary; commercial.

○━ This agency specializes in nonfiction, particularly books on history, popular science, biography, social issues, and narrative nonfiction, as well as cooking, gardening, and literary and commercial fiction. Does not want romance, fantasy, science fiction, poetry or screenplays.

How to Contact Query with SASE, outline. No e-mail or fax queries. Considers simultaneous queries. Returns materials only with SASE. Obtains most new clients through recommendations from others, solicitations.

Recent Sales Sold 25-30 titles in the last year. *More Fast Food My Way*, by Jacques Pepin (Houghton Mifflin); *Entertaining Simple*, by Matthew Mead (John Wiley & Sons); *International Grilling*, by Chris Schlesinger and John Willoughby (Dorling Kindersley); *The Setpoint Solution*, by George Blackburn (HarperCollins Publishers); *You're Never Too Old To Start Something New*, by Martha Manglesdorf (Ten Speed Press); *Openwork*, by Adria Bernardi (SMU Press); *See What You Can Be*, by Liz Suneby and Diane Heiman (American Girl). *Movie/TV MOW script(s) optioned/sold:* *A Crime in the Neighborhood*, by Suzanne Berne; *Mr. White's Confession*, by

Robert Clark. Other clients include WGBH, New England Aquarium, Blue Balliett, Deborah Madison, Rick Bayless, Molly Stevens, David Allen, Adria Bernardi, Paula Poundstone.
Terms Agent receives 15% commission on domestic sales; 10% of original advance commission on foreign sales.

⊘ CORNERSTONE LITERARY, INC.

4525 Wilshire Blvd., Ste. 208, Los Angeles CA 90010. (323)930-6037. Fax: (323)930-0407. E-mail: hb@cornersto neliterary.com. Web site: www.cornerstoneliterary.com. **Contact:** Helen Breitwieser. Estab. 1998. Member of AAR, Author's Guild, MWA, RWA, PEN, Poets & Writers. Represents 40 clients. 30% of clients are new/ unpublished writers.

- Prior to founding her own boutique agency, Ms. Breitwieser was a literary agent at The William Morris Agency.

Represents Nonfiction books, novels. **Considers these fiction areas:** Detective/police/crime; erotica; ethnic; family saga; glitz; historical; literary; mainstream/contemporary; multicultural; mystery/suspense; romance; thriller; women's.

- ○⇥ "We are not taking new clients at this time. We do not respond to unsolicited e-mail inquiries. All unsolicited manuscripts will be returned unopened." Does not want to receive science fiction, West-ern's, poetry, screenplays, fantasy, gay/lesbian, horror, self-help, psychology, business or diet.

How to Contact Obtains most new clients through recommendations from others.
Recent Sales Sold 37 titles in the last year. *The Bright Side of Disaster*, by Katherine Center (Random House); *We'll Never Tell*, by Kayla Perrin (St. Martin's Press); *When Gods Die*, by C.S. Harris (NAL). Other clients include Catherine O'Connell, Danielle Girard, Rachel Lee, Marilyn Jaye Lewis, Carole Matthews, Ahmet Zappa.
Terms Agent receives 15% commission on domestic sales; 20% commission on foreign sales. Offers written contract, binding for 1 year; 2-month notice must be given to terminate contract.

⊿ THE CREATIVE CULTURE, INC.

72 Spring St., Suite 304, New York NY 10012. (212)680-3510. Fax: (212)680-3509. Web site: www.thecreativecul ture.com. **Contact:** Debra Goldstein. Estab. 1998. Member of AAR.

- Prior to opening her agency, Ms. Goldstein and Ms. Gerwin were agents at the William Morris Agency; Ms. Naples was a senior editor at Simon & Schuster.

Member Agents Debra Goldstein (self-help, creativity, fitness, inspiration, lifestyle); Mary Ann Naples (health/ nutrition, lifestyle, narrative nonfiction, practical nonfiction, literary fiction, animals/vegetarianism); Laura Nolan (literary fiction, parenting, self-help, psychology, women's studies, current affairs, science); Karen Ger-win; Emmanuelle Alspaugh (romance, general nonfiction, fiction).
Represents Nonfiction books, novels.

- ○⇥ Does not want to receive children's, poetry, screenplays or science fiction.

How to Contact Query with bio, book description, 5-7 sample pages (fiction only), SASE. Accepts e-mail queries. No fax queries. Responds in 2 months to queries.
Recent Sales *Dr. Neal Barnard's Program for Reversing Diabetes*, by Neil Barnard (Rodale); *The Power of Patience: How to Slow the Rush and Enjoy More Happiness, Success, and Peace of Mind Every Day*, by M.J. Ryan (Broadway Books); *The Secret Lives of Curious Virgins: My Life as a Reluctant Good Girl*, by Carlene Bauer (HarperCollins). Other clients include David Awbrey, Tom Hughes, Brenda McClain, Paula Chaffee Scardamalia.

Ⓝ ⊿ CRICHTON & ASSOCIATES

6940 Carroll Ave., Takoma Park MD 20912. (301)495-9663. Fax: (202)318-0050. E-mail: cricht1@aol.com; queries@crichton-associates.com. Web site: www.crichton-associates.com. **Contact:** Sha-Shana Crichton. Es-tab. 2002. 90% of clients are new/unpublished writers. Currently handles: 20% nonfiction books; 80% novels.

- Prior to becoming an agent, Ms. Crichton did commercial litigation for a major law firm.

Represents Nonfiction books, novels. **Considers these nonfiction areas:** Child guidance/parenting; ethnic/ cultural interests; gay/lesbian issues; government/politics/law; true crime/investigative; women's issues/stud-ies; Caribbean, Hispanic and Latin-American studies, African-American studies. **Considers these fiction areas:** Ethnic; feminist; literary; mainstream/contemporary; mystery/suspense; religious/inspirational; romance.

- ○⇥ Seeking women's fiction, romance, and chick lit. No poetry.

How to Contact Accepts e-mail queries (no attachments). Responds in 3-5 weeks to queries. Returns materials only with SASE.
Recent Sales *Driven*, by Eve Kenin (Dorchester); *His Dark Prince*, by Eve Silver (Kensington); *Demon Kiss*, by Eve Silver (Warner); *Wish Club*, by Kim Strickland (Crown); *How to Salsa In a Sari*, by Dona Sakar (Kimani TRU); *My Soul Cries Out*, by Sherri Lewis (Urban Christian); *Dead Broke*, by Trista Russell (Simon & Schuster); *Give Me More*, by PJ Mellor (Kensington); *Spirit of Our Ancestors*, by Natalie Robertson (Praeger). Other clients include Dirk Gibson, Kimberley White, Beverly Long, Jessica Trap, Altonya Washington, Ann Christopher.

Terms Agent receives 15% commission on domestic sales; 20% commission on foreign sales. Offers written contract, binding for 45 days. Only charges fees for postage and photocopying.
Writers' Conferences Silicon Valley RWA; BookExpo America.

◉ RICHARD CURTIS ASSOCIATES, INC.

171 E. 74th St., New York NY 10021. (212)772-7363. Fax: (212)772-7393. Web site: www.curtisagency.com. Estab. 1979. Member of RWA, MWA, SFWA; signatory of WGA. Represents 100 clients. 1% of clients are new/unpublished writers. Currently handles: 70% nonfiction books; 20% genre fiction, 10% fiction.

- Prior to opening his agency, Mr. Curtis was an agent with the Scott Meredith Literary Agency for seven years. He has also authored more than 50 published books.

Represents Commercial nonfiction and fiction. **Considers these nonfiction areas:** Health/medicine; history; science/technology.
How to Contact Send 1-page query letter and no more than a 5-page synopsis. Don't send ms unless specifically requested. If requested, submission must be accompanied by a SASE. No e-mail or fax queries. Returns materials only with SASE.
Recent Sales Sold 150 titles in the last year. *The Terror*, by Dan Simmons; *The Side-Effects Solution*, by Dr. Frederic Vagnini and Barry Fox; *Quantico*, by Greg Bear. Other clients include Janet Dailey, Jennifer Blake, Leonard Maltin, D.J. MacHale, John Altman, Beverly Barton, Earl Mindell, Barbara Parker.
Terms Agent receives 15% commission on domestic sales; 25% commission on foreign sales. Offers written contract. Charges for photocopying, express mail, international freight, book orders.
Writers' Conferences SFWA Conference; HWA Conference; RWA National Conference; World Fantasy Convention; Backspace Writers Conference.

◎ JAMES R. CYPHER, THE CYPHER AGENCY

816 Wolcott Ave., Beacon NY 12508-4261. Phone/Fax: (845)831-5677. E-mail: jim@jimcypher.com. Web site: www.jimcypher.com. **Contact:** James R. Cypher. Estab. 1993. Member of AAR, Authors Guild. Represents 23 clients. 56% of clients are new/unpublished writers. Currently handles: 100% nonfiction books.

- Prior to opening his agency, Mr. Cypher worked as a corporate public relations manager for a Fortune 500 multi-national computer company for 28 years.

Represents Nonfiction books. **Considers these nonfiction areas:** Current affairs; health/medicine; history; memoirs; popular culture; science/technology; sports (NASCAR, golf, baseball); true crime/investigative; biography.

- ⟶ This agent is semi-retired, and taking on few new clients. Does not want to receive humor, sewing, computer books, children's, gardening, cookbooks, spiritual, religious, or New Age topics.

How to Contact Query with SASE, proposal package, 2 sample chapters. Accepts e-mail queries. Considers simultaneous queries. Responds in 2 weeks to queries; 6 weeks to mss. Obtains most new clients through recommendations from others, conferences, networking on online computer service.
Recent Sales Sold 9 titles in the last year. *Courting the Media: Public Relations for the Accused and the Accuser*, by Margaret A. Mackenzie (Praeger Publishers); *The Great Sex Secret: What Satisfied Women and Men Know That No One Talks About*, by Kim Marshall (Sourcebooks, Inc.); *Terrorism on American Soil: A Concise History of Plots and Perpetrators from the Famous to the Forgotten*, by Joseph T. McCann (Sentient Publications); *The National Wrestling Alliance: The Untold Story of the Monopoly That Controlled Pro Wrestling*, by Timothy M. Hornbaker (ECW Press). Other clients include Walter Harvey, Mark Horner, Charles Hustmyre, Glenn Puit, Robert L. Snow.
Terms Agent receives 15% commission on domestic sales; 20% commission on foreign sales. Offers written contract; 1-month notice must be given to terminate contract. 100% of business is derived from commissions on ms sales.

◉ D4EO LITERARY AGENCY

7 Indian Valley Road, Weston CT 06883. (203)544-7180. Fax: (203)544-7160. E-mail: d4eo@optonline.net. **Contact:** Bob Diforio. Estab. 1991. Represents more than 100 clients. 50% of clients are new/unpublished writers. Currently handles: 70% nonfiction books; 25% novels; 5% juvenile books.

- Prior to opening his agency, Mr. Diforio was a publisher.

Represents Nonfiction books, novels. **Considers these nonfiction areas:** Art/architecture/design; biography/autobiography; business/economics; child guidance/parenting; current affairs; gay/lesbian issues; health/medicine; history; how-to; humor/satire; juvenile nonfiction; memoirs; military/war; money/finance; psychology; religious/inspirational; science/technology; self-help/personal improvement; sports; true crime/investigative; women's issues/studies. **Considers these fiction areas:** Action/adventure; detective/police/crime; erotica; historical; horror; humor/satire; juvenile; literary; mainstream/contemporary; mystery/suspense; picture books; romance; science fiction; sports; thriller; westerns/frontier; young adult.

How to Contact Query with SASE. Accepts and prefers e-mail queries. Prefers to read material exclusively. Responds in 1 week to queries. Returns materials only with SASE. Obtains most new clients through recommendations from others.

Recent Sales Sold 125 titles in the last year. *Jaywalker* plus 2 novels, by Joseph Teller; *Skeleton Coast*, by Jack Du Brul; *Revenge* (Butch Karp #20), by Robert K. Tanenbaum; *Secrets of the Alchemist Dar*, by Michael Stadther; The Pleasure Series, by Cathryn Fox; *The Valorian Journals*, by Tawny Stokes. Other clients include Robert K. Tanenbaum, Andrea DaRif, Tawny Stokes, Cathy Verge, Lynn Kerston, Bob Bly, Michael Levine, Mark Wiskup, George Parker, Michael Stodther, Evie Rhoder, Charlie Stella, Kathy Tracy.

Terms Agent receives 15% commission on domestic sales; 25% commission on foreign sales. Offers written contract, binding for 2 years; 60-day notice must be given to terminate contract. Charges for photocopying and submission postage.

🌑 LAURA DAIL LITERARY AGENCY, INC.

350 Seventh Ave., Suite 2003, New York NY 10010. (212)239-7477. Fax: (212)947-0460. E-mail: queries@ldlainc .com. Web site: www.ldlainc.com. Member of AAR.

Member Agents Talia Cohen; Laura Dail; Tamar Ellman.

Represents Nonfiction books, novels.

> ⚬⚮ "Due to the volume of queries and manuscripts received, we apologize for not answering every e-mail and letter." Specializes in historical, literary and some young adult fiction, as well as both practical and idea-driven nonfiction.

How to Contact Query with SASE. This agency prefers e-queries.

Recent Sales *This Year's Model*, by Carol Alt and Nina Malkin (Regan); *Skinny Bitch in the Kitch and Skinny Mama*, by Rory Freedman and Kim Barnoin (Running Press); *The Lost Memoirs of Jane Austin: A Novel*, by Syrie James (Avon).

🌑 DARHANSOFF, VERRILL, FELDMAN LITERARY AGENTS

236 W. 26th St., Suite 802, New York NY 10001. (917)305-1300. Fax: (917)305-1400. Web site: www.dvagency.c om. Estab. 1975. Member of AAR. Represents 120 clients. 10% of clients are new/unpublished writers. Currently handles: 25% nonfiction books; 60% novels; 15% story collections.

Member Agents Liz Darhansoff; Charles Verrill; Leigh Feldman.

Represents Nonfiction books, novels, short story collections.

How to Contact Obtains most new clients through recommendations from others.

ⓃⓌ🌑 CAROLINE DAVIDSON LITERARY AGENCY

5 Queen Anne's Gardens, London England W4 ITU, United Kingdom. (44)(208)995-5768. Fax: (44)(208)994-2770. E-mail: caroline@cdla.co.uk. Web site: www.cdla.co.uk. **Contact:** Caroline Davidson. Estab. 1988.

> • Prior to her current position, Ms. Davidson was a journalist with Reuters News Agency; she also worked for BBC television and edited publications for the Library of Congress.

Represents Nonfiction books, novels.

> ⚬⚮ Does not want to receive autobiographies, children's, crime, erotica, fantasy, murder mysteries, occult, sci-fi, thrillers, individual short stories, textbooks, memoirs, self-help, poetry, war stories or local history.

How to Contact Query with SASE. Thorough submission guidelines are online. No fax queries. Responds in 2 weeks to queries. Obtains most new clients through recommendations from others, solicitations.

Recent Sales *The Light Revolution*, by Richard Hobday; *Champagne and Shambles*, by Catherine Beale; *Touchy Subjects*, by Emma Donoghue. Other clients include Danny Boothe, Saskia Sarginson, Andrew Balby, Richard Hibday, David Saffery, Cindy Engel.

Tips Specific submission guidelines regarding fiction and nonfiction genres as well as what to include are online. Read them before submitting.

🌑 LIZA DAWSON ASSOCIATES

350 Seventh Ave., Ste. 2003, New York NY 10001. (212)465-9071. Member of AAR, MWA, Women's Media Group. Represents 50 + clients. 15% of clients are new/unpublished writers. Currently handles: 60% nonfiction books; 40% novels.

> • Prior to becoming an agent, Ms. Dawson was an editor for 20 years, spending 11 years at William Morrow as vice president and 2 years at Putnam as executive editor. Ms. Bladell was a senior editor at HarperCollins and Avon. Ms. Miller is an *Essence*-bestselling author and niche publisher. Ms. Olswanger is an author.

Member Agents Liza Dawson; Anna Olswanger; Havis Dawson. izadawsonassociates.com.

Represents Nonfiction books, novels and gift books (Olswanger only). **Considers these nonfiction areas:**

Biography/autobiography; health/medicine; history; memoirs; psychology; sociology; women's issues/studies; politics; business; parenting. **Considers these fiction areas:** Fantasy (Blasdell only); historical; literary; mystery/suspense; regional; science fiction (Blasdell only); thriller; African-American (Miller only).

> O— This agency specializes in readable literary fiction, thrillers, mainstream historicals, women's fiction, academics, historians, business, journalists and psychology. Does not want to receive Western, sports, computers or juvenile.

How to Contact Query with SASE. Responds in 3 weeks to queries; 6 weeks to mss. Obtains most new clients through recommendations from others, conferences.

Recent Sales Sold 40 titles in the last year. *Going for It*, by Karen E. Quinones Miller (Warner); *Mayada: Daughter of Iraq*, by Jean Sasson (Dutton); *It's So Much Work to Be Your Friend: Social Skill Problems at Home and at School*, by Richard Lavoie (Touchstone); *WORDCRAFT: How to Write Like a Professional*, by Jack Hart (Pantheon); *...And a Time to Die: How Hospitals Shape the End of Life Experience*, by Dr. Sharon Kaufman (Scribner); *Zeus: A Biography*, by Tom Stone (Bloomsbury).

Terms Agent receives 15% commission on domestic sales; 20% commission on foreign sales. Offers written contract. Charges clients for photocopying and overseas postage.

☑ THE JENNIFER DECHIARA LITERARY AGENCY

31 East 32nd St., Suite 300, New York NY 10016. (212)481-8484. E-mail: jenndec@aol.com. Web site: www.jdlit.com. **Contact:** Jennifer DeChiara. Estab. 2001. Represents 100 clients. 50% of clients are new/unpublished writers. Currently handles: 50% nonfiction books; 25% novels; 25% juvenile books.

• Prior to becoming an agent, Ms. DeChiara was a writing consultant, freelance editor at Simon & Schuster and Random House, and a ballerina and an actress.

Represents Nonfiction books, novels, juvenile books. **Considers these nonfiction areas:** Biography/autobiography; child guidance/parenting; cooking/foods/nutrition; crafts/hobbies; current affairs; education; ethnic/cultural interests; gay/lesbian issues; government/politics/law; health/medicine; history; how-to; humor/satire; interior design/decorating; juvenile nonfiction; language/literature/criticism; memoirs; military/war; money/finance; music/dance; nature/environment; photography; popular culture; psychology; science/technology; self-help/personal improvement; sociology; sports; theater/film; true crime/investigative; women's issues/studies. **Considers these fiction areas:** Confession; detective/police/crime; ethnic; family saga; fantasy; feminist; gay/lesbian; historical; horror; humor/satire; juvenile; literary; mainstream/contemporary; mystery/suspense; picture books; regional; sports; thriller; young adult; chick lit; psychic/supernatural; glitz.

> O— "We represent both children's and adult books in a wide range of ages and genres. We are a full-service agency and fulfill the potential of every book in every possible medium—stage, film, television, etc. We help writers every step of the way, from creating book ideas to editing and promotion. We are passionate about helping writers further their careers, but are just as eager to discover new talent, regardless of age or lack of prior publishing experience. This agency is committed to managing a writer's entire career. For us, it's not just about selling books, but about making dreams come true. We are especially attracted to the downtrodden, the discouraged, and the downright disgusted." Actively seeking literary fiction, chick lit, young adult fiction, self-help, pop culture, and celebrity biographies. Does not want westerns, poetry, or short stories.

How to Contact Query with SASE. Considers simultaneous queries. Responds in 3-6 months to queries; 3-6 months to mss. Returns materials only with SASE. Obtains most new clients through recommendations from others, conferences, query letters.

Recent Sales Sold 30 titles in the last year. *I Was a Teenage Popsicle*, by Bev Katz Rosenbaum (Berkley/JAM); *Hazing Meri Sugarman*, by M. Apostolina (Simon Pulse); *The 10-Minute Sexual Solution* and *Virgin Sex: A Guy's Guide to Sex*, by Dr. Darcy Luadzers (Hatherleigh Press). ***Movie/TV MOW script(s) optioned/sold:*** *Geography Club*, by Brent Hartinger (East of Doheny). Other clients include Adam Meyer, Herbie J. Pilato, Chris Demarest, Jeff Lenburg, Joe Cadora, Tiffani Amber Thiessen, Bonnie Neubauer.

Terms Agent receives 15% commission on domestic sales; 20% commission on foreign sales. Offers written contract.

☑ DEFIORE & CO.

72 Spring St., Suite 304, New York NY 10012. (212)925-7744. Fax: (212)925-9803. E-mail: info@defioreandco.com. Web site: www.defioreandco.com. **Contact:** Brian DeFiore. Estab. 1999. Member of AAR. Represents 55 clients. 50% of clients are new/unpublished writers. Currently handles: 70% nonfiction books; 30% novels.

• Prior to becoming an agent, Mr. DeFiore was publisher of Villard Books (1997-1998), editor-in-chief of Hyperion (1992-1997), and editorial director of Delacorte Press (1988-1992).

Member Agents Brian DeFiore (popular nonfiction, business, pop culture, parenting, commercial fiction); Laurie Abkemeier (memoir, parenting, business, how-to/self-help, popular science); Kate Garrick (literary fiction, crime, pop culture, politics, history, psychology, narrative nonfiction).

Represents Nonfiction books, novels. **Considers these nonfiction areas:** Biography/autobiography; business/economics; child guidance/parenting; cooking/foods/nutrition; money/finance; multicultural; popular culture; psychology; religious/inspirational; self-help/personal improvement; sports. **Considers these fiction areas:** Ethnic; literary; mainstream/contemporary; mystery/suspense; thriller.

How to Contact Query with SASE. Considers simultaneous queries. Responds in 3 weeks to queries; 2 months to mss. Returns materials only with SASE. Obtains most new clients through recommendations from others.

Recent Sales Sold 35 titles in the last year. *Marley and Me*, by John Grogan; *Post Secret*, by Frank Warren; *Bitter Is the New Black*, by Jen Lancaster; *All for a Few Perfect Waves*, by David Rensin; *Seemed Like a Good Idea at the Time*, by David Goodwillie; *Lights Out*, by Jason Starr; *The Alpha Solution*, by Dr Ronald Glassman; *The $64 Tomato*, by Bill Alexander; *The Extraordinary Adventures of Alfred Kropp*, by Rick Yancey. Other clients include Loretta LaRoche, Joel Engel, Robin McMillan, Jessica Teich, Ronna Lichtenberg, Jimmy Lerner, Lou Manfredini, Norm Green, Lisa Kusel, Michael Walter, Stephen Graham Jones.

Terms Agent receives 15% commission on domestic sales; 20% commission on foreign sales. Offers written contract; 10-day notice must be given to terminate contract. Charges clients for photocopying and overnight delivery (deducted only after a sale is made).

Writers' Conferences Maui Writers Conference; Pacific Northwest Writers Conference; North Carolina Writers' Network Fall Conference.

🜨 JOELLE DELBOURGO ASSOCIATES, INC.

516 Bloomfield Ave., Suite 5, Montclair NJ 07042. (973)783-6800. Fax: (973)783-6802. E-mail: info@delbourgo.com. Web site: www.delbourgo.com. **Contact:** Joelle Delbourgo, Molly Lyons. Estab. 2000. Represents 80 clients. 40% of clients are new/unpublished writers. Currently handles: 75% nonfiction books; 25% novels.

• Prior to becoming an agent, Ms. Delbourgo was an editor and senior publishing executive at HarperCollins and Random House.

Member Agents Joelle Delbourgo (parenting, self-help, psychology, business, serious nonfiction, narrative nonfiction, quality fiction); Molly Lyons (practical and narrative nonfiction, memoir, quality fiction).

Represents Nonfiction books, novels, short story collections. **Considers these nonfiction areas:** Biography/autobiography; business/economics; child guidance/parenting; cooking/foods/nutrition; current affairs; education; ethnic/cultural interests; gay/lesbian issues; government/politics/law; health/medicine; history; how-to; money/finance; music/dance; nature/environment; popular culture; psychology; religious/inspirational; science/technology; self-help/personal improvement; sociology; theater/film; true crime/investigative; women's issues/studies; New Age/metaphysics, interior design/decorating. **Considers these fiction areas:** Historical; literary; mainstream/contemporary; mystery/suspense; regional.

🔑 "We are former publishers and editors, with deep knowledge and an insider perspective. We have a reputation for individualized attention to clients, strategic management of authors' careers, and creating strong partnerships with publishers for our clients." Actively seeking history, narrative nonfiction, science/medicine, memoir, literary fiction, psychology, parenting and biographies. Does not want to receive genre fiction or screenplays.

How to Contact Query with SASE. No e-mail or fax queries. Considers simultaneous queries. Responds in 3 weeks to queries; 2 months to mss. Returns materials only with SASE.

Recent Sales Sold 26 titles in the last year. *Washashores*, by Lynn Bonasia (Touchstone/Fireside); *Leftovers: The New Food Underclass and the Fight Against Obesity*, by Hank J. Cardello with Doug Garr (Regan/HarperCollins); *Mad Fish*, by Charlie Moore (St. Martin's Press); *Three Little Words*, by Ashley Rhodes Courer (Simon & Schuster); *Kissing Snowflakes*, by Abby Sher (Scholastic). Other clients include Pamela Duncan, Geeta Anand, Philip Mitchell Freeman, Roy Hoffman, Chris Farrell, David Cole, Marc Siegel, Joan Wester Anderson, Julie Fenster.

Terms Agent receives 15% commission on domestic sales; 20% commission on foreign sales. Offers written contract. Charges clients for postage and photocopying.

Tips "Do your homework. Do not cold call. Read and follow submission guidelines before contacting us. Do not call to find out if we received your material. No e-mail queries. Treat agents with respect, as you would any other professional, such as a doctor, lawyer or financial advisor."

🜨 DH LITERARY, INC.

P.O. Box 805, Nyack NY 10960-0990. E-mail: dhendin@aol.com. **Contact:** David Hendin. Estab. 1993. Member of AAR. Represents 10 clients. Currently handles: 80% nonfiction books; 10% novels; 10% scholarly books.

• Prior to opening his agency, Mr. Hendin served as president and publisher for Pharos Books/World Almanac, as well as senior VP and COO at sister company United Feature Syndicate.

🔑 "We are not accepting new clients. Please do not send queries or submissions."

Recent Sales *No Vulgar Hotel*, by Judith Martin (Norton); *Murder Between the Covers*, by Elaine Viets (Penguin/Putnam); *Coined by God*, by Jeffrey McQuain and Stanley Malless (Norton).

Literary Agents

Terms Agent receives 15% commission on domestic sales; 20% commission on foreign sales. Offers written contract, binding for 1 year. Charges for out-of-pocket expenses for overseas postage specifically related to the sale.

◯ DHS LITERARY, INC.

10711 Preston Road, Suite 100, Dallas TX 75230. (214)363-4422. Fax: (214)363-4423. E-mail: submissions@dhsliterary.com. Web site: www.dhsliterary.com. **Contact:** David Hale Smith, president. Estab. 1994. Represents 35 clients. 15% of clients are new/unpublished writers. Currently handles: 60% nonfiction books; 40% novels.

● Prior to opening his agency, Mr. Smith was an agent at Dupree/Miller & Associates.

Represents Nonfiction books, novels. **Considers these nonfiction areas:** Biography/autobiography; business/economics; child guidance/parenting; cooking/foods/nutrition; current affairs; ethnic/cultural interests; popular culture; sports; true crime/investigative. **Considers these fiction areas:** Detective/police/crime; ethnic; literary; mainstream/contemporary; mystery/suspense; thriller; westerns/frontier.

○➡ This agency specializes in commercial fiction and nonfiction for the adult trade market. Actively seeking thrillers, mysteries, suspense, etc., and narrative nonfiction. Does not want to receive poetry, short fiction or children's books.

How to Contact Accepts new material by referral only and only responds if interested. *No unsolicited mss.* No fax queries.

Recent Sales *Officer Down*, by Theresa Schwegel; *Private Wars*, by Greg Rucka; *The Lean Body Promise*, by Lee Labrada.

Terms Agent receives 15% commission on domestic sales; 25% commission on foreign sales. Offers written contract; 10-day notice must be given to terminate contract. This agency charges for postage and photocopying.

Tips "Remember to be courteous and professional, and to treat marketing your work and approaching an agent as you would any formal business matter. If you have a referral, always query first via e-mail. Sorry, but we cannot respond to queries sent via mail, even with a SASE. Visit our Web site for more information."

◯ SANDRA DIJKSTRA LITERARY AGENCY

1155 Camino del Mar, PMB 515, Del Mar CA 92014. (858)755-3115. Fax: (858)794-2822. E-mail: sdla@dijkstraagency.com. **Contact:** Taryn Fagerness. Estab. 1981. Member of AAR, Authors Guild, PEN West, Poets and Editors, MWA. Represents 100+ clients. 30% of clients are new/unpublished writers. Currently handles: 50% nonfiction books; 45% novels; 5% juvenile books.

Member Agents Sandra Dijkstra; Jill Marsal; Taryn Fagerness.

Represents Nonfiction books, novels. **Considers these nonfiction areas:** Americana; animals (pets); anthropology/archaeology; business/economics; child guidance/parenting; cooking/foods/nutrition; ethnic/cultural interests; gay/lesbian issues; government/politics/law; health/medicine; history; juvenile nonfiction; language/literature/criticism; military/war; money/finance; nature/environment; psychology; regional; religious/inspirational; science/technology; self-help/personal improvement; sociology; travel; women's issues/studies; Asian studies; art; accounting; biography; environmental studies; technology; transportation. **Considers these fiction areas:** Erotica; ethnic; literary; mainstream/contemporary; mystery/suspense; picture books; thriller.

○➡ This agency specializes in quality fiction including women's and multicultural fiction, mystery/thrillers, children's literature, narrative nonfiction, psychology, self-help, science, health, business, memoirs, biography, current affairs and history. Does not want to receive Western, sci-fi or poetry.

How to Contact Submit for fiction, send brief synopsis and 50 sample pages, SASE. No e-mail or fax queries. Responds in 4-6 weeks to queries. Obtains most new clients through recommendations from others, solicitations, conferences.

Recent Sales *Firewife*, by Tinling Choong; *Palace of Illusions*, by Chitra Divakaruni; *The Longevity Bible*, by Dr. Gary Small; *The American Resting Place*, by Marilyn Yalom.

Terms Agent receives 15% commission on domestic sales; 20% commission on foreign sales. Offers written contract. Charges clients for expenses "to cover domestic costs so that we can spend time selling books instead of accounting expenses. We also charge for the photocopying of the full manuscript or nonfiction proposal and for foreign postage."

Writers' Conferences "We have attended Squaw Valley Writers' Workshop, Santa Barbara Writers' Conference, Asilomar, Southern California Writers' Conference, and Rocky Mountain Fiction Writers' Colorado Gold, to name a few. We also speak regularly for writers groups such as PEN West and the Independent Writers Association."

Tips "Be professional and learn the standard procedures for submitting your work. Be a regular patron of bookstores, and study what kind of books are being published. Read. Check out your local library and bookstores—you'll find lots of books on writing and the publishing industry that will help you. At conferences, ask published writers about their agents. Don't believe the myth that an agent has to be in New York to be successful—we've already disproved it!"

◉ THE JONATHAN DOLGER AGENCY

49 E. 96th St., Suite 9B, New York NY 10128. Fax: (212)369-7118. Estab. 1980. Member of AAR.
Represents Nonfiction books, novels. **Considers these nonfiction areas:** Biography/autobiography; history; women's issues/studies; cultural/social. **Considers these fiction areas:** Women's; commercial.
How to Contact Query with SASE. No e-mail queries.
Recent Sales This agency prefers not to share information on specific sales.
Terms Agent receives 15% commission on domestic sales; 25% commission on foreign sales.
Tips "Writers must have been previously published if submitting fiction. We prefer to work with published/established authors, and work with a small number of new/previously unpublished writers."

◎ DONADIO & OLSON, INC.

121 W. 27th St., Suite 704, New York NY 10001. (212)691-8077. Fax: (212)633-2837. E-mail: mail@donadio.com. Member of AAR.
Member Agents Neil Olson (no queries); Ira Silverberg (query via snail mail for general fiction, history, biography, pop culture); Edward Hibbert (no queries); Darren Web (query via snail mail).
Represents Nonfiction books, novels.
   O─ This agency represents mostly fiction, and is very selective.
How to Contact Query by snail mail is preferred; only send submissions to open agents. No fax queries. Obtains most new clients through recommendations from others.
Recent Sales *Kings of Infinite Space*, by James Hynes (St. Martin's Press); *Shifting Through Neutral*, by Bridgett M. Davis (Amistad); *The Faithful Narrative of a Pastor's Disappearance: A Novel*, by Benjamin Anastas (Straus Giroux).

◉ JANIS A. DONNAUD & ASSOCIATES, INC.

525 Broadway, Second Floor, New York NY 10012. (212)431-2664. Fax: (212)431-2667. E-mail: jdonnaud@aol.com; donnaudassociate@aol.com. **Contact:** Janis A. Donnaud. Member of AAR; signatory of WGA. Represents 40 clients. 5% of clients are new/unpublished writers. Currently handles: 100% nonfiction books.
   • Prior to opening her agency, Ms. Donnaud was vice president and associate publisher of Random House Adult Trade Group.
Represents Nonfiction books. **Considers these nonfiction areas:** Biography/autobiography; child guidance/parenting; cooking/foods/nutrition; current affairs; health/medicine; humor/satire; psychology (pop); women's issues/studies; lifestyle.
   O─ This agency specializes in health, medical, cooking, humor, pop psychology, narrative nonfiction, biography, parenting, and current affairs. "We give a lot of service and attention to clients." Actively seeking serious narrative nonfiction, cookbooks, and books on health and medical topics—all written by experts with an already established national platform in their area of specialty. Does not want to receive fiction, poetry, mysteries, juvenile books, romances, science fiction, young adult, religious or fantasy.
How to Contact Query with SASE, submit description of book, 2-3 pages of sample material. Prefers to read materials exclusively. No phone calls. Accepts e-mail queries. No fax queries. Responds in 1 month to queries; 1 month to mss. Obtains most new clients through recommendations from others.
Recent Sales Sold 25 titles in the last year. *Inventing the Rest of Our Lives*, by Suzanne Braun Levine; *Southern Fried Divorce: A Woman Unleashes Her Hound and His Dog in the Big Easy*, by Judy Conner (Light of New Orleans Publishing); *Inventing The Rest Of Our Lives: Women In Second Adulthood*, by Susanne Braun Levine (Viking Books).
Terms Agent receives 15% commission on domestic sales; 20% commission on foreign sales; 20% commission on dramatic rights sales. Offers written contract; 1-month notice must be given to terminate contract. Charges clients for messengers, photocopying and purchase of books.

◖ JIM DONOVAN LITERARY

4515 Prentice St., Suite 109, Dallas TX 75206. **Contact:** Jim Donovan, president. Estab. 1993. Currently handles: 70% nonfiction books; 30% novels.
Represents Nonfiction books, novels.
   O─ This agency specializes in commercial fiction and nonfiction. Does not want to receive poetry, humor, short stories, sci-fi/fantasy, juvenile, romance, or religious work.
How to Contact For nonfiction, send query letter. For fiction, send outline (2-5 pages), 3 sample chapters, SASE. No e-mail or fax queries. Considers simultaneous queries. Obtains most new clients through recommendations from others, solicitations.
Terms Agent receives 15% commission on domestic sales. Offers written contract, binding for 1 year; written notice must be given to terminate contract.
Tips "The vast majority of material I receive, particularly fiction, is not ready for publication. Do everything

you can to get your fiction work in top shape before you try to find an agent. I've been in the book business since 1981, in retail (as a chain buyer), as an editor, and as a published author. I'm open to working with new writers if they're serious about their writing and are prepared to put in the work necessary—the rewriting—to become publishable.''

◙ DOYEN LITERARY SERVICES, INC.

1931 660th St., Newell IA 50568-7613. (712)272-3300. Web site: www.barbaradoyen.com. **Contact:** (Ms.) B.J. Doyen, president. Estab. 1988. Represents over 100 clients. 20% of clients are new/unpublished writers. Currently handles: 95% nonfiction books; 5% novels.

- Prior to opening her agency, Ms. Doyen worked as a published author, teacher, guest speaker, and wrote and appeared in her own weekly TV show airing in 7 states. She is also the co-author of *The Everything Guide to Writing a Book Proposal* (Adams 2005) and *The Everything Guide to Getting Published* (Adams 2006).

Represents Nonfiction books, novels. **Considers these nonfiction areas:** Agriculture/horticulture; americana; animals; anthropology/archaeology; art/architecture/design; biography/autobiography; business/economics; child guidance/parenting; computers/electronic; cooking/foods/nutrition; crafts/hobbies; current affairs; education; ethnic/cultural interests; gardening; government/politics/law; health/medicine; history; how-to; interior design/decorating; language/literature/criticism; memoirs; military/war; money/finance; multicultural; music/ dance; nature/environment; New Age/metaphysics; philosophy; photography; popular culture; psychology; recreation; regional; religious/inspirational; science/technology; self-help/personal improvement; sex; sociology; software; spirituality; theater/film; travel; true crime/investigative; women's issues/studies; young adult; creative nonfiction. **Considers these fiction areas:** Family saga; historical; literary; mainstream/contemporary.

- This agency specializes in nonfiction and occasionally handles mainstream fiction for adults. Actively seeking business, health, how-to, self-help—all kinds of adult nonfiction suitable for the major trade publishers. Does not want to receive pornography, children's books, or poetry.

How to Contact Query with SASE. No e-mail or fax queries. Considers simultaneous queries. Responds in 3 weeks to mss. Responds immediately to queries. Returns materials only with SASE.

Recent Sales *The Birth Order Effect for Couples*, by Isaacson/Schneider (Fairwinds); *1,000 Best Casino Tips*, by Bill Burton (Sourcebooks).

Terms Agent receives 15% commission on domestic sales; 20% commission on foreign sales. Offers written contract, binding for 2 years.

Tips ''Our authors receive personalized attention. We market aggressively, undeterred by rejection. We get the best possible publishing contracts. We are very interested in nonfiction book ideas at this time and will consider most topics. Many writers come to us from referrals, but we also get quite a few who initially approach us with query letters. Do not call us regarding queries. It is best if you do not collect editorial rejections prior to seeking an agent, but if you do, be upfront and honest about it. Do not submit your manuscript to more than 1 agent at a time—querying first can save you (and us) much time. We're open to established or beginning writers— just send us a terrific letter with a SASE!''

◙ DUNHAM LITERARY, INC.

156 Fifth Ave., Suite 625, New York NY 10010-7002. (212)929-0994. Web site: www.dunhamlit.com. **Contact:** Jennie Dunham. Estab. 2000. Member of AAR. Represents 50 clients. 15% of clients are new/unpublished writers. Currently handles: 25% nonfiction books; 25% novels; 50% juvenile books.

- Prior to opening her agency, Ms. Dunham worked as a literary agent for Russell & Volkening. The Rhoda Weyr Agency is now a division of Dunham Literary, Inc.

Represents Nonfiction books, novels, short story collections, juvenile books. **Considers these nonfiction areas:** Anthropology/archaeology; biography/autobiography; ethnic/cultural interests; government/politics/law; health/medicine; history; language/literature/criticism; nature/environment; popular culture; psychology; science/technology; women's issues/studies. **Considers these fiction areas:** Ethnic; juvenile; literary; mainstream/contemporary; picture books; young adult.

How to Contact Query with SASE. No e-mail or fax queries. Responds in 1 week to queries; 2 months to mss. Obtains most new clients through recommendations from others, solicitations.

Recent Sales *America the Beautiful*, by Robert Sabuda; *Dahlia*, by Barbara McClintock; *Living Dead Girl*, by Tod Goldberg; *In My Mother's House*, by Margaret McMulla; *Black Hawk Down*, by Mark Bowden; *Look Back All the Green Valley*, by Fred Chappell; *Under a Wing*, by Reeve Lindbergh; *I Am Madame X*, by Gioia Diliberto.

Terms Agent receives 15% commission on domestic sales; 20% commission on foreign sales.

◙ DUNOW, CARLSON, & LERNER AGENCY

27 W. 20th St., #1107, New York NY 10011. **Contact:** Jennifer Carlson, Henry Dunow, Betsy Lerner. Member of AAR.

How to Contact Query with SASE.
Recent Sales *Black Olives*, by Martha Tod Dudman (Simon & Schuster).

DUPREE/MILLER AND ASSOCIATES INC. LITERARY

100 Highland Park Village, Suite 350, Dallas TX 75205. (214)559-BOOK. Fax: (214)559-PAGE. E-mail: editorial@ dupreemiller.com. **Contact:** Submissions Department. Estab. 1984. Member of ABA. Represents 200 clients. 20% of clients are new/unpublished writers. Currently handles: 90% nonfiction books; 10% novels.
Member Agents Jan Miller, president/CEO; Shannon Miser-Marven, senior executive VP; Annabelle Baxter; Nena Madonia; Cheri Gillis.
Represents Nonfiction books, novels, scholarly books, syndicated material (1), religious.inspirational/spirituality. **Considers these nonfiction areas:** Americana; animals; anthropology/archaeology; art/architecture/design; biography/autobiography; business/economics; child guidance/parenting; cooking/foods/nutrition; crafts/hobbies; creative nonfiction (1); current affairs; education; ethnic/cultural interests; gardening; government/politics/law; health/medicine; history; how-to; humor/satire; interior design/decorating; language/literature/criticism; memoirs; money/finance; multicultural; music/dance; nature/environment; New Age/metaphysics; philosophy; photography; popular culture; psychology; recreation; regional; science/technology; self-help/personal improvement; sex; sociology; sports; theater/film; translation; true crime/investigative; women's issues/studies. **Considers these fiction areas:** Action/adventure; detective/police/crime; ethnic; experimental; family saga; feminist; glitz; historical; humor/satire; literary; mainstream/contemporary; mystery/suspense; picture books; psychic/supernatural; religious/inspirational; sports; thriller.
  ⊶ This agency specializes in commercial fiction and nonfiction.
How to Contact Submit 1-page query, outline, SASE. Obtains most new clients through recommendations from others, conferences, lectures.
Recent Sales Sold 30 titles in the last year. *It's All About You: Get the Life You're Craving*, by Mary Goulet and Heather Reider (Free Press). Other clients include Dr. Phil Mcgraw, Robin Mcgraw, Maria Shriver, Catherine Crier, Anthony Robbins, Dr. Stephen Covey, Pastor Joel Osteen, Deborah Norville, Dr. Creflo Dollar, Dr. Frank Lawlis, Dr. Bill Dorfman.
Terms Agent receives 15% commission on domestic sales. Offers written contract.
Writers' Conferences Aspen Summer Words Literary Festival.
Tips "If interested in agency representation, it is vital to have the material in the proper working format. As agents' policies differ, it is important to follow their guidelines. The best advice I can give is to work on establishing a strong proposal that provides sample chapters, an overall synopsis (fairly detailed), and some biographical information on yourself. Do not send your proposal in pieces; it should be complete upon submission. Remember you are trying to sell your work, and it should be in its best condition."

DYSTEL & GODERICH LITERARY MANAGEMENT

1 Union Square W., Suite 904, New York NY 10003. (212)627-9100. Fax: (212)627-9313. E-mail: miriam@dystel. com. Web site: www.dystel.com. **Contact:** Miriam Goderich. Estab. 1994. Member of AAR. Represents 300 clients. 50% of clients are new/unpublished writers. Currently handles: 65% nonfiction books; 25% novels; 10% cookbooks.
  • Dystel & Goderich Literary Management recently acquired the client list of Bedford Book Works.
Member Agents Stacey Glick; Jane Dystel; Miriam Goderich; Michael Bourret; Jim McCarthy; Lauren Abramo; Adina Kahn.
Represents Nonfiction books, novels, cookbooks. **Considers these nonfiction areas:** Animals; anthropology/archaeology; biography/autobiography; business/economics; child guidance/parenting; cooking/foods/nutrition; current affairs; education; ethnic/cultural interests; gay/lesbian issues; government/politics/law; health/medicine; history; humor/satire; military/war; money/finance; New Age/metaphysics; popular culture; psychology; religious/inspirational; science/technology; true crime/investigative; women's issues/studies. **Considers these fiction areas:** Action/adventure; detective/police/crime; ethnic; family saga; gay/lesbian; literary; mainstream/contemporary; mystery/suspense; thriller.
  ⊶ This agency specializes in cookbooks and commercial and literary fiction and nonfiction.
How to Contact Query with SASE. Considers simultaneous queries. Responds in 1 month to queries; 6 weeks to mss. Obtains most new clients through recommendations from others, solicitations, conferences.
Terms Agent receives 15% commission on domestic sales; 19% commission on foreign sales. Offers written contract. Charges for photocopying. Galley charges and book charges from the publisher are passed on to the author.
Writers' Conferences Whidbey Island Writers' Conference; Backspace Writers' Conference; Iowa Summer Writing Festival; Pacific Northwest Writers' Association; Pike's Peak Writers' Conference; Santa Barbara Writers' Conference; Harriette Austin Writers' Conference; Sandhills Writers' Conference; Denver Publishing Institute; Love Is Murder.

Tips "Work on sending professional, well-written queries that are concise and addressed to the specific agent the author is contacting. No dear Sirs/Madam."

N ⬛ 🖉 TOBY EADY ASSOCIATES

Third Floor, 9 Orme Court, London England W2 4RL, United Kingdom. (44)(207)792-0092. Fax: (44)(207)792-0879. E-mail: Jamie@tobyeady.demon.co.uk. Web site: www.tobyeadyassociates.co.uk. **Contact:** Jamie Coleman. Estab. 1968. Represents 53 clients. 13% of clients are new/unpublished writers. Currently handles: 50% nonfiction books; 50% novels.

Member Agents Toby Eady (China, the Middle East, Africa, politics of a Swiftian nature); Laetitia Rutherford (fiction and nonfiction from around the world).

Represents Nonfiction books, novels, short story collections, novellas, anthologies. **Considers these nonfiction areas:** Art/architecture/design; cooking/foods/nutrition; current affairs; ethnic/cultural interests; government/politics/law; health/medicine; history; memoirs; popular culture. **Considers these fiction areas:** Action/adventure; confession; historical; literary; mainstream/contemporary.

> **O—** "We handle fiction and nonfiction for adults and we specialize in China, the Middle East and Africa." Actively seeking stories that demand to be heard. Does not want to receive poetry, screenplays or children's books.

How to Contact Query with synopsis/outline, bio, 2 sample chapters, SASE. Considers simultaneous queries. Responds in 2 weeks to queries; 2 weeks to mss. Returns materials only with SASE. Obtains most new clients through recommendations from others, solicitations, conferences.

Recent Sales *My Name Is Salma*, by Fadia Faquir (Doubleday); *Speaking to the Heart*, by Sister Wendy Beckett (Constable & Robinson); *February Flowers*, by Fan Wu (Picador Asia). Other clients include Bernard Cornwell, Chris Cleave, Rana Dasgupta, Julia Lovell and Rachel Seiffert.

Terms Agent receives 15% commission on domestic sales; 20% commission on foreign sales. Offers written contract; 3-month notice must be given to terminate contract.

Writers' Conferences City Lit; Winchester Writers' Festival.

Tips "Do your research!"

N 🖉 EBELING AND ASSOCIATES

P.O. Box 790267, Pala HI 96779. (808)579-6414. Fax: (808)579-9294. E-mail: ebothat@yahoo.com. Web site: www.ebelingagency.com. **Contact:** Michael Ebeling or Kristina Holmes. Estab. 2003. Represents 6 clients. 50% of clients are new/unpublished writers. Currently handles: 100% nonfiction books.

> ● Prior to becoming an agent, Mr. Ebeling worked in sales and marketing, working one-on-one with authors to develop their platform and position themselves in the marketplace.

Member Agents Michael Ebeling (platform building and marketing of clients; considers self help and business titles); Kristina Holmes (health/wellness, spirituality, self help, environmental/social issues).

Represents Nonfiction books. **Considers these nonfiction areas:** Animals; anthropology/archaeology; art/architecture/design; biography/autobiography; business/economics; child guidance/parenting; computers/electronic; cooking/foods/nutrition; current affairs; education; ethnic/cultural interests; gay/lesbian issues; government/politics/law; health/medicine; history; how-to; humor/satire; money/finance; music/dance; nature/environment; photography; popular culture; psychology; religious/inspirational; science/technology; self-help/personal improvement; sports; women's issues/studies.

> **O—** "We accept very few clients for representation. We represent nonfiction authors, most predominantly in the areas of business and self-help. We are very committed to our authors and their messages, which is a main reason we have such a high placement rate. We are always looking at new ways to help our authors gain the exposure they need to not only get published, but develop a successful literary career." Actively seeking well written nonfiction material with fresh perspectives written by writers with established platforms. Does not want to receive fiction.

How to Contact Query with SASE, submit outline/proposal, SASE. Accepts e-mail queries. No fax queries. Considers simultaneous queries. Responds in 2-4 weeks to queries. Returns materials only with SASE. Obtains most new clients through recommendations from others, solicitations.

Recent Sales Sold 10 titles in the last year. *Relax Into Wealth: How to Get More by Doing Less*, by Alan Cohen (Tarcher/Penguin); *The Advantage Makers*, by Steven Feinberg (Pearson Education); *Gimme! The Human Nature of Successful Marketing* by John Hallward (John Wiley and Sons); *The Relationship Emergency Kit* by Chuck Spezzano (Random House/Germany).

Terms Agent receives 15% commission on domestic sales; 15% commission on foreign sales. Offers written contract; 60-day notice must be given to terminate contract. There is a charge for normal out-of-pocket fees, not to exceed $200 without client approval.

Writers' Conferences BookExpo America; San Francisco Writers' Conference.

Tips "Approach agents when you're already building your platform, you have a well written book, you've done a lot of research about the publishing process, and have come up with a complete competitive proposal. Know the name of the agent you are contacting, and equally important, make sure the agent represents the category of writing your work falls into."

⬤ ANNE EDELSTEIN LITERARY AGENCY

20 W. 22nd St., Suite 1603, New York NY 10010. (212)414-4923. Fax: (212)414-2930. E-mail: info@aeliterary.c om. Web site: www.aeliterary.com. Estab. 1990. Member of AAR.
Member Agents Anne Edelstein; Emilie Stewart.
Represents Nonfiction books, novels. **Considers these nonfiction areas:** History; memoirs; psychology; religious/inspirational; Buddhist thought. **Considers these fiction areas:** Commercial.
   O⚓ This agency specializes in fiction and narrative nonfiction.
How to Contact Query with SASE; submit 25 sample pages. No e-mail or fax queries.
Recent Sales *I Just Want My Pants Back*, by David J. Rosen (Broadway).

◎ EDUCATIONAL DESIGN SERVICES, LLC

7238 Treviso Ln., Boynton Beach FL 33437-7338. (561)739-9402. Fax: (561)739-9402. E-mail: blinder@educatio naldesignservices.com. Web site: www.educationaldesignservices.com. **Contact:** Bertram L. Linder, president. Estab. 1981. Represents 14 clients. 95% of clients are new/unpublished writers. Currently handles: 100% textbooks and professional materials for education.
   ● Prior to becoming an agent, Mr. Linder was an author and a teacher.
Member Agents Bertram Linder (textbooks and professional materials for education).
Represents Scholarly books, textbooks.
   O⚓ "We are one of the few agencies that specialize exclusively in materials for the education market. We handle text materials for grades preK-12, text materials for college/university use, and materials for professionals in the field of education, staff development and education policy." Does not want children's fiction and nonfiction, picture books.
How to Contact Query with SASE, submit proposal package, outline, outline/proposal, 2-3 sample chapter(s), SASE. Accepts e-mail queries. No fax queries. Considers simultaneous queries. Responds in 3-4 weeks to queries; 3-4 weeks to mss. Returns materials only with SASE. Obtains most new clients through recommendations from others, solicitations, conferences.
Recent Sales Sold 4 titles in the last year. *No Parent Left Behind*, by P. Petrosino and L. Spiegel (Rowman & Littlefield Education); *Preparing for the 8th Grade Test in Social Studies*, by E. Farran and A. Paci (Amsco Book Company); *Teaching Test-Taking Skills by G. Durham* (Rowman & Littlefield Education); *Teachers's Quick Guide to Communicating*, by G. Sundem (Corwin Press).
Terms Agent receives 15% commission on domestic sales; 25% commission on foreign sales. Offers written contract; 30 days notice must be given to terminate contract. Charges clients for extraordinary expenses in postage and shipping, as well as long distance telephone calls.

⚙ ◻ JUDITH EHRLICH LITERARY MANAGEMENT, LLC

880 Third Ave., Eighth Floor, New York NY 10022. (646)505-1570. Web site: www.judithehrlichliterary.com. Estab. 2002. Member of Author's Guild, the American Society of Journalists and Authors.
   ● Prior to her current position, Ms. Ehrlich was an award-winning journalist; she is the co-author of *The New Crowd: The Changing of the Jewish Guard on Wall Street* (Little, Brown). Ms. Hoffman worked at Harold Matson Company and as a freelance editor.
Member Agents Judith Ehrlich, jehrlich@judithehrlichliterary.com; Sophia Seidner, sseidner@judithehrlichliterary.com; Martha Hoffman, mhoffman@judithehrlichliterary.com (psychology, cultural commentary, and historical work that ties unique perspectives to strong narrative).
Represents Nonfiction books, novels.
   O⚓ "Special areas of interest include compelling narrative nonfiction, outstanding biographies and memoirs, lifestyle books, works that reflect our changing culture, women's issues, psychology, science, social issues, current events, parenting, health, history, business, and prescriptive books offering fresh information and advice." Actively seeking stellar fiction (literary, quality and commercial) with an intriguing story line, strong characters and distinctive style. Among our special interests are women's fiction, humorous novels, mysteries, thrillers and historicals.
How to Contact Query with SASE. Queries should include a synopsis and some sample pages. Send e-queries to jehrlich@judithehrlichliterary.com. The agency will respond only if interested. Accepts e-mail queries. No fax queries. Returns materials only with SASE.
Recent Sales *Up and Running: The Jami Goldman Story*, by Andrea Cagan (Pocket Books); *Forewarned: Why the Government Is Failing to Protect Us—and What We Can Do to Protect Ourselves*, by Michael Cherkasky

(Ballantine); *Let the Baby Drive: Navigating the Road of New Motherhood*, by Lu Hanessian (St. Martin's); *Marriage from the Heart: Eight Commitments of a Spiritually Fulfilling Life Together*, by Lois Kellerman and Nelly Bly (Viking).

◎ LISA EKUS PUBLIC RELATIONS CO., LLC
57 North St., Hatfield MA 01038. (413)247-9325. Fax: (413)247-9873. Web site: www.lisaekus.com. **Contact:** Lisa Ekus. Estab. 1982. Member of AAR.

Represents Nonfiction books. **Considers these nonfiction areas:** Cooking/foods/nutrition; occasionally health/well-being and women's issues.

How to Contact Submit a hard copy proposal with title page, proposal contents, concept, author bio, marketing and promotion, competition, TOC, chapter summaries, complete sample chapter (include tested recipes).

Recent Sales Please see the regularly updated client listing at www.lisaekus.com.

◪ ETHAN ELLENBERG LITERARY AGENCY
548 Broadway, #5-E, New York NY 10012. (212)431-4554. Fax: (212)941-4652. E-mail: agent@ethanellenberg.com. Web site: www.ethanellenberg.com. **Contact:** Ethan Ellenberg. Estab. 1983. Represents 80 clients. 10% of clients are new/unpublished writers. Currently handles: 25% nonfiction books; 75% novels.

• Prior to opening his agency, Mr. Ellenberg was contracts manager of Berkley/Jove and associate contracts manager for Bantam.

Represents Nonfiction books, novels, children's books. **Considers these nonfiction areas:** Biography/autobiography; current affairs; health/medicine; history; military/war; science/technology; narrative. **Considers these fiction areas:** Commerical fiction—specializing in romance/fiction for women, science fiction and fantasy, thrillers, suspense and mysteries, children's books (all types: picture books, middle grade and YA).

O—π This agency specializes in commercial fiction—especially thrillers, romance/women's, and specialized nonfiction. "We also do a lot of children's books, commercial fiction as noted above—romance/fiction for women, science fiction and fantasy, thrillers, suspense and mysteries. Our other two main areas of interest are children's books and narrative nonfiction. We are actively seeking clients, follow the directions on our Web site." Does not want to receive poetry, short stories, Western's, autobiographies or screenplays.

How to Contact For fiction, send introductory letter, outline, first 3 chapters, SASE. For nonfiction, send query letter, proposal, 1 sample chapter, SASE. For children's books, send introductory letter, up to 3 picture book mss, outline, first 3 chapters, SASE. No fax queries. Accepts e-mail queries (no attachments). Will only respond to e-mail queries if interested. Considers simultaneous queries. Responds in 4-6 weeks to mss. Returns materials only with SASE.

Recent Sales *Sleeping With the Fishes and Dead and Loving It*, by Maryjanice Davidson (Berkley); *The Summoner*, by Gail Martin (Solaris); *Empress of Mijak*, by Karen Miller (Harper Australia); *Hellgate: London*, by Mel Odom (Pocket Books); *The Last Colony* and *Android's Dream*, by John Scalzi (Tor Books); *General Winston's Daughter*, by Sharon Shinn (Ace Books); *Dead Sexy*, by Amanda Ashley (Kensington). Other clients include Mel Odom, MaryJanice Davidson, Amanda Ashley, Rebecca York, Bertrice Small, Eric Rohmann.

Terms Agent receives 15% commission on domestic sales; 10% commission on foreign sales. Offers written contract. Charges clients (with their consent) for direct expenses limited to photocopying and postage.

Writers' Conferences RWA National Conference; Novelists, Inc; and other regional conferences.

Tips "We do consider new material from unsolicited authors. Write a good, clear letter with a succinct description of your book. We prefer the first 3 chapters when we consider fiction. For all submissions, you must include a SASE or the material will be discarded. It's always hard to break in, but talent will find a home. Check our Web site for complete submission guidelines. We continue to see natural storytellers and nonfiction writers with important books."

◪ THE NICHOLAS ELLISON AGENCY
Affiliated with Sanford J. Greenburger Associates, 55 Fifth Ave., 15th Floor, New York NY 10003. (212)206-6050. Fax: (212)463-8718. Web site: www.greenburger.com. **Contact:** Nicholas Ellison. Estab. 1983. Represents 70 clients. Currently handles: 50% nonfiction books; 50% novels.

• Prior to becoming an agent, Mr. Ellison was an editor at Minerva Editions and Harper & Row, and editor-in-chief at Delacorte.

Member Agents Nicholas Ellison; Sarah Dickman.

Represents Nonfiction books, novels. **Considers these nonfiction areas:** Considers most nonfiction areas. **Considers these fiction areas:** Literary; mainstream/contemporary.

How to Contact Query with SASE. Responds in 6 weeks to queries.

Recent Sales *School of Fortune*, by Amanda Brown and Janice Weber (St. Martin's); *You Suck*, by Christopher Moore (HarperCollins); *I'm Not Myself*, by Sarah Dunn (Little, Brown); next 3 Nelson DeMille Books (Warner).

Other clients include Olivia Goldsmith, P.T. Deutermann, Nancy Geary, Jeff Lindsay, Thomas Christopher Greene, Bill Mason, Geoff Emerick, Howard Massey, Emily Benedek, Alan Weisman, Matthew Scott Hansen.
Terms Agent receives 15% commission on domestic sales; 20% commission on foreign sales.

ANN ELMO AGENCY, INC.

60 E. 42nd St., New York NY 10165. (212)661-2880. Fax: (212)661-2883. **Contact:** Lettie Lee. Estab. 1959. Member of AAR, Authors Guild.
Member Agents Lettie Lee; Mari Cronin (plays); A.L. Abecassis (nonfiction).
Represents Nonfiction books, novels. **Considers these nonfiction areas:** Biography/autobiography; current affairs; health/medicine; history; how-to; popular culture; science/technology. **Considers these fiction areas:** Ethnic; family saga; mainstream/contemporary; romance (contemporary, gothic, historical, regency); thriller; women's.
How to Contact Only accepts mailed queries with SASE. Do not send full ms unless requested. No fax queries. Responds in 3 months to queries. Obtains most new clients through recommendations from others.
Recent Sales This agency prefers not to share information on specific sales.
Terms Agent receives 15% commission on domestic sales; 20% commission on foreign sales. Offers written contract. This agency charges clients for special mailings, shipping, multiple international calls. There is no charge for usual cost of doing business.
Tips "Query first, and only when asked send properly prepared manuscript. A double-spaced, readable manuscript is the best recommendation. Include a SASE, of course."

THE ELAINE P. ENGLISH LITERARY AGENCY

4701 41st St. NW, Suite D, Washington DC 20016. (202)362-5190. Fax: (202)362-5192. E-mail: elaine@elaineeng lish.com. Web site: www.elaineenglish.com. **Contact:** Elaine English. Member of AAR. Represents 16 clients. 25% of clients are new/unpublished writers. Currently handles: 100% novels.
● Ms. English has been working in publishing for more than 20 years. She is also an attorney specializing in media and publishing law.
Represents Novels. **Considers these fiction areas:** Historical; multicultural; mystery/suspense; romance (single title, historical, contemporary, romantic, suspense, chick lit, erotic); thriller; general women's fiction. The agency is slowly but steadily acquiring in all mentioned areas.
○➡ Actively seeking women's fiction, including single-title romances. Does not want to receive any science fiction, time travel, children's, or young adult.
How to Contact Prefers e-queries sent to queries@elaineenglish.com. If requested, submit synopsis, first 3 chapters, SASE. Accepts e-mail queries. No fax queries. Responds in 6-12 weeks to queries; 6 months to requested ms. Returns materials only with SASE. Obtains most new clients through recommendations from others, conferences, submissions.
Recent Sales *The Blue-Eyed Devil*, by Diane Whiteside (Kensington).
Terms Agent receives 15% commission on domestic sales; 20% commission on foreign sales. Offers written contract; 30-day notice must be given to terminate contract. Charges only for copying and postage; generally taken from proceeds.
Writers' Conferences RWA National Conference; SEAK Medical & Legal Fiction Writing Conference; Novelists, Inc; Malice Domestic; Washington Romance Writers Retreat, among others.

THE EPSTEIN LITERARY AGENCY

P.O. Box 356, Avon MA 02368. (781)718-4025. E-mail: kate@epsteinliterary.com. Web site: www.epsteinliterar y.com. **Contact:** Kate Epstein. Estab. 2005. Represents 20 clients. 70% of clients are new/unpublished writers. Currently handles: 100% nonfiction books.
● Prior to opening her literary agency, Ms. Epstein was an acquisitions editor at Adams Media.
Represents Nonfiction books. **Considers these nonfiction areas:** Animals; biography/autobiography; business/economics; child guidance/parenting; cooking/foods/nutrition; current affairs; health/medicine; how-to; humor/satire; memoirs; popular culture; psychology; self-help/personal improvement; sociology; women's issues/studies; New Age/metaphysics.
○➡ "My background as an editor means that I'm extremely good at selling to them. It also means I'm a careful and thorough line editor. I'm particularly skilled at hardening concepts to make them sellable and proposing the logical follow-up for any book. Most of my list is practical nonfiction, and I have a particular affinity for pets." Actively seeking commercial nonfiction for adults. Does not want scholarly works.
How to Contact Query via e-mail (no attachments). Considers simultaneous queries. Returns materials only with SASE. Obtains most new clients through solicitations.
Recent Sales *Everything I Needed to Know, I Learned from Watching Television*, by Jeff Alexander (Berkley);

The Dog Who's Always Welcome, by Lorie Long (Howell House); *Herding Cats*, by Dusty Rainbolt (Lyons Press); *The Log Home Owner's Handbook*, by Mary Beth Temple (Storey); *The Rookie Reiner*, by Heather Cook (Trafalgar Square); *Whatever You Do Don't Run*, by Peter Allison (Globe Pequot); *Knitting Is Better Than Therapy*, by Mary Beth Temple (Andrews McMeel). Other clients include Tena Bastian, Jennifer Keene, The Segullah Group/Kathryn Lynard Soper.

Terms Agent receives 15% commission on domestic sales; 20% commission on foreign sales. Offers written contract; 30-day notice must be given to terminate contract.

Writers' Conferences Grub Stret's Annual Muse & the Marketplace Conference.

⬤ FELICIA ETH LITERARY REPRESENTATION

555 Bryant St., Suite 350, Palo Alto CA 94301-1700. (650)375-1276. Fax: (650)401-8892. E-mail: feliciaeth@aol.com. **Contact:** Felicia Eth. Estab. 1988. Member of AAR. Represents 25-35 clients. Currently handles: 85% nonfiction books; 15% adult novels.

Represents Nonfiction books, novels. **Considers these nonfiction areas:** Animals; anthropology/archaeology; biography/autobiography; business/economics; child guidance/parenting; current affairs; ethnic/cultural interests; gay/lesbian issues; government/politics/law; health/medicine; history; nature/environment; popular culture; psychology; science/technology; sociology; true crime/investigative; women's issues/studies. **Considers these fiction areas:** Ethnic; feminist; gay/lesbian; literary; mainstream/contemporary; thriller.

    O→ This agency specializes in high-quality fiction (preferably mainstream/contemporary) and provocative, intelligent, and thoughtful nonfiction on a wide array of commercial subjects.

How to Contact Query with SASE, outline. Considers simultaneous queries. Responds in 3 weeks to queries; 4-6 weeks to mss.

Recent Sales Sold 7-10 titles in the last year. *Jane Austen in Boca*, by Paula Marantz Cohen (St. Martin's Press); *Why Gender Matters*, by Dr. Leonard Sax (Doubleday/Random House); *Anna Maria Violino*, by Barbara Quick (HarperCollins).

Terms Agent receives 15% commission on domestic sales; 20% commission on foreign sales; 20% commission on dramatic rights sales. Charges clients for photocopying and express mail service.

Writers' Conferences National Coalition of Independent Scholars Conference.

Tips "For nonfiction, established expertise is certainly a plus—as is magazine publication—though not a prerequisite. I am highly dedicated to those projects I represent, but highly selective in what I choose."

⬤ MARY EVANS, INC.

242 E. Fifth St., New York NY 10003. (212)979-0880. Fax: (212)979-5344. Member of AAR.

Member Agents Mary Evans, merrylit@aol.com (no unsolicited queries); Tanya McKinnon, tanyamckinnon@yahoo.com (children's, humor, journalism, multicultural, graphic novels, African-American fiction and nonfiction); Devin McIntyre.

Represents Nonfiction books, novels.

How to Contact Query with SASE. Query by snail mail. No fax queries. Obtains most new clients through recommendations from others, solicitations.

Recent Sales *The Bitch Posse*, by Martha O'Connor (St. Martin's Press); *Li'l Dan, the Drummer Boy: A Civil War Story*, by Romare Bearden (Simon & Schuster Children's).

Ⓝ ⬤ FAIRBANK LITERARY REPRESENTATION

199 Mount Auburn St., Suite 1, Cambridge MA 02138-4809. (617)576-0030. Fax: (617)576-0030. E-mail: queries @fairbankliterary.com. Web site: www.fairbankliterary.com. **Contact:** Sorche Fairbank. Estab. 2002. Represents 40 clients. 20% of clients are new/unpublished writers. Currently handles: 60% nonfiction books; 22% novels; 3% story collections; 15% other.

Member Agents Sorche Fairbank (narrative nonfiction, literary fiction, memoir, food and wine); Matthew Frederick (sports, architecture, design).

Represents Nonfiction books, novels, short story collections. **Considers these nonfiction areas:** Agriculture/horticulture; art/architecture/design; biography/autobiography; cooking/foods/nutrition; crafts/hobbies; current affairs; ethnic/cultural interests; gay/lesbian issues; government/politics/law; history; how-to; interior design/decorating; language/literature/criticism; memoirs; military/war; nature/environment; photography; popular culture; science/technology; sociology; sports; true crime/investigative; women's issues/studies. **Considers these fiction areas:** Action/adventure; feminist; gay/lesbian; literary; mainstream/contemporary; mystery/suspense; sports; thriller; women's; Southern voices.

    O→ "I have a small agency in Harvard Square, where I tend to gravitate toward literary fiction and narrative nonfiction, with a strong interest in women's issues and women's voices, South American and Latina/Latina voices, class and race issues, and projects that simply teach me something new about the greater world and society around us. We have a good reputation for working closely and developmentally with our authors and love what we do.'' Actively seeking literary fiction, international and culturally diverse voices, narrative nonfiction (including one-subject material a la Mark Kurlansky), topical subjects (politics, current affairs), history, sports, architecture/design and pop culture. Does not want to receive romance, poetry, science fiction, young adult or children's works.

How to Contact Query with SASE, submit author bio. Accepts e-mail queries. No fax queries. Considers simultaneous queries. Responds in 2-6 weeks to queries; 4-8 weeks to mss. Returns materials only with SASE. Obtains most new clients through recommendations from others, solicitations, conferences, ideas generated in-house.

Recent Sales Sold 19 titles in the last year. *To Full Term: A Mother's Triumph Over Miscarriage*, by Darci Hamilton-Klein (Berkley/Penguin); *Spirit of Summer: At Home in the Thousand Islands*, by Kathleen Quigley (Rizzoli); *The Uncommon Quilter*, by Jeanne Williamson (Potter Craft/Crown); *Solar Revolution*, by Travis Bradford (The MIT Press). Other clients include Robin Moore, Xaviera Hollander, Rex Burns, John McAleer (estate of), David Yonke, Charlotte Forbes, Banny Golson, Dr. Kim Hardin, Wendy Madar, Leslie Lytle, Man Martin, Larry Schooler, Penny Rudolph, Michael Siverling.

Terms Agent receives 15% commission on domestic sales; 20% commission on foreign sales. Offers written contract, binding for 12 months; 30-day notice must be given to terminate contract. Charges postage and mailing fees, printing at cost, deducted from sale of work.

Writers' Conferences San Francisco Writers' Conference, Midwest Literary Festival, Muse and the Marketplace/Grub Street Conference, Washington Independent Writers' Conference.

Tips ''Have a reason for contacting me about your project other than I was the next name listed on some Web site. Please do not use form query software! Believe me, we can get a dozen or so a day that look identical—we know when you are using a form. Show me that you know your audience—and your competition. Have the writing and/or proposal at the very, very best it can be before starting the querying process. Don't assume that if someone likes it enough they'll 'fix' it. The biggest mistake new writers make is starting the querying process before they—and the work—are ready.''

⬛ FARBER LITERARY AGENCY, INC.

14 E. 75th St., #2E, New York NY 10021. (212)861-7075. Fax: (212)861-7076. E-mail: farberlit@aol.com. Web site: www.donaldfarber.com. **Contact:** Ann Farber, Dr. Seth Farber. Estab. 1989. Represents 40 clients. 50% of clients are new/unpublished writers. Currently handles: 25% nonfiction books; 35% novels; 15% scholarly books; 25% stage plays.

Member Agents Ann Farber (novels); Seth Farber (plays, scholarly books, novels); Donald C. Farber (attorney, all entertainment media).

Represents Nonfiction books, novels, juvenile books, textbooks, stage plays. **Considers these nonfiction areas:** Child guidance/parenting; cooking/foods/nutrition; music/dance; psychology; theater/film. **Considers these fiction areas:** Action/adventure; humor/satire; juvenile; literary; mainstream/contemporary; mystery/suspense; thriller; young adult.

How to Contact Submit outline, 3 sample chapters, SASE. Prefers to read materials exclusively. Responds in 1 month to queries; 2 months to mss. Obtains most new clients through recommendations from others.

Terms Agent receives 15% commission on domestic sales; 20% commission on foreign sales. Offers written contract, binding for 1 year. Client must furnish copies of ms, treatments, and any other items for submission.

Tips ''Our attorney, Donald C. Farber, is the author of many books. His services are available to the agency's clients as part of the agency service at no additional charge.''

⬛ FARRIS LITERARY AGENCY, INC.

P.O. Box 570069, Dallas TX 75357. (972)203-8804. E-mail: farris1@airmail.net. Web site: www.farrisliterary.com. **Contact:** Mike Farris, Susan Morgan Farris. Estab. 2002. Represents 30 clients. 60% of clients are new/unpublished writers.

• Both Mr. Farris and Ms. Farris are attorneys.

Represents Nonfiction books, novels. **Considers these nonfiction areas:** Biography/autobiography; business/economics; child guidance/parenting; cooking/foods/nutrition; current affairs; government/politics/law; health/medicine; history; how-to; humor/satire; memoirs; military/war; music/dance; popular culture; religious/inspirational; self-help/personal improvement; sports; women's issues/studies. **Considers these fiction areas:** Action/adventure; detective/police/crime; historical; humor/satire; mainstream/contemporary; mystery/suspense; religious/inspirational; romance; sports; thriller; westerns/frontier.

    ⚬⇥ ''We specialize in both fiction and nonfiction books. We are particularly interested in discovering unpublished authors. We adhere to AAR guidelines.'' Does not consider science fiction, fantasy, gay and lesbian, erotica, young adult, or children's.

How to Contact Query with SASE. Considers simultaneous queries. Responds in 2-3 weeks to queries; 4-8 weeks to mss. Returns materials only with SASE. Obtains most new clients through recommendations from others, solicitations, conferences.

Recent Sales Sold 4 titles in the last year. *The Show Must Go On*, by Doug Snauffer (McFarland).

Terms Agent receives 15% commission on domestic sales; 20% commission on foreign sales. Offers written contract; 30-day notice must be given to terminate contract. Charges clients for postage and photocopying.

Writers' Conferences Oklahoma Writers Federation Conference; The Screenwriting Conference in Santa Fe; Pikes Peak Writers Conference; Women Writing the West Annual Conference.

Ⓝ Ⓐ THE FIELDING AGENCY, LLC

269 S. Beverly Drive, No. 341, Beverly Hills CA 90212. (323)461-4791. E-mail: wlee@fieldingagency.com. Web site: www.fieldingagency.com. **Contact:** Whitney Lee. Estab. 2003. Currently handles: 25% nonfiction books; 35% novels; 35% juvenile books; 5% other.

● Prior to her current position, Ms. Lee worked at other agencies in different capacities.

Represents Nonfiction books, novels, short story collections, juvenile books. **Considers these nonfiction areas:** Animals; anthropology/archaeology; art/architecture/design; biography/autobiography; business/economics; child guidance/parenting; cooking/foods/nutrition; crafts/hobbies; current affairs; education; ethnic/cultural interests; gay/lesbian issues; government/politics/law; health/medicine; history; how-to; humor/satire; interior design/decorating; juvenile nonfiction; language/literature/criticism; memoirs; military/war; money/finance; nature/environment; popular culture; psychology; science/technology; self-help/personal improvement; sociology; sports; translation; true crime/investigative; women's issues/studies. **Considers these fiction areas:** Action/adventure; comic books/cartoon; detective/police/crime; ethnic; family saga; fantasy; feminist; gay/lesbian; glitz; historical; horror; humor/satire; juvenile; literary; mainstream/contemporary; mystery/suspense; picture books; romance; thriller; young adult; women's.

○➤ "We specialize in representing books published abroad and have strong relationships with foreign co-agents and publishers. For books we represent in the U.S., we have to be head-over-heels passionate about it because we are involved every step of the way." Does not want to receive scripts for TV or film.

How to Contact Query with SASE, submit synopsis, author bio. Accepts queries by e-mail and snail mail. No fax queries. Considers simultaneous queries. Returns materials only with SASE. Obtains most new clients through recommendations from others.

Recent Sales *Every Crooked Pot*, by Renee Rosen (St. Martin's); *It's Vintage, Darling!*, by Christa Weil (Hodder & Stoughton) *He Just Thinks He's Not That Into You*, by Danielle Whitman (Running Press); *Mother Mayhem*, by Sue Ann Jaffarian (Midnight Ink).

Terms Agent receives 15% commission on domestic sales; 20% commission on foreign sales. Offers written contract, binding for 9-12 months.

Writers' Conferences London Book Fair; Frankfurt Book Fair.

Ⓐ DIANA FINCH LITERARY AGENCY

116 W. 23rd St., Suite 500, New York NY 10011. (646)375-2081. E-mail: diana.finch@verizon.net. **Contact:** Diana Finch. Estab. 2003. Member of AAR. Represents 45 clients. 20% of clients are new/unpublished writers. Currently handles: 65% nonfiction books; 25% novels; 5% juvenile books; 5% multimedia.

● Prior to opening her agency, Ms. Finch worked at Ellen Levine Literary Agency for 18 years.

Represents Nonfiction books, novels, scholarly books. **Considers these nonfiction areas:** Biography/autobiography; business/economics; child guidance/parenting; computers/electronic; current affairs; ethnic/cultural interests; government/politics/law; health/medicine; history; how-to; humor/satire; juvenile nonfiction; memoirs; military/war; money/finance; music/dance; nature/environment; photography; popular culture; psychology; science/technology; self-help/personal improvement; sports; theater/film; translation; true crime/investigative; women's issues/studies. **Considers these fiction areas:** Action/adventure; detective/police/crime; ethnic; historical; literary; mainstream/contemporary; thriller; young adult.

○➤ Actively seeking narrative nonfiction, popular science, and health topics. Does not want romance, mysteries, or children's picture books.

How to Contact Query with SASE or via e-mail (no attachments). No phone or fax queries. Considers simultaneous queries. Returns materials only with SASE. Obtains most new clients through recommendations from others.

Recent Sales *Armed Madhouse*, by Greg Palast (Penguin US/UK); *The Bush Agenda*, by Antonia Juhasz; *Journey of the Magi*, by Tudor Parfitt (Farrar, Straus & Giroux); *Radiant Days*, by Michael FitzGerald (Shoemaker & Hoard); *The Queen's Soprano*, by Carol Dines (Harcourt Young Adult); *Was the 2004 Election Stolen?*, by Steven Freeman and Joel Bleifuss (Seven Stories); *Lipstick Jihad*, by Azadeh Moaveni (Public Affairs); *Great Customer Connections*, by Rich Gallagher (Amacom). Other clients include Daniel Duane, Thomas Goltz, Hugh Pope, Owen Matthews, Dr. Robert Marion.

Terms Agent receives 15% commission on domestic sales; 20% commission on foreign sales. Offers written contract. "I charge for photocopying, overseas postage, galleys, and books purchased, and try to recap these costs from earnings received for a client, rather than charging outright."

Tips "Do as much research as you can on agents before you query. Have someone critique your query letter before you send it. It should be only 1 page and describe your book clearly—and why you are writing it—but also demonstrate creativity and a sense of your writing style."

FIREBRAND LITERARY

701 President St., #4, Brooklyn NY 11215. (347)689-4762. Fax: (347)689-4762. E-mail: info@firebrandliterary.c om. Web site: www.firebrandliterary.com. **Contact:** Nadia Cornier. Estab. 2005. Represents 30 clients. 50% of clients are new/unpublished writers. Currently handles: 10% nonfiction books; 85% novels; 5% novellas.

- Before becoming an agent, Ms. Cornier started her own publicity firm and currently channels her interest and skill in marketing into her work with authors.

Member Agents Nadia Cornier, nadia@firebrandliterary.com (young adult, adult commercial, adult genre romance, nonfiction, some middle grade).

Represents Nonfiction books, novels, novellas, juvenile books. **Considers these nonfiction areas:** Business/economics; how-to; humor/satire; juvenile nonfiction; language/literature/criticism; money/finance. **Considers these fiction areas:** Erotica; fantasy; historical; juvenile; literary; mainstream/contemporary; romance; young adult; women's.

- "Firebrand endeavors to be a perfect fit for a few authors rather than a good fit for every author—we do so by working with our writers with editing and marketing direction alongside the usual responsibilities of selling their properties. Most of all, we want the author to be excited about what they're doing and what they're writing. While we in turn want to be excited to work with them. That kind of enthusiasm is contagious and we feel it is an important foundation to have when it comes to pitching an author's ideas not only to publishers and the industry, but to the world." Does not want to receive children's books, screenplays, poetry or anything about terrorists.

How to Contact This agency prefers its submissions made through the Web site form. See the site for all details. Send ms only by request. No e-mail or fax queries. Considers simultaneous queries. Responds in 2 weeks to queries; 2 months to mss. Returns materials only with SASE. Obtains most new clients through recommendations from others, solicitations.

Recent Sales *Austenland*, by Shannon Hale (Bloomsbury); *How To Get Suspended & Influence People*, by Adam Selzer (Random House/Delacorte); *Bitterwood*, by James Maxey (Solaris); Salem Witch Tryouts (series), by Kelly McClymer (Simon & Schuster).

Terms Agent receives 15% commission on domestic sales; 20% commission on foreign sales. Offers written contract; 30-day notice must be given to terminate contract.

Tips "Send a short query letter and let the work stand on its own."

JAMES FITZGERALD AGENCY

80 E. 11th St., Suite 301, New York NY. (212)308-1122. E-mail: submissions@jfitzagency.com. Web site: www.jf itzagency.com. **Contact:** James Fitzgerald. Estab. 2003.

- Prior to his current position, Mr. Fitzgerald was an editor at St. Martin's Press and Doubleday. Ms. Garrett held positions at Cambridge University Press and Seven Stories Press.

Member Agents James Fitzgerald; Anne Garrett.

Represents Nonfiction books, novels.

- Does not want to receive poetry or screenplays.

How to Contact Query with SASE, submit proposal package, outline/proposal, publishing history, author bio, overview. Accepts e-mail queries. No fax queries.

Recent Sales A biography of film director David Lynch, by Dennis Lim (Wiley); *But Princes Don't Moonwalk: Essays on Rock, Pop, Country, and Rap's Most Famous, Infamous, Underappreciated, and Unthought-of Rivalries*, by Sean Manning (Three Rivers Press); *To the End of East Bay*, by Jack Boulware and Silke Tudor's (Viking Penguin); *Pocket Karaoke*, by Sarah Lewitinn (Simon Spotlight Entertainment); *The Art of the Creche: Folk Art Nativities from Around the World*, by James L. Govan (Merrell). Other clients include Dennis Hopper, Sonny Barger, Andy Greenwald, Osho, Ed Sanders, David Carradine, Blair Tindall, Dale Maharidge, Nat Finkelstein, Legs McNeil, Marc Spitz.

Tips "As an agency, we primarily represent books that reflect the popular culture of today being in the forms of fiction, nonfiction, graphic and packaged books. Please submit all information in English, even if your manuscript is in Spanish."

FLAMING STAR LITERARY ENTERPRISES

320 Riverside Drive, New York NY 10025. E-mail: flamingstarlit@aol.com. Web site: flamingstarlit.com. **Contact:** Joseph B. Vallely, Janis C. Vallely. Estab. 1985. Represents 100 clients. 25% of clients are new/unpublished writers. Currently handles: 100% nonfiction books.

• Prior to opening the agency, Mr. Vallely served as national sales manager for Dell; Ms. Vallely was vice president of Doubleday.

Represents Nonfiction books. **Considers these nonfiction areas:** Current affairs; government/politics/law; health/medicine; nature/environment; science/technology; self-help/personal improvement; spirituality; sports.

O⊷ This agency specializes in upscale commercial nonfiction.

How to Contact E-mail only (no attachments). Obtains most new clients through recommendations from others, solicitations.

Recent Sales *His and Hers*, by Daniel Monti and Anthony Bazzan (Collins).

Terms Agent receives 15% commission on domestic sales; 20% commission on foreign sales. Offers written contract. Charges clients for photocopying and postage only.

⦿ FLANNERY LITERARY

1155 S. Washington St., Suite 202, Naperville IL 60540. (630)428-2682. Fax: (630)428-2683. **Contact:** Jennifer Flannery. Estab. 1992. Represents 40 clients. 50% of clients are new/unpublished writers. Currently handles: 100% juvenile books.

O⊷ This agency specializes in children's and young adult fiction and nonfiction. It also accepts picture books.

How to Contact Query with SASE. No fax or e-mail queries. Responds in 2 weeks to queries; 1 month to mss. Obtains most new clients through recommendations from others, submissions.

Recent Sales Sold 50 titles in the last year. This agency prefers not to share information on specific sales.

Terms Agent receives 15% commission on domestic sales; 20% commission on foreign sales. Offers written contract, binding for life of book in print; 1-month notice must be given to terminate contract. 100% of business is derived from commissions on ms sales.

Tips "Write an engrossing, succinct query describing your work. We are always looking for a fresh new voice."

⦿ PETER FLEMING AGENCY

P.O. Box 458, Pacific Palisades CA 90272. (310)454-1373. **Contact:** Peter Fleming. Estab. 1962. Currently handles: 100% nonfiction books.

O⊷ This agency specializes in nonfiction books that unearth innovative and uncomfortable truths with bestseller potential. Greatly interested in journalists in the free press (the Internet).

How to Contact Query with SASE. Obtains most new clients through "a different, one-of-a-kind idea for a book often backed by the writer's experience in that area of expertise."

Recent Sales *Rulers of Evil*, by F. Tupper Saussy (HarperCollins); *Why Is It Always About You—Saving Yourself from the Narcissists in Your Life*, by Sandy Hotchkiss (Free Press).

Terms Agent receives 15% commission on domestic sales; 25% commission on foreign sales. Offers written contract, binding for 1 year. Charges clients only those fees agreed to in writing.

Tips "You can begin by starting your own Web site."

⦿ FLETCHER & PARRY

78 Fifth Ave., 3rd Floor, New York NY 10011. (212)614-0778. Fax: (212)614-0728. **Contact:** Christy Fletcher, Emma Parry. Estab. 2003. Member of AAR.

Represents Nonfiction books, novels. **Considers these nonfiction areas:** Current affairs; history; memoirs; sports; travel; African American; narrative; science; biography; business; health; lifestyle. **Considers these fiction areas:** Literary; young adult; commercial.

O⊷ Does not want genre fiction.

How to Contact Query with SASE. Responds in 4-6 weeks to queries.

Recent Sales *Let Them In: The Case for Open Borders*, by Jason Riley (Gotham); *The Vanishing Act of Esme Lennox*, by Maggie O'Farrell (Harcourt).

◗ THE FOGELMAN LITERARY AGENCY

5420 LBJ Freeway to Lincoln Center, Suite 1900, Dallas TX 75240. (972)661-5114. Fax: (972)661-5691. Web site: www.fogelman.com. Alternate address: 415 Park Ave., New York NY 10022. (212)836-4803. **Contact:** Evan Fogelman. Estab. 1990. Member of AAR. Represents 100 clients. 2% of clients are new/unpublished writers. Currently handles: 40% nonfiction books; 40% novels; 10% scholarly books; 10% TV scripts.

• Prior to opening his agency, Mr. Fogelman was an entertainment lawyer. He is still active in the field and serves as chairman of the Texas Entertainment and Sports Lawyers Association. The Fogelman Literary Agency is associated with the law firm Underwood, Perkins & Ralstan.

Represents Nonfiction books, novels. **Considers these nonfiction areas:** Biography/autobiography; business/economics; child guidance/parenting; current affairs; education; ethnic/cultural interests; government/politics/

law; health/medicine; popular culture; psychology; sports; true crime/investigative; women's issues/studies. **Considers these fiction areas:** Historical; literary; mainstream/contemporary; romance (all genres).

⚐ This agency specializes in women's fiction and nonfiction. "Zealous advocacy makes this agency stand apart from others." No children's/juvenile.

How to Contact Query with SASE. Send queries by snail mail. Considers simultaneous queries. Responds in 1 week to queries; 3 months to mss. Returns materials only with SASE. Obtains most new clients through recommendations from others.

Recent Sales *Bulletproof Princess*, by Vicki Hinze (Silhouette Bombshell); *Surf Girl School*, by Cathy Yardley (Harlequin Signature Spotlight); *The Dark One*, by Ronda Thompson (St. Martin's Press).

Terms Agent receives 15% commission on domestic sales; 10% commission on foreign sales. Offers written contract.

Writers' Conferences RWA National Conference; Novelists, Inc.

Tips "Finish your manuscript, then see our Web site."

⚐ THE FOLEY LITERARY AGENCY

34 E. 38th St., New York NY 10016-2508. (212)686-6930. **Contact:** Joan Foley, Joseph Foley. Estab. 1961. Represents 10 clients. Currently handles: 75% nonfiction books; 25% novels.

Represents Nonfiction books, novels.

How to Contact Query with letter, brief outline, SASE. Responds promptly to queries. Obtains most new clients through recommendations from others (rarely taking on new clients).

Recent Sales This agency prefers not to share information on specific sales.

Terms Agent receives 10% commission on domestic sales; 15% commission on foreign sales. 100% of business is derived from commissions on ms sales.

Ⓝ ⚐ FOLIO LITERARY MANAGEMENT, LLC

505 Eighth Ave., Suite 603, New York NY 10018. Web site: www.foliolit.com. Alternate address: 1627 K St. NW, Suite 1200, Washington DC 20006. Estab. 2006. Member of AAR. Represents 100+ clients.

● Prior to creating Folio Literary Management, Mr. Hoffman worked for several years at another agency; Mr. Kleinman was an agent at Graybill & English; Ms. Wheeler was an agent at Creative Media Agency; Ms. Fine was an agent at Vigliano Associates and Trident Media Group; Ms. Cartwright-Niumata was an editor at Simon & Schuster, HarperCollins, and Avalon Books; Ms. Becker worked as a copywriter, journalist and author.

Member Agents Scott Hoffman; Jeff Kleinman; Paige Wheeler; Celeste Fine; Erin Cartwright-Niumata, Laney K. Becker.

Represents Nonfiction books, novels, short story collections. **Considers these nonfiction areas:** Animals (equestrian); business/economics; child guidance/parenting; history; how-to; humor/satire; memoirs; military/war; nature/environment; popular culture; psychology; religious/inspirational; science/technology; self-help/personal improvement; women's issues/studies; narrative nonfiction; art; espionage; biography; crime; politics; health/fitness; lifestyle; relationship; culture; cookbooks. **Considers these fiction areas:** Erotica; fantasy; literary; mystery/suspense; religious/inspirational; romance; science fiction; thriller (psychological); young adult; women's; Southern; legal; edgy crime.

How to Contact Query with SASE or via e-mail (no attachments). Read agent bios online for specific submission guidelines. Responds in 1 month to queries.

Recent Sales Sold more than 100 titles in the last year. *Finn*, by Jon Clinch (Random House); *A Killing Tide*, by P.J. Alderman (Dorchester); *The Inn on Half Moon Bay*, by Diane Tyrrel (Berkley); *The Biography of Kenny Chesney*, by Holly Gleason (Center Street); *Color of the Sea*, by John Hamamura (Thomas Dunne Books/St. Martin's Press); *The 30-Day Diabetes Miracle* (Perigee); *Meow Is for Murder*, by Linda O. Johnston (Berkley Prime Crime); *Wildlife's Scotland Yard*, by Laurel Neme (Joseph Henry Press); *Mockingbird*, by Charles J. Shields (Henry Holt); *Under the Mask*, by Heidi Ardizzone (Norton); *The Culture Code*, by Dr. Clotaire Rapaille (Doubleday).

⚐ LYNN C. FRANKLIN ASSOCIATES, LTD.

1350 Broadway, Suite 2015, New York NY 10018. (212)868-6311. Fax: (212)868-6312. **Contact:** Lynn Franklin, Claudia Nys. Estab. 1987. Member of PEN America. Represents 30-35 clients. 50% of clients are new/unpublished writers. Currently handles: 90% nonfiction books; 10% novels.

Represents Nonfiction books, novels. **Considers these nonfiction areas:** Biography/autobiography; current affairs; health/medicine; history; memoirs; New Age/metaphysics; psychology; religious/inspirational; self-help/personal improvement; spirituality. **Considers these fiction areas:** Literary; mainstream/contemporary (commercial).

○━ This agency specializes in general nonfiction with a special interest in self-help, biography/memoir, alternative health, and spirituality.

How to Contact Query with SASE. *No unsolicited mss.* Considers simultaneous queries. Responds in 2 weeks to queries; 6 weeks to mss. Obtains most new clients through recommendations from others, solicitations.

Recent Sales *Dalai Lama: Man, Monk, Mystic,* by Mayank Chhaya (Doubleday); *Grandmothers Counsel the World: Indigenous Women Elders Offer Their Vision for Our Planet,* by Carol Schaefer (Shambhala Publications); *Intuitive Wellness: Using Your Body's Inner Wisdom to Heal,* by Laura Alden Kamm (Atria Books/Beyond Words); *Rabble-Rouser for Peace: The Authorized Biography of Desmond Tutu,* by John Allen (Free Press); *Healing Invisible Wounds: Paths to Hope and Recovery in a Violent World,* by Richard Mollica (Harcourt).

Terms Agent receives 15% commission on domestic sales; 20% commission on foreign sales. Offers written contract; 100% of business is derived from commissions on ms sales. Charges clients for postage, photocopying, long distance telephone (if significant).

✪ JEANNE FREDERICKS LITERARY AGENCY, INC.

221 Benedict Hill Road, New Canaan CT 06840. (203)972-3011. Fax: (203)972-3011. E-mail: jeanne.fredericks@gmail.com. **Contact:** Jeanne Fredericks. Estab. 1997. Member of AAR, Authors Guild. Represents 90 clients. 10% of clients are new/unpublished writers. Currently handles: 100% nonfiction books.

● Prior to opening her agency, Ms. Fredericks was an agent and acting director with the Susan P. Urstadt, Inc. Agency.

Represents Nonfiction books. **Considers these nonfiction areas:** Animals; biography/autobiography; child guidance/parenting; cooking/foods/nutrition; gardening; health/medicine (alternative health); history; how-to; interior design/decorating; money/finance; nature/environment; photography; psychology; self-help/personal improvement; sports (not spectator sports); women's issues/studies.

○━ This agency specializes in quality adult nonfiction by authorities in their fields. Does not want to receive children's books or fiction.

How to Contact Query first with SASE, then send outline/proposal, 1-2 sample chapters, SASE. No fax queries. Accepts short e-mail queries (no attachments). Considers simultaneous queries. Responds in 3-5 weeks to queries; 2-4 months to mss. Returns materials only with SASE. Obtains most new clients through recommendations from others, solicitations, conferences.

Recent Sales *American Quilts,* by Robert Shaw (Sterling); *Lilias! Yoga Gets Better with Age,* by Lilias Folan (Rodale); *Homescaping,* by Anne Halpin (Rodale); *The Big Steal,* by Emyl Jenkins (Algonquin); *Creating Optimism in Your Child,* by Bob Murray, PhD, and Alice Fortinberry, MS (McGraw-Hill); *Waking the Warrior Goddess,* by Christine Horner, MD (Basic Health).

Terms Agent receives 15% commission on domestic sales; 25% commission on foreign sales with co-agent; without co-agent receives 20% commission on foreign sales. Offers written contract, binding for 9 months; 2-month notice must be given to terminate contract. Charges client for photocopying of whole proposals and mss, overseas postage, priority mail, express mail services.

Writers' Conferences Connecticut Press Club Biennial Writer's Conference; ASJA Writers' Conference; BookExpo America; Garden Writers' Association Annual Symposium.

Tips "Be sure to research competition for your work and be able to justify why there's a need for your book. I enjoy building an author's career, particularly if he/she is professional, hardworking, and courteous. Aside from 17 years of agenting experience, I've had 10 years of editorial experience in adult trade book publishing that enables me to help an author polish a proposal so that it's more appealing to prospective editors. My MBA in marketing also distinguishes me from other agents."

Ⓝ ✪ GRACE FREEDSON'S PUBLISHING NETWORK

375 North Broadway, Suite 103, Jericho NY 11375. (516)931-7757. Fax: (516)931-7759. E-mail: gfreedson@world.att.net. **Contact:** Grace Freedson. Estab. 2000. Represents 100 clients. 10% of clients are new/unpublished writers. Currently handles: 90% nonfiction books; 10% juvenile books.

● Prior to becoming an agent, Ms. Freedson was a managing editor and director of acquisition for Barron's Educational Series.

Represents Nonfiction books, juvenile books. **Considers these nonfiction areas:** Animals; business/economics; cooking/foods/nutrition; current affairs; education; health/medicine; history; how-to; humor/satire; money/finance; nature/environment; popular culture; psychology; religious/inspirational; science/technology; self-help/personal improvement; sports; craft/hobbies.

○━ "In addition to representing many qualified authors, I work with publishers as a packager of unique projects—mostly series." Does not want to receive fiction.

How to Contact Query with SASE, submit synopsis, SASE. Responds in 2-6 weeks to queries. Returns materials only with SASE. Obtains most new clients through recommendations from others.

Recent Sales Sold 50 titles in the last year. *Women Who Launch,* by Karin Abarbival and Bruce Freeman (Ten

Speed Press); *Privacy Lost*, by David Holtzman (Jossey-Bass/Wiley); *The Connected Father*, by Carl Pickhacer (Palgrave-MacMillan).

Terms Agent receives 15% commission on domestic sales. Offers written contract; 30-day notice must be given to terminate contract.

Writers' Conferences BookExpo of America.

Tips "At this point, I am only reviewing proposals on nonfiction topics by credentialed authors with platforms."

Ⓝ ☑ ◎ FRESH BOOKS LITERARY AGENCY

231 Diana St., Placerville CA 95667. E-mail: matt@fresh-books.com. Web site: www.fresh-books.com. **Contact:** Matt Wagner. Estab. 2005. Represents 30+ clients. 5% of clients are new/unpublished writers. Currently handles: 95% nonfiction books; 5% multimedia.

• Prior to becoming an agent, Mr. Wagner was with Waterside Productions for 15 years.

Represents Nonfiction books. **Considers these nonfiction areas:** Animals; anthropology/archaeology; art/architecture/design; business/economics; child guidance/parenting; computers/electronic; cooking/foods/nutrition; crafts/hobbies; current affairs; education; ethnic/cultural interests; gay/lesbian issues; government/politics/law; health/medicine; history; how-to; humor/satire; military/war; money/finance; music/dance; nature/environment; photography; popular culture; psychology; science/technology; sports.

☋ "I specialize in tech and how-to. I love working with books and authors, and I've repped many of my clients for upwards of 15 years now." Actively seeking popular science, natural history, adventure, how-to, business, education and reference. Does not want to receive fiction, children's books or poetry.

How to Contact Query with SASE. No phone calls. Accepts e-mail queries. No fax queries. Considers simultaneous queries. Responds in 1-4 weeks to queries; 1-4 weeks to mss. Returns materials only with SASE. Obtains most new clients through recommendations from others.

Recent Sales Sold 30+ titles in the last year. *Macs for Dummies*, by Edward Baig (Wiley); *Skin: The Complete Guide to Digitally Lighting, Photographing and Retouching Faces and Bodies*, by Lee Varis (Sybex); *Stereotyped: Hip Hop's Unsung Graphic Design Heroes*, by Darius Wilmore (HOW Design Books); *How to Make Love in a Tent*, by Michelle Waitzman (Wilderness Press). Other clients include Dan Gookin, Andy Rathbone, Gary Bouton, Harold Davis, Taz Tally, Christopher Spencer, Kevin Epstein.

Terms Agent receives 15% commission on domestic sales; 20% commission on foreign sales.

Tips "Do your research. Find out what sorts of books and authors an agent represents. Go to conferences. Make friends with other writers—most of my clients come from referrals."

♡ SARAH JANE FREYMANN LITERARY AGENCY

59 W. 71st St., Suite 9B, New York NY 10023. (212)362-9277. E-mail: sarah@sarahjanefreymann.com. Web site: www.sarahjanefreymann.com. **Contact:** Sarah Jane Freymann, Steve Schwartz. Represents 100 clients. 20% of clients are new/unpublished writers. Currently handles: 75% nonfiction books; 23% novels; 2% juvenile books.

Member Agents Sarah Jane Freymann; Steve Schwartz, steve@sarahjanefreymann.com (historical novels, thrillers, crime, sports, humor, food, travel).

Represents Nonfiction books, novels, illustrated books. **Considers these nonfiction areas:** Animals; anthropology/archaeology; art/architecture/design; biography/autobiography; business/economics; child guidance/parenting; cooking/foods/nutrition; current affairs; ethnic/cultural interests; health/medicine; history; interior design/decorating; memoirs (narrative); nature/environment; psychology; religious/inspirational; self-help/personal improvement; women's issues/studies; lifestyle. **Considers these fiction areas:** Ethnic; literary; mainstream/contemporary.

How to Contact Query with SASE. Responds in 2 weeks to queries; 6 weeks to mss. Obtains most new clients through recommendations from others.

Recent Sales *Girl Stories*, by Lauren Weinstein (Henry Holt); *The Good, Good Pig*, by Sy Montgomery (Ballantine/Random House); *The Man Who Killed the Whale*, by Linda Hogan (W.W. Norton); *Writing the Fire! Yoga and the Art of Making Your Words Come Alive*, by Gail Sher (Harmoney/Bell Tower); *Mexicocina*, by Melba Levick and Betsy McNair (Chronicle); *Holy Play*, by Kirk Byron Jones (Jossey Bass).

Terms Agent receives 15% commission on domestic sales; 20% commission on foreign sales. Offers written contract. Charges clients for long distance, overseas postage, photocopying. 100% of business is derived from commissions on ms sales.

Tips "I love fresh, new, passionate works by authors who love what they are doing and have both natural talent and carefully honed skill."

Ⓝ ☑ FREDRICA S. FRIEDMAN AND CO., INC.

136 E. 57th St., 14th Floor, New York NY 10022. (212)829-9600. Fax: (212)829-9669. E-mail: fsfsubmissions@yahoo.com. **Contact:** Lee Bacon. Estab. 2001. Represents 75+ clients. 50% of clients are new/unpublished writers. Currently handles: 95% nonfiction books; 5% novels.

Represents Nonfiction books, novels, anthologies. **Considers these nonfiction areas:** Art/architecture/design; biography/autobiography; business/economics; child guidance/parenting; cooking/foods/nutrition; current affairs; education; ethnic/cultural interests; gay/lesbian issues; government/politics/law; health/medicine; history; how-to; humor/satire; language/literature/criticism; memoirs; money/finance; music/dance; photography; popular culture; psychology; self-help/personal improvement; sociology; theater/film; true crime/investigative; women's issues/studies; interior design/decorating. **Considers these fiction areas:** Literary.

○→ "We represent a select group of outstanding nonfiction and fiction writers. We are particularly interested in helping writers expand their readership and develop their careers." Does not want religious/inspirational, computers, textbooks, or juvenile.

How to Contact Submit query, synopsis. Considers simultaneous queries. Responds in 2-4 weeks to queries; 4-6 weeks to mss. Obtains most new clients through recommendations from others.

Recent Sales Sold 30-40 titles in the last year. *Just This Once*, by Frances Kuffel (Basic Books); *Footpaths in the Painted City*, by Sadia Shepard (Penguin Press); *China Ghosts*, by Jeff Gammage (William Morrow); *Seducing the Boys' Club*, by Nina DiSesa (Random House).

Terms Agent receives 15% commission on domestic sales; 25% commission on foreign sales. Offers written contract. Charges for photocopying and messenger/shipping fees for proposals.

Tips "Spell the agent's name correctly on your query letter."

[N] ● THE FRIEDRICH AGENCY

136 East 57th St., 18th Floor, New York NY 10022. Web site: www.friedrichagency.com. **Contact:** Molly Friedrich. Estab. 2006. Member of AAR. Represents 50+ clients.

● Prior to her current position, Ms. Friedrich was an agent at the Aaron Priest Literary Agency.

Member Agents Molly Friedrich, founder and agent (not open to queries); Paul Cirone, agent (open to queries, mostly literary fiction, memoirs and narrative nonfiction); Andy Marino, assistant.

Represents Nonfiction books, novels.

How to Contact Query with SASE. Query Mr. Cirone through snail mail only.

Recent Sales *Paranoia : A Novel*, by Joseph Finder (St. Martin's Press); *The Rug Merchant*, by Meg Mullins (Viking Adult); *Girls of Tender Age: A Memoir*, by Mary-Ann Tirone Smith (Free Press). Other clients include Esmerelda Santiago, Terry McMillan, Frank McCourt, Sue Grafton, Jane Smiley, Laura Cunningham, John Murray and more.

● FULL CIRCLE LITERARY, LLC

7676 Hazard Center Dr., Suite 500, San Diego CA 92108. E-mail: info@fullcircleliterary.com. Web site: www.fullcircleliterary.com. **Contact:** Lilly Ghahremani, Stefanie Von Borstel. Estab. 2004. Represents 40 clients. 80% of clients are new/unpublished writers. Currently handles: 70% nonfiction books; 10% novels; 20% juvenile books.

● Before forming Full Circle, Ms. Von Borstel worked in both marketing and editorial capacities at Penguin and Harcourt; Ms. Ghahremani received her law degree from UCLA, and has experience in representing authors on legal affairs.

Member Agents Lilly Ghahremani (pop culture, crafts, useful humor, how-to, narrative nonfiction, cookbooks, business, relationships, health, Middle Eastern interest, performing arts, multicultural); Stefanie Von Borstel (Latino interest, crafts, cookbooks, parenting, wedding/relationships, how-to, self help, middle grade/teen fiction, multicultural/bilingual picture books).

Represents Nonfiction books, juvenile books, graphic novels. **Considers these nonfiction areas:** Animals; biography/autobiography; business/economics; child guidance/parenting; cooking/foods/nutrition; crafts/hobbies; current affairs; ethnic/cultural interests; health/medicine; how-to; humor/satire; juvenile nonfiction; music/dance; popular culture; religious/inspirational; self-help/personal improvement; sports; theater/film; translation; women's issues/studies. **Considers these fiction areas:** Comic books/cartoon; ethnic; literary; young adult.

○→ "Our full-service boutique agency, representing a range of nonfiction and children's books (limited fiction), provides a one-stop resource for authors. Our extensive experience in the realms of law and marketing provide Full Circle clients with a unique edge." Actively seeking nonfiction by authors with a unique and strong platform, projects that offer new and diverse viewpoints, and literature with a global or multicultural perspective. "We are particularly interested in books with a Latino or Middle Eastern angle and books related to pop culture, music, or the arts." Does not want to receive screenplays, poetry, commercial fiction or genre fiction (horror, thriller, mystery, Western, sci-fi, fantasy, romance).

How to Contact For nonfiction, send hard copy of outline, 1 sample chapter. Send children's/middle grade/YA queries to kidsquery@fullcircleliterary.com; fiction/nonfiction queries to query@fullcircleliterary.com. Considers simultaneous queries. Responds in 1-2 weeks to queries; 4-6 weeks to mss. Returns materials only with SASE. Obtains most new clients through recommendations from others, solicitations, conferences.

Recent Sales Sold 20 titles in the last year. *The Grilled Cheese Madonna & 99 Other of the Weirdest, Wackiest, Most Famous eBay Auctions Ever*, by Christopher Cihlar (Broadway/Random House); *The Bilingual Edge: The Ultimate Guide to Why, When and How to Teach Your Child a Second Language*, by Kendall King and Alison Mackey (HarperCollins); *Baby Read-Aloud Basics*, by Caroline Blakemore and Barbara Weston Ramirez (Amacom); *Isabel's Cantina*, by Isabel Cruz (Clarkson Potter); *The Craftster Guide to Nifty, Thrifty & Kitschy Crafts*, by Leah Kramer (Ten Speed Press); *The Softies Crafting Book* by Therese Laskey (Chronicle Books); *The Non-Runner's Marathon Training Guide*, by Dawn Dais (Seal Press); *Poetry Zoo/Zoologico de Poemas*, by Margarita Montalvo (Scholastic).

Terms Agent receives 15% commission on domestic sales; 20% commission on foreign sales. Offers written contract; up to 60-day notice must be given to terminate contract. Charges for copying and postage.

Writers' Conferences San Diego State University Writers; Conference, San Francisco Writers' Conference; Pikes Peak Writers' Conference; National Latino Writers' Conference; Santa Barbara Writers' Conference; Willamette Writers' Conference; La Jolla Writers' Conference; Surrey International Writers' Conference; Writers League of Texas Conference; Pacific Northwest Writers' Conference.

Tips "Put your best foot forward. Contact us when you simply can't make your project any better on your own, and please be sure your work fits with what the agent you're approaching represents. Little things count, so copyedit your work. Join a writing group and attend conferences to get objective and constructive feedback before submitting. Be active about building your platform as an author before, during, and after publication. Remember this is a business and your agent is a business partner. Be prepared to work together every step of the way. Be patient—this publishing thing takes time."

[N] [◎] NANCY GALLT LITERARY AGENCY

273 Charlton Ave., South Orange NJ 07079. (973)761-6358. Fax: (973)761-6318. E-mail: ngallt@aol.com. **Contact:** Nancy Gallt. Estab. 2000. Represents 40 clients. 30% of clients are new/unpublished writers. Currently handles: 100% juvenile books.

• Prior to opening her agency, Ms. Gallt was subsidiary rights director of the children's book division at Morrow, Harper and Viking.

Member Agents Nancy Gallt, Craig Virden.

Represents Juvenile books.

O—¬ "I only handle children's books." Actively seeking middle-grade and young adult novels. Does not want to receive rhyming picture book texts.

How to Contact Query with 3 sample chapters, SASE. If an author wants the ms returned, include a large SASE. Considers simultaneous queries. Responds in 3 months to queries; 3 months to mss. Obtains most new clients through recommendations from others, solicitations.

Recent Sales Sold 50 titles in the last year. Percy Jackson series, by Rick Riordan (Hyperion); A-Z Mysteries Super-Edition, by Ron Roy (Random House Books for Young Readers); *Little Gnome* (Simon & Schuster); *My Bar Mitzvah* (Simon & Schuster).

Terms Agent receives 10% commission on domestic sales; 20% commission on foreign sales. Offers written contract; 30-day notice must be given to terminate contract.

Tips "A book stands on its own, so a submission should be as close to perfect as the author can make it."

[◎] MAX GARTENBERG LITERARY AGENCY

912 N. Pennsylvania Ave., Yardley PA 19067. (215)295-9230. Web site: www.maxgartenberg.com. **Contact:** Max Gartenberg, Anne Devlin, Will Devlin. Estab. 1954. Represents 30 clients. 5% of clients are new/unpublished writers. Currently handles: 90% nonfiction books; 10% novels.

Member Agents Max Gartenberg, president, gartenbook@att.net (biography, military history, environment, and narrative nonfiction); Anne G. Devlin, agent, agdevlin@aol.com (politics, current events, women's issues, health, literary fiction and mysteries); Will Devlin, agent, wad411@hotmail.com (commercial fiction, sports, popular culture, humor and politics).

Represents Nonfiction books, novels. **Considers these nonfiction areas:** Agriculture/horticulture; animals; art/architecture/design; biography/autobiography; child guidance/parenting; current affairs; health/medicine; history; military/war; money/finance; music/dance; nature/environment; psychology; science/technology; self-help/personal improvement; sports; theater/film; true crime/investigative; women's issues/studies.

How to Contact Query with SASE. Send queries via snail mail. Considers simultaneous queries. Responds in 2 weeks to queries; 6 weeks to mss. Obtains most new clients through recommendations from others, following up on good query letters.

Recent Sales *What Patients Taught Me*, by Audrey Young, MD (Sasquatch Books); *Unorthodox Warfare: The Chinese Experience*, by Ralph D. Sawyer (Westview Press); *Encyclopedia of Earthquakes and Volcanoes*, by Alexander E. Gates (Facts on File).

Terms Agent receives 15% commission on domestic sales; 15-20% commission on foreign sales.
Tips "We have recently expanded to allow more access for new writers."

N ☑ DON GASTWIRTH & ASSOCIATES

265 College St., New Haven CT 06510. (203)562-7600. Fax: (203)562-4300. E-mail: Donlit@snet.net. **Contact:** Don Gastwirth. Estab. 1986. Signatory of WGA. Represents 26 clients. 10% of clients are new/unpublished writers. Currently handles: 30% nonfiction books; 60% scholarly books; 10% other.
    ● Prior to becoming an agent, Mr. Gastwirth was an entertainment lawyer and law professor.
Represents Nonfiction books, scholarly books. **Considers these nonfiction areas:** Business/economics; current affairs; history; military/war; money/finance; music/dance; nature/environment; popular culture; psychology; translation; true crime/investigative. **Considers these fiction areas:** Mystery/suspense; thriller.
    ○╼ This is a selective agency and is rarely open to new clients that do not come through a referral.
How to Contact Query with SASE. No fax queries.
Recent Sales Sold 11 titles in the last year. This agency prefers not to share information on specific sales.
Terms Agent receives 15% commission on domestic sales; 10% commission on foreign sales.

☑ GELFMAN SCHNEIDER LITERARY AGENTS, INC.

250 W. 57th St., Suite 2515, New York NY 10107. (212)245-1993. Fax: (212)245-8678. E-mail: mail@gelfmansch neider.com. **Contact:** Jane Gelfman, Deborah Schneider. Estab. 1981. Member of AAR. Represents 300+ clients. 10% of clients are new/unpublished writers.
Represents Nonfiction books, novels. **Considers these nonfiction areas:** Biography; health; lifestyle; politics; science. **Considers these fiction areas:** Literary; mainstream/contemporary; mystery/suspense; women's.
    ○╼ Does not want to receive romance, science fiction, westerns, or children's books.
How to Contact Query with SASE. Send queries via snail mail only. No e-mail or fax queries. Responds in 1 month to queries; 2 months to mss.
Terms Agent receives 15% commission on domestic sales; 20% commission on foreign sales; 15% commission on dramatic rights sales. Offers written contract. Charges clients for photocopying and messengers/couriers.

N ☑ THE GERNERT COMPANY

136 East 57th St., 15th Floor, New York NY 10022. (212)838-7777. Fax: (212)838-6020. **Contact:** Sarah Burnes.
    ● Prior to her current position, Ms. Burnes was with Burnes & Clegg, Inc.
Member Agents Sarah Burnes, sburnes@thegernertco.com (commercial fiction, adventure and true story); Stephanie Cabot (literary fiction, commercial fiction, historical fiction); Chris Parris-Lamb, clamb@thegernert-co.com.
Represents Nonfiction books, novels.
How to Contact Query with SASE. Snail mail queries are preferred. No fax queries. Obtains most new clients through recommendations from others, solicitations.
Recent Sales *House of Joy*, by Sarah-Kate Lynch (Plume); *Mudbound*, by Hillary Jordan (Algonquin); *The Reluctant Diplomat: Peter Paul Rubens and His Secret Mission to Save Europe from Itself*, by Mark Lamster (Talese).

N ⊕ ☑ GILLON AITKEN ASSOCIATES

18-21 Cavaye Place, London England SW10 9PT, United Kingdom. (44)(207)373-8672. Fax: (44)(207)373-6002. E-mail: recep@gillonaitken.co.uk. Web site: www.gillonaitkenassociates.co.uk. **Contact:** Submissions Department. Estab. 1977. Represents 300+ clients. 10% of clients are new/unpublished writers.
Member Agents Gillon Aitken, agent; Clare Alexander, agent; Kate Shaw, foreign rights; Lesley Thorne, film/television.
Represents Nonfiction books, novels, short story collections, novellas, movie scripts, TV scripts. **Considers these nonfiction areas:** Current affairs; government/politics/law; history; memoirs; popular culture. **Considers these fiction areas:** Historical; literary.
    ○╼ "We specialize in literary fiction and nonfiction."
How to Contact Query with SASE. Submit synopsis, first 30 pages, SASE via fax, e-mail or mail. Send screenplay submissions to Lesley Thorne. Responds in 6-8 weeks to queries. Returns materials only with SASE. Obtains most new clients through recommendations from others, solicitations.
Recent Sales Sold 35+ titles and sold 4+ scripts in the last year. *My Life With George*, by Judith Summers (Voice); *The Separate Hearth*, by Simon Robson (Cape); *The Fall of the House of Wittynstein*, by Alexander Vaugh (Bloomsbury); *Shakespeare's Life*, by Germane Greer; *Occupational Hazards*, by Rory Stewart. Other clients include Caroline Alexander, Pat Barker, Nicholas Blincoe, Gordon Burn, John Cornwell, Josephine Cox, Sarah Dunant, Susan Elderkin, Sebastian Faulks, Helen Fielding, John Fowles, Germaine Greer, Mark Haddon, Susan Howatch, Liz Jensen, V.S. Naipaul, Jonathan Raban, Colin Thubron, A.N. Wilson.

Terms Agent receives 10% commission on domestic sales; 20% commission on foreign sales. Offers written contract; 28-day notice must be given to terminate contract. Charges for photocopying and postage.

Tips "Before submitting to us, we advise you to look at our existing client list to establish whether your work will be of interest. Equally, you should consider whether the material you have written is ready to submit to a literary agency. If you feel your work qualifies, then send us a letter introducing yourself: Keep it relevant to your writing (e.g., tell us about any previously published work, be it a short story or journalism; you may be studying or have completed a post-graduate qualification in creative writing; when it comes to nonfiction, we would want to know what qualifies you to write about the subject)."

◳ THE GISLASON AGENCY

219 Main St. SE, Suite 506, Minneapolis MN 55414-2160. (612)331-8033. Fax: (612)331-8115. E-mail: gislasonbj @aol.com. Web site: www.thegislasonagency.com. **Contact:** Barbara J. Gislason. Estab. 1992. Member of Minnesota State Bar Association, American Bar Association, Art & Entertainment Law Section, Animal Law, Minnesota Intellectual Property Law Association Copyright Committee; Icelandic Association of Minnesota, American Academy of Acupuncture and Oriental Medicine. 80% of clients are new/unpublished writers. Currently handles: 10% nonfiction books; 90% novels.

• Ms. Gislason became an attorney in 1980, and continues to practice art and entertainment law. She has been nationally recognized as a Leading American Attorney and a Super Lawyer.

Represents Nonfiction books, novels. **Considers these nonfiction areas:** Animals; companion animals/pets, feral animals, working and service animals, domestic and farm animals, laboratory animals, caged animals and wild animals. **Considers these fiction areas:** Animals (companion animals/pets, feral animals, working and service animals, domestic and farm animals, laboratory animals, caged animals and wild animals).

○┓ Do not send personal memoirs, poetry, short stories, screenplays, or children's books.

How to Contact For fiction, query with synopsis, first 3 chapters, SASE. For nonfiction, query with proposal, sample chapters. No e-mail or fax queries. Responds in 1 months to queries; 6 months to mss. Obtains most new clients through recommendations from others, conferences, *Guide to Literary Agents*, *Literary Market Place*, other reference books.

Terms Agent receives 15% commission on domestic sales; 20% commission on foreign sales. Offers written contract, binding for 1 year with option to renew. Charges clients for photocopying and postage.

Writers' Conferences Southwest Writers Conference; Willamette Writers Conference; Wrangling with Writing; other state and regional conferences.

Tips "We are looking for manuscripts for adults that express ideas and tell stories powerful enough to change people's views about animals, without overt sentimentality. Your cover letter should be well written and include a detailed synopsis (fiction) or proposal (nonfiction), the first 3 chapters, and author bio. Appropriate SASE required. If submitting nonfiction work, explain how the submission differs from and adds to previously published works in the field. Remember to proofread. If the work was written with a specific publisher in mind, this should be communicated."

◳ BARRY GOLDBLATT LITERARY, LLC

320 Seventh Ave., #266, Brooklyn NY 11215. Fax: (718)360-5453. **Contact:** Barry Goldblatt. Member of AAR.
Represents Juvenile books. **Considers these fiction areas:** Picture books; young adult; middle grade.
How to Contact Query with SASE. No e-mail queries.
Recent Sales The Chasing Yesterday trilogy, by Robin Wasserman (Scholastic); *Rabbit and Squirrel*, by Kara LaReau (Harcourt); *Go Go Gorillas*, by Julia Durango (Simon & Schuster Children's).

◳ FRANCES GOLDIN LITERARY AGENCY, INC.

57 E. 11th St., Suite 5B, New York NY 10003. (212)777-0047. Fax: (212)228-1660. E-mail: agency@goldinlit.com. Web site: www.goldinlit.com. Estab. 1977. Member of AAR. Represents over 100 clients.
Member Agents Frances Goldin, principal/agent; Ellen Geiger, agent (commercial and literary fiction and nonfiction, cutting-edge topics of all kinds); Matt McGowan, agent/rights director (innovative works of fiction and nonfiction); Sam Stoloff, agent (literary fiction, memoir, history, accessible sociology and philosophy, cultural studies, serious journalism, narrative and topical nonfiction with a progressive orientation); Josie Schoel, agent/office manager (literary fiction and nonfiction).
Represents Nonfiction books, novels. **Considers these nonfiction areas:** Serious, controversial nonfiction with a progressive political orientation. **Considers these fiction areas:** Adult literary.

○┓ "We are hands on and we work intensively with clients on proposal and manuscript development." Does not want anything that is racist, sexist, agist, homophobic, or pornographic. No screenplays, children's books, art books, cookbooks, business books, diet books, self-help, or genre fiction.

How to Contact Query with SASE. No unsolicited mss or work previously submitted to publishers. Prefers hard-copy queries. Responds in 4-6 weeks to queries.

Recent Sales *Skin Deep*, by Dalton Conley (Pantheon); *Conned: How Millions Have Lost the Right to Vote*, by Sasha Abramsky (New Press); *Gotham II*, by Mike Wallace; *Animal, Vegetable, Miracle*, by Barbara Kingslover; an untitled memoir by Staceyann Chin.

ⓝ ◑ THE SUSAN GOLOMB LITERARY AGENCY

875 Avenue of the Americas, Suite 2302, New York NY 10001. Fax: (212)239-9503. E-mail: susan@sgolombagen cy.com. **Contact:** Corey Ferguson. Estab. 1991. Represents 100 clients. 20% of clients are new/unpublished writers. Currently handles: 50% nonfiction books; 40% novels; 10% story collections.
Represents Nonfiction books, novels, short story collections, novellas. **Considers these nonfiction areas:** Animals; anthropology/archaeology; biography/autobiography; business/economics; current affairs; government/politics/law; health/medicine; history; memoirs; military/war; money/finance; nature/environment; popular culture; psychology; science/technology; sociology; women's issues/studies. **Considers these fiction areas:** Ethnic; historical; humor/satire; literary; mainstream/contemporary; thriller; young adult; women's/chick lit.
> ⚬━ "We specialize in literary and upmarket fiction and nonfiction that is original, vibrant and of excellent quality and craft. Nonfiction should be edifying, paradigm-shifting, fresh and entertaining." Actively seeking writers with strong voices. Does not want to receive genre fiction.

How to Contact Query with SASE, submit outline/proposal, synopsis, 1 sample chapter(s), author bio, SASE. Query via mail or e-mail. Accepts e-mail queries. No fax queries. Responds in 1 week to queries; 6 weeks to mss. Returns materials only with SASE. Obtains most new clients through recommendations from others, solicitations.
Recent Sales Sold 20 titles in the last year. *The Discomfort Zone*, by Jonathan Franzen (Farrar, Straus & Giroux); *Imperial*, by William T. Vollmann (Viking); *All We Ever Wanted Was Everything*, by Janelle Brown (Spiegel & Grau). Other clients include Glen David Gold, Sarah Shun-lien Bynum, Marisha Pessl, Thomas Mullen.
Terms Agent receives 15% commission on domestic sales; 20% commission on foreign sales. Offers written contract.

▦ ◑ GOLVAN ARTS MANAGEMENT

P.O. Box 766, Kew VIC 3101 Australia. E-mail: golvan@ozemail.com.au. Web site: www.golvanarts.com.au.
Contact: Colin Golvan.
Represents Nonfiction books, novels, juvenile books, poetry books, movie scripts, TV scripts, stage plays.
How to Contact Query with author bio, SASE.
Recent Sales *The Runaway Circus*, by Gordon Reece (Lothian Books); *Two for the Road*, by Shirly Hardy-Rix and Brian Rix (Macmillan); *The Catch*, by Marg Vandeleur (Penguin).
Terms Agent receives 11% commission on domestic sales.

◑ GOODMAN ASSOCIATES

500 West End Ave., New York NY 10024-4317. (212)873-4806. **Contact:** Elise Simon Goodman. Estab. 1976. Member of AAR. Represents 50 clients.
> ● Mr. Goodman is the former chair of the AAR Ethics Committee.

Member Agents Elise Simon Goodman; Arnold P. Goodman.
Represents Nonfiction books, novels.
> ⚬━ Accepting new clients by recommendation only. Does not want to receive poetry, articles, individual stories, children's or young adult material.

How to Contact Query with SASE. Responds in 10 days to queries; 1 month to mss.
Recent Sales *Urban Preservation*, by Eugenia Bone (Clarkson Potter).
Terms Agent receives 15% commission on domestic sales; 20% commission on foreign sales. Charges clients for certain expenses: faxes, toll calls, overseas postage, photocopying, book purchases.

◑ IRENE GOODMAN LITERARY AGENCY

80 Fifth Ave., Suite 1101, New York NY 10011. Web site: www.irenegoodman.com. **Contact:** Irene Goodman, Miriam Kriss. Member of AAR.
Represents Nonfiction books, novels. **Considers these nonfiction areas:** History; parenting, social issues, francophilia, anglophilia, Judaica, lifestyles, cooking, memoir. **Considers these fiction areas:** Historical; literary; mystery/suspense; romance; thriller; young adult; women's; chick lit; modern urban fantasies.
How to Contact Query with 1-3 chapters, synopsis, SASE. No e-mail or fax queries. Accepts e-mail queries. No fax queries. Responds in 1 month to mss.

ⓝ ▦ ◑ ◎ GOUMEN & SMIRNOVA LITERARY AGENCY

Nauki pr., 19/2 fl. 293, St. Petersburg 195220, Russia. E-mail: info@gs-agency.com. Web site: www.gs-agency.c om. **Contact:** Julia Goumen, Natalia Smirnova. Estab. 2006. Represents 20 clients. 10% of clients are new/

unpublished writers. Currently handles: 10% nonfiction books; 80% novels; 5% story collections; 5% juvenile books.

- Prior to becoming agents, both Ms. Goumen and Ms. Smirnova worked as foreign rights managers with an established Russian publisher selling translation rights for literary fiction.

Member Agents Julia Goumen (translation rights, Russian language rights, film rights); Natalia Smirnova (translation rights, Russian language rights, film rights).

Represents Nonfiction books, novels, short story collections, novellas, movie scripts, TV scripts, TV movie of the week, sitcom. **Considers these nonfiction areas:** Biography/autobiography; current affairs; ethnic/cultural interests; humor/satire; memoirs; music/dance. **Considers these fiction areas:** Action/adventure; experimental; family saga; historical; horror; literary; mainstream/contemporary; mystery/suspense; romance; thriller; young adult; women's. **Considers these script subject areas:** Action/adventure; comedy; detective/police/crime; family saga; mainstream; romantic comedy; romantic drama; teen; thriller.

- O—¬ "We are the first full-service agency in Russia, representing our authors in book publishing, film, television, and other areas. We are also the first agency, representing Russian authors worldwide, based in Russia. The agency also represents international authors, agents and publishers in Russia. Our philosophy is to provide an individual approach to each author, finding the right publisher both at home and across international cultural and linguistic borders, developing original marketing and promotional strategies for each title." Actively seeking manuscripts written in Russian, both literary and commercial; and foreign publishers and agents with the high-profile fiction and general nonfiction list—to represent in Russia. Does not want to receive unpublished manuscripts in languages other then Russian, or any information irrelevant to our activity.

How to Contact Query with SASE, submit synopsis, author bio. Accepts e-mail queries. No fax queries. Considers simultaneous queries. Responds in 14 days to mss. Obtains most new clients through recommendations from others, solicitations.

Recent Sales Sold 15+ titles in the last year. *Geographer Drank Away His Globe*, by Alexei Ivanov (Meulenhoff, The Netherlands); *Scary Fairy Tales*, by Ludmilla Petrushevskaya (Penguin, U.S.); *Solitude-12*, by Arsen Revazov (Bertelsmann, Germany); *Mazes of Echo*, by Max Frei (Overlook Press, U.S.). Other clients include Garros-Evdokimov, Mikhail Veller, Daniil Kharms, Pavel Vadimov, Andrei Turgenev, Anna Starobinets.

Terms Agent receives 20% commission on domestic sales; 20% commission on foreign sales. Offers written contract, binding for 1 year; 2-month notice must be given to terminate contract.

Ⓝ ⊕ ◯ GRAHAM MAW LITERARY AGENCY

16 De Beauvoir Square, London England N1 4LD, United Kingdom. (44)(207)812-9937. E-mail: enquiries@grahammawagency.com. Web site: www.grahammawagency.com. Estab. 2005. Represents 20 clients. 30% of clients are new/unpublished writers. Currently handles: 100% nonfiction books.

- Prior to opening her agency, Ms. Graham Maw was a publishing director at HarperCollins and worked in rights, publicity and editorial. She has ghostwritten several nonfiction books, which gives her an insider's knowledge of both the publishing industry and the pleasures and pitfalls of authorships. Ms. Christie has a background in advertising and journalism.

Member Agents Jane Graham Maw; Jennifer Christie.

Represents Nonfiction books. **Considers these nonfiction areas:** Biography/autobiography; child guidance/parenting; cooking/foods/nutrition; health/medicine; how-to; memoirs; popular culture; psychology; self-help/personal improvement.

- O—¬ "We aim to make the publishing process easier and smoother for authors. We work hard to ensure that publishing proposals are watertight before submission. We aim for collaborative relationships with publishers so that we provide the right books to the right editor at the right time. We represent ghostwriters as well as authors." Does not want to receive fiction, poetry, plays or e-mail submissions.

How to Contact Query with synopsis, chapter outline, bio, SASE. No e-mail or fax queries. Responds in 2 weeks to queries. Returns materials only with SASE. Obtains most new clients through recommendations from others.

Recent Sales Sold 6 titles in the last year. *Jack Osbourne: 21 Years Gone*, by Jack Osbourne (Macmillan); *Nourish*, by Jennifer Harper-Deacon (Rodale); *For the Love of My Son*, by Margaret Davis (Hodder).

Terms Agent receives 15% commission on domestic sales; 20% commission on foreign sales. Offers written contract; 30-day notice must be given to terminate contract.

Writers' Conferences London Book Fair, Frankfurt Book Fair.

Ⓝ ◙ THE GRANT AGENCY

3621 Huntwick Drive, Orange TX 77632. E-mail: query@thegrantagency.com. Web site: www.thegrantagency.com. **Contact:** Steven Grant; adheres to AAR canon of ethics.

Represents Novels. **Considers these fiction areas:** Erotica; romance (all sub-genres).

O→ Romance. Does not want to receive self-help, poetry, nonfiction or children's books.

How to Contact Query with SASE, submit contact information, first 5 pages of ms. This agency prefers e-queries. No fax queries. Responds in 4 weeks to queries; 12 weeks to mss. Obtains most new clients through recommendations from others, solicitations.

Recent Sales *The Druid's Glen 2: Highland Nights*, by Donna Grant; *Project Daddy*, by Kate Perry (Kensington Books). Other clients include Renee Field, Renee Halverson, Judith Leger, Allie McCormack.

Terms Agent receives 15% commission on domestic sales; 20% commission on foreign sales. Offers written contract.

Tips "If you are concerned as to receipt of your material, please inquire through e-mail. Only send one project at a time. Do not send unsolicited mss. Please put 'query' or 'submission' in the subject heading of the e-mail."

◘ ASHLEY GRAYSON LITERARY AGENCY

1342 18th St., San Pedro CA 90732. Fax: (310)514-1148. E-mail: graysonagent@earthlink.net. Estab. 1976. Member of AAR. Represents 100 clients. 5% of clients are new/unpublished writers. Currently handles: 20% nonfiction books; 50% novels; 30% juvenile books.

Member Agents Ashley Grayson (fantasy, mystery, thrillers, young adult); Carolyn Grayson (chick lit, mystery, children's, nonfiction, women's fiction, romance, thrillers); Denise Dumars (mind/body/spirit, women's fiction, dark fantasy/horror); Lois Winston (women's fiction, chick lit, mystery).

Represents Nonfiction books, novels. **Considers these nonfiction areas:** Business/economics; computers/electronic; history; popular culture; science/technology; self-help/personal improvement; sports; true crime/investigative; mind/body/spirit; health; lifestyle. **Considers these fiction areas:** Fantasy; juvenile; multicultural; mystery/suspense; romance; science fiction; young adult; women's; chick lit.

O→ "We prefer to work with published (traditional print), established authors. We will give first consideration to authors who come recommended to us by our clients or other publishing professionals. We accept a very small number of new, previously unpublished authors."

How to Contact Query with SASE, first 3 pages of ms or overview of the nonfiction proposal. Accepts e-mail queries (no attachments).

Recent Sales *Ball Don't Lie*, by Matt de la Pena (Delacorte); *Heaven*, by Jack Cohen and Ian Stewart (Warner Books); *I Wish I Never Met You*, by Denise Wheatley (Touchstone/Simon & Schuster). Other clients include Isaac Adamson, John Barnes, Andrew Fox, Barb and J.C. Hendee, Geoffrey Landis, Bruce Coville, J.B. Cheaney, David Lubar and Christopher Pike.

Terms Agent receives 15% commission on domestic sales; 20% commission on foreign sales.

ℕ ◘ KATHRYN GREEN LITERARY AGENCY, LLC

250 West 57th St., Suite 2302, New York NY 10107. (212)245-2445. Fax: (212)245-2040. E-mail: query@kgreenagency.com. **Contact:** Kathy Green. Estab. 2004. Member of Women's Media Group. Represents 20 clients. 50% of clients are new/unpublished writers. Currently handles: 50% nonfiction books; 25% novels; 25% juvenile books.

● Prior to becoming an agent, Ms. Green was a book and magazine editor.

Represents Nonfiction books, novels, short story collections, juvenile books. **Considers these nonfiction areas:** Biography/autobiography; business/economics; child guidance/parenting; cooking/foods/nutrition; current affairs; education; history; how-to; humor/satire; memoirs; popular culture; psychology; self-help/personal improvement; sports; true crime/investigative; women's issues/studies; interior design, juvenile. **Considers these fiction areas:** Detective/police/crime; family saga; historical; humor/satire; juvenile; literary; mainstream/contemporary; mystery/suspense; romance; thriller; young adult; women's.

O→ "Keeping the client list small means that writers receive my full attention throughout the process of getting their project published." Does not want to receive science fiction or fantasy.

How to Contact Query with SASE, submit synopsis, 3 sample chapter(s), author bio. Accepts e-mail queries. No fax queries. Considers simultaneous queries. Responds in 1-2 months to mss. Returns materials only with SASE. Obtains most new clients through recommendations from others, solicitations, conferences.

Recent Sales This agency prefers not to share information on specific sales.

Terms Agent receives 15% commission on domestic sales; 20% commission on foreign sales. Offers written contract.

◘ SANFORD J. GREENBURGER ASSOCIATES, INC.

55 Fifth Ave., New York NY 10003. (212)206-5600. Fax: (212)463-8718. E-mail: firstinitiallastname@sjga.com. Web site: www.greenburger.com. Estab. 1932. Member of AAR. Represents 500 clients.

Member Agents Heide Lange; Faith Hamlin; Dan Mandel; Peter McGuigan; Matthew Bialer; Jeremy Katz; Tricia Davey.

Represents Nonfiction books, novels. **Considers these nonfiction areas:** Agriculture/horticulture; americana;

animals; anthropology/archaeology; art/architecture/design; biography/autobiography; business/economics; child guidance/parenting; computers/electronic; cooking/foods/nutrition; crafts/hobbies; current affairs; education; ethnic/cultural interests; gardening; gay/lesbian issues; government/politics/law; health/medicine; history; how-to; humor/satire; interior design/decorating; juvenile nonfiction; language/literature/criticism; memoirs; military/war; money/finance; multicultural; music/dance; nature/environment; New Age/metaphysics; philosophy; photography; popular culture; psychology; recreation; regional; religious/inspirational; science/technology; self-help/personal improvement; sex; sociology; software; sports; theater/film; translation; travel; true crime/investigative; women's issues/studies; young adult. **Considers these fiction areas:** Action/adventure; detective/police/crime; ethnic; family saga; feminist; gay/lesbian; glitz; historical; humor/satire; literary; mainstream/contemporary; mystery/suspense; psychic/supernatural; regional; sports; thriller.

○→ No romances or Westerns.

How to Contact Submit query, first 3 chapters, synopsis, brief bio, SASE. Accepts e-mail and fax queries. Considers simultaneous queries. Responds in 2 months to queries and mss. Returns materials only with SASE. Obtains most new clients through recommendations from others.

Recent Sales Sold 200 titles in the last year. This agency prefers not to share information on specific sales.

Terms Agent receives 15% commission on domestic sales; 20% commission on foreign sales. Charges for photocopying and books for foreign and subsidiary rights submissions.

🌐 ☑ GREGORY & CO. AUTHORS' AGENTS

3 Barb Mews, Hammersmith, London W6 7PA, England. (44)(207)610-4676. Fax: (44)(207)610-4686. E-mail: maryjones@gregoryandcompany.co.uk. Web site: www.gregoryandcompany.co.uk. **Contact:** Mary Jones. Estab. 1987. Member of AAA. Represents 60 clients. Currently handles: 10% nonfiction books; 90% novels.

Represents Nonfiction books, novels. **Considers these nonfiction areas:** Biography/autobiography; history. **Considers these fiction areas:** Detective/police/crime; historical; literary; mainstream/contemporary; thriller; contemporary women's fiction.

○→ "As a British agency, we do not generally take on American authors." Actively seeking well-written, accessible modern novels. Does not want to receive horror, science fiction, fantasy, mind/body/spirit, children's books, screenplays, plays, short stories or poetry.

How to Contact Query with SASE, submit outline, 3 (or fewer than 10 pages if sending by e-mail) sample chapter(s), publishing history, author bio. Considers simultaneous queries. Returns materials only with SASE. Obtains most new clients through recommendations from others, conferences.

Recent Sales *Tokyo*, by Mo Hayder (Bantam UK/Gove Atlantic); *The Torment of Others*, by Val McDermid (HarperCollins UK/St. Martin's Press); *Disordered Minds*, by Minette Walters (MacMillan UK/Putnam USA); *The Lover*, by Laura Wilson (Orion UK/Bantam USA); *Gagged & Bound*, by Natasha Cooper (Simon & Schuster UK/St. Martin's Press); *Demon of the Air*, by Simon Levack (Simon & Schuster/St. Martin's Press).

Terms Agent receives 15% commission on domestic sales; 20% commission on foreign sales. Offers written contract; 3-month notice must be given to terminate contract. Charges clients for photocopying of whole typescripts and copies of book for submissions.

Writers' Conferences CWA Conference; Bouchercon.

Ⓝ ☑ GREGORY LITERARY AGENCY, LLC

Birmingham AL 35242. (205)799-0380. Fax: (205)278-8572. E-mail: gregoryliteraryagency@yahoo.com. **Contact:** Steven P. Gregory. Estab. 2006. Currently handles: 50% nonfiction books; 50% novels.

● Prior to becoming an agent, Mr. Gregory was an attorney.

Represents Nonfiction books, novels. **Considers these nonfiction areas:** Biography/autobiography; current affairs; ethnic/cultural interests; government/politics/law; memoirs; military/war; money/finance; New Age/metaphysics; religious/inspirational; sports. **Considers these fiction areas:** Action/adventure; detective/police/crime; ethnic; glitz; literary; mainstream/contemporary; mystery/suspense; sports; thriller; women's.

○→ Actively seeking mainstream fiction, mystery/thriller, memoir, biography, African-American fiction/nonfiction, military history, money/finance/economics, law/government/politics, economics/current affairs, New Age/Buddhist. Does not want children's, science fiction, cookbooks, how-to, general nonfiction, humor or religious/inspirational.

How to Contact Query with SASE. Send no unsolicited mss of any kind. Accepts e-mail queries. No fax queries. Considers simultaneous queries. Responds in 1 month to queries; 2 months to mss. Obtains most new clients through recommendations from others, solicitations. Agent receives 15% commission on domestic sales; 20% commission on foreign sales. Offers written contract. This agency charges for postage, overnight delivery and travel; costs are charged against advance after sales.

Tips "Write the best book you can then polish and edit the final version. Do not waste money on a 'professional editor.' Edit the manuscript yourself. If you write in first person, the narrator must exhibit a compelling and unique voice. My agency strongly prefers to receive queries and requested samples by e-mail and by pdf attachments."

☑ BLANCHE C. GREGORY, INC.

2 Tudor City Place, New York NY 10017. (212)697-0828. E-mail: info@bcgliteraryagency.com, query@bcgliterar yagency.com. Web site: www.bcgliteraryagency.com. Member of AAR.

Represents Nonfiction books, novels, juvenile books.

○➡ This agency specializes in adult fiction and nonfiction; children's literature is also considered. Does not want to receive screenplays, stage plays or teleplays.

How to Contact Submit query, brief synopsis, bio, SASE. No e-mail queries. No fax queries. Obtains most new clients through recommendations from others.

Recent Sales *Chilly Scenes of Winter Distortions*, a short story collection by Ann Beattie; *Loose Ends*, by Neal Bowers; *It Happened in Boston*, by Russell H. Greenan.

Ⓝ ☑ GREYSTONE LITERARY AGENCY

1512 Allison St. NW, Washington DC 20011. (202)234-2299. E-mail: mike@greystonelit.com. Web site: www.gr eystonelit.com. **Contact:** Michael Mancilla. Estab. 2003. Represents 15 clients. 25% of clients are new/unpublished writers. Currently handles: 60% nonfiction books; 15% novels; 25% juvenile books.

● Prior to opening his agency, Mr. Mancilla worked with literary agent Peter Rubie via New York University's book publishing program. He is also a nonfiction writer who earned a Lambda Literary Award nomination and has 15 years of experience as a therapist and clinical social worker.

Represents Nonfiction books, novels, juvenile books, scholarly books. **Considers these nonfiction areas:** Anthropology/archaeology; art/architecture/design; biography/autobiography; business/economics; child guidance/parenting; computers/electronic; current affairs; education; ethnic/cultural interests; gay/lesbian issues; health/medicine; history; how-to; psychology; interior design/decorating. **Considers these fiction areas:** Ethnic; gay/lesbian; mystery/suspense; picture books; young adult.

○➡ "We are dedicated to both cultivating the voices and perspectives from the authors we represent and acting as a liason to the publishing community. As a published author, I can provide a unique perspective on what to expect through the complete cycle—from acceptance by a publisher to post-publication marketing." Actively seeking narrative nonfiction by credentialed and recognized leaders in their fields and fact-based fiction that allows readers to learn about another land or time through solid research that both educates and entertains. Does not want to receive poetry, Western, romance or screenplays. "While I love a good memoir, I don't want to see writing that is more autopathology than autobiography (i.e., books that list the terrible things you have gone through without a strong redemptive focus)."

How to Contact Query with SASE. Considers simultaneous queries. Responds in 1 week to queries; 4-6 weeks to mss. Returns materials only with SASE. Obtains most new clients through solicitations, conferences.

Recent Sales Sold 8 titles in the last year. *The Boys and the Bees*, by Joe Babcock (Carroll & Graf); *A Death at the Rose Paperworks*, by M.J. Zellnik (Midnight Ink); *The Everything Seed*, by Carole Martignacco; illustrated by Joy Troyer (Tricycle Press); *The Two Second Commute: A Career in Virtual Assistance*, by Christine Durst and Michael Haaren (Career Press).

Terms Agent receives 15% commission on domestic sales; 20% commission on foreign sales. Offers written contract, binding for 1 year; 30-day notice must be given to terminate contract. Charges for copying mss and priority mailing.

Writers' Conferences BEA/Writer's Digest Books Writers' Conference; Washington Independent Writers Spring Writers' Conference.

Tips "Effective Jan. 1, 2008, our new address will be 437 New York Ave., Suite 211, Washington, D.C. 20001."

Ⓝ ◻ JILL GRINBERG LITERARY AGENCY

244 Fifth Ave., Floor 11, New York NY 10011. (212)620-5883. Fax: (212)627-4725. E-mail: jillgrin@aol.com. Web site: www.grinbergliterary.com.

● Prior to her current position, Ms. Grinberg was at Anderson Grinberg Literary Management.

Member Agents Jill Grinberg; Kirsten Wolf (foreign rights).

Represents Nonfiction books, novels. **Considers these nonfiction areas:** Biography/autobiography; business/ economics; current affairs; government/politics/law; health/medicine; history; multicultural; psychology; science/technology; spirituality; travel; women's issues/studies. **Considers these fiction areas:** Fantasy; historical; romance; science fiction; young adult; women's; literary fiction, commercial fiction, children's, middle grade.

How to Contact Query with SASE, submit Send a proposal and author bio for nonfiction; send a query, synopsis and the first 50 pages for fiction. No e-mail or fax queries.

Recent Sales *Red Sky in Mourning*, by Jill Grinberg (Hyperion); *Strange Angel*, by George Pendle (Harcourt); *Jesse James: Last Rebel of the Civil War*, by T.J. Stiles (Vintage); *Searching for El Dorado*, by Marc Herman (Nan A. Talese).

Tips "We prefer submissions by mail."

☑ JILL GROSJEAN LITERARY AGENCY

1390 Millstone Road, Sag Harbor NY 11963-2214. (631)725-7419. Fax: (631)725-8632. E-mail: jill6981@aol.com. **Contact:** Jill Grosjean. Estab. 1999. Represents 33 clients. 100% of clients are new/unpublished writers.

- Prior to becoming an agent, Ms. Grosjean was manager of an independent bookstore. She has also worked in publishing and advertising.

Represents Novels. **Considers these fiction areas:** Historical; literary; mainstream/contemporary; mystery/ suspense; regional; romance.

- O— This agency offers some editorial assistance (i.e., line-by-line edits). Actively seeking literary novels and mysteries.

How to Contact Query with SASE. No cold calls, please. Considers simultaneous queries. Responds in 1 week to queries; 1 month to mss. Returns materials only with SASE. Obtains most new clients through recommendations from others, solicitations.

Recent Sales *Beating the Babushka,* by Tim Maleeny *(Midnight Ink); Whispers Within,* by Don Locke (Nav Press); *Rivers Edge,* by Marie Bostwick (Kensington Publishing); *Stealing the Dragon,* by Tim Maleeny (Midnight Ink); *I Love You Like a Tomato,* by Marie Giordano (Forge Books); *Nectar,* by David C. Fickett (Forge Books); *Cycling* and *Sanctuary,* by Greg Garrett (Kensington); *The Smoke,* by Tony Broadbent (St. Martin's Press/ Minotaur); *Fields of Gold,* by Marie Bostwick (Kensington); *Spectres in the Smoke,* by Tony Broadbent (St. Martin's Press/Minotaur).

Terms Agent receives 15% commission on domestic sales; 20% commission on foreign sales. No written contract. Charges clients for photocopying and mailing expenses.

Writers' Conferences Book Passage's Mystery Writers' Conference; Agents and Editors Conference; Texas Writers' and Agents' Conference.

☑ THE GROSVENOR LITERARY AGENCY

5510 Grosvenor Lane, Bethesda MD 20814. Fax: (301)581-9401. E-mail: deb@gliterary.com. Web site: www.glit erary.com. Alternate address: 1627 K St., Suite 1200, Washington DC 20006. **Contact:** Deborah C. Grosvenor. Estab. 1996. Represents 40 clients. 10% of clients are new/unpublished writers. Currently handles: 60% nonfiction books; 40% novels.

- Prior to opening her agency, Ms. Grosvenor was a book editor for 16 years.

Represents Nonfiction books, novels. **Considers these nonfiction areas:** Animals; anthropology/archaeology; art/architecture/design; biography/autobiography; business/economics; child guidance/parenting; current affairs; government/politics/law; health/medicine; history; how-to; language/literature/criticism; military/war; money/finance; music/dance; nature/environment; photography; popular culture; psychology; religious/inspirational; science/technology; self-help/personal improvement; sociology; spirituality; theater/film; translation; true crime/investigative; women's issues/studies. **Considers these fiction areas:** Detective/police/crime; family saga; historical; literary; mainstream/contemporary; mystery/suspense; romance (contemporary, gothic, historical); thriller.

How to Contact For nonfiction, send outline/proposal. For fiction, send query, 3 sample chapters. No fax queries. Responds in 1 month to queries; 2 months to mss. Returns materials only with SASE. Obtains most new clients through recommendations from others.

Terms Agent receives 15% commission on domestic sales; 20% commission on foreign sales. Offers written contract; 10-day notice must be given to terminate contract.

☑ REECE HALSEY NORTH

98 Main St., #704, Tiburon CA 94920. Fax: (415)789-9177. E-mail: info@reecehalseynorth.com. Web site: www.reecehalseynorth.com. **Contact:** Kimberley Cameron. Estab. 1957 (Reece Halsey Agency); 1993 (Reece Halsey North). Member of AAR. Represents 40 clients. 30% of clients are new/unpublished writers. Currently handles: 75% fiction, 25% nonfiction.

- The Reece Halsey Agency has had an illustrious client list of established writers, including the estate of Aldous Huxley, and has represented Upton Sinclair, William Faulkner, and Henry Miller.

Member Agents Kimberley Cameron, Elizabeth Evans.

Represents Nonfiction books, novels. **Considers these nonfiction areas:** Biography/autobiography; current affairs; history; language/literature/criticism; popular culture; science/technology; true crime/investigative; women's issues/studies. **Considers these fiction areas:** Action/adventure; contemporary issues; detective/ police/crime; ethnic; family saga; historical; horror; literary; mainstream/contemporary; mystery/suspense; science fiction; thriller; women's.

- O— "We are looking for a unique and heartfelt voice that conveys a universal truth."

How to Contact Query with SASE, first 50 pages of novel. Please do not fax queries. Responds in 3-6 weeks to queries; 1 month to mss. Obtains most new clients through recommendations from others, solicitations.

Terms Agent receives 15% commission on domestic sales; 10% commission on dramatic rights sales. Offers written contract, binding for 1 year. Requests 6 copies of ms if representing an author.

Writers' Conferences Maui Writers Conference; Aspen Summer Words Literary Festival; Willamette Writers Conference, numerous others.

Tips "Always send a polite, well-written query and please include a SASE with it."

N ☪ ◪ THE HARDING AGENCY

P.O. Box 76003, Vancouver BC V6E 4T2, Canada. (604)331-9330. Fax: (604)331-9328. E-mail: reception@theharding agency.com. Web site: www.thehardingagency.com. **Contact:** Sally Harding. Represents 20 clients.

● Prior to her current position, Ms. Harding spent eight years in editing, bookselling and publishing in New Zealand and Australia, and three years as a literary agent with Seventh Avenue Literary Agency.

Represents Nonfiction books (narrative), novels (commercial and literary fiction).

○☞ "The Harding Agency is an energetic boutique agency. We work closely and collaboratively with our authors as we fine-tune their manuscripts, submit their writing to publishers, negotiate contracts on their behalf, and build their careers. We respond promptly and personally to resolve any difficulties or concerns our clients may have. We maintain an international perspective representing clients from Canada, the United States and New Zealand. Our authors are published by independent and large international publishers, and we regularly travel to major publishing centers and book fairs to foster those relationships and take care of our authors' interests. Our clients are further represented through our extensive network of skilled, specialist sub-agents." Actively seeking commercial and literary fiction, and narrative nonfiction. Does not want to receive children's books, plays, poetry or screenplays.

How to Contact Query with SASE, submit a full submission package, if querying by snail mail. Look online to learn more. Send query only, if using e-mail,. No fax queries. Considers simultaneous queries. Responds in 6-8 weeks to queries; 6-8 weeks to mss. Returns materials only with SASE. Obtains most new clients through recommendations from others, solicitations.

Recent Sales *Inside* and *The Town That Forgot How to Breathe*, by Kenneth J. Harvey; *In the Palace of Repose*, by Holly Phillips.

Tips "Please note that due to the very large number of email queries we receive, we do not respond to email queries unless we intend to further consider your work."

◪ THE JOY HARRIS LITERARY AGENCY, INC.

156 Fifth Ave., Suite 617, New York NY 10010. (212)924-6269. Fax: (212)924-6609. **Contact:** Joy Harris. Member of AAR. Represents more than 100 clients. Currently handles: 50% nonfiction books; 50% novels.

Represents Nonfiction books, novels. **Considers these fiction areas:** Ethnic; experimental; family saga; feminist; gay/lesbian; glitz; hi-lo; historical; humor/satire; literary; mainstream/contemporary; multicultural; multimedia; mystery/suspense; regional; short story collections; spiritual; translation; young adult; women's.

○☞ No screenplays.

How to Contact Query with sample chapter, outline/proposal, SASE. Accepts fax queries. No e-mail queries. Considers simultaneous queries. Responds in 2 months to queries. Returns materials only with SASE. Obtains most new clients through recommendations from clients and editors.

Recent Sales This agency prefers not to share information on specific sales.

Terms Agent receives 15% commission on domestic sales; 20% commission on foreign sales. Charges clients for some office expenses.

◪ HARTLINE LITERARY AGENCY

123 Queenston Dr., Pittsburgh PA 15235-5429. (412)829-2495. Fax: (412)829-2432. E-mail: joyce@hartlinelitera ry.com. Web site: www.hartlineliterary.com. **Contact:** Joyce A. Hart. Estab. 1990. Represents 40 clients. 20% of clients are new/unpublished writers. Currently handles: 40% nonfiction books; 60% novels.

Member Agents Joyce A. Hart, principal agent; Andrea Boeshaar; Terry Burns; Tamela Hancock Murray.

Represents Nonfiction books, novels. **Considers these nonfiction areas:** Business/economics; child guidance/parenting; cooking/foods/nutrition; money/finance; religious/inspirational; self-help/personal improvement; women's issues/studies. **Considers these fiction areas:** Action/adventure; contemporary issues; family saga; historical; literary; mystery/suspense (amateur sleuth, cozy); regional; religious/inspirational; romance (contemporary, gothic, historical, regency); thriller.

○☞ This agency specializes in the Christian bookseller market. Actively seeking adult fiction, self-help, nutritional books, devotional, and business. Does not want to receive erotica, gay/lesbian, fantasy, horror, etc.

How to Contact Submit summary/outline, author bio, 3 sample chapters. Accepts e-mail and fax queries. Considers simultaneous queries. Responds in 2 months to queries; 3 months to mss. Returns materials only with SASE. Obtains most new clients through recommendations from others.

Recent Sales *I'm Not OK and Neither Are You*, by David E. Clarke, PhD (Barbour Publishers); *Along Came Love*, by Carrie Turansky (Steeple Hill); *Glory Be*, by Ron and Janet Benrey (Steeple Hill); *Overcoing the Top Ten Reasons Singles Stay Single*, by Tom and Beverly Rodgers (NavPress); *A Clearing in the Wild*, by Jane Kirkpatrick (Waterbrook); *The Mothers-in-Law*, by Andrea Boeshaar and Jeri Odel (Focus on the Family); *Ties to Home*, by Kim Sawyer (Bethany House); The Reluctant 3-book series, by Jill Nelson (Harvest House).
Terms Agent receives 15% commission on domestic sales. Offers written contract.

⊕ ◑ ANTONY HARWOOD LIMITED

103 Walton St., Oxford OX2 6EB, England. (44)(186)555-9615. Fax: (44)(186)531-0660. E-mail: mail@antonyharwood.com. Web site: www.antonyharwood.com. **Contact:** Antony Harwood, James Macdonald Lockhart. Estab. 2000. Represents 52 clients.

● Prior to starting this agency, Mr. Harwood and Mr. Lockhart worked at publishing houses and other literary agencies.

Represents Nonfiction books, novels. **Considers these nonfiction areas:** Agriculture/horticulture; americana; animals; anthropology/archaeology; art/architecture/design; biography/autobiography; business/economics; child guidance/parenting; computers/electronic; cooking/foods/nutrition; creative nonfiction (1); current affairs; education; ethnic/cultural interests; gardening; gay/lesbian issues; government/politics/law; health/medicine; history; how-to; humor/satire; language/literature/criticism; memoirs; military/war; money/finance; multicultural; music/dance; nature/environment; philosophy; photography; popular culture; psychology; recreation; regional; religious/inspirational; science/technology; self-help/personal improvement; sex; sociology; software; spirituality; sports; theater/film; translation; travel; true crime/investigative; women's issues/studies. **Considers these fiction areas:** Action/adventure; comic books/cartoon; confession; detective/police/crime; erotica; ethnic; experimental; family saga; fantasy; feminist; gay/lesbian; gothic; hi-lo; historical; horror; humor/satire; literary; mainstream/contemporary; military/war; multicultural; multimedia; mystery/suspense; occult; picture books; plays; regional; religious/inspirational; romance; science fiction; spiritual; sports; thriller; translation; westerns/frontier; young adult.

⊙┐ "We accept every genre of fiction and nonfiction except for children's fiction for readers ages 10 and younger." No poetry or screenplays.

How to Contact Submit outline, 2-3 sample chapters via e-mail or postal mail (include SASE or IRC). No fax queries. Responds in 2 months to queries.
Terms Agent receives 15% commission on domestic sales; 20% commission on foreign sales.

◑ JOHN HAWKINS & ASSOCIATES, INC.

71 W. 23rd St., Suite 1600, New York NY 10010. (212)807-7040. Fax: (212)807-9555. E-mail: jha@jhalit.com. Web site: www.jhalit.com. **Contact:** Moses Cardona (moses@jhalit.com). Estab. 1893. Member of AAR. Represents over 100 clients. 5-10% of clients are new/unpublished writers. Currently handles: 40% nonfiction books; 40% novels; 20% juvenile books.
Member Agents Moses Cardona; Warren Frazier; Anne Hawkins; John Hawkins; William Reiss.
Represents Nonfiction books, novels, young adult. **Considers these nonfiction areas:** Agriculture/horticulture; americana; anthropology/archaeology; art/architecture/design; biography/autobiography; business/economics; current affairs; education; ethnic/cultural interests; gardening; gay/lesbian issues; government/politics/law; health/medicine; history; how-to; interior design/decorating; language/literature/criticism; memoirs; money/finance; multicultural; nature/environment; philosophy; popular culture; psychology; recreation; science/technology; self-help/personal improvement; sex; sociology; software; theater/film; travel; true crime/investigative; young adult; music, creative nonfiction. **Considers these fiction areas:** Action/adventure; detective/police/crime; ethnic; experimental; family saga; feminist; gay/lesbian; glitz; gothic; hi-lo; historical; literary; mainstream/contemporary; military/war; multicultural; multimedia; mystery/suspense; psychic/supernatural; religious/inspirational; short story collections; sports; thriller; translation; westerns/frontier; young adult; women's.
How to Contact Submit query, proposal package, outline, SASE. Considers simultaneous queries. Responds in 1 month to queries. Returns materials only with SASE. Obtains most new clients through recommendations from others.
Recent Sales *Catching Genius*, by Kristy Kiernan; *Raven Black*, by Ann Cleeves; *The Museum of Dr. Moses*, by Joyce Carol Oates; *Waltzing With Alligators*, by Lorelle Marinello (Avon).
Terms Agent receives 15% commission on domestic sales; 20% commission on foreign sales. Charges clients for photocopying.

◑ HEACOCK LITERARY AGENCY, INC.

West Coast Office, 11740 Big Tujunga Canyon Road, Tujunga CA 91042. E-mail: catt@heacockliteraryagency.com. Web site: www.heacockliteraryagency.com. **Contact:** Catt LeBaigue. Estab. 1978. Member of AAR, SCBWI.

• Prior to becoming an agent, Ms. LeBaigue spent 18 years with Sony Pictures and Warner Bros.

Member Agents Rosalie Grace Heacock Thompson (semi-retired, no queries at this time); Catt LeBaigue (middle grade children's fiction, children's chapter books, young adult fiction, a limited number of picture books; nonfiction including art, anthropology, animals, body, mind and spirit, health, nature, travel, indigenous cultures, and material that makes a new connection between formal science and the inner man).

Represents Nonfiction books, juvenile books.

How to Contact Query with SASE. E-mail queries only. No unsolicited manuscripts. No e-mail attachments. Returns materials only with SASE. Obtains most new clients through recommendations from others, solicitations.

Recent Sales Other clients include Don and Audrey Wood, Stephen Cosgrove, Larry Dane Brimner, Elliot Abravanel, E.A. King, E. Joseph Cossman, Joseph Bark. Offers written contract.

Tips "Take time to write an informative query letter expressing your book idea, the market for it, your qualifications to write the book, the 'hook' that would make a potential reader buy the book."

N ✉ HELEN HELLER AGENCY INC.

892 Avenue Road, Toronto Ontario M5P 2K6, Canada. (416)631-0968. E-mail: info@helenhelleragency.com. Web site: www.helenhelleragency.com. **Contact:** Helen Heller. Estab. 1988. Represents 30+ clients.

• Prior to her current position, Ms. Heller worked for Cassell & Co. (England), was an editor for Harlequin Books, a senior editor for Avon Books, and editor-in-chief for Fitzhenry & Whiteside.

Member Agents Helen Heller, helen@helenhelleragency.com; Daphne Hart, daphne.hart@sympatico.ca; Sarah Heller, sarah@helenhelleragency.com.

Represents Nonfiction books, novels.

O— Actively seeking adult fiction and nonfiction (excluding children's literature, screenplays or genre fiction). Does not want to receive children's literature, screenplays or genre fiction such as fantasy and science fiction.

How to Contact Query with SASE, submit synopsis, publishing history, author bio. Obtains most new clients through recommendations from others, solicitations.

Recent Sales *Break on Through*, by Jill Murray (Doubleday Canada); *Womankind: Faces of Change Around the World*, by Donna Nebenzahl (Raincoast Books); *One Dead Indian: The Premier, The Police and the Ipperwash Crisis*, by Peter Edwards (McClelland & Stewart); a full list of deals is available online.

Tips "Whether you are an author searching for an agent, or whether an agent has approached you, it is in your best interest to first find out who the agent represents, what publishing houses has that agent sold to recently and what foreign sales have been made. You should be able to go to the bookstore, or search online and find the books the agent refers to. Many authors acknowledge their agents in the front or back or their books."

✉ RICHARD HENSHAW GROUP

22 West 23rd St., Fifth Floor, New York NY 10010. (212)414-1172. Fax: (212)414-1182. E-mail: submissions@he nshaw.com. Web site: www.rich.henshaw.com. **Contact:** Rich Henshaw. Estab. 1995. Member of AAR, SinC, MWA, HWA, SFWA, RWA. Represents 35 clients. 20% of clients are new/unpublished writers. Currently handles: 35% nonfiction books; 65% novels.

• Prior to opening his agency, Mr. Henshaw served as an agent with Richard Curtis Associates, Inc.

Represents Nonfiction books, novels. **Considers these nonfiction areas:** Animals; biography/autobiography; business/economics; child guidance/parenting; computers/electronic; cooking/foods/nutrition; current affairs; gay/lesbian issues; government/politics/law; health/medicine; how-to; humor/satire; military/war; money/finance; music/dance; nature/environment; New Age/metaphysics; popular culture; psychology; science/technology; self-help/personal improvement; sociology; sports; true crime/investigative; women's issues/studies. **Considers these fiction areas:** Action/adventure; detective/police/crime; ethnic; family saga; fantasy; glitz; historical; horror; humor/satire; literary; mainstream/contemporary; mystery/suspense; psychic/supernatural; romance; science fiction; sports; thriller.

O— This agency specializes in thrillers, mysteries, science fiction, fantasy and horror.

How to Contact Query with SASE. Responds in 3 weeks to queries; 6 weeks to mss. Obtains most new clients through recommendations from others, solicitations, conferences.

Recent Sales *Blindfold Game*, by Dana Stabenow (St. Martin's Press); *A Deeper Sleep*, by Dana Stabenow (St. Martin's Press); *The Drowning Man*, by Margaret Coel (Berkley); *The History of the Ancient World*, by Susan Wise Bauer (Norton); *Stone Butterfly*, by James D. Doss (St. Martin's Press); *Box Like the Pros*, by Joe Frazier and William Dettloff (HarperCollins); *The Raven Prince*, by Elizabeth Hoyt (Warner). Other clients include Jessie Wise, Peter van Dijk, Jay Caselberg, Judith Laik.

Terms Agent receives 15% commission on domestic sales; 20% commission on foreign sales. No written contract. 100% of business is derived from commissions on ms sales. Charges clients for photocopying and book orders.

Tips "While we do not have any reason to believe that our submission guidelines will change in the near future, writers can find up-to-date submission policy information on our Web site. Always include a SASE with correct return postage."

☑ THE JEFF HERMAN AGENCY, LLC

P.O. Box 1522, Stockbridge MA 01262. (413)298-0077. Fax: (413)298-8188. E-mail: jeff@jeffherman.com. Web site: www.jeffherman.com. **Contact:** Jeffrey H. Herman. Estab. 1985. Represents 100 clients. 10% of clients are new/unpublished writers. Currently handles: 85% nonfiction books; 5% scholarly books; 5% textbooks.

● Prior to opening his agency, Mr. Herman served as a public relations executive.

Member Agents Deborah Levine, vice president (nonfiction book doctor); Jeff Herman.

Represents Nonfiction books. **Considers these nonfiction areas:** Business/economics; government/politics/law; health/medicine (recovery issues); history; how-to; self-help/personal improvement; spirituality; popular reference; technology; popular psychology.

☛ This agency specializes in adult nonfiction.

How to Contact Query with SASE. Accepts e-mail and fax queries. Considers simultaneous queries.

Recent Sales Sold 35 titles in the last year. This agency prefers not to share information on specific sales.

Terms Agent receives 15% commission on domestic sales. Offers written contract. Charges clients for copying and postage.

⬛ ☑ HIDDEN VALUE GROUP

1240 E. Ontario Ave., Ste. 102-148, Corona CA, 92881. (951)549-8891. Fax: (951)549-8891. E-mail: bookquery@hiddenvaluegroup.com. Web site: www.hiddenvaluegroup.com. **Contact:** Jeff Jernigan. Estab. 2001. Represents 20 clients. 20% of clients are new/unpublished writers.

Member Agents Jeff Jernigan, jjernigan@hiddenvaluegroup.com (men's nonfiction, fiction, Bible studies/curriculum, marriage and family); Nancy Jernigan, njernigan@hiddenvaluegroup.com (nonfiction, women's issues, inspiration, marriage and family, fiction).

Represents Nonfiction books, novels, juvenile books. **Considers these nonfiction areas:** Biography/autobiography; business/economics; child guidance/parenting; history; how-to; juvenile nonfiction; language/literature/criticism; memoirs; money/finance; psychology; religious/inspirational; self-help/personal improvement; women's issues/studies. **Considers these fiction areas:** Action/adventure; detective/police/crime; fantasy; literary; religious/inspirational; thriller; westerns/frontier; women's.

☛ "The Hidden Value Group specializes in helping authors throughout their publishing career. We believe that every author has a special message to be heard and we specialize in getting that message heard." Actively seeking established fiction authors, and authors who are focusing on women's issues. Does not want to receive poetry or short stories.

How to Contact Query with SASE, submit synopsis, 3 sample chapter(s), author bio. Accepts e-mail queries. No fax queries. Considers simultaneous queries. Responds in 1 month to queries; 1 month to mss. Returns materials only with SASE. Obtains most new clients through recommendations from others, solicitations.

Recent Sales *More Than a Match*, by Michael and Amy Smalley (Waterbrook Press); *Body, Beauty, Boys*, by Sarah Bragg; *The DNA of Relationships*, by Gary Smalley; *A Happier, Healthier You*, by Lorraine Bosse Smith.

Terms Agent receives 15% commission on domestic sales; 15% commission on foreign sales. Offers written contract.

Writers' Conferences Glorieta Christian Writers' Conference; CLASS Publishing Conference.

☑ FREDERICK HILL BONNIE NADELL, INC.

1842 Union St., San Francisco CA 94123. (415)921-2910. Fax: (415)921-2802. **Contact:** Elise Proulx. Estab. 1979. Represents 100 clients.

Member Agents Fred Hill, president; Bonnie Nadell, vice president; Elise Proulx, associate.

Represents Nonfiction books, novels. **Considers these nonfiction areas:** Current affairs; health/medicine; history; language/literature/criticism; nature/environment; popular culture; science/technology; biography; government/politics, narrative. **Considers these fiction areas:** Literary; mainstream/contemporary.

How to Contact Query with SASE. No e-mail or fax queries. Considers simultaneous queries. Returns materials only with SASE.

Recent Sales *It Might Have Been What He Said*, by Eden Collinsworth; *Consider the Lobster and Other Essays*, by David Foster Wallace; *The Underdog*, by Joshua Davis.

Terms Agent receives 15% commission on domestic sales; 20% commission on foreign sales; 15% commission on dramatic rights sales. Charges clients for photocopying and foreign mailings.

Ⓝ ♥ HILL MEDIA

1155 Camino Del Mar, #530, Del Mar CA 92014. (858)259-2595. Fax: (858)259-2777. **Contact:** Julie Hill. Estab. 1994. Represents 50 clients. 20% of clients are new/unpublished writers. Currently handles: 90% nonfiction books; 5% story collections; 5% books that accompany films.

Member Agents Julie Hill, agent/publicist; Anette Farrell, agent.

Represents Nonfiction books, short story collections, anthologies. **Considers these nonfiction areas:** Art/architecture/design; biography/autobiography; cooking/foods/nutrition; ethnic/cultural interests; health/medicine; history; how-to; interior design/decorating; language/literature/criticism; memoirs; music/dance; New Age/metaphysics; popular culture; psychology; religious/inspirational; self-help/personal improvement; women's issues/studies.

> ⚬━ "Check your ego at the door. If we love your book, we mean it. If we are so-so, we also mean that. If we cannot place it, we tell you ASAP." Actively seeking nonfiction: travel, health, media tie-ins. Does not want to receive horror, juvenile, sci-fi, thrillers or autobiographies or any kind.

How to Contact Submit outline/proposal, SASE. Send all submissions via snail mail. See the Web site for more instructions. Never send a complete ms unless requested. No e-mail or fax queries. Considers simultaneous queries. Responds in 4-6 weeks to queries. Obtains most new clients through recommendations from others, solicitations, conferences.

Recent Sales Sold 21 titles in the last year. *Sunshines, The Astrology of Happiness*, by Michael Lutin (Simon and Schuster); *Images from the Film: Memoirs of a Geisha* (Newmarket Press); *Return to Naples*, by Robert Zweig (Dusty Spark). Other clients include Peggy Mulloy, Barbara Ganim, Susan Fox, Joe Wolff, David W. Morrow, Suzi Doll, Darlene Trew Crist, Roger Paperno, Robert Llewellyn, Timothy Jordan, Linda Noble Topf, Laura Lea Miller, Andrea Joy Cohen.

♥ BARBARA HOGENSON AGENCY

165 West End Ave., Suite 19-C, New York NY 10023. (212)874-8084. Fax: (212)362-3011. E-mail: bhogenson@aol.com. **Contact:** Barbara Hogenson, Nicole Verity. Member of AAR.

How to Contact Query with SASE. No e-mail or fax queries. Obtains most new clients through recommendations from other clients.

♥ HOPKINS LITERARY ASSOCIATES

2117 Buffalo Rd., Suite 327, Rochester NY 14624-1507. (585)352-6268. **Contact:** Pam Hopkins. Estab. 1996. Member of AAR, RWA. Represents 30 clients. 5% of clients are new/unpublished writers. Currently handles: 100% novels.

Represents Novels. **Considers these fiction areas:** Romance (historical, contemporary, category); women's.

> ⚬━ This agency specializes in women's fiction, particularly historical, contemporary, and category romance, as well as mainstream work.

How to Contact Submit outline, 3 sample chapters. No e-mail or fax queries. Considers simultaneous queries. Responds in 2 weeks to queries; 1 month to mss. Returns materials only with SASE. Obtains most new clients through recommendations from others, solicitations, conferences.

Recent Sales Sold 50 titles in the last year. *Lady of Sin*, by Madeline Hunter (Bantam); *Silent in the Grave*, by Deanna Raybourn (Mira); *Passion*, by Lisa Valdez (Berkley).

Terms Agent receives 15% commission on domestic sales; 20% commission on foreign sales. No written contract.

Writers' Conferences RWA National Conference.

♥ HORNFISCHER LITERARY MANAGEMENT

P.O. Box 50544, Austin TX 78763. E-mail: jim@hornfischerlit.com. Web site: www.hornfischerlit.com. **Contact:** James D. Hornfischer, president. Estab. 2001. Represents 45 clients. 10% of clients are new/unpublished writers. Currently handles: 98% nonfiction books; 2%.

> • Prior to opening his agency, Mr. Hornfischer was an agent with Literary Group International and held editorial positions at HarperCollins and McGraw-Hill. "My New York editorial background working with a variety of bestselling authors, such as Erma Bombeck, Jared Diamond, and Erica Jong, is useful in this regard. In 14 years as an agent, I've handled eight *New York Times* nonfiction bestsellers, including two No. 1's."

Represents Nonfiction books. **Considers these nonfiction areas:** Anthropology/archaeology; biography/autobiography; business/economics; child guidance/parenting; current affairs; government/politics/law; health/medicine; history; how-to; humor/satire; memoirs; military/war; money/finance; multicultural; nature/environment; popular culture; psychology; religious/inspirational; science/technology; self-help/personal improvement; sociology; sports; true crime/investigative.

○┐ Actively seeking the best work of terrific writers. Does not want poetry or genre fiction.

How to Contact Submit proposal package, outline, 2 sample chapters. Considers simultaneous queries. Responds in 6-8 weeks to queries. Returns materials only with SASE. Obtains most new clients through referrals from clients, reading books and magazines, pursuing ideas with New York editors.

Recent Sales *Cosmotopia: The Shaping of American Thought and Culture*, by William H. Goetzmann (Basic); see this agency's Web site for more sales information.

Terms Agent receives 15% commission on domestic sales; 25% commission on foreign sales. Offers written contract. Reasonable expenses deducted from proceeds after book is sold.

Tips "When you query agents and send out proposals, present yourself as someone who's in command of his material and comfortable in his own skin. Too many writers have a palpable sense of anxiety and insecurity. Take a deep breath and realize that—if you're good—someone in the publishing world will want you."

☒ ⬛ ANDREA HURST LITERARY MANAGEMENT

P.O. Box 19010, Sacramento CA 95819. E-mail: (agentfirstname)@andreahurst.com. Web site: www.andreahurst.com. **Contact:** Andrea Hurst, president; Judy Mikalonis, associate agent. Estab. 2002. Represents 50+ clients. 50% of clients are new/unpublished writers. Currently handles: 75% nonfiction books; 10% novels; 15% juvenile books.

• Prior to becoming an agent, Ms. Hurst was an acquisitions editor as well as a freelance editor and writer; Ms. Mikalonis was in marketing and branding consulting.

Member Agents Andrea Hurst, andrea@andreahurst.com (nonfiction—including personal growth, health and wellness, science, business, parenting, relationships, women's issues, animals, spirituality, women's issues, metaphysical, psychological and self help; fiction interests include adult fiction); Judy Mikalonis, judy@andreahurst.com (YA fiction, Christian fiction, Christian nonfiction).

Represents Nonfiction books, novels, juvenile books. **Considers these nonfiction areas:** Animals; art/architecture/design; biography/autobiography; business/economics; child guidance/parenting; cooking/foods/nutrition; crafts/hobbies; education; health/medicine; how-to; humor/satire; interior design/decorating; juvenile nonfiction; memoirs; military/war; money/finance; music/dance; nature/environment; New Age/metaphysics; photography; popular culture; psychology; religious/inspirational; science/technology; self-help/personal improvement; sociology; true crime/investigative; women's issues/studies; gift books. **Considers these fiction areas:** Juvenile; literary; mainstream/contemporary; psychic/supernatural; religious/inspirational; romance; thriller; young adult; women's.

○┐ Actively seeking well written nonfiction by authors with a strong platform; superbly crafted fiction with depth that touches the mind and heart and all of our listed subjects. Does not want to receive sci-fi, mystery, horror, Western, poetry or screenplays.

How to Contact Query with SASE, submit outline/proposal, synopsis, 2 sample chapter(s), author bio. Accepts e-mail queries. No fax queries. Considers simultaneous queries. Obtains most new clients through recommendations from others, solicitations, conferences.

Recent Sales Sold 20 titles in the last year. *Love, Magic, and Mudpies*, by Bernie Siegel (Rodale); *The Lazy Dog's Guide to Enlightenment*, by Andrea Hurst and Beth Wilson (New World Library); *Favorite Recipes from America's Best Food Festivals*, by James Fraioli (Penguin); *True Self—True Wealth*, by Peter Cole and Daisy Reese; *The Complete Idiot's Guide to Evangelical Christianity*, by David Cobia (Penguin); *Soldier's Heart: Close-up with PTSD in Vietnam Veterans*, by Ronald Dawe and William Schroeder (Praeger Security International).

Terms Agent receives 15% commission on domestic sales; 20% commission on foreign sales. Offers written contract, binding for 6 to 12 months; 30-day notice must be given to terminate contract. This agency charges for postage.

Writers' Conferences San Francisco Writers' Conference; Willamette Writers' Conference; Santa Barbara Writers' Conference; Surrey International; PNWA.

Tips "Do your homework and submit a professional package. Get to know the agent you are submitting to by researching their Web site or meeting them at a conference. Perfect your craft: Write well and edit ruthlessly over and over again before submitting to an agent. Be realistic: Understand that publishing is a business and be prepared to prove why your book is marketable and how you will market it on your own. Be Persistent!"

⬛ IMPRINT AGENCY, INC.

240 West 35th St., Suite 500, New York NY 10001. Web site: www.imprintagency.com. **Contact:** Stephany Evans, president. Member of AAR.

• Prior to her current position, Ms. Evans began agenting in 1990 with Sandra Martin/Paraview; Ms. Reid formerly ran her own agency, JetReid.

Member Agents Stephany Evans, sevans@imprintagency.com (health and wellness, spirituality, psychology/self-help, mind/body, pregnancy and parenting, lifestyle, popular reference, narrative nonfiction, women's fiction, both literary and commercial—including chick lit, mystery and light suspense); Gary Heidt, gheidt@imprintagency.com (mystery, thriller, romance, literary fiction, multicultural, speculative, humorous, satirical); Mhays@imprintagency.com (sophisticated women's fiction—think urban chick lit, pop culture, lifestyle, animals, and absorbing nonfiction accounts); Janet Reid, jreid@imprintagency.com.

Represents Nonfiction books, novels. **Considers these nonfiction areas:** Government/politics/law; health/medicine; history; music/dance; psychology; self-help/personal improvement; spirituality; relationship, parapsychology, parenting, pregancy, narrative nonfiction, lifestyle. **Considers these fiction areas:** Literary; multicultural; mystery/suspense; thriller; young adult; women's (chick-lit); commercial.

> O⚲ "Special areas of interest include alternative health and healing, spirituality, popular psychology, transpersonal psychology, parapsychology, pets, women's issues, history, popular science, parenting, multicultural issues, home decor and narrative nonfiction. We are not looking for historicals, Western's, fantasies, science fiction, plays, poetry or children's books."

How to Contact Query with SASE, proposal package, outline, outline/proposal, publishing history, author bio. No attachments on e-mails. If interested, the agency will contact you. Accepts e-mail queries. No fax queries. Sold more than 25 titles in the last year. *Baby Proof*, by Emily Giffin (St. Martin's Press); *Crossing Into Medicine Country*, by David Carson (Arcade); *Rollergirl: Totally True Tales From the Track*, by Melissa Joulwan (Simon & Schuster); *The Pirate Primer*, by George Choundras (Writer's Digest Books). Agent receives 15% commission on domestic sales; 20% commission on foreign sales.

◑ INKWELL MANAGEMENT, LLC

521 Fifth Ave., 26th Floor, New York NY 10175. (212)922-3500. Fax: (212)922-0535. E-mail: submissions@inkwellmanagement.com. Web site: www.inkwellmanagement.com. Estab. 2004. Represents 500 clients. Currently handles: 60% nonfiction books; 40% novels.

Member Agents Michael Carlisle; Richard Pine; Kimberly Witherspoon; George Lucas; Catherine Drayton; David Forrer; Eleanor Jackson; Alexis Hurley; Pilar Queen; Elisa Petrini; Libby O'Neill.

Represents Nonfiction books, novels.

How to Contact Query with SASE or via e-mail. Obtains most new clients through recommendations from others.

Recent Sales Sold 100 titles in the last year. *300 Bucks an Hour*, by Eliot Schrefer (Gotham).

Terms Agent receives 15% commission on domestic sales; 20% commission on foreign sales. Offers written contract.

Tips "We will not read manuscripts before receiving a letter of inquiry."

◐ INTERNATIONAL CREATIVE MANAGEMENT

825 Eighth Ave., New York NY 10019. (212)556-5600. Web site: www.icmtalent.com. **Contact:** Literary Department. Member of AAR; signatory of WGA.

Member Agents Christine Earle, cearle@icmtalent.com (fiction interests include: young adult, children's, middle grade; nonfiction interests include: dating/relationships, pop culture); Lisa Bankoff, lbankoff@icmtalent.com (fiction interests include: literary fiction, family saga, historical fiction, offbeat/quirky; nonfiction interests include: history, biography, parenting, memoirs, narrative, humor); Sam Cohn; Patrick Herold, pherold@icmtalent.com; Jennifer Joel, jjoel@icmtalent.com (fiction interests include: literary fiction, commercial fiction, historical fiction, thrillers/suspense; nonfiction interests include: history, sports, art, adventure/true story, pop culture); Esther Newberg; Sloan Harris; Amanda "Binky" Urban; Mitch Douglas; Heather Schroder; Kristine Dahl; Andrea Barzvi, abarzvi@icmtalent.com (fiction interests include: chick lit, commercial fiction, women's fiction, thrillers/suspense; nonfiction interests include: sports, celebrity, self-help, dating/relationships, women's issues, pop culture, health and fitness); Tina Dubois Wexler, twexler@icmtalent.com (literary fiction, chick lit, young adult, middle grade, memoir, narrative nonfiction); Katharine Cluverius; Kate Lee, klee@icmtalent.com (mystery, commercial fiction, short stories, memoir, dating/relationships, pop culture, humor, journalism).

Represents Nonfiction books, novels.

> O⚲ "We do not accept unsolicited submissions."

How to Contact Query with SASE. Send queries via snail mail and include an SASE. Target a specific agent. No fax queries. Obtains most new clients through recommendations from others.

Terms Agent receives 15% commission on domestic sales; 20% commission on foreign sales.

ℕ ◐ INTERNATIONAL LITERARY ARTS

RR 5, Box 5391 A, Moscow PA, 18444. E-mail: query@InternationalLiteraryArts.com. Web site: www.InternationalLiteraryArts.com. **Contact:** Pamela K. Brodowsky. Estab. 2000.

> • Prior to her current position, Ms. Fazio worked at Prentice Hall, Random House, M.E. Sharpe and Baker & Taylor; Ms. Brodowsky is a public speaker, as well as the author of *Secrets of Successful Query Letters* and *Bulletproof Book Proposals*.

Member Agents Pamela K. Brodowsky; Evelyn Fazio.

Represents Nonfiction books, movie scripts. **Considers these nonfiction areas:** Biography/autobiography; business/economics; cooking/foods/nutrition; current affairs; health/medicine; history; humor/satire; money/finance; science/technology; self-help/personal improvement; sports; travel; reference, parenting, lifestyle.

- **O–** "ILA is a full service literary property agency representing authors in all areas of nonfiction across the creative spectrum. The agency is committed to the clients it represents and to the publishers with whom we match our talent. Our goal is to provide for our publishers talented authors with long-term career goals. Our mission is to create the continuance of the discovery of new talent and thriving careers for our represented clients." Does not want to receive fiction at this time.

How to Contact Query with SASE. For nonfiction, send an e-mail cover letter, contact info, proposal and sample chapter. Send no e-attachments. Accepts e-mail queries. No fax queries. Responds in 4-6 weeks to queries.

Recent Sales *Planning for Disaster*, by William Ramroth (Kaplan); *PR on a Budget*, by Leonard Saffir (Dearborn Trade); *The Five Jerks You Meet on Earth*, by Ray Zardetto (Andrews McMeel); *How to Raise Kids You Want to Keep*, by Jerry Day (Sourcebooks).

Writers' Conferences BookExpo America.

Tips "If you are inquiring about a nonfiction book project, please address your material to the attention of the Book Department. For screenplays, please address your material to the attention of the Motion Picture Department. Due to the enormous amount of submissions we receive, we will only respond to queries that we feel are a good fit for our agency."

Ⓝ ⊘ Ⓜ INTERNATIONAL TRANSACTIONS, INC.

P.O. Box 420, Wassaic NY 12592. (845)373-9696. Fax: (845)373-7868. E-mail: info@intltrans.com. Web site: www.intltrans.com; www.itincusa.com. **Contact:** Peter Riva. Estab. 1975. Represents 40 clients. 10% of clients are new/unpublished writers. Currently handles: 40% nonfiction books; 45% novels; 5% story collections; 5% juvenile books; 5% scholarly books.

Member Agents Peter Riva (nonfiction, fiction, illustrated; television and movie rights placement); Sandra Riva (fiction, juvenile, biographies); JoAnn Collins (fiction, women's fiction, medical fiction).

Represents Nonfiction books, novels, short story collections, juvenile books, scholarly books, illustrated books, anthologies. **Considers these nonfiction areas:** Anthropology/archaeology; art/architecture/design; biography/autobiography; computers/electronic; cooking/foods/nutrition; current affairs; ethnic/cultural interests; gay/lesbian issues; government/politics/law; health/medicine; history; humor/satire; language/literature/criticism; memoirs; military/war; music/dance; nature/environment; photography; science/technology; self-help/personal improvement; sports; translation; true crime/investigative; women's issues/studies. **Considers these fiction areas:** Action/adventure; detective/police/crime; erotica; experimental; family saga; feminist; gay/lesbian; historical; humor/satire; literary; mainstream/contemporary; mystery/suspense; sports; thriller; young adult; women's/chick lit.

- **O–** "We specialize in large and small projects, helping qualified authors perfect material for publication." Actively seeking intelligent, well-written innovative material that breaks new ground. Does not want to receive material influenced by TV (too much dialogue); a rehash of previous successful novels' themes or poorly prepared material.

How to Contact Query with an outline or synopsis. E-queries preferred. No fax queries. Responds in 2 weeks to queries; 5 weeks to mss. Obtains most new clients through recommendations from others, solicitations.

Recent Sales Sold 12 titles in the last year. *Colt*, by Dennis Adler (Book Sales Inc.); *Penguins*, by Brutus Ostling (HarperCollins); *Road to Damascus*, by Lena Einhorn (Lyons Press); *Tao of Daily Life*, by Derek Lin (Penguin). Other clients include Ake Edwardson, Stieg Larsson, R.L. Wilson, Ulf Nordfjell, Richard Novak, John Enright, Ed Harris, Ron Lealos, Allan Levine, Eric Maisel, Ed Mattingly, Rob Ogus, Paul Popp, Ted Riccardi, Edgar Nicaud, Herb Warden, Eric Caren, Tom Claytor, Chris King, Mark Lender, Maria Riva, Sam Moses, Norstedts Publishing House, Prisma Publishing House, Martin Nweeia, Seren Publishing.

Terms Agent receives 15% (25% on illustrated books) commission on domestic sales; 5% commission on foreign sales. Offers written contract; 180-day notice must be given to terminate contract.

Tips " 'Book'—a published work of literature. That last word is the key. Not a string of words, not a book of (TV or film) 'scenes,' and never a stream of consciousness unfathomable by anyone outside of the writer's coterie. A writer should only begin to get 'interested in getting an agent' if the work is polished, literate and ready to be presented to a publishing house."

Ⓜ J DE S ASSOCIATES, INC.

9 Shagbark Road, Wilson Point, South Norwalk CT 06854. (203)838-7571. **Contact:** Jacques de Spoelberch. Estab. 1975. Represents 50 clients. Currently handles: 50% nonfiction books; 50% novels.

- Prior to opening his agency, Mr. de Spoelberch was an editor with Houghton Mifflin.

Represents Nonfiction books, novels. **Considers these nonfiction areas:** Biography/autobiography; business/economics; current affairs; ethnic/cultural interests; government/politics/law; health/medicine; history; military/war; New Age/metaphysics; self-help/personal improvement; sociology; sports; translation. **Considers these fiction areas:** Detective/police/crime; historical; juvenile; literary; mainstream/contemporary; mystery/suspense; New Age; westerns/frontier; young adult.

How to Contact Query with SASE. Responds in 2 months to queries. Obtains most new clients through recommendations from authors and other clients.

Terms Agent receives 15% commission on domestic sales; 20% commission on foreign sales. Charges clients for foreign postage and photocopying.

⊘ JABBERWOCKY LITERARY AGENCY

P.O. Box 4558, Sunnyside NY 11104-0558. (718)392-5985. Web site: www.awfulagent.com. **Contact:** Joshua Bilmes. Estab. 1994. Member of SFWA. Represents 40 clients. 15% of clients are new/unpublished writers. Currently handles: 15% nonfiction books; 75% novels; 5% scholarly books; 5% other.

Represents Nonfiction books, novels, scholarly books. **Considers these nonfiction areas:** Biography/autobiography; business/economics; cooking/foods/nutrition; current affairs; gay/lesbian issues; government/politics/law; health/medicine; history; humor/satire; language/literature/criticism; military/war; money/finance; nature/environment; popular culture; science/technology; sociology; sports; theater/film; true crime/investigative; women's issues/studies. **Considers these fiction areas:** Action/adventure; contemporary issues; detective/police/crime; ethnic; family saga; fantasy; gay/lesbian; glitz; historical; horror; humor/satire; literary; mainstream/contemporary; psychic/supernatural; regional; science fiction; sports; thriller.

> ○ₓ This agency represents quite a lot of genre fiction and is actively seeking to increase the amount of nonfiction projects. It does not handle juvenile or young adult. Book-length material only—no poetry, articles, or short fiction.

How to Contact Query with SASE. Do not send mss unless requested. No e-mail or fax queries. Considers simultaneous queries. Responds in 2 weeks to queries. Returns materials only with SASE. Obtains most new clients through solicitations, recommendation by current clients.

Recent Sales Sold 30 US and 100 foreign titles in the last year. *All Together Dead*, by Charlaine Harris (Ace); *Command Decision*, by Elizabeth Moon (Del Rey); *Poltergeist*, by Kat Richardson (Ace); *Mistborn* series and *Alcatraz* series, by Brandon Sanderson (Scholastic). Other clients include Simon Green, Tanya Huff, Tobias Buckell.

Terms Agent receives 15% commission on domestic sales; 20% commission on foreign sales. Offers written contract, binding for 1 year. Charges clients for book purchases, photocopying, international book/ms mailing.

Writers' Conferences Malice Domestic; World Fantasy Convention.

Tips "In approaching with a query, the most important things to me are your credits and your biographical background to the extent it's relevant to your work. I (and most agents) will ignore the adjectives you may choose to describe your own work."

⊘ JAMES PETER ASSOCIATES, INC.

P.O. Box 358, New Canaan CT 06840. (203)972-1070. E-mail: gene_brissie@msn.com. **Contact:** Gene Brissie. Estab. 1971. Represents 75 individual and 6 corporate clients. 15% of clients are new/unpublished writers. Currently handles: 100% nonfiction books.

Represents Nonfiction books. **Considers these nonfiction areas:** Anthropology/archaeology; art/architecture/design; biography/autobiography; business/economics; child guidance/parenting; current affairs; ethnic/cultural interests; gay/lesbian issues; government/politics/law; health/medicine; history; language/literature/criticism; memoirs (political, business); military/war; money/finance; music/dance; popular culture; psychology; self-help/personal improvement; theater/film; travel; women's issues/studies.

> ○ₓ "We are especially interested in general, trade and reference nonfiction." Does not want to receive children's/young adult books, poetry or fiction.

How to Contact Submit proposal package, outline, SASE. Prefers to read materials exclusively. No e-mail or fax queries. Responds in 1 month to queries. Returns materials only with SASE. Obtains most new clients through recommendations from others, solicitations, contact with people who are doing interesting things.

Recent Sales Sold 50 titles in the last year. *Nothing to Fear*, by Alan Axelrod (Prentice-Hall); *The Right Way*, by Mark Smith (Regnery); *Churchill's Folly*, by Christopher Catherwood (Carroll & Graf); *The Encyclopedia of Cancer*, by Carol Turkington (Facts on File); *The Lazy Person's Guide to Investing*, by Paul Farrell (Warner Books); *The Subject Is Left-Handed*, by Barney Rosset (Algonquin Books); *It's OK to Be Neurotic*, by Frank Bruno (Adams Media).

Terms Agent receives 15% commission on domestic sales; 20% commission on foreign sales. Offers written contract.

⊘ JCA LITERARY AGENCY

174 Sullivan St., New York NY 10012. (212)807-0888. E-mail: mel@jcalit.com. Web site: www.jcalit.com. **Contact:** Melanie Meyers Cushman. Estab. 1978. Member of AAR. Represents 100 clients.

Member Agents Tom Cushman; Melanie Meyers Cushman; Tony Outhwaite.

Represents Nonfiction books, novels. **Considers these nonfiction areas:** Biography/autobiography; current affairs; government/politics/law; history; language/literature/criticism; memoirs; popular culture; sociology; sports; theater/film; translation; true crime/investigative. **Considers these fiction areas:** Action/adventure; contemporary issues; detective/police/crime; family saga; historical; literary; mainstream/contemporary; mystery/suspense; sports; thriller.

> ⚬ Does not want to receive screenplays, poetry, children's books, science fiction/fantasy or genre romance. Agent receives 15% commission on domestic sales; 20% commission on foreign sales. No written contract.

N ⊘ JET LITERARY ASSOCIATES

2570 Camino San Patricio, Santa Fe NM 87505. (505)474-9139. Fax: (505)474-9139. E-mail: etp@jetliterary.com. Web site: www.jetliterary.com. **Contact:** Liz Trupin-Pulli. Estab. 1975. Represents 75 clients. 35% of clients are new/unpublished writers.

Member Agents Liz Trupin-Pulli (adult and YA fiction/nonfiction; romance, mysteries, parenting); Jim Trupin (adult fiction/nonfiction, military history, pop culture).

Represents Nonfiction books, novels, short story collections. **Considers these nonfiction areas:** Biography/autobiography; business/economics; child guidance/parenting; current affairs; ethnic/cultural interests; gay/lesbian issues; government/politics/law; humor/satire; memoirs; military/war; popular culture; sports; true crime/investigative; women's issues/studies. **Considers these fiction areas:** Action/adventure; detective/police/crime; erotica; ethnic; gay/lesbian; glitz; historical; humor/satire; literary; mainstream/contemporary; mystery/suspense; romance; thriller; young adult; women's.

> ⚬ "JET was founded in New York in 1975, so we bring a wealth of knowledge and contacts, as well as quite a bit of expertise to our representation of writers." Actively seeking women's fiction, mysteries and narrative nonfiction. Does not want to receive sci-fi, fantasy, horror, poetry, children's or religious.

How to Contact An e-query is preferred; if sending by snail mail, include an SASE. No fax queries. Responds in 1 week to queries; 8 weeks to mss. Returns materials only with SASE. Obtains most new clients through recommendations from others, solicitations, conferences.

Recent Sales Sold 20 titles in the last year. *Virtually His*, by Gennita Lowe (MIRA/Harlequin); *Uncontrollable*, by Charlotte Mede (Kensington/BRAVA); *Over Exposéd*, by Joanna Campbell Slan (Midnight Ink); *For Thine Is the Kingdom*, by Sarah Posner (Polipoint Press).

Terms Agent receives 15% commission on domestic sales; 10% commission on foreign sales. Offers written contract, binding for 3 years. This agency charges for reimbursement of mailing and any photocopying.

Writers' Conferences Ozark Creative Writers; Women Writing the West.

Tips "Do not write 'cute' queries—stick to a straightforward message that includes the title and what your book is about, why you are suited to write this particular book, and what you have written in the past (if anything), along with a bit of a bio."

N ♡ CAREN JOHNSON LITERARY AGENCY

132 East 43rd St., No. 216, New York NY 10017. Fax: (718)228-8785. E-mail: carenjla@gmail.com. Web site: www.Cjla.squarespace.com. **Contact:** Caren Johnson. Estab. 2006. Represents 20 clients. 50% of clients are new/unpublished writers. Currently handles: 10% nonfiction books; 70% novels; 20% juvenile books.

> ● Prior to her current position, Ms. Johnson was with Firebrand Literary.

Represents Nonfiction books, novels. **Considers these nonfiction areas:** History; popular culture; science/technology. **Considers these fiction areas:** Detective/police/crime; erotica; ethnic; mainstream/contemporary; mystery/suspense; romance; young adult; women's.

> ⚬ Does not want to receive picture books, plays or screenplays/scripts.

How to Contact Query with SASE, submit outline/proposal, synopsis, 1 sample chapter(s), author bio. This agency only accepts e-queries. Considers simultaneous queries. Responds in 4-6 weeks to queries; 6-8 weeks to mss. Obtains most new clients through recommendations from others.

Recent Sales Sold 15 titles in the last year. This agency prefers not to share information on specific sales. Other clients include A.E. Roman, Kelley St. John, Dianna Love Snell, Caridad Pineiro, Barbara Ferrer, Irene Peterson, Karen Anders, Rob Preece, Stephanie Kuehnert, L. Faye Hughes, Anne Elizabeth, Terri Molina, Lori Avocato, Lee Roland, Jennifer Echols.

Terms Agent receives 15% commission on domestic sales; 20% commission on foreign sales. Offers written contract; 30-day notice must be given to terminate contract. This agency charges for postage and photocopying, though the author is consulted before any charges are incurred.

Writers' Conferences RWA National; Romantic Times Conference; Backspace; BookExpo America; Moonlight and Magnolias.

Ⓝ Ⓜ Ⓞ KELLER MEDIA INC.—FORTHWRITE LITERARY AGENCY AND SPEAKERS BUREAU

23852 West Pacific Coast Hwy., Suite 701, Malibu CA 90265. (310)857-6828. Fax: (310)857-6373. E-mail: query @KellerMedia.com. Web site: www.KellerMedia.com. **Contact:** Wendy Keller, senior editor. Estab. 1989. Member of National Speakers Association. 65% of clients are new/unpublished writers. Currently handles: 100% nonfiction books.

- Prior to becoming an agent, Ms. Keller was an award-winning journalist at PR Newswire and associate editor of a large L.A. County daily paper (until 1984).

Represents Nonfiction books, scholarly books. **Considers these nonfiction areas:** Agriculture/horticulture; animals; anthropology/archaeology; biography/autobiography; business/economics; child guidance/parenting; current affairs; education; ethnic/cultural interests; government/politics/law; health/medicine; history; how-to; language/literature/criticism; memoirs; money/finance; nature/environment; New Age/metaphysics; popular culture; psychology; religious/inspirational; science/technology; self-help/personal improvement; sociology; women's issues/studies. **Considers these fiction areas:** Historical.

- O→ "We focus a great deal of attention on authors who want to also become paid professional speakers, and speakers who want to become authors." Actively seeking nonfiction by highly credible experts, who have or want a significant platform (such as media, syndication, speaking, etc.).

How to Contact Query with SASE, submit proposal package, author bio, the first chapter and whatever is most prescriptive to the book. Include marketing plans. Accepts e-mail and fax queries. Considers simultaneous queries. Responds in 7 days to queries; 2 weeks to mss. Returns materials only with SASE. Obtains most new clients through recommendations from others.

Recent Sales Sold 16 titles in the last year. *Our Own Worst Enemy: Fighting Terrorism From the Oval Office to Your Kitchen Table*, by Col. Randall J. Larsen (Warner Books); *The Top Ten Distinctions Between Millionaires and the Middle Class*, by Keith Cameron Smith (Random House); *Inner Wisdom: Trusting Your Own Intuition in Life, Love and Business*, by Char Margolis (Simon & Schuster); *The Confident Millionaire*, by Kelvin Boston (Wiley).

Terms Agent receives 15% commission on domestic sales; 20% commission on foreign sales.

Tips "Know that the person you're querying really does the type of book you're writing. 80% of what we reject is because it doesn't fit our established, advertised, printed, touted guidelines. Be organized! Have your proposal in order. Never make apologies for 'bad writing' or sloppy content—get it right before you waste your one shot with us. Write a solid proposal."

Ⓜ NATASHA KERN LITERARY AGENCY

P.O. Box 1069, White Salmon WA 98672. (509)493-3803. Web site: www.natashakern.com. **Contact:** Natasha Kern. Estab. 1986. Member of RWA, MWA, SinC.

- Prior to opening her agency, Ms. Kern worked as an editor and publicist for Simon & Schuster, Bantam, and Ballantine. "This agency has sold more than 700 books."

Represents Adult commercial nonfiction and fiction. **Considers these nonfiction areas:** Animals; child guidance/parenting; current affairs; ethnic/cultural interests; gardening; health/medicine; nature/environment; New Age/metaphysics; popular culture; psychology; religious/inspirational; self-help/personal improvement; spirituality; women's issues/studies; investigative journalism. **Considers these fiction areas:** Women's; chick lit; lady lit; romance (contemporary, historical); historical; mainstream/contemporary; multicultural; mystery/suspense; religious/inspirational; thriller.

- O→ This agency specializes in commercial fiction and nonfiction for adults. "We are a full-service agency." Does not represent sports, true crime, scholarly works, coffee table books, war memoirs, software, scripts, literary fiction, photography, poetry, short stories, children's, horror, fantasy, genre science fiction, stage plays, or traditional westerns.

How to Contact See submission instructions online. Query with submission history, writing credits and length of ms. Don't include SASE. Considers simultaneous queries. Responds in 3 weeks to queries.

Recent Sales Sold 56 titles in the last year. *China Dolls*, by Michelle Yu and Blossom Kan (St. Martin's); *Bastard Tongues*, by Derek Bickerton (Farrar Strauss); *Bone Rattler*, by Eliot Pattison; *Wicked Pleasure*, by Nina Bangs (Berkley); *Inviting God In*, by David Aaron (Shambhala); *Perfect Killer*, by Lewis Perdue (Tor); *Unlawful Contact*, by Pamela Clare (Berkley); *Dead End Dating*, by Kimberly Raye (Ballantine); *A Scent of Roses*, by Nikki Arana (Baker Book House); *The Sexiest Man Alive*, by Diana Holquist (Warner Books).

Terms Agent receives 15% commission on domestic sales; 20% commission on foreign sales; 15% commission on dramatic rights sales.

Writers' Conferences RWA National Conference; MWA National Conference; ACFW Conference; and many regional conferences.

Tips "Your chances of being accepted for representation will be greatly enhanced by going to our Web site first. If we know what you need and want, we can help you achieve it. A dream client has a storytelling gift, a commitment to a writing career, a desire to learn and grow, and a passion for excellence. This client understands that many people have to work together for a book to succeed and that everything in publishing takes far longer than one imagines. Trust and communication are truly essential.''

☑ LOUISE B. KETZ AGENCY

1485 First Ave., Suite 4B, New York NY 10021-1363. (212)535-9259. Fax: (212)249-3103. E-mail: ketzagency@aol.com. **Contact:** Louise B. Ketz. Estab. 1983. Represents 25 clients. 15% of clients are new/unpublished writers. Currently handles: 100% nonfiction books.

Represents Nonfiction books. **Considers these nonfiction areas:** Current affairs; history; military/war; science/technology; economics.

  ○→ This agency specializes in science, history and reference.

How to Contact Query with SASE, submit outline, 1 sample chapter, author bio (with qualifications for authorship of work). Responds in 6 weeks to mss. Obtains most new clients through recommendations from others, idea development.

Terms Agent receives 15% commission on domestic sales.

◑ VIRGINIA KIDD AGENCY, INC.

538 E. Harford St., P.O. Box 278, Milford PA 18337. (570)296-6205. Fax: (570)296-7266. Web site: www.vk-agency.com. Estab. 1965. Member of SFWA, SFRA. Represents 80 clients.

Member Agents Christine Cohen; Vaughne Hansen.

Represents Novels. **Considers these fiction areas:** Fantasy; historical; mystery/suspense; science fiction; women's; speculative; mainstream.

  ○→ This agency specializes in science fiction and fantasy.

How to Contact Submit synopsis (1-3 pages), cover letter, first chapter, SASE. Responds in 4-6 weeks to queries.

Recent Sales *Sagramanda*, by Alan Dean Foster (Pyr); *Incredible Good Fortune*, by Ursula K. Le Guin (Shambhala); *The Wizard* and *Soldier of Sidon*, by Gene Wolfe (Tor); *Voices* and *Powers*, by Ursula K. Le Guin (Harcourt); *Galileo's Children*, by Gardner Dozois (Pyr); *The Light Years Beneath My Feet* and *Running From the Deity*, by Alan Dean Foster (Del Ray); *Chasing Fire*, by Michelle Welch. Other clients include Eleanor Arnason, Ted Chiang, Jack Skillingstead, Daryl Gregory, Nick DiChario, Patricia Briggs, and the estates for James Tiptree Jr., Murray Leinster, E.E. ''Doc'' Smith, R.A. Lafferty.

Terms Agent receives 15% commission on domestic sales; 20-25% commission on foreign sales; 20% commission on dramatic rights sales. Offers written contract; 2-month notice must be given to terminate contract. Charges clients occasionally for extraordinary expenses.

Tips ''If you have a completed novel that is of extraordinary quality, please send us a query.''

◎ KIRCHOFF/WOHLBERG, INC., AUTHORS' REPRESENTATION DIVISION

866 United Nations Plaza, #525, New York NY 10017. (212)644-2020. Fax: (212)223-4387. **Contact:** Liza Pulitzer Voges. Estab. 1930s. Member of AAR, AAP, Society of Illustrators, SPAR, Bookbuilders of Boston, New York Bookbinders' Guild, AIGA. Represents 50 clients. 10% of clients are new/unpublished writers. Currently handles: 5% nonfiction books; 25% novels; 5% young adult; 65% picture books.

  • Kirchoff/Wohlberg has been in business for more than 60 years..

  ○→ This agency specializes in only juvenile through young adult trade books.

How to Contact For novels, query with SASE, outline, a few sample chapters. For picture books, send entire ms, SASE. No e-mail or fax queries. Considers simultaneous queries. Responds in 1 month to queries; 2 months to mss. Returns materials only with SASE. Obtains most new clients through recommendations from authors, illustrators, and editors.

Recent Sales Sold more than 50 titles in the last year. *Dizzy*, by Jonah Winter (Scholastic); *Homework Machine*, by Dan Gutman (Simon and Schuster); Princess Power series, by Suzanne Williams (HarperCollins); My Weird School series, by Dan Gutman (HarperCollins); *Biscuit*, by Alyssa Capucilli (HarperCollins).

Terms Offers written contract, binding for at least 1 year. Agent receives standard commission, depending upon whether it is an author only, illustrator only, or an author/illustrator book.

🅽 ◑ KLEINWORKS AGENCY

2814 Brooks Ave., No. 635, Missoula MT 59801. E-mail: judyklein@kleinworks.com. Web site: www.kleinworks.com. **Contact:** Judy Klein. Estab. 2005. Represents 10 clients. Currently handles: 25% nonfiction books; 50% novels; 25% juvenile books.

  • Prior to becoming an agent, Ms. Klein spent a dozen years with Farrar, Straus & Giroux; she also held the position of editor-in-chief at The Literary Guild Book Club and later, at Booksonline.com.

Represents Nonfiction books, novels. **Considers these nonfiction areas:** Biography/autobiography; business/economics; health/medicine; how-to; memoirs; money/finance; nature/environment; popular culture; self-help/personal improvement. **Considers these fiction areas:** Ethnic; experimental; humor/satire; literary; young adult; women's/chick lit.

> ☞ "Kleinworks Agency may be geographically removed from the red-hot center of New York publishing, but our credentials and connections keep us close to New York's best publishers and editors. As a publishing veteran with two decades of book experience, intimate knowledge of the industry and expertise in domestic and international negotiations, I provide my clients with an edge in getting their books published well. Kleinworks offers dedicated services to a small, select group of writers and publishers so that we can guarantee spirited and undivided attention."

How to Contact Query with SASE, submit proposal package, outline/proposal, synopsis, author bio, sample chapters. No phone queries. Accepts e-mail and fax queries. Considers simultaneous queries. Responds in 2-3 weeks to queries; 1-2 months to mss. Returns materials only with SASE. Obtains most new clients through recommendations from others.

Recent Sales This agency prefers not to share information on specific sales.

Terms Agent receives 15% commission on domestic sales; 20% commission on foreign sales. Offers written contract, binding for optional, for 1 year; 3-month notice must be given to terminate contract. Charges for postage and photocopying fees after six months.

Writers' Conferences Montana Festival of the Book, Yellowstone Nature Writers' Field Conference.

▣ HARVEY KLINGER, INC.

300 W. 55th St., New York NY 10019. (212)581-7068. E-mail: queries@harveyklinger.com. Web site: www.harveyklinger.com. **Contact:** Harvey Klinger. Estab. 1977. Member of AAR. Represents 100 clients. 25% of clients are new/unpublished writers. Currently handles: 50% nonfiction books; 50% novels.

Member Agents David Dunton (popular culture, music-related books, literary fiction, crime novels, thrillers); Sara Crowe (children's and young adult authors, adult fiction and nonfiction, foreign rights sales); Andrea Somberg (literary fiction, commercial fiction, romance, sci-fi/fantasy, mysteries/thrillers, young adult, middle grade, quality narrative nonfiction, popular culture, how-to, self-help, humor, interior design, cookbooks, health/fitness); Nikki Van De Car (science fiction/fantasy, horror, romance, literary fiction, popular culture, how-to, memoir).

Represents Nonfiction books, novels. **Considers these nonfiction areas:** Biography/autobiography; cooking/foods/nutrition; health/medicine; psychology; science/technology; self-help/personal improvement; spirituality; sports; true crime/investigative; women's issues/studies. **Considers these fiction areas:** Action/adventure; detective/police/crime; family saga; glitz; literary; mainstream/contemporary; mystery/suspense; thriller.

> ☞ This agency specializes in big, mainstream, contemporary fiction and nonfiction.

How to Contact Query with SASE. No phone or fax queries. Accepts e-mail queries. No fax queries. Responds in 2 months to queries and mss. Obtains most new clients through recommendations from others.

Recent Sales *Breakable You*, By Brian Morton; *The Money In You!*, by Julie Stav; *The Mercy Seller*, by Brenda Vantrease; *A Country Music Christmas*, by Edie Hand and Buddy Killen; *Keep Climbing*, by Sean Swarner; *The Cubicle Survival Guide*, by James F. Thompson; *Cookie Sensations*, by Meaghan Mountford; *Stranger*, by Justine Musk; *Laird Of The Mist*, by Paula Quinn. Other clients include Barbara Wood, Terry Kay, Barbara De Angelis, Jeremy Jackson.

Terms Agent receives 15% commission on domestic sales; 25% commission on foreign sales. Offers written contract. Charges for photocopying mss and overseas postage for mss.

▣ KNEERIM & WILLIAMS

225 Franklin St., Boston MA 02110. (617)542-5070. Fax: (617)542-8906. Web site: www.fr.com/kwfr. **Contact:** Melissa Grella. Estab. 1990. Represents 200 clients. 5% of clients are new/unpublished writers. Currently handles: 80% nonfiction books; 15% novels; 5% movie scripts.

> ● Prior to becoming an agent, Mr. Williams was a lawyer; Ms. Kneerim was a publisher and editor; Mr. Wasserman was an editor and journalist.

Member Agents John Taylor Williams; Jill Kneerim; Steve Wasserman; Bretthe Bloom.

Represents Nonfiction books, novels. **Considers these nonfiction areas:** Anthropology/archaeology; biography/autobiography; business/economics; child guidance/parenting; current affairs; government/politics/law; health/medicine; history; language/literature/criticism; memoirs; nature/environment; popular culture; psychology; religious/inspirational; science/technology; sociology; sports; women's issues/studies. **Considers these fiction areas:** Historical; literary; mainstream/contemporary.

> ☞ This agency specializes in narrative nonfiction, history, science, business, women's issues, commercial and literary fiction, film, and television. "We have 7 agents and 2 scouts in Boston, New York, and Santa Fe." Actively seeking distinguished authors, experts, professionals, intellectuals, and serious writers. Does not want to receive blanket multiple submissions, genre fiction, children's literature, or original screenplays.

How to Contact Query with SASE. Responds in 2 weeks to queries; 2 months to mss. Returns materials only with SASE. Obtains most new clients through recommendations from others.

Recent Sales *Frank Gehry and the Bilbao Museum*, by Nicolai Ouroussoff (Basic); *Nuclear Terrorism*, by Graham Allison (Times Books); *Beggar at the Gate*, by Thalassa Ali (Bantam); *The Future of Life*, by E.O. Wilson (Knopf); *Savage Mountain: The Women of K2*, by Jennifer Jordan (Morrow).

☻ LINDA KONNER LITERARY AGENCY

10 W. 15th St., Suite 1918, New York NY 10011-6829. (212)691-3419. E-mail: ldkonner@cs.com. **Contact:** Linda Konner. Estab. 1996. Member of AAR, ASJA; signatory of WGA. Represents 85 clients. 30-35% of clients are new/unpublished writers. Currently handles: 100% nonfiction books.

Represents Nonfiction books. **Considers these nonfiction areas:** Biography/autobiography (celebrity); gay/lesbian issues; health/medicine (diet/nutrition/fitness); how-to; money/finance (personal finance); popular culture; psychology; self-help/personal improvement; women's issues; African American and Latino issues; business; parenting; relationships.

O⊷ This agency specializes in health, self-help, and how-to books.

How to Contact Query with SASE, synopsis, author bio, sufficient return postage. Prefers to read materials exclusively for 2 weeks. Considers simultaneous queries. Obtains most new clients through recommendations from others, occasional solicitation among established authors/journalists.

Recent Sales Sold 30 titles in the last year. *The Modern Bride Survival Guide*, by the editors of *Modern Bride Magazine* (Wiley); *The 7-Step Diabetes Fitness Plan*, by Sheri Colberg (Avalon); *Chuck That Schmuck: From Doormat to Diva in 6 Weeks*, by Debra Mandel (HarperCollins).

Terms Agent receives 15% commission on domestic sales; 25% commission on foreign sales. Offers written contract. Charges $85 one-time fee for domestic expenses; additional expenses may be incurred for foreign sales.

Writers' Conferences ASJA Writers Conference.

☻ ELAINE KOSTER LITERARY AGENCY, LLC

55 Central Park W., Suite 6, New York NY 10023. (212)362-9488. Fax: (212)712-0164. **Contact:** Elaine Koster, Stephanie Lehmann. Member of AAR, MWA; Author's Guild, Women's Media Group. Represents 40 clients. 10% of clients are new/unpublished writers. Currently handles: 30% nonfiction books; 70% novels.

● Prior to opening her agency in 1998, Ms. Koster was president and publisher of Dutton NAL, part of the Penguin Group.

Represents Nonfiction books, novels. **Considers these nonfiction areas:** Biography/autobiography; business/economics; child guidance/parenting; cooking/foods/nutrition; current affairs; ethnic/cultural interests; health/medicine; history; how-to; money/finance; nature/environment; popular culture; psychology; self-help/personal improvement; spirituality; women's issues/studies. **Considers these fiction areas:** Contemporary issues; detective/police/crime; ethnic; family saga; feminist; historical; literary; mainstream/contemporary; mystery/suspense (amateur sleuth, cozy, culinary, malice domestic); regional; thriller; young adult; chick lit.

O⊷ This agency specializes in quality fiction and nonfiction. Does not want to receive juvenile, screenplays, or science fiction.

How to Contact Query with SASE, outline, 3 sample chapters. Prefers to read materials exclusively. No e-mail or fax queries. Responds in 3 weeks to queries; 1 month to mss. Returns materials only with SASE. Obtains most new clients through recommendations from others.

Recent Sales Sold 50 titles in the last year. *The Opposite of Love*, by Julie Buxbaum (Dial Press); *Secret Sins*, by Francis Ray (St. Martin's); *No One Needs a Husband Seven Days a Week*, by Nina Foxx (Avon).

Terms Agent receives 15% commission on domestic sales. Bills back specific expenses incurred doing business for a client.

Tips "We prefer exclusive submissions. Don't e-mail or fax submissions. Please include biographical information and publishing history."

☻ BARBARA S. KOUTS, LITERARY AGENT

P.O. Box 560, Bellport NY 11713. (631)286-1278. Fax: (631) 286-1538. **Contact:** Barbara Kouts. Estab. 1980. Member of AAR. Represents 50 clients. 10% of clients are new/unpublished writers.

Represents Juvenile books.

O⊷ This agency specializes in children's books.

How to Contact Query with SASE. Considers simultaneous queries. Responds in 1 week to queries; 2 months to mss. Obtains most new clients through recommendations from others, solicitations, conferences.

Terms Agent receives 10% commission on domestic sales; 20% commission on foreign sales. This agency charges clients for photocopying.

Tips "Write, do not call. Be professional in your writing."

☑ KRAAS LITERARY AGENCY

E-mail: irene@kraasliteraryagency.com. Web site: www.kraasliteraryagency.com. **Contact:** Irene Kraas. Estab. 1990. Represents 40 clients. 75% of clients are new/unpublished writers. Currently handles: 5% nonfiction books; 95% novels.

Member Agents Irene Kraas, principal (psychological thrillers, medical thrillers, literary fiction, young adult).

☞ Actively seeking books that are well written with commercial potential. No short stories, plays or poetry.

How to Contact Please refer to this agency's Web site, as its submission guidelines are in flux. No e-mail or fax queries. Considers simultaneous queries. Returns materials only with SASE.

Recent Sales See Web site for a list of recent sales. Offers written contract.

Writers' Conferences Southwest Writers Conference, Wrangling with Writing.

Tips "Material by unpublished authors will be accepted in the above areas only. Pay attention to the submission guidelines as they apply to all submissions."

☒ ☑ BERT P. KRAGES

6665 SW Hampton St., Suite 200, Portland OR 97223. (503)597-2525. E-mail: krages@onemain.com. Web site: www.krages.com. **Contact:** Bert Krages. Estab. 2001. Represents 10 clients. 80% of clients are new/unpublished writers. Currently handles: 95% nonfiction books; 5% scholarly books.

● Mr. Krages is also an attorney.

Represents Nonfiction books. **Considers these nonfiction areas:** Agriculture/horticulture; animals; anthropology/archaeology; art/architecture/design; biography/autobiography; business/economics; child guidance/parenting; computers/electronic; current affairs; education; ethnic/cultural interests; health/medicine; history; memoirs; military/war; nature/environment; psychology; science/technology; self-help/personal improvement; sociology.

☞ "I handle a small number of literary clients and concentrate on trade nonfiction (science, history)."

How to Contact Submit a book proposal. Considers simultaneous queries. Responds in 1-6 weeks to queries. Obtains most new clients through solicitations. Sold 2 titles in the last year.

Terms Agent receives 15% commission on domestic sales; 20% commission on foreign sales. Offers written contract, binding for 1 year; 60-day notice must be given to terminate contract. Charges for photocopying and postage only if the book is placed.

Tips "Read at least 2 books on how to prepare book proposals before sending material. An extremely well-prepared proposal will make your material stand out."

☑ STUART KRICHEVSKY LITERARY AGENCY, INC.

381 Park Ave. S., Suite 914, New York NY 10016. (212)725-5288. Fax: (212)725-5275. E-mail: query@skagency.com. Member of AAR.

Member Agents Stuart Krichevsky; Shana Cohen (science fiction, fantasy); Kathryne Wick.

Represents Nonfiction books, novels.

How to Contact Submit query, synopsis, 1 sample page via e-mail (no attachments). Snail mail queries also acceptable. No fax queries. Obtains most new clients through recommendations from others, solicitations.

Recent Sales *Untitled*, by C.J. Chivers (Simon & Schuster); *American Islam*, by Paul M. Barrett (Farrar, Straus and Giroux); *The Nabokov's Nutcracker: Knowing and Loving the Parts of Speech*, by Ben Yagoda (Broadway Books).

☒ ◎ EDITE KROLL LITERARY AGENCY, INC.

20 Cross St., Saco ME 04072. (207)283-8797. Fax: (207)283-8799. E-mail: ekroll@maine.rr.com. **Contact:** Edite Kroll. Estab. 1981. Represents 45 clients. 20% of clients are new/unpublished writers. Currently handles: 40% nonfiction books; 5% novels; 40% juvenile books; 5% scholarly books; 10% commercial/merchandising.

● Prior to opening her agency, Ms. Kroll served as a book editor and translator.

Represents Nonfiction books, novels (very selective), juvenile books, scholarly books. **Considers these nonfiction areas:** Biography/autobiography; current affairs; ethnic/cultural interests; gay/lesbian issues; government/politics/law; health/medicine (no diet books); humor/satire; juvenile nonfiction (selectively); memoirs (selectively); popular culture; psychology; religious/inspirational (selectively); self-help/personal improvement (selectively); women's issues/studies; issue-oriented nonfiction. **Considers these fiction areas:** Juvenile; picture books; young adult; middle grade.

☞ "We represent writers and writer-artists of both adult and children's books. We have a special focus on international feminist writers, women writers and artists who write their own books (including children's and humor books)." Actively seeking artists who write their own books and international feminists who write in English. Does not want to receive genre (mysteries, thrillers, diet, cookery, etc.), photography books, coffee table books, romance or commercial fiction.

How to Contact Query with SASE, submit outline/proposal, synopsis, 1-2 sample chapter(s), author bio, entire ms if sending picture book. No phone queries. Accepts e-mail and fax queries. Responds in 2-4 weeks to queries; 4-8 weeks to mss. Returns materials only with SASE. Obtains most new clients through recommendations from others.

Recent Sales Sold 13 domestic/10 foreign titles in the last year. This agency prefers not to share information on specific sales. Other clients include Shel Silverstein Estate, Suzy Becker, Geoffrey Hayes, Henrik Drescher, Charlotte Kasl, Gloria Skurzynski.

Terms Agent receives 15% commission on domestic sales; 20% commission on foreign sales. Offers written contract; 30-day notice must be given to terminate contract. Charges clients for photocopying and legal fees with prior approval from writer.

Tips ''Please do your research so you won't send me books/proposals I specifically excluded.''

☐ KT PUBLIC RELATIONS & LITERARY SERVICES

1905 Cricklewood Cove, Fogelsville PA 18051. (610)395-6298. Fax: (610)395-6299. E-mail: kae@ktpublicrelations.com or jon@ktpublicrelations.com. Web site: www.ktpublicrelations.com. **Contact:** Kae Tienstra, Jon Tienstra. Estab. 2005. Represents 12 clients. 75% of clients are new/unpublished writers. Currently handles: 50% nonfiction books; 50% novels.

- Prior to becoming an agent, Ms. Tienstra was publicity director for Rodale, Inc. for 13 years and then founded her own publicity agency; Mr. Tienstra joined the firm in 1995 with varied corporate experience and a master's degree in library science.

Member Agents Kae Tienstra (health, parenting, psychology, how-to, crafts, foods/nutrition, beauty, women's fiction, general fiction); Jon Tienstra (nature/environment, history, cooking/foods/nutrition, war/military, automotive, health/medicine, gardening, general fiction, science fiction/fantasy, popular fiction).

Represents Nonfiction books, novels, novellas. **Considers these nonfiction areas:** Agriculture/horticulture; animals; child guidance/parenting; cooking/foods/nutrition; crafts/hobbies; health/medicine; history; how-to; military/war; nature/environment; popular culture; psychology; science/technology; self-help/personal improvement; interior design/decorating. **Considers these fiction areas:** Action/adventure; detective/police/crime; family saga; fantasy; historical; literary; mainstream/contemporary; mystery/suspense; romance; science fiction; thriller.

> ⟳ Specializes in parenting, history, cooking/foods/nutrition, crafts, beauty, war, health/medicine, psychology, how-to, gardening, science fiction, fantasy, women's fiction, and popular fiction. Does not want to see unprofessional material.

How to Contact Query with SASE. Accepts e-mail and fax queries. Considers simultaneous queries. Responds in 2 weeks to queries; 3 months to mss. Returns materials only with SASE. Obtains most new clients through recommendations from others.

Terms Agent receives 15% commission on domestic sales; 20% commission on foreign sales. Offers written contract. Charges clients for long-distance phone calls, fax, postage, photocopying (only when incurred). No advance payment for these out-of-pocket expenses.

◑ THE LA LITERARY AGENCY

P.O. Box 46370, Los Angeles CA 90046. (323)654-5288. E-mail: laliteraryag@aol.com. **Contact:** Ann Cashman, Eric Lasher. Estab. 1980.

- Prior to becoming an agent, Mr. Lasher worked in publishing in New York and Los Angeles.

Represents Nonfiction books, novels. **Considers these nonfiction areas:** Animals; anthropology/archaeology; art/architecture/design; biography/autobiography; business/economics; child guidance/parenting; cooking/foods/nutrition; current affairs; ethnic/cultural interests; government/politics/law; health/medicine; history; how-to; nature/environment; popular culture; psychology; science/technology; self-help/personal improvement; sociology; sports; true crime/investigative; women's issues/studies; narrative nonfiction. **Considers these fiction areas:** Action/adventure; detective/police/crime; family saga; feminist; historical; literary; mainstream/contemporary; sports; thriller.

How to Contact Query with SASE, outline, 1 sample chapter. No e-mail or fax queries.

Recent Sales *Full Bloom: The Art and Life of Georgia O'Keeffe,* by Hunter Drohojowska-Philp (Norton); *And the Walls Came Tumbling Down,* by H. Caldwell (Scribner); *Italian Slow & Savory,* by Joyce Goldstein (Chronicle); *A Field Guide to Chocolate Chip Cookies,* by Dede Wilson (Harvard Common Press); *Teen Knitting Club* (Artisan); *The Framingham Heart Study,* by Dr. Daniel Levy (Knopf).

Ⓝ ◐ LADNERBOND LITERARY MANAGEMENT

12A Longfellow Ave., Brunswick ME 04011. (207)841-9634. E-mail: query@ladnerbondlm.com. Web site: ladnerbondlm.com. **Contact:** Christopher Ladner. Estab. 2002; adheres to AAR canon of ethics.

- Prior to his current position, Mr. Ladner began his career in publishing as an associate at Writers House.

Represents Nonfiction books, novels. **Considers these nonfiction areas:** Biography/autobiography; health/medicine; history; memoirs; popular culture; sports; lifestyle.

O→ Actively seeking nonfiction.

How to Contact Query with SASE, submit author bio, description of the project and a complete outline. This agency is only seeking nonfiction queries currently. Accepts e-mail queries. No fax queries. Responds in 4 weeks to queries; 6-8 weeks to mss. Returns materials only with SASE. Obtains most new clients through recommendations from others, solicitations.

Recent Sales *Smart Moves: Career Lessons from Liberal Arts Graduates*, by Sheila Curran and Suzanne Greenwald (Ten Speed Press); *Summer Snow*, by William Hathaway (Avatar Publications).

Tips "While we supply our clients with project development and editorial expertise, we expect that all prospective work has undergone scrupulous revison or professional editing prior to our consideration."

N ⬤ ALBERT LaFARGE LITERARY AGENCY

Fax: (270)512-5179. E-mail: lafargeliterary@gmail.com. **Contact:** Albert LaFarge. Estab. 2003. Represents 24 clients. 50% of clients are new/unpublished writers. Currently handles: 90% nonfiction books; 10% novels.

• Prior to becoming an agent, Mr. LaFarge was an editor.

Represents Nonfiction books, novels. **Considers these nonfiction areas:** Art/architecture/design; biography/autobiography; current affairs; health/medicine; history; memoirs; music/dance; nature/environment; photography; psychology; sports. **Considers these fiction areas:** Literary.

O→ This agency specializes in helping clients to develop nonfiction.

How to Contact Query with SASE, submit outline and sample chapters. Accepts e-mail queries. No fax queries. Obtains most new clients through recommendations from others.

Recent Sales This agency prefers not to share information on specific sales.

Terms Agent receives 15% commission on domestic sales; 20% commission on foreign sales. No written contract. Charges for photocopying.

⬤ PETER LAMPACK AGENCY, INC.

551 Fifth Ave., Suite 1613, New York NY 10176-0187. (212)687-9106. Fax: (212)687-9109. E-mail: alampack@verizon.net. **Contact:** Andrew Lampack. Estab. 1977. Represents 50 clients. 10% of clients are new/unpublished writers. Currently handles: 20% nonfiction books; 80% novels.

Member Agents Peter Lampack (president); Rema Delanyan (foreign rights); Andrew Lampack (new writers).

Represents Nonfiction books, novels. **Considers these fiction areas:** Action/adventure; detective/police/crime; family saga; historical; literary; mainstream/contemporary; mystery/suspense; thriller; contemporary relationships.

O→ This agency specializes in commercial fiction and nonfiction by recognized experts. Actively seeking literary and commercial fiction, thrillers, mysteries, suspense, and psychological thrillers. Does not want to receive horror, romance, science fiction, westerns, historical literary fiction or academic material.

How to Contact Query with SASE. *No unsolicited mss.* Accepts e-mail queries. No fax queries. Considers simultaneous queries. Responds in 2 months to queries and mss. Obtains most new clients through referrals made by clients.

Recent Sales *Inner Workings*, by J.M. Coetzee; *Treasure of Kahn*, by Clive Cussler and Dick Cussler; *Skeleton Coast*, by Clive Cussler and Jack Du Brul; *The Navigator*, by Clive Cussler with Paul Kemprecos; *Dust*, by Martha Grimes; *Bloodthirsty Bitches and Pious Pimps of Power*, by Gerry Spence.

Terms Agent receives 15% commission on domestic sales; 20% commission on foreign sales.

Writers' Conferences BookExpo America.

Tips "Submit only your best work for consideration. Have a very specific agenda of goals you wish your prospective agent to accomplish for you. Provide the agent with a comprehensive statement of your credentials—educational and professional."

⬤ LAURA LANGLIE, LITERARY AGENT

239 Carroll St., Garden Apartment, Brooklyn NY 11231. (718)855-8102. Fax: (718)855-4450. E-mail: laura@lauralanglie.com. **Contact:** Laura Langlie. Estab. 2001. Represents 25 clients. 50% of clients are new/unpublished writers. Currently handles: 25% nonfiction books; 48% novels; 2% story collections; 25% juvenile books.

• Prior to opening her agency, Ms. Langlie worked in publishing for 7 years and as an agent at Kidde, Hoyt & Picard for 6 years.

Represents Nonfiction books, novels, short story collections, novellas, juvenile books. **Considers these nonfiction areas:** Animals (not how-to); anthropology/archaeology; biography/autobiography; current affairs; ethnic/cultural interests; gay/lesbian issues; government/politics/law; history; humor/satire; memoirs; nature/environment; popular culture; psychology; theater/film; women's issues/studies; history of medicine and science; language/literature. **Considers these fiction areas:** Detective/police/crime; ethnic; feminist; gay/lesbian; historical; humor/satire; juvenile; literary; mystery/suspense; romance; thriller; young adult; mainstream.

o—¬ "I love working with first-time authors. I'm very involved with and committed to my clients. I also employ a publicist to work with all my clients to make the most of each book's publication. Most of my clients come to me via recommendations from other agents, clients and editors. I've met very few at conferences. I've often sought out writers for projects, and I still find new clients via the traditional query letter." Does not want to receive children's picture books, science fiction, poetry, men's adventure or erotica.

How to Contact Query with SASE. Accepts queries via fax. Considers simultaneous queries. Responds in 1 week to queries; 1 month to mss. Returns materials only with SASE. Obtains most new clients through recommendations, submissions.

Recent Sales Sold 30 titles in the last year. *Pants on Fire* by Meg Cabot (HarperCollins Children's); *It's About Your Husband*, by Lauren Lipton (Warner Books); *Price of Admission*, by Leslie Margolis (Simon Pulse); *Island of the Lost*, by Joan Druett (Algonguin Books of Chapel Hill). Other clients include Renee Ashley, Mignon F. Ballard, Jessica Benson, Jack El-Hai, Sarah Elliott, Fiona Gibson, Robin Hathaway, Melanie Lynne Hauser, Mary Hogan, Jonathan Neale, Eric Pinder, Delia Ray, Cheryl L. Reed, Jennifer Sturman.

Terms Agent receives 15% commission on domestic sales; 20% commission on foreign sales. No written contract.

Tips "Be complete, forthright and clear in your communications. Do your research as to what a particular agent represents."

[N] ☑ LANGTONS INTERNATIONAL AGENCY

240 West 35th St., Suite 500, New York NY 10001. (212)929-1937. E-mail: langtonsinternational@gmail.com. Web site: www.langtonsinternational.com. **Contact:** Linda Langton.

• Prior to becoming an agent, Ms. Langton was a founding director of the international greeting card and calendar company, The Ink Group.

Represents Nonfiction books, novels.

o—¬ "Langtons International Agency is a multi-media literary and licensing agency specializing in nonfiction, thrillers and children's books as well as the the visual world of photography, illustrative art, gift books, calendars, greeting cards, posters and other related products."

How to Contact Query with SASE, submit outline/proposal, synopsis, publishing history, author bio. Only published authors should query this agency. No fax queries. Considers simultaneous queries.

Recent Sales *The Great Expectations School*, by Daniel Brown (Arcade); the Beatle Mania books, by Hal Pollack; *Cockpit From Hell*, by Dror Rishpy; *Spies*, by Yossi Melman and Eitan Habber; *Celebutante*, by Kira Coplin.

☑ MICHAEL LARSEN/ELIZABETH POMADA, LITERARY AGENTS

1029 Jones St., San Francisco CA 94109-5023. (415)673-0939. E-mail: larsenpoma@aol.com. Web site: www.larsen-pomada.com. **Contact:** Mike Larsen, Elizabeth Pomada. Estab. 1972. Member of AAR, Authors Guild, ASJA, PEN, WNBA, California Writers Club, National Speakers Association. Represents 100 clients. 40-45% of clients are new/unpublished writers. Currently handles: 70% nonfiction books; 30% novels.

• Prior to opening their agency, Mr. Larsen and Ms. Pomada were promotion executives for major publishing houses. Mr. Larsen worked for Morrow, Bantam and Pyramid (now part of Berkley); Ms. Pomada worked at Holt, David McKay and The Dial Press. Mr. Larsen is the author of the third editions of *How to Write a Book Proposal* and *How to Get a Literary Agent*.

Member Agents Michael Larsen (nonfiction); Elizabeth Pomada (fiction, narrative nonfiction, nonfiction for women); Laurie McLean, laurie@agentsavant.com (fantasy, science, romance, middle-grade and YA fiction).

Represents Adult book-length fiction and nonfiction that will interest New York publishers or are irresistibly written or conceived. **Considers these nonfiction areas:** Anthropology/archaeology; art/architecture/design; biography/autobiography; business/economics; cooking/foods/nutrition; current affairs; ethnic/cultural interests; gay/lesbian issues; government/politics/law; health/medicine; history; how-to; humor/satire; memoirs; money/finance; music/dance; nature/environment; New Age/metaphysics; popular culture; psychology; religious/inspirational; science/technology; self-help/personal improvement; sociology; sports; theater/film; travel; true crime/investigative; women's issues/studies; futurism. **Considers these fiction areas:** Action/adventure; contemporary issues; detective/police/crime; ethnic; experimental; family saga; fantasy; feminist; gay/lesbian; glitz; historical; humor/satire; literary; mainstream/contemporary; mystery/suspense; religious/inspirational; romance (contemporary, gothic, historical); chick lit.

o—¬ "We have diverse tastes. We look for fresh voices and new ideas. We handle literary, commercial and genre fiction, and the full range of nonfiction books." Actively seeking commercial, genre and literary fiction. Does not want to receive children's books, plays, short stories, screenplays, pornography, poetry or stories of abuse.

How to Contact Query with SASE, submit first 10 pages of completed novel, 2-page synopsis, SASE. Make sure the query is 1 page. For nonfiction, send a promotion plan done according to the advice on the Web site. Accepts e-mail queries. No fax queries. Responds in 2 weeks to queries; 2 months to mss.

Recent Sales Sold at least 15 titles in the last year. *Banana Hear Summer*, by Merlinda Bobis (Bantam); *Guerilla Marketing: Secrets for Making Big Profits from Your Small Business, 4th edition*, by Jay Levinson (Houghton Mifflin); *The Tender Carnivore: How to Be a Thoughtful Meat-Eater*, by Catherine Friend (Marlowe).

Terms Agent receives 15% commission on domestic sales; 20% (30% for Asia) commission on foreign sales. May charge for printing, postage for multiple submissions, foreign mail, foreign phone calls, galleys, books, legal fees.

Writers' Conferences BookExpo America; Santa Barbara Writers' Conference; San Francisco Writers' Conference.

Tips ''We love helping writers get the rewards and recognition they deserve. If you can write books that meet the needs of the marketplace and you can promote your books, now is the best time ever to be a writer. We must find new writers to make a living, so we are very eager to hear from new writers whose work will interest large houses, and nonfiction writers who can promote their books. For a list of recent sales, helpful info, and three ways to make yourself irresistible to any publisher, please visit our Web site.''

◎ THE STEVE LAUBE AGENCY

5501 N. Seventh Ave., #502, Phoenix AZ 85013. (602)336-8910. Fax: (602)532-7123. E-mail: krichards@stevelaube.com. Web site: www.stevelaube.com. **Contact:** Steve Laube. Estab. 2004. Member of CBA. Represents 60+ clients. 5% of clients are new/unpublished writers. Currently handles: 48% nonfiction books; 48% novels; 2% novellas; 2% scholarly books.

- Prior to becoming an agent, Mr. Laube worked 11 years as a Christian bookseller and 11 years as editorial director of nonfiction with Bethany House Publishers.

Represents Nonfiction books, novels. **Considers these nonfiction areas:** Religious/inspirational. **Considers these fiction areas:** Religious/inspirational.

- O→ ''We primarily serve the Christian market (CBA).'' Actively seeking Christian fiction and religious nonfiction. Does not want to receive children's picture books, poetry or cookbooks.

How to Contact Submit proposal package, outline, 3 sample chapters, SASE. No e-mail submissions. Consult Web site for guidelines. Considers simultaneous queries. Responds in 6-8 weeks to queries. Returns materials only with SASE. Obtains most new clients through recommendations from others, solicitations, conferences.

Recent Sales Sold 80 titles in the last year. *Day With a Perfect Stranger*, by David Gregory (Kelly's Filmworks). Other clients include Deborah Raney, Bright Media, Allison Bottke, H. Norman Wright, Ellie Kay, Jack Cavanaugh, Karen Ball, Tracey Bateman, Clint Kelly, Susan May Warren, Lisa Bergren, John Rosemond, David Gregory, Cindy Woodsmall.

Terms Agent receives 15% commission on domestic sales; 20% commission on foreign sales. Offers written contract; 30-day notice must be given to terminate contract.

Writers' Conferences Mount Hermon Christian Writers' Conference; American Christian Fiction Writers' Conference; Glorieta Christian Writers' Conference.

🅽 🅭 LAUNCHBOOKS LITERARY AGENCY

566 Sweet Pea Place, Encinitas CA 92024. (760)944-9909. E-mail: david@launchbooks.com. Web site: www.launchbooks.com. **Contact:** David Fugate. Estab. 2005. Represents 35 clients. 35% of clients are new/unpublished writers. Currently handles: 85% nonfiction books; 5% novels; 10% multimedia.

- Prior to his current position, Mr. Fugate was hired by the Margret McBride Agency to handle its submissions. In 1994, he moved to Waterside Productions, Inc., where he was an agent for 11 years and successfully represented more than 600 book titles before leaving to form LaunchBooks.

Represents Nonfiction books, novels, textbooks. **Considers these nonfiction areas:** Anthropology/archaeology; biography/autobiography; business/economics; child guidance/parenting; computers/electronic; cooking/foods/nutrition; current affairs; education; ethnic/cultural interests; government/politics/law; health/medicine; history; how-to; humor/satire; memoirs; military/war; money/finance; music/dance; nature/environment; popular culture; science/technology; sociology; sports; true crime/investigative. **Considers these fiction areas:** Action/adventure; humor/satire; mainstream/contemporary; science fiction; thriller.

- O→ Actively seeking a wide variety of nonfiction, including business, technology, adventure, popular culture, creative nonfiction, current events, history, politics, reference, memoirs, health, how-to, lifestyle, parenting and more. Mr. Fugate is also interested in hard science fiction.

How to Contact Query with SASE, submit outline/proposal, synopsis, 1 sample chapter(s), author bio. Accepts e-mail queries. No fax queries. Considers simultaneous queries. Responds in 1 week to queries; 4 weeks to mss. Returns materials only with SASE. Obtains most new clients through recommendations from others, solicitations.

Recent Sales Sold 49 titles in the last year. *Notes from the New World*, by Wagner James Au (HarperCollins);

Ghetto Rising, by John Jeter (W.W. Norton); *Branding is Dead*, by Jonathan S. Baskin (Warner Books); *Lifehacker*, by Gina Trapani (John Wiley & Sons); *U.S. Military History for Dummies*, by John McManus (John Wiley & Sons); *Transcending CSS*, by Andy Clarke (Pearson). Other clients include Kevin Mitnick, Molly Holzschlag, Eric Meyer, Jill Gilbert Welytok, Paul Nielsen.

Terms Agent receives 15% commission on domestic sales; 25% commission on foreign sales. Offers written contract; 30-day notice must be given to terminate contract. Charges occur very seldom and typically only if the author specifically requests overnight or something of that nature. This agency's agreement limits any charges to $50 unless the author gives a written consent.

◨ LAZEAR AGENCY, INC.

431 Second St., Suite 300, Hudson WI 54016. (715)531-0012. Fax: (715)531-0016. E-mail: admin@lazear.com. Web site: www.lazear.com. **Contact:** Editorial Board. Estab. 1984. 20% of clients are new/unpublished writers. Currently handles: 55% nonfiction books; 40% novels; 5% juvenile books.

• The Lazear Agency opened a New York office in September 1997.

Member Agents Jonathon Lazear; Christi Cardenas; Julie Mayo; Anne Blackstone.

Represents Nonfiction books, novels, short story collections, novellas, juvenile books, graphic novels. **Considers these nonfiction areas:** Agriculture/horticulture; americana; animals; anthropology/archaeology; art/architecture/design; biography/autobiography; business/economics; child guidance/parenting; computers/electronic; cooking/foods/nutrition; current affairs; education; ethnic/cultural interests; gardening; gay/lesbian issues; government/politics/law; health/medicine; history; how-to; humor/satire; interior design/decorating; juvenile nonfiction; language/literature/criticism; memoirs; military/war; money/finance; multicultural; music/dance; nature/environment; New Age/metaphysics; philosophy; photography; popular culture; psychology; recreation; regional; religious/inspirational; science/technology; self-help/personal improvement; sex; sociology; software; spirituality; sports; theater/film; travel; true crime/investigative; women's issues/studies; young adult; creative nonfiction. **Considers these fiction areas:** Action/adventure; confession; detective/police/crime; ethnic; family saga; fantasy; feminist; gay/lesbian; gothic; hi-lo; historical; humor/satire; juvenile; literary; mainstream/contemporary; military/war; multicultural; multimedia; mystery/suspense; New Age; occult; picture books; plays; poetry; poetry in translation; psychic/supernatural; religious/inspirational; romance; science fiction; short story collections; spiritual; sports; thriller; translation; westerns/frontier; young adult; women's.

O➡ Actively seeking new voices in commercial fiction and nonfiction. "It's all in the writing, no matter the subject matter." Does not want to receive horror, poetry, scripts and/or screenplays.

How to Contact Query with SASE, submit outline/proposal, synopsis, author bio, SASE. No phone calls or faxes. We prefer snail mail queries. Responds in 2 weeks to queries; 3 weeks to mss. Returns materials only with SASE. Obtains most new clients through recommendations from others, solicitations.

Recent Sales Sold more than 50 titles in the last year. Untitled book, by Jane Goodall (Warner); Untitled book, by Tony Hendra (Holt); Untitled YA series, by Will Weaver (FSG); *The Truth (with Jokes)*, by Al Franken (Dutton); *Harvest for Hope*, by Jane Goodall with Gary McAvoy and Gail Hudson (Warner); *Mommy Knows Worst*, by James Lileks (Crown); *The Prop*, by Pete Hautman (Simon & Schuster). Other clients include Margaret Weis, Gerry Gross, Noah Adams, and many more.

Terms Agent receives 15% commission on domestic sales; 20% commission on foreign sales. Offers written contract. Charges clients for photocopying, international express mail, bound galleys, books used for subsidiary rights sales. No fees charged if book is not sold.

Tips "The writer should first view himself as a salesperson in order to obtain an agent. Sell yourself, your idea, your concept. Do your homework. Notice what is in the marketplace. Be sophisticated about the arena in which you are writing. Please note that we also have a New York office, but the primary office remains in Hudson, Wis., for the receipt of any material."

ⓃⓌ◎ SUSANNA LEA ASSOCIATES

28, rue Bonaparte, 75006 Paris, France. E-mail: postmaster@susannalea.com. Web site: www.susannaleaassociates.com. **Contact:** Submissions Department.

Represents Nonfiction books, novels.

O➡ "We pride ourselves in keeping our list small: We prefer to focus our energies on a limited number of projects rather than spreading our energies thin. The company is currently developing new international projects: always selective, yet broad in their reach, they all remain faithful to the slogan, 'Published in Europe, Read by the World.'" Does not want to receive poetry, plays, screenplays, science fiction, educational text books, short stories or illustrated works.

How to Contact Send a query letter, brief synopsis, the first three chapters and/or proposal to this agency via snail mail. If the author wants work returned, include a SASE/IRC and sufficient postage. No e-mail or fax queries.

Recent Sales *Heroines of the Bible*, by Marek Halter; *Incas*, by A.B. Daniel; *In Our Strange Gardens*, by Michel

Quint; *The Phoenix*, by Henning Boetius; *Until Death Do Us Part*, by Ingrid Betancourt. Other clients include Marc Levy, Carmen Bin Ladin, Stephen Clarke, Frederic Lenoir, Marie-France Etchegoin and more.

Tips "Your query letter should be concise and include any pertinent information about yourself, relevant writing history, etc."

Ⓝ Ⓞ LEATHER BOUND WORDS

1493 Campton Court, St. Louis MO 63368. (314)346-3548. E-mail: thomas@leatherboundwords.com. Web site: www.leatherboundwords.com. **Contact:** Thomas Grady. Estab. 2004. 50% of clients are new/unpublished writers. Currently handles: 90% nonfiction books; 10% novels.

• In addition to agenting, Mr. Grady is a Partner "Emeritus" at a leading family wealth management firm in St. Louis. He is the author of two books, as well as numerous articles and columns.

Represents Nonfiction books, novels. **Considers these nonfiction areas:** Business/economics; money/finance; any topic related directly to baby boomers. **Considers these fiction areas:** Finance/money, any topic related to baby boomers.

How to Contact Query with SASE, submit synopsis, author bio, SASE. This agency prefers e-queries. No fax queries. Considers simultaneous queries. Responds in 10 days to queries; 3 months to mss. Obtains most new clients through recommendations from others, solicitations.

Terms Agent receives 15% commission on domestic sales; 20% commission on foreign sales. Offers written contract. This agency charges for copying and misc. office fees until book is published.

Ⓞ THE NED LEAVITT AGENCY

70 Wooster St., Suite 4F, New York NY 10012. (212)334-0999. Web site: www.nedleavittagency.com. **Contact:** Ned Leavitt. Member of AAR. Represents 40+ clients.

Member Agents Ned Leavitt, founder and agent; Britta Alexander, agent; Jill Beckman, editorial assistant.

Represents Nonfiction books, novels.

○┓ "We are small in size, but intensely dedicated to our authors and to supporting excellent and unique writing."

How to Contact This agency now only takes queries/submissions through referred clients. Do *not* cold query. No fax queries.

Recent Sales *In Time of War*, by Allen Appel (Carroll & Graf); *From Father to Son*, by Allen Appel (St. Martin's); *The Way of Song*, by Shawna Carol (St. Martin's); *Alchemy of Illness*, by Kat Duff (Pantheon); *Are You Getting Enlightened or Losing Your Mind?*, by Dennis Gersten (Harmony).

Tips Look online for this agency's recently changed submission guidelines.

Ⓝ Ⓞ ROBERT LECKER AGENCY

4055 Melrose Ave., Montreal QC H4A 2S5 Canada. (514)830-4818. Fax: (514)483-1644. E-mail: leckerlink@aol.com. Web site: www.leckeragency.com. **Contact:** Robert Lecker. Estab. 2004. Represents 15 clients. 20% of clients are new/unpublished writers. Currently handles: 80% nonfiction books; 10% novels; 10% scholarly books.

• Prior to becoming an agent, Mr. Lecker was the co-founder and publisher of ECW Press and professor of English literature at McGill University. He has 30 years of experience in book and magazine publishing.

Member Agents Robert Lecker (popular culture, music); Mary Williams (travel, food, popular science).

Represents Nonfiction books, novels, scholarly books, syndicated material. **Considers these nonfiction areas:** Biography/autobiography; cooking/foods/nutrition; ethnic/cultural interests; how-to; language/literature/criticism; music/dance; popular culture; science/technology; theater/film. **Considers these fiction areas:** Action/adventure; detective/police/crime; erotica; literary; mainstream/contemporary; mystery/suspense; thriller.

○┓ RLA specializes in books about popular culture, music, entertainment, food and travel. The agency responds to articulate, innovative proposals within 2 weeks. Actively seeking original book mss only after receipt of outlines and proposals.

How to Contact Submit proposal package, outline. Accepts e-mail queries. No fax queries. Considers simultaneous queries. Responds in 2 weeks to queries; 1 month to mss. Obtains most new clients through recommendations from others, conferences, interest in Web site.

Terms Agent receives 15% commission on domestic sales; 15-20% commission on foreign sales. Offers written contract, binding for 1 year; 6-month notice must be given to terminate contract.

Ⓞ LESCHER & LESCHER, LTD.

47 E. 19th St., New York NY 10003. (212)529-1790. Fax: (212)529-2716. **Contact:** Robert Lescher, Susan Lescher. Estab. 1966. Member of AAR. Represents 150 clients. Currently handles: 80% nonfiction books; 20% novels.

Represents Nonfiction books, novels. **Considers these nonfiction areas:** Current affairs; history; memoirs;

popular culture; biography; cookbooks/wines; law; contemporary issues; narrative nonfiction. **Considers these fiction areas:** Literary; mystery/suspense; commercial.

O→ Does not want to receive screenplays, science fiction or romance.

How to Contact Query with SASE. Obtains most new clients through recommendations from others.

Recent Sales Sold 35 titles in the last year. This agency prefers not to share information on specific sales. Clients include Neil Sheehan, Madeleine L'Engle, Calvin Trillin, Judith Viorst, Thomas Perry, Anne Fadiman, Frances FitzGerald, Paula Fox, Robert M. Parker Jr.

Terms Agent receives 15% commission on domestic sales; 20% commission on foreign sales.

N © LEVELFIVEMEDIA, LLC

130 W. 42nd St., Suite 1901-02, New York NY 10036. (212)575-3096. Fax: (212)575-7797. E-mail: levelfivemedia @l5m.net; submissions@l5m.net. Web site: www.l5m.net. **Contact:** Stephen Hanselman. Estab. 2005.

• Prior to becoming an agent, Ms. Hemming served as president of HarperCollins General Books. Mr. Hanselman served as senior VP and publisher of HarperBusiness, HarperResource and HarperSanFrancisco.

Member Agents Stephen Hanselman; Cathy Hemming.

Represents Nonfiction books, novels. **Considers these nonfiction areas:** Business/economics; cooking/foods/ nutrition; health/medicine; history; money/finance; psychology; religious/inspirational; self-help/personal improvement; fitness/exercise, inspiration, popular science, investigative journalism, lifestyle, how-to, popular reference, parenting, cultural studies. **Considers these fiction areas:** Commercial, literary, children's.

O→ "Our commitment is to focus on fewer authors and to provide more of these missing services, including media development and marketing consultation, by building their benefits into each project that is offered to publishers. Given this choice of focus, we are not accepting submissions except from published authors, credentialed speakers, established journalists, media personalities, leading scholars and religious figures, prominent science and health professionals, and high-level business consultants."

How to Contact Query with SASE, submit synopsis, publishing history, author bio, cover letter. No snail mail queries. Qualified fiction authors must have a previously published book or be referred. Accepts e-mail queries. No fax queries. Obtains most new clients through recommendations from others.

Recent Sales *The Message*, by William Griffin (NavPress); *The Saint & The Sultan*, by Paul Moses; *On the Night You Were Born*, by Nancy Tillman (Feiwel & Friends).

© LEVINE GREENBERG LITERARY AGENCY, INC.

307 Seventh Ave., Suite 2407, New York NY 10001. (212)337-0934. Fax: (212)337-0948. Web site: www.levinegr eenberg.com. Estab. 1989. Member of AAR. Represents 250 clients. 33% of clients are new/unpublished writers. Currently handles: 70% nonfiction books; 30% novels.

• Prior to opening his agency, Mr. Levine served as vice president of the Bank Street College of Education.

Member Agents James Levine; Arielle Eckstut; Daniel Greenberg; Stephanie Kip Rostan; Jenoyne Adams.

Represents Nonfiction books, novels. **Considers these nonfiction areas:** Animals; art/architecture/design; biography/autobiography; business/economics; child guidance/parenting; computers/electronic; cooking/ foods/nutrition; gardening; gay/lesbian issues; health/medicine; money/finance; nature/environment; New Age/metaphysics; religious/inspirational; science/technology; self-help/personal improvement; sociology; spirituality; sports; women's issues/studies. **Considers these fiction areas:** Literary; mainstream/contemporary; mystery/suspense; thriller (psychological); women's.

O→ This agency specializes in business, psychology, parenting, health/medicine, narrative nonfiction, spirituality, religion, women's issues, and commercial fiction.

How to Contact See Web site for full submission procedure. Prefers e-mail queries. Obtains most new clients through recommendations from others.

Recent Sales *Sharp Objects*, by Gillian Flynn; *Love is a Mix Tape*, by Rob Sheffield; *Growing Great Employees*, Erika Anderson.

Terms Agent receives 15% commission on domestic sales; 20% commission on foreign sales. Offers written contract. Charges clients for out-of-pocket expenses—telephone, fax, postage, photocopying—directly connected to the project.

Writers' Conferences ASJA Writers' Conference.

Tips "We focus on editorial development, business representation, and publicity and marketing strategy."

© PAUL S. LEVINE LITERARY AGENCY

1054 Superba Ave., Venice CA 90291-3940. (310)450-6711. Fax: (310)450-0181. E-mail: pslevine@ix.netcom.c om. Web site: www.paulslevine.com. **Contact:** Paul S. Levine. Estab. 1996. Member of the State Bar of California. Represents over 100 clients. 75% of clients are new/unpublished writers. Currently handles: 30% nonfiction books; 30% novels; 10% movie scripts; 30% TV scripts.

Represents Nonfiction books, novels, movie scripts, feature film, TV scripts, TV movie of the week, episodic drama, sitcom, animation, documentary, miniseries, syndicated material. **Considers these nonfiction areas:** Art/architecture/design; biography/autobiography; business/economics; child guidance/parenting; computers/electronic; cooking/foods/nutrition; crafts/hobbies; current affairs; education; ethnic/cultural interests; gay/lesbian issues; government/politics/law; health/medicine; history; how-to; humor/satire; interior design/decorating; language/literature/criticism; memoirs; military/war; money/finance; music/dance; nature/environment; New Age/metaphysics; photography; popular culture; psychology; religious/inspirational; science/technology; self-help/personal improvement; sociology; sports; theater/film; true crime/investigative; women's issues/studies; creative nonfiction. **Considers these fiction areas:** Action/adventure; comic books/cartoon; confession; detective/police/crime; erotica; ethnic; experimental; family saga; feminist; gay/lesbian; glitz; historical; humor/satire; literary; mainstream/contemporary; mystery/suspense; regional; religious/inspirational; romance; sports; thriller; westerns/frontier. **Considers these script subject areas:** Action/adventure; biography/autobiography; cartoon/animation; comedy; contemporary issues; detective/police/crime; erotica; ethnic; experimental; family saga; feminist; gay/lesbian; glitz; historical; horror; juvenile; mainstream; multimedia; mystery/suspense; religious/inspirational; romantic comedy; romantic drama; sports; teen; thriller; western/frontier.

O➥ Actively seeking commercial fiction and nonfiction. Also handles children's and young adult fiction and nonfiction. Does not want to receive science fiction, fantasy, or horror.

How to Contact Query with SASE. Accepts e-mail and fax queries. Considers simultaneous queries. Responds in 1 day to queries; 2 months to mss. Returns materials only with SASE. Obtains most new clients through conferences, referrals, listings on various Web sites and in directories.

Recent Sales Sold 25 titles in the last year. This agency prefers not to share information on specific sales.

Terms Agent receives 15% commission on domestic sales; 20% commission on foreign sales. Offers written contract. Charges clients for messengers, long distance calls, postage (only when incurred). No advance payment necessary.

Writers' Conferences California Lawyers for the Arts Workshops; Selling to Hollywood Conference; Willamette Writers Conference; and many others.

◎ ROBERT LIEBERMAN ASSOCIATES

400 Nelson Rd., Ithaca NY 14850-9440. (607)273-8801. Fax: (801)749-9682. E-mail: rhl10@cornell.edu. Web site: www.people.cornell.edu/pages/rhl10. **Contact:** Robert Lieberman. Estab. 1993. Represents 30 clients. 50% of clients are new/unpublished writers. Currently handles: 20% nonfiction books.

Represents Nonfiction books (trade), scholarly books, textbooks (college/high school/middle school). **Considers these nonfiction areas:** Agriculture/horticulture; anthropology/archaeology; art/architecture/design; business/economics; computers/electronic; education; health/medicine; memoirs (by authors with high public recognition); money/finance; music/dance; nature/environment; psychology; science/technology; sociology; theater/film.

O➥ This agency only accepts nonfiction ideas and specializes in university/college-level textbooks, CD-ROM/software for the university/college-level textbook market, and popular trade books in math, engineering, economics, and other subjects. Does not want to receive fiction, self-help, or screenplays.

How to Contact Query with SASE or by e-mail. Prefers to read materials exclusively. Prefers e-mail queries. Responds in 2 weeks to queries; 1 month to mss. Returns materials only with SASE. Obtains most new clients through referrals.

Recent Sales Sold 15 titles in the last year. *The Theory of Almost Everything*, by Robert Oerter (Plume Press); *Fundamentals in Voice Quality Engineering in Wireless Networks*, by Avi Perry (Cambridge University Press); *C++ Programming*, by John Mason (Prentice Hall); *College Physics*, by Giambattist and Richardson (McGraw-Hill); *Conflict Resolution*, by Baltos and Weir (Cambridge University Press).

Terms Agent receives 15% commission on domestic sales; 20% commission on foreign sales. Offers written contract; 1-month notice must be given to terminate contract. 100% of business is derived from commissions on ms sales. Fees are sometimes charged to clients for shipping and when special reviewers are required.

Tips "The trade books we handle are by authors who are highly recognized in their fields of expertise. Our client list includes Nobel Prize winners and others with high name recognition, either by the public or within a given area of expertise."

▦ ◎ LIMELIGHT MANAGEMENT

33 Newman St., London W1T 1PY England. (44)(207)637-2529. E-mail: Submissions@limelightmanagement.com. Web site: www.limelightmanagement.com. **Contact:** Fiona Lindsay. Estab. 1990. Member of AAA. Represents 70 clients. Currently handles: 100% nonfiction books; multimedia.

● Prior to becoming an agent, Ms. Lindsay was a public relations manager at the Dorchester and was working on her law degree.

Represents Nonfiction books. **Considers these nonfiction areas:** Art/architecture/design; cooking/foods/nutrition; crafts/hobbies; gardening (agriculture/horticulture); health/medicine; interior design/decorating; nature/environment; New Age/metaphysics; photography; self-help/personal improvement; sports; travel.

O→ "We are celebrity agents for TV celebrities, broadcasters, writers, journalists, celebrity speakers and media personalities, after dinner speakers, motivational speakers, celebrity chefs, TV presenters and TV chefs."

How to Contact Prefers to read materials exclusively. Query with SASE/IRC via e-mail. Agents will be in contact if they want to see more. Accepts e-mail queries. No fax queries. Responds in 1 week to queries. Returns materials only with SASE. Obtains most new clients through recommendations from others.

Recent Sales This agency prefers not to share information on specific sales. Clients include Oz Clarke, Antony Worrall Thompson, David Stevens, Linda Barker, James Martin.

Terms Agent receives 15% commission on domestic sales; 20% commission on foreign sales. Offers written contract; 2-month notice must be given to terminate contract.

[N] [✎] LINDSTROM LITERARY MANAGEMENT, LLC

871 N. Greenbrier St., Arlington VA 22205. Fax: (703)527-7624. E-mail: lindlitgrp@aol.com. **Contact:** Kristin Lindstrom. Estab. 1993. Member of Author's Guild. Represents 7 clients. 75% of clients are new/unpublished writers. Currently handles: 30% nonfiction books; 70% novels.

• Prior to her current position, Ms. Lindstrom was an editor of a monthly magazine in the energy industry.

Represents Nonfiction books, novels. **Considers these nonfiction areas:** Animals; biography/autobiography; business/economics; current affairs; history; memoirs; popular culture; science/technology; true crime/investigative. **Considers these fiction areas:** Action/adventure; detective/police/crime; erotica; mainstream/contemporary; mystery/suspense; religious/inspirational; thriller; women's.

O→ "In 2006, I decided to add my more specific promotion/publicity skills to the mix in order to support the marketing efforts of my published clients." Actively seeking commercial fiction and narrative nonfiction. Does not want to receive juvenile or children's books.

How to Contact Query with SASE, submit author bio, synopsis and first four chapters if submitting fiction. For nonfiction, send the first 4 chapters, synopsis, proposal, outline and mission statement. Accepts e-mail queries. No fax queries. Considers simultaneous queries. Responds in 5 weeks to queries; 8 weeks to mss. Returns materials only with SASE. Obtains most new clients through recommendations from others, solicitations.

Recent Sales Sold 4 titles in the last year. *Veterinary Confidential*, by Nick Trout (Broadway Books); *When the Guillotine Fell*, by Jeremy Mercer (St. Martin's); three mysteries, by Julia Buckley (Midnight Ink).

Terms Agent receives 15% commission on domestic sales; 20% commission on foreign sales. Offers written contract. This agency charges for postage, UPS, copies and other basic office expenses.

Tips "Do your homework on accepted practices; make sure you know what kind of book the agent handles."

[N] [✎] LINN PRENTIS LITERARY

155 East 116th St., #2F, New York NY 10029. (212)875-8557. Fax: (212)875-5565. E-mail: linnprentis@earthlink. net. **Contact:** Linn Prentis, Greg Parasmo. Estab. 2000. Represents 18-20 clients. 25% of clients are new/unpublished writers. Currently handles: 5% nonfiction books; 65% novels; 7% story collections; 10% novellas; 10% juvenile books; 3% scholarly books.

• Prior to becoming an agent, Ms. Prentis was a nonfiction writer and editor, mostly for magazines; she also worked for the Virginia Kidd Agency and in book promotion.

Member Agents Linn Prentis (fiction: novels, YA and middle-reader fiction, mainstream, women's, men's, mystery, sci-fi, literary, historical); Greg Parasmo (fiction targeting ages 18-30+).

Represents Nonfiction books, novels, short story collections, novellas (from authors whose novels I already represent), juvenile books (for older juveniles), scholarly books, anthology. **Considers these nonfiction areas:** Animals; art/architecture/design; biography/autobiography; current affairs; education; ethnic/cultural interests; government/politics/law; how-to; humor/satire; juvenile nonfiction; language/literature/criticism; memoirs; music/dance; photography; popular culture; sociology; women's issues/studies. **Considers these fiction areas:** Action/adventure; ethnic; family saga; fantasy; feminist; gay/lesbian; glitz; historical; horror; humor/satire; juvenile; literary; mainstream/contemporary; mystery/suspense; science fiction; thriller; westerns/frontier; young adult; women's.

O→ "Because of the Virginia Kidd connection and the clients I brought with me at the start, I have a special interest in sci-fi and fantasy, but, really, fiction is what interests me. As for my nonfiction projects, they are books I just couldn't resist." Actively seeking science fiction, family saga, mystery, memoir, mainstream, literary, women's. Does not want to receive books for little kids.

How to Contact Query with SASE, submit synopsis. No phone or fax queries. Snail mail is best. Considers simultaneous queries. Obtains most new clients through recommendations from others, solicitations.

Recent Sales Sold 15 titles in the last year. *The Sons of Heaven*, by Kage Baker (Tor); *Indigo Springs* and a sequel, by A.M. Dellamonica (Tor); *Stable Strategies and Others*, a story collection, by Eileen Gunn (Tachyon); *Moon Called; Blood Bound*, by Patricia Briggs (Ace).

Terms Agent receives 15% commission on domestic sales; 20% commission on foreign sales. Offers written contract; 60-day notice must be given to terminate contract.

Tips "Consider query letters and synopses as writing assignments. Spell names correctly."

◐ WENDY LIPKIND AGENCY

120 E. 81st St., New York NY 10028. (212)628-9653. Fax: (212)585-1306. E-mail: lipkindag@aol.com. **Contact:** Wendy Lipkind. Estab. 1977. Member of AAR. Represents 50 clients. Currently handles: 100% nonfiction books.
Represents Nonfiction books. **Considers these nonfiction areas:** Biography/autobiography; current affairs; health/medicine; history; science/technology; women's issues/studies; social history; narrative nonfiction.

    ○➼ This agency specializes in adult nonfiction.

How to Contact Prefers to read materials exclusively. Accepts e-mail queries only (no attachments). Obtains most new clients through recommendations from others.

Recent Sales Sold 10 titles in the last year. *One Small Step*, by Robert Mauner (Workman); *Kingdom of Strangers: A Muslim Woman's Journey Through Fear and Faith in Saudi Arabia*, by Dr. Qanta Amhed (Sourcebooks).

Terms Agent receives 15% commission on domestic sales; 20% commission on foreign sales. Sometimes offers written contract. Charges clients for foreign postage, messenger service, photocopying, transatlantic calls, faxes.

Tips "Send intelligent query letter first. Let me know if you've submitted to other agents."

◐ LIPPINCOTT MASSIE MCQUILKIN

80 Fifth Ave., Suite 1101, New York NY 10011. (212)337-2044. Fax: (212)352-2059. E-mail: info mqlit.com. Web site: www.lmqlit.com. **Contact:** Molly Lindley, assistant. Estab. 2003. Represents 90 clients. 30% of clients are new/unpublished writers. Currently handles: 40% nonfiction books; 40% novels; 10% story collections; 5% scholarly books; 5% poetry.
Member Agents Maria Massie (fiction, memoir, cultural criticism); Will Lippincott (politics, current affairs, history); Rob McQuilkin (fiction, history, psychology, sociology, graphic material).
Represents Nonfiction books, novels, short story collections, scholarly books, graphic novels. **Considers these nonfiction areas:** Animals; anthropology/archaeology; art/architecture/design; biography/autobiography; business/economics; child guidance/parenting; current affairs; ethnic/cultural interests; gay/lesbian issues; government/politics/law; health/medicine; history; language/literature/criticism; memoirs; military/war; money/finance; music/dance; nature/environment; popular culture; psychology; religious/inspirational; science/technology; self-help/personal improvement; sociology; theater/film; true crime/investigative; women's issues/studies. **Considers these fiction areas:** Action/adventure; comic books/cartoon; confession; family saga; feminist; gay/lesbian; historical; humor/satire; literary; mainstream/contemporary; regional.

    ○➼ LMQ focuses on bringing new voices in literary and commercial fiction to the market, as well as popularizing the ideas and arguments of scholars in the fields of history, psychology, sociology, political science, and current affairs. Actively seeking fiction writers who already have credits in magazines and quarterlies, as well as nonfiction writers who already have a media platform or some kind of a university affiliation. Does not want to receive romance, genre fiction, or children's material.

How to Contact Send query via e-mail. Only send additional materials if requested. Considers simultaneous queries. Responds in 1 week to queries; 1 month to mss. Obtains most new clients through recommendations from others, solicitations, conferences.

Recent Sales Sold 27 titles in the last year. *The Abstinence Teacher*, by Tom Perrotta (St. Martins); *Queen of Fashion*, by Caroline Weber (Henry Holt); *Whistling Past Dixie*, by Tom Schaller (Simon & Schuster); *Pretty Little Dirty*, by Amanda Boyden (Vintage). Other clients include Peter Ho Davies, Kim Addonizio, Don Lee, Natasha Trethewey, Anatol Lieven, Sir Michael Marmot, Anne Carson, Liza Ward, David Sirota, Anne Marie Slaughter, Marina Belozerskaya, Kate Walbert.

Terms Agent receives 15% commission on domestic sales; 20% commission on foreign sales. Offers written contract; 30-day notice must be given to terminate contract. Only charges for reasonable business expenses upon successful sale.

Ⓝ ◐ LITERARY AGENCY FOR SOUTHERN AUTHORS

2123 Paris Metz Road, Chattanooga TN 37421. E-mail: southernlitagent@aol.com. **Contact:** Lantz Powell. Estab. 2001. Represents 20 clients. 60% of clients are new/unpublished writers. Currently handles: 50% nonfiction books; 50% novels.

    ● Prior to becoming an agent, Mr. Powell was in sales and contract negotiation.

Represents Nonfiction books, novels, juvenile books (for ages 14 and up). **Considers these nonfiction areas:** Art/architecture/design; biography/autobiography; business/economics; crafts/hobbies; current affairs; education; ethnic/cultural interests; government/politics/law; history; how-to; humor/satire; interior design/decorating; language/literature/criticism; military/war; New Age/metaphysics; photography; popular culture; religious/inspirational; self-help/personal improvement; true crime/investigative. **Considers these fiction areas:** Comic books/cartoon; horror; humor/satire; literary; mainstream/contemporary; regional (Southern); religious/inspirational; young adult.

O→ "We focus on authors that live in the southern United States. We have the ability to translate and explain complexities of publishing for the southern author." Actively seeking quality projects by authors with a vision of where they want to be in 10 years and a plan of how to get there. Does not want to receive unfinished, unedited projects that do not follow the standard presentation conventions of the trade. No romance.

How to Contact Query via e-mail first and include a synopsis. Accepts e-mail queries. No fax queries. Considers simultaneous queries. Responds in 2-3 days to queries; 1 week to mss. Obtains most new clients through recommendations from others.

Recent Sales Sold 10 + titles in the last year. List of other clients and books sold will be available to authors pre-signing, but is not for public knowledge.

Terms Agent receives 15% commission on domestic sales; 25% commission on foreign sales. Offers written contract. "We charge when a publisher wants a hard copy overnight or the like. We get it done at Kinkos and charge their cost plus 15%. The client always knows this beforehand."

Writers' Conferences Conference for Southern Literature; Tennessee Book Fair.

Tips "If you are an unpublished author, join a writers group, even if it is on the Internet. You need good honest feedback. Don't send a manuscript that has not been read by at least five people. Don't send a manuscript cold to any agent without first asking if they want it. Try to meet the agent face to face before signing. Make sure the fit is right."

◙ LITERARY AND CREATIVE ARTISTS, INC.

3543 Albemarle St. NW, Washington DC 20008-4213. (202)362-4688. Fax: (202)362-8875. E-mail: query@lcadc. com. Web site: www.lcadc.com. **Contact:** Muriel Nellis. Estab. 1981. Member of AAR, Authors Guild, American Bar Association. Represents 75 clients. Currently handles: 70% nonfiction books; 30% novels.

Member Agents Muriel Nellis; Jane Roberts.

Represents Nonfiction books, novels. **Considers these nonfiction areas:** Biography/autobiography; business/economics; cooking/foods/nutrition; government/politics/law; health/medicine; how-to; memoirs; philosophy; human drama; lifestyle.

How to Contact Query with SASE. *No unsolicited mss.* Send no e-mail attachments. Accepts e-mail queries. No fax queries. Responds in 3 months to queries.

Recent Sales *Lady Cottington's Pressed Fairy Book*, by Brian Froud and Terry Jones (Pavilion); *The New Feminine Brain*, by Mona Lisa Schulz (Free Press); *Al Qaeda in Europe*, by Lorenzo Vidino (Prometheus Books); *What Type of Leader Am I?*, by Ginger Lapid-Bogda (McGraw-Hill); *The Longest Ride*, by Emilio Scotto (MBI Publishing).

Terms Agent receives 15% commission on domestic sales; 20% commission on foreign sales; 25% commission on dramatic rights sales. Charges clients for long-distance phone/fax, photocopying, shipping.

Tips "While we prefer published writers, publishing credits are not required if the proposed work has great merit."

◙ THE LITERARY GROUP

51 E. 25th St., Suite 401, New York NY 10010. (212)274-1616. Fax: (212)274-9876. E-mail: fweimann@theliterar ygroup.com. Web site: www.theliterarygroup.com. **Contact:** Frank Weimann. Estab. 1985. 65% of clients are new/unpublished writers. Currently handles: 50% nonfiction books; 50% fiction.

Member Agents Frank Weimann; Ian Kleinert.

Represents Nonfiction books, novels. **Considers these nonfiction areas:** Animals; anthropology/archaeology; biography/autobiography; business/economics; child guidance/parenting; crafts/hobbies; current affairs; education; ethnic/cultural interests; government/politics/law; health/medicine; history; how-to; humor/satire; juvenile nonfiction; language/literature/criticism; memoirs; military/war; money/finance; multicultural; music/dance; nature/environment; popular culture; psychology; religious/inspirational; science/technology; self-help/personal improvement; sociology; sports; theater/film; true crime/investigative; women's issues/studies; creative nonfiction. **Considers these fiction areas:** Action/adventure; contemporary issues; detective/police/crime; ethnic; family saga; fantasy; feminist; horror; humor/satire; mystery/suspense; psychic/supernatural; romance (contemporary, gothic, historical, regency); sports; thriller; westerns/frontier.

O→ This agency specializes in nonfiction (memoir, military, history, biography, sports, how-to).

How to Contact Query with SASE, outline, 3 sample chapters. Prefers to read materials exclusively. Only responds if interested. Returns materials only with SASE. Obtains most new clients through referrals, writers' conferences, query letters.

Recent Sales Sold 150 titles in the last year. *The Alchemyst*, by Michael Scott; *Dog and Bear*, by Laura Vaccaro Seeger; *How To Be Sexy*, by Carmen Electra; *Ship of Ghosts*, by James Hornfischer; *Push*, by Relentless Aaron; *Falling Out of Fashion*, by Karen Yampolsky. Other clients include Robert Anderson, Michael Reagan, J.L. King.
Terms Agent receives 15% commission on domestic sales; 20% commission on foreign sales. Offers written contract; 30-day notice must be given to terminate contract.
Writers' Conferences San Diego State University Writers' Conference; Maui Writers' Conference; Agents and Editors Conference.

ⓝ 🕮 LITERARY SERVICES, INC.

P.O. Box 888, Barnegat NJ 08005. (609)698-7162. Fax: (609)698-7163. E-mail: john@LiteraryServicesInc.com. Web site: www.LiteraryServicesInc.com. **Contact:** John Willig. Estab. 1991. Member of Author's Guild. Represents 85 clients. 25% of clients are new/unpublished writers. Currently handles: 100% nonfiction books.
Member Agents John Willig (business, personal growth, narratives, history, health); Cynthia Zigmund (personal finance, investments, entreprenuership); Joel Margulis (business).
Represents Nonfiction books. **Considers these nonfiction areas:** Art/architecture/design; biography/autobiography; business/economics; child guidance/parenting; cooking/foods/nutrition; crafts/hobbies; health/medicine; history; how-to; humor/satire; language/literature/criticism; money/finance; New Age/metaphysics; popular culture; psychology; science/technology; self-help/personal improvement; sports; true crime/investigative.

> ⊶ "Our publishing experience and 'inside' knowledge of how companies and editors really work sets us apart from many agencies; our specialties are noted above, but we are open to unique presentations in all nonfiction topic areas." Actively seeking business, work/life topics, story-driven narratives. Does not want to receive fiction, children's books, science fiction, religion or memoirs.

How to Contact Query with SASE, submit proposal package, synopsis, 3 sample chapter(s), author bio. For starters, a one-page outline sent via e-mail is acceptable. See our Web site to learn more. Accepts e-mail queries. No fax queries. Considers simultaneous queries. Responds in 2 weeks to queries; 4 weeks to mss. Returns materials only with SASE. Obtains most new clients through recommendations from others, solicitations, conferences.
Recent Sales Sold 22 titles in the last year. *The Energy Cure: How to Recharge Your Life Every Day*, by Kimberly Kinsley (New Page Books); A full list of new books are noted on the Web site.
Terms Agent receives 15% commission on domestic sales; 20% commission on foreign sales. Offers written contract. This agency charges fees for copying, postage, etc.
Writers' Conferences Author 101; Mega Book Marketing; Publicity Summit.
Tips "Be focused. In all likelihood, your work is not going to be of interest to 'a very broad audience' or 'every parent,' so I appreciate when writers put aside their passion and do some homework, i.e. positioning, special features and benefits of your work. Be a marketer. How have you tested your ideas and writing (beyond your inner circle of family and friends)? Have you received any key awards for your work or endorsements from influential persons in your field? What steps have you taken to increase your presence in the market?"

ⓝ LJK LITERARY MANAGEMENT

708 Third Ave., 16th Floor, New York NY 10018. (212)221-8797. Fax: (212)221-8722. E-mail: submissions@ljklit erary.com. Web site: www.ljkliterary.com. Represents 20+ clients.

> • Prior to becoming an agent, Mr. Laghi worked for ICM; Mr. Kirshbaum worked for Random House; Ms. Einstein was a senior executive at Maria Campbell Associates.

Member Agents Larry Kirshbaum; Susanna Einstein (contemporary fiction, literary fiction, romance, suspense, historical fiction, middle grade, young adult, crime fiction, narrative nonfiction, memoir and biography); Jud Laghi (celebrity, pop culture, humor, journalism).
Represents Nonfiction books, novels.

> ⊶ "We are not considering picture books at this time."

How to Contact Query with SASE, submi. E-mail queries are preferred. The only attachment should be the writing sample. No fax queries. Responds in 8 weeks to queries; 8 weeks to mss.
Recent Sales *In the Company of Liars*, by David Ellis (Putnam); *Brainiac: Adventures in the Curious, Competitive, Compulsive World of Trivia*, by Ken Jennings (Villard); *Found II*, by Davy Rothbart (Fireside).
Tips "All submissions will receive a response from us if they adhere to our submission guidelines. Please do not contact us to inquire about the submission unless 10 weeks have passed since you submitted it."

ⓦ JULIA LORD LITERARY MANAGEMENT

38 W. Ninth St., #4, New York NY 10011. (212)995-2333. Fax: (212)995-2332. E-mail: julialordliterary@nyc.rr.c om. Estab. 1999. Member of AAR.
Member Agents Julia Lord, owner; Riley Kellogg, subagent.
Represents Nonfiction books, novels. **Considers these nonfiction areas:** Biography/autobiography; history;

sports; travel; African-American; lifestyle; narrative nonfiction. **Considers these fiction areas:** Action/adventure; historical; literary; mainstream/contemporary; mystery/suspense.

How to Contact Query with SASE or via e-mail. Obtains most new clients through recommendations from others, solicitations.

STERLING LORD LITERISTIC, INC.

65 Bleecker St., 12th Floor, New York NY 10012. (212)780-6050. Fax: (212)780-6095. E-mail: info@sll.com. Web site: www.sll.com. Estab. 1952. Member of AAR; signatory of WGA. Represents 600 clients. Currently handles: 50% nonfiction books; 50% novels.

Member Agents Marcy Posner; Philippa Brophy; Laurie Liss; Chris Calhoun; Peter Matson; Sterling Lord; Claudia Cross; Neeti Madan; George Nicholson; Jim Rutman; Charlotte Sheedy (affiliate); Douglas Stewart; Robert Guinsler.

Represents Nonfiction books, novels.

How to Contact Query with SASE. Query by snail mail. No e-mail or fax queries. Responds in 1 month to mss. Obtains most new clients through recommendations from others.

Recent Sales This agency prefers not to share information on specific sales. Other clients include Kent Haruf, Dick Francis, Mary Gordon, Sen. John McCain, Simon Winchester, James McBride, Billy Collins, Richard Paul Evans, Dave Pelzer.

Terms Agent receives 15% commission on domestic sales; 20% commission on foreign sales. Offers written contract. Charges clients for photocopying.

NANCY LOVE LITERARY AGENCY

250 E. 65th St., New York NY 10021-6614. (212)980-3499. Fax: (212)308-6405. E-mail: nloveag@aol.com. **Contact:** Nancy Love. Estab. 1984. Member of AAR. Represents 60-80 clients. 25% of clients are new/unpublished writers. Currently handles: 90% nonfiction books; 10% novels.

• This agency is not taking on any new fiction writers at this time.

Represents Nonfiction books. **Considers these nonfiction areas:** Biography/autobiography; child guidance/parenting; cooking/foods/nutrition; current affairs; ethnic/cultural interests; government/politics/law; health/medicine; history; how-to; nature/environment; popular culture; psychology; religious/inspirational; science/technology; self-help/personal improvement; sociology; spirituality; travel (armchair only, no how-to); true crime/investigative; women's issues/studies.

○━ This agency specializes in adult nonfiction. Actively seeking narrative nonfiction.

How to Contact Query with SASE. No e-mail or fax queries. Considers simultaneous queries. Responds in 3 weeks to queries; 6 weeks to mss. Returns materials only with SASE. Obtains most new clients through recommendations from others, solicitations.

Recent Sales Sold 18 titles in the last year. *Say Good-bye to Knee Pain*, by Marian Betancourt and Joe Hofannin (Pocket); *Texas Hill Country Cookbook*, by Scott Cohen and Marian Betancourt (Globe Pequot); *The Monster in the Corner Office*, by Patricia King (Adams); *Shooting Star*, by Cynthia Riggs (St. Martin's); *Indian Pipes*, by Cynthia Riggs (St. Martin's Press); *Overthrow*, by Stephen Kinzer (Henry Holt); *Don't Panic*, by Stanton Peele (Crown); *Overcoming Obesity with Surgery*, by James Weber (M. Evans/Rowman & Littlefield); *How to Think Like a Terrorist*, by Mike German (Potomac Books).

Terms Agent receives 15% commission on domestic sales; 20% commission on foreign sales. Offers written contract. Charges clients for photocopying if it runs more than $20.

Tips "Nonfiction authors and/or collaborators must be an authority in their subject area and have a platform. Send an SASE if you want a response."

LOWENSTEIN-YOST ASSOCIATES

121 W. 27th St., Suite 601, New York NY 10001. (212)206-1630. Fax: (212)727-0280. Web site: www.lowenstein yost.com. **Contact:** Barbara Lowenstein or Nancy Yost. Estab. 1976. Member of AAR. Represents 150 clients. 20% of clients are new/unpublished writers. Currently handles: 60% nonfiction books; 40% novels.

Member Agents Barbara Lowenstein, president (nonfiction interests include narrative nonfiction, health, money, finance, travel, multicultural, popular culture and memoir; fiction interests include literary fiction and women's fiction); Nancy Yost, vice president (mainstream/contemporary fiction, mystery, suspense, contemporary/historical romance, thriller, women's fiction); Norman Kurz, business affairs; Zoe Fishman, foreign rights (young adult, literary fiction, narrative nonfiction); Rachel Vater (fantasy, young adult, women's fiction); Natanya Wheeler (narrative nonfiction, literary fiction, historical, women's fiction, birds).

Represents Nonfiction books, novels. **Considers these nonfiction areas:** Animals; anthropology/archaeology; biography/autobiography; business/economics; child guidance/parenting; current affairs; education; ethnic/cultural interests; government/politics/law; health/medicine; history; how-to; language/literature/criticism; memoirs; money/finance; multicultural; nature/environment; popular culture; psychology; self-help/personal improvement; sociology; travel; women's issues/studies; music; narrative nonfiction; science; film. **Considers these fiction areas:** Detective/police/crime; erotica; ethnic; feminist; historical; literary; mainstream/contemporary; mystery/suspense; romance (contemporary, historical, regency); thriller; women's; fantasy, young adult.

O→ This agency specializes in health, business, creative nonfiction, literary fiction and commercial fiction—especially suspense, crime and women's issues. "We are a full-service agency, handling domestic and foreign rights, film rights and audio rights to all of our books."

How to Contact Query with SASE. Prefers to read materials exclusively. For fiction, send outline and first chapter. *No unsolicited mss.* Responds in 4 weeks to queries. Returns materials only with SASE. Obtains most new clients through recommendations from others, solicitations, conferences.

Recent Sales *Body After Baby*, by Jackie Keller (Avery); *Creating Competitive Advantage*, by Jaynie Smith & Bill Flanagan (Doubleday); *To Keep a Husband*, by Lindsay Graves (Ballantine); *The Notorious Mrs. Winston*, by Mary Mackey (Berkley); *Gleason's Gym Total Body Boxing Workout for Women*, by Hector Roca & Bruce Silverglade (Fireside); *More Than A Champion: A Biography of Mohammed Ali*, by Ishmael Reed (Shaye Areheart); *Dreams of A Caspian Rain*, by Gina Nahai; *House of Dark Delights*, by Louisa Burton (Bantam); a new thriller by Perri O'Shaugnessy (Pocket); the debut thriller by N.P.R. writer Susan Arnout Smith (St. Martin's); *Sworn to Silence*, by Linda Castillo; *Thinner or Pretty on the Outside*, by Valerie Frankel; *In the Stars*, by Eileen Cook; *The Dark Lantern*, by Gerri Brightwell. Other clients include Stephanie Laurens, Dr. Ro, Penny McFall, Deborah Crombie, Liz Carlyle, Suzanne Enoch, Gaelen Foley, Tamar Myers, Sandi K. Shelton, Kathryn Smith, Cheyenne McCray, Barbara Keesling.

Terms Agent receives 15% commission on domestic sales; 20% commission on foreign sales. Offers written contract. Charges for large photocopy batches, messenger service, international postage.

Writers' Conferences Malice Domestic; Bouchercon; RWA National Conference.

Tips "Know the genre you are working in and read! Also, please see our Web site for details on which agent to query for your project."

⊕ ☑ ANDREW LOWNIE LITERARY AGENCY, LTD.

36 Great Smith St., London SW1P 3BU, England. (44)(207)222-7574. Fax: (44)(207)222-7576. E-mail: lownie@globalnet.co.uk. Web site: www.andrewlownie.co.uk. **Contact:** Andrew Lownie. Estab. 1988. Member of AAA. Represents 130 clients. 20% of clients are new/unpublished writers. Currently handles: 90% nonfiction books; 10% novels.

● Prior to becoming an agent, Mr. Lownie was a journalist, bookseller, publisher, author of 12 books and director of the Curtis Brown Agency.

Represents Nonfiction books. **Considers these nonfiction areas:** Biography/autobiography; current affairs; government/politics/law; history; memoirs; military/war; popular culture; true crime/investigative.

O→ This agent has wide publishing experience, extensive journalistic contacts, and a specialty in showbiz/celebrity memoir. Showbiz memoirs, narrative histories, and biographies. No poetry, short stories, children's fiction, academic or scripts.

How to Contact Query with SASE and/or IRC. Submit outline, 1 sample chapter. Accepts e-mail and fax queries. Considers simultaneous queries. Responds in 1 week to queries; 1 month to mss. Returns materials only with SASE. Obtains most new clients through recommendations from others.

Recent Sales Sold 50 titles in the last year. *Avenging Justice*, by David Stafford (Time Warner); *Shadow of Solomon*, by Laurence Gardner; David Hasselhoff's autobiography. Other clients include Norma Major, Guy Bellamy, Joyce Cary estate, Lawrence James, Juliet Barker, Patrick McNee, Sir John Mills, Peter Evans, Desmond Seward, Laurence Gardner, Richard Rudgley, Timothy Good, Tom Levine.

Terms Agent receives 15% commission on domestic sales; 15% commission on foreign sales. Offers written contract; 30-day notice must be given to terminate contract. This agency charges clients for copying, postage, books for submission.

Tips "I prefer submissions in writing by letter."

ℕ ☑ LYONS & PANDE INTERNATIONAL, LLC

55 West 116th St., Suite 314, New York NY 10026. (212)368-2812 for Jennifer; (212)368-2813 for Ayesha. Web site: www.lyonspande.com.

● Prior to her current position, Ms. Lyons was a senior agent for Writers House; Ms. Pande was an editor for 15 years.

Member Agents Jennifer Lyons, Jennifer@lyonspande.com (commercial fiction, memoirs, women's issues, pop culture, narrative, photography); Ayesha Pande, Ayesha@lyonspande.com (general fiction, juvenile fiction, biography, business/investing/finance, history, mind/body/spirit, health).

Represents Nonfiction books, novels.

How to Contact Query with SASE. Send your snail mail query to the attention of either Ms. Lyons or Ms.

Pande, not both. No e-mail or fax queries. Obtains most new clients through recommendations from others, solicitations.

Recent Sales *Evening is the Whole Day*, by Preeta Samarasan (Houghton Mifflin); *Mexican High*, by Liza Monroy (Spiegel & Grau); *Christmas in America*, by Peter Guttman (Skyhorse); *The Dairy-Free Gourmet*, by Levana Kerschenbaum (Skyhorse); *Skunk Girl*, by Sheba Karim (Farrar, Straus Children's).

⚏ ✉ LYONS LITERARY, LLC

116 West 23rd St., Suite 500, New York NY 10011. (212)851-8428. Fax: (212)851-8405. E-mail: info@lyonsliterary.com. Web site: www.lyonsliterary.com. **Contact:** Jonathan Lyons. Estab. 2007. Member of AAR, The Author's Guild, American Bar Association, New York State Bar Associaton, New York State Intellectual Property Law Section. Represents 36 clients. 15% of clients are new/unpublished writers. Currently handles: 60% nonfiction books; 36% novels; 2% story collections; 2% poetry.

Represents Nonfiction books, novels, short story collections. **Considers these nonfiction areas:** Animals; biography/autobiography; business/economics; child guidance/parenting; cooking/foods/nutrition; crafts/hobbies; current affairs; ethnic/cultural interests; gay/lesbian issues; government/politics/law; health/medicine; history; how-to; humor/satire; memoirs; military/war; money/finance; multicultural; music/dance; nature/environment; popular culture; psychology; science/technology; self-help/personal improvement; sociology; sports; translation; travel; true crime/investigative; women's issues/studies. **Considers these fiction areas:** Action/adventure; comic books/cartoon; confession; detective/police/crime; ethnic; experimental; family saga; fantasy; feminist; gay/lesbian; glitz; historical; horror; humor/satire; literary; mainstream/contemporary; mystery/suspense; psychic/supernatural; regional; science fiction; sports; thriller; women's; chick lit.

> ☛ "With my legal expertise and experience selling domestic and foreign language book rights, paperback reprint rights, audio rights, film/TV rights and permissions, I am able to provide substantive and personal guidance to my clients in all areas relating to their projects. In addition, with the advent of new publishing technology, Lyons Literary, LLC is situated to address the changing nature of the industry while concurrently handling authors' more traditional needs."

How to Contact Query with SASE, submit outline, synopsis, author bio, SASE. No phone queries. Accepts e-mail queries. No fax queries. Considers simultaneous queries. Responds in 8 weeks to queries; 12 weeks to mss. Returns materials only with SASE. Obtains most new clients through recommendations from others.

Recent Sales Sold more than 30 titles in the last year. This agency prefers not to share information on specific sales.

Terms Agent receives 15% commission on domestic sales; 20% commission on foreign sales. Offers written contract.

Writers' Conferences Agents and Editors Conference.

Tips "Please submit electronic queries through our Web site submission form."

⚏ DONALD MAASS LITERARY AGENCY

121 W. 27th St., Suite 801, New York NY 10001. (212)727-8383. Web site: www.maassagency.com. Estab. 1980. Member of AAR, SFWA, MWA, RWA. Represents more than 100 clients. 5% of clients are new/unpublished writers. Currently handles: 100% novels.

> • Prior to opening his agency, Mr. Maass served as an editor at Dell Publishing (New York) and as a reader at Gollancz (London). He also served as the president of AAR.

Member Agents Donald Maass (mainstream, literary, mystery/suspense, science fiction); Jennifer Jackson (commercial fiction, romance, science fiction, fantasy, mystery/suspense); Cameron McClure (literary, mystery/suspense, urban, fantasy, narrative nonfiction and projects with multicultural, international, and environmental themes, gay/lesbian); Stephen Barbara (literary fiction, young adult novels, middle grade, narrative nonfiction, historical nonfiction, mainstream, genre).

Represents Novels. **Considers these nonfiction areas:** Young adult. **Considers these fiction areas:** Detective/police/crime; fantasy; historical; horror; literary; mainstream/contemporary; mystery/suspense; psychic/supernatural; romance (historical, paranormal, time travel); science fiction; thriller; women's.

> ☛ This agency specializes in commercial fiction, especially science fiction, fantasy, mystery and suspense. Actively seeking to expand in literary fiction and women's fiction. Does not want to receive nonfiction, picture books, prescriptive nonfiction, or poetry.

How to Contact Query with SASE, synopsis, first 5 pages. Returns material only with SASE. Considers simultaneous queries. Responds in 2 weeks to queries; 3 months to mss.

Recent Sales *Afternoons With Emily*, by Rose MacMurray (Little, Brown); *Denial: A Lew Fonesca Mystery*, by Stuart Kaminsky (Forge); *The Shifting Tide*, by Anne Perry (Ballantine); *Midnight Plague*, by Gregg Keizer (G.P. Putnam's Sons); *White Night: A Novel of The Dresden Files*, by Jim Butcher (Roc).

Terms Agent receives 15% commission on domestic sales; 20% commission on foreign sales.

Writers' Conferences Donald Maass: World Science Fiction Convention; Frankfurt Book Fair; Pacific Northwest

Writers Conference; Bouchercon. Jennifer Jackson: World Science Fiction Convention; RWA National Conference.

Tips "We are fiction specialists, also noted for our innovative approach to career planning. Few new clients are accepted, but interested authors should query with a SASE. Works with subagents in all principle foreign countries and Hollywood. No prescriptive nonfiction, picture books or poetry will be considered."

☺ GINA MACCOBY LITERARY AGENCY

P.O. Box 60, Chappaqua NY 10514. (914)238-5630. **Contact:** Gina Maccoby. Estab. 1986. Represents 25 clients. Currently handles: 33% nonfiction books; 33% novels; 33% juvenile books; illustrators of children's books.

Represents Nonfiction books, novels, juvenile books. **Considers these nonfiction areas:** Biography/autobiography; current affairs; ethnic/cultural interests; history; juvenile nonfiction; popular culture; women's issues/studies. **Considers these fiction areas:** Juvenile; literary; mainstream/contemporary; mystery/suspense; thriller; young adult.

How to Contact Query with SASE. Considers simultaneous queries. Responds in 3 months to queries. Returns materials only with SASE. Obtains most new clients through recommendations from clients and publishers.

Recent Sales Sold 21 titles in the last year.

Terms Agent receives 15% commission on domestic sales; 25% commission on foreign sales. Charges clients for photocopying. May recover certain costs, such as legal fees or the cost of shipping books by air to Europe or Japan.

Ⓝ ☺ MACGREGOR LITERARY

2373 N.W. 185th Ave., Suite 165, Hillsboro OR 97214. (503)277-8308. E-mail: submissions@macgregorliterary.com. Web site: www.macgregorliterary.com. **Contact:** Chip MacGregor. Signatory of WGA. Represents 25 clients. 10% of clients are new/unpublished writers. Currently handles: 40% nonfiction books; 60% novels.

- Prior to his current position, Mr. MacGregor was the senior agent with Alive Communications. Most recently, he was associate publisher for Time-Warner Book Group's Faith Division, and helped put together their Center Street imprint.

Represents Nonfiction books, novels, short story collections, scholarly books. **Considers these nonfiction areas:** Biography/autobiography; business/economics; child guidance/parenting; current affairs; history; how-to; humor/satire; popular culture; religious/inspirational (and inspirational); self-help/personal improvement; sports. **Considers these fiction areas:** Detective/police/crime; historical; mainstream/contemporary; mystery/suspense; religious/inspirational; romance; thriller; women's/chick lit.

- ⃟ "My specialty has been in career planning with authors—finding commercial ideas, then helping authors bring them to market, and in the midst of that assisting the authors as they get firmly established in their writing careers. I'm probably best known for my work with Christian books over the years, but I've done a fair amount of general market projects as well." Actively seeking authors with a Christian worldview and a growing platform. Does not want to receive fantasy, sci-fi, children's books, poetry or screenplays.

How to Contact Query with SASE. Accepts e-mail queries. No fax queries. Considers simultaneous queries. Responds in 3 weeks to queries. Obtains most new clients through recommendations from others.

Recent Sales *The Seven Decisions*, by Andy Andrews; *A is for Atticus*, by Lorilee Craker (Hachette Book Group USA); The Amanda Bell Browne series, by Claudia Mair Burney (Simon & Schuster); *The Clear Light of Day*, by Penelope Wilcock (Cook Communications). Other clients include Ginger Garrett, Lisa Samson, Susan Meissner, Irene Hannon, Brandt Dodson, Jenn Doucette, Sandra Glahn, Susan Page Davis, Gina Holmes, Scott Jeffrey, Ann Tatlock, Kimberly Stuart.

Terms Agent receives 15% commission on domestic sales; 15% commission on foreign sales. Offers written contract; 30-day notice must be given to terminate contract. Charges for "exceptional fees" after receiving authors' permission.

Writers' Conferences Mount Hermon Christian Writers' Conference; Blue Ridge Christian Writers' Conference; Write to Publish.

Tips "Seriously consider attending a good writers' conference. It will give you the chance to be face-to-face with people in the industry. Also, if you're a novelist, consider joining one of the national writers' organizations. The American Christian Fiction Writers (ACFW) is a wonderful group for new as well as established writers. And if you're a Christian writer of any kind, check into The Writers View, an online writing group. All of these have proven helpful to writers."

Ⓝ ☒ GILLIAN MACKENZIE AGENCY

328 West 101st, 3A, New York NY 10025. E-mail: query@gillianmackenzieagency.com. Web site: www.gillianmackenzieagency.com. **Contact:** Gillian MacKenzie.

- Prior to her current position, Ms. MacKenzie was vice president of Jane Startz Productions, Inc. She began her literary career at Curtis Brown.

Represents Nonfiction books, juvenile books.

o— Actively seeking adult nonfiction and select children's titles.

How to Contact Query with SASE. Query via e-mail. No fax queries. Obtains most new clients through recommendations from others, solicitations.

Recent Sales *Eight Pieces of Empire*, by Lawrence Scott Sheets (Crown); *The Last Single Woman in America*, by Cindy Guidry (Dutton); The Go Pop series, by Bob Staake (LB Kids).

RICIA MAINHARDT AGENCY (RMA)

612 Argyle Road, #L5, Brooklyn NY 11230. (718)434-1893. Fax: (718)434-2157. E-mail: ricia@ricia.com. Web site: www.ricia.com. **Contact:** Ricia Mainhardt. Estab. 1986. Represents 10 clients. 50% of clients are new/unpublished writers. Currently handles: 40% nonfiction books; 50% novellas; 10% juvenile books.

Represents Nonfiction books, novels, juvenile books. **Considers these nonfiction areas:** Any area of nonfiction that seems commercial enough to sell. **Considers these fiction areas:** Action/adventure; confession; detective/police/crime; erotica; ethnic; family saga; fantasy; feminist; gay/lesbian; glitz; historical; horror; humor/satire; juvenile; literary; mainstream/contemporary; mystery/suspense; psychic/supernatural; regional; romance; science fiction; sports; thriller; westerns/frontier; young adult; women's.

o— "We are a small boutique agency that provides hands-on service and attention to clients." Actively seeking adult and young adult fiction, nonfiction, picture books for early readers. Does not want to receive poetry, children's books or screenplays.

How to Contact Query with SASE, submit first 2 sample chapter(s), publishing history, author bio, No attachments or diskettes. Accepts e-mail queries. No fax queries. Considers simultaneous queries. Responds in 1 month to queries; 4 months to mss. Returns materials only with SASE. Obtains most new clients through recommendations from others, solicitations.

Recent Sales A full list of this agency's sales is available online.

Terms Agent receives 15% commission on domestic sales. Offers written contract; 90-day notice must be given to terminate contract.

Writers' Conferences Science Fiction Worldcon; Lunacon.

Tips "Be professional; be patient. It takes a long time for me to evaluate all the submissions that come through the door. Pestering phone calls and e-mails are not appreciated. Write the best book you can in your own style and keep an active narrative voice."

KIRSTEN MANGES LITERARY AGENCY

115 West 29th St., Third Floor, New York NY 10001. E-mail: kirsten@mangeslit.com. Web site: www.mangeslit. com. **Contact:** Kirsten Manges.

- Prior to her current position, Ms. Manges was an agent at Curtis Brown.

Represents Nonfiction books, novels, juvenile books. **Considers these nonfiction areas:** Cooking/foods/nutrition; history; memoirs; multicultural; psychology; science/technology; spirituality; sports; travel; women's issues/studies; journalism, narrative. **Considers these fiction areas:** Young adult; women's; commercial, chick lit.

o— This agency has a focus on women's issues. Actively seeking high quality fiction and nonfiction. "I'm looking for strong credentials, an original point of view and excellent writing skills. With fiction, I'm looking for well written commercial novels, as well as compelling and provocative literary works."

How to Contact Query with SASE. Accepts e-mail queries. No fax queries. Obtains most new clients through recommendations from others, solicitations.

Recent Sales *A Rose for the Crown*, by Anne Easter Smith (Touchstone); *Flip-Flopped*, by Jill Smolinski (Griffin); *Financial Identity*, by Bonnie Eaker Weil (Hudson Street Press/Plume). Other clients include Jennifer Vandever, Olympia Vernon.

CAROL MANN AGENCY

55 Fifth Ave., New York NY 10003. (212)206-5635. Fax: (212)675-4809. E-mail: will@carolmannagency.com. **Contact:** Will Sherlin. Estab. 1977. Member of AAR. Represents roughly 200 clients. 15% of clients are new/unpublished writers. Currently handles: 90% nonfiction books; 10% novels.

Member Agents Carol Mann; Will Sherlin; Laura Yorke.

Represents Nonfiction books, novels. **Considers these nonfiction areas:** Anthropology/archaeology; art/architecture/design; biography/autobiography; business/economics; child guidance/parenting; current affairs; ethnic/cultural interests; government/politics/law; health/medicine; history; money/finance; popular culture; psychology; self-help/personal improvement; sociology; sports; women's issues/studies; music. **Considers these fiction areas:** Literary; commercial.

O⚷ This agency specializes in current affairs, self-help, popular culture, psychology, parenting, and history. Does not want to receive genre fiction (romance, mystery, etc.).

How to Contact Query with outline/proposal, SASE. Responds in 3 weeks to queries.

Recent Sales Clients include novelists Paul Auster and Marita Golden; National Book Award Winner Tim Egan, Hannah Storm, and Willow Bay; Pulitzer Prize-winner Fox Butterfield; bestselling essayist Shelby Steele; sociologist Dr. William Julius Wilson; economist Thomas Sowell; bestselling diet doctors Mary Dan and Michael Eades; ACLU president Nadine Strossen; pundit Mona Charen; memoirist Lauren Winner; photography project editors Rick Smolan and David Cohen (*America 24/7*); Kevin Liles, executive vice president of Warner Music Group and former president of Def Jam Records; and Jermaine Dupri.

Terms Agent receives 15% commission on domestic sales; 20% commission on foreign sales. Offers written contract.

🔲 ◎ SARAH MANSON LITERARY AGENT

6 Totnes Walk, London N2 0AD United Kingdom. (44)(208)442-0396. E-mail: info@sarahmanson.com. Web site: www.sarahmanson.com. **Contact:** Sarah Manson. Estab. 2002. Currently handles: 100% juvenile books.

• Prior to opening her agency, Ms. Manson worked in academic and children's publishing for 10 years and was a chartered school librarian for 8 years.

O⚷ This agency specializes in fiction for children and young adults. No picture books. Does not want to receive submissions from writers outside the United Kingdom and the Republic of Ireland.

How to Contact See Web site for full submission guidelines.

Recent Sales This agency prefers not to give information on specific sales.

Terms Agent receives 10% commission on domestic sales; 20% commission on foreign sales. Offers written contract, binding for 1-month.

🔲 MANUS & ASSOCIATES LITERARY AGENCY, INC.

425 Sherman Ave., Suite 200, Palo Alto CA 94306. (650)470-5151. Fax: (650)470-5159. E-mail: manuslit@manus lit.com. Web site: www.manuslit.com. 445 Park Ave., New York NY 10022. (212)644-8020. Fax (212)644-3374. **Contact:** Janet Manus. **Contact:** Jillian Manus, Jandy Nelson, Stephanie Lee, Donna Levin, Penny Nelson. Estab. 1985. Member of AAR. Represents 75 clients. 30% of clients are new/unpublished writers. Currently handles: 70% nonfiction books; 30% novels.

• Prior to becoming an agent, Ms. Manus was associate publisher of two national magazines and director of development at Warner Bros. and Universal Studios; she has been a literary agent for 20 years.

Member Agents Jandy Nelson, jandy@manuslit.com (self-help, health, memoirs, narrative nonfiction, women's fiction, literary fiction, multicultural fiction, thrillers); Stephanie Lee, slee@manuslit.com (self-help, narrative nonfiction, commercial literary fiction, quirky/edgy fiction, pop culture, pop science); Jillian Manus, jillian-@manuslit.com (political, memoirs, self-help, history, sports, women's issues, Latin fiction and nonfiction, thrillers); Penny Nelson, penny@manuslit.com (memoirs, self-help, sports, nonfiction); Dena Fischer (literary fiction, mainstream/commercial fiction, chick lit, women's fiction, historical fiction, ethnic/cultural fiction, narrative nonfiction, parenting, relationships, pop culture, health, sociology, psychology).

Represents Nonfiction books, novels. **Considers these nonfiction areas:** Biography/autobiography; business/economics; child guidance/parenting; current affairs; ethnic/cultural interests; health/medicine; how-to; memoirs; money/finance; nature/environment; popular culture; psychology; science/technology; self-help/personal improvement; women's issues/studies; Gen X and Gen Y issues; creative nonfiction. **Considers these fiction areas:** Literary; mainstream/contemporary; multicultural; mystery/suspense; thriller; women's; quirky/edgy fiction.

O⚷ "Our agency is unique in the way that we not only sell the material, but we edit, develop concepts, and participate in the marketing effort. We specialize in large, conceptual fiction and nonfiction, and always value a project that can be sold in the TV/feature film market." Actively seeking high-concept thrillers, commercial literary fiction, women's fiction, celebrity biographies, memoirs, multicultural fiction, popular health, women's empowerment and mysteries. No horror, romance, science fiction, fantasy, Western, young adult, children's, poetry, cookbooks or magazine articles.

How to Contact Query with SASE. If requested, submit outline, 2-3 sample chapters. All queries should be sent to the California office. Accepts e-mail queries. No fax queries. Considers simultaneous queries. Responds in 3 months to queries; 3 months to mss. Returns materials only with SASE. Obtains most new clients through recommendations from others, solicitations, conferences.

Recent Sales *Nothing Down for the 2000s* and *Multiple Streams of Income for the 2000s*, by Robert Allen; *Missed Fortune* and *Missed Fortune 101*, by Doug Andrew; *Cracking the Millionaire Code*, by Mark Victor Hansen and Robert Allen; *Stress Free for Good*, by Dr. Fred Luskin and Dr. Ken Pelletier; *The Mercy of Thin Air*, by Ronlyn Domangue; *The Fine Art of Small Talk*, by Debra Fine; *Bone Man of Bonares*, by Terry Tarnoff.

Terms Agent receives 15% commission on domestic sales; 20-25% commission on foreign sales. Offers written contract, binding for 2 years; 60-day notice must be given to terminate contract. Charges for photocopying and postage/UPS.

Writers' Conferences Maui Writers' Conference; San Diego State University Writers' Conference; Willamette Writers' Conference; BookExpo America; MEGA Book Marketing University.

Tips "Research agents using a variety of sources."

◐ MARCH TENTH, INC.

4 Myrtle St., Haworth NJ 07641-1740. (201)387-6551. Fax: (201)387-6552. E-mail: hchoron@aol.com. Web site: www.marchtenthinc.com. **Contact:** Harry Choron, vice president. Estab. 1982. Represents 40 clients. 30% of clients are new/unpublished writers. Currently handles: 75% nonfiction books; 25% novels.

Represents Nonfiction books, novels. **Considers these nonfiction areas:** Biography/autobiography; current affairs; health/medicine; history; humor/satire; language/literature/criticism; music/dance; popular culture; theater/film. **Considers these fiction areas:** Confession; ethnic; family saga; historical; humor/satire; literary; mainstream/contemporary.

 ➜ "We prefer to work with published/established writers."

How to Contact Query with SASE. Considers simultaneous queries. Responds in 1 month to queries. Returns materials only with SASE.

Recent Sales Sold 24 titles in the last year. *Art of the Chopper*, by Tom Zimberoff; *Bruce Springstein Live*, by Dave Marsh; *Complete Annotated Grateful Dead Lyrics*, by David Dodd.

Terms Agent receives 15% commission on domestic sales; 20% commission on foreign sales; 20% commission on dramatic rights sales. Charges clients for postage, photocopying, overseas phone expenses. Does not require expense money upfront.

◐ THE DENISE MARCIL LITERARY AGENCY, INC.

156 Fifth Ave., Suite 625, New York NY 10010. (212)337-3402. Fax: (212)727-2688. Web site: www.DeniseMarci lAgency.com. **Contact:** Denise Marcil, Maura Kye-Casella. Estab. 1977. Member of AAR. Represents 50 clients. 10% of clients are new/unpublished writers.

 • Prior to opening her agency, Ms. Marcil served as an editorial assistant with Avon Books and as an assistant editor with Simon & Schuster.

Member Agents Denise Marcil (women's commercial fiction, thrillers, suspense, popular reference, how-to, self-help, health, business, and parenting. "I am looking for fresh, new voices in commercial women's fiction—stories that capture women's experiences today. I'd love to find a well-written historical novel about a real-life woman from another century"); Maura Kye-Casella (narrative nonfiction, adventure, pop culture, parenting, cookbooks, humor, memoir; and for fiction: multicultural, paranormal, suspense, well-written novels with an edgy voice, quirky characters, and/or unique plots and settings); Anne Marie O'Farrell (manuscripts in the following areas: quantum physics, New Age, business, human potential, personal growth/self-help, healing, children's books and books about drama and acting); Chris Morehouse (manuscripts in the following areas: sports, memoirs, biography, historical fiction and young adult fiction and nonfiction).

How to Contact Query with SASE.

Recent Sales Sold 43 titles in the last year. *My Next Phase*, by Eric Sundstrom, Michael Burnham and J. Randolph Burnham; *How Women are Getting Ahead by Working Abroad*, by Stacie Nevadomski Berdan and C. Perry Yeatman; *Diet for a Pain Free Life*, by Dr. Harris McIlwain and Debra Fulghum Bruce; *Feels Like Family* and *Mending Fences* by Sherryl Woods; *Devour* by Melina Morel; and *Red Cat* by Peter Spiegelman.

Terms Agent receives 15% commission on domestic sales; 20% commission on foreign sales. Offers written contract, binding for 2 years; 100% of business is derived from commissions on ms sales. Charges $100/year for postage, photocopying, long-distance calls, etc.

Writers' Conferences Pacific Northwest Writers' Conference; RWA National Conference; Oregon Writers' Colony.

Ⓝ ◉ THE MARSH AGENCY, LTD

11/12 Dover Street, London England W1S 4LJ, United Kingdom. (44)(207)399-2800. Fax: (44)(207)399-2801. Web site: www.marsh-agency.co.uk. Estab. 1994.

Member Agents Caroline Hardman, rights executive and junior agent (caroline@marsh-agency.co.uk); Jessica Woollard, agent (jessica@marsh-agency.co.uk, specialties: literary fiction, narrative nonfiction, international literature—especially from the Far East); Geraldine Cooke, agent (geraldine@marsh-agency.co.uk); Leyla Mogh-adam, agent (leyla@marsh-agency.co.uk; she is concentrating on English-language sales).

Represents Novels.

 ➜ This agency was founded "as an international rights specialist for literary agents and publishers in the United Kingdom, the U.S., Canada and New Zealand, for whom we sell foreign rights on a commission basis. We work directly with publishers in all the major territories and in the majority of the smaller ones; sometimes in conjunction with local representatives." Actively seeking crime novels.

How to Contact Query with SASE. No fax queries. Obtains most new clients through recommendations from others, solicitations.

Recent Sales A full list of clients and sales is available online.

Tips Use this agency's online form to send a generic e-mail message.

☑ THE EVAN MARSHALL AGENCY

Six Tristam Place, Pine Brook NJ 07058-9445. (973)882-1122. Fax: (973)882-3099. E-mail: evanmarshall@theno velist.com. **Contact:** Evan Marshall. Estab. 1987. Member of AAR, MWA, RWA, Sisters in Crime. Currently handles: 100% novels.

> • Prior to opening his agency, Mr. Marshall served as an editor with Houghton Mifflin, New American Library, Everest House, and Dodd, Mead & Co., and then worked as a literary agent at The Sterling Lord Agency.

Represents Novels. **Considers these fiction areas:** Action/adventure; erotica; ethnic; historical; horror; humor/satire; literary; mainstream/contemporary; mystery/suspense; religious/inspirational; romance (contemporary, gothic, historical, regency); science fiction; westerns/frontier.

How to Contact Query first with SASE; do not enclose material. No e-mail queries. Responds in 1 week to queries; 3 months to mss. Obtains most new clients through recommendations from others.

Recent Sales *Last Known Victim*, by Erica Spindler (Mira); *Julia's Chocolates*, by Cathy Lamb (Kensington); *Maverick*, by Joan Hohl (Silhouette).

Terms Agent receives 15% commission on domestic sales; 20% commission on foreign sales. Offers written contract.

ℕ ☑ THE MARTELL AGENCY

545 Madison Ave., Seventh Floor, New York NY 10022-4219. Fax: (212)317-2676. E-mail: afmartell@aol.com. **Contact:** Alice Martell.

Represents Nonfiction books, novels. **Considers these nonfiction areas:** Business/economics; health/medicine (fitness); history; memoirs; multicultural; psychology; self-help/personal improvement; women's issues/studies. **Considers these fiction areas:** Mystery/suspense; thriller (espionage); women's; suspense, commercial.

> ⍾ Actively seeking mysteries.

How to Contact Query with SASE, submit sample chapters, SASE. No e-mail or fax queries.

Recent Sales *Peddling Peril: The Secret Nuclear Arms Trade*, by David Albright and Joel Wit (Free Press); *Hunger Point: A Novel*, by Jillian Medoff (Harpercollins); *America's Women: Four Hundred Years of Dolls, Drudges, Helpmates, and Heroines*, by Gail Collins (William Morrow). Other clients include Serena Bass, Thomas E. Ricks, Janice Erlbaum.

☑ MARTIN LITERARY MANAGEMENT

17328 Ventura Blvd., Suite 138, Encino (LA) CA 91316. (818)595-1130. Fax: (818)715-0418. E-mail: sharlene@m artinliterarymanagement.com. Web site: www.MartinLiteraryManagement.com. **Contact:** Sharlene Martin. Estab. 2002. Member of AAR. 75% of clients are new/unpublished writers. Currently handles: 100% nonfiction books.

> • Prior to becoming an agent, Ms. Martin worked in film/TV production and acquisitions.

Represents Nonfiction books. **Considers these nonfiction areas:** Biography/autobiography; business/economics; child guidance/parenting; current affairs; health/medicine; history; how-to; humor/satire; memoirs; popular culture; psychology; religious/inspirational; self-help/personal improvement; true crime/investigative; women's issues/studies.

> ⍾ This agency has strong ties to film/TV. Actively seeking nonfiction that is highly commercial and that can be adapted to film.

How to Contact Query with SASE, submit outline, 2 sample chapters. Prefers e-mail queries. Will request supporting materials if interested. No phone queries. Do not send materials unless requested. Submission guidelines defined on Web site. Accepts e-mail queries. No fax queries. Considers simultaneous queries. Responds in 1 week to queries; 3-4 weeks to mss. Returns materials only with SASE. Obtains most new clients through recommendations from others.

Recent Sales *Prince of Darkness—Richard Perle: The Kingdom, The Power, and the End of Empire in America*, by Alan Weisman (Union Square Press/Sterling); *Truth At Last: The Real Story of James Earl Ray*, by John Larry Ray with Lyndon Barsten (Lyons Press).

Terms Agent receives 15% commission on domestic sales; 25% commission on foreign sales. Offers written contract, binding for 1 year; 1-month notice must be given to terminate contract. Charges author for postage and copying if material is not sent electronically. 99 percent of materials are sent electronically to minimize charges to author for postage and copying.

Tips "Have a strong platform for nonfiction. Please don't call. I welcome e-mail. I'm very responsive when I'm interested in a query and work hard to get my clients materials in the best possible shape before submissions. Do your homework prior to submission and only submit your best efforts. Please review our Web site carefully to make sure we're a good match for your work."

⚂ MARGRET MCBRIDE LITERARY AGENCY

7744 Fay Ave., Suite 201, La Jolla CA 92037. (858)454-1550. Fax: (858)454-2156. E-mail: staff@mcbridelit.com. Web site: www.mcbrideliterary.com. **Contact:** Michael Daley, submissions manager. Estab. 1980. Member of AAR, Authors Guild. Represents 55 clients.

• Prior to opening her agency, Ms. McBride worked at Random House, Ballantine Books, and Warner Books.

Represents Nonfiction books, novels. **Considers these nonfiction areas:** Biography/autobiography; business/economics; cooking/foods/nutrition; current affairs; ethnic/cultural interests; government/politics/law; health/medicine; history; how-to; money/finance; music/dance; popular culture; psychology; science/technology; self-help/personal improvement; sociology; women's issues/studies; style. **Considers these fiction areas:** Action/adventure; detective/police/crime; ethnic; historical; humor/satire; literary; mainstream/contemporary; mystery/suspense; thriller; westerns/frontier.

○┰ This agency specializes in mainstream fiction and nonfiction. Does not want to receive screenplays, romance, poetry, or children's/young adult.

How to Contact Query with synopsis, bio, SASE. No e-mail or fax queries. Considers simultaneous queries. Responds in 4-6 weeks to queries; 6-8 weeks to mss. Returns materials only with SASE.

Recent Sales *Accelerants*, by Michael Boylan (Portfolio); *You Call the Shots*, by Cameron Johnson; *From Hope to Higher Ground*, by Gov. Mike Huckabee; *Extraordinary Weddings*, by Colin Cowie.

Terms Agent receives 15% commission on domestic sales; 25% commission on foreign sales. Charges for overnight delivery and photocopying.

⚂ THE MCCARTHY AGENCY, LLC

7 Allen St., Rumson NJ 07660. Phone/Fax: (732)741-3065. E-mail: mccarthylit@aol.com; ntfrost@hotmail.com. 101 Clinton Ave., Apt. #2, Brooklyn NY 11205 **Contact:** Shawna McCarthy. Estab. 1999. Member of AAR. Currently handles: 25% nonfiction books; 75% novels.

Member Agents Shawna McCarthy (New Jersey address); Nahvae Frost (Brooklyn address).

Represents Nonfiction books, novels. **Considers these nonfiction areas:** Biography/autobiography; history; philosophy; science/technology. **Considers these fiction areas:** Fantasy; juvenile; mystery/suspense; romance; science fiction; women's.

How to Contact Query via e-mail. Accepts e-mail queries. No fax queries. Considers simultaneous queries.

◖ HELEN MCGRATH

1406 Idaho Court, Concord CA 94521. (925)672-6211. Fax: (925)672-6383. E-mail: hmcgrath_lit@yahoo.com. **Contact:** Helen McGrath. Estab. 1977. Currently handles: 50% nonfiction books; 50% novels.

Represents Nonfiction books, novels. **Considers these nonfiction areas:** Biography/autobiography; business/economics; current affairs; health/medicine; history; how-to; military/war; psychology; self-help/personal improvement; sports; women's issues/studies. **Considers these fiction areas:** Detective/police/crime; literary; mainstream/contemporary; mystery/suspense; psychic/supernatural; romance; science fiction; thriller.

How to Contact Submit proposal with SASE. *No unsolicited mss.* Responds in 2 months to queries. Obtains most new clients through recommendations from others.

Terms Agent receives 15% commission on domestic sales. Offers written contract. Charges clients for photocopying.

◖ MENDEL MEDIA GROUP, LLC

115 West 30th St., Suite 800, New York NY 10001. (646)239-9896. Fax: (212)685-4717. E-mail: scott@mendelme dia.com. Web site: www.mendelmedia.com. Estab. 2002. Member of AAR. Represents 40-60 clients.

• Prior to becoming an agent, Mr. Mendel was an academic. "I taught American literature, Yiddish, Jewish studies, and literary theory at the University of Chicago and the University of Illinois at Chicago while working on my PhD in English. I also worked as a freelance technical writer and as the managing editor of a healthcare magazine. In 1998, I began working for the late Jane Jordan Browne, a long-time agent in the book publishing world."

Represents Nonfiction books, novels, scholarly books (with potential for broad/popular appeal). **Considers these nonfiction areas:** Americana; animals; anthropology/archaeology; art/architecture/design; biography/autobiography; business/economics; child guidance/parenting; cooking/foods/nutrition; current affairs; education; ethnic/cultural interests; gardening; gay/lesbian issues; government/politics/law; health/medicine; history; how-to; humor/satire; language/literature/criticism; memoirs; military/war; money/finance; multicultural; music/dance; nature/environment; philosophy; popular culture; psychology; recreation; regional; religious/inspirational; science/technology; self-help/personal improvement; sex; sociology; software; spirituality; sports; true crime/investigative; women's issues/studies; Jewish topics; creative nonfiction. **Considers these fiction areas:** Action/adventure; contemporary issues; detective/police/crime; erotica; ethnic; feminist; gay/lesbian; glitz; historical; humor/satire; juvenile; literary; mainstream/contemporary; mystery/suspense; picture books; religious/inspirational; romance; sports; thriller; young adult; Jewish fiction.

> ⊶ "I am interested in major works of history, current affairs, biography, business, politics, economics, science, major memoirs, narrative nonfiction, and other sorts of general nonfiction." Actively seeking new, major or definitive work on a subject of broad interest, or a controversial, but authoritative, new book on a subject that affects many people's lives.

How to Contact Query with SASE. Do not e-mail or fax queries. For nonfiction, include a complete, fully-edited book proposal with sample chapters. For fiction, include a complete synopsis and no more than 20 pages of sample text. Responds in 2 weeks to queries; 4-6 weeks to mss. Returns materials only with SASE. Obtains most new clients through recommendations from others.

Terms Agent receives 15% commission on domestic sales; 20% commission on foreign sales. Offers written contract, binding for 2 years; 1-month notice must be given to terminate contract. Charges clients for ms duplication, expedited delivery services (when necessary), any overseas shipping, telephone calls/faxes necessary for marketing the author's foreign rights.

Writers' Conferences BookExpo America; Frankfurt Book Fair; London Book Fair; RWA National Conference; Modern Language Association Convention; Jerusalem Book Fair.

Tips "While I am not interested in being flattered by a prospective client, it does matter to me that she knows why she is writing to me in the first place. Is one of my clients a colleague of hers? Has she read a book by one of my clients that led her to believe I might be interested in her work?"

⦿ MENZA-BARRON AGENCY

1170 Broadway, Suite 807, New York NY 10001. (212)889-6850. **Contact:** Claudia Menza, Manie Barron. Estab. 1983. Member of AAR. Represents 100 clients. 50% of clients are new/unpublished writers.

Represents Nonfiction books, novels. **Considers these nonfiction areas:** Current affairs; education; ethnic/cultural interests (especially African-American); health/medicine; history; multicultural; music/dance; photography; psychology; theater/film.

> ⊶ This agency specializes editorial assistance and African-American fiction and nonfiction.

How to Contact Query with SASE. Responds in 2-4 weeks to queries; 2-4 months to mss. Returns materials only with SASE.

Recent Sales This agency prefers not to share information on specific sales.

Terms Agent receives 15% commission on domestic sales; 20% (if co-agent is used) commission on foreign sales; 20% commission on dramatic rights sales. Offers written contract.

⟦Ⓝ⟧ ⦿ SCOTT MEREDITH LITERARY AGENCY

200 W. 57th St., Suite 904, New York NY 10019. (646)274-1970. Fax: (212)977-5997. E-mail: aklebanoff@rosettabooks.com. Web site: www.scottmeredith.com. **Contact:** Arthur Klebanoff, CEO. Estab. 1946; adheres to the AAR canon of ethics. Represents 20 clients. 0% of clients are new/unpublished writers. Currently handles: 90% nonfiction books; 5% novels; 5% textbooks.

> • Prior to becoming an agent, Mr. Klebanoff was a lawyer.

Represents Nonfiction books, textbooks. **Considers these nonfiction areas:** Any category leading entry.

> ⊶ This agency's specialty lies in category nonfiction publishing programs. Actively seeking category leading nonfiction. Does not want to receive first fiction projects.

How to Contact Query with SASE, submit proposal package, author bio. Accepts e-mail queries. No fax queries. Considers simultaneous queries. Responds in 1 week to queries; 2 weeks to mss. Returns materials only with SASE. Obtains most new clients through recommendations from others.

Recent Sales Sold 10 titles in the last year. *Positively American*, by U.S. Sen. Chuck Schumer (Rodale); *The Story We Are Told*, by Bill Bradley (Random House); *The Silver Palate Cookbook: 25th Anniversary Edition*, by Julee Rosso and Sheila Lukins (Workman); *Michel Thomas Language Program*, by Michel Thomas (Hodder and Stoughton McGraw Hill); *Roots: 30th Anniversary Edition*, by Alex Haley (Vanguard Press/Perseus). Other clients include Paul Krugman, Mayo Clinic, Roger Tory Peterson, Linda Goodman, Janson Family (Janson's History of Art), Michael Steinhardt.

Terms Agent receives 15% commission on domestic sales; 25% commission on foreign sales. Offers written contract.

⟦Ⓝ⟧ ⦿ METROPOL LITERARY

115 W. 29th St., New York NY 10001. E-mail: contact@metlit.com. Web site: www.metlit.com. 9663 Santa Monica Blvd., Beverly Hills CA 90210 Estab. 2002; adheres to AAR canon of ethics.

Represents Nonfiction books, novels, juvenile books. **Considers these nonfiction areas:** Biography/autobiography; business/economics; computers/electronic; health/medicine; history; juvenile nonfiction; multicultural; religious/inspirational; science/technology; sports; lifestyle. **Considers these fiction areas:** Fantasy; mystery/suspense; romance; science fiction.

○→ This agency has offices in New York as well as Beverly Hills. Actively seeking nonfiction sports, celebrity, pop culture and current affairs—including biographies, authorized or objective. This agency is also interested in books with an emphasis on prescriptive (books that offer a solution to a problem), exposé and nonfiction narrative. Books that offer an insider's perspective to a unique environment (e.g., *The Nanny Diaries, The Devil Wears Prada, How to Lose Friends and Alienate People*) are also sought.

How to Contact Query with SASE, submit 5 pages of sample material (for fiction), résumé, 1-2 page overview; for nonfiction, send résumé, 2-5 page project overview. E-queries only. No e-mail attachments. This agency only responds if interested. Responds in 1 week to queries. Obtains most new clients through recommendations from others, solicitations.

Recent Sales *The Quit-Day Plan*, by Sandra Rutter (Hazelden Press); *Betting the House: The Agassi Story*, by Mike Agassi (ECW); *Blind Run: Rebel Without a Cause—How James Dean and Nicholas Ray Invented the Teenager*, by Lawrence Frascella and Al Weisel (Simon and Schuster).

Tips "Please ensure that your work has been edited and is stylistically flawless."

◙ DORIS S. MICHAELS LITERARY AGENCY, INC.

1841 Broadway, Suite 903, New York NY 10023. (212)265-9474. Fax: (212)265-9480. E-mail: query@dsmagency .com. Web site: www.dsmagency.com. **Contact:** Doris S. Michaels, president. Estab. 1994. Member of AAR, WNBA.

Represents Novels. **Considers these fiction areas:** Literary (with commercial appeal and strong screen potential).

How to Contact Query by e-mail; see submission guidelines on Web site. Obtains most new clients through recommendations from others, conferences.

Recent Sales *Cheap and Easy: Fast Food for Fast Girls*, by Sandra Bark and Alexis Kanfer; *Why Did I Marry You Anyway?*, by Barbara Bartlein; *You Look Too Young to be a Mom*, by Deborah Davis.

Terms Agent receives 15% commission on domestic sales; 20% commission on foreign sales. Offers written contract, binding for 1 year; 1-month notice must be given to terminate contract. 100% of business is derived from commissions on ms sales. Charges clients for office expenses, not to exceed $150 without written permission.

Writers' Conferences BookExpo America; Frankfurt Book Fair; London Book Fair; Maui Writers Conference.

◙ MARTHA MILLARD LITERARY AGENCY

50 W. 67th St., #1G, New York NY 10023. (212)787-7769. Fax: (212)787-7867. **Contact:** Martha Millard. Estab. 1980. Member of AAR, SFWA. Represents 50 clients. Currently handles: 25% nonfiction books; 65% novels; 10% story collections.

• Prior to becoming an agent, Ms. Millard worked in editorial departments of several publishers and was vice president at another agency for more than four years.

Represents Nonfiction books, novels. **Considers these nonfiction areas:** Art/architecture/design; biography/autobiography; business/economics; child guidance/parenting; cooking/foods/nutrition; current affairs; education; ethnic/cultural interests; health/medicine; history; how-to; juvenile nonfiction; memoirs; money/finance; music/dance; New Age/metaphysics; photography; popular culture; psychology; self-help/personal improvement; theater/film; true crime/investigative; women's issues/studies. **Considers these fiction areas:** Fantasy; mystery/suspense; romance; science fiction.

How to Contact No unsolicited queries. **Referrals only**. No e-mail or fax queries. Returns materials only with SASE. Obtains most new clients through recommendations from others.

Recent Sales *The Dragons of Babel*, by Michael Swanwick (Tor); *Nazi Art: The Secret of Post-War History*, by Gregory Maertz (Yale University Press); *Playing With the HP Way*, by Peter Burrows (John Wiley & Sons); *Restore Yourself*, by James Simm and Victoria Houston (Berkley).

Terms Agent receives 15% commission on domestic sales; 20% commission on foreign sales. Offers written contract.

◙ THE MILLER AGENCY

Film Center, 630 Ninth Ave., Suite 1102, New York NY 10036. (212) 206-0913. Fax: (212) 206-1473. E-mail: angela@milleragency.net. Web site: www.milleragency.net. **Contact:** Angela Miller, Sharon Bowers, Jennifer Griffin. Estab. 1990. Represents 100 clients. 5% of clients are new/unpublished writers.

Represents Nonfiction books. **Considers these nonfiction areas:** Anthropology/archaeology; art/architecture/ design; biography/autobiography; business/economics; child guidance/parenting; cooking/foods/nutrition;

current affairs; ethnic/cultural interests; gay/lesbian issues; health/medicine; language/literature/criticism; New Age/metaphysics; psychology; self-help/personal improvement; sports; women's issues/studies.

O→ This agency specializes in nonfiction, multicultural arts, psychology, self-help, cookbooks, biography, travel, memoir, and sports. Fiction is considered selectively.

How to Contact Query with SASE, outline, a few sample chapters. Considers simultaneous queries. Responds in 1 week to queries. Obtains most new clients through referrals.

Recent Sales Sold 25 titles in the last year.

Terms Agent receives 15% commission on domestic sales; 20-25% commission on foreign sales. Offers written contract, binding for 2 years; 2-month notice must be given to terminate contract. 100% of business is derived from commissions on ms sales. Charges clients for postage (express mail or messenger services) and photocopying.

◎ MOORE LITERARY AGENCY

10 State St., Newburyport MA 01950. (978)465-9015. Fax: (978)465-8817. E-mail: cmoore@moorelit.com. **Contact:** Claudette Moore. Estab. 1989. 10% of clients are new/unpublished writers. Currently handles: 100% nonfiction books.

Represents Nonfiction books. **Considers these nonfiction areas:** Computers/electronic; technology.

O→ This agency specializes in trade computer books (90% of titles).

How to Contact Query with SASE, submit proposal package. Query by e-mail. Send proposals by snail mail. Accepts e-mail queries. No fax queries. Obtains most new clients through recommendations from others, conferences.

Recent Sales *Windows XP Timesaving Techniques for Dummies*, by Woody Leonhard (Wiley); *Expert One-on-One Microsoft Access Application Development*, by Helen Feddema (Wiley); *Thinking in C++, Vol. 2*, by Bruce Eckel and Chuck Allison (Prentice Hall); *Microsoft Windows XP Inside Out, 2nd Ed.*, by Ed Bolt, Carl Siechert, and Craig Stinson (Microsoft Press).

Terms Agent receives 15% commission on domestic sales; 15% commission on foreign sales; 15% commission on dramatic rights sales. Offers written contract.

◐ PATRICIA MOOSBRUGGER LITERARY AGENCY

165 Bennet Ave., #6M, New York NY 10040. Web site: www.pmagency.net. **Contact:** Patricia Moosbrugger. Member of AAR.

Represents Nonfiction books.

How to Contact Query with SASE.

Recent Sales *Indiana, Indiana*, by Laird Hunt (Coffee House Press); *Surrendered Child: A Birth Mother's Journey*, by Karen Salyer McElmurray (University of Georgia Press).

◐ HOWARD MORHAIM LITERARY AGENCY

30 Pierrepont St., Brooklyn NY 11201. (718)222-8400. Fax: (718)222-5056. Member of AAR.

Member Agents Howard Morhaim; John Michel; Kate McKean (contemporary women's fiction, paranormal romance, urban fantasy, literary fiction, narrative nonfiction, sports-related books, pop culture, and health and wellness).

Represents Fiction, young adult fiction, nonfiction.

O→ Actively seeking fiction, nonfiction and young-adult novels.

How to Contact Query with SASE, submit outline/proposal, 3 sample chapter(s), publishing history, author bio, SASE.

Recent Sales *Dancing With Werewolves*, by Carole Nelson Douglas (Juno).

◐ WILLIAM MORRIS AGENCY, INC.

1325 Avenue of the Americas, New York NY 10019. (212)586-5100. Fax: (212)246-3583. Web site: www.wma.c om. Alternate address: One William Morris Place, Beverly Hills CA 90212. (310)859-4000. Fax: (310)859-4462. **Contact:** Literary Department Coordinator. Member of AAR.

Member Agents Owen Laster; Jennifer Rudolph Walsh; Suzanne Gluck; Joni Evans; Tracy Fisher; Mel Berger; Jay Mandel; Peter Franklin; Lisa Grubka; Jonathan Pecursky.

Represents Nonfiction books, novels.

O→ Does not want to receive screenplays.

How to Contact Query with synopsis, publication history, SASE. Send book queries to the NYC address. Considers simultaneous queries.

Recent Sales This agency prefers not to share information on specific sales.

Terms Agent receives 15% commission on domestic sales; 20% commission on foreign sales.

⦿ HENRY MORRISON, INC.

105 S. Bedford Road, Suite 306A, Mt. Kisco NY 10549. (914)666-3500. Fax: (914)241-7846. **Contact:** Henry Morrison. Estab. 1965. Signatory of WGA. Represents 53 clients. 5% of clients are new/unpublished writers. Currently handles: 5% nonfiction books; 95% novels.

Represents Nonfiction books, novels. **Considers these nonfiction areas:** Anthropology/archaeology; biography/autobiography; government/politics/law; history. **Considers these fiction areas:** Action/adventure; detective/police/crime; family saga; historical.

How to Contact Query with SASE. Responds in 2 weeks to queries; 3 months to mss. Obtains most new clients through recommendations from others.

Recent Sales Sold 15 titles in the last year. *The Bourne Betrayal*, by Eric Lustbader (Warner Books/Hachette); *The Vampire of New York*, by R.L. Stevens (Signet); *Glass Tiger*, by Joe Gores (Penzler Harcourt); *Prion*, by Daniel Kalla (Forge); *Dark Reflections*, by Samuel R. Delany (Carroll & Graf); *City of Glory*, by Beverly Swerling (Simon & Schuster). Other clients include Daniel Cohen, Joel Ross, Dan Kalla, Christopher Hyde, Charles W. Henderson.

Terms Agent receives 15% commission on domestic sales; 25% commission on foreign sales. Charges clients for ms copies, bound galleys, finished books for submissions to publishers, movie producers and foreign publishers.

ⓝ ⊘ MORTIMER LITERARY AGENCY

52645 Paui Road, Aguanga CA 92536. Fax: (951)332-8209. E-mail: mla@mtpalomar.net. Web site: www.mortimerliterary.com. **Contact:** Kelly L. Mortimer. Estab. 2006. Member of RWA. Represents 10 clients. 70% of clients are new/unpublished writers. Currently handles: 5% nonfiction books; 90% novels; 5% juvenile books.

● Prior to becoming an agent, Ms. Mortimer was a freelance writer and the CFO of Microvector, Inc.

Represents Nonfiction books, novels, novellas, juvenile books (young adult). **Considers these nonfiction areas:** Religious/inspirational; self-help/personal improvement; relationship advice. **Considers these fiction areas:** Action/adventure; detective/police/crime; fantasy; historical; horror; mainstream/contemporary; mystery/suspense; psychic/supernatural; religious/inspirational; romance; thriller; young adult.

   ○━ "I keep a short client list to give my writers personal attention. I do a complete line edit of every manuscript. I send manuscripts out to pre-selected editors the day after I receive them. I am not seeking new clients now, but will be in the future."

How to Contact Query with SASE. E-queries only. Responds to partials in weeks. Query only after reading Web site guidelines. Considers simultaneous queries. Responds in 2-3 months to mss. Returns materials only with SASE. Obtains most new clients through recommendations from others, solicitations, conferences.

Recent Sales Sold 3 titles in the last year. Other clients include Debra Holland, Natalie Ellis, Pam Hillman, Dineen Miller, Sheila Raye, Charlene Sands, R.J. Sullivan, Steven Guerrero.

Terms Agent receives 15% commission on domestic sales; 20% commission on foreign sales. Offers written contract. "I charge for postage—only the amount I pay and it comes out of the author's advance. The writer provides me with copies of their manuscripts."

Writers' Conferences RWA, ACFW.

Tips "Follow submission guidelines on the Web site or your query will be ignored. Don't send material or mss that aren't requested."

⊘ DEE MURA LITERARY

269 West Shore Drive, Massapequa NY 11758-8225. (516)795-1616. Fax: (516)795-8797. E-mail: samurai5@ix.netcom.com. **Contact:** Dee Mura, Karen Roberts, Bobbie Sokol, Brian Hertler, Kimiko Nakamura. Estab. 1987. Signatory of WGA. 50% of clients are new/unpublished writers.

● Prior to opening her agency, Ms. Mura was a public relations executive with a roster of film and entertainment clients and worked in editorial for major weekly news magazines.

Represents Nonfiction books, novels, juvenile books, scholarly books, feature film, TV scripts, episodic drama, sitcom, animation, documentary, miniseries, variety show. **Considers these nonfiction areas:** Agriculture/horticulture; animals; anthropology/archaeology; biography/autobiography; business/economics; child guidance/parenting; computers/electronic; current affairs; education; ethnic/cultural interests; gay/lesbian issues; government/politics/law; health/medicine; history; how-to; humor/satire; juvenile nonfiction; memoirs; military/war; money/finance; nature/environment; science/technology; self-help/personal improvement; sociology; sports; travel; true crime/investigative; women's issues/studies. **Considers these fiction areas:** Action/adventure; contemporary issues; detective/police/crime (and espionage); ethnic; experimental; family saga; fantasy; feminist; gay/lesbian; glitz; historical; humor/satire; juvenile; literary; mainstream/contemporary; mystery/suspense; psychic/supernatural; regional; romance (contemporary, gothic, historical, regency); science fiction; sports; thriller; westerns/frontier; young adult; political. **Considers these script subject areas:** Action/adventure; cartoon/animation; comedy; contemporary issues; detective/police/crime (and espionage); family saga; fantasy; feminist; gay/lesbian; glitz; historical; horror; juvenile; mainstream; mystery/suspense;

psychic/supernatural; religious/inspirational; romantic comedy; romantic drama; science fiction; sports; teen; thriller; western/frontier.

   O→ "We work on everything, but are especially interested in literary fiction, commercial fiction/nonfiction, thrillers/espionage, humor/drama (we love to laugh and cry), self-help, inspirational, medical, scholarly, true life stories, true crime, war/military and women's stories/issues." Actively seeking unique nonfiction mss and proposals, novelists who are great storytellers, and contemporary writers with distinct voices and passion. Does not want to receive ideas for sitcoms, novels, films, etc., or queries without SASEs.

How to Contact Query with SASE. Accepts e-mail queries (no attachments). No fax queries. Considers simultaneous queries. Only responds if interested. Returns materials only with SASE. Obtains most new clients through recommendations from others, queries.

Recent Sales Sold more than 40 titles and sold 35 scripts in the last year.

Terms Agent receives 15% commission on domestic sales; 20% commission on foreign sales. Offers written contract. Charges clients for photocopying, mailing expenses, overseas/long distance phone calls/faxes.

Tips "Please include a paragraph on your background, even if you have no literary background, and a brief synopsis of the project. We enjoy well-written query letters that tell us about the project and the author."

[N] Ⓩ RANDI MURRAY LITERARY AGENCY, INC.

1325 Howard Ave., PMB 619, Burlingame CA 94010. E-mail: randi@murrayagency.com. Web site: www.murray agency.com. **Contact:** Randi Murray.

Represents Nonfiction books, novels. **Considers these nonfiction areas:** Biography/autobiography; business/economics; current affairs; government/politics/law; history; humor/satire; memoirs; psychology; science/technology; sports; women's issues/studies; narrative, prescriptive (relationships, lifestyle, health). **Considers these fiction areas:** Historical; literary; mystery/suspense; women's; chick lit.

   O→ Does not want to receive children's and young adult books, horror, poetry, Western, romance, academic books, science fiction, techno-thrillers.

How to Contact Query with SASE, submit synopsis, publishing history, author bio, first 30 pp. (for fiction), or proposal and 50 pages (for nonfiction). Use the online query form for quickest response. Note if your submission is exclusive. Accepts e-mail queries. No fax queries. Responds in 4 weeks to queries. Obtains most new clients through recommendations from others, solicitations.

Recent Sales *My Cousin the Saint*, by Justin Catanoso (ReganMedia); *Pornology*, by Ayn Carillo Gailey (Running Press); *Talking With My Mouth Full: Crabcakes, Bundt Cakes and Other Kitchen Stories*, by Bonny Wolf (St. Martin's Press).

Terms Agent receives 15% commission on domestic sales; 20% commission on foreign sales. Offers written contract.

Tips "Follow our submission guidelines and send only what we ask for, including all of your contact information on the cover letter."

Ⓩ MUSE LITERARY MANAGEMENT

189 Waverly Place, #4, New York NY 10014. (212)925-3721. E-mail: museliterarymgmt@aol.com. **Contact:** Deborah Carter. Estab. 1998. Member of MediaBistro, Author's Guild, SCBWI, International Thriller Writers. Represents 10 clients. 80% of clients are new/unpublished writers.

   ● Prior to starting her agency, Ms. Carter trained with an AAR literary agent and worked in the music business and as a talent scout for record companies in artist management. She has a BA in English and music from Washington Square University College at NYU.

Represents Novels, short story collections, novellas, juvenile books. **Considers these nonfiction areas:** Narrative-only nonfiction (memoir, outdoors, music, writing). Please query other narrative nonfiction subjects. **Considers these fiction areas:** Action/adventure; detective/police/crime; picture books; young adult; espionage; middle-grade novels; literary short story collections, literary fiction with popular appeal, mystery/suspense/thriller (no cozies).

   O→ Specializes in manuscript development, the sale and administration of print, performance, and foreign rights to literary works, and post-publication publicity and appearances. Actively seeking progressive, African-American, and multicultural fiction for adults and children in the U.S. market. Does not want to receive category fiction (romance, chick lit, fantasy, science fiction, horror), or fiction/nonfiction with religious/spiritual matter, illness or victimhood.

How to Contact Query with SASE. Query via e-mail (no attachments). Discards unwanted queries. Responds in 2 weeks to queries; 2-3 weeks to mss. Obtains most new clients through recommendations from others, conferences.

Recent Sales Sold 2 titles in the last year. Untitled children's folktale collection, by Anne Shelby (UNC Press); foreign rights sales: *The Fund*, by Wes DeMott in Russian. Other clients include various new writers.

Terms Agent receives 15% commission on domestic sales; 20% commission on foreign sales. Offers written contract, binding for 1 year; 1-day notice must be given to terminate contract. Sometimes charges for postage and photocopying. All expenses are subject to client approval.
Writers' Conferences BookExpo America.

⚫ JEAN V. NAGGAR LITERARY AGENCY, INC.

216 E. 75th St., Suite 1E, New York NY 10021. (212)794-1082. E-mail: jvnla@jvnla.com. Web site: www.jvnla.com. **Contact:** Jean Naggar. Estab. 1978. Member of AAR, PEN, Women's Media Group, Women's Forum. Represents 80 clients. 20% of clients are new/unpublished writers. Currently handles: 35% nonfiction books; 45% novels; 15% juvenile books; 5% scholarly books.

• Ms. Naggar has served as president of AAR.

Member Agents Jean Naggar (mainstream fiction, nonfiction); Jennifer Weltz, director (subsidiary rights, children's books); Alice Tasman, senior agent (commercial and literary fiction, thrillers, narrative nonfiction); Mollie Glick, agent (specializes in literary and practical nonfiction); Jessica Regel, agent (young adult fiction and nonfiction).

Represents Nonfiction books, novels. **Considers these nonfiction areas:** Biography/autobiography; child guidance/parenting; current affairs; government/politics/law; health/medicine; history; juvenile nonfiction; memoirs; New Age/metaphysics; psychology; religious/inspirational; self-help/personal improvement; sociology; travel; women's issues/studies. **Considers these fiction areas:** Action/adventure; detective/police/crime; ethnic; family saga; feminist; historical; literary; mainstream/contemporary; mystery/suspense; psychic/supernatural; thriller.

○➔ This agency specializes in mainstream fiction and nonfiction and literary fiction with commercial potential.

How to Contact Query with SASE. Prefers to read materials exclusively. No e-mail or fax queries. Responds in 1 day to queries; 2 months to mss. Returns materials only with SASE. Obtains most new clients through recommendations from others.

Recent Sales *Dark Angels*, by Karleen Koen; *Poison*, by Susan Fromberg Schaeffer; *Unauthorized*, by Kristin McCloy; *Voyage of the Sea Turtle: The Search for the Last Dinosaurs*, by Carl Safina; *Enola Holmes*, by Nancy Springer; *The Liar's Diary*, by Patry Francis; *Closing Costs*, by Seth Margolis; *Blind Faith*, by Richard Sloan.

Terms Agent receives 15% commission on domestic sales; 20% commission on foreign sales. Offers written contract. Charges for overseas mailing, messenger services, book purchases, long-distance telephone, photocopying—all deductible from royalties received.

Writers' Conferences Willamette Writers Conference; Pacific Northwest Writers Conference; Bread Loaf Writers Conference; Marymount Manhattan Writers Conference; SEAK Medical & Legal Fiction Writing Conference.

Tips "We will now only guarantee to read and respond to queries from writers who come recommended by someone we know. Our areas are general fiction and nonfiction—no children's books by unpublished writers, no multimedia, no screenplays, no formula fiction, and no mysteries by unpublished writers."

⚫ NANCY COFFEY LITERARY & MEDIA REPRESENTATION

240 W. 35th St., Suite 500, New York NY 10001. **Contact:** Nancy Coffey. Member of AAR. Currently handles: 5% nonfiction books; 90% novels; 5% juvenile books.

Represents Nonfiction books, novels, juvenile books (young adult, from cutting edge material to fantasy). **Considers these fiction areas:** Family saga; fantasy; military/war (espionage); mystery/suspense; romance; science fiction; thriller; young adult; women's.

How to Contact Query with SASE.

Recent Sales *The Gardens of Covington*, by Joan A. Medlicott (Thomas Dunne Books); *The Sixth Fleet*, by David E. Meadows (Berkley).

Ⓝ ⚫ NAPPALAND LITERARY AGENCY

P.O. Box 1674, Loveland CO 80539-1674. Fax: (970)635-9869. E-mail: Literary@nappaland.com. Web site: www.nappaland.com/literary.htm. **Contact:** Mike Nappa, senior agent. Estab. 1995. Represents 8 clients. 0% of clients are new/unpublished writers. Currently handles: 45% nonfiction books; 50% novels; 5% scholarly books.

• Prior to becoming an agent, Mr. Nappa served as an acquisition editor for three major Christian publishing houses.

Represents Nonfiction books, novels. **Considers these nonfiction areas:** Child guidance/parenting; current affairs; popular culture; religious/inspirational; women's issues/studies. **Considers these fiction areas:** Action/adventure; detective/police/crime; literary; mainstream/contemporary; religious/inspirational; thriller.

○➔ "Nappaland Literary Agency is a deliberately small agency that has been active within the Christian publishing industry since 1995. We represent only authors with whom we have worked in the past, or who come to us with glowing recommendations from our current network of industry friends.'' Actively seeking thoughtful, vivid, nonfiction works on religious and cultural themes. Also, fast-paced, well-crafted fiction (suspense, literary, women's) that reads like a work of art. Does not want to receive children's books, movie or television scripts, textbooks, short stories, stage plays or poetry.

How to Contact Query with SASE, submit author bio. Include the name of the person referring you to us. Do *not* send entire proposal unless requested. Send query and bio only. E-queries preferred and given first priority. No attachments please. Accepts e-mail and fax queries. Considers simultaneous queries. Responds in 1 month to queries; 3 months to mss.

Recent Sales Sold 3 titles in the last year. *Misquoting Truth*, by Timothy Paul Jones (InterVarsity Press); *Zachary's Zoo*, by Mike and Amy Nappa (Zondervan); *The Christ Conspiracies*, by Timothy Paul Jones (Strang Book Group).

Terms Agent receives 15% commission on domestic sales; 20% commission on foreign sales. Offers written contract; 30-day notice must be given to terminate contract.

Writers' Conferences Colorado Christian Writers' Conference in Estes Park.

🄽 🄬 THE NASHVILLE AGENCY

P.O. Box 110909, Nashville TN 37222. (615)263-4143. Fax: (866)333-8663. E-mail: info@nashvilleagency.com; submissions@nashvilleagency.com. Web site: www.nashvilleagency.com. **Contact:** Taylor Joseph. Estab. 2002. Represents 18 clients. 50% of clients are new/unpublished writers. Currently handles: 40% nonfiction books; 15% novels; 5% novellas; 40% juvenile books.

Member Agents Tim Grable (business books); Jonathan Clements (nonfiction, juvenile); Taylor Joseph (fiction, novels, memoirs).

Represents Nonfiction books, novels, novellas, juvenile books, scholarly books, movie scripts, documentary. **Considers these nonfiction areas:** Biography/autobiography; business/economics; child guidance/parenting; cooking/foods/nutrition; crafts/hobbies; current affairs; education; history; how-to; humor/satire; juvenile nonfiction; memoirs; military/war; music/dance; popular culture; religious/inspirational; self-help/personal improvement; sports; true crime/investigative; women's issues/studies. **Considers these fiction areas:** Action/adventure; fantasy; historical; humor/satire; juvenile; literary; mainstream/contemporary; mystery/suspense; regional; religious/inspirational; thriller; young adult; women's. **Considers these script subject areas:** Action/adventure; contemporary issues.

> ⊶ ''Our agency looks not as much for specific genres or stylings. Rather, we look for far-reaching potentials (i.e., brands, properties) to branch outside a token specific market.'' Actively seeking novels, nonfiction, religious/spiritual material. Does not want to receive poetry, stage plays or textbooks.

How to Contact Query with SASE, submit proposal package, synopsis, publishing history, author bio, Description of how your relationship with The Nashville Agency was initiated. Query via e-mail. No fax queries. Considers simultaneous queries. Responds in 3 weeks to queries; 3 months to mss. Returns materials only with SASE. Obtains most new clients through recommendations from others.

Recent Sales This agency prefers not to share information on specific sales.

Terms Agent receives 15% commission on domestic sales; 20% commission on foreign sales. Offers written contract, binding for 5 years; 30-day notice must be given to terminate contract. This agency charges for standard office fees.

Writers' Conferences Blue Ridge Writers' Conference.

🄬 NELSON LITERARY AGENCY

1020 15th St., Suite 26L, Denver CO 80202. (303)463-5301. E-mail: query@nelsonagency.com. Web site: www.nelsonagency.com. **Contact:** Kristin Nelson. Estab. 2002. Member of AAR.

> ● Prior to opening her own agency, Ms. Nelson worked as a literary scout and subrights agent for agent Jody Rein.

Represents Novels, select nonfiction. **Considers these nonfiction areas:** Memoirs; narrative nonfiction. **Considers these fiction areas:** Literary; romance (includes fantasy with romantic elements, science fiction, fantasy, young adult); women's; chick lit (includes mysteries); commercial/mainstream.

> ⊶ NLA specializes in representing commercial fiction and high caliber literary fiction. Actively seeking Latina writers who tackle contemporary issues in a modern voice (think *Dirty Girls Social Club*). Does not want short story collections, mysteries (except chick lit), thrillers, Christian, horror, or children's picture books.

How to Contact Query by e-mail only.

Recent Sales *Schemes of Love*, by Sherry Thomas (Bantam Dell); *The Camelot Code*, by Mari Mancusi (Dutton Children's); *Magic Lost, Trouble Found*, by Lisa Shearin (Ace); *Magellan's Witch*, by Carolyn Jewel (Hachette/Warner); *No Place Safe*, by Kim Reid (Kensington); *Plan B*, by Jennifer O'Connell (MTV/Pocket Books); *Code of Love*, by Cheryl Sawyer (NAL/Penguin Group); *Once Upon Stilettos*, by Shanna Swendson (Ballantine); *I'd*

Tell You I Love You But Then I'd Have to Kill You, by Ally Carter (Hyperion Children's); *An Accidental Goddess*, by Linnea Sinclair (Bantam Spectra). Other clients include Paula Reed, Becky Motew, Jack McCallum, Jana Deleon.

N ◑ THE NEVILLE AGENCY

E-mail: info@nevilleagency.com. Web site: www.nevilleagency.com. **Contact:** Barret Neville. Currently handles: 90% nonfiction books; 10% novels.

- Prior to his current position, Mr. Neville was an editor, and spent 10 years acquiring and developing books, including several national and *New York Times* bestsellers, for publishers such as Penguin, St. Martin's Press and McGraw-Hill. He is also the author, with John Salka, of *First In, Last Out: Leadership Lessons of the New York Fire Department*.

Represents Nonfiction books, novels. **Considers these nonfiction areas:** Biography/autobiography; business/economics; health/medicine; history; humor/satire; popular culture; self-help/personal improvement; narrative, parenting. **Considers these fiction areas:** Historical; mystery/suspense; thriller.

- O⇥ "The Neville Agency is a boutique literary agency specializing in nonfiction. We seek out authors who are experts in their fields; who have a unique voice or vision; and who are poised to contribute something new or provocative to the cultural dialogue. We also handle a select number of mysteries and thrillers."

How to Contact Send a brief e-query with a bio and any relevant publishing history. No snail mail queries or phone calls. No fax queries. Responds in 3 days to queries.

Recent Sales *Run Less, Run Faster: Become a Faster, Stronger Runner with the Revolutionary FIRST Training Program*, by William Pierce, et al (Rodale); *Adoption 101: Secrets to a Fast, Safe and Affordable Adoption*, by Randall Hicks (Penguin/Perigee); *Flipping the Switch*, by John Miller; *The Dictionary of Corporate Bullshit*, by Lois Beckwith; *The Baby Game*, by Randall Hicks.

Tips "For mysteries and thrillers, our ideal partners are authors who have a clear understanding of their book's appeal (for example, it's a cozy, a police procedural, romantic suspense, etc.) and who are bringing something new to the genre, be it an unusual protagonist, unique setting or unforgettable voice."

◎ NEW ENGLAND PUBLISHING ASSOCIATES, INC.

P.O. Box 361, Chester CT 06412-0645. (860)345-READ or (860)345-4976. Fax: (860)345-3660. E-mail: nepa@nepa.com. Web site: www.nepa.com. **Contact:** Elizabeth Frost-Knappman, Edward W. Knappman, Victoria Harlow. Estab. 1983. Member of AAR. Represents 125-150 clients. 15% of clients are new/unpublished writers.

Member Agents Ed Knappman.

Represents Nonfiction books. **Considers these nonfiction areas:** Biography/autobiography; business/economics; child guidance/parenting; government/politics/law; health/medicine; history; language/literature/criticism; military/war; money/finance; nature/environment; psychology; science/technology; self-help/personal improvement; sports; true crime/investigative; women's issues/studies; reference.

- O⇥ This agency specializes in adult nonfiction of serious purpose. Currently, this agency is only taking on 2-3 new clients per year.

How to Contact Send outline/proposal, SASE. Accepts e-mail and fax queries. Considers simultaneous queries. Responds in 1 month to queries; 5 weeks to mss. Returns materials only with SASE.

Recent Sales Sold 45 titles in the last year. *When Asia Was the World*, by Stewart Gordon (Da Capo); *The Anatomy of Trends*, by Henrik Vejlgaard (McGraw Hill); *Poincare's Prize*, by George Szpiro (Dutton); *A Brief History of History*, by Colin Wells (Lyons Press); *The Network Marketing Success Handbook*, by Mary Christensen (Amacom); *Armed America*, by Clayton Cramer (Thomas Nelson); *Businomics*, by William Conerly (Adams).

Terms Agent receives 15% commission on domestic sales; 20% commission on foreign sales. Offers written contract, binding for 6 months. Charges clients for copying.

Writers' Conferences BookExpo America; London Book Fair.

Tips "Send us a well-written proposal that clearly identifies your audience—who will buy this book and why. Check our Web site for tips on proposals and advice on how to market your books."

◑ NINE MUSES AND APOLLO, INC.

525 Broadway, Suite 201, New York NY 10012. (212)431-2665. **Contact:** Ling Lucas. Estab. 1991. Represents 50 clients. 10% of clients are new/unpublished writers. Currently handles: 100% nonfiction books.

- Prior to her current position, Ms. Lucas served as vice president, sales/marketing director and associate publisher of Warner Books.

Represents Nonfiction books.

- O⇥ This agency specializes in nonfiction. Does not want to receive children's or young adult material.

How to Contact Submit outline, 2 sample chapters, SASE. Prefers to read materials exclusively.

Terms Agent receives 15% commission on domestic sales; 20-25% commission on foreign sales. Offers written contract. Charges clients for photocopying, postage.

Tips "Your outline should already be well developed, cogent, and reveal clarity of thought about the general structure and direction of your project."

[N] ◑ NORTHERN LIGHTS LITERARY SERVICES, LLC

306 North Center Valley Road, Sandpoint ID 83864. (888)558-4354. Fax: (208)265-1948. E-mail: agent@northern lightsls.com. Web site: www.northernlightsls.com. **Contact:** Sammie Justesen. Estab. 2005. Represents 25 clients. 35% of clients are new/unpublished writers. Currently handles: 90% nonfiction books; 10% novels.

Member Agents Sammie Justesen (fiction and nonfiction); Vorris Dee Justesen (business and current affairs).

Represents Nonfiction books, novels. **Considers these nonfiction areas:** Animals; biography/autobiography; business/economics; child guidance/parenting; cooking/foods/nutrition; crafts/hobbies; current affairs; ethnic/cultural interests; health/medicine; how-to; memoirs; nature/environment; New Age/metaphysics; popular culture; psychology; religious/inspirational; self-help/personal improvement; sports; true crime/investigative; women's issues/studies. **Considers these fiction areas:** Action/adventure; detective/police/crime; ethnic; family saga; feminist; glitz; historical; mainstream/contemporary; mystery/suspense; psychic/supernatural; regional; religious/inspirational; romance; thriller; women's.

    ○╼ "As a young agency, our goal is to provide personalized service to clients and create a bond that will endure throughout the writer's career. We seriously consider each query we receive and will accept hardworking new authors who are willing to develop their talents and skills. We enjoy working with healthcare professionals and writers who clearly understand their market and have a platform." Actively seeking general nonfiction—especially if the writer has a platform. Does not want to receive fantasy, horror, erotica, children's books, screenplays, poetry or short stories.

How to Contact Query with SASE, submit outline/proposal, synopsis, 3 sample chapter(s), author bio. E-queries preferred. No phone queries. No fax queries. Considers simultaneous queries. Responds in 2 months to queries; 2 months to mss. Returns materials only with SASE. Obtains most new clients through solicitations, conferences.

Recent Sales *Unraveling the Mystery of Fibromyalgia and Chronic Fatigue Syndrome*, by Daniel Dantini (Addicus); *Boots 'N Beans*, by Roy "Boots" Reynolds (Keokee); *Special Effects*, by Michael Slone (Michael Wiese Productions); *Rearview Regrets: Tips to Avoid Ticket Trouble with the Cops*, by Steve Pomper (Lyons Press).

Terms Agent receives 15% commission on domestic sales; 20% commission on foreign sales. Offers written contract; 30-day notice must be given to terminate contract.

Tips "If you're fortunate enough to find an agent who answers your query and asks for a printed manuscript, always include a letter and cover page containing your name, physical address, e-mail address and phone number. Be professional!"

◑ HAROLD OBER ASSOCIATES

425 Madison Ave., New York NY 10017. (212)759-8600. Fax: (212)759-9428. **Contact:** Craig Tenney. Estab. 1929. Member of AAR. Represents 250 clients. 10% of clients are new/unpublished writers. Currently handles: 35% nonfiction books; 50% novels; 15% juvenile books.

Member Agents Phyllis Westberg; Pamela Malpas; Craig Tenney (few new clients, mostly Ober backlist).

Represents Nonfiction books, novels, juvenile books.

    ○╼ "We consider all subjects/genres of fiction and nonfiction."

How to Contact Submit query letter only with SASE. No e-mail or fax queries. Responds as promptly as possible. Obtains most new clients through recommendations from others.

Terms Agent receives 15% commission on domestic sales; 20% commission on foreign sales. Charges clients for photocopying and express mail/package services.

◑ FIFI OSCARD AGENCY, INC.

110 W. 40th St., 21st Floor, New York NY 10018. (212)764-1100. Fax: (212)840-5019. E-mail: agency@fifioscard. com. Web site: www.fifioscard.com. **Contact:** Literary Department. Estab. 1978. Signatory of WGA.

Member Agents Peter Sawyer; Carmen La Via; Kevin McShane; Carolyn French; Jerry Rudes.

Represents Nonfiction books, novels, stage plays. **Considers these nonfiction areas:** Business/economics (finance); history; religious/inspirational; science/technology; sports; women's issues/studies; African American; biography; body/mind/spirit; health; lifestyle; cookbooks. **Considers these fiction areas:** Fantasy; mystery/suspense; science fiction.

How to Contact Query through online submission form preferred, though snail mail queries are acceptable. *No unsolicited mss.* Responds in 2 weeks to queries.

Recent Sales *Beating Around the Bush*, by Art Buchwald (Seven Stories); *To the Mountaintop*, by Stewart

Burns (HarperSanFrancisco); *Perfect ... I'm Not*, by David Wells and Chris Kreski (Wm. Morrow). Other clients include This agency's client list is available online.

Terms Agent receives 15% commission on domestic sales; 20% commission on foreign sales; 10% commission on dramatic rights sales. Charges clients for photocopying expenses.

◉ PARAVIEW, INC.

40 Florence Circle, Bracey VA 23919. Phone/Fax: (434)636-4138. E-mail: lhagan@paraview.com. Web site: www.paraview.com. **Contact:** Lisa Hagan. Estab. 1988. Represents 75 clients. 15% of clients are new/unpublished writers. Currently handles: 100% nonfiction books.

Represents Nonfiction books. **Considers these nonfiction areas:** Agriculture/horticulture; animals; anthropology/archaeology; art/architecture/design; biography/autobiography; business/economics; cooking/foods/nutrition; current affairs; education; ethnic/cultural interests; gay/lesbian issues; government/politics/law; health/medicine; history; how-to; humor/satire; language/literature/criticism; memoirs; military/war; money/finance; multicultural; nature/environment; New Age/metaphysics; philosophy; popular culture; psychology; recreation; regional; religious/inspirational; science/technology; self-help/personal improvement; sex; sociology; spirituality; travel; true crime/investigative; women's issues/studies; Americana; creative nonfiction.

   O→ This agency specializes in business, science, gay/lesbian, spiritual, New Age, and self-help nonfiction.

How to Contact Submit query, synopsis, author bio via e-mail. Responds in 1 month to queries; 3 months to mss. Obtains most new clients through recommendations from editors and current clients.

Recent Sales Sold 40 titles in the last year. *The High Purpose Company*, by Christine Arena (Collins Business); *Never Throw Rice at a Pisces*, by Stacey Wolf (Thomas Dunne Books); *The Whole World Was Watching*, by Romaine Patterson and Patrick Hinds (Alyson Books); *Babylon's Ark*, by Graham Spence and Lawrence Anthony (Thomas Dunne Books); *From Zero to Zillionaire*, by Chellie Campbell (Sourcebooks); *The Encyclopedia of Magickal Ingredients*, by Lexa Rosean (Pocket Books).

Terms Agent receives 15% commission on domestic sales; 20% commission on foreign sales.

Writers' Conferences BookExpo America; London Book Fair; E3—Electronic Entertainment Exposition.

Tips "New writers should have their work edited, critiqued, and carefully reworked prior to submission. First contact should be via e-mail."

Ⓝ ◉ PARK LITERARY GROUP, LLC

156 Fifth Ave., Suite 1134, New York NY 10010. (212)691-3500. Fax: (212)691-3540. E-mail: info@parkliterary.com. Web site: www.parkliterary.com. Estab. 2005.

   • Prior to their current positions, Ms. Park and Ms. O'Keefe were literary agents at Sanford J. Greenburger Associates.

Member Agents Theresa Park (plot-driven fiction and serious nonfiction); Shannon O'Keefe (literary and commercial fiction—including modern love stories, social comedies, mysteries, graphic novels and young adult novels—as well as nonfiction, including cookbooks, sports, music, education, travel, memoir and popular culture); Abigail Koons (quirky, edgy and commercial fiction, as well as superb thrillers and mysteries; adventure and travel narrative nonfiction, exceptional memoirs, popular science, history, politics and art).

Represents Nonfiction books, novels.

   O→ "The Park Literary Group represents fiction and nonfiction with a boutique approach: an emphasis on servicing a relatively small number of clients, with the highest professional standards and focused personal attention." Does not want to receive poetry or screenplays.

How to Contact Query with SASE, submit synopsis, SASE. Send all submissions through the mail. No e-mail or fax queries. Responds in 4-6 weeks to queries.

Recent Sales Other clients include Nicholas Sparks, Robert Whitaker, Laura Zigman, Lee Silver, Dominika Dery, B.R. Myers, Frank Partnoy, Linda Nichols, and Thomas Levenson.

◉ THE RICHARD PARKS AGENCY

Box 693, Salem NY 12865. Web site: www.richardparksagency.com. **Contact:** Richard Parks. Estab. 1988. Member of AAR. Currently handles: 55% nonfiction books; 40% novels; 5% story collections.

Represents Nonfiction books, novels. **Considers these nonfiction areas:** Animals; anthropology/archaeology; art/architecture/design; biography/autobiography; business/economics; child guidance/parenting; cooking/foods/nutrition; crafts/hobbies; current affairs; ethnic/cultural interests; gardening; gay/lesbian issues; government/politics/law; health/medicine; history; how-to; humor/satire; language/literature/criticism; memoirs; military/war; money/finance; music/dance; nature/environment; popular culture; psychology; science/technology; self-help/personal improvement; sociology; theater/film; travel; women's issues/studies.

   O→ Actively seeking nonfiction. Considers fiction by referral only. Does not want to receive unsolicited material.

How to Contact Query with SASE. No e-mail or fax queries. Considers simultaneous queries Responds in 2 weeks to queries. Returns materials only with SASE. Obtains most new clients through recommendations/ referrals.

Terms Agent receives 15% commission on domestic sales; 20% commission on foreign sales. Charges clients for photocopying or any unusual expense incurred at the writer's request.

● KATHI J. PATON LITERARY AGENCY

P.O. Box 2240, New York NY 10101. (212)265-6586. E-mail: kjplitbiz@optonline.net. **Contact:** Kathi Paton. Estab. 1987. Currently handles: 85% nonfiction books; 15% novels.

Represents Nonfiction books, novels, short story collections, book-based film rights. **Considers these nonfiction areas:** Business/economics; child guidance/parenting; humor/satire; money/finance (personal investing); nature/environment; psychology; religious/inspirational; personal investing. **Considers these fiction areas:** Literary; mainstream/contemporary; multicultural.

   O¬ This agency specializes in adult nonfiction.

How to Contact Accepts e-mail queries only. Considers simultaneous queries. Obtains most new clients through recommendations from other clients.

Recent Sales *Zero Day Threat* by Byron Acohido and Jon Swartz (Carroll & Graf/Avalon); *Unraveling the Mystery of Autism*, by Karyn Seroussi (Simon & Schuster); *Bury My Heart at Cooperstown*, by Frank Russo and Gene Racz (Triumph/Random House).

Terms Agent receives 15% commission on domestic sales; 20% commission on foreign sales. Offers written contract. Charges clients for photocopying.

Writers' Conferences Attends major regional panels, seminars and conferences.

N ◎ PAVILION LITERARY MANAGEMENT

660 Massachusetts Ave., Suite 4, Boston MA 02118. (617)792-5218. E-mail: query@pavilionliterary.com. Web site: www.pavilionliterary.com. **Contact:** Jeff Kellogg.

   • Prior to his current position, Mr. Kellogg was a literary agent with The Stuart Agency, and an acquiring editor with HarperCollins.

Represents Nonfiction books, novels, memoir. **Considers these nonfiction areas:** Biography/autobiography; computers/electronic; health/medicine; history; military/war; multicultural; nature/environment; psychology; science/technology; sports; travel; neuroscience, medicine, physics/astrophysics. **Considers these fiction areas:** Action/adventure; fantasy; juvenile; mystery/suspense; thriller; general fiction, genre-blending fiction.

   O¬ "We are presently accepting fiction submissions only from previously published authors and/or by client referral. Nonfiction projects, specifically narrative nonfiction and cutting-edge popular science from experts in their respective fields, are most welcome."

How to Contact Query first by e-mail (no attachments). Your subject line should specify fiction or nonfiction and include the title of the work. If submitting nonfiction, include a book proposal (no longer than 75 pages), with sample chapters. No fax queries.

Recent Sales *I'm With Stupid.* by Elaine Szewczyk (Warner 5 Spot); *Grievances*, by Mark Ethridge (New South Books); *The Other Brain*, by R. Douglas Fields (S&S); *The Fourth Horseman*, by Robert Koenig (Public Affairs); *Knowing: The Deceptive Biology of Convinction*, by Robert Burton, (SMP). Other clients include Steve Almond, Mark Ethridge, R. Douglas Fields, Juliana Hatfield, Robert Koenig, George Rabasa, Dennis Drayna.

N ◯ PEARSON, MORRIS & BELT

3000 Connecticut Ave., NW, Suite 317, Washington DC 20008. (202)723-6088. E-mail: dpm@morrisbelt.com; llb@morrisbelt.com. Web site: www.morrisbelt.com.

   • Prior to their current positions, Ms. Belt and Ms. Morris were agents with Adler & Robin Books, Inc.

Member Agents Laura Belt (nonfiction and computer books); Djana Pearson Morris (fiction, nonfiction, and computer books. Her favorite subjects are self-help, narrative nonfiction, African-American fiction and nonfiction, health and fitness, women's fiction, technology and parenting).

Represents Nonfiction books, novels, computer books.

   O¬ This agency specializes in nonfiction, computer books and exceptional fiction. Actively seeking women's commercial fiction, literary fiction, and African-American literary and commercial fiction. Does not want to receive poetry, children's literature or screenplays. Regarding fiction, this agency does not accept science fiction, thrillers or mysteries.

How to Contact Query with SASE, submit proposal (nonfiction); detailed synopsis and 2-3 sample chapters (fiction). Only query with a finished ms. No e-mail attachments. Accepts e-mail queries. No fax queries. Responds in 6-8 weeks to queries. Returns materials only with SASE. Obtains most new clients through recommendations from others, solicitations.

Recent Sales *The New Color of Success*, by Niki Butler-Michell (Prima Publishing); *Mid-Life Motherhood*, by Jann Blackstone Ford (St. Martin's Press); *Hour to Hour*, by Shelly Marshall (Pocket Books); *Fried, Dyed, and*

Laid to the Side, by Michele Collison (Amistad/HarperCollins); *It's All Good*, by Michele Collison (Amistad/HarperCollins); *Everything Monsters*, by Shannon Turlington (Adams Media).

Tips "Many of our books come from ideas and proposals we generate in-house. We retain a proprietary interest in and control of all ideas we create and proposals we write."

Ⓝ Ⓔ PELHAM LITERARY AGENCY

2451 Royal St. James Drive, El Cajon CA, 92019-4408. (619)447-4468. E-mail: jmeals@pelhamliterary.com. Web site: pelhamliterary.com. **Contact:** Jim Meals. Estab. 1993. Currently handles: 10% nonfiction books; 90% novels.

● Before becoming agents, both Mr. Pelham and Mr. Meals were writers.

Member Agents Howard Pelham; Jim Meals.

Represents Nonfiction books, novels.

   O⊸ "Every manuscript that comes to our agency receives a careful reading and assessment. When a writer submits a promising manuscript, we work extensively with the author until the work is ready for marketing."

How to Contact Query by mail or e-mail first; do not send unsolicited mss. No fax queries.

Recent Sales *The Complete Guide to Foreign Adoption*, by Barbara Bascom and Carole McKelvey; *The General*, by Patrick A. Davis; *The Highest Bidder*, by B.H.B. Harper.

Terms Agent receives 15% commission on domestic sales. Offers written contract. Charges for photocopying and postage.

Tips "Only phone if it's necessary."

Ⓔ L. PERKINS ASSOCIATES

5800 Arlington Ave., Riverdale NY 10471. (718)543-5344. Fax: (718)543-5354. E-mail: lperkinsagency@yahoo.com. **Contact:** Lori Perkins, Amy Stout (jrlperkinsagency@yahoo.com). Estab. 1990. Member of AAR. Represents 90 clients. 10% of clients are new/unpublished writers.

● Ms. Perkins has been an agent for 20 years. She is also the author of *The Insider's Guide to Getting an Agent* (Writer's Digest Books), as well as three other nonfiction books. She has also edited two anthologies.

Represents Nonfiction books, novels. **Considers these nonfiction areas:** Popular culture. **Considers these fiction areas:** Erotica; fantasy; horror; literary (dark); science fiction.

   O⊸ Most of Ms. Perkins' clients write both fiction and nonfiction. "This combination keeps my clients publishing for years. I am also a published author, so I know what it takes to write a good book." Actively seeking a Latino *Gone With the Wind* and *Waiting to Exhale*, and urban ethnic horror. Does not want to receive anything outside of the above categories (westerns, romance, etc.).

How to Contact Query with SASE. Considers simultaneous queries. Responds in 12 weeks to queries; 3-6 months to mss. Returns materials only with SASE. Obtains most new clients through recommendations from others, solicitations, conferences.

Recent Sales Sold 100 titles in the last year. *How to Make Love Like a Porn Star: A Cautionary Tale*, by Jenna Jameson (Reagan Books); *Everything But ...?*, by Rachel Krammer Bussel (Bantam); *Dear Mom, I Always Wanted You to Know*, by Lisa Delman (Perigee Books); *The Illustrated Ray Bradbury*, by Jerry Weist (Avon); *The Poet in Exile*, by Ray Manzarek (Avalon); *Behind Sad Eyes: The Life of George Harrison*, by Marc Shapiro (St. Martin's Press).

Terms Agent receives 15% commission on domestic sales; 20% commission on foreign sales. No written contract. Charges clients for photocopying.

Writers' Conferences San Diego State University Writers' Conference; NECON; BookExpo America; World Fantasy Convention.

Tips "Research your field and contact professional writers' organizations to see who is looking for what. Finish your novel before querying agents. Read my book, *An Insider's Guide to Getting an Agent*, to get a sense of how agents operate. Read agent blogs—litsoup.blogspot.com and missnark.blogspot.com."

Ⓔ STEPHEN PEVNER, INC.

382 Lafayette St., Eighth Floor, New York NY 10003. (212)674-8403. Fax: (212)529-3692. E-mail: spevner@aol.com. **Contact:** Stephen Pevner.

Represents Nonfiction books, novels, feature film, TV scripts, TV movie of the week, episodic drama, animation, documentary, miniseries. **Considers these nonfiction areas:** Biography/autobiography; ethnic/cultural interests; gay/lesbian issues; history; humor/satire; language/literature/criticism; memoirs; music/dance; New Age/metaphysics; photography; popular culture; religious/inspirational; sociology; travel. **Considers these fiction areas:** Comic books/cartoon; erotica; ethnic; experimental; gay/lesbian; glitz; horror; humor/satire; literary; mainstream/contemporary; psychic/supernatural; thriller; urban. **Considers these script subject areas:**

Comedy; contemporary issues; detective/police/crime; gay/lesbian; glitz; horror; romantic comedy; romantic drama; thriller.

☞ This agency specializes in motion pictures, novels, humor, pop culture, urban fiction, and independent filmmakers.

How to Contact Query with SASE, outline/proposal. Prefers to read materials exclusively. No e-mail or fax queries. Responds in 2 weeks to queries; 1 month to mss. Obtains most new clients through recommendations from others.

Recent Sales *Matt and Ben*, by Mindy Kaling and Brenda Withers; *In the Company of Men* and *Bash: Latterday Plays*, by Neil Labote; *Guide to Life*, by The Five Lesbian Brothers; *Noise From Underground*, by Michael Levine. Other clients include Richard Linklater, Gregg Araki, Tom DiCillo, Genvieve Turner/Rose Troche, Todd Solondz, Neil LaBute.

Terms Agent receives 15% commission on domestic sales; 20% commission on foreign sales. Offers written contract, binding for 1 year; 6-week notice must be given to terminate contract. 100% of business is derived from commissions on ms sales.

Tips "Be persistent, but civilized."

▣ ☺ PFD NEW YORK

373 Park Ave. S, Fifth Floor, New York NY 10016. (917)256-0707. Fax: (212)685-9635. E-mail: email@pfdny.com. Web site: www.pfdny.com. **Contact:** Submissions Department. Estab. 2003 (NYC office).

• Prior to his current position, Mr. Reiter worked at IMG; Ms. Pagnamenta was with the Wylie Agency.

Member Agents Zoe Pagnamenta (U.S. authors), ajump@pfdgroup.com; Mark Reiter (U.S. authors), mreiter@pfdgroup.com.

Represents Nonfiction books, novels, short story collections (if the author has other written works), poetry books.

☞ This agency has offices in New York as well as the United Kingdom.

How to Contact Query with SASE, submit proposal package, synopsis, 2-3 sample chapter(s), publishing history, author bio, cover letter. Submit via snail mail. See online submission guidelines for more information. No e-mail or fax queries. Responds in 1 month to queries. Returns materials only with SASE. Obtains most new clients through recommendations from others, solicitations.

Recent Sales *Seize the Fire*, by Adam Nicolson; *Have Glove, Will Travel*, by Bill "Spaceman" Lee and Richard Lally; *Crippen*, by John Boyne; *The First Scientific American: Benjamin Franklin and the Pursuit of Genius*, by Joyce Chaplin.

☺ PINDER LANE & GARON-BROOKE ASSOCIATES, LTD.

159 W. 53rd St., Suite 14C, New York NY 10019. Member of AAR; signatory of WGA.

Member Agents Robert Thixton, pinderl@interport.net; Dick Duane, pinderl@interport.net.

☞ This agency specializes in mainstream fiction and nonfiction. Does not want to receive screenplays, TV series teleplays, or dramatic plays.

How to Contact Query with SASE. *No unsolicited mss.* Obtains most new clients through referrals.

Terms Agent receives 15% commission on domestic sales; 30% commission on foreign sales. Offers written contract.

◉ PIPPIN PROPERTIES, INC.

155 E. 38th St., Suite 2H, New York NY 10016. (212)338-9310. Fax: (212)338-9579. E-mail: info@pippinproperties.com. Web site: www.pippinproperties.com. **Contact:** Holly McGhee. Estab. 1998. Represents 40 clients. Currently handles: 100% juvenile books.

• Prior to becoming an agent, Ms. McGhee was an editor for 7 years and in book marketing for 4 years. Prior to becoming an agent, Ms. van Beek worked in children's book editorial for 4 years.

Member Agents Holly McGhee; Emily van Beek; John Sellers.

Represents Juvenile books.

☞ "We are strictly a children's literary agency devoted to the management of authors and artists in all media. We are small and discerning in choosing our clientele." Actively seeking middle-grade and young-adult novels.

How to Contact Query with SASE. Accepts e-mail queries. Considers simultaneous queries. Responds in 6 weeks to queries; 10 weeks to mss. Obtains most new clients through recommendations from others.

Terms Agent receives 15% commission on domestic sales; 25% commission on foreign sales. Offers written contract; 30-day notice must be given to terminate contract. Charges for color copying and UPS/FedEx.

Tips "Please do not start calling after sending a submission."

ALICKA PISTEK LITERARY AGENCY, LLC

302A W. 12th St., #124, New York NY 10014. E-mail: info@apliterary.com. Web site: www.apliterary.com. **Contact:** Alicka Pistek. Estab. 2003. Represents 15 clients. 50% of clients are new/unpublished writers. Currently handles: 60% nonfiction books; 40% novels.

• Prior to opening her agency, Ms. Pistek worked at ICM and as an agent at Nicholas Ellison, Inc.

Represents Nonfiction books, novels. **Considers these nonfiction areas:** Animals; anthropology/archaeology; biography/autobiography; child guidance/parenting; current affairs; government/politics/law; health/medicine; history; how-to; language/literature/criticism; memoirs; military/war; money/finance; nature/environment; psychology; science/technology; self-help/personal improvement; travel; creative nonfiction. **Considers these fiction areas:** Detective/police/crime; ethnic; family saga; historical; literary; mainstream/contemporary; mystery/suspense; romance; thriller.

○→ Does not want to receive fantasy, science fiction or Western.

How to Contact Send e-query to info@apliterary.com. The agency will only respond if interested. Accepts e-mail queries. No fax queries. Considers simultaneous queries. Responds in 2 months to queries; 8 weeks to mss. Returns materials only with SASE.

Recent Sales *The Animal Girl*, by John Fulton; *Elephants on Acid*, by Alex Boese; *Living on the Fly*, by Amanda Switzer and Daniel A. Shaw. Other clients include Matthew Zapruder, Steven R. Kinsella, Julie Tilsner, Michael Christopher Carroll, Quinton Skinner, Erin Grady.

Terms Agent receives 15% commission on domestic sales; 20% commission on foreign sales. Offers written contract. This agency charges for photocopying more than 40 pages and international postage.

Tips "Be sure you are familiar with the genre you are writing in and learn standard procedures for submitting your work. A good query will go a long way."

PMA LITERARY AND FILM MANAGEMENT, INC.

45 West 21st St., Fourth Floor, New York NY 10010. (212)929-1222. Fax: (212)206-0238. E-mail: queries@pmalitfilm.com. Web site: www.pmalitfilm.com. Address for packages is P.O. Box 1817, Old Chelsea Station, New York NY 10113 **Contact:** Kelly Skillen. Represents more than 100 clients. 50% of clients are new/unpublished writers. Currently handles: 40% nonfiction books; 30% novels; 5% juvenile books; 25% movie scripts.

• In his time in the literary world, Mr. Miller has successfully managed more than 1,000 books and dozens of motion picture and television properties. He is the author of *Author! Screenwriter!*; Ms. Skillen was previously in the restaurant and nightclub industry.

Member Agents Peter Miller ("big" nonfiction, business, true crime, religion); Kelly Skillen, kelly@pmalitfilm.com (literary fiction, narrative nonfiction, pop culture); Adrienne Rosado (literary and commercial fiction, young adult).

Represents Nonfiction books, novels, juvenile books, movie scripts, TV scripts, TV movie of the week. **Considers these nonfiction areas:** Biography/autobiography; business/economics; child guidance/parenting; cooking/foods/nutrition; current affairs; ethnic/cultural interests; humor/satire; memoirs; money/finance; popular culture; religious/inspirational; self-help/personal improvement; sports; true crime/investigative. **Considers these fiction areas:** Action/adventure; detective/police/crime; erotica; ethnic; experimental; gay/lesbian; historical; humor/satire; juvenile; literary; mainstream/contemporary; mystery/suspense; psychic/supernatural; religious/inspirational; romance; thriller; young adult; women's. **Considers these script subject areas:** Action/adventure; comedy; mainstream; romantic comedy; romantic drama; thriller.

○→ "PMA believes in long-term relationships with professional authors. We manage an author's overall career—hence the name—and have strong connections to Hollywood." Actively seeking new ideas beautifully executed. Does not want to receive poetry, stage plays, picture books and clichés.

How to Contact Query with SASE, submit publishing history, author bio. Send no attachments or mss of any kind unless requested. Accepts e-mail queries. No fax queries. Considers simultaneous queries. Responds in 4-6 weeks to mss. 5-7 days for e-mail queries; six months for paper submissions Returns materials only with SASE. Obtains most new clients through recommendations from others, solicitations, conferences.

Recent Sales *For the Sake of Liberty*, by M. William Phelps (Thomas Dunne Books); *The Haunting of Cambria*, by Richard Taylor (Tor); *Cover Girl Confidential*, by Beverly Bartlett (5 Spot); *Ten Prayers God Always Says Yes To!*, by Anthony DeStefano (Doubleday); *Miss Fido Manners: The Complete Book of Dog Etiquette*, by Charlotte Reed (Adams Media); film rights to *Murder in the Heartland*, by M. William Phelps (Mathis Entertainment); film rights to *The Killer's Game*, by Jay Bonansinga (Andrew Lazar/Mad Chance, Inc.).

Terms Agent receives 15% commission on domestic sales; 25% commission on foreign sales. Offers written contract; 30-day notice must be given to terminate contract. This agency charges for approved expenses, such as photocopies and overnight delivery.

Writers' Conferences A full list of Mr. Miller's speaking engagements is available online.

Tips "Don't approach agents before your work is ready, and always approach them as professionally as possible. Don't give up."

◢ AARON M. PRIEST LITERARY AGENCY

708 Third Ave., 23rd Floor, New York NY 10017-4103. (212)818-0344. Fax: (212)573-9417. Estab. 1974. Member of AAR. Currently handles: 25% nonfiction books; 75% novels.

Member Agents Aaron Priest, querypriest@aaronpriest.com (thrillers and fiction); Lisa Erbach Vance, queryvance@aaronpriest.com (general fiction, mystery, thrillers, historical fiction, up market women's fiction, narrative nonfiction, memoir); Lucy Childs, querychilds@aaronpriest.com (literary and commercial fiction, memoir, historical fiction, upscale commercial women's fiction); Nicole Kenealy, querykenealy@aaronpriest.com (chicklit/commercial women's fiction, literary fiction, young adult fiction and nonfiction).

Represents Commercial fiction, literary fiction, some nonfiction.

How to Contact Query with SASE, submit publishing history, author bio. Make sure your query is one page. Paste first chapter into body e-mail. Do not query more than one agent here. Accepts e-mail queries. No fax queries. Considers simultaneous queries. Responds in 3 weeks, only if interested.

Recent Sales *She is Me*, by Kathleen Schine; *Killer Smile*, by Lisa Scottoline.

Terms Agent receives 15% commission on domestic sales. This agency charges for photocopying and postage expenses.

◢ PROSPECT AGENCY LLC

285 Fifth Ave., PMB 445, Brooklyn NY 11215. (718)788-3217. E-mail: esk@prospectagency.com. Web site: www.prospectagency.com. **Contact:** Emily Sylvan Kim. Estab. 2005. Represents 15 clients. 50% of clients are new/unpublished writers. Currently handles: 66% novels; 33% juvenile books.

• Prior to starting her agency, Ms. Kim briefly attended law school and worked for another literary agency.

Represents Nonfiction books, novels, juvenile books. **Considers these nonfiction areas:** Memoirs; science/technology; juvenile. **Considers these fiction areas:** Action/adventure; detective/police/crime; erotica; ethnic; family saga; juvenile; literary; mainstream/contemporary; mystery/suspense; picture books; romance; science fiction; thriller; westerns/frontier; young adult.

☞ "We are currently looking for the next generation of writers to shape the literary landscape. Our clients receive professional and knowledgeable representation. We are committed to offering skilled editorial advice and advocating our clients in the marketplace." Actively seeking romance, literary fiction, and young adult submissions. Does not want to receive poetry, short stories, textbooks, or most nonfiction.

How to Contact Upload outline and 3 sample chapters to the Web site. Considers simultaneous queries. Responds in 3 weeks to queries; 1 month to mss. Obtains most new clients through recommendations from others, conferences, unsolicited mss.

Recent Sales *Love Potion #10*, by Janice Maynard (NAL); *God's Own Drunk*, by Tim Tharp (Knopf Children). Other clients include Diane Perkins, Regina Scott, Opal Carew, Marissa Doyle, Meagan Brothers, Elizabeth Scott, Bonnie Edwards.

Terms Agent receives 15% commission on domestic sales; 20% commission on foreign sales. Offers written contract.

Writers' Conferences SCBWI Annual Winter Conference; Pikes Peak Writers Conference; RWA National Conference.

◢ PSALTIS LITERARY

Post Office: Park West Finance, P.O. Box 20736, New York NY 10025. E-mail: psaltisliterary@mpsaltis.com. Web site: www.mpsaltis.com. **Contact:** Michael Psaltis. Member of AAR. Represents 30-40 clients.

Represents Nonfiction books, novels. **Considers these nonfiction areas:** Biography/autobiography; business/economics; cooking/foods/nutrition; health/medicine; history; memoirs; popular culture; psychology; science/technology. **Considers these fiction areas:** Mainstream/contemporary.

How to Contact Submit outline/proposal. Responds in 2-4 weeks to queries; 6-8 weeks to mss.

Recent Sales *Hometown Appetites*, by Kelly Alexander and Cindy Harris (Gotham Books); *A Life in Twilight*, by Mark Wolverton (Joseph Henry Press); *Cooked*, by Jeff Henderson (William Morrow).

Terms Agent receives 15% commission on domestic sales; 20% commission on foreign sales. Offers written contract.

N ◢ QUEEN LITERARY AGENCY

850 Seventh Ave., Suite 704, New York NY 10019. (212)974-8333. Fax: (212)974-8347. Web site: www.queenliterary.com. Mr. Murphy's address: 115 Hosea Ave., Cincinnati OH 45220 (201)704-2483 **Contact:** Lisa Queen, Michael Murphy. Estab. 2006.

• Prior to her current position, Ms. Queen was a former publishing executive and most recently head of IMG Worldwide's literary division; Mr. Murphy was a vice president at Random House and has 26 years experience in book publishing.

Member Agents Lisa Queen, Michael Murphy (interested in new and established writers; interests are narrative nonfiction, humor and visual books).

Represents Nonfiction books, novels.

> O— Ms. Queen's specialties: "While our agency represents a wide range of nonfiction titles, we have a particular interest in business books, food writing, science and popular psychology, as well as books by well-known chefs, radio and television personalities and sports figures."

How to Contact Query with SASE. No fax queries.

Recent Sales *Hero of the Underground*, by Jason Peter (St. Martin's); *Change Your Life in Seven Days*, by Paul McKenna; *Pig Perfect*, by Peter Kaminsky.

QUICKSILVER BOOKS: LITERARY AGENTS

508 Central Park Ave., #5101, Scarsdale NY 10583. Phone/Fax: (914)722-4664. Web site: www.quicksilverbooks .com. **Contact:** Bob Silverstein. Estab. 1973 as packager; 1987 as literary agency. Represents 50 clients. 50% of clients are new/unpublished writers. Currently handles: 75% nonfiction books; 25% novels.

> ● Prior to opening his agency, Mr. Silverstein served as senior editor at Bantam Books and Dell Books/ Delacorte Press.

Represents Nonfiction books, novels. **Considers these nonfiction areas:** Anthropology/archaeology; biography/autobiography; business/economics; child guidance/parenting; cooking/foods/nutrition; current affairs; ethnic/cultural interests; health/medicine; history; how-to; language/literature/criticism; memoirs; nature/environment; New Age/metaphysics; popular culture; psychology; religious/inspirational; science/technology; self-help/personal improvement; sociology; sports; true crime/investigative; women's issues/studies. **Considers these fiction areas:** Action/adventure; glitz; mystery/suspense; thriller.

> O— This agency specializes in literary and commercial mainstream fiction and nonfiction, especially psychology, New Age, holistic healing, consciousness, ecology, environment, spirituality, reference, self-help, cookbooks and narrative nonfiction. Does not want to receive science fiction, pornography, poetry or single-spaced mss.

How to Contact Query with SASE. Authors are expected to supply SASE for return of ms and for query letter responses. No fax queries. Considers simultaneous queries. Responds in 2 weeks to queries; 1 month to mss. Returns materials only with SASE. Obtains most new clients through recommendations, listings in sourcebooks, solicitations, workshop participation.

Recent Sales Sold more than 20 titles in the last year. *See Jane Lead*, by Lois Frankel (Warner); *28-Day Shapeover*, by Brad Schoenfeld (Human Kinetics); *Don't Sabotage Your Career*, by Lois Frankel (Warner); *Beyond the Indigo Children*, by P.M.H. Atwater (Bear & Company); *Dinner at Mr. Jefferson's*, by Charles Cerami (Wiley); *Nice Girls Don't Get Rich*, by Lois P. Frankel (Warner Books); *The Young Patriots*, by Charles Cerami (Sourcebooks); *The Coming of the Beatles*, by Martin Goldsmith (Wiley); *The Real Food Daily Cookbook*, by Ann Gentry (Ten Speed Press); *The Complete Book of Vinyasa Yoga*, by Srivatsa Ramaswami (Marlowe & Co.).

Terms Agent receives 15% commission on domestic sales; 20% commission on foreign sales. Offers written contract.

Writers' Conferences National Writers Union.

Tips "Write what you know. Write from the heart. Publishers print, authors sell."

SUSAN RABINER, LITERARY AGENT, INC.

240 W. 35th St., Suite 500, New York NY 10001. (212)279-0316. Fax: (212)279-0932. E-mail: susan@rabiner.net. Web site: www.rabiner.net. **Contact:** Susan Rabiner.

> ● Prior to becoming an agent, Ms. Rabiner was editorial director of Basic Books. She is also the co-author of *Thinking Like Your Editor: How to Write Great Serious Nonfiction and Get it Published* (W.W. Norton).

Member Agents Susan Rabiner; Susan Arellano; Sydelle Kramer; Annie Rhodes; Helena Schwarz.

Represents Nonfiction books, novels, textbooks. **Considers these nonfiction areas:** Biography/autobiography; business/economics; education; government/politics/law; health/medicine; history; philosophy; psychology; religious/inspirational; science/technology; sociology; sports; biography, law/politics.

How to Contact Query with proposal, sample chapter, SASE. No fax or phone queries. Considers simultaneous queries. Responds in 3 weeks to queries. Returns materials only with SASE. Obtains most new clients through recommendations from editors.

Recent Sales *The Bodies on the Mountain: The Story of May 2006 on Mt. Everest*, by Myles Gregory Osborne (Viking); *Love Life: A Case Study*, by Allison Bechdel (Houghton Mifflin); *Madness: A Life*, by Marya Hornbaeher (Houghton Mifflin); *Is God a Mathematician?*, by Mario Livio (Simon & Schuster); *Teapot in a Tempest: The Boston Tea Party*, by Benjamin Carp (Yale University Press).

Terms Agent receives 15% commission on domestic sales; 20% commission on foreign sales. Offers written contract; 1-month notice must be given to terminate contract.

ⓃⓄ LYNNE RABINOFF AGENCY

72-11 Austin St., No. 201, Forest Hills NY 11375. (718)459-6894. E-mail: Lynne@lynnerabinoff.com. **Contact:** Lynne Rabinoff. Estab. 1991. Represents 50 clients. 50% of clients are new/unpublished writers. Currently handles: 99% nonfiction books; 1% novels.

* Prior to becoming an agent, Ms. Rabinoff was in publishing and dealt with foreign rights.

Represents Nonfiction books. **Considers these nonfiction areas:** Anthropology/archaeology; biography/autobiography; business/economics; current affairs; ethnic/cultural interests; government/politics/law; history; memoirs; military/war; popular culture; psychology; religious/inspirational; science/technology; women's issues/studies.

O↝ This agency specializes in history, political issues, current affairs and religion.

How to Contact Query with SASE, submit proposal package, synopsis, 1 sample chapter(s), author bio, SASE. Accepts e-mail queries. No fax queries. Responds in 1 month to mss. Obtains most new clients through recommendations from others.

Recent Sales *War of Ideas*, by Walid Phares (Palgrave); *Flying Solo*, by Robert Vaughn (Thomas Dunne); *Thugs*, by Micah Halpern (Thomas Nelson); *Cleared for Charge*, by James Lacey (St. Martin's Press). Other clients include Edwin Black, Abraham Foxman, Brigitte Gabriel, Nonie Darwish, Mitch Bard, Robin Young, Darin Rubin, Ariel Cohen, Steve Binder, Rose Eichenbaum.

Terms Agent receives 15% commission on domestic sales; 20% commission on foreign sales. Offers written contract; 60-day notice must be given to terminate contract. This agency charges for postage.

Ⓞ RAINES & RAINES

103 Kenyon Road, Medusa NY 12120. (518)239-8311. Fax: (518)239-6029. **Contact:** Theron Raines (member of AAR); Joan Raines; Keith Korman. Represents 100 clients.

Represents Nonfiction books, novels. **Considers these nonfiction areas:** All subjects. **Considers these fiction areas:** Action/adventure; detective/police/crime; fantasy; historical; mystery/suspense; picture books; science fiction; thriller; westerns/frontier.

How to Contact Query with SASE. Responds in 2 weeks to queries.

Terms Agent receives 15% commission on domestic sales; 20% commission on foreign sales. Charges for photocopying.

Ⓞ CHARLOTTE CECIL RAYMOND, LITERARY AGENT

32 Bradlee Rd., Marblehead MA 01945. **Contact:** Charlotte Cecil Raymond. Estab. 1983. Currently handles: 90% nonfiction books; 10% novels.

Represents Nonfiction books. **Considers these nonfiction areas:** Current affairs; ethnic/cultural interests; history; nature/environment; psychology; sociology; biography, gender interests.

O↝ Does not want to receive self-help/personal improvement, science fiction, fantasy, young adult, juvenile, poetry, or screenplays.

How to Contact Query with SASE, proposal package, outline. Responds in 2 weeks to queries; 6 weeks to mss.

Terms Agent receives 15% commission on domestic sales. 100% of business is derived from commissions on ms sales.

ⓃⓄ RED WRITING HOOD INK

2019 Attala Road 1990, Kosciusko MS 39090. (662)674-0636. Fax: (662)796-3095. E-mail: info@redwritinghoodink.net; submissions@redwritinghoodink.net. Web site: www.redwritinghoodink.net. **Contact:** Sheri Ables. Estab. 2005; adheres to AAR canon. Currently handles: 100% nonfiction books.

* Prior to her current position, Ms. Ables was an agent of the Williams Agency. In addition, she worked for an agency in Oregon from 1996-1997. Collectively, the staff of RWHI has more than 25 years experience in the publishing industry.

Member Agents Sheri Ables, agent; Terri Dunlap, literary assistant (terri@redwritinghoodink.net).

Represents Nonfiction books. **Considers these nonfiction areas:** Reference, history, religious, mind/body/spirit, investigative, controversial topics.

O↝ This agency's goal is "one-on-one service with our clients, making each feel that he/she is the only client. We limit the number of clients we take on at a given time for this reason. We also believe personalized attention is important in maintaining a good business relationship. We specialize in nonfiction projects. Our motto: Don't be afraid to go against the grain. Controversy entices. Tell the world what others are too scared to reveal!"

How to Contact Send cover letter and synopsis only. Queries accepted via e-mail or postal mail. No phone calls. No fax queries.

Recent Sales *The Thunder of Angels: The Montgomery Bus Boycott and the People Who Broke the Back of Jim*

Crow, by Donnie Williams and Wayne Greenhaw (Chicago Review Press); *War Elephants*, by John Kistler (Praeger).

Terms Agent receives 15% commission on domestic sales; 20% commission on foreign sales.

Tips "Writers: View submission guidelines prior to making contact."

⃞ ⊕ ⃞ REDHAMMER MANAGEMENT, LTD.

186 Bickenhall Mansions, London England W1U 6BX, United Kingdom. (44)(207)487-3465. E-mail: info@redha mmer.info. Web site: www.redhammer.info. **Contact:** Peter Cox, managing director. Estab. 1999. Represents 24 clients. 65% of clients are new/unpublished writers. Currently handles: 40% nonfiction books; 10% novels; 30% juvenile books; 10% movie scripts; 10% TV scripts.

- Prior to becoming an agent, Mr. Cox was a bestselling author. He was also the managing director of an advertising agency.

Represents Nonfiction books, novels, juvenile books, movie scripts, TV scripts, TV movie of the week, documentary. **Considers these nonfiction areas:** Biography/autobiography; business/economics; current affairs; gay/lesbian issues; government/politics/law; health/medicine; history; how-to; humor/satire; language/literature/criticism; memoirs; military/war; money/finance; music/dance; nature/environment; popular culture; psychology; religious/inspirational; science/technology; self-help/personal improvement; sociology; sports; true crime/investigative. **Considers these fiction areas:** Action/adventure; erotica; family saga; feminist; gay/lesbian; historical; horror; humor/satire; juvenile; literary; mainstream/contemporary; mystery/suspense; romance; science fiction; sports; thriller; young adult; women's/chick lit. **Considers these script subject areas:** Action/adventure; biography/autobiography; comedy; contemporary issues; detective/police/crime; fantasy; glitz; historical; horror; juvenile; mainstream; mystery/suspense; romantic comedy; romantic drama; science fiction; thriller.

- ⃞ "We handle a small number of clients and give them unparalleled attention, help them plan their writing careers, fulfill their goals and dreams, and leverage maximum value out of all aspects of their creative output." Actively seeking committed, top-flight authors with distinctive voices and extraordinary talent. Does not want to receive bulk e-mail submissions. "Read our Web site if you are serious about submitting work to us."

How to Contact See the Web site for submission information. Considers simultaneous queries. Responds in 6 weeks to queries; 6 weeks to mss. Returns materials only with SASE.

Recent Sales Sold 20 titles and sold 4 scripts in the last year. *Jack Flint and the Redthorn Sword*, by Joe Donnelly (Orion Children's Books); *Perfect Hostage*, by Justin Wintle (Hutchinson); *Dave Allen: The Biography*, by Carolyn Soutar (Orion); *The God Effect*, by Brian Clegg (St. Martin's Press). Other clients include Martin Bell, Nicolas Booth, John Brindley, Audrey Eyton, Maria Harris, U.S. Sen. Orrin Hatch, Amanda Lees, Nicholas Monson, Michelle Paver, Donald Trelford, David Yelland.

Terms Agent receives 17.5% commission on domestic sales; 20% commission on foreign sales. Offers written contract; 90-day notice must be given to terminate contract. "We charge reimbursement for couriers and FedEx but these fees are applied only once the writer has started earning royalty."

⃞ ⃞ THE REDWOOD AGENCY

474 Wellesley Ave., Mill Valley CA, 94941. (415)381-2269 ext. 2. Fax: (415)381-2719. E-mail: info@redwoodage ncy.com. Web site: www.redwoodagency.com. **Contact:** Catherine Fowler, founder; adheres to AAR canon of ethics. Currently handles: 100% nonfiction books.

- Prior to becoming an agent, Ms. Fowler was an editor, subsidiary rights director and associate publisher for Doubleday, Simon & Schuster and Random House.

Represents Nonfiction books. **Considers these nonfiction areas:** Business/economics; cooking/foods/nutrition; health/medicine; humor/satire; memoirs; nature/environment; popular culture; psychology; self-help/personal improvement; women's issues/studies; narrative, parenting, aging, reference, lifestyle, cultural technology.

- ⃞ "Along with our love of books and publishing, we have the desire and commitment to work with fun, interesting and creative people, to do so with respect and professionalism, but also with a sense of humor." Actively seeking high-quality, nonfiction works created for the general consumer market, as well as projects with the potential to become book series. Does not want to receive fiction. Do not send packages that require signature for delivery.

How to Contact Query with SASE. Accepts e-mail queries. No fax queries. Obtains most new clients through recommendations from others, solicitations.

Recent Sales *The Absent Savior*, by Sandra Kring (Bantam Dell); *The Girl & the Fig Cookbook: More than 100 Recipes from the Acclaimed California Wine Country Restaurant*, by Sondra Bernstein (Simon & Schuster); Students Helping Students series (Perigee). Offers written contract. Charges for copying and delivery charges as specified in author/agency agreement.

Literary Agents *(side margin)*

⊘ HELEN REES LITERARY AGENCY

376 North St., Boston MA 02113-2013. (617)227-9014. Fax: (617)227-8762. E-mail: reesagency@reesagency.c om. **Contact:** Joan Mazmanian, Ann Collette, Helen Rees, Lorin Rees. Estab. 1983. Member of AAR, PEN. Represents more than 100 clients. 50% of clients are new/unpublished writers. Currently handles: 60% nonfiction books; 40% novels.

Member Agents Ann Collette (literary fiction, women's studies, health, biography, history); Helen Rees (business, money/finance/economics, government/politics/law, contemporary issues, literary fiction); Lorin Rees (business, money/finance, management, history, narrative nonfiction, science, literary fiction, memoir).

Represents Nonfiction books, novels. **Considers these nonfiction areas:** Biography/autobiography; business/economics; current affairs; government/politics/law; health/medicine; history; money/finance; women's issues/studies. **Considers these fiction areas:** Historical; literary; mainstream/contemporary; mystery/suspense; thriller.

How to Contact Query with SASE, outline, 2 sample chapters. No unsolicited e-mail submissions. No multiple submissions. No e-mail or fax queries. Responds in 3-4 weeks to queries. Obtains most new clients through recommendations from others, conferences, submissions.

Recent Sales Sold more than 35 titles in the last year. *Get Your Shipt Together*, by Capt. D. Michael Abrashoff; *Overpromise and Overdeliver*, by Rick Berrara; *Opacity*, by Joel Kurtzman; *America the Broke*, by Gerald Swanson; *Murder at the B-School*, by Jeffrey Cruikshank; *Bone Factory*, by Steven Sidor; *Father Said*, by Hal Sirowitz; *Winning*, by Jack Welch; *The Case for Israel*, by Alan Dershowitz; *As the Future Catches You*, by Juan Enriquez; *Blood Makes the Grass Grow Green*, by Johnny Rico; *DVD Movie Guide*, by Mick Martin and Marsha Porter; *Words That Work*, by Frank Luntz; *Stirring It Up*, by Gary Hirshberg; *Hot Spots*, by Martin Fletcher; *Andy Grove: The Life and Times of an American*, by Richard Tedlow; *Girls Most Likely To*, by Poonam Sharma.

Terms Agent receives 15% commission on domestic sales; 20% commission on foreign sales.

⊘ REGAL LITERARY AGENCY

1140 Broadway, Penthouse, New York NY 10001. (212)684-7900. Fax: (212)684-7906. E-mail: Shannon@regal-literary.com. Web site: www.regal-literary.com. **Contact:** Shannon Firth, Marcus Hoffmann. Estab. 2002. Member of AAR. Represents 100 clients. 20% of clients are new/unpublished writers. Currently handles: 48% nonfiction books; 46% novels; 6% poetry.

- Prior to becoming agents, Mr. Regal was a musician; Mr. Steinberg was a filmmaker and screenwriter; Ms. Reid and Ms. Schott Pearson were magazine editors; Mr. Hoffman worked in the publishing industry in London.

Member Agents Joseph Regal (literary fiction, science, history, memoir); Peter Steinberg (literary and commercial fiction, history, humor, memoir, narrative nonfiction, young adult); Bess Reed (literary fiction, narrative nonfiction, self-help); Lauren Schott Pearson (literary fiction, commercial fiction, memoir, narrative nonfiction, thrillers, mysteries); Markus Hoffmann (foreign rights manager, literary fiction, mysteries, thrillers, international fiction, science, music). Michael Psaltis of Psaltis Literary also works with Regal Literary agents to form the Culinary Cooperative—a joint-venture agency dedicated to food writing, cookbooks, and all things related to cooking. Recent sales include *Cooked* (William Morrow); *Carmine's Family Style* (St. Martin's Press); *Fish On a First-Name Basis* (St. Martin's Press); *The Reverse Diet* (John Wiley & Sons); and *The Seasoning of a Chef* (Doubleday/Broadway).

Represents Nonfiction books, novels, short story collections, novellas. **Considers these nonfiction areas:** Anthropology/archaeology; art/architecture/design; biography/autobiography; business/economics; cooking/foods/nutrition; current affairs; ethnic/cultural interests; gay/lesbian issues; history; humor/satire; language/literature/criticism; memoirs; military/war; music/dance; nature/environment; photography; popular culture; psychology; religious/inspirational; science/technology; sports; translation; women's issues/studies. **Considers these fiction areas:** Comic books/cartoon; detective/police/crime; ethnic; historical; literary; mystery/suspense; thriller; contemporary.

- ⊶ "We have discovered more than a dozen successful literary novelists in the last 5 years. We are small, but are extraordinarily responsive to our writers. We are more like managers than agents, with an eye toward every aspect of our writers' careers, including publicity and other media." Actively seeking literary fiction and narrative nonfiction. Does not want romance, science fiction, horror, or screenplays.

How to Contact Query with SASE, 5-15 sample pages. No phone calls. No e-mail or fax queries. Considers simultaneous queries. Responds in 2-3 weeks to queries; 4-12 to mss. Returns materials only with SASE. Obtains most new clients through recommendations from others, unsolicited submissions.

Recent Sales Sold 20 titles in the last year. *The Stolen Child*, by Keith Donohue (Nan Talese/Doubleday); *What Elmo Taught Me*, by Kevin Clash (HarperCollins); *The Affected Provincial's Companion*, by Lord Breaulove Swells Whimsy (Bloomsbury); *The Three Incestuous Sisters*, by Audrey Niffenegger (Abrams); *The Traveler*, by John Twelve Hawks (Doubleday). Other clients include James Reston Jr., Tony Earley, Dennie Hughes, Mark Lee, Jake Page, Cheryl Bernard, Daniel Wallace, John Marks, Keith Scribner, Cathy Day, Alicia Erian, Gregory

David Roberts, Dallas Hudgens, Tim Winton, Ian Spiegelman, Brad Barkley, Heather Hepler, Gavin Edwards, Sara Voorhees, Alex Abella.

Terms Agent receives 15% commission on domestic sales; 20% commission on foreign sales. No written contract. Charges clients for typical/major office expenses, such as photocopying and foreign postage.

N ♥ THE AMY RENNERT AGENCY

98 Main St., #302, Tiburon CA 94920. E-mail: queries@amyrennert.com. Web site: www.amyrennert.com. **Contact:** Amy Rennert.

Represents Nonfiction books, novels. **Considers these nonfiction areas:** Biography/autobiography; health/medicine; history; memoirs; sports; lifestyle, narrative nonfiction. **Considers these fiction areas:** General fiction, mystery.

> ○→ "The Amy Rennert Agency specializes in books that matter. We provide career management for established and first-time authors, and our breadth of experience in many genres enables us to meet the needs of a diverse clientele."

How to Contact Query via e-mail. For nonfiction, send cover letter and attach a Word file with proposal/first chapter. For fiction, send cover letter and attach file with 10-20 pages.

Recent Sales *A Salty Piece of Land*, by Jimmy Buffett; *Maisie Dobbs*, by Jacqueline Winspear; *The Prize Winner of Defiance, Ohio*, by Terry Ryan; *The Travel Detective*, by Peter Greenberg; *Offer of Proof*, by Robert Heilbrun; *No Place to Hide*, by Robert O'Harrow; *The Poet of Tolstoy Park*, by Sonny Brewer. Other clients include Elliot Jaspin, Beth Kephart, Kris Kristofferson, Adam Phillips, Don Lattin, Kathryn Shevelow, Cynthia Kaplan, Frank Viviano, Amy Krouse Rosenthal, Kim Severson, Pat Walsh, John Shannon, Brian Copeland, Tony Broadbent, Janis Cooke Newman.

Tips "Due to the high volume of submissions, it is not possible to respond to each and every one. Please understand that we are only able to respond to queries that we feel may be a good fit with our agency."

♥ JODIE RHODES LITERARY AGENCY

8840 Villa La Jolla Drive, Suite 315, La Jolla CA 92037-1957. **Contact:** Jodie Rhodes, president. Estab. 1998. Member of AAR. Represents 50 clients. 60% of clients are new/unpublished writers. Currently handles: 60% nonfiction books; 35% novels; 5% middle grade/young adult books.

> • Prior to opening her agency, Ms. Rhodes was a university-level creative writing teacher, workshop director, published novelist, and vice president/media director at the N.W. Ayer Advertising Agency.

Member Agents Jodie Rhodes; Clark McCutcheon (fiction); Bob McCarter (nonfiction).

Represents Nonfiction books, novels. **Considers these nonfiction areas:** Biography/autobiography; child guidance/parenting; ethnic/cultural interests; government/politics/law; health/medicine; history; memoirs; military/war; science/technology; women's issues/studies. **Considers these fiction areas:** Ethnic; family saga; historical; literary; mainstream/contemporary; mystery/suspense; thriller; young adult; women's.

> ○→ Actively seeking witty, sophisticated women's books about career ambitions and relationships; edgy/trendy YA and teen books; narrative nonfiction on groundbreaking scientific discoveries, politics, economics, military and important current affairs by prominent scientists and academic professors. Does not want to receive erotica, horror, fantasy, romance, science fiction, religious/inspirational, or children's books (does accept young adult/teen).

How to Contact Query with brief synopsis, first 30-50 pages, SASE. Do not call. Do not send complete ms unless requested. This agency does not return unrequested material weighing a pound or more that requires special postage. Include e-mail address with query. No e-mail or fax queries. Considers simultaneous queries. Responds in 3 weeks to queries. Returns materials only with SASE. Obtains most new clients through recommendations from others, agent sourcebooks.

Recent Sales Sold 40 titles in the last year. *A Matter of Gravity*, by John Moffat (HarperCollins); *A Girl Named Indie*, by Kavita Daswani (Simon and Schuster); *First Six Minutes of Life on Earth*, by Christina Reed (John Wiley & Sons); *Flak Jacket Rock*, by Dean Kohler (HarperCollins); *Roots and Wings*, by Many Ly (Random House); *The Art of Solving Crime*, by Max Houck (Praeger); *Murder at the Universe*, by Dan Craig (Midnight Ink); *Into Jerusalem*, by Craig Eisendrath (The Permanent Press); *Preventing Alzheimer's* by Marwan Sabbagh (John Wiley & Sons); *The Genie Machine*, by Robert Plotkin (Stanford University Press); *Take Charge of Your Diabetes*, by Sarfraz Zaidi (Da Capo Press).

Terms Agent receives 15% commission on domestic sales; 20% commission on foreign sales. Offers written contract; 1-month notice must be given to terminate contract. Charges clients for fax, photocopying, phone calls, postage. Charges are itemized and approved by writers upfront.

Tips "Think your book out before you write it. Do your research, know your subject matter intimately, and write vivid specifics, not bland generalities. Care deeply about your book. Don't imitate other writers. Find your own voice. We never take on a book we don't believe in, and we go the extra mile for our writers. We welcome talented, new writers."

RICHARDS LITERARY AGENCY

P.O. Box 31 240, Milford Auckland 1309 New Zealand. (64)(9)410-5681. E-mail: rla.richards@clear.net.nz. **Contact:** Ray Richards. Estab. 1977. Member of NZALA. Represents 100 clients. 20% of clients are new/unpublished writers. Currently handles: 20% nonfiction books; 15% novels; 5% story collections; 40% juvenile books; 5% scholarly books; 15% movie rights.

- Prior to opening his agency, Mr. Richards was a book publisher, managing director and vice chairman..

"We offer a high quality of experience, acceptances and client relationships." Does not want to receive short stories, articles or poetry.

How to Contact Submit outline/proposal. Do not send full ms until requested. Responds in 1 week to queries; 1 month to mss. Returns materials only with SASE. Obtains most new clients through referrals.

Recent Sales *Blindsight*, by Maurice Gee (Penguin/Faber); *The Whale Rider*, by Witi Ihimaera (Reed Publishing); *Margaret Mahy: A Writer's Life*, by Tessa Duder (HarperCollins); Wild Cards: *New Zealand Eccentrics*, by John Dunmore (New Holland). ***Movie/TV MOW script(s) optioned/sold:*** Buzzy Bee TV animation series.

Terms Agent receives 15% commission on domestic sales; 20% commission on foreign sales. Offers written contract. Charges clients for overseas postage and photocopying.

Tips "We first need a full book proposal, outline of 2-10 pages, author statement of experience and published works."

RIGHTS UNLIMITED, INC.

6 W. 37th St., Fourth Floor, New York NY 10018. E-mail: submissions@rightsunlimited.com. Web site: www.rightsunlimited.com. Estab. 1985. Member of AAR. Represents 100+ clients.

Member Agents Desmond Sansevere; Diane Dreher; Ben Salmon; Ryan Dreher.

Represents Nonfiction books, novels. **Considers these nonfiction areas:** Business/economics; current affairs; health/medicine; history; humor/satire; memoirs; popular culture; self-help/personal improvement; sociology; travel; women's issues/studies; celebrity biography; career development; alternative culture; diet/fitness; alternative medicine; inspiration; relationships; gender/sexuality; lifestyle; cookbooks; gift books. **Considers these fiction areas:** Fantasy; literary; multicultural; mystery/suspense; romance (contemporary); science fiction; thriller (international); women's (mainstream); chick lit; mommy lit; quirky/edgy fiction; crime.

No textbooks or poetry.

How to Contact Query with SASE or via e-mail (no attachments). For nonfiction, send query letter, bio, outline, SASE. For fiction, send query letter, bio, synopsis, first 10 pages, SASE. Responds in 1 month to queries.

Recent Sales *Driving the Career Highway*, by Janice Reals-Ellig and William J. Morin (Nelson Business); *101 Things To Do Before You Get a Job*, by Lindsey Pollak (Harper Business); *Health by Water*, by Alexa Fleckenstein and Roanne Weisman (Contemporary).

Terms Agent receives 15% commission on domestic sales; 20% commission on foreign sales; 20% commission on dramatic rights sales.

ANGELA RINALDI LITERARY AGENCY

P.O. Box 7877, Beverly Hills CA 90212-7877. (310)842-7665. Fax: (310)837-8143. E-mail: amr@rinaldiliterary.com. Web site: www.rinaldiliterary.com. **Contact:** Angela Rinaldi. Estab. 1994. Member of AAR. Represents 50 clients. Currently handles: 50% nonfiction books; 50% novels.

- Prior to opening her agency, Ms. Rinaldi was an editor at NAL/Signet, Pocket Books and Bantam, and the manager of book development for *The Los Angeles Times*.

Represents Nonfiction books, novels, TV and motion picture rights (for clients only). **Considers these nonfiction areas:** Biography/autobiography; business/economics; health/medicine; money/finance; self-help/personal improvement; true crime/investigative; women's issues/studies; books by journalists and academics. **Considers these fiction areas:** Literary; commercial; upmarket women's fiction; suspense.

Actively seeking commercial and literary fiction. Does not want to receive scripts, poetry, category romances, children's books, Western's, science fiction/fantasy, technothrillers or cookbooks.

How to Contact For fiction, send first 3 chapters, brief synopsis, SASE. For nonfiction, query with SASE or send outline/proposal, SASE. Do not send certified or metered mail. Brief e-mail inquiries are OK (no attachments). Considers simultaneous queries. Please advise if it is a multiple submission. Responds in 6 weeks to queries. Returns materials only with SASE.

Recent Sales *My First Crush*, by Linda Kaplan (Lyons Press); *Rescue Me*, by Megan Clark (Kensington); *The Blood Orange Tree*, by Drusilla Campbell (Kensington); *Indivisible by Two: Great Tales of Twins, Triplets and Quads*, by Dr. Nancy Segal (Harvard University Press); *Zen Putting*, by Dr. Joseph Parent (Gotham Books); *Bone Lake*, by Drusilla Campbell (Madison Park Press).

Terms Agent receives 15% commission on domestic sales; 20% commission on foreign sales. Offers written contract. Charges clients for photocopying.

◐ ANN RITTENBERG LITERARY AGENCY, INC.

30 Bond St., New York NY 10012. (212)684-6936. Fax: (212)684-6929. Web site: www.rittlit.com. **Contact:** Ann Rittenberg, president. Estab. 1992. Member of AAR. Currently handles: 50% nonfiction books; 50% novels.
Represents Nonfiction books, novels. **Considers these nonfiction areas:** Biography/autobiography; history (social/cultural); memoirs; women's issues/studies. **Considers these fiction areas:** Literary.
  ○┐ This agent specializes in literary fiction and literary nonfiction.
How to Contact Query with SASE, submit outline, 3 sample chapters, SASE. Query via snail mail *only*. No e-mail or fax queries. Considers simultaneous queries. Responds in 6 weeks to queries; 2 months to mss. Obtains most new clients through referrals from established writers and editors.
Recent Sales *Bad Cat*, by Jim Edgar (Workman); *A Certain Slant of Light*, by Laura Whitcomb (Houghton Mifflin); *New York Night*, by Mark Caldwell (Scribner); *In Plain Sight*, by C.J. Box (Putnam); *Improbable*, by Adam Fawer; *Colleges That Change Lives*, by Loren Pope.
Terms Agent receives 15% commission on domestic sales; 20% commission on foreign sales. Offers written contract. This agency charges clients for photocopying only.

◐ RIVERSIDE LITERARY AGENCY

41 Simon Keets Road, Leyden MA 01337. (413)772-0067. Fax: (413)772-0969. E-mail: rivlit@sover.net. **Contact:** Susan Lee Cohen. Estab. 1990. Represents 40 clients. 20% of clients are new/unpublished writers.
Represents Adult nonfiction, adult novels.
How to Contact Query with SASE, outline. Accepts e-mail queries. No fax queries. Considers simultaneous queries. Responds in 2 weeks to queries. Obtains most new clients through referrals.
Recent Sales *Writing to Change the World*, by Mary Pipher (Riverhead/Penguin Putnam); *The Sociopath Next Door: The Ruthless Versus the Rest of Us*, by Martha Stout (Broadway); *The Secret Magdalene*, by Ki Longfellow (Crown); *Buddha is as Buddha Does*, by Lama Surya Das (Broadway).
Terms Agent receives 15% commission on domestic sales. Offers written contract. Charges clients for foreign postage, photocopying large mss, express mail deliveries, etc.

◖ RLR ASSOCIATES, LTD.

Literary Department, 7 W. 51st St., New York NY 10019. (212)541-8641. Fax: (212)541-6052. E-mail: info@rlrass ociates.net. Web site: www.rlrliterary.net. **Contact:** Jennifer Unter, Tara Mark, Scott Gould. Member of AAR. Represents 50 clients. 25% of clients are new/unpublished writers. Currently handles: 70% nonfiction books; 25% novels; 5% story collections.
Represents Nonfiction books, novels, short story collections, scholarly books. **Considers these nonfiction areas:** Animals; anthropology/archaeology; art/architecture/design; biography/autobiography; business/economics; child guidance/parenting; cooking/foods/nutrition; current affairs; education; ethnic/cultural interests; gay/lesbian issues; government/politics/law; health/medicine; history; humor/satire; interior design/decorating; language/literature/criticism; memoirs; money/finance; multicultural; music/dance; nature/environment; photography; popular culture; psychology; religious/inspirational; science/technology; self-help/personal improvement; sociology; sports; translation; travel; true crime/investigative; women's issues/studies. **Considers these fiction areas:** Action/adventure; comic books/cartoon; detective/police/crime; ethnic; experimental; family saga; feminist; gay/lesbian; historical; horror; humor/satire; literary; mainstream/contemporary; multicultural; mystery/suspense; sports; thriller.
  ○┐ "We provide a lot of editorial assistance to our clients and have connections." Actively seeking fiction, current affairs, history, art, popular culture, health and business. Does not want to receive science fiction, fantasy, screenplays or illustrated children's stories.
How to Contact Query with SASE. Considers simultaneous queries. Responds in 4-8 weeks to queries. Returns materials only with SASE. Obtains most new clients through recommendations from others.
Recent Sales Other clients include Shelby Foote, The Grief Recovery Institute, Don Wade, Don Zimmer, The Knot.com, David Plowden, PGA of America, Danny Peary, Goerge Kalinsky, Peter Hyman, Daniel Parker, Lee Miller, Elise Miller, Nina Planck, Karyn Bosnak.
Terms Agent receives 15% commission on domestic sales; 20% commission on foreign sales. Offers written contract.
Tips "Please check out our Web site for more details on our agency."

◖ B.J. ROBBINS LITERARY AGENCY

5130 Bellaire Ave., North Hollywood CA 91607-2908. (818)760-6602. E-mail: robbinsliterary@aol.com. **Contact:** (Ms.) B.J. Robbins. Estab. 1992. Member of AAR. Represents 40 clients. 50% of clients are new/unpublished writers. Currently handles: 50% nonfiction books; 50% novels.
Represents Nonfiction books, novels. **Considers these nonfiction areas:** Biography/autobiography; current affairs; ethnic/cultural interests; health/medicine; how-to; humor/satire; memoirs; music/dance; popular cul-

ture; psychology; self-help/personal improvement; sociology; sports; theater/film; travel; true crime/investigative; women's issues/studies. **Considers these fiction areas:** Detective/police/crime; ethnic; literary; mainstream/contemporary; mystery/suspense; sports; thriller.

How to Contact Query with SASE, submit outline/proposal, 3 sample chapters, SASE. Accepts e-mail queries (no attachments). No fax queries. Considers simultaneous queries. Responds in 2-6 weeks to queries; 6-8 weeks to mss. Returns materials only with SASE. Obtains most new clients through conferences, referrals.

Recent Sales Sold 15 titles in the last year. *Getting Stoned with Savages*, by J. Maarten Troost (Broadway); *Hot Water*, by Kathryn Jordan (Berkley); *Between the Bridge and the River*, by Craig Ferguson (Chronicle); *I'm Proud of You*, by Tim Madigan (Gotham); *Man of the House*, by Chris Erskine (Rodale); *Bird of Another Heaven*, by James D. Houston (Knopf); *Tomorrow They Will Kiss*, by Eduardo Santiago (Little, Brown).

Terms Agent receives 15% commission on domestic sales; 20% commission on foreign sales. Offers written contract; 3-month notice must be given to terminate contract. 100% of business is derived from commissions on ms sales. This agency charges clients for postage and photocopying (only after sale of ms).

Writers' Conferences Squaw Valley Writers Workshop; San Diego State University Writers' Conference; Santa Barbara Writers' Conference.

N ⊕ ☑ ROGERS, COLERIDGE & WHITE

20 Powis Mews, London England W11 1JN, United Kingdom. (44)(207)221-3717. Fax: (44)(207)229-9084. E-mail: info@rcwlitagency.co.uk. Web site: www.rcwlitagency.co.uk. Estab. 1987.

• Prior to opening the agency, Ms. Rogers was an agent with Peter Janson-Smith; Ms. Coleridge worked at Sidgwick & Jackson, Chatto & Windus, and Anthony Sheil Associates; Ms. White was an editor and rights director for Simon & Schuster; Mr. Straus worked at Hodder and Stoughton, Hamish Hamilton, and Macmillan; Mr. Miller worked as Ms. Rogers' assistant and was treasurer of the AAA; Ms. Waldie worked with Carole Smith.

Member Agents Deborah Rogers; Gill Coleridge; Pat White (illustrated and children's books); Peter Straus; David Miller; Zoe Waldie (fiction, biography, current affairs, narrative history); Laurence Laluyaux (foreign rights); Stephen Edwards (foreign rights).

Represents Nonfiction books, novels, juvenile books. **Considers these nonfiction areas:** Cooking/foods/nutrition; current affairs; history (narrative); humor/satire; sports; biography. **Considers these fiction areas:** Most fiction categories.

O→ Does not want to receive plays, screenplays, technical books or educational books.

How to Contact Submit synopsis, proposal, sample chapters, bio, SAE by mail. Responds in 6-8 weeks to queries. Obtains most new clients through recommendations from others, solicitations, conferences.

Recent Sales *Where They Were Missed*, by Lucy Caldwell (Viking); *Theft: A Love Story*, by Peter Carey (Faber); *Nefertiti*, by Nick Drake (Transworld); *Kept: A Victorian Mystery*, by D.J. Taylor (Chatto).

Terms Agent receives 15% commission on domestic sales; 20% commission on foreign sales. Offers written contract.

☑ LINDA ROGHAAR LITERARY AGENCY, LLC

133 High Point Drive, Amherst MA 01002. (413)256-1921. Fax: (413)256-2636. E-mail: contact@lindaroghaar.com. Web site: www.lindaroghaar.com. **Contact:** Linda L. Roghaar. Estab. 1996. Represents 50 clients. 10% of clients are new/unpublished writers. Currently handles: 90% nonfiction books; 10% novels.

• Prior to opening her agency, Ms. Roghaar worked in retail bookselling for 5 years and as a publishers' sales rep for 15 years.

Represents Nonfiction books, novels. **Considers these nonfiction areas:** Animals; anthropology/archaeology; biography/autobiography; education; history; nature/environment; popular culture; religious/inspirational; self-help/personal improvement; women's issues/studies. **Considers these fiction areas:** Mystery/suspense (amateur sleuth, cozy, culinary, malice domestic).

How to Contact Query with SASE. Accepts e-mail queries. No fax queries. Considers simultaneous queries. Responds in 2 months to queries; 4 months to mss.

Recent Sales *Awakened Writer*, by Laraine Herring (Shambhala); *Starting From Scratch*, by Pam Johnson Bennett (Penguin); *Knitting Yarn and The Truth About How Things Are*, by Stephanie Pearl-McPhee (Andrews McMeel).

Terms Agent receives 15% commission on domestic sales; negotiable commission on foreign sales. Offers written contract.

N ⊕ ◎ MERCEDES ROS LITERARY AGENCY

Castell 38, 08329 Teia, Barcelona, Spain. (34)(93)540-1353. Fax: (34)(93)540-1346. E-mail: info@mercedesros.com. Web site: www.mercedesros.com. **Contact:** Mercedes Ros.

Member Agents Mercedes Ros; Mercé Segarra.

Represents Juvenile books.

    O→ "Gemser Publications publishes nonfiction and religious illustrated books for the 0-7 age group. Our products, basically aimed to convey concepts, habits, attitudes and values that are close to the child's environment, always adopting an open mentality in a globalized world. We combine excellent quality with competitive prices and good texts and beautiful illustrations to educate and inspire our young readers."

How to Contact Accepts submissions by e-mail or on disc. No fax queries.

Writers' Conferences Frankfurt Book Fair; London Book Fair; Bologna Book Fair; BookExpo of America; Tokyo Book Fair; Beijing International Book Fair; Frankfurt Book Fair 2007.

Tips "Try to read or look at as many books a publisher has published before sending in your material, to get a feel for their list and whether your manuscript, idea or style of illustration is likely to fit."

◪ THE ROSENBERG GROUP

23 Lincoln Ave., Marblehead MA 01945. (781)990-1341. Fax: (781)990-1344. Web site: www.rosenberggroup.com. **Contact:** Barbara Collins Rosenberg. Estab. 1998. Member of AAR, recognized agent of the RWA. Represents 25 clients. 15% of clients are new/unpublished writers. Currently handles: 30% nonfiction books; 30% novels; 10% scholarly books; 30% college textbooks.

    • Prior to becoming an agent, Ms. Rosenberg was a senior editor for Harcourt.

Represents Nonfiction books, novels, textbooks (college textbooks only). **Considers these nonfiction areas:** Current affairs; popular culture; psychology; sports; women's issues/studies; women's health; food/wine/beverages. **Considers these fiction areas:** Romance; women's.

    O→ Ms. Rosenberg is well-versed in the romance market (both category and single title). She is a frequent speaker at romance conferences. Actively seeking romance category or single title in contemporary chick lit, romantic suspense, and the historical subgenres. Does not want to receive inspirational or spiritual romances.

How to Contact Query with SASE. No e-mail or fax queries. Responds in 2 weeks to queries; 4-6 weeks to mss. Returns materials only with SASE. Obtains most new clients through recommendations from others, solicitations, conferences.

Recent Sales Sold 21 titles in the last year.

Terms Agent receives 15% commission on domestic sales; 15% commission on foreign sales. Offers written contract; 1-month notice must be given to terminate contract. Charges maximum of $350/year for postage and photocopying.

Writers' Conferences RWA National Conference; BookExpo America.

◪ RITA ROSENKRANZ LITERARY AGENCY

440 West End Ave., Suite 15D, New York NY 10024-5358. (212)873-6333. **Contact:** Rita Rosenkranz. Estab. 1990. Member of AAR. Represents 30 clients. 30% of clients are new/unpublished writers. Currently handles: 99% nonfiction books; 1% novels.

    • Prior to opening her agency, Ms. Rosenkranz worked as an editor in major New York publishing houses.

Represents Nonfiction books. **Considers these nonfiction areas:** Animals; anthropology/archaeology; art/architecture/design; biography/autobiography; business/economics; child guidance/parenting; computers/electronic; cooking/foods/nutrition; crafts/hobbies; current affairs; ethnic/cultural interests; gay/lesbian issues; government/politics/law; health/medicine; history; how-to; humor/satire; interior design/decorating; language/literature/criticism; military/war; money/finance; music/dance; nature/environment; New Age/metaphysics; photography; popular culture; psychology; religious/inspirational; science/technology; self-help/personal improvement; sports; theater/film; women's issues/studies.

    O→ This agency focuses on adult nonfiction, stresses strong editorial development and refinement before submitting to publishers, and brainstorms ideas with authors. Actively seeking authors who are well paired with their subject, either for professional or personal reasons.

How to Contact Submit proposal package, outline, SASE. No e-mail or fax queries. Considers simultaneous queries. Responds in 2 weeks to queries. Obtains most new clients through solicitations, conferences, word of mouth.

Recent Sales Sold 35 titles in the last year. *Forbidden Fruit: True Love Stories from the Underground Railroad*, by Betty DeRamus (Atria Books); *Business Class: Etiquette Essentials for Success at Work*, by Jacqueline Whitmore (St. Martin's Press); *Olive Trees and Honey: A Treasury of Vegetarian Recipes from Jewish Communities Around the World*, by Gil Marks (Wiley); *20 Strengths Adoptive Parents Must Discover*, by Sherrie Eldridge (Bantom Dell); *Baseball Hall of Fame Museum*, by Bert Sugar (Running Press).

Terms Agent receives 15% commission on domestic sales; 20% commission on foreign sales. Offers written contract, binding for 3 years; 3-month written notice must be given to terminate contract. 100% of business is derived from commissions on ms sales. Charges clients for photocopying. Makes referrals to editing services.

Literary Agents

Tips ''Identify the current competition for your project to make sure the project is valid. A strong cover letter is very important.''

◐ ROSENSTONE/WENDER

38 E. 29th St., 10th Floor, New York NY 10016. (212)725-9445. Fax: (212)725-9447. **Contact:** Phyllis Wender. Member of AAR. Currently handles: 100% stage plays.

Member Agents Phyllis Wender; Sonia Pabley.

Represents Theatrical stage play.

    ○➔ Interested in literary, adult and dramatic material.

How to Contact Query with SASE. No e-mail or fax queries. Obtains most new clients through recommendations from others.

Recent Sales *River of Heaven*, by Lee Martin (Shaye Areheart Books).

◐ THE GAIL ROSS LITERARY AGENCY

1666 Connecticut Ave. NW, #500, Washington DC 20009. (202)328-3282. Fax: (202)328-9162. E-mail: jennifer@gailross.com. Web site: www.gailross.com. **Contact:** Jennifer Manguera. Estab. 1988. Member of AAR. Represents 200 clients. 75% of clients are new/unpublished writers. Currently handles: 95% nonfiction books.

Represents Nonfiction books. **Considers these nonfiction areas:** Anthropology/archaeology; biography/autobiography; business/economics; education; ethnic/cultural interests; gay/lesbian issues; government/politics/law; health/medicine; money/finance; nature/environment; psychology; religious/inspirational; science/technology; self-help/personal improvement; sociology; sports; true crime/investigative.

    ○➔ This agency specializes in adult trade nonfiction.

How to Contact Query with SASE. Considers simultaneous queries. Responds in 1 month to queries. Obtains most new clients through recommendations from others.

Recent Sales Sold 50 titles in the last year. *Facing the 40 or 50: The No-Knife Solution to Fixing Your Face*, by Brandith Irwin (Da Capo).

Terms Agent receives 15% commission on domestic sales; 25% commission on foreign sales. Charges for office expenses.

◑ CAROL SUSAN ROTH, LITERARY & CREATIVE

P.O. Box 620337, Woodside CA 94062. (650)323-3795. E-mail: carol@authorsbest.com. Web site: www.authorsbest.com. **Contact:** Carol Susan Roth. Estab. 1995. Represents 50 clients. 15% of clients are new/unpublished writers. Currently handles: 100% nonfiction books.

    ● Prior to becoming an agent, Ms. Roth was trained as a psychotherapist and worked as a motivational coach, conference producer, and promoter for best-selling authors (e.g., Scott Peck, Bernie Siegal, John Gray) and the 1987 Heart of Business conference (the first business and spirituality conference).

Represents Nonfiction books. **Considers these nonfiction areas:** Business/economics; health/medicine; money/finance (personal finance/investing); popular culture; religious/inspirational; self-help/personal improvement; spirituality; Buddhism, yoga, humor, real estate, entrepreneurship, beauty, social action, wellness.

    ○➔ This agency specializes in health, science, pop culture, spirituality, personal growth, personal finance, entrepreneurship and business. Actively seeking previously published, media saavy journalists, authors, and experts with an established audience in pop culture, history, the sciences, health, spirituality, personal growth, and business. Does not want to receive fiction or children's books.

How to Contact Submit proposal package, media kit, promotional video, SASE. Accepts e-mail queries (no attachments). Considers simultaneous queries. Responds in 2 days to queries. Returns materials only with SASE. Obtains most new clients through recommendations from others, solicitations.

Recent Sales Sold 17 titles in the last year. *Way of the Fertile Soul*, by Randine Lewis (Atria/S&S); *Teachings of the Adventure Rabbi*, by Rabbi Jamie Korngold (Doubleday); *Seven Stones That Rocked the World*, by Patrick Hunt (University of California Press); *Ten Discoveries That Rewrote History*, by Patrick Hunt (Penguin Plume); *Snooze or Lose!*, by Helene Emsellem (Joseph Henry Press).

Terms Agent receives 15% commission on domestic sales; 15% commission on foreign sales. Offers written contract, binding for 3 years (only for work with the acquiring publisher); 60-day notice must be given to terminate contract. This agency asks the client to provide postage (FedEx airbills) and do copying. Refers to book doctor for proposal development and publicity service on request.

Writers' Conferences Stanford Professional Publishing Course, MEGA Book Marketing University, Maui Writers Conference, Jack London Writers' Conference, San Francisco Writers' Conference.

Tips ''Have charisma, content, and credentials—solve an old problem in a new way. I prefer experts with extensive teaching and speaking experience.''

◉ JANE ROTROSEN AGENCY LLC

318 E. 51st St., New York NY 10022. (212)593-4330. Fax: (212)935-6985. E-mail: firstinitiallastname@janerotros
en.com. Estab. 1974. Member of AAR, Authors Guild. Represents over 100 clients. Currently handles: 30%
nonfiction books; 70% novels.

Member Agents Jane R. Berkey; Andrea Cirillo; Annelise Robey; Margaret Ruley; Kelly Harms; Christina Ho-
grebe; Peggy Gordijn, director of translation rights.

Represents Nonfiction books, novels. **Considers these nonfiction areas:** Biography/autobiography; business/
economics; child guidance/parenting; cooking/foods/nutrition; current affairs; health/medicine; how-to; hu-
mor/satire; money/finance; nature/environment; popular culture; psychology; self-help/personal improvement; sports; true crime/investigative; women's issues/studies. **Considers these fiction areas:** Action/adven-
ture; detective/police/crime; family saga; historical; horror; mainstream/contemporary; mystery/suspense;
romance; thriller; women's.

How to Contact Query with SASE. No e-mail or fax queries. Responds in 2 months to mss. Responds in 2 weeks
to writers who have been referred by a client or colleague. Returns materials only with SASE. Obtains most
new clients through referrals.

Recent Sales This agency prefers not to share information on specific sales.

Terms Agent receives 15% commission on domestic sales; 20% commission on foreign sales. Offers written
contract, binding for 3-5 years; 2-month notice must be given to terminate contract. Charges clients for photocopying, express mail, overseas postage, book purchase.

◉ THE PETER RUBIE LITERARY AGENCY

240 W. 35th St., Suite 500, New York NY 10001. (212)279-1776. Fax: (212)279-0927. E-mail: peterrubie@prlit.c
om. Web site: www.prlit.com. **Contact:** Peter Rubie (peterrubie@prlit.com); June Clark (pralit@aol.com); and
Amy Tipton (assist@prlit.com). Estab. 2000. Member of AAR. Represents 130 clients. 20% of clients are new/
unpublished writers.

• Prior to opening his agency, Mr. Rubie authored two novels and a number of nonfiction books. He was
also the fiction editor at Walker and Co. Ms. Clark is the author of several books and plays, and previously
worked in cable TV marketing and promotion. Ms. Tipton is also a writer and has worked as a literary
assistant and office manager at several agencies.

Member Agents Peter Rubie (crime, science fiction, fantasy, literary fiction, thrillers, narrative/serious nonfiction, business, self-help, how-to, popular, food/wine, history, commercial science, music, education, parenting); June Clark (celebrity biographies, parenting, pets, women's issues, teen nonfiction, how-to, self-help,
offbeat business, food/wine, commercial New Age, pop culture, entertainment, gay/lesbian); Amy Tipton
(edgy/gritty fiction, urban, women's fiction, memoir and young adult).

Represents Nonfiction books, novels. **Considers these nonfiction areas:** Business/economics; current affairs;
ethnic/cultural interests; gay/lesbian issues; how-to; popular culture; science/technology; self-help/personal
improvement; TV; creative nonfiction (narrative); health/nutrition; cooking/food/wine; music; theater/film;
prescriptive New Age; parenting/education; pets; commercial academic material. **Considers these fiction areas:**
Fantasy; historical; literary; science fiction; thriller.

How to Contact For fiction, submit short synopsis, first 30-40 pages. For nonfiction, submit 1-page overview
of the book, TOC, outline, 1-2 sample chapters. Accepts e-mail queries. No fax queries. Responds in 2 months
to queries; 3 months to mss. Returns materials only with SASE. Obtains most new clients through recommendations from others.

Recent Sales Sold 50 titles in the last year. *Walking Money*, by James Born (Putnam); *Atherton*, by Patrick
Carman (Little, Brown); *One Nation Under God*, by James P. Moore (Doubleday); *28 Days*, by Gabrielle Lichter-
man (Adams); *Shattered Dreams*, by Harlan Ullman (Carroll & Graf); *Chef on Fire*, by Joseph Carey (Taylor);
Laughing with Lucy, by Madelyn Pugh Davis (Emis); *Read My Hips*, by Eve Marx (Adams); *Black Comedians*,
Black Comedy, by Darryl Littleton.

Terms Agent receives 15% commission on domestic sales; 20% commission on foreign sales. Offers written
contract. Charges clients for photocopying and some foreign mailings.

Tips "We look for writers who are experts, have a strong platform and reputation in their field, and have an
outstanding prose style. Be professional and open-minded. Know your market and learn your craft. Go to our
Web site for up-to-date information on clients and sales."

ⓝ ◉ ◎ THE RUDY AGENCY

825 Wildlife Lane, Estes Park CO 80517. (970)577-8500. Fax: (970)577-8600. E-mail: mak@rudyagency.com.
Web site: www.rudyagency.com. **Contact:** Maryann Karinch. Estab. 2003; adheres to AAR canon of ethics.
Represents 12 clients. 50% of clients are new/unpublished writers. Currently handles: 100% nonfiction books.

• Prior to becoming an agent, Ms. Karinch was, and continues to be, an author of nonfiction books—
covering the subjects of health/medicine and human behavior. Prior to that, she was in public relations and
marketing: areas of expertise she also applies in her practice as an agent.

Member Agents Maryann Karinch (nonfiction: health/medicine, culture/values, history, biography, memoir, science/technology, military/intelligence).

Represents Nonfiction books, textbooks (with consumer appeal). **Considers these nonfiction areas:** Anthropology/archaeology; biography/autobiography; business/economics; child guidance/parenting; computers/electronic; current affairs; education; ethnic/cultural interests; gay/lesbian issues; government/politics/law; health/medicine; history; how-to; language/literature/criticism; memoirs; military/war; money/finance; music/dance; nature/environment; popular culture; psychology; science/technology; self-help/personal improvement; sociology; sports; true crime/investigative; women's issues/studies.

O→ Actively seeking projects with social value, projects that open minds to new ideas and interesting lives, and projects that entertain through good storytelling. Does not want to receive poetry, children's/juvenile books, screenplays/plays, art/photo books, novels/novellas, religion books, and joke books or books that fit in to the impulse buy/gift book category.

How to Contact Query us. If we like the query, we will invite a complete proposal. No phone queries. Accepts e-mail and fax queries. Considers simultaneous queries. Responds in 8 weeks to mss. Returns materials only with SASE. Obtains most new clients through recommendations from others, solicitations.

Recent Sales Sold 8 titles in the last year. *Live from Jordan: Letters Home from My Journal Through the Middle East*, by Benjamin Orbach (Amacom); *Finding Center: Strategies to Build Strong Girls & Women*, by Maureen Mack (New Horizon Press); *Crossing Fifth Avenue to Bergdorf Goodman: An Insider's Account on the Rise of Luxury Retailing*, by Ira Neimark (SPI Books); *The First American: The Suppressed Story of the People Who Discovered the New World*, by Christopher Hardaker (Career Press/New Page Books). Other clients include Gregory Hartley, Jackson Brooks, Savo Heleta, Vanessa Vega, Peter Richichi, Janai Lowenstein, David Chacko, Samuel Crompton.

Terms Agent receives 15% commission on domestic sales. Offers written contract, binding for 1 year.

Writers' Conferences BookExpo America; industry events.

Tips "Present yourself professionally. I tell people all the time: Subscribe to *Writer's Digest* (I do), because you will get good advice about how to approach an agent."

N ◯ MARLY RUSOFF & ASSOCIATES, INC.

P.O. Box 524, Bronxville NY 10708. (914)961-7939. Web site: www.rusoffagency.com. **Contact:** Marly Rusoff.

• Prior to her current position, Ms. Rusoff held positions at Houghton Mifflin, Doubleday and William Morrow. Ms. Hansen worked for Crown, Simon & Schuster and Doubleday.

Member Agents Marly Rusoff; Judith Hansen.

Represents Nonfiction books, novels. **Considers these nonfiction areas:** Art/architecture/design; biography/autobiography; business/economics; health/medicine; history; memoirs; money/finance; popular culture; psychology. **Considers these fiction areas:** Historical; literary; commercial.

O→ "While we take delight in discovering new talent, we are particularly interested in helping established writers expand readership and develop their careers."

How to Contact Query with SASE, submit synopsis, publishing history, author bio, contact information. For e-queries, include no attachments or pdf files. This agency only responds if interested. No fax queries. Obtains most new clients through recommendations from others.

Recent Sales *Ellington Boulevard*, by Adam Langer (Spiegel & Grau); *Confessions of a Jane Austen Addict*, by Laurie Viera Rigler; *My Father's Bonus March*, by Adam Langer; *The Decency Rules and Regulations*, by Susan and Frank Fuller.

◯ RUSSELL & VOLKENING

50 W. 29th St., #7E, New York NY 10001. (212)684-6050. Fax: (212)889-3026. Web site: www.randvinc.com. **Contact:** Timothy Seldes, Jesseca Salky. Estab. 1940. Member of AAR. Represents 140 clients. 20% of clients are new/unpublished writers. Currently handles: 45% nonfiction books; 50% novels; 3% story collections; 2% novellas.

Represents Nonfiction books, novels, short story collections. **Considers these nonfiction areas:** Anthropology/archaeology; art/architecture/design; biography/autobiography; business/economics; cooking/foods/nutrition; current affairs; education; ethnic/cultural interests; gay/lesbian issues; government/politics/law; health/medicine; history; language/literature/criticism; military/war; money/finance; music/dance; nature/environment; photography; popular culture; psychology; science/technology; sociology; sports; theater/film; true crime/investigative; women's issues/studies; creative nonfiction. **Considers these fiction areas:** Action/adventure; detective/police/crime; ethnic; literary; mainstream/contemporary; mystery/suspense; picture books; sports; thriller.

O→ This agency specializes in literary fiction and narrative nonfiction.

How to Contact Query with SASE, submit synopsis, several pages. No e-mail or fax queries. Responds in 4 weeks to queries.

Recent Sales *Digging to America*, by Anne Tyler (Knopf); *Get a Life*, by Nadine Gardiner; *The Franklin Affair*, by Jim Lehrer (Random House).

Terms Agent receives 15% commission on domestic sales; 20% commission on foreign sales. Charges clients for standard office expenses relating to the submission of materials.

Tips "If the query is cogent, well written, well presented, and is the type of book we'd represent, we'll ask to see the manuscript. From there, it depends purely on the quality of the work."

◖ REGINA RYAN PUBLISHING ENTERPRISES, INC.

251 Central Park W., 7D, New York NY 10024. (212)787-5589. E-mail: queryreginaryanbooks@rcn.com. **Contact:** Regina Ryan. Estab. 1976. Currently handles: 100% nonfiction books.

- Prior to becoming an agent, Ms. Ryan was an editor at Alfred A. Knopf, editor-in-chief of Macmillan Adult Trade, and a book producer.

Represents Nonfiction books. **Considers these nonfiction areas:** Gardening; history; psychology; travel; women's issues/studies; narrative nonfiction; natural history (especially birds and birding); popular science; parenting; adventure; architecture.

How to Contact Query by e-mail or mail with SASE. No telephone queries. Does not accept queries for juvenile or fiction. Considers simultaneous queries. Tries to respond in 1 month to queries. Returns materials only with SASE. Obtains most new clients through recommendations from others.

Recent Sales *Chronicles: The 750-Year History of an Eastern European Jewish Family*, by Michael Karpin (Wiley); *The Legacy: The Rockefellers and Their Museums*, by Suzanne Loebl (Smithsonian Press); *Passport to Your National Parks Field Guides*, by Randi Minetor (Globe Pequot); *Trapped by Toxic Guilt? Five Steps to Freedom*, by Susan Carrell (McGraw Hill); *The Last Leaf: The Uncollected Works of Dorothy West, edited by Lionel Bascom (St. Martin's Press); The Serotonin Diet*, by Judith Wurtman, PhD and Nina Marquis, MD (Rodale); *Autopsy of a Suicidal Mind*, by Edwin Shneidman, PhD (Oxford University Press); *Surviving Hitler*, by Andrea Warren (HarperCollins Books for Young Readers); *The Bomb in the Basement: The Israeli Nuclear Option*, by Michael Karpin (Simon & Schuster).

Terms Agent receives 15% commission on domestic sales; 15% commission on foreign sales. Offers written contract. Charges clients for all out-of-pocket expenses (e.g., long distance calls, messengers, freight, copying) if it's more than just a nominal amount.

Tips "An analysis of why your proposed book is different and better than the competition is essential; a sample chapter is helpful."

◖ THE SAGALYN AGENCY

4922 Fairmont Ave., Suite 200, Bethesda MD 20814. (301)718-6440. Fax: (301)718-6444. E-mail: query@sagalyn.com. Web site: www.sagalyn.com. Estab. 1980. Member of AAR. Currently handles: 85% nonfiction books; 5% novels; 10% scholarly books.

- Prior to becoming an agent, Ms. Sagalyn worked for ICM and had her own agency in Washington, D.C.

Member Agents Raphael Sagalyn

Represents Nonfiction books. **Considers these nonfiction areas:** Biography/autobiography; business/economics; history; memoirs; popular culture; religious/inspirational; science/technology; journalism.

- ⊶ Does not want to receive stage plays, screenplays, poetry, science fiction, fantasy, romance, children's books or young adult books.

How to Contact Please send e-mail queries only (no attachments). Include 1 of these words in the subject line: query, submission, inquiry. Accepts e-mail queries. No fax queries.

Recent Sales *Intrinsic Motivation: The New Logic of Rewards*, by Daniel Pink (Riverhead); *Sexpertise*, by Robin Sawyer (Simon Spotlight Entertainment); see Web site for more sales information.

Tips "We receive 1,000-1,200 queries a year, which in turn lead to 2 or 3 new clients. Query via e-mail only."

Ｎ ◖ SALKIND LITERARY AGENCY

Part of Studio B, 734 Indiana St., Lawrence KS 66044. (913)538-7113. Fax: (516)706-2369. E-mail: neil@studiob.com. Web site: www.salkindagency.com. **Contact:** Neil Salkind. Estab. 1995. Represents 100 clients. 25% of clients are new/unpublished writers. Currently handles: 60% nonfiction books; 20% scholarly books; 20% textbooks.

- Prior to becoming an agent, Mr. Salkind authored numerous trade textbooks.

Represents Nonfiction books, scholarly books, textbooks. **Considers these nonfiction areas:** Business/economics; child guidance/parenting; computers/electronic; cooking/foods/nutrition; crafts/hobbies; education; ethnic/cultural interests; gay/lesbian issues; health/medicine; how-to; money/finance; photography; popular culture; psychology; religious/inspirational; science/technology; self-help/personal improvement; sports.

- ⊶ Actively seeking distinct nonfiction that takes risks and explores new ideas from authors who have, or can establish, a significant platform. Does not want to receive book proposals based on ideas where potential authors have not yet researched what has been published.

How to Contact Query with SASE, submit publishing history, author bio. Accepts e-mail queries. No fax queries. Responds in 1 week to queries; 1 week to mss. Obtains most new clients through recommendations from others.
Recent Sales Sold 120 titles in the last year. *Googlinaire*, by Anthony Boreilli (Wiley); *Clinical Psychology*, by Dean McKay (Blackwell); *The American Dream*, by Ralph Roberts (Kaplan); *Microsoft 2007 Exchange Admin Companion*, by Walter Glenn (Microsoft Press).
Terms Agent receives 15% commission on domestic sales; 15% commission on foreign sales.
Tips "Present a unique idea based on a thorough knowledge of the market, be it a trade or textbook."

⬤ VICTORIA SANDERS & ASSOCIATES

241 Avenue of the Americas, Suite 11 H, New York NY 10014. (212)633-8811. Fax: (212)633-0525. E-mail: queriesvsa@hotmail.com. Web site: www.victoriasanders.com. **Contact:** Victoria Sanders, Diane Dickensheid. Estab. 1993. Member of AAR; signatory of WGA. Represents 135 clients. 25% of clients are new/unpublished writers. Currently handles: 50% nonfiction books; 50% novels.
Represents Nonfiction books, novels. **Considers these nonfiction areas:** Biography/autobiography; current affairs; ethnic/cultural interests; gay/lesbian issues; government/politics/law; history; humor/satire; language/literature/criticism; music/dance; popular culture; psychology; theater/film; translation; women's issues/studies. **Considers these fiction areas:** Action/adventure; contemporary issues; ethnic; family saga; feminist; gay/lesbian; literary; thriller.
How to Contact Query by e-mail only.
Recent Sales Sold 20+ titles in the last year. *Faithless, Triptych & Skin Privilege*, by Karin Slaughter (Delacorte); *Jewels: 50 Phenomenal Black Women Over 50*, by Connie Briscoe and Michael Cunningham (Bulfinch); *B Mother*, by Maureen O'Brien (Harcourt); *Vagablonde*, by Kim Green (Warner); *Next Elements*, by Jeff Chang (Basic Civitas); *The Ties That Bind*, by Dr. Bertice Berry.
Terms Agent receives 15% commission on domestic sales; 20% commission on foreign sales. Offers written contract. Charges for photocopying, messenger, express mail. If in excess of $100, client approval is required.
Tips "Limit query to letter (no calls) and give it your best shot. A good query is going to get a good response."

⬤ SCHIAVONE LITERARY AGENCY, INC.

236 Trails End, West Palm Beach FL 33413-2135. (561)966-9294. Fax: (561)966-9294. E-mail: profschia@aol.com. New York office: 3671 Hudson Manor Terrace, No. 11H, Bronx, NY, 10463-1139, phone: (718)548-5332; fax: (718)548-5332; e-mail: jendu77@aol.com **Contact:** Dr. James Schiavone. CEO, corporate offices in Florida; Jennifer DuVall, president, New York office. Estab. 1996. Member of National Education Association. Represents 60+ clients. 2% of clients are new/unpublished writers. Currently handles: 50% nonfiction books; 49% novels; 1% textbooks.

- Prior to opening his agency, Dr. Schiavone was a full professor of developmental skills at the City University of New York and author of 5 trade books and 3 textbooks. Jennifer DuVall has many years of combined experience in office management and agenting.

Represents Nonfiction books, novels, juvenile books, scholarly books, textbooks. **Considers these nonfiction areas:** Animals; anthropology/archaeology; biography/autobiography; child guidance/parenting; current affairs; education; ethnic/cultural interests; gay/lesbian issues; government/politics/law; health/medicine; history; how-to; humor/satire; juvenile nonfiction; language/literature/criticism; military/war; nature/environment; popular culture; psychology; science/technology; self-help/personal improvement; sociology; spirituality (mind and body); true crime/investigative. **Considers these fiction areas:** Ethnic; family saga; historical; horror; humor/satire; juvenile; literary; mainstream/contemporary; science fiction; young adult.

⊶ This agency specializes in celebrity biography and autobiography and memoirs. Does not want to receive poetry.

How to Contact Query with SASE. Do not send unsolicited materials or parcels requiring a signature. Send no e-attachments. Accepts e-mail queries. No fax queries. Considers simultaneous queries. Responds in 2 weeks to queries; 6 weeks to mss. Returns materials only with SASE. Obtains most new clients through recommendations from others, solicitations, conferences.
Terms Agent receives 15% commission on domestic sales; 20% commission on foreign sales. Offers written contract. Charges clients for postage only.
Writers' Conferences Key West Literary Seminar; South Florida Writers' Conference; Tallahassee Writers' Conference, Million Dollar Writers' Conference.
Tips "We prefer to work with established authors published by major houses in New York. We will consider marketable proposals from new/previously unpublished writers."

⬤ ◎ SUSAN SCHULMAN LITERARY AGENCY

454 West 44th St., New York NY 10036. (212)713-1633. Fax: (212)581-8830. E-mail: schulman@aol.com. Web site: www.schulmanagency.com. **Contact:** Susan Schulman. Estab. 1980. Member of AAR, Dramatists Guild;

signatory of WGA. 10% of clients are new/unpublished writers. Currently handles: 50% nonfiction books; 25% novels; 15% juvenile books; 10% stage plays.

Member Agents Eleanora Tevis, director of foreign rights; Linda Migali, theater; Emily Uhry, submissions editor.

Represents Nonfiction books, novels, juvenile books, scholarly books. **Considers these nonfiction areas:** Anthropology/archaeology; biography/autobiography; business/economics; child guidance/parenting; cooking/foods/nutrition; current affairs; education; ethnic/cultural interests; gay/lesbian issues; government/politics/law; health/medicine; history; how-to; language/literature/criticism; memoirs; money/finance; music/dance; nature/environment; popular culture; psychology; religious/inspirational; self-help/personal improvement; sociology; sports; true crime/investigative; women's issues/studies. **Considers these fiction areas:** Action/adventure; detective/police/crime; feminist; historical; humor/satire; juvenile; literary; mainstream/contemporary; mystery/suspense; picture books; religious/inspirational; young adult; women's.

- ⊶ "We specialize in books for, by and about women and women's issues including nonfiction self-help books, fiction and theater projects. We also handle the film, television and allied rights for several small agencies as well as foreign rights for several small publishing houses." Actively seeking new nonfiction. Considers plays. Does not want to receive poetry, television scripts or concepts for television.

How to Contact Query with SASE, submit outline, synopsis, 3 sample chapter(s), author bio, SASE. Accepts email queries. No fax queries. Considers simultaneous queries. Responds in 6 weeks to queries; 6 weeks to mss. Returns materials only with SASE. Obtains most new clients through recommendations from others, solicitations, conferences.

Recent Sales Sold 50 titles and sold 5 scripts in the last year. *Who's Your City?* (HarperCollins); *Better Than Yesterday*, by Robyn Schneider (Delacorte Knopf).

Terms Agent receives 15% commission on domestic sales; 20% commission on foreign sales. Offers written contract; 30-day notice must be given to terminate contract.

Writers' Conferences Geneva Writers' Conference (Switzerland); Columbus Writers' Conference; Skidmore Conference of the Independent Women's Writers Group.

Tips "Keep writing!"

Ⓝ ⬛ JONATHAN SCOTT, INC

933 West Van Buren, Suite 510, Chicago IL 60607. (847)557-2365. Fax: (847)557-8408. E-mail: jon@jonathanscott.us; scott@jonathanscott.us. Web site: www.jonathanscott.us. **Contact:** Jon Malysiak, Scott Adlington. Estab. 2005. Represents 40 clients. 75% of clients are new/unpublished writers. Currently handles: 90% nonfiction books; 10% novels.

Member Agents Scott Adlington (narrative nonfiction, sports, health, wellness, fitness, environmental issues); Jon Malysiak (narrative nonfiction and fiction, current affairs, history, memoir, business).

Represents Nonfiction books. **Considers these nonfiction areas:** Biography/autobiography; business/economics; current affairs; ethnic/cultural interests; gay/lesbian issues; government/politics/law; health/medicine; history; humor/satire; memoirs; military/war; nature/environment; popular culture; self-help/personal improvement; sociology; sports; true crime/investigative.

- ⊶ "We are very hands-on with our authors in terms of working with them to develop their proposals and manuscripts. Since both of us come from publishing backgrounds—editorial and sales—we are able to give our authors a perspective of what goes on within the publishing house from initial consideration through the entire development, publication, marketing and sales processes."

How to Contact Query with SASE, submit proposal package, synopsis, 2-3 sample chapter(s), author bio. Accepts e-mail queries. No fax queries. Considers simultaneous queries. Responds in 1-2 weeks to queries; 4-6 weeks to mss. Obtains most new clients through recommendations from others, solicitations, contacting good authors for representation.

Recent Sales Sold 9 titles in the last year. *Here's What We'll Say*, by Reichen Lehmkuhl (Carroll & Graf); *The Loss of Innocence*, by Ron and Carren Clem (Virgin Books); *Entrepreneurship Undercover*, by Wesley Moss (Prentice Hall); *Harvey Walden's No Excuses! Workout*, by Harvey Walden IV (Rodale).

Terms Agent receives 15% commission on domestic sales; 20% commission on foreign sales. Offers written contract; 30-day notice must be given to terminate contract.

Tips "Platform, platform, platform. We can't emphasize this enough. Without a strong national platform, it is nearly impossible to get the interest of a publisher. Also, be organized in your thoughts and your goals before contacting an agent. Think of the proposal as your business plan. What do you hope to achieve by publishing your book. How can your book change the world?"

⬛ SCOVIL CHICHAK GALEN LITERARY AGENCY

276 Fifth Ave., Suite 708, New York NY 10001. (212)679-8686. Fax: (212)679-6710. E-mail: info@scglit.com. Web site: www.scglit.com. **Contact:** Russell Galen. Estab. 1992. Member of AAR. Represents 300 clients. Currently handles: 70% nonfiction books; 30% novels.

Member Agents Jack Scovil, jackscovil@scglit.com; Russell Galen, russellgalen@scglit.com (fiction novels that stretch the bounds of reality; strong, serious nonfiction books on almost any subject that teach something new; no books that are merely entertaining, such as diet or pop psych books; serious interests include science, history, journalism, biography, business, memoir, nature, politics, sports, contemporary culture, literary nonfiction, etc.); Anna Ghosh, annaghosh@scglit.com (strong nonfiction proposals on all subjects as well as adult commercial and literary fiction by both unpublished and published authors; serious interests include investigative journalism, literary nonfiction, history, biography, memoir, popular culture, science, adventure, art, food, religion, psychology, alternative health, social issues, women's fiction, historical novels and literary fiction); Danny Baror, dannybaror@scglit.com (foreign rights).

Represents Nonfiction books, novels.

How to Contact Query with SASE or via e-mail. Considers simultaneous queries.

Recent Sales *Nefertiti: A Novel*, by Michelle Moran (Crown); *The Marketing of the Fittest: DNA and the Record of Evolution*, by Sean B. Carroll; *Why Marines Fight*, by James Brady.

Terms Charges clients for photocopying and postage.

☑ SCRIBBLERS HOUSE, LLC LITERARY AGENCY

P.O. Box 1007, Cooper Station, New York NY 10276-1007. (212)714-7744. E-mail: query@scribblershouse.net. Web site: www.scribblershouse.net. **Contact:** Stedman Mays, Garrett Gambino. Estab. 2003. 25% of clients are new/unpublished writers.

Represents Nonfiction books, novels (occasionally). **Considers these nonfiction areas:** Business/economics; health/medicine; history; how-to; language/literature/criticism; memoirs; popular culture; psychology; self-help/personal improvement; sex; spirituality; diet/nutrition; the brain; personal finance; biography; politics; writing books; relationships; gender issues; parenting. **Considers these fiction areas:** Historical; literary; women's; suspense; crime; thrillers.

How to Contact Query via e-mail. Put "nonfiction query" or "fiction query" in the subject line followed by the title of your project. Considers simultaneous queries.

Recent Sales *Perfect Balance: Dr. Robert Greene's Breakthrough Program for Getting the Hormone Health You Deserve*, by Robert Greene and Leah Feldon (Clarkson Potter/Random House); *Age-Proof Your Mind*, by Zaldy Tan (Warner); *The Okinawa Program* and *The Okinawa Diet Plan*, by Bradley Willcox, Craig Willcox and Makoto Suzuki (Clarkson Potter/Random House); *The Emotionally Abusive Relationship*, by Beverly Engel (Wiley); *Help Your Baby Talk*, by Dr. Robert Owens with Leah Feldon (Perigee).

Terms Agent receives 15% commission on domestic sales. Charges clients for postage, shipping and copying.

Tips "We prefer e-mail queries, but if you must send by snail mail, we will return material or respond to a United States Postal Service-accepted SASE. (No international coupons or outdated mail strips, please.) Presentation means a lot. A well-written query letter with a brief author bio and your credentials is important. Consult our Web site for the most up-to-date information on submitting."

◻ SCRIBE AGENCY, LLC

5508 Joylynne Dr., Madison WI 53716. E-mail: queries@scribeagency.com. Web site: www.scribeagency.com. **Contact:** Kristopher O'Higgins. Estab. 2004. Represents 8 clients. 50% of clients are new/unpublished writers. Currently handles: 100% novels.

● "We have 15 years of experience in publishing and have worked on both agency and editorial sides in the past, with marketing expertise to boot. We love books as much or more than anyone you know. Check our Web site to see what we're about and to make sure you jive with the Scribe vibe."

Member Agents Kristopher O'Higgins; Jesse Vogel.

Represents Nonfiction books, novels, short story collections, novellas, juvenile books, poetry books. **Considers these nonfiction areas:** Cooking/foods/nutrition; ethnic/cultural interests; gay/lesbian issues; humor/satire; memoirs; music/dance; popular culture; true crime/investigative; women's issues/studies. **Considers these fiction areas:** Action/adventure; comic books/cartoon; detective/police/crime; erotica; ethnic; experimental; fantasy; feminist; gay/lesbian; horror; humor/satire; literary; mainstream/contemporary; mystery/suspense; psychic/supernatural; science fiction; thriller; young adult.

⊶ Actively seeking excellent writers with ideas and stories to tell. Does not want cat mysteries or anything not listed above.

How to Contact Query with SASE. Responds in 3-4 weeks to queries; 3-4 months to mss. Returns materials only with SASE.

Recent Sales Sold 2 titles in the last year.

Terms Agent receives 15% commission on domestic sales; 20% commission on foreign sales. Offers written contract. Charges for postage and photocopying.

Writers' Conferences BookExpo America; The Writer's Institute; Spring Writer's Festival; WisCon; Wisconsin Book Festival; World Fantasy Convention.

[N] [●] SECRET AGENT MAN

P.O. Box 1078, Lake Forest CA 92609-1078. (949)463-1638. Fax: (949)831-4648. E-mail: scott@secretagentman. net; seagman@msn.com. Web site: www.secretagentman.net. **Contact:** Scott Mortenson. Estab. 1999.
Represents Novels. **Considers these fiction areas:** Detective/police/crime; mystery/suspense; religious/inspirational; thriller.

O┳ Actively seeking selective mystery, thriller, suspense and detective fiction.

How to Contact Query with SASE. Query via e-mail or snail mail; sample chapter optional. Obtains most new clients through recommendations from others, solicitations.
Recent Sales *Head Shots* (Dalen).

[●] LYNN SELIGMAN, LITERARY AGENT

400 Highland Ave., Upper Montclair NJ 07043. (973)783-3631. **Contact:** Lynn Seligman. Estab. 1985. Member of Women's Media Group. Represents 32 clients. 15% of clients are new/unpublished writers. Currently handles: 60% nonfiction books; 40% novels.

• Prior to opening her agency, Ms. Seligman worked in the subsidiary rights department of Doubleday and Simon & Schuster, and served as an agent with Julian Bach Literary Agency (which became IMG Literary Agency). Foreign rights are represented by Books Crossing Borders, Inc.

Represents Nonfiction books, novels. **Considers these nonfiction areas:** Anthropology/archaeology; art/architecture/design; biography/autobiography; business/economics; child guidance/parenting; cooking/foods/nutrition; current affairs; education; ethnic/cultural interests; government/politics/law; health/medicine; history; how-to; humor/satire; interior design/decorating; language/literature/criticism; money/finance; music/dance; nature/environment; photography; popular culture; psychology; science/technology; self-help/personal improvement; sociology; theater/film; true crime/investigative; women's issues/studies. **Considers these fiction areas:** Detective/police/crime; ethnic; fantasy; feminist; gay/lesbian; historical; horror; humor/satire; literary; mainstream/contemporary; mystery/suspense; romance (contemporary, gothic, historical, regency); science fiction.

O┳ This agency specializes in general nonfiction and fiction. "I also do illustrated and photography books and have represented several photographers for books." This agency does not handle children's or young adult books.

How to Contact Query with SASE, sample chapters, outline/proposal. Prefers to read materials exclusively. No e-mail or fax queries. Considers simultaneous queries. Responds in 2 weeks to queries; 2 months to mss. Returns materials only with SASE. Obtains most new clients through referrals from other writers and editors.
Recent Sales Sold 15 titles in the last year. *Naughty in Deed* by Barbara Pierce; *Morbid Curiousity*, by Deborah Leblanc.

Terms Agent receives 15% commission on domestic sales; 25% commission on foreign sales. Charges clients for photocopying, unusual postage, express mail, telephone expenses (checks with author first).

[●] SERENDIPITY LITERARY AGENCY, LLC

305 Gates Ave., Brooklyn NY 11216. (718)230-7689. Fax: (718)230-7829. E-mail: rbrooks@serendipitylit.com. Web site: www.serendipitylit.com. **Contact:** Regina Brooks. Estab. 2000. Represents 50 clients. 50% of clients are new/unpublished writers. Currently handles: 50% nonfiction books; 50% fiction.

• Prior to becoming an agent, Ms. Brooks was an acquisitions editor for John Wiley & Sons, Inc. and McGraw-Hill Companies.

Represents Nonfiction books, novels, juvenile books, scholarly books, children's books. **Considers these nonfiction areas:** Business/economics; current affairs; education; ethnic/cultural interests; history; juvenile nonfiction; memoirs; money/finance; multicultural; New Age/metaphysics; popular culture; psychology; religious/inspirational; science/technology; self-help/personal improvement; sports; women's issues/studies; health/medical; narrative; popular science; biography; politics; crafts/design; food/cooking; contemporary culture. **Considers these fiction areas:** Action/adventure; confession; ethnic; historical; juvenile; literary; multicultural; picture books; thriller; suspense; mystery; romance.

O┳ African-American nonfiction, commercial fiction, young adult novels with an urban flair and juvenile books. No stage plays, screenplays or poetry.

How to Contact Prefers to read materials exclusively. For nonfiction, submit outline, 1 sample chapter, SASE. Responds in 2 months to queries; 3 months to mss. Obtains most new clients through conferences, referrals.
Recent Sales This agency prefers not to share information on specific sales. Recent sales available upon request.
Terms Agent receives 15% commission on domestic sales; 20% commission on foreign sales. Offers written contract; 2-month notice must be given to terminate contract. Charges clients for office fees, which are taken from any advance.
Tips "We are eagerly looking for young adult books and fiction and nonfiction targeted to 20- and 30-year-old's. We also represent illustrators."

N ⚑ ◐ SEVENTH AVENUE LITERARY AGENCY

1663 West Seventh Ave., Vancouver British Columbia V6J 1S4, Canada. (604)734-3663. Fax: (604)734-8906. E-mail: info@seventhavenuelit.com. Web site: www.seventhavenuelit.com. **Contact:** Robert Mackwood, director. Currently handles: 85% nonfiction books; 15% novels.

Represents Nonfiction books, novels. **Considers these nonfiction areas:** Biography/autobiography; business/economics; computers/electronic; health/medicine; history; science/technology; sports; travel; lifestyle.

> **⎯** "Seventh Avenue Literary Agency is one of Canada's largest and most venerable literary and personal management agencies." (The agency was originally called Contemporary Management.) Actively seeking nonfiction. Does not want to receive poetry, screenplays, children's books, young adult titles, or genre writing such as science fiction, fantasy or erotica.

How to Contact Query with SASE, submit outline, synopsis, 1 (nonfiction) sample chapter(s), publishing history, author bio, table of contents with proposal or query. Send 1-2 chapters and submission history if sending fiction. No e-mail attachments. Provide full contact information. Accepts e-mail queries. No fax queries. Obtains most new clients through recommendations from others, solicitations.

Recent Sales *The Taxman is Watching*, by Paul DioGuardio and Philippe DioGuardio (Harper Canada); *Confessions of an Innocent Man: Torture and Survival in a Saudi Prison*, by William Sampson; *Bud, Inc.*, by Ian Mulgrew; *The Rainbow Bridge*, by Adrian Raeside (Raincoast Books).

Tips "If you want your material returned, please include an SASE with adequate postage; otherwise, material will be recycled. (U.S. stamps are not adequate; they do not work in Canada.)"

◐ THE SEYMOUR AGENCY

475 Miner St., Canton NY 13617. (315)386-1831. E-mail: marysue@slic.com. Web site: www.theseymouragency .com. **Contact:** Mary Sue Seymour. Estab. 1992. Member of AAR, RWA, Authors Guild; signatory of WGA. Represents 50 clients. 5% of clients are new/unpublished writers. Currently handles: 50% nonfiction books; 50% fiction.

> • Ms. Seymour is a retired New York State certified teacher.

Represents Nonfiction books, novels. **Considers these nonfiction areas:** Business/economics; health/medicine; how-to; self-help/personal improvement; Christian books; cookbooks; any well-written nonfiction that includes a proposal in standard format and 1 sample chapter. **Considers these fiction areas:** Religious/inspirational (Christian books); romance (any type).

How to Contact Query with SASE, synopsis, first 50 pages for romance. Accepts e-mail queries. No fax queries. Considers simultaneous queries. Responds in 1 month to queries; 3 months to mss. Returns materials only with SASE.

Recent Sales Two romance books, by Tracy Willouer; two romance books, by Kimberly Kaye Terry; Maryanne Raphael's authorized biograohy of Mother Teresa; *Interference*, by Shelley Wernlein; *The Doctor's Daughter*, by Donna MacQuigg.

Terms Agent receives 12-15% commission on domestic sales.

Writers' Conferences BookExpo America; Start Your Engines; Romantic Times Convention; ICE Escape Writers Conference; Spring Into Romance; Silicon Valley RWA Conference; Put Your Heart in a Book; RWA National.

◐ DENISE SHANNON LITERARY AGENCY, INC.

20 W. 22nd St., Suite 1603, New York NY 10010. (212)414-2911. Fax: (212)414-2930. E-mail: info@deniseshann onagency.com. Web site: www.deniseshannonagency.com. **Contact:** Denise Shannon. Estab. 2002. Member of AAR.

> • Prior to opening her agency, Ms. Shannon worked for 16 years with Georges Borchardt and International Creative Management.

Represents Nonfiction books, novels. **Considers these nonfiction areas:** Biography/autobiography; business/economics; health/medicine; narrative nonfiction; politics; journalism; social history. **Considers these fiction areas:** Literary.

> **⎯** "We are a boutique agency with a distinguished list of fiction and nonfiction authors."

How to Contact Query with SASE. Submit query with description of project, bio, SASE. Accepts e-mail queries (submissions@deniseshannonagency.com).

Recent Sales *The God of Animals*, by Aryn Kyle (Scribner); *Organic, Inc.: The Marketing of Innocence*, by Samuel Fromartz (Harcourt); *Absurdistan*, by Gary Shteyngart (Random House); *The Visible World*, by Mark Slouka (Houghton Mifflin).

Tips Query to the e-mail address submissions@deniseshannonagency.com.

◐ THE ROBERT E. SHEPARD AGENCY

1608 Dwight Way, Berkeley CA 94703-1804. (510)849-3999. E-mail: mail@shepardagency.com. Web site: www. shepardagency.com. **Contact:** Robert Shepard. Estab. 1994. Member of Authors Guild. Represents 60 clients.

15% of clients are new/unpublished writers. Currently handles: 90% nonfiction books; 10% scholarly books.

• Prior to opening his agency, Mr. Shepard was an editor and a sales and marketing manager in book publishing; he now writes, teaches courses for nonfiction authors, and speaks at many writers' conferences.

Represents Nonfiction books, scholarly books (appropriate for trade publishers). **Considers these nonfiction areas:** Business/economics; current affairs; gay/lesbian issues; government/politics/law; history; popular culture; sports; Judaica; narrative nonfiction; health; cultural issues; science for laypeople.

O→ This agency specializes in nonfiction, particularly key issues facing society and culture. Actively seeking works by experts recognized in their fields whether or not they're well-known to the general public, and books that offer fresh perspectives or new information even when the subject is familiar. Does not want to receive autobiographies, art books, or fiction.

How to Contact Query with SASE. E-mail queries encouraged. Fax and phone queries strongly discouraged. Considers simultaneous queries. Responds in 2-3 weeks to queries; 6 weeks to proposals or mss. Returns materials only with SASE. Obtains most new clients through recommendations from others, solicitations.

Recent Sales Sold 10 titles in the last year. *A Few Seconds of Panic*, by Stefan Fatsis (Houghton-Mifflin); *American Band*, by Kristen Laine (Gotham Books); *Find Your Focus Zone*, by Lucy Jo Palladino (Free Press); *Up Your Energy From Lo to Go*, by Laura Stack (Broadway); *Night Draws Near*, by Pulitzer-Prize-winner Anthony Shadid (Henry Holt); *Champagne: How the World's Most Glamorous Wine Overcame War and Hard Times*, by Don and Petie Kladstrup (William Morrow); *Word Freak: Heartbreak, Triumph, Genius, and Obsession in the World of Competitive Scrabble Players*, by Stefan Fatsis (Houghton Mifflin HC/Penguin PB); *The Root of Wild Madder: Chasing the History, Mystery, and Lore of the Persian Carpet*, by Brian Murphy (Simon & Schuster).

Terms Agent receives 15% commission on domestic sales; 20% commission on foreign sales. Offers written contract, binding for term of project or until canceled; 30-day notice must be given to terminate contract. Charges clients for phone/fax, photocopying, postage (if and when the project sells).

Tips "Please do your homework! There's no substitute for learning all you can about similar or directly competing books and presenting a well-reasoned competitive analysis in your proposal. Be sure to describe what's new and fresh about your work, why you are the best person to be writing on your subject, and how the book will serve the needs or interests of your intended readers."

⬛ WENDY SHERMAN ASSOCIATES, INC.

450 Seventh Ave., Suite 2307, New York NY 10123. (212)279-9027. Fax: (212)279-8863. Web site: www.wsherman.com. **Contact:** Wendy Sherman. Estab. 1999. Member of AAR. Represents 50 clients. 30% of clients are new/unpublished writers. Currently handles: 50% nonfiction books; 50% novels.

• Prior to opening the agency, Ms. Sherman worked for The Aaron Priest agency and served as vice president, executive director, associate publisher, subsidary rights director, and sales and marketing director in the publishing industry.

Member Agents Wendy Sherman; Michelle Brower.

Represents Nonfiction books, novels. **Considers these nonfiction areas:** Psychology; narrative; practical. **Considers these fiction areas:** Literary; women's (suspense).

O→ "We specialize in developing new writers, as well as working with more established writers. My experience as a publisher has proven to be a great asset to my clients."

How to Contact Query with SASE or send outline/proposal, 1 sample chapter. No e-mail queries. Considers simultaneous queries. Responds in 1 month to queries. Returns materials only with SASE. Obtains most new clients through recommendations from others.

Recent Sales *America's Boy: A Memoir*, by Wade Rouse; *Marked Man*, by William Lashner; *The Vanishing Point*, by Mary Sharratt; *Spooning: The Cooking Club Divas Turn Up The Heat*, by Darri Stephens and Megan DeSales; *The Kindergarten Wars: The Battle To Get Into America's Best Private Schools*, by Alan Eisenstock; *The Judas Field: A Novel Of The Civil War*, by Howard Bahr. Other clients include Fiction clients include: William Lashner, Nani Power, DW Buffa, Howard Bahr, Suzanne Chazin, Sarah Stonich, Ad Hudler, Mary Sharratt, Libby Street, Heather Estay, Darri Stephens, Megan Desales. Nonfiction clients include: Rabbi Mark Borovitz, Alan Eisenstock, Esther Perel, Clifton Leaf, Maggie Estep, Greg Baer, Martin Friedman, Lundy Bancroft, Alvin Ailey Dance, Lise Friedman, Liz Landers, Vicky Mainzer.

Terms Agent receives 15% commission on domestic sales; 20% commission on foreign sales. Offers written contract.

Tips "The bottom line is: Do your homework. Be as well prepared as possible. Read the books that will help you present yourself and your work with polish. You want your submission to stand out."

⬛ ⬛ JEFFREY SIMMONS LITERARY AGENCY

15 Penn House, Mallory St., London NW8 8SX England. (44)(207)224-8917. E-mail: jasimmons@btconnect.com. **Contact:** Jeffrey Simmons. Estab. 1978. Represents 43 clients. 40% of clients are new/unpublished writers. Currently handles: 65% nonfiction books; 35% novels.

- Prior to becoming an agent, Mr. Simmons was a publisher. He is also an author.

Represents Nonfiction books, novels. **Considers these nonfiction areas:** Biography/autobiography; current affairs; government/politics/law; history; language/literature/criticism; memoirs; music/dance; popular culture; sociology; sports; theater/film; translation; true crime/investigative. **Considers these fiction areas:** Action/adventure; confession; detective/police/crime; family saga; literary; mainstream/contemporary; mystery/suspense; thriller.

O—¬ This agency seeks to handle good books and promising young writers. "My long experience in publishing and as an author and ghostwriter means I can offer an excellent service all around, especially in terms of editorial experience where appropriate." Actively seeking quality fiction, biography, autobiography, showbiz, personality books, law, crime, politics, and world affairs. Does not want to receive science fiction, horror, fantasy, juvenile, academic books, or specialist subjects (e.g., cooking, gardening, religious).

How to Contact Submit sample chapter, outline/proposal, SASE (IRCs if necessary). Prefers to read materials exclusively. Responds in 1 week to queries; 1 month to mss. Obtains most new clients through recommendations from others, solicitations.

Terms Agent receives 10-15% commission on domestic sales; 15% commission on foreign sales. Offers written contract, binding for lifetime of book in question or until it becomes out of print.

Tips "When contacting us with an outline/proposal, include a brief biographical note (listing any previous publications, with publishers and dates). Preferably tell us if the book has already been offered elsewhere."

ⓝ ◨ SLIGO LITERARY AGENCY, LLC

425 Poa Place, San Luis Obispo CA 93405. (805)550-1667. Fax: (805)783-2317. E-mail: ric@mckennapubgrp.com. Web site: sligolitagency.com. **Contact:** Eric Bollinger. Estab. 1997. Represents 30-40 clients. 50% of clients are new/unpublished writers. Currently handles: 50% nonfiction books; 50% novels.

Member Agents Eric Bollinger (fiction and nonfiction); Bill Dawson (fiction); Jydith Markham (fiction); Wanda Shaw (nonfiction).

Represents Nonfiction books, novels. **Considers these nonfiction areas:** Biography/autobiography; business/economics; current affairs; education; gay/lesbian issues; government/politics/law; how-to; humor/satire; memoirs; self-help/personal improvement; sports; true crime/investigative; women's issues/studies. **Considers these fiction areas:** Action/adventure; detective/police/crime; erotica; feminist; gay/lesbian; glitz; literary; mainstream/contemporary; mystery/suspense; romance; thriller; women's.

O—¬ "We specialize in nonfiction, but have strong editing backgrounds for taking on fiction as well. We are all editors and ghostwriters." Actively seeking nonfiction and fiction. Does not want to receive children's, poetry, cookbooks or short stories.

How to Contact Query with SASE, submit proposal package, synopsis, author bio. Accepts e-mail queries. No fax queries. Considers simultaneous queries. Responds in 2 weeks to mss. Obtains most new clients through recommendations from others, solicitations.

Recent Sales Sold 16 titles in the last year. This agency prefers not to share information on specific sales.

Terms Agent receives 15% commission on domestic sales; 20% commission on foreign sales. Offers written contract, binding for 6 months. This agency charges for postage, photocopying, overseas mailings. $175 is deducted from commission from advance of royalties.

Tips "Read our submission guidelines prior to making a submission."

ⓜ ◨ BEVERLEY SLOPEN LITERARY AGENCY

131 Bloor St. W., Suite 711, Toronto ON M5S 1S3 Canada. (416)964-9598. Fax: (416)921-7726. E-mail: beverly@slopenagency.ca. Web site: www.slopenagency.ca. **Contact:** Beverley Slopen. Estab. 1974. Represents 70 clients. 20% of clients are new/unpublished writers. Currently handles: 60% nonfiction books; 40% novels.

- Prior to opening her agency, Ms. Slopen worked in publishing and as a journalist.

Represents Nonfiction books, novels, scholarly books, textbooks (college). **Considers these nonfiction areas:** Anthropology/archaeology; biography/autobiography; business/economics; current affairs; psychology; sociology; true crime/investigative; women's issues/studies. **Considers these fiction areas:** Literary; mystery/suspense.

O—¬ This agency has a strong bent toward Canadian writers. Actively seeking serious nonfiction that is accessible and appealing to the general reader. Does not want to receive fantasy, science fiction, or children's books.

How to Contact Query with SAE and IRCs. Returns materials only with SASE (Canadian postage only). Accepts short e-mail queries. Considers simultaneous queries. Responds in 2 months to queries.

Recent Sales Sold over 40 titles in the last year. *Court Lady* and *Country Wife*, by Lita-Rose Betcherman (HarperCollins Canada/Morrow/Wiley UK); *Vermeer's Hat*, by Timothy Brook (HarperCollins Canada); *Midnight Cab*, by James W. Nichol (Canongate US/Droemer); *Lady Franklin's Revenge*, by Ken McGoogan (HarperCollins Canada/Bantam UK); *Understanding Uncertainty*, by Jeffrey Rosenthal (HarperCollins Canada); *Dam-*

aged *Angels*, by Bonnie Buxton (Carroll & Graf US); *Sea of Dreams*, by Adam Mayers (McClelland & Stewart Canada); *Memory Book*, by Howard Engel (Carroll & Graf); *Written in the Flesh*, by Edward Shorter (University of Toronto Press); *Punch Line*, by Joey Slinger. Other clients include Modris Eksteins, Michael Marrus, Robert Fulford, Morley Torgov, Elliott Leyton, Don Gutteridge, Joanna Goodman, Roberta Rich, Jennifer Welsh, Margaret Wente, Frank Wydra.

Terms Agent receives 15% commission on domestic sales; 10% commission on foreign sales. Offers written contract, binding for 2 years; 3-month notice must be given to terminate contract.

Tips "Please, no unsolicited manuscripts."

N ◎ SLW LITERARY AGENCY

4100 Ridgeland Ave., Northbrook IL 60062. (847)509-0999. Fax: (847)509-0996. E-mail: shariwenk@aol.com. **Contact:** Shari Wenk. Currently handles: 100% nonfiction books.

Represents Nonfiction books. **Considers these nonfiction areas:** Sports.

O→ This agency specializes in representing books written by sports celebrities and sports writers.

Recent Sales *The NBA Crisis*, by Harvey Araton; *I'm Just Gettin' Started*, by Jack McKeon; *Buckeye Madness: Ohio State Football from Woody Hayes to a National Championship* (Simon & Schuster); Untitled, by Joe Menzer (Wiley). Other clients include Filip Bondy, Sam Smith, Skip Bayless, Ric Bucher, Earl Woods, Tiger Woods Foundation, Randy Johnson, Nolan Ryan, Jackie Joyner-Kersee, Joe Theismann, Terry Bradshaw, Joe Garagiola, Tony Gwynn, Mike Singletary, Jay Johnstone, Steve Garvey, Rickey Henderson.

⊞ ◐ ROBERT SMITH LITERARY AGENCY, LTD.

12 Bridge Wharf, 156 Caledonian Rd., London NI 9UU England. (44)(207)278-2444. Fax: (44)(207)833-5680. E-mail: robertsmith.literaryagency@virgin.net. **Contact:** Robert Smith. Estab. 1997. Member of AAA. Represents 25 clients. 10% of clients are new/unpublished writers. Currently handles: 80% nonfiction books; 20% syndicated material.

• Prior to becoming an agent, Mr. Smith was a book publisher.

Represents Nonfiction books, syndicated material. **Considers these nonfiction areas:** Biography/autobiography; cooking/foods/nutrition; health/medicine; memoirs; music/dance; New Age/metaphysics; popular culture; self-help/personal improvement; theater/film; true crime/investigative.

O→ This agency offers clients full management service in all media. Clients are not necessarily book authors. "Our special expertise is in placing newspaper series internationally." Actively seeking autobiographies.

How to Contact Submit outline/proposal, SASE (IRCs if necessary). Prefers to read materials exclusively. Accepts e-mail and fax queries. Responds in 2 weeks to queries. Returns materials only with SASE. Obtains most new clients through recommendations from others, direct approaches to prospective authors.

Recent Sales Sold 25 titles in the last year. *Bill Hicks*, by Kevin Booth and Michael Bertin (HarperCollins); *For Better or Worse: Her Story*, by Christine Hamilton (Robson Books); *Himmler's Secret War*, by Martin Allen (Constable and Robinson). Other clients include Kate Adie (serialisations), Amanda Barrie (serialisations), Judy Cook, Stewart Evans, Neil Hamilton, James Haspiel, Lois Jenkins, Roberta Kray, Ann Ming, Mike Reid, Keith Skinner.

Terms Agent receives 15% commission on domestic sales; 20% commission on foreign sales. Offers written contract, binding for 3 months; 3-month notice must be given to terminate contract. Charges clients for couriers, photocopying, overseas mailings of mss (subject to client authorization).

N ◑ VALERIE SMITH, LITERARY AGENT

1746 Route 44/55, Modena NY 12548. **Contact:** Valerie Smith. Estab. 1978. Represents 17 clients. Currently handles: 2% nonfiction books; 75% novels; 1% story collections; 20% juvenile books; 1% scholarly books; 1% textbooks.

Represents Nonfiction books, novels, juvenile books, textbooks. **Considers these nonfiction areas:** Agriculture/horticulture; cooking/foods/nutrition; how-to; self-help/personal improvement. **Considers these fiction areas:** Fantasy; historical; juvenile; literary; mainstream/contemporary; mystery/suspense; science fiction; young adult; women's/chick lit.

O→ "This is a small, personalized agency with a strong long-term commitment to clients interested in building careers. I have strong ties to science fiction, fantasy and young adult projects. I look for serious, productive writers whose work I can be passionate about." Does not want to receive unsolicited mss.

How to Contact Query with synopsis, bio, 3 sample chapters, SASE. Contact by snail mail only. No e-mail or fax queries. Returns materials only with SASE. Obtains most new clients through recommendations from others.

Recent Sales *Brokedown Palace*, by Steven Brust (Tor); *Inda*, by Sherwood Smith (DAW); *Going North*, by Pamela Dean (Penguin).

Terms Agent receives 15% commission on domestic sales; 20% commission on foreign sales. Offers written contract; 6-week notice must be given to terminate contract.

◪ MICHAEL SNELL LITERARY AGENCY

P.O. Box 1206, Truro MA 02666-1206. (508)349-3718. **Contact:** Michael Snell. Estab. 1978. Represents 200 clients. 25% of clients are new/unpublished writers. Currently handles: 90% nonfiction books; 10% novels.

• Prior to opening his agency, Mr. Snell served as an editor at Wadsworth and Addison-Wesley for 13 years.

Member Agents Michael Snell (business, leadership, pets, sports); Patricia Snell (pets, relationships, health, communication, parenting, self-help, how-to).

Represents Nonfiction books. **Considers these nonfiction areas:** Agriculture/horticulture; animals (pets); anthropology/archaeology; art/architecture/design; business/economics; child guidance/parenting; computers/electronic; cooking/foods/nutrition; crafts/hobbies; current affairs; education; ethnic/cultural interests; gardening; gay/lesbian issues; government/politics/law; health/medicine; history; how-to; humor/satire; interior design/decorating; language/literature/criticism; military/war; money/finance; music/dance; nature/environment; New Age/metaphysics; photography; popular culture; psychology; recreation; religious/inspirational; science/technology; self-help/personal improvement; sex; spirituality; sports (fitness); theater/film; travel; true crime/investigative; women's issues/studies; creative nonfiction.

> ⊶ This agency specializes in how-to, self-help, and all types of business and computer books, from low-level how-to to professional and reference. Especially interested in business, health, law, medicine, psychology, science, and women's issues. Actively seeking strong book proposals in any nonfiction area where a clear need exists for a new book—especially self-help and how-to books on all subjects, from business to personal well-being. Does not want to receive fiction, children's books, or complete mss (considers proposals only).

How to Contact Query with SASE. Prefers to read materials exclusively. Responds in 1 week to queries; 2 weeks to mss. Obtains most new clients through unsolicited mss, word of mouth, *Literary Market Place, Guide to Literary Agents.*

Recent Sales *The Art of Woo*, by Richard Shell (Penguin/Portfolio); *The Happy Breastfed Baby*, by Stacy Rubin (Amalom); *Talent IQ*, by Emmitt Murphy (Adams Media); *Your Inner CEO*, by Allan Cox; *The Mortgage Originator's Handbook*, by Barbara Osurb (Wiley).

Terms Agent receives 15% commission on domestic sales; 15% commission on foreign sales.

Tips "Send a maximum 1-page query with SASE. Brochure on 'How to Write a Book Proposal' is available on request with SASE. We suggest prospective clients read Michael Snell's book, *From Book Idea to Bestseller* (Prima 1997), or purchase a model proposal directly from the company."

◪ SPECTRUM LITERARY AGENCY

320 Central Park W., Suite 1-D, New York NY 10025. Fax: (212)362-4562. Web site: www.spectrumliteraryagency.com. **Contact:** Eleanor Wood, president. Represents 90 clients. Currently handles: 10% nonfiction books; 90% novels.

Member Agents Lucienne Diver.

Represents Nonfiction books, novels. **Considers these fiction areas:** Fantasy; historical; mainstream/contemporary; mystery/suspense; romance; science fiction.

How to Contact Query with SASE, submit author bio, publishing credits. No unsolicited mss will be read. Snail mail queries **only**. No e-mail or fax queries. Responds in 1-3 months to queries. Obtains most new clients through recommendations from authors.

Recent Sales Sold more than 100 titles in the last year. Sales available on this agency's Web site.

Terms Agent receives 15% commission on domestic sales. Deducts for photocopying and book orders.

◪ SPENCERHILL ASSOCIATES

P.O. Box 374, Chatham NY 12037. (518)392-9293. Fax: (518)392-9554. E-mail: ksolem@klsbooks.com; jennifer@klsbooks.com. **Contact:** Karen Solem or Jennifer Schober. Estab. 2001. Member of AAR. Represents 40 clients. 5% of clients are new/unpublished writers. Currently handles: 5% nonfiction books; 90% novels; 5% novellas.

• Prior to becoming an agent, Ms. Solem was editor-in-chief at HarperCollins and an associate publisher.

Member Agents Karen Solem; Jennifer Schober (new agent actively seeking clients).

Represents Nonfiction books, novels. **Considers these nonfiction areas:** Animals; religious/inspirational. **Considers these fiction areas:** Detective/police/crime; historical; mainstream/contemporary; religious/inspirational; romance; thriller.

> ⊶ "We handle mostly commercial women's fiction, historical novels, romance (historical, contemporary, paranormal), thrillers, and mysteries. We also represent Christian fiction and nonfiction." No poetry, science fiction, juvenile, or scripts.

How to Contact Query with SASE, proposal package, outline. Responds in 1 month to queries. Returns materials only with SASE.

Recent Sales Sold 225 titles in the last year.

Terms Agent receives 15% commission on domestic sales; 20% commission on foreign sales. Offers written contract; 3-month notice must be given to terminate contract.

◙ THE SPIELER AGENCY

154 W. 57th St., Suite 135, New York NY 10019. **Contact:** Katya Balter. Estab. 1981. Represents 160 clients. 2% of clients are new/unpublished writers.
  ● Prior to opening his agency, Mr. Spieler was a magazine editor.
Member Agents Joe Spieler; John Thornton (nonfiction); Lisa M. Ross (fiction, nonfiction); Deirdre Mullane (nonfiction); Eric Myers (nonfiction, fiction); Victoria Shoemaker (fiction, nonfiction).
Represents Nonfiction books, novels, children's books. **Considers these nonfiction areas:** Biography/autobiography; business/economics; child guidance/parenting; current affairs; gay/lesbian issues; government/politics/law; history; memoirs; money/finance; music/dance; nature/environment; religious/inspirational; sociology; spirituality; theater/film; travel; women's issues/studies. **Considers these fiction areas:** Detective/police/crime; feminist; gay/lesbian; literary; mystery/suspense.
How to Contact Query with SASE. Prefers to read materials exclusively. Returns materials only with SASE; otherwise materials are discarded when rejected. No fax queries. Considers simultaneous queries. Responds in 2 weeks to queries; 2 months to mss. Obtains most new clients through recommendations, listing in *Guide to Literary Agents*.
Recent Sales *Tilt-A-Whirl*, by Chris Grabenstein (Carroll and Graf); *What's the Matter with Kansas*, by Thomas Frank (Metropolitan/Holt); *Natural History of the Rich*, by Richard Conniff (W.W. Norton); *Juicing the Game*, by Howard Bryant (Viking).
Terms Agent receives 15% commission on domestic sales. Charges clients for messenger bills, photocopying, postage.
Writers' Conferences London Book Fair.

◙ PHILIP G. SPITZER LITERARY AGENCY, INC

50 Talmage Farm Ln., East Hampton NY 11937. (631)329-3650. Fax: (631)329-3651. E-mail: spitzer516@aol.com. **Contact:** Philip Spitzer, Lukas Ortiz. Estab. 1969. Member of AAR. Represents 60 clients. 10% of clients are new/unpublished writers. Currently handles: 50% nonfiction books; 50% novels.
  ● Prior to opening his agency, Mr. Spitzer served at New York University Press, McGraw-Hill, and the John Cushman Associates literary agency.
Represents Nonfiction books, novels. **Considers these nonfiction areas:** Biography/autobiography; business/economics; current affairs; ethnic/cultural interests; government/politics/law; health/medicine; history; language/literature/criticism; military/war; music/dance; nature/environment; popular culture; psychology; sociology; sports; theater/film; true crime/investigative. **Considers these fiction areas:** Detective/police/crime; literary; mainstream/contemporary; mystery/suspense; sports; thriller.
  ○━ This agency specializes in mystery/suspense, literary fiction, sports and general nonfiction (no how-to).
How to Contact Query with SASE, outline, 1 sample chapter. Responds in 1 week to queries; 6 weeks to mss. Obtains most new clients through recommendations from others.
Recent Sales *The Overlook*, by Michael Connelly; *Acts of Nature*, by Jonathon King; *Dead Connections*, by Alafair Burke; *Pegasus Descending*, by James Lee Burke; *Four Kinds of Rain*, by Robert Ward; *Ty & Babe*, by Tom Stanton; *Con Ed*, by Matthew Klein; *Kidnapped*, by Jan Burke.
Terms Agent receives 15% commission on domestic sales; 20% commission on foreign sales. Charges clients for photocopying.
Writers' Conferences BookExpo America.

◙ STEELE-PERKINS LITERARY AGENCY

26 Island Ln., Canandaigua NY 14424. (585)396-9290. Fax: (585)396-3579. E-mail: pattiesp@aol.com. **Contact:** Pattie Steele-Perkins. Member of AAR, RWA. Currently handles: 100% novels.
Represents Novels. **Considers these fiction areas:** Romance and women's, including multicultural and inspirational.
How to Contact Submit outline, 3 sample chapters, SASE. Considers simultaneous queries. Responds in 6 weeks to queries. Returns materials only with SASE. Obtains most new clients through recommendations from others, queries/solicitations.
Recent Sales This agency prefers not to share information on specific sales.
Terms Agent receives 15% commission on domestic sales. Offers written contract, binding for 1 year; 1-month notice must be given to terminate contract.
Writers' Conferences RWA National Conference; BookExpo America; CBA Convention; Romance Slam Jam.
Tips "Be patient. E-mail rather than call. Make sure what you are sending is the best it can be."

◉ STERNIG & BYRNE LITERARY AGENCY

2370 S. 107th St., Apt. #4, Milwaukee WI 53227-2036. (414)328-8034. Fax: (414)328-8034. E-mail: jackbyrne@h otmail.com. Web site: www.sff.net/people/jackbyrne. **Contact:** Jack Byrne. Estab. 1950s. Member of SFWA, MWA. Represents 30 clients. 10% of clients are new/unpublished writers. Currently handles: 5% nonfiction books; 85% novels; 10% juvenile books.

Represents Nonfiction books, novels, juvenile books. **Considers these fiction areas:** Fantasy; horror; mystery/ suspense; science fiction.

> ○➔ "Our client list is comfortably full and our current needs are therefore quite limited." Actively seeking science fiction/fantasy and mystery by established writers. Does not want to receive romance, poetry, textbooks, or highly specialized nonfiction.

How to Contact Query with SASE. Prefers e-mail queries (no attachments); hard copy queries also acceptable. Accepts e-mail queries. No fax queries. Responds in 3 weeks to queries; 3 months to mss. Returns materials only with SASE.

Recent Sales Sold 16 titles in the last year. *Cybermancy*, by Kelly McCullough; *Ha'Penny*, by Jo Walton; *Mirador*, by Sarah Monette. Other clients include Lyn McConche, Betty Ren Wright, Jo Walton, Moira Moore, Sarah Monette, John C. Wright, Bill Gagliani.

Terms Agent receives 15% commission on domestic sales; 20% commission on foreign sales. Offers written contract; 2-month notice must be given to terminate contract.

Tips "Don't send first drafts, have a professional presentation (including cover letter), and know your field. Read what's been done—good and bad."

◉ STIMOLA LITERARY STUDIO, LLC

306 Chase Court, Edgewater NJ 07020. Phone/Fax: (201)945-9353. E-mail: LTRYstudio@aol.com. **Contact:** Rosemary B. Stimola. Member of AAR.

Represents Preschool through young adult fiction and nonfiction.

How to Contact Query with SASE or via e-mail (no unsolicited attachments). Responds in 3 weeks to queries; 2 months to mss. Obtains most new clients through referrals. Unsolicited submissions are still accepted.

Recent Sales The Hunger Games trilogy, by Suzanne Collins (Scholastic); *Rucker Park*, by Paul Volponi (Viking); *The V.O.E. of Merilee Marvelous*, by Suzanne Crowley (Greenwillow/Harper); *Breathe My Name*, by R.A. Nelson (Razorbill/Penguin); *A Little Friendly Advice*, by Siobhan Vivian (Scholastic); *Max and Pinky, Super Heroes*, by Maxwell Eaton III (Random House); *Pilot Pups*, by Michelle Meadows (Simon and Schuster).

Terms Agent receives 15% commission on domestic sales; 20% (if subagents are employed) commission on foreign sales.

Ⓝ ◉ STRACHAN LITERARY AGENCY

P.O. Box 2091, Annapolis MD 21404. E-mail: query@strachanlit.com. Web site: www.strachanlit.com. **Contact:** Laura Strachan.

> • Prior to becoming an agent, Ms. Strachan was (and still is) an attorney.

Represents Nonfiction books, novels. **Considers these nonfiction areas:** Cooking/foods/nutrition; gardening; interior design/decorating; memoirs; photography; psychology; self-help/personal improvement; travel; narrative, parenting, arts. **Considers these fiction areas:** Literary; mystery/suspense; legal and pyschological thrillers, children's.

> ○➔ This agency specializes in literary fiction and narrative nonfiction. Actively seeking new, fresh voices.

How to Contact Query with cover letter outlining your professional experience and a brief synopsis. Send no e-mail attachments. Accepts e-mail queries. No fax queries.

Recent Sales *Serpent Box*, by Vincent Carrella (HarperPerennial); *Swan Town: The Secret Journal of Susanna Shakespeare*, by Michael Ortiz (HarperCollins Children's); *Little Star of Bela Lua*, by Luana Monteiro (Delphinium Books); *The Good Man*, by Ed Jae-Suk Lee (Bridge Works Publishing).

◉ PAM STRICKLER AUTHOR MANAGEMENT

1 Water St., New Paltz NY 12561. (845)255-0061. Web site: www.pamstrickler.com. **Contact:** Pamela Dean Strickler. Member of AAR.

> • Prior to opening her agency, Ms. Strickler was senior editor at Ballantine Books..

> ○➔ Specializes in romance and women's fiction. Does not want to receive nonfiction or children's books.

How to Contact Query via e-mail with 1-page letter including brief plot description and first 10 pages of ms (no attachments). *No unsolicited mss.*

Recent Sales *Lady Dearing's Masquerade*, by Elena Greene (New American Library); *Her Body of Work*, by Marie Donovan (Harlequin/Blaze); *Deceived*, by Nicola Cornick (Harlequin/HQN).

◎ REBECCA STRONG INTERNATIONAL LITERARY AGENCY

235 W. 108th St., #35, New York NY 10025. (212)865-1569. **Contact:** Rebecca Strong. Estab. 2003.

• Prior to opening her agency, Ms. Strong was an industry executive with experience editing and licensing in the US and UK. She has worked at Crown/Random House, Harmony/Random House, Bloomsbury, and Harvill.

Represents Nonfiction books, novels. **Considers these nonfiction areas:** Biography/autobiography; business/economics; health/medicine; history; memoirs; science/technology; travel. **Considers these fiction areas:** General fiction.

O–¬ "We are a consciously small agency dedicated to established and building writers' book publishing careers rather than representing one-time projects." Does not want to receive poetry, screenplays or any unsolicited mss.

How to Contact Query with SASE. No e-mail or fax queries. Considers simultaneous queries. Responds in 2 months to queries. Returns materials only with SASE. Obtains most new clients through recommendations from others, conferences.

Terms Agent receives 15% commission on domestic sales; 20% commission on foreign sales. Offers written contract, binding for 10 years; 30-day notice must be given to terminate contract.

Tips "I represent writers with prior publishing experience only: journalists, magazine writers or writers of fiction who have been published in anthologies or literary magazines. There are exceptions to this guideline, but not many."

◎ THE STROTHMAN AGENCY, LLC

One Faneuil Hall Marketplace, Third Floor, Boston MA 02109. (617)742-2011. Fax: (617)742-2014. Web site: www.strothmanagency.com. **Contact:** Wendy Strothman, Dan O'Connell. Estab. 2003. Represents 50 clients. Currently handles: 70% nonfiction books; 10% novels; 20% scholarly books.

• Prior to becoming an agent, Ms. Strothman was head of Beacon Press (1983-1995) and executive vice president of Houghton Mifflin's Trade & Reference Division (1996-2002).

Member Agents Wendy Strothman; Dan O'Connell.

Represents Nonfiction books, novels, scholarly books. **Considers these nonfiction areas:** Current affairs; government/politics/law; history; language/literature/criticism; nature/environment. **Considers these fiction areas:** Literary.

O–¬ "Because we are highly selective in the clients we represent, we increase the value publishers place on our properties. We seek out public figures, scholars, journalists and other acknowledged and emerging experts in their fields. We specialize in narrative nonfiction, memoir, history, science and nature, arts and culture, literary travel, current affairs and some business. We have a highly selective practice in literary fiction and children's literature." Does not want to receive commercial fiction, romance, science fiction or self-help.

How to Contact Query with SASE. Considers simultaneous queries. Responds in 3 weeks to queries; 1 month to mss. Returns materials only with SASE. Obtains most new clients through recommendations from others.

Recent Sales Sold 25 titles in the last year. *Flights Against the Sunset,* by Kenn Kaufman (Houghton Mifflin); *Guantanamo Bay: A History,* by Jonathan Hansen (Random House); *Backcast: A Memoir of Fly Fishing, Fatherhood, and Divorce,* by Lou Ureneck (St. Martin's); *Model-Wives: Madame Cezanne, Madame Monet, Madame Rodin,* by Ruth Butler (Yale University Press); *Smithsonian Ocean,* by Deborah Cramer (Smithsonian Books); *Free Fall: The Rising Economic Risk Facing America's Working Families,* by Peter Gosselin (Basic Books).

Terms Agent receives 15% commission on domestic sales; 20% commission on foreign sales. Offers written contract; 30-day notice must be given to terminate contract.

N ◎ THE STUART AGENCY

260 W. 52 St., #24C, New York NY 10019. (212)586-2711. Fax: (212)977-1488. Web site: www.stuartagency.com. **Contact:** Andrew Stuart. Estab. 2002.

• Prior to his current position, Mr. Stuart was an agent with Literary Group International for five years. Prior to becoming an agent, he was an editor at Random House and Simon & Schuster.

Represents Nonfiction books, novels. **Considers these nonfiction areas:** Biography/autobiography; ethnic/cultural interests; government/politics/law; history; memoirs; multicultural; psychology; science/technology; sports; narrative nonfiction. **Considers these fiction areas:** General fiction.

How to Contact Query with SASE. Do not send any materials besides query/SASE unless requested. Accepts e-mail queries. No fax queries.

Recent Sales *The New New Rich: The Secret World of the Haves and the Haves Mores,* by David Callahan (Wiley); *The Darwin Awards: Evolution in Action and The Darwin Awards II: Unnatural Selection,* by Wendy Northcutt (Dutton); *You're Only As Good As Your Next One,* by Mike Medavoy (Atria); *The Boys of Winter,* by Wayne Coffey (Crown).

❤ MARK CHRISTIAN SUBIAS AGENCY

331 W. 57th St., #462, New York NY 10019. (212)445-1091. Fax: (212)898-0375. E-mail: marksubias@earthlink. net. **Contact:** Mark Subias. Estab. 2002. Represents 18 clients. Currently handles: 100% stage plays.

Represents Stage plays.

○➡ This agency is not currently representing movie scripts.

How to Contact Query with SASE.

🔲 ⦿ THE SUSIJN AGENCY

64 Great Titchfield St., London W1W 7QH England, United Kingdom. (44)(207)580-6341. Fax: (44)(207)580-8626. Web site: www.thesusijnagency.com. **Contact:** Laura Susijn, Nicola Barr. Currently handles: 25% nonfiction books; 75% novels.

● Prior to becoming an agent, Ms. Susijn was a rights director at Sheil Land Associates and at Fourth Estate; Ms. Barr was a commissioning editor at Flamingo (literary imprint of HarperCollins).

Represents Nonfiction books, novels. **Considers these nonfiction areas:** Biography/autobiography; memoirs; multicultural; popular culture; science/technology; travel. **Considers these fiction areas:** Literary.

○➡ Does not want to receive romance, sagas, fantasy or screenplays.

How to Contact Submit outline, 2 sample chapters, SASE/IRC. Returns materials only with SASE. Obtains most new clients through recommendations from others.

Recent Sales Sold 120 titles in the last year. Clients include Dubravka Ugresic, Peter Ackroyd, Robin Baker, BI Feiyu, Jeffrey Moore, Podium, De Arbeiderspers, Van Oorschot.

Terms Agent receives 15% commission on domestic sales; 15-20% commission on foreign sales. Offers written contract; 6-week notice must be given to terminate contract. Charges clients for photocopying (only if sale is made).

🔲 ⦿ EMMA SWEENEY AGENCY, LLC

245 East 80th St., New York NY 10021. E-mail: queries@emmasweeneyagency.com; info@emmasweeneyagency.com. Web site: www.emmasweeneyagency.com. **Contact:** Eva Talmadge. Estab. 2006. Member of AAR, Women's Media Group. Represents 50 clients. 5% of clients are new/unpublished writers. Currently handles: 30% nonfiction books; 70% novels.

● Prior to becoming an agent, Ms. Sweeney was a subsidiary rights assistant at William Morrow. Since 1990, she has been a literary agent, and was most recently an agent with Harold Ober Associates.

Member Agents Emma Sweeney, president; Eva Talmadge, rights manager; Lauren Carnali, editorial assistant (lauren@emmasweeneyagency.com).

Represents Nonfiction books, novels. **Considers these nonfiction areas:** Agriculture/horticulture; animals; biography/autobiography; cooking/foods/nutrition; memoirs. **Considers these fiction areas:** Literary; mystery/suspense; thriller; women's.

○➡ "Please note that we specialize in quality fiction and nonfiction. Our primary areas of interest include literary and women's fiction, mysteries and thrillers, science, history, biography, memoir, religious studies and the natural sciences." Does not want to receive romance, Western's or screenplays.

How to Contact See Web site for submission and contact information. No snail mail queries. Accepts e-mail queries. No fax queries.

Recent Sales *Water for Elephants*, by Sara Gruen (Algonquin); *The Joy of Living*, by Yongey Mingyur Rinpoche (Harmony Books); *The River Wife*, by Jonis Agee (Random House).

Terms Agent receives 15% commission on domestic sales; 10% commission on foreign sales.

Writers' Conferences Nebraska Writers' Conference; Words and Music Festival in New Orleans.

⦿ THE SWETKY AGENCY

2150 Balboa Way, No. 29, St. George UT 84770. E-mail: fayeswetky@amsaw.org. Web site: www.amsaw.org/swetkyagency/index.html. **Contact:** Faye M. Swetky. Estab. 2000. Member of American Society of Authors and Writers. Represents 40+ clients. 80% of clients are new/unpublished writers. Currently handles: 30% nonfiction books; 30% novels; 20% movie scripts; 20% TV scripts.

● Prior to becoming an agent, Ms. Swetky was an editor and corporate manager. She has also raised and raced thoroughbred horses.

Represents Nonfiction books, novels, short story collections, juvenile books, movie scripts, feature film, TV scripts, TV movie of the week, sitcom, documentary. **Considers these nonfiction areas:** All major nonfiction genres. **Considers these fiction areas:** All major fiction genres. **Considers these script subject areas:** Action/adventure; biography/autobiography; cartoon/animation; comedy; contemporary issues; detective/police/crime; erotica; ethnic; experimental; family saga; fantasy; feminist; gay/lesbian; glitz; historical; horror; juvenile; mainstream; multicultural; multimedia; mystery/suspense; psychic/supernatural; regional; religious/inspirational; romantic comedy; romantic drama; science fiction; sports; teen; thriller; western/frontier.

o→ "We handle only book-length fiction and nonfiction and feature-length movie and television scripts. Please visit our Web site before submitting. All agency-related information is there, including a sample contract, e-mail submission forms, policies, clients, etc." Actively seeking young adult material. Do not send unprofessionally prepared mss and/or scripts.

How to Contact See Web site for submission instructions. Accepts e-mail queries only. Considers simultaneous queries. Response time varies. Obtains most new clients through queries.

Recent Sales *Zen and the Art of Pond Building*, by J.D. Herda (Sterling); *Solid Stiehl*, by D.J. Herda (Archebooks); *24/7*, by Susan Diplacido (Zumaya Publications); *House on the Road to Salisbury*, by Lisa Adams (Archebooks). ***Movie/TV MOW script(s) optioned/sold:*** *Demons 5*, by Jim O'Rear (Katzir Productions); *Detention* and *Instinct Vs. Reason*, by Garrett Hargrove (Filmjack Productions).

Terms Agent receives 15% commission on domestic sales; 20% commission on foreign sales; 20% commission on dramatic rights sales. Offers written contract, binding for 1 year; 30-day notice must be given to terminate contract.

Tips "Be professional. Have a professionally prepared product."

☑ TALCOTT NOTCH LITERARY

276 Forest Road, Milford CT 06460. (203)877-1146. Fax: (203)876-9517. E-mail: gpanettieri@talcottnotch.net; rdowen@talcottnotch.net. Web site: www.talcottnotch.net. **Contact:** Gina Panettieri, president. Estab. 2003. Represents 25 clients. 30% of clients are new/unpublished writers.

• Prior to becoming an agent, Ms. Panettieri was a freelance writer and editor.

Member Agents Gina Panettieri (nonfiction, mystery); Rachel Dowen (children's fiction, mystery).

Represents Nonfiction books, novels, juvenile books, scholarly books, textbooks. **Considers these nonfiction areas:** Agriculture/horticulture; animals; anthropology/archaeology; art/architecture/design; biography/autobiography; business/economics; child guidance/parenting; computers/electronic; cooking/foods/nutrition; current affairs; education; ethnic/cultural interests; gay/lesbian issues; government/politics/law; health/medicine; history; how-to; memoirs; military/war; money/finance; music/dance; nature/environment; popular culture; psychology; science/technology; self-help/personal improvement; sociology; sports; true crime/investigative; women's issues/studies; New Age/metaphysics, interior design/decorating, juvenile nonfiction. **Considers these fiction areas:** Action/adventure; detective/police/crime; juvenile; mystery/suspense; thriller; young adult.

o→ Actively seeking prescriptive nonfiction, children's fiction and mysteries. Does not want to receive poetry or picture books.

How to Contact Query via e-mail (preferred) or with SASE. Considers simultaneous queries. Responds in 1 week to queries; 2 weeks to mss. Returns materials only with SASE.

Recent Sales Sold 24 titles in the last year. *The Connected Child*, by Dr. Karyn Purvis, Dr. David Cross and Wendy Sunshine (Mcgraw-Hill); *Parenting Your Defiant Child*, by Dr. Philip Hall And Dr. Nancy Hall (Amacom); *Fall: The Rape and Murder of Innocence in a Small Town*, by Ron Franscell (New Horizon Press); *The New Supervisor's Handbook*, by Brette Sember and Terry Sember (Career Press); *The Executive's Guide To E-mail Correspondance*, by Dr. Dawn-Michelle Baude (Career Press). Other clients include Dr. Leslie Young, Moira Mccarthy, Corrie Lynne Player, David Evans Katz, Erik Lawrence, Dagmara Scalise, Nancy Whitney Reiter, A.E. Rought/Savannah Jordan.

Terms Agent receives 15% commission on domestic sales; 20% commission on foreign sales. Offers written contract, binding for 1 year.

Tips "Present your book or project effectively in your query. Don't include links to a Web page rather than a traditional query, and take the time to prepare a thorough but brief synopsis of the material. Make the effort to prepare a thoughtful analysis of comparison titles. How is your work different, yet would appeal to those same readers?"

☑ ROSLYN TARG LITERARY AGENCY, INC.

105 W. 13th St., New York NY 10011. (212)206-9390. Fax: (212)989-6233. E-mail: roslyn@roslyntargagency.com. **Contact:** Roslyn Targ. Member of AAR. Represents 100 clients.

• In 1970, Roslyn Targ purchased the Franz J. Horch Agency (founded in 1945) and changed the agency's name.

How to Contact Query with SASE, outline/proposal, curriculum vitae. No mss without query first. Accepts e-mail queries. No fax queries. Obtains most new clients through recommendations from others, solicitations.

Terms Agent receives 15% commission on domestic sales; 20% commission on foreign sales. Charges standard agency fees (bank charges, long distance, postage, photocopying, shipping of books, overseas long distance, shipping, etc.).

◐ PATRICIA TEAL LITERARY AGENCY

2036 Vista Del Rosa, Fullerton CA 92831-1336. Phone/Fax: (714)738-8333. **Contact:** Patricia Teal. Estab. 1978. Member of AAR. Represents 20 clients. Currently handles: 10% nonfiction books; 90% fiction.

Represents Nonfiction books, novels. **Considers these nonfiction areas:** Animals; biography/autobiography; child guidance/parenting; health/medicine; how-to; psychology; self-help/personal improvement; true crime/investigative; women's issues/studies. **Considers these fiction areas:** Glitz; mainstream/contemporary; mystery/suspense; romance (contemporary, historical).

    O→ This agency specializes in women's fiction, commercial how-to, and self-help nonfiction. Does not want to receive poetry, short stories, articles, science fiction, fantasy, or regency romance.

How to Contact Published authors only may query with SASE. No e-mail or fax queries. Considers simultaneous queries. Responds in 10 days to queries; 6 weeks to mss. Returns materials only with SASE. Obtains most new clients through conferences, recommendations from authors and editors.

Recent Sales Sold 30 titles in the last year. *Texas Rose*, by Marie Ferrarella (Silhouette); *Watch Your Language*, by Sterling Johnson (St. Martin's Press); *The Black Sheep's Baby*, by Kathleen Creighton (Silhouette); *Man With a Message*, by Muriel Jensen (Harlequin).

Terms Agent receives 10-15% commission on domestic sales; 20% commission on foreign sales. Offers written contract, binding for 1 year. Charges clients for postage.

Writers' Conferences RWA Conferences; Asilomar; BookExpo America; Bouchercon; Maui Writers Conference.

Tips "Include SASE with all correspondence. I am taking on published authors only."

◐ TESSLER LITERARY AGENCY, LLC

27 W. 20th St., Suite 1003, New York NY 10011. (212)242-0466. Fax: (212)242-2366. Web site: www.tessleragency.com. **Contact:** Michelle Tessler. Member of AAR.

    ● Prior to forming her own agency, Ms. Tessler worked at Carlisle & Co. (now a part of Inkwell Management). She has also worked at the William Morris Agency and the Elaine Markson Literary Agency..

    O→ The Tessler Agency is a full-service boutique agency that represents writers of high-quality nonfiction and literary and commercial fiction.

How to Contact Submit query through Web site only.

N ⊕ ◐ THE TFS LITERARY AGENCY

P.O. Box 46-031, Lower Hutt 5044, New Zealand. E-mail: tfs@elseware.co.nz. Web site: www.elseware.co.nz. **Contact:** Chris Else, Barbara Else. Estab. 1988. Member of NZALA.

    O→ Seeks general fiction, nonfiction, and children's books from New Zealand authors only. No poetry, individual short stories, or articles.

How to Contact Send query and brief author bio via e-mail.

◐ 3 SEAS LITERARY AGENCY

P.O. Box 8571, Madison WI 53708. (608)221-4306. E-mail: queries@threeseaslit.com. Web site: www.threeseaslit.com. **Contact:** Michelle Grajkowski, Cori Deyoe. Estab. 2000. Member of RWA, Chicago Women in Publishing. Represents 40 clients. 10% of clients are new/unpublished writers. Currently handles: 5% nonfiction books; 80% novels; 15% juvenile books.

    ● Prior to becoming an agent, Ms. Grajkowski worked in both sales and purchasing for a medical facility. She has a degree in journalism from the University of Wisconsin-Madison. Prior to joining the agency in 2006, Ms. Deyoe was a multi-published author. She is excited to be part of the agency and is actively building her client list.

Member Agents Michelle Grajkowski; Cori Deyoe.

Represents Nonfiction books, novels, juvenile books, scholarly books.

    O→ 3 Seas focuses on romance (including category, historical, regency, Western, romantic suspense, paranormal), women's fiction, mysteries, nonfiction, young adult and children's stories. No poetry, screenplays or short stories.

How to Contact For fiction and young adult, query with first 3 chapters, synopsis, bio, SASE. For nonfiction, query with complete proposal, first 3 chapters, word count, bio, SASE. For picture books, query with complete ms. Considers simultaneous queries. Responds in 1 month to queries. Responds in 3 months to partials. Returns materials only with SASE. Obtains most new clients through recommendations from others, conferences.

Recent Sales Sold 75 titles in the last year. *Even Vampires Get the Blues* and *Light My Fire*, by Katie MacAlister (NAL); *Vamps in the City*, by Kerrelyn Sparks (Avon); *Date Me Baby, One More Time* and *Must Love Dragons*, by Stephanie Rowe (Warner); *From the Dark*, by Michelle Hauf (Harlequin Nocturne); *The Runaway Daughter*, by Anna DeStefano; *Calamity Jayne Rides Again*, by Kathleen Bacus (Leisure); *Daddy Daycare*, by Laura Marie Altom (Harlequin American); *Dark Protector*, by Alexis Morgan (Pocket); *Seduced By the Night*, by Robin T. Popp (Warner); *What Happens In Paris*, by Nancy Robards Thompson (Harlequin NEXT). Other clients include

Naomi Neale, Brenda Mott, Winnie Griggs, Barbara Jean Hicks, Cathy McDavid, Lisa Mondello, R. Barri Flowers, Dyanne Davis, Catherine Kean, Pat White, Mary Buckham.

Terms Agent receives 15% commission on domestic sales; 20% commission on foreign sales. Offers written contract.

Writers' Conferences RWA National Conference.

ANN TOBIAS: A LITERARY AGENCY FOR CHILDREN'S BOOKS

520 E. 84th St., Apt. 4L, New York NY 10028. **Contact:** Ann Tobias. Estab. 1988. Represents 25 clients. 10% of clients are new/unpublished writers. Currently handles: 100% juvenile books.

- Prior to opening her agency, Ms. Tobias worked as a children's book editor at Harper, William Morrow and Scholastic.

Represents Juvenile books. **Considers these nonfiction areas:** Juvenile nonfiction. **Considers these fiction areas:** Picture books; poetry (for children); young adult; illustrated mss; mid-level novels.

O→ This agency specializes in books for children.

How to Contact For all age groups and genres: Send a one-page letter of inquiry accompanied by a one-page writing sample, double-spaced. No e-mail or fax queries. Considers simultaneous queries, but requires 1-month exclusive on all requested mss. Responds in 2 months to mss. Returns materials only with SASE. Obtains most new clients through recommendations from editors.

Recent Sales This agency prefers not to share information on specific sales.

Terms Agent receives 15% commission on domestic sales; 20% commission on foreign sales. No written contract. This agency charges clients for photocopying, overnight mail, foreign postage, foreign telephone.

Tips ''Read at least 200 children's books in the age group and genre in which you hope to be published. Follow this by reading another 100 children's books in other age groups and genres so you will have a feel for the field as a whole.''

LYNDA TOLLS LITERARY AGENCY

P.O. Box 1884, Bend OR 97709. (541)388-3510. E-mail: blswarts@juno.com. **Contact:** Lynda Tolls Swarts. Estab. 1995. Represents 8 clients. 20% of clients are new/unpublished writers. Currently handles: 90% nonfiction books; 10% novels.

Represents Nonfiction books, novels. **Considers these nonfiction areas:** Education; ethnic/cultural interests; health/medicine; history; self-help/personal improvement; travel; biography; global interests; religious/spiritual. **Considers these fiction areas:** Mystery/suspense (and its subgenres).

How to Contact For nonfiction, query with book concept, market, competing titles, author expertise. For fiction, query with synopsis, first 10 pages.

Writers' Conferences Willamette Writers Conference; Surrey International Writers' Conference; Idaho Writers' Conference.

TRANSATLANTIC LITERARY AGENCY

72 Glengowan Road, Toronto Ontario M4N 1G4, Canada. E-mail: info@tla1.com. Web site: www.tla1.com. **Contact:** Lynn Bennett. Estab. 1993. Represents 250 clients. 10% of clients are new/unpublished writers. Currently handles: 30% nonfiction books; 15% novels; 50% juvenile books; 5% textbooks.

Member Agents Lynn Bennett, Lynn@tla1.com, (juvenile and young adult fiction); Shaun Bradley, Shaun@tla-1.com (literary fiction and narrative nonfiction); Marie Campbell, Marie@tla1.com (literary juvenile and young adult fiction); Andrea Cascardi, Andrea@tla1.com (literary juvenile and young adult fiction); Samantha Haywood, Sam@tla1.com (literary fiction, narrative nonfiction and graphic novels); Karen Klockner, Karen@tla1.com (juvenile nonfiction and illustration); Don Sedgwick, Don@tla1.com (literary fiction and narrative nonfiction); Leona Trainer, Leona@tla1.com (adult mysteries and literary young adult fiction).

Represents Nonfiction books, novels, juvenile books. **Considers these nonfiction areas:** Biography/autobiography; business/economics; current affairs; nature/environment. **Considers these fiction areas:** Juvenile; literary; mainstream/contemporary; mystery/suspense; young adult.

O→ ''In both children's and adult literature, we market directly into the United States, the United Kingdom and Canada.'' Actively seeking literary children's and adult fiction, nonfiction. Does not want to receive poetry, screenplays or stage plays.

How to Contact Query with SASE, submit synopsis, 2 sample chapter(s), author bio. Accepts e-mail queries. No fax queries. Responds in 2 weeks to queries; 4 weeks to mss. Obtains most new clients through recommendations from others.

Recent Sales Sold 330 titles in the last year. *Sports Series*, by John Coy (Henry Holt); *The Perilous Realm*, by Thomas Wharton (Doubleday Canada); *A Brief History of Natural Calamities*, by Marq de Villiers and Sheila Hirtle (Penguin Canada); *Uncle Bobby's Wedding*, by Sarah Brannen (G.P. Putnam & Sons); *Shadowdancers*, by Bernice Morgan (Random House Canada); *The Story of Olive*, by Kim Kane (Doubleday Canada); *Mega Disasters*, by Florin Diacu (Princeton University Press).

Terms Agent receives 15% commission on domestic sales; 20% commission on foreign sales. Offers written contract; 45-day notice must be given to terminate contract. This agency charges for photocopying and postage when it exceeds $100.

S©OTT TREIMEL NY

434 Lafayette St., New York NY 10003. (212)505-8353. Fax: (212)505-0664. E-mail: st.ny@verizon.net. **Contact:** Maryleigh Krasniewicz. Estab. 1995. Member of AAR, Authors Guild, SCBWI. 10% of clients are new/unpublished writers. Currently handles: 100% junvenile/teen books.

- Prior to becoming an agent, Mr. Treimel was an assistant to Marilyn E. Marlow at Curtis Brown, a rights agent for Scholastic, a book packager and rights agent for United Feature Syndicate, a freelance editor, a rights consultant for HarperCollins Children's Books, and the founding director of Warner Bros. Worldwide Publishing.

Represents Nonfiction books, novels, juvenile books (children's, picture books, young adult).

O→ This agency specializes in tightly focused segments of the trade and institutional markets. Career clients.

How to Contact Send query/outline, SASE, sample chapters of no more than 50 pages. No multiple submissions. Queries without SASE will be recycled. No fax queries.

Recent Sales Sold 23 titles in the last year. *What Happened to Cass McBride?*, by Gail Gailes (Little, Brown); *Fragments*, by Jeff Johnston (Simon & Schuster); *The Ugliest Beast*, by Pat Hughes (Farrar, Straus & Giroux); *But That's Another Story*, by Mary Hanson (Random House/Schwartz & Wade); *Megiddo's Shadow*, by Art Slade (Random House/Wendy Lamb Books); *Death & Me*, by Richard Scrimger (Tundra Books).

Terms Agent receives 15% commission on domestic sales; 20% commission on foreign sales. Offers verbal or written contract. Charges clients for photocopying, express postage, messengers, and books ordered to sell foreign, film, and other rights.

Writers' Conferences SCBWI; The New School; Southwest Writers Conference; Pikes Peak Writers Conference.

TRIADA U.S. LITERARY AGENCY, INC.

P.O. Box 561, Sewickley PA 15143. (412)401-3376. E-mail: uwe@triadaus.com. Web site: www.triadaus.com. **Contact:** Dr. Uwe Stender. Estab. 2004. Represents 47 clients. 58% of clients are new/unpublished writers. Currently handles: 45 nonfiction books; 45 novels; 12 juvenile books; 3 scholarly books.

Member Agents Paul Hudson (science fiction, fantasy).

Represents Nonfiction books, novels, short story collections, juvenile books, scholarly books. **Considers these nonfiction areas:** Biography/autobiography; business/economics; child guidance/parenting; education; how-to; humor/satire; memoirs; popular culture; self-help/personal improvement; sports. **Considers these fiction areas:** Action/adventure; detective/police/crime; ethnic; fantasy; historical; horror; juvenile; literary; mainstream/contemporary; mystery/suspense; romance; science fiction; sports; thriller; young adult.

O→ "We are now focusing on self-help and how-to. Additionally, we specialize in literary novels and suspense. Education, business, popular culture, and narrative nonfiction are other strong suits. Our response time is fairly unique. We recognize that neither we nor the authors have time to waste, so we guarantee a 5-day response time. We usually respond within 24 hours." Actively looking for nonfiction, especially self-help, how-to, and prescriptive nonfiction. De-emphasizing fiction, although great writing will always be considered.

How to Contact E-mail queries preferred; otherwise query with SASE. Considers simultaneous queries. Responds in 1-5 weeks to queries; 2-6 weeks to mss. Returns materials only with SASE. Obtains most new clients through recommendations from others, conferences.

Recent Sales *Unlocking the Secret of Lost*, by Poter/Robson/Lavery (Sourcebooks); *Confessions of Emergency Room Doctors*, by Rocky Lang (Andrew McMeel); *365 Ways to Save Gas*, by Ron Weiers (DK Publishing); *Parenting Beyond Belief*, by Dale McGowan (Amacom); *Yellowstone Drift*, by John Holt (Univ. of Nebraska Press); *Out of the Pocket*, by Tony Moss (Univ. of Nebraska Press); *Lost World*, by Lynnette Porter and David Lavery (Sourcebooks); *Cinderella*, by Michael Lito (Sourcebooks); *Joss Whedon: Wonder Boy*, by David Lavery (IB Tauris).

Terms Agent receives 15% commission on domestic sales; 20% commission on foreign sales. Offers written contract; 30-day notice must be given to terminate contract.

Tips "I comment on all requested manuscripts which I reject."

TRIDENT MEDIA GROUP

41 Madison Ave., 36th Floor, New York NY 10010. E-mail: levine.assistant@tridentmediagroup.com. Web site: www.tridentmediagroup.com. **Contact:** Ellen Levine. Member of AAR.

Member Agents Jenny Bent; Scott Miller; Paul Fedorko; Alex Glass; Melissa Flashman; Eileen Cope.

O⊸ Actively seeking new or established authors in a variety of fiction and nonfiction genres.
How to Contact Query with SASE or via e-mail. Check Web site for more details.

🙂 2M COMMUNICATIONS, LTD.

121 W. 27 St., #601, New York NY 10001. (212)741-1509. Fax: (212)691-4460. E-mail: morel@bookhaven.com. Web site: www.2mcommunications.com. **Contact:** Madeleine Morel. Estab. 1982. Member of AAR. Represents 100 clients. 20% of clients are new/unpublished writers. Currently handles: 100% nonfiction books.

• Prior to becoming an agent, Ms. Morel worked at a publishing company.

Represents Nonfiction books. **Considers these nonfiction areas:** Biography/autobiography; child guidance/parenting; ethnic/cultural interests; health/medicine; history; self-help/personal improvement; women's issues/studies; music; cookbooks.

O⊸ This agency specializes in exclusively and non-exclusively representing professional ghostwriters and collaborators. This agency's writers have penned multiple bestsellers. They work closely with other leading literary agents and editors whose high-profile authors require confidential associations.

How to Contact Query with SASE, submit outline, 3 sample chapters. Considers simultaneous queries. Responds in 1 week to queries; 1 month to mss. Obtains most new clients through recommendations from others, solicitations.

Recent Sales Sold 25 titles in the last year. *How Do You Compare?*, by Andy Williams (Penguin Putnam); *Hormone Wisdom*, by Theresa Dale (John Wiley); *Irish Dessert Cookbook*, by Margaret Johnson (Chronicle).

Terms Agent receives 15% commission on domestic sales; 20% commission on foreign sales. Offers written contract, binding for 2 years. Charges clients for postage, photocopying, long-distance calls, faxes.

🅽 🔾 VANGUARD LITERARY AGENCY

81 E. Jefryn Blvd., Suite E, Deer Park NY 11729. (631)964-0030. Fax: (718)504-4541. E-mail: sandylu@vanguardliterary.com. Web site: www.vanguardliterary.com. **Contact:** Sandy Lu. Estab. 2006. Represents 10 clients. 60% of clients are new/unpublished writers. Currently handles: 20% nonfiction books; 80% novels.

• Prior to becoming an agent, Ms. Lu held managerial positions in commercial theater.

Represents Nonfiction books, novels, short story collections, novellas. **Considers these nonfiction areas:** Anthropology/archaeology; biography/autobiography; cooking/foods/nutrition; ethnic/cultural interests; gay/lesbian issues; history; memoirs; music/dance; popular culture; psychology; science/technology; sociology; translation; true crime/investigative; women's issues/studies. **Considers these fiction areas:** Action/adventure; confession; detective/police/crime; ethnic; historical; horror; humor/satire; literary; mainstream/contemporary; mystery/suspense; regional; thriller; women's (no chick lit).

O⊸ "Very few agents in the business still edit their clients' manuscripts, especially when it comes to fiction. Vanguard Literary Agency is different. I care about the quality of my clients' works and will not send anything out to publishers without personally going through each page first to ensure that when the manuscript is sent out, it is in the best possible shape." Actively seeking literary and commercial fiction with a unique voice. Does not want to receive movie or TV scripts, stage plays or poetry; unwanted fiction genres include science fiction/fantasy, Western, YA, children's; unwanted nonfiction genres include self-help, how-to, parenting, sports, dating/relationship, military/war, religion/spirituality, New Age, gift books.

How to Contact Query with SASE, submit outline/proposal, synopsis, author bio, 10-15 sample pp. Accepts e-mail queries. No fax queries. Considers simultaneous queries. Responds in 2 weeks to queries; 6-8 weeks to mss. Returns materials only with SASE. Obtains most new clients through recommendations from others, solicitations, conferences.

Terms Agent receives 15% commission on domestic sales; 20% commission on foreign sales. Offers written contract, binding for 1 year; 30-day notice must be given to terminate contract. This agency charges for photocopying and postage, and discusses larger costs (in excess of $100) with authors prior to charging.

Tips "Do your research. Do not query an agent for a genre he or she does not represent. Personalize your query letter. Start with an interesting hook. Learn how to write a succinct yet interesting synopsis or proposal."

🙂 VENTURE LITERARY

8895 Towne Centre Drive, Suite 105, #141, San Diego CA 92122. (619)807-1887. Fax: (772)365-8321. E-mail: submissions@ventureliterary.com. Web site: www.ventureliterary.com. **Contact:** Frank R. Scatoni. Estab. 1999. Represents 50 clients. 40% of clients are new/unpublished writers. Currently handles: 80% nonfiction books; 20% novels.

• Prior to becoming an agent, Mr. Scatoni worked as an editor at Simon & Schuster.

Member Agents Frank R. Scatoni (general nonfiction, biography, memoir, narrative nonfiction, sports, serious nonfiction, graphic novels, narratives); Greg Dinkin (general nonfiction, how-to, business, gambling); Jennifer de la Fuente (literary, commercial and women's fiction, women's nonfiction, pop culture).

Represents Nonfiction books, novels, graphic novels, narratives. **Considers these nonfiction areas:** Animals; anthropology/archaeology; biography/autobiography; business/economics; current affairs; ethnic/cultural interests; government/politics/law; history; memoirs; military/war; money/finance; multicultural; music/dance; nature/environment; popular culture; psychology; science/technology; sports; true crime/investigative; gambling. **Considers these fiction areas:** Action/adventure; detective/police/crime; literary; mainstream/contemporary; mystery/suspense; sports; thriller; women's.

   O⊶ Specializes in nonfiction, sports, biography, gambling and nonfiction narratives. Actively seeking nonfiction, graphic novels and narratives.

How to Contact Considers e-mail queries only. *No unsolicited mss.* See Web site for complete submission guidelines. Obtains most new clients through recommendations from others.

Recent Sales *The 9/11 Report: A Graphic Adaptation*, by Sid Jacobson and Ernie Colon (FSG); *Untitled on Infertility*, by Cindy Margolis (Perigee/Penguin); *Phil Gordon's Little Blue Book*, by Phil Gordon (Simon & Schuster); *Super Critical*, by Todd Tucker (Free Press); *The Making of Michelle Wie*, by Eric Adelson (ESPN Books); *Online Ace*, by Scott Fischman (ESPN Books).

Terms Agent receives 15% commission on domestic sales; 20% commission on foreign sales. Offers written contract.

⊘ VERITAS LITERARY AGENCY

510 Sand Hill Circle, Menlo Park CA 94025. E-mail: agent@veritasliterary.com. Web site: www.veritasliterary.com. **Contact:** Katherine Boyle. Member of AAR.

Represents Nonfiction books, novels. **Considers these nonfiction areas:** Current affairs; government/politics/law; memoirs; popular culture; women's issues/studies; narrative nonfiction, art and music biography, natural history, health and wellness, psychology, serious religion (no New Age) and popular science. **Considers these fiction areas:** Contemporary and literary fiction only.

   O⊶ Does not want to receive romance, sci-fi, poetry or children's books.

How to Contact Query with SASE. This agency prefers a short query letter with no attachments. Accepts e-mail queries. No fax queries.

⊘ BETH VESEL LITERARY AGENCY

80 Fifth Ave., Suite 1101, New York NY 10011. (212)924-4252. Fax: (212)675-1381. E-mail: mlindley@bvlit.com. **Contact:** Molly Lindley, assistant. Estab. 2003. Represents 65 clients. 10% of clients are new/unpublished writers. Currently handles: 75% nonfiction books; 10% novels; 5% story collections; 10% scholarly books.

   • Prior to becoming an agent, Ms. Vesel was a poet and a journalist.

Represents Nonfiction books, novels. **Considers these nonfiction areas:** Biography/autobiography; business/economics; ethnic/cultural interests; health/medicine; how-to; memoirs; photography; psychology; self-help/personal improvement; true crime/investigative; women's issues/studies; cultural criticism. **Considers these fiction areas:** Detective/police/crime; literary.

   O⊶ "My specialties include serious nonfiction, psychology, cultural criticism, memoir, and women's issues." Actively seeking cultural criticism, literary psychological thrillers, and sophisticated memoirs. No uninspired psychology or run-of-the-mill first novels.

How to Contact Query with SASE. Considers simultaneous queries. Responds in 2 weeks to queries; 1 month to mss. Returns materials only with SASE. Obtains most new clients through referrals, reading good magazines, contacting professionals with ideas.

Recent Sales Sold 10 titles in the last year. *The Female Thing*, by Laura Kipnis (Pantheon); *The Little Book of Plagarism*, by Richard Posner; *Meet*, by Virginia Vitzthum (Little, Brown). Other clients include Martha Beck, Linda Carroll, Tracy Thompson, Vicki Robin, Paul Raeburn, John Head, Joe Graves.

Terms Agent receives 15% commission on domestic sales; 20% commission on foreign sales. Offers written contract.

Writers' Conferences Squaw Valley Writers Workshop, Iowa Summer Writing Festival.

Tips "Try to find out if you fit on a particular agent's list by looking at his/her books and comparing yours. You can almost always find who represents a book by looking at the acknowledgements."

⊘ MARY JACK WALD ASSOCIATES, INC.

111 E. 14th St., New York NY 10003. (212)254-7842. **Contact:** Danis Sher. Estab. 1985. Member of AAR, Authors Guild, SCBWI. Represents 35 clients. 5% of clients are new/unpublished writers.

Member Agents Mary Jack Wald; Danis Sher; Alvin Wald.

Represents Nonfiction books, novels, short story collections, novellas, juvenile books, clients' movie/TV scripts. **Considers these nonfiction areas:** Biography/autobiography; current affairs; ethnic/cultural interests; history; juvenile nonfiction; language/literature/criticism; music/dance; nature/environment; photography; sociology; theater/film; translation; true crime/investigative. **Considers these fiction areas:** Action/adventure;

contemporary issues; detective/police/crime; ethnic; experimental; family saga; feminist; gay/lesbian; glitz; historical; juvenile; literary; mainstream/contemporary; mystery/suspense; picture books; thriller; young adult; satire.

    O— This agency is not accepting mss at this time. This agency specializes in literary works and juvenile works.

Recent Sales *Ghost Walk*, by Richie Tankersley Cusick (Speak/Penguin); *Gates of Hades*, by Gregg Loomis (Leisure Books/Dorchester); *Escape From Castle Cant*, by K.P. Bath (Recorded Books).

Terms Agent receives 15% commission on domestic sales; 15-30% commission on foreign sales. Offers written contract, binding for 1 year.

◢ WALES LITERARY AGENCY, INC.

P.O. Box 9428, Seattle WA 98109-0428. (206)284-7114. E-mail: waleslit@waleslit.com. Web site: www.waleslit. com. **Contact:** Elizabeth Wales, Josie di Bernardo. Estab. 1988. Member of AAR, Book Publishers' Northwest, Pacific Northwest Booksellers Association, PEN. Represents 65 clients. 10% of clients are new/unpublished writers. Currently handles: 60% nonfiction books; 40% novels.

    ● Prior to becoming an agent, Ms. Wales worked at Oxford University Press and Viking Penguin.

Member Agents Elizabeth Wales; Neal Swain.

    O— This agency specializes in narrative nonfiction and quality mainstream and literary fiction. Does not handle screenplays, children's literature, genre fiction, or most category nonfiction.

How to Contact Query with cover letter, writing sample (about 30 pages), SASE. No phone or fax queries. Prefers regular mail queries, but accepts 1-page e-mail queries with no attachments. Considers simultaneous queries. Responds in 3 weeks to queries; 6 weeks to mss. Returns materials only with SASE.

Recent Sales *Fashion Statements*, edited by Michelle Tea (Seal Press/Avalon); *The Mom and Pop Store: Minding the American Dream*, by Robert Specter (Walker Books); *The Million Dollar Chicken: How I Won the Grand Prize at the Pillsbury Bake-Off*, by Ellie Mathews (Berkley/Penguin).

Terms Agent receives 15% commission on domestic sales; 20% commission on foreign sales.

Writers' Conferences Pacific Northwest Writers Conference; Willamette Writers Conference.

Tips ''We are especially interested in work that espouses a progressive cultural or political view, projects a new voice, or simply shares an important, compelling story. We also encourage writers living in the Pacific Northwest, West Coast, Alaska, and Pacific Rim countries, and writers from historically underrepresented groups, such as gay and lesbian writers and writers of color, to submit work (but does not discourage writers outside these areas). Most importantly, whether in fiction or nonfiction, the agency is looking for talented storytellers.''

◢ JOHN A. WARE LITERARY AGENCY

392 Central Park W., New York NY 10025-5801. (212)866-4733. Fax: (212)866-4734. **Contact:** John Ware. Estab. 1978. Represents 60 clients. 40% of clients are new/unpublished writers. Currently handles: 75% nonfiction books; 25% novels.

    ● Prior to opening his agency, Mr. Ware served as a literary agent with James Brown Associates/Curtis Brown, Ltd., and as an editor for Doubleday & Co.

Represents Nonfiction books, novels. **Considers these nonfiction areas:** Anthropology/archaeology; biography/autobiography; current affairs; health/medicine (academic credentials required); history (oral history, Americana, folklore); language/literature/criticism; music/dance; nature/environment; popular culture; psychology (academic credentials required); science/technology; sports; true crime/investigative; women's issues/studies; social commentary; investigative journalism; bird's eye views of phenomena. **Considers these fiction areas:** Detective/police/crime; mystery/suspense; thriller; accessible literary noncategory fiction.

    O— Does not want personal memoirs.

How to Contact Query with SASE. Send a letter only. No e-mail or fax queries. Considers simultaneous queries. Responds in 2 weeks to queries.

Recent Sales Untitled on Afghanistan, by Jon Krakauer (Doubleday); *High School*, by Jennifer Niven (Simon Spotlight Entertainment); *The Man Who Made the Blues: A Biography of W.C. Handy*, by David Robertson (Knopf); *Abundance of Valor*, by Will Irwin (Presidio); *Ledyard*, by Bill Gifford (Harcourt); *The Star Garden*, by Nancy E. Turner (Thomas Dunne/St. Martin's); *Sunday*, by Craig Harline (Doubleday); *The Family Business: The Story of Tabasco*, by Jeff Rothfeder (HarperBusiness); *Hawking the Empire*, by Tim Shorrock (Simon & Schuster); *The Jedburghs*, by Will Irwin (PublicAffairs).

Terms Agent receives 15% commission on domestic sales; 20% commission on foreign sales; 15% commission on dramatic rights sales. Charges clients for messenger service and photocopying.

Tips ''Writers must have appropriate credentials for authorship of proposal (nonfiction) or manuscript (fiction); no publishing track record required. I am open to good writing and interesting ideas by new or veteran writers.''

◓ WATERSIDE PRODUCTIONS, INC.

2376 Oxford Ave., Cardiff-by-the-Sea CA 92007. (760)632-9190. Fax: (760)632-9295. E-mail: admin@waterside.com. Web site: www.waterside.com. Estab. 1982.

Member Agents Bill Gladstone; Margot Maley Hutchison; Carole McClendon; William E. Brown; Lawrence Jackel; Ming Russell; Neil Gudovitz; Kimberly Valentini, Chris Van Buren.

Represents Nonfiction books. **Considers these nonfiction areas:** Art/architecture/design; biography/autobiography; business/economics; child guidance/parenting; computers/electronic; ethnic/cultural interests; health/medicine; how-to; humor/satire; money/finance; nature/environment; popular culture; psychology; sociology; sports; cookbooks.

   O⚊ Specializes in computer books, how-to, business, and health titles.

How to Contact Query via mail or online form. Phone queries are not accepted. Obtains most new clients through referrals from established client and publisher list.

Recent Sales "We have represented bestselling authors ranging from Eckhart Tolle to Kevin Trudeau, Mellisa Rossi, Ken Milbern, Randy Fitzgerald, and David Karlins."

Tips "For new writers, a quality proposal and a strong knowledge of the market you're writing for goes a long way toward helping us turn you into a published author. We like to see a strong author platform."

◓ WATKINS LOOMIS AGENCY, INC.

133 E. 35th St., Suite 1, New York NY 10016. (212)532-0080. Fax: (212)889-0506. **Contact:** Jacqueline S. Hackett. Estab. 1908. Represents 150 clients.

Member Agents Gloria Loomis, president; Jacqueline S. Hackett, agent.

Represents Nonfiction books, novels, short story collections. **Considers these nonfiction areas:** Art/architecture/design; biography/autobiography; current affairs; ethnic/cultural interests; history; nature/environment; popular culture; science/technology; investigative journalism. **Considers these fiction areas:** Literary.

   O⚊ This agency specializes in literary fiction and nonfiction.

How to Contact *No unsolicited mss.*

Recent Sales This agency prefers not to share information on specific sales. Clients include Walter Mosley and Cornel West.

Terms Agent receives 15% commission on domestic sales; 20% commission on foreign sales.

◔ WAXMAN LITERARY AGENCY, INC.

80 Fifth Ave., Suite 1101, New York NY 10011. Web site: www.waxmanagency.com. **Contact:** Scott Waxman. Estab. 1997. Represents 60 clients. 50% of clients are new/unpublished writers. Currently handles: 80% nonfiction books; 20% novels.

   ● Prior to opening his agency, Mr. Waxman was an editor at HarperCollins.

Member Agents Scott Waxman (all categories of nonfiction, commercial fiction); Byrd Leavell; Farley Chase.

Represents Nonfiction books, novels. **Considers these nonfiction areas:** Narrative nonfiction. **Considers these fiction areas:** Literary.

   O⚊ "We're looking for serious journalists and novelists with published works."

How to Contact All unsolicited mss returned unopened. Query through Web site. Considers simultaneous queries. Responds in 2 weeks to queries; 6 weeks to mss. Returns materials only with SASE. Obtains most new clients through recommendations from others, solicitations, conferences.

Recent Sales *Grip It and Sip It*, by John Daly (Harper); *That First Season*, by John Eisenberg (Houghton Mifflin); *The Fighting 69th: The Remarkable Journey of New York's Weekend Warriors From Ground Zero to Baghdad*, by Sean Michael Flynn (Viking Penguin).

Terms Agent receives 15% commission on domestic sales; 25% commission on foreign sales. Offers written contract; 2-month notice must be given to terminate contract.

🅽 ◎ IRENE WEBB LITERARY

9255 Sunset Blvd., Suite 500, Los Angeles CA 90069. E-mail: webblit@verizon.net. Web site: www.irenewebb.com. **Contact:** Irene Webb. Estab. 2003.

Represents Nonfiction books, novels. **Considers these nonfiction areas:** Memoirs; popular culture; sports. **Considers these fiction areas:** Mystery/suspense; thriller; literary and commercial fiction.

   O⚊ "Irene Webb Literary is known as one of the top boutique agencies selling books and scripts to film and TV. We have close relationships with top film producers and talent in Hollywood." Does not want to receive unsolicited manuscripts or screenplays.

How to Contact Query with SASE. Accepts e-mail queries. No fax queries. Obtains most new clients through recommendations from others, solicitations.

Recent Sales Film rights to *Mystery*, by Peter Straub (Seven Over Seven Productions); film rights to *Flirting With Forty*, by Jane Porter (Sony Pictures).

◑ THE WENDY WEIL AGENCY, INC.

232 Madison Ave., Suite 1300, New York NY 10016. (212)685-0030. Fax: (212)685-0765. E-mail: wweil@wendy weil.com. Web site: www.wendyweil.com. Member of AAR. Currently handles: 20% nonfiction books; 80% novels.

Member Agents Wendy Weil (commercial fiction, women's fiction, family saga, historical fiction, short stories); Emily Forland; Emma Patterson.

Represents Nonfiction books, novels.

How to Contact Query with SASE. Snail mail queries are preferred. No fax queries. Obtains most new clients through recommendations from others, solicitations.

Recent Sales *What's the Girl Worth?: A Novel*, by Christina Fitzpatrick (HarperCollins); *Miss American Pie: A Diary*, by Margaret Sartor (Bloomsbury USA); *Devil in the Details: Scenes from an Obsessive Girlhood*, by Jennifer Traig (Little, Brown).

◑ CHERRY WEINER LITERARY AGENCY

28 Kipling Way, Manalapan NJ 07726-3711. (732)446-2096. Fax: (732)792-0506. E-mail: cherry8486@aol.com. **Contact:** Cherry Weiner. Estab. 1977. Represents 40 clients. 10% of clients are new/unpublished writers. Currently handles: 10-20% nonfiction books; 80-90% novels.

Represents Nonfiction books, novels. **Considers these nonfiction areas:** Self-help/personal improvement. **Considers these fiction areas:** Action/adventure; contemporary issues; detective/police/crime; family saga; fantasy; historical; mainstream/contemporary; mystery/suspense; psychic/supernatural; romance; science fiction; thriller; westerns/frontier.

    ⊶ This agency is currently not accepting new clients except by referral or by personal contact at writers' conferences. Specializes in fantasy, science fiction, Western's, mysteries (both contemporary and historical), historical novels, Native-American works, mainstream and all genre romances.

How to Contact Query with SASE. Prefers to read materials exclusively. No fax queries. Responds in 1 week to queries; 2 months to mss. Returns materials only with SASE.

Recent Sales Sold 75 titles in the last year. This agency prefers not to share information on specific sales.

Terms Agent receives 15% commission on domestic sales; 15% commission on foreign sales. Offers written contract. Charges clients for extra copies of mss, first-class postage for author's copies of books, express mail for important documents/mss.

Tips "Meet agents and publishers at conferences. Establish a relationship, then get in touch with them and remind them of the meeting and conference."

◑ THE WEINGEL-FIDEL AGENCY

310 E. 46th St., 21E, New York NY 10017. (212)599-2959. **Contact:** Loretta Weingel-Fidel. Estab. 1989. Currently handles: 75% nonfiction books; 25% novels.

    ● Prior to opening her agency, Ms. Weingel-Fidel was a psychoeducational diagnostician.

Represents Nonfiction books, novels. **Considers these nonfiction areas:** Art/architecture/design; biography/ autobiography; memoirs; music/dance; psychology; science/technology; sociology; women's issues/studies; investigative journalism. **Considers these fiction areas:** Literary; mainstream/contemporary.

    ⊶ This agency specializes in commercial and literary fiction and nonfiction. Actively seeking investigative journalism. Does not want to receive genre fiction, self-help, science fiction, or fantasy.

How to Contact Accepts writers by referral only. *No unsolicited mss.*

Terms Agent receives 15% commission on domestic sales; 20% commission on foreign sales. Offers written contract, binding for 1 year with automatic renewal. Bills sent back to clients are all reasonable expenses, such as UPS, express mail, photocopying, etc.

Tips "A very small, selective list enables me to work very closely with my clients to develop and nurture talent. I only take on projects and writers about which I am extremely enthusiastic."

◑ TED WEINSTEIN LITERARY MANAGEMENT

307 Seventh Ave., Suite 2407, Dept. GLA, New York NY 10001. Web site: www.twliterary.com. **Contact:** Ted Weinstein. Estab. 2001. Member of AAR. Represents 50 clients. 50% of clients are new/unpublished writers. Currently handles: 100% nonfiction books.

Represents Nonfiction books by a wide range of journalists, academics, and other experts. **Considers these nonfiction areas:** Biography/autobiography; business/economics; current affairs; government/politics/law; health/medicine; history; popular culture; science/technology; self-help/personal improvement; travel; lifestyle, narrative journalism, popular science.

How to Contact Please visit Web site for detailed guidelines before submitting. Accepts e-mail queries. No fax queries. Responds in 3 weeks to queries.

Terms Agent receives 15% commission on domestic sales; 20% commission on foreign sales; 20% commission on dramatic rights sales. Offers written contract, binding for 1 year. Charges clients for photocopying and express shipping.

Tips "Send e-queries only. See the Web site for guidelines."

⬛ ◪ ◉ WESTWOOD CREATIVE ARTISTS, LTD.

94 Harbord St., Toronto Ontario M5S 1G6, Canada. (416)964-3302. Fax: (416)975-9209. E-mail: wca_office@wc altd.com. Web site: www.wcaltd.com. Represents 200+ clients.
Member Agents Deborah Wood, book-to-film agent; Aston Westwood, book-to-film agent; Linda McKnight, literary agent; Jackie Kaiser, literary agent; Hilary McMahon, literary agent; Natasha Daneman, subsidiary rights director; Michael Levine, film & TV agent.
Represents Nonfiction books, novels, movie scripts, feature film, TV scripts, TV movie of the week.
How to Contact Query with SASE. Use a referral to break into this agency. Accepts e-mail queries. No fax queries. Considers simultaneous queries.
Recent Sales A biography of Richard Nixon, by Conrad Black (Public Affairs); *The New Cold War: Revolutions, Rigged Elections and Pipeline Politics in the Former Soviet Union*, by Mark MacKinnon (Carroll & Graf).

⬛ ◯ ◪ WHIMSY LITERARY AGENCY, LLC

310 East 12th St., Suite 2C, New York NY 10003. Fax: (212)674-1060. E-mail: whimsynyc@aol.com. **Contact:** Jackie Meyer. Estab. 2006. Member of Small Press Center Advisory Board. Represents 10 clients. 50% of clients are new/unpublished writers. Currently handles: 80% nonfiction books; 10% novels; 5% juvenile books; 5% other.
  ● Prior to becoming an agent, Ms. Meyer was with Warner Books for 19 years; Ms. Vezeris has 30 years experience at various book publishers.
Member Agents Jackie Meyer (nonfiction); Olga Vezeris (rights and all types of editorial).
Represents Nonfiction books, novels. **Considers these nonfiction areas:** Agriculture/horticulture; art/architecture/design; biography/autobiography; business/economics; child guidance/parenting; cooking/foods/nutrition; education; health/medicine; history; how-to; humor/satire; interior design/decorating; memoirs; money/finance; New Age/metaphysics; popular culture; psychology; religious/inspirational; self-help/personal improvement; true crime/investigative; women's issues/studies. **Considers these fiction areas:** Mainstream/contemporary; religious/inspirational; thriller; women's.
  ⚷ "Whimsy looks for projects that are concept and platform driven. We seek books that educate, inspire and entertain." Actively seeking experts in their field with good platforms.
How to Contact Send a query letter via e-mail. Send a synopsis, sample chapters, bio and proposal. No snail mail submissions. Accepts e-mail queries. No fax queries. Responds in 5 days to queries; 30 days to mss. Obtains most new clients through recommendations from others, solicitations.
Recent Sales *The Boy Who Cried Wolf*, by Scott Deming (Wiley); *You Can Never Be Too Rich*, by Alan Haft (Wiley); *God Made Easy*, by Patrice Karst (Cider Mill Press). Other clients include Heather Hummel, Valerie Ramsey, Paul Wisenthal, Gerald Celente, Alison Leopold, Dale Patterson, Barney Leason, Jaclynn Demas.
Terms Agent receives 15% commission on domestic sales; 20% commission on foreign sales. Offers written contract. Charges for posting and photocopying.

◉ WIESER & ELWELL, INC.

80 Fifth Ave., Suite 1101, New York NY 10010. (212)260-0860. Fax: (212)675-1381. **Contact:** Jake Elwell. Estab. 1975. 30% of clients are new/unpublished writers. Currently handles: 50% nonfiction books; 50% novels.
Member Agents Jake Elwell (history, military, mysteries, romance, sports, thrillers, psychology, fiction, pop medical).
Represents Nonfiction books, novels. **Considers these nonfiction areas:** Business/economics; cooking/foods/nutrition; current affairs; health/medicine; history; money/finance; nature/environment; psychology; sports; true crime/investigative. **Considers these fiction areas:** Detective/police/crime; historical; literary; mainstream/contemporary; mystery/suspense; romance; thriller.
  ⚷ This agency specializes in mainstream fiction and nonfiction.
How to Contact For nonfiction, query with proposal, SASE. For fiction, query with synopsis, first 2-10 pages, SASE. Accepts e-mail and fax queries. Responds in 2 weeks to queries. Obtains most new clients through recommendations from others, solicitations.
Recent Sales *Stolen Tomorrows*, by Steven Levenkron (Norton); *The Wire: Truth Be Told*, by Rafael Alvarez (Pocket); *Freemasons*, by H. Paul Jeffers (Citadel).
Terms Agent receives 15% commission on domestic sales; 20% commission on foreign sales. Offers written contract. Charges clients for photocopying and overseas mailing.
Writers' Conferences BookExpo America; Frankfurt Book Fair.

◢ WINSUN LITERARY AGENCY

3706 NE Shady Lane Dr., Gladstone MO 64119. Phone/Fax: (816)459-8016. E-mail: mlittleton@earthlink.net. Estab. 2004. Represents 20 clients. 50% of clients are new/unpublished writers. Currently handles: 75% nonfiction books; 20% novels; 5% juvenile books.

- Prior to becoming an agent, Mr. Littleton was a writer and a speaker.

Represents Nonfiction books, novels, juvenile books. **Considers these nonfiction areas:** Biography/autobiography; child guidance/parenting; current affairs; how-to; humor/satire; memoirs; religious/inspirational; self-help/personal improvement. **Considers these fiction areas:** Action/adventure; detective/police/crime; family saga; humor/satire; juvenile; literary; mainstream/contemporary; mystery/suspense; picture books; psychic/supernatural; religious/inspirational; romance; thriller.

　　○━ "We mainly serve Christian clients in the CBA."

How to Contact Query with SASE. E-queries accepted. Considers simultaneous queries. Responds in 6 weeks to queries; 3 months to mss. Returns materials only with SASE. Obtains most new clients through recommendations from others, conferences.

Recent Sales Sold 8 titles in the last year. Sold several titles in 2006 to Howard Publishing, Adams Media, Jordan House, Bethany House and others.

Terms Agent receives 15% commission on domestic sales; 20% commission on foreign sales. Offers written contract, binding for 1 year; 30-day notice must be given to terminate contract.

◢ WOLGEMUTH & ASSOCIATES, INC

8600 Crestgate Circle, Orlando FL 32819. (407)909-9445. Fax: (407)909-9446. E-mail: ewolgemuth@cfl.rr.com. **Contact:** Erik Wolgemuth. Estab. 1992. Member of AAR. Represents 40 clients. 10% of clients are new/unpublished writers. Currently handles: 90% nonfiction books; 2% novellas; 5% juvenile books; 3% multimedia.

- "We have been in the publishing business since 1976, having been a marketing executive at a number of houses, a publisher, an author, and a founder and owner of a publishing company."

Member Agents Robert D. Wolgemuth; Andrew D. Wolgemuth; Erik S. Wolgemuth.

　　○━ "We are not considering any new material at this time."

Recent Sales Sold 35-40 titles in the last year. Works by prominent Christian pastors and lay leaders.

Terms Agent receives 15% commission on domestic sales. Offers written contract, binding for 2-3 years; 30-day notice must be given to terminate contract.

◢ WORDSERVE LITERARY GROUP

10152 S. Knoll Circle, Highlands Ranch CO 80130. (303)471-6675. Web site: www.wordserveliterary.com. **Contact:** Greg Johnson. Estab. 2003. Represents 30 clients. 25% of clients are new/unpublished writers. Currently handles: 30% nonfiction books; 40% novels; 10% story collections; 5% novellas; 10% juvenile books; 5% multimedia.

- Prior to becoming an agent in 1994, Mr. Johnson was a magazine editor and freelance writer of more than 20 books and 200 articles.

Represents Primarily religious books in these categories: nonfiction, fiction, short story collections, novellas. **Considers these nonfiction areas:** Biography/autobiography; child guidance/parenting; memoirs; religious/inspirational.

　　○━ Materials with a faith-based angle.

How to Contact Query with SASE, proposal package, outline, 2-3 sample chapters. Considers simultaneous queries. Responds in 1 week to queries; 2 months to mss. Returns materials only with SASE. Obtains most new clients through recommendations from others.

Recent Sales Sold 1,300 titles in the last 10 years. Redemption series, by Karen Kingsbury (Tyndale); *Loving God Up Close*, by Calvin Miller (Warner Faith); *Christmas in My Heart*, by Joe Wheeler (Tyndale). Other clients include Steve Arterburn, Wanda Dyson, Catherine Martin, David Murrow, Leslie Haskin, Gilbert Morris, Calvin Miller, Robert Wise, Jim Burns, Wayne Cordeiro, Denise George, Susie Shellenberger, Tim Smith, Joe Wheeler, Athol Dickson, Bob DeMoss, Patty Kirk, John Shore.

Terms Agent receives 15% commission on domestic sales; 10-15% commission on foreign sales. Offers written contract; up to 60-day notice must be given to terminate contract.

Tips "We are looking for good proposals, great writing, and authors willing to market their books, as appropriate. Also, we're only looking for projects with a faith element bent. See the Web site before submitting."

◢ WRITERS HOUSE

21 W. 26th St., New York NY 10010. (212)685-2400. Fax: (212)685-1781. Web site: www.writershouse.com. Estab. 1974. Member of AAR. Represents 440 clients. 50% of clients are new/unpublished writers. Currently handles: 25% nonfiction books; 40% novels; 35% juvenile books.

Member Agents Albert Zuckerman (major novels, thrillers, women's fiction, important nonfiction); Amy Berkower (major juvenile authors, women's fiction, art/decorating, psychology); Merrilee Heifetz (quality children's fiction, science fiction/fantasy, popular culture, literary fiction); Susan Cohen (juvenile/young adult fiction and nonfiction, Judaism, women's issues); Susan Ginsburg (serious and popular fiction, true crime, narrative nonfiction, personality books, cookbooks); Michele Rubin (serious nonfiction); Robin Rue (commercial fiction and nonfiction, young adult fiction); Jodi Reamer (juvenile/young adult fiction and nonfiction, adult commercial fiction, popular culture); Simon Lipskar (literary and commercial fiction, narrative nonfiction); Steven Malk (juvenile/young adult fiction and nonfiction); Dan Lazar (commercial and literary fiction, pop culture, narrative nonfiction, women's interest, memoirs, Judaica and humor); Rebecca Sherman (juvenile, young adult); Ken Wright (juvenile, young adult).

Represents Nonfiction books, novels, juvenile books. **Considers these nonfiction areas:** Animals; art/architecture/design; biography/autobiography; business/economics; child guidance/parenting; cooking/foods/nutrition; health/medicine; history; humor/satire; interior design/decorating; juvenile nonfiction; military/war; money/finance; music/dance; nature/environment; psychology; science/technology; self-help/personal improvement; theater/film; true crime/investigative; women's issues/studies. **Considers these fiction areas:** Action/adventure; contemporary issues; detective/police/crime; erotica; ethnic; family saga; fantasy; feminist; gay/lesbian; gothic; hi-lo; historical; horror; humor/satire; juvenile; literary; mainstream/contemporary; military/war; multicultural; mystery/suspense; New Age; occult; picture books; psychic/supernatural; regional; romance; science fiction; short story collections; spiritual; sports; thriller; translation; westerns/frontier; young adult; women's; cartoon.

O── This agency specializes in all types of popular fiction and nonfiction. Does not want to receive scholarly, professional, poetry, plays, or screenplays.

How to Contact Query with SASE. No e-mail or fax queries. Responds in 1 month to queries. Obtains most new clients through recommendations from authors and editors.

Recent Sales Sold 200-300 titles in the last year. *Moneyball*, by Michael Lewis (Norton); *Cut and Run*, by Ridley Pearson (Hyperion); *Report from Ground Zero*, by Dennis Smith (Viking); *Northern Lights*, by Nora Roberts (Penguin/Putnam); Captain Underpants series, by Dav Pilkey (Scholastic); Junie B. Jones series, by Barbara Park (Random House). Other clients include Francine Pascal, Ken Follett, Stephen Hawking, Linda Howard, F. Paul Wilson, Neil Gaiman, Laurel Hamilton, V.C. Andrews, Lisa Jackson, Michael Gruber, Chris Paolini, Barbara Delinsky, Ann Martin, Bradley Trevor Greive, Erica Jong, Kyle Mills, Andrew Guess, Tim Willocks.

Terms Agent receives 15% commission on domestic sales; 20% commission on foreign sales. Offers written contract, binding for 1 year. Agency charges fees for copying mss/proposals and overseas airmail of books.

Tips "Do not send manuscripts. Write a compelling letter. If you do, we'll ask to see your work."

WRITERS' PRODUCTIONS LITERARY AGENCY
P.O. Box 630, Westport CT 06881-0630. (203)227-8199. E-mail: dlm67@mac.com. **Contact:** David L. Meth. Estab. 1982. Represents 25 clients. Currently handles: 40% nonfiction books; 60% novels.

Represents Nonfiction books, novels, quality literary fiction.

O── "We are not accepting new clients at this time."

How to Contact No e-mail or fax queries. Obtains most new clients through recommendations from others.

Recent Sales This agency prefers not to share information on specific sales.

Terms Agent receives 15% commission on domestic sales; 25% commission on foreign sales. Offers written contract. Charges clients for electronic transmissions, long-distance phone calls, express or overnight mail, courier service, etc.

Tips "Send only your best, most professionally prepared work. Do not send it before it is ready. We must have a SASE for all correspondence and return of manuscripts. Do not waste time sending work to agencies or editors who are not accepting new clients."

WRITERS' REPRESENTATIVES, LLC
116 W. 14th St., 11th Floor, New York NY 10011-7305. (212)620-9009. Fax: (212)620-0023. E-mail: transom@writersreps.com. Web site: www.writersreps.com. Estab. 1985. Represents 130 clients. 10% of clients are new/unpublished writers. Currently handles: 90% nonfiction books; 10% novels.

● Prior to becoming an agent, Ms. Chu was a lawyer; Mr. Hartley worked at Simon & Schuster, Harper & Row, and Cornell University Press.

Member Agents Lynn Chu; Glen Hartley; Farah Peterson.

Represents Nonfiction books, novels. **Considers these fiction areas:** Literary.

O── Serious nonfiction and quality fiction. No motion picture or television screenplays.

How to Contact Query with SASE. Prefers to read materials exclusively. Considers simultaneous queries, but must be informed at time of submission.

Recent Sales Sold 30 titles in the last year. *War Made New*, by Max Boot; *Book by Book*, by Michael Dirda; *Dangerous Nation*, by Robert Kagan; *Power, Faith and Fantasy*,by Michael B. Oren.
Terms Agent receives 15% commission on domestic sales; 20% commission on foreign sales.
Tips "Always include a SASE; it will ensure a response from the agent and the return of your submitted material."

⬤ WYLIE-MERRICK LITERARY AGENCY

1138 S. Webster St., Kokomo IN 46902-6357. (765)459-8258. Web site: www.wylie-merrick.com. **Contact:** Sharene Martin, Robert Brown. Estab. 1999. Member of AAR, SCBWI. Currently handles: 10% nonfiction books; 85% novels; 5% juvenile books.
- Ms. Martin holds a master's degree in language education and is a writing and technology curriculum specialist; Mr. Brown holds a degree in communication and English.
Member Agents Sharene Martin (juvenile, picture books, young adult); Robert Brown (adult fiction and nonfiction, young adult).
 ○➔ "We prefer writers who understand the writing craft and have thoroughly researched and have a firm understanding of the publishing industry. We specialize in highly commercial literature."
How to Contact Correspond via e-mail only. No phone queries, please. No fax queries. Obtains most new clients through recommendations from others, conferences.
Recent Sales *Death for Dessert*, by Dawn Richard (Harlequin Worldwide Mystery); *Mineral Spirits*, by Heather Sharfeddin (Bridge Works); *Whiskey and Tonic*, by Nina Wright (Midnight Ink); *Discreet Young Gentlemen*, by M.J. Pearson (Seventh Window); *Epoch*, by Tim Carter (Flux); *The Love of His Brother*, by Jennifer Allee (Five Star).
Terms Agent receives 15% commission on domestic sales; 20% commission on foreign sales; 20% commission on dramatic rights sales. Offers written contract.
Writers' Conferences Florida Writers Association.
Tips "Please see Web site for contact information. Please refer to our Web site for the most updated information about our agency. We changed the way we take queries in September 2006, and queries that don't follow our guidelines will be discarded. No phone or snail mail queries accepted."

Ⓝ ⬛ YATES & YATES, LLP

1100 Town & Country Road, Suite 1300, Orange CA 92868. (714)480-4000. Web site: yates-yates.com. **Contact:** Curtis Yates. Estab. 1989. Represents 60 clients.
Represents Nonfiction books, novels. **Considers these nonfiction areas:** Business/economics; current affairs; government/politics/law; memoirs; religious/inspirational. **Considers these fiction areas:** Literary; regional; religious/inspirational; thriller; women's.
Recent Sales *No More Mondays*, by Dan Miller (Doubleday Currency).

⬤ ZACHARY SHUSTER HARMSWORTH

1776 Broadway, Suite 1405, New York NY 10019. (212)765-6900. Fax: (212)765-6490. E-mail: kfleury@zshlitera ry.com; reception@zshliterary.com. Web site: www.zshliterary.com. Alternate address: 535 Boylston St., 11th Floor. (617)262-2400. Fax: (617)262-2468. **Contact:** Kathleen Fleury. Estab. 1996. Represents 125 clients. 20% of clients are new/unpublished writers. Currently handles: 45% nonfiction books; 45% novels; 5% story collections; 5% scholarly books.
- "Our principals include two former publishing and entertainment lawyers, a journalist, and an editor/agent."
Member Agents Esmond Harmsworth (commercial mysteries, literary fiction, history, science, adventure, business); Todd Shuster (narrative and prescriptive nonfiction, biography, memoirs); Lane Zachary (biography, memoirs, literary fiction); Jennifer Gates (literary fiction, nonfiction).
Represents Nonfiction books, novels. **Considers these nonfiction areas:** Animals; biography/autobiography; business/economics; current affairs; gay/lesbian issues; government/politics/law; health/medicine; history; how-to; language/literature/criticism; memoirs; money/finance; music/dance; psychology; science/technology; self-help/personal improvement; sports; true crime/investigative; women's issues/studies. **Considers these fiction areas:** Detective/police/crime; ethnic; feminist; gay/lesbian; historical; literary; mainstream/contemporary; mystery/suspense; thriller.
 ○➔ This agency specializes in journalist-driven narrative nonfiction and literary and commercial fiction. No poetry.
How to Contact Query with SASE. *No unsolicited manuscripts.* No e-mail or fax queries. Obtains most new clients through recommendations from others.
Recent Sales *Can You Tell a Sunni from a Shiite?*, by Jeff Stein (Hyperion); *Christmas Hope*, by Donna Van Liere; *Female Chauvinist Pigs*, by Ariel Levy; *War Trash*, by Ha Jin; *Women Who Think Too Much*, by Susan

Nolen-Hoeksema, PhD; *The Red Carpet*, by Lavanya Sankaran; *Grapevine*, by David Balter and John Butman.
Terms Agent receives 15% commission on domestic sales; 20% commission on foreign sales. Offers written contract, binding for 1 work only; 30-day notice must be given to terminate contract. Charges clients for postage, copying, courier, telephone. "We only charge expenses if the manuscript is sold."
Tips "We work closely with all our clients on all editorial and promotional aspects of their works."

N ● KAREN GANTZ ZAHLER LITERARY AGENCY

860 Fifth Ave., Suite 7J, New York NY 10021. (212)734-3619. E-mail: karen@karengantzlit.com. Web site: www.karengantzlit.com. **Contact:** Karen Gantz Zahmen. Currently handles: 95% nonfiction books; 5% novels.
- Prior to her current position, Ms. Zahler wrote two cookbooks, *Taste of New York* (Addison-Wesley) and *Superchefs* (John Wiley & Sons). She also participated in a Presidential Advisory Committee on Intellectual Property, U.S. Department of Commerce.

Represents Nonfiction books, novels (very selective).
- ⊶ "We are hired for two purposes, one as lawyers to negotiate publishing agreements, option agreements and other entertainment deals and two as literary agents to help in all aspects of the publishing field. Ms. Zahler is both a literary agent and a literary property lawyer. Thus, she involves herself in all stages of a book's development, including the collaboration agreement with the writer, advice regarding the book proposal, presentations to the publisher, negotiations including the legal work for the publishing agreement and other rights to be negotiated, and work with the publisher and public relations firm so that the book gets the best possible media coverage." Actively seeking nonfiction.

How to Contact Query with SASE. Include a summary. Check the Web site for complete submission information. Accepts e-mail queries. No fax queries. Responds in 4 weeks to queries. Obtains most new clients through recommendations from others, solicitations.
Recent Sales *Life After Divorce*, by Alec Baldwin (St. Martin's Press); *Take the Lead, Lady! Kathleen Turner's Life Lessons*, by Kathleen Turner in collaboration with Gloria Feldt (Springboard Press); *Tales of a Neo-Con*, by Benjamin Wattenberg(John Wiley and Sons); more sales can be found online.
Tips "Our dream client is someone who is a professional writer and a great listener. What writers can do to increase the likelihood of our retainer is to write an excellent summary and provide a great marketing plan for their proposal in an excellent presentation. Any typos or grammatical mistakes do not resonate well. If we want to read it, we will ask you to send a copy by snail mail with an envelope and return postage enclosed. We don't call people unless we have something to report."

● SUSAN ZECKENDORF ASSOC., INC.

171 W. 57th St., New York NY 10019. (212)245-2928. **Contact:** Susan Zeckendorf. Estab. 1979. Member of AAR. Represents 15 clients. 25% of clients are new/unpublished writers. Currently handles: 50% nonfiction books; 50% novels.
- Prior to opening her agency, Ms. Zeckendorf was a counseling psychologist.

Represents Nonfiction books, novels. **Considers these nonfiction areas:** Biography/autobiography; child guidance/parenting; health/medicine; history; music/dance; psychology; science/technology; sociology; women's issues/studies. **Considers these fiction areas:** Detective/police/crime; ethnic; historical; literary; mainstream/contemporary; mystery/suspense; thriller.
- ⊶ Actively seeking mysteries, literary fiction, mainstream fiction, thrillers, social history, parenting, classical music, and biography. Does not want to receive science fiction, romance, or children's books.

How to Contact Query with SASE. No e-mail or fax queries. Considers simultaneous queries. Responds in 10 days to queries; 3 weeks to mss. Returns materials only with SASE.
Recent Sales *How to Write a Damn Good Mystery*, by James N. Frey (St. Martin's Press); *The Handscrabble Chronicles* (Berkley); *Haunted Heart: A Biography of Susannah McCorkle*, by Linda Dahl (University of Michigan Press); *Garden of Aloes*, by Gayle Jandrey (Permanent Press).
Terms Agent receives 15% commission on domestic sales; 20% commission on foreign sales. Charges for photocopying and messenger services.
Writers' Conferences Frontiers in Writing Conference; Oklahoma Festival of Books.
Tips "We are a small agency giving lots of individual attention. We respond quickly to submissions."

N ● HELEN ZIMMERMANN LITERARY AGENCY

3 Emmy Lane, New Paltz NY 12561. (845)256-0977. Fax: (845)256-0979. E-mail: helen@zimmagency.com. **Contact:** Helen Zimmermann. Estab. 2004. Represents 25 clients. 50% of clients are new/unpublished writers. Currently handles: 80% nonfiction books; 20% novels.
- Prior to opening her agency, Ms. Zimmermann was the director of advertising and promotion at Random House and the events coordinator at an independent bookstore.

Represents Nonfiction books, novels. **Considers these nonfiction areas:** Animals; child guidance/parenting;

cooking/foods/nutrition; how-to; humor/satire; memoirs; nature/environment; popular culture; sports. **Considers these fiction areas:** Family saga; historical; literary; mystery/suspense.

⁕ ''As an agent who has experience at both a publishing house and a bookstore, I have a keen insight for viable projects. This experience also helps me ensure every client gets published well, through the whole process.'' Actively seeking memoirs, nature, pop culture, women's issues and accessible literary fiction. Does not want to receive science fiction, poetry or romance.

How to Contact Query with proposal (about 50 pages), SASE. Considers simultaneous queries. Responds in 2 weeks to queries; 1 month to mss. Returns materials only with SASE. Obtains most new clients through recommendations from others, solicitations.

Recent Sales Sold 7 titles in the last year. *The First Season*, by Charley Rosen (McGraw Hill); *The Cosmic Navigator*(Red Wheel Weiser); *Let the Dog Lead*, by Deborah Potter (Samstone Press); *Chosen By a Horse*, by Susan Richards (Soho Press); *101 Things Not To Do Before You Die*, by Robert Harris (St. Martin's Press); *Truth Catcher*, by Anna Salter (Pegasus Books); *The Mini Ketchup Cookbook*, by Cameron Pearl (Running Press). Other clients include Mary Ann McGuigan, Dave Belden, Sonya Sheptaugh and Claire Miller.

Terms Agent receives 15% commission on domestic sales. Offers written contract; 30-day notice must be given to terminate contract. Charges for photocopying and postage (reimbursed if project is sold).

Writers' Conferences BEA/Writer's Digest Books Writers' Conference

N ☞ BARBARA J. ZITWER AGENCY

525 West End Ave., Suite 11H, New York NY 10024. (212)501-8423. Fax: (212)501-8462. E-mail: zitwer@gmail.com. Web site: www.Barbarajzitweragency.com. **Contact:** Barbara J. Zitwer. Estab. 1994. Represents 40 clients. 85% of clients are new/unpublished writers. Currently handles: 30% nonfiction books; 70%.

• Prior to becoming an agent, Ms. Zitwer was (and still is) a film producer, produced playwright and author of novels.

Represents Nonfiction books, novels.

⁕ ''We specialize in discovering new authors, working with writers from all over the world in translation, selling international rights, selling Hollywood movie rights and also developing books with writers. We have strong editorial experience. We are a 100% international agency that happens to have its homebase in New York City, but we are very, very strong in selling international rights of American authors and representing authors from every part of the globe.'' Actively seeking fiction and nonfiction. Does not want to receive business, cookbooks, science, sports, YA, illustrated, health or religion.

How to Contact E-queries only. Only send query unless more is requested. Responds in 1 week to queries; 3 weeks to mss. Obtains most new clients through recommendations from others.

Recent Sales *The Friday Night Knitting Club*, by Kate Jacobs (Putnam and 17 countries around the world); *Empire of Light*, by Young ha Kim and Philipe Picquier (Harcourt and other countries); *Tales From the Crib*, by Risa Green (Marabout, NAL/Dutton & others countries); *Nightingales*, by Catherine Bourne (Blanvalet); *Inside the Red Mansion*, by Oliver August (Houghton Mifflin and others). Other clients include Sharon Krum, Risa Green, Paul Hond, Catherine Bourne, Kate Jacobs, Jeff Povey, Drew Lerman, David Bowker, Oliver August, Eileen Borris-Dunchstang.

Terms Agent receives 15% commission on domestic sales; 25% commission on foreign sales. Offers written contract; 60-day notice must be given to terminate contract.

Tips ''Find an agent who represents works that you admire.''

Script Agents

This section contains agents who sell feature film scripts, television scripts and theatrical stage plays. Many of the script agents listed here are signatories to the Writers Guild of America (WGA) Artists' Manager Basic Agreement. They have paid a membership fee and agree to abide by the WGA's standard code of behavior.

It's a good idea to register your script before sending it out, and the WGA offers a registration service to members and nonmembers alike. Membership in the WGA is earned through the accumulation of professional credits and carries a number of significant benefits.

A few of the listings in this section are actually management companies. The role of managers is quickly changing in Hollywood. Actors and the occasional writer were once the only ones to use them. Now many managers are actually selling scripts to producers.

Like the literary agents listed in this book, some script agencies ask that clients pay for some or all of the office fees accrued when sending out scripts. Always have a clear understanding of any fee an agent asks you to pay.

SUBHEADS

Each listing is broken down into subheads to make locating specific information easier. In the first section, you'll find contact information for each agency. You'll also learn if the agent is a WGA signatory or a member of any other professional organizations. Other information provided indicates the agency's size, its willingness to work with a new or unpublished writer, and a percentage breakdown of the general types of scripts the agency will consider.

Member Agents: Agencies comprised of more than one agent list member agents and their individual specialties to help you determine the person to whom you should send your query letter.

Represents: In this section, agents specify what type of scripts they represent. Make sure you query only agents who represent the type of material you write.

⊶ Look for the key icon to quickly learn an agent's areas of specialization. In this portion of the listing, agents mention the specific subject areas they're currently seeking, as well as those subject areas they do not consider.

How to Contact: Most agents open to submissions prefer an initial query letter that briefly describes your work. Script agents usually discard material sent without a SASE. In this section, agents also mention if they accept queries by fax or e-mail; if they consider simultaneous submissions; and how they prefer to solicit new clients.

Recent Sales: Reflecting the different ways scriptwriters work, agents list scripts optioned or sold and scripting assignments procured for clients. The film industry is very secretive about sales, but you may be able to get a list of clients or other references upon request—especially if the agency is interested in representing your work.

Terms: Most agents' commissions range from 10-15 percent, and WGA signatories may not earn more than 10 percent from WGA members.

Writers' Conferences: A great way to meet an agent is at a writers' conference. Here agents list the conferences they usually attend. For more information about a specific conference, check the Conferences section starting on page 253.

Tips: In this section, agents offer advice and additional instructions for writers seeking representation.

SPECIAL INDEXES

Script Agents Specialties Index: This index (page 337) organizes agencies according to the subjects they are interested in receiving. This index should help you compose a list of agents specializing in your areas. Cross-referencing categories and concentrating on agents interested in two or more aspects of your manuscript might increase your chances of success.

Script Agents Format Index: This index (page 342) organizes agents according to the script types they consider, such as TV movie of the week (MOW), sitcom or episodic drama.

Agents Index: This index (page 344) provides a list of agents' names in alphabetical order along with the name of the agency for which they work. Find the name of the person you would like to contact, and then check the agency listing.

General Index: This index (page 356) lists all agencies, publicists and conferences appearing in the book.

Quick Reference Icons

At the beginning of some listings, you will find one or more of the following symbols:

N   Agency new to this edition

≈   Canadian agency

⊕   International agency

○   Agency actively seeking clients

◑   Agency seeking both new and established writers

◐   Agency seeking mostly established writers through referrals

◎   Agency specializing in certain types of work

⊘   Agency not currently seeking new clients

Find a pull-out bookmark with a key to symbols on the inside cover of this book.

☑ ABOVE THE LINE AGENCY

468 N. Camden Drive, #200, Beverly Hills CA 90210. (310)859-6115. Fax: (310)859-6119. Web site: www.anet. net/users/rima/web/agency.html. **Contact:** Bruce Bartlett; Rima Bauer Greer, owner. Estab. 1994. Signatory of WGA. Represents 35 clients. 10% of clients are new/unpublished writers. Currently handles: 100% movie scripts.

> • Prior to opening her agency, Ms. Greer served as president of Writers & Artists Agency.

Represents Feature film. **Considers these script subject areas:** Cartoon/animation.

How to Contact This agency accepts clients by referral only and does not guarantee a response.

Recent Sales *The Great Cookie Wars*, by Greg Taylor and Jim Strain (Fox); *Velveteen Rabbit*, by Greg Taylor (Disney); *Wing and a Prayer*, by David Engelbach and John Wolff (Franchise).

Terms Agent receives 10% commission on domestic sales; 10% commission on foreign sales.

☑ ABRAMS ARTISTS AGENCY

275 Seventh Ave., 26th Floor, New York NY 10001.

Member Agents Beth Blickers; Sarah Douglas; Morgan Jenness; Charles Kopelman; Kate Navin; Maura Teitelbaum.

Represents Stage plays, screenplays, books. **Considers these script subject areas:** Action/adventure; biography/autobiography; comedy; contemporary issues; detective/police/crime; ethnic; experimental; family saga; fantasy; feminist; gay/lesbian; glitz; historical; horror; juvenile; mainstream; multicultural; multimedia; mystery/suspense; psychic/supernatural; regional; religious/inspirational; romantic comedy; romantic drama; science fiction; sports; teen; thriller; western/frontier.

> ○━ This agency specializes in musicals and stage plays.

How to Contact Query with SASE. Prefers to read materials exclusively. Referrals needed for new materials. *No unsolicited mss.* No e-mail or fax queries.

☑ ACME TALENT & LITERARY

4727 Wilshire Blvd., Suite #333, Los Angeles CA 90010. (323)602-0330. Fax: (323)954-2262. E-mail: mickeyasst @acmeagents.com. Web site: www.acmetalentandliterary.com. **Contact:** Mickey Frieberg, head of literary division. Estab. 1993. Signatory of WGA. Represents 50 clients.

Member Agents Mickey Freiberg (books, film scripts).

Represents Movie scripts, TV scripts, video game rights. **Considers these script subject areas:** Action/adventure; biography/autobiography; cartoon/animation; comedy; contemporary issues; detective/police/crime; erotica; ethnic; experimental; family saga; fantasy; feminist; gay/lesbian; glitz; historical; horror; juvenile; mainstream; multicultural; multimedia; mystery/suspense; psychic/supernatural; regional; religious/inspirational; romantic comedy; romantic drama; science fiction; sports; teen; thriller; western/frontier.

> ○━ This agency specializes in feature films and completed specs or pitches by established/produced writers and new writers. Actively seeking great feature scripts. Does not want to receive unsolicited screenplays.

How to Contact Only query through the mail with an SASE. No e-mail or fax queries. Obtains most new clients through recommendations from established industry contacts, production companies of note and reputable entertainment attorneys.

Recent Sales Film rights to *Flags of Our Fathers*, by Ron Powers.

Terms Agent receives 10% commission on domestic sales; 15% commission on foreign sales. Offers written contract, binding for 2 years.

☒ ☑ AEI: ATCHITY EDITORIAL/ENTERTAINMENT INTERNATIONAL, INC. MOTION PICTURE PRODUCTION & LITERARY MANAGEMENT

9601 Wilshire Blvd., Box #1202, Beverly Hills CA 90210. (323)932-0407. Fax: (323)932-0321. E-mail: submission s@aeionline.com. Web site: www.aeionline.com. **Contact:** Jennifer Pope. Estab. 1995. Member of Producers Guild of America. Represents 65 clients. 50% of clients are new/unpublished writers. Currently handles: 25% nonfiction books; 25% novels; 5% juvenile books; 40% movie scripts; 5% TV scripts.

Member Agents Ken Atchity (books and film); Chi-Li Wong (TV and film); Brenna Lui (books); Mike Kuciak (films and TV); Greg F. Dix (uplifting stories, inspirational, faith-based work).

Represents Nonfiction books, novels, juvenile books, animation, miniseries, Web sites, games for dramatic exploitation. **Considers these nonfiction areas:** Animals; biography/autobiography; business/economics; computers/electronic; current affairs; ethnic/cultural interests; government/politics/law; health/medicine; history; how-to; humor/satire; memoirs; military/war; money/finance; nature/environment; popular culture; psychology; religious/inspirational; science/technology; self-help/personal improvement; translation; true crime/investigative; women's issues/studies. **Considers these fiction areas:** Action/adventure; confession; detective/police/crime; ethnic; family saga; fantasy; historical; horror; humor/satire; juvenile; literary; mainstream/contemporary; mystery/suspense; religious/inspirational; science fiction; thriller; westerns/frontier; young adult; African-American, ethnic, psychic/supernatural. **Considers these script subject areas:** Action/adventure; biography/autobiography; cartoon/animation; comedy; contemporary issues; detective/police/crime; fantasy; horror; juvenile; mainstream; mystery/suspense; psychic/supernatural; religious/inspirational; romantic comedy; teen; thriller.

☌ "We've developed the niche of focusing on storytellers instead of 'projects' or 'writers,' and helping them tell their stories (whether fiction or nonfiction) for all possible markets (book, film, Web, etc.). Actively seeking young adult novels, nonfiction, mom lit, minority lit, action screenplays, broad comedy screenplays. Does not want to receive poetry, children's books or photo books.

How to Contact Query with SASE, submit proposal package, synopsis. Accepts e-mail queries. No fax queries. Considers simultaneous queries. Responds in 2-4 weeks to queries; 4-6 weeks to mss. Returns materials only with SASE. Obtains most new clients through recommendations from others, solicitations, conferences, referrals from our books, Web site.

Recent Sales Sold 10 titles and sold 5 scripts in the last year. *Demon Keeper*, by Royce Buckingham (Putnam/ Fox 2000); *Dark Gold*, by David Angsten (Thomas Dunne); *Arm Bone Flute*, by Alaya Johnson (Agate).

Terms Agent receives 15% commission on domestic sales; 30% commission on foreign sales. Offers written contract, binding for 1 year; 30-day notice must be given to terminate contract. Agency charges for misc. expenses, but costs not to exceed $500 from any publication advance, with the balance recoupable from other gross proceeds.

Writers' Conferences Santa Barbara Writers' Conference; Midwest Literary Festival; Pacific Northwest Writers' Conference.

Tips "Respect what we do as story merchants, and treat us, from the beginning, as business partners who can help you build the creative life of your dreams. Find out who we are and know what we like and believe in even before you approach us. It's all on our Web site. Most of all, think outside the box and take an entrepreneurial approach to both your career and your relationship with us."

◎ THE ALPERN GROUP

15645 Royal Oak Road, Encino CA 91436. (818)528-1111. E-mail: mail@alperngroup.com. **Contact:** Jeff Alpern. Estab. 1994. Represents 50 clients. 10% of clients are new/unpublished writers. Currently handles: 30% movie scripts; 60% TV scripts; 10% stage plays.

• Prior to opening his agency, Mr. Alpern was an agent with William Morris.

Member Agents Jeff Alpern, president; Elana Trainoff; Jeff Aghassi.

Represents Movie scripts, feature film, TV scripts, TV movie of the week, episodic drama, miniseries. **Considers these script subject areas:** Action/adventure; biography/autobiography; comedy; contemporary issues; detective/police/crime; ethnic; fantasy; feminist; gay/lesbian; horror; juvenile; mainstream; multicultural; mystery/ suspense; regional; romantic comedy; science fiction; teen; thriller; family; supernatural.

How to Contact Query with SASE or via e-mail. Only responds to e-mail queries if interested. Responds to all mail queries that include a SASE. Responds in 1 month to queries.

Terms Agent receives 10% commission on domestic sales. Offers written contract.

◖ AMATO THEATRICAL ENTERPRISE

1650 Broadway, Suite 307, New York NY 10019. (212)247-4456 or (212)247-4457. **Contact:** Michael Amato. Estab. 1970. Member of SAG, AFTRA. Represents 6 clients.

Represents Feature film, TV movie of the week, episodic drama, animation, documentary, miniseries. **Considers these script subject areas:** Action/adventure.

How to Contact Query with SASE. Responds in 1 month to queries. Obtains most new clients through recommendations from others.

Recent Sales This agency prefers not to share information on specific sales.

◖ THE ARTISTS AGENCY

1180 S. Beverly, Suite 400, Los Angeles CA 90035. (310)277-7779. Fax: (310)785-9338. **Contact:** Richard Shepherd. Estab. 1974. Signatory of WGA. Represents 50 clients. 20% of clients are new/unpublished writers. Currently handles: 70% movie scripts; 30% TV scripts.

Represents Movie scripts (feature film), TV movie of the week. **Considers these script subject areas:** Action/ adventure; comedy; contemporary issues; detective/police/crime; mystery/suspense; romantic comedy; romantic drama; thriller.

How to Contact Query with SASE. Responds in 2 weeks to queries. Obtains most new clients through recommendations from others.

Recent Sales This agency prefers not to share information on specific sales.

Terms Agent receives 10% commission on dramatic rights sales. Offers written contract, binding for 1-2 years.

� ✄ ◎ AURORA ARTISTS

19 Wroxeter Ave., Toronto ON M4K 1J5, Canada. (416)463-4634. Fax: (416)463-4889. E-mail: aurora.artists@sympatico.ca. **Contact:** Janine S. Cheeseman. Estab. 1990.
Member Agents Janine S. Cheeseman, principal agent; Tracy Essex-Simpson, associate agent.
Represents Movie scripts, TV scripts, stage plays.
How to Contact Query with SASE, submit synopsis, publishing history, author bio, up to 3 pages of a screenplay, SASE. Accepts e-mail queries. No fax queries.

◎ BASKOW AGENCY

2948 E. Russell Road, Las Vegas NV 89120. (702)733-7818. Fax: (702)733-2052. E-mail: jaki@baskow.com. Web site: www.baskow.com. **Contact:** Jaki Baskow. Estab. 1976. Represents 8 clients. 40% of clients are new/unpublished writers. Currently handles: 5% nonfiction books; 5% novels; 20% movie scripts; 70% TV scripts.
Member Agents Jaki Baskow (true life stories and comedies).
Represents Feature film, TV movie of the week, episodic drama, sitcom, documentary, miniseries, variety show. **Considers these script subject areas:** Action/adventure; biography/autobiography; comedy; contemporary issues; family saga; glitz; mystery/suspense; religious/inspirational; romantic comedy; romantic drama; science fiction (juvenile only); thriller.
> ☞ Actively seeking unique scripts, all-American true stories, kids' projects, and movies of the week. Looking for light, comedic and family-oriented work. Does not want to receive scripts with heavy violence or scripts that require animation.

How to Contact Query with SASE, submit outline, proposal, treatments. Accepts e-mail and fax queries. Responds in 1 month to queries; 60 days to mss. Obtains most new clients through recommendations from others.
Recent Sales Sold 3 movie/TV MOW scripts in the last year. *Dying to be Young*, by Eric Katlan (Nightengale Books); *Malpractice*, by Larry Leirketen (Blakely); *Angel of Death* (CBS). Other clients include Cheryl Anderson, Camisole Prods, Michael Store.
Terms Agent receives 10% commission on domestic sales; 10% commission on foreign sales. Offers written contract.

◎ THE BOHRMAN AGENCY

8899 Beverly Blvd., Suite 811, Los Angeles CA 90048. **Contact:** Michael Hruska, Caren Bohrman. Signatory of WGA.
Represents Novels, feature film, TV scripts. **Considers these script subject areas:** Action/adventure; biography/autobiography; cartoon/animation; comedy; contemporary issues; detective/police/crime; erotica; ethnic; experimental; family saga; fantasy; feminist; gay/lesbian; glitz; historical; horror; juvenile; mainstream; multicultural; multimedia; mystery/suspense; psychic/supernatural; regional; religious/inspirational; romantic comedy; romantic drama; science fiction; sports; teen; thriller; western/frontier.
How to Contact *Absolutely no unsolicited mss.* Query only by U.S. Mail with an accompanying self-addressed, stamped postcard. No phone calls. Obtains most new clients through recommendations from others.
Recent Sales This agency prefers not to share information on specific sales.

◎ ◎ ALAN BRODIE REPRESENTATION LTD.

Fairgate House, 78 New Oxford St., Sixth Floor, London England WC1A 1HB, United Kingdom. Web site: www.alanbrodie.com. Member of PMA. 10% of clients are new/unpublished writers.
Member Agents Alan Brodie; Sarah McNair; Lisa Foster.
Represents Theater, television, film, new media, radio.
> ☞ Does not want to receive fiction, nonfiction or poetry.

How to Contact Does not accept unsolicited mss. North American writers accepted only in exceptional circumstances. Accepts e-mail and fax queries. Responds in 3 months to queries. Returns materials only with SASE. Obtains most new clients through recommendations from others.
Recent Sales See this agency's Web site for clients and sales.
Terms Charges clients for photocopying.
Tips "Biographical details can be helpful. Generally only playwrights whose work has been performed will be considered, provided they come recommended by an industry professional. Please be aware that all submissions are treated as strictly confidential. Be advised: From time to time, two writers will come up with very similar ideas; this is the nature of the business and is purely coincidence. In submitting your material to us you are relying on our professional integrity."

◎ DON BUCHWALD & ASSOCIATES, INC.

6500 Wilshire Blvd., 22nd Floor, Los Angeles CA 90048. (323)655-7400. Fax: (323)655-7470. Web site: www.donbuchwald.com. Estab. 1977. Signatory of WGA. Represents 50 clients.

Represents Movie scripts, feature film, TV scripts, TV movie of the week, episodic drama, sitcom, documentary, miniseries.
How to Contact Query with SASE. See the Web site and secure a good referral before contacting this agency. Considers simultaneous queries. Obtains most new clients through recommendations from others.

KELVIN C. BULGER AND ASSOCIATES

4540 W. Washington Blvd., Suite 101, Chicago IL 60624. (312)218-1943. E-mail: kcbwoi@aol.com. **Contact:** Kelvin Bulger. Estab. 1992. Signatory of WGA. Represents 25 clients. 90% of clients are new/unpublished writers. Currently handles: 75% movie scripts; 25% TV scripts.
Represents Feature film, TV movie of the week, documentary, syndicated material. **Considers these script subject areas:** Action/adventure; cartoon/animation; comedy; contemporary issues; ethnic; family saga; religious/inspirational.
How to Contact Query with SASE, 1-page logline, 1-page plot synopsis (beginning/middle/end), first 10 pages of screenplay. Accepts e-mail and fax queries. Considers simultaneous queries. Responds in 3 weeks to queries; 2 months to mss. Returns materials only with SASE. Obtains most new clients through recommendations from others, solicitations.
Recent Sales *Severed Ties*, by David Johnson (Maverick Entertainment).
Terms Agent receives 10% commission on domestic sales; 10% commission on foreign sales. Offers written contract, binding for 6-12 months.
Tips "Proofread before submitting to an agent. We only reply to letters of inquiry if an SASE is enclosed."

CEDAR GROVE AGENCY ENTERTAINMENT

P.O. Box 1692, Issaquah WA 98027-0068. (425)837-1687. Fax: (425)391-7907. E-mail: cedargroveagency@msn. com. **Contact:** Samantha Powers. Estab. 1995. Member of Cinema Seattle. Represents 7 clients. 100% of clients are new/unpublished writers. Currently handles: 90% movie scripts; 10% TV scripts.
- Prior to becoming an agent, Ms. Taylor worked for Morgan Stanley Dean Witter.
Member Agents Amy Taylor, senior vice president of motion picture division; Samantha Powers, executive vice president of motion picture division.
Represents Feature film, TV movie of the week, sitcom. **Considers these script subject areas:** Action/adventure; biography/autobiography; comedy; detective/police/crime; family saga; juvenile; mystery/suspense; romantic comedy; science fiction; sports; thriller; western/frontier.
- Cedar Grove Agency Entertainment was formed in the Pacific Northwest to take advantage of the rich and diverse culture, as well as the many writers who reside there. Does not want to receive period pieces, horror writing, children's scripts dealing with illness, or scripts dealing with excessive substance abuse.
How to Contact Submit 1-page synopsis via mail with SASE or via e-mail (no attachments). No phone calls, please. Responds in 10 days to queries; 2 months to mss. Obtains most new clients through referrals, Web site.
Recent Sales This agency prefers not to share information on specific sales.
Terms Agent receives 10% commission on domestic sales. Offers written contract, binding for 6-12 months; 30-day notice must be given to terminate contract.
Tips "We focus on finding that rare gem, the undiscovered, multi-talented writer, no matter where they live. Write, write, write! Find time every day to write. Network with other writers when possible, and write what you know. Learn the craft through books. Read scripts of your favorite movies. Enjoy what you write!"

THE CHARACTERS TALENT AGENCY

8 Elm St., Toronto ON M5G 1G7 Canada. (416)964-8522. Fax: (416)964-6349. E-mail: clib5@aol.com. Web site: www.thecharacters.com. **Contact:** Carl Liberman. Estab. 1968; Signatory of WGC. Represents 1,000 clients (writers, actors, directors). 5% of clients are new/unpublished writers.
- Before becoming an agent, Mr. Liberman was an advertising executive, writer and actor.
Member Agents Brent Jordan Sherman (film/TV writers and directors); Geoff Brooks (animation, children's writers); Ben Silverman (writers).
Represents Movie scripts, feature film, TV scripts, TV movie of the week, episodic drama, sitcom, animation, documentary, miniseries, soap opera, syndicated material. **Considers these script subject areas:** Action/adventure; biography/autobiography; cartoon/animation; comedy; contemporary issues; detective/police/crime; erotica (no porn); ethnic; family saga; fantasy; feminist; gay/lesbian; glitz; historical; horror; juvenile; mainstream; mystery/suspense; psychic/supernatural; romantic comedy; romantic drama; science fiction; sports; teen; thriller; western/frontier.
- Actively seeking romantic comedy features, comedy features, family comedy features, and strong female leads in thrillers (MOW/features). Does not want to receive stage plays.
How to Contact Query with SASE. include a 1-page synopsis. Accepts e-mail and fax queries. Considers simulta-

neous queries. Responds in 2 days to queries if by e-mail; 60 days to ms if query is accepted. Obtains most new clients through recommendations from others.

Recent Sales *Ada*, by Ronalda Jones (Milagro Films); *13th Apostle*, by Paul Margolis (Stallion Films); *Drake Diamond: Exorcist for Hire*, by Arne Olsen (Montecito Pictures); *Grounded in Eire*, by Ralph Keefer (Amaze Film & TV).

Terms Agent receives 10% commission on domestic sales; 10% commission on foreign sales. No written contract.

Tips "To reach or get information about each individual agent, please call for an e-mail address. All agents are based in Toronto, except one in Vancouver."

◖ CIRCLE OF CONFUSION

Fax: (212)572-8304 or (212)975-7748. E-mail: queries@circleofconfusion.com. Web site: www.circleofconfusion.com. Estab. 1990.

Represents Movie scripts.

> ○→ This agency specializes in comic books, video games and screenplays (science fiction, action, fantasy, thrillers, urban, horror).

How to Contact Submit query and brief synopsis via e-mail. Obtains most new clients through recommendations from others, writing contests, queries.

Recent Sales *Movie/TV MOW script(s) optioned/sold:* *The Matrix*, by Wachowski Brothers (Warner Brothers); *Reign of Fire*, by Chabot/Peterka (Dreamworks); *Mr. & Mrs. Smith*, by Simon Kinberg.

Terms Agent receives 10% commission on domestic sales; 10% commission on foreign sales. Offers written contract, binding for 1 year.

Tips "We look for writing that shows a unique voice, especially one which puts a fresh spin on commercial Hollywood genres."

◖ COMMUNICATIONS AND ENTERTAINMENT, INC.

4201 N. Ocean Blvd., #303-C, Boca Raton FL 33431-5359. (561)391-9575. Fax: (561)391-7922. E-mail: jlbearde@bellsouth.net. **Contact:** James L. Bearden. Estab. 1989. Represents 10 clients. 50% of clients are new/unpublished writers. Currently handles: 10% novels; 5% juvenile books; 40% movie scripts; 40% TV scripts.

> • Prior to opening his agency, Mr. Bearden worked as a producer/director and an entertainment attorney.

Member Agents James Bearden (TV, film); Joyce Daniels (literary).

Represents Novels, juvenile books, movie scripts, TV scripts, syndicated material. **Considers these nonfiction areas:** History; music/dance; theater/film. **Considers these fiction areas:** Action/adventure; comic books/cartoon; fantasy; historical; mainstream/contemporary; science fiction; thriller.

How to Contact For scripts, query with SASE. For books, query with outline/proposal or send entire ms. Responds in 1 month to queries; 3 months to mss. Obtains most new clients through recommendations from others.

Recent Sales This agency prefers not to share information on specific sales.

Terms Agent receives 10% commission on domestic sales; 5% commission on foreign sales. Offers written contract.

Tips "Be patient."

◖◖ THE CORE GROUP TALENT AGENCY, INC.

89 Bloor St. W., Suite 300, Toronto ON M5S 1M1 Canada. (416)955-0819. Fax: (416)955-0825. E-mail: literary@coregroupta.com. **Contact:** Charles Northcote, literary agent/co-owner. Estab. 1989. Member of WGC. Represents 60 clients. 10% of clients are new/unpublished writers. Currently handles: 25% movie scripts; 25% TV scripts; 50% stage plays.

Represents Movie scripts, feature film, TV scripts, TV movie of the week, episodic drama, sitcom, animation, documentary, miniseries, soap opera, stage plays. **Considers these script subject areas:** Action/adventure; biography/autobiography; cartoon/animation; comedy; contemporary issues; detective/police/crime; erotica; ethnic; experimental; family saga; fantasy; feminist; gay/lesbian; glitz; historical; horror; juvenile; mainstream; multicultural; mystery/suspense; psychic/supernatural; regional; romantic comedy; romantic drama; sports; teen; thriller; western/frontier.

> ○→ Seeks previously-produced writers with Canadian status. Does not want queries from international writers without Canadian status.

How to Contact Query with SASE. Responds in 1 week to queries. Returns materials only with SASE.

Terms Agent receives 10% commission on domestic sales. Offers written contract, binding for 1 year; 60-day notice must be given to terminate contract.

☒ ☑ DEITER LITERARY AGENCY

6207 Fushsimi Court, Burke VA 22015-3451. **Contact:** Mary A. Deiter. Estab. 1995. Signatory of WGA. Represents 12 clients.

Member Agents Mary A. Deiter (general fiction, general nonfiction, general interest screenplays).

Represents Nonfiction books, novels, movie scripts.

 ☐☎ This is a small agency with a set list of clients. While the agency will consider new work, Ms. Deiter is very selective.

How to Contact Query with SASE, submit synopsis, publishing history, author bio. No e-mail or fax queries. Returns materials only with SASE. Offers written contract.

Tips ''We usually don't take on TV writers because it's a hard sell, but if the work is good, we will consider it.''

☑ DRAMATIC PUBLISHING

311 Washington St., Woodstock IL 60098. (815)338-7170. Fax: (815)338-8981. E-mail: plays@dramaticpublishin g.com. Web site: www.dramaticpublishing.com. **Contact:** Linda Habjan. Estab. 1885. Currently handles: 2% textbooks; 98% stage plays.

Represents Stage plays.

 ☐☎ This agency specializes in a full range of stage plays, musicals, adaptations and instructional books about theater.

How to Contact Query with SASE, submit complete ms, SASE. Reports in 10-12 weeks to mss.

Recent Sales This agency prefers not to share information on specific sales.

☑ THE E S AGENCY

6612 Pacheco Way, Citrus Heights CA 95610. (916)723-2794. Fax: (916)723-2796. E-mail: edley07@cs.com. **Contact:** Ed Silver, president. Estab. 1995. Represents 50-75 clients. 70% of clients are new/unpublished writers. Currently handles: 50% nonfiction books; 25% novels; 25% movie scripts.

 • Prior to becoming an agent, Mr. Silver was an entertainment business manager.

Represents Nonfiction books, novels, movie scripts, feature film, TV movie of the week. **Considers these nonfiction areas:** General nonfiction. **Considers these fiction areas:** Action/adventure; detective/police/crime; erotica; experimental; historical; humor/satire; literary; mainstream/contemporary; mystery/suspense; thriller; young adult. **Considers these script subject areas:** Action/adventure; comedy; contemporary issues; detective/ police/crime; erotica; ethnic; experimental; family saga; mainstream; mystery/suspense; romantic comedy; romantic drama; sports; thriller.

 ☐☎ This agency specializes in theatrical screenplays, MOW, and miniseries. Actively seeking anything unique and original.

How to Contact Query with SASE. Considers simultaneous queries. Returns materials only with SASE. Obtains most new clients through recommendations from others, queries from WGA agency list.

Terms Agent receives 15% commission on domestic sales; 20% commission on foreign sales; 10% commission on dramatic rights sales. Offers written contract; 30-day notice must be given to terminate contract.

☑ EVATOPIA, INC.

400 S. Beverly Drive, Suite 214, Beverly Hills CA 90212. E-mail: submissions@evatopia.com. Web site: www.ev atopia.com. **Contact:** Margery Walshaw. Estab. 2004. Represents 15 clients. 85% of clients are new/unpublished writers. Currently handles: 100% movie scripts.

 • Prior to becoming an agent, Ms. Walshaw was a writer and publicist for the entertainment industry.

Member Agents Mary Kay (story development); Stacy Glenn (story development); Jamie Davis (story assistant); Jill Jones (story editor).

Represents Movie scripts. **Considers these script subject areas:** Action/adventure; biography/autobiography; cartoon/animation; comedy; contemporary issues; detective/police/crime; ethnic; family saga; fantasy; historical; horror; juvenile; mainstream; mystery/suspense; psychic/supernatural; romantic comedy; romantic drama; science fiction; sports; teen; thriller.

 ☐☎ ''We specialize in promoting and developing the careers of first-time screenwriters. All of our staff members have strong writing and entertainment backgrounds, making us sympathetic to the needs of our clients.'' Actively seeking dedicated and hard-working writers.

How to Contact Submit via online submission form. Considers simultaneous queries. Responds in 2 weeks to queries; 3 weeks to mss. Returns materials only with SASE. Obtains most new clients through recommendations from others, solicitations.

Terms Agent receives 15% commission on domestic sales; 15% commission on foreign sales. Offers written contract, binding for up to 2 years; 30-day notice must be given to terminate contract.

Tips ''Remember that you only have one chance to make that important first impression. Make your loglines original and your synopses concise. The secret to a screenwriter's success is creating an original story and telling it in a manner that we haven't heard before.''

◖ FITZGERALD LITERARY MANAGEMENT

84 Monte Alto Road, Santa Fe NM 87505. (505)466-1186. **Contact:** Lisa FitzGerald. Estab. 1994. Represents 12 clients. 75% of clients are new/unpublished writers. Currently handles: 15% film rights novels; 85% movie scripts.
- Prior to opening her agency, Ms. FitzGerald headed development at Universal Studios for Oscar-nominated writers/producers Bruce Evans and Raynold Gideon. She also served as executive story analyst at CBS, and held positions at Curtis Brown in New York, as well as Adams, Ray & Rosenberg Talent Agency in Los Angeles.

Represents Feature film, TV movie of the week, film rights to novels. **Considers these fiction areas:** Mainstream/contemporary (novels with film potential). **Considers these script subject areas:** Action/adventure; biography/autobiography; comedy; contemporary issues; detective/police/crime; ethnic; family saga; fantasy; historical; horror; mainstream; mystery/suspense; psychic/supernatural; romantic comedy; romantic drama; science fiction; sports; teen; thriller; western/frontier.
- O⚊ This agency specializes in screenwriters and selling film rights to novels. Actively seeking mainstream feature film scripts. Does not want to receive true stories.

How to Contact We are not accepting new clients except by referral.

Recent Sales Sold 7 titles and sold 5 scripts in the last year.

Terms Agent receives 15% commission on domestic sales. Offers written contract, binding for 1-2 years. Charges clients for photocopying and postage.

Tips "Know your craft. Read produced screenplays. Enter screenplay contests. Educate yourself on the business in general (read *The Hollywood Reporter* or *Daily Variety*). Learn how to pitch. Keep writing and don't be afraid to get your work out there.''

◖ ROBERT A. FREEDMAN DRAMATIC AGENCY, INC.

1501 Broadway, Suite 2310, New York NY 10036. (212)840-5760. Fax: (212)840-5776. **Contact:** Robert A. Freedman. Estab. 1928. Member of AAR; signatory of WGA.
- Mr. Freedman has served as vice president of the dramatic division of AAR.

Member Agents Robert A. Freedman, president; Selma Luttinger, senior vice president; Robin Kaver, vice president (movie/TV scripts); Marta Praeger, agent (stage plays).

Represents Movie scripts, TV scripts, stage plays.
- O⚊ This agency works with both new and established authors who write plays and movie and TV scripts.

How to Contact Query with SASE. All unsolicited mss returned unopened. Responds in 2 weeks to queries; 3 months to mss.

Recent Sales "We will speak directly with any prospective client concerning sales that are relevant to his/her specific script.''

Terms Agent receives 10% commission on domestic sales. Charges clients for photocopying.

◖ SAMUEL FRENCH, INC.

45 W. 25th St., New York NY 10010-2751. (212)206-8990. Fax: (212)206-1429. E-mail: info@samuelfrench.com. Web site: samuelfrench.com. **Contact:** Lawrence Harbison, senior editor. Estab. 1830. Member of AAR.

Member Agents Leon Embry.

Represents Theatrical stage play, musicals. **Considers these script subject areas:** Comedy; contemporary issues; detective/police/crime; ethnic; fantasy; horror; mystery/suspense; thriller.
- O⚊ This agency specializes in publishing plays which it also licenses for production.

How to Contact Query with SASE, or submit complete ms to Lawrence Harbison. Accepts e-mail and fax queries. Considers simultaneous queries. Responds in 2-8 months to mss. Responds immediately to queries.

Recent Sales This agency prefers not to share information on specific sales.

Terms Agent receives variable commission on domestic sales.

◖ THE GAGE GROUP

14724 Ventura Blvd., Suite 505, Sherman Oaks CA 91403. (818)905-3800. Fax: (818)905-3322. E-mail: Literary.GageGroupLA@gmail.com. Estab. 1976. Member of DGA; signatory of WGA.

Member Agents Jonathan Westover (feature, television); Joshua Orenstein (TV).

Represents Movie scripts, feature film, TV scripts, theatrical stage play.
- O⚊ Considers all script subject areas.

How to Contact Snail mail queries preferred. Accepts e-mail queries. No fax queries. Considers simultaneous queries. Responds in 1 month to queries; 1 month to mss.

Recent Sales This agency prefers not to share information on specific sales.

Terms Agent receives 10% commission on domestic sales; 10% commission on foreign sales. This agency charges clients for photocopying.

◪ GRAHAM AGENCY

311 W. 43rd St., New York NY 10036. **Contact:** Earl Graham. Estab. 1971. Represents 40 clients. 30% of clients are new/unpublished writers.

Represents Theatrical stage play, musicals.

> ⚭ This agency specializes in playwrights. "We're interested in commercial material of quality." Does not want to receive one-acts or material for children.

How to Contact Query with SASE. No e-mail or fax queries. Responds in 3 months to queries; 6 weeks to mss. Obtains most new clients through recommendations from others, solicitations.

Recent Sales This agency prefers not to share information on specific sales.

Terms Agent receives 10% commission on dramatic rights sales.

Tips "Write a concise, intelligent letter giving the gist of what you are offering."

◪ THE SUSAN GURMAN AGENCY, LLC

865 West End Ave., # 15A, New York NY 10025. (212)749-4618. Fax: (212)864-5055. E-mail: susan@gurmanagency.com. Web site: www.gurmanagency.com. Estab. 1993. Signatory of WGA.

Represents Playwrights, directors, composers, lyricists.

How to Contact Obtains new clients by referral only. No e-mail or fax queries.

◪ ◪ CHARLENE KAY AGENCY

901 Beaudry St., Suite 6, St.Jean/Richelieu QC J3A 1C6 Canada. E-mail: lmchakay@hotmail.com. **Contact:** Louise Meyers, director of development. Estab. 1992. Member of BMI; signatory of WGA. 50% of clients are new/unpublished writers. Currently handles: 50% movie scripts; 50% TV scripts.

> • Prior to opening her agency, Ms. Kay was a screenwriter.

Member Agents Louise Meyers; Karen Forsyth.

Represents Feature film, TV scripts, TV movie of the week, episodic drama, sitcom. **Considers these script subject areas:** Action/adventure; biography/autobiography; family saga; fantasy; psychic/supernatural; romantic comedy; romantic drama; science fiction.

> ⚭ This agency specializes in teleplays and screenplays. "We seek stories that are out of the ordinary, something we don't see too often. A well-written and well-constructed script is important." Does not want to receive thrillers, barbaric/erotic films, novels, books or mss.

How to Contact Query with SASE, submit outline/proposal. Does not return materials. Rejected mss are shredded. Responds in 1 month to queries; 10 weeks to mss.

Recent Sales This agency prefers not to share information on specific sales.

Terms Agent receives 10% commission on domestic sales; 10% commission on foreign sales. Offers written contract, binding for 1 year.

Tips "This agency is on the WGA lists, and query letters arrive by the dozens every week. As our present clients understand, success comes with patience. A sale rarely happens overnight, especially when you are dealing with totally unknown writers. We are not impressed by the credentials of a writer, amateur or professional, or by his/her pitching techniques, but by his/her story ideas and ability to build a well-crafted script."

◪ EDDIE KRITZER PRODUCTIONS

10221 Marcus Ave., Tujunga CA 91042-2007. E-mail: producedby@aol.com. Web site: www.eddiekritzer.com. **Contact:** Executive Story Editor. Estab. 1974.

Member Agents Eddie Kritzer (producer who also secures publishing agreements).

Represents Nonfiction books, movie scripts, feature film, TV scripts, TV movie of the week.

How to Contact Query with SASE. Prefers to read materials exclusively. Discards unwanted queries and mss. Obtains most new clients through recommendations from others, solicitations.

Recent Sales *Gmen & Gangsters* (Seven Locks Press/in development at Mandeville Films); *The Practical Patient* (Seven Locks Press); *The Making of a Surgeon in the 21st Century*, by Craig Miller (Blue Dolphin Press); *Kids Say the Darndest Things*, by Art Linkletter (Ten Speed Press/produced by Nick@Nite); *Live Ten Years Longer*, by Clarence Agrees (Ten Speed Press); *Take Back a Scary Movie* (currently at auction).

Terms Agent receives 15% commission on domestic sales; 20% commission on foreign sales. Offers written contract.

Tips "Contact by e-mail. I am only looking for the most compelling stories. Be succinct, but compelling."

◐ THE LANTZ OFFICE

200 W. 57th St., Suite 503, New York NY 10019. (212)586-0200. Fax: (212)262-6659. E-mail: rlantz@lantzoffice. com. Web site: www.lantzoffice.com. **Contact:** Robert Lantz. Member of AAR.
Represents Movie scripts, feature film, theatrical stage play.
How to Contact Query with SASE. Obtains most new clients through recommendations from others.
Terms Agent receives 10% commission on domestic sales; 10% commission on foreign sales.
Tips This is a very selective agency.

◪ THE LUEDTKE AGENCY

1674 Broadway, Suite 7A, New York NY 10019. (212)765-9564. Fax: (212)765-9582. **Contact:** Penny Luedtke.
• Prior to becoming an agent, Ms. Luedtke was in classical music management.
Represents Movie scripts, TV scripts (pilots), stage plays, musicals.
  O➔ Actively seeking well-written material with originality. Works closely with writers and offers editorial assistance, if desired. Does not want to receive any project with graphic or explicit violence.
How to Contact Query with SASE. No e-mail or fax queries. Considers simultaneous queries. Returns materials only with SASE. Obtains most new clients through recommendations from others, workshops.
Recent Sales This agency prefers not to share information on specific sales.
Terms Agent receives 10% commission on domestic sales; 15% commission on foreign sales. Offers written contract.

◎ THE MANAGEMENT CO.

1337 Ocean Ave., Suite F, Santa Monica CA 90401. **Contact:** Tom Klassen. Represents 15 clients.
• Prior to starting his agency, Mr. Klassen was an agent with International Creative Management.
Member Agents Tom Klassen; Helene Taber; Paul Davis; Steve Gamber; Veronica Hernandez.
Represents Feature film, TV scripts, episodic drama, sitcom, miniseries.
  O➔ Actively seeking studio-quality, action-drama scripts and really good comedies. No horror scripts.
How to Contact Submit query letter with synopsis. No e-mail or fax queries. Responds in 2-3 weeks to queries. Returns materials only with SASE. Obtains most new clients through recommendations from others, conferences.
Recent Sales Sold 11 scripts in the last year.
Terms Agent receives 10% commission on domestic sales; 10% commission on foreign sales. Offers written contract, binding for 2 years.
Writers' Conferences Sundance Film Festival; film festivals in New York, Telluride, Atlanta, Chicago, Minnesota.
Tips "We only accept query letters with a short, 1-page synopsis. We will request a full manuscript with an SASE if interested. We rarely take on nonreferred material, but do review query letters and occasionally take on new writers. We have done very well with those we have taken on."

N ◉ ◪ MARJACQ SCRIPTS, LTD

34 Devonshire Place, London England W1G 6JW, United Kingdom. (44)(207)935-9499. Fax: (44)(207)935-9115. E-mail: philip@marjacq.com; luke@marjacq.com. Web site: www.marjacq.com. **Contact:** Philip Patterson (literary); Luke Speed (film). Estab. 1974. Represents 80 clients. 40% of clients are new/unpublished writers. Currently handles: 10% nonfiction books; 40% novels; 5% juvenile books; 20% movie scripts; 25% TV scripts.
  • Prior to becoming an agent, Mr. Patterson was a film, TV and theatre agent at Curtis Brown and sold rights at HarperCollins; Mr. Speed worked in film production with Civilian Content and worked at Saatchi and Saatchi.
Member Agents Philip Patterson, literary agent; Luke Speed, film/TV agent.
  O➔ "We are a young and vibrant agency always looking for clients. We handle all rights—print publishing, film, TV, radio, translation and intellectual property." Actively seeking quality fiction, nonfiction, children's books and young adult books. Does not want to receive plays, poetry or short stories.
How to Contact Submit outline, synopsis, 3 sample chapters, bio, covering letter, SASE. Do not bother with fancy bindings and folders. Keep synopses, bio and covering letter short. Accepts e-mail queries via Word attachment. Considers simultaneous queries. Responds in 3 days to queries; 4-6 weeks to mss. Returns materials only with SASE. Obtains most new clients through recommendations from others, solicitations, conferences.
Recent Sales Sold 40 titles in the last year. *Second Time Round*, by Sophie King (Hodder & Stoughton); 3-book deal for Stuart MacBride (HarperCollins UK); 3-book deal for Catrin Collier (Orion Books); 2-book deal for Jack Sheffield (Transworld); 2-book deal for John Connor (Orion Books). Other clients include Katherine John, Rosie Goodwin, R.D. Wingfield, Christopher Goffard, Giulio Leoni, Ben Pastor, James Follett, George Markstein, Richard Lambert, Michael Taylor, Pat Mills, Graham Oakley, Richard Craze, Ros Jay, Richard Asplin, Stewart Hennessey, Claes Johansen, David Clayton.

Terms Agent receives 10% commission on domestic sales; 20% commission on foreign sales. Offers written contract. Charges for bank fees for money transfers.

Tips "Keep trying! If one agent rejects you, that is his/her opinion."

◢ THE STUART M. MILLER CO.

11684 Ventura Blvd., #225, Studio City CA 91604-2699. (818)506-6067. Fax: (818)506-4079. E-mail: smmco@aol .com. **Contact:** Stuart Miller. Estab. 1977; Signatory of WGA, DGA. Currently handles: 50% movie scripts; 10% multimedia; 40% books.

Represents Nonfiction books, novels, movie scripts. **Considers these nonfiction areas:** Biography/autobiography; computers/electronic; current affairs; government/politics/law; health/medicine; history; how-to; memoirs; military/war; self-help/personal improvement; true crime/investigative. **Considers these fiction areas:** Action/adventure; detective/police/crime; historical; literary; mainstream/contemporary; mystery/suspense; science fiction; sports; thriller. **Considers these script subject areas:** Action/adventure; biography/autobiography; cartoon/animation; comedy; contemporary issues; detective/police/crime; family saga; historical; mainstream; multimedia; mystery/suspense; romantic comedy; romantic drama; science fiction; sports; teen; thriller.

How to Contact For screenplays, query with SASE, narrative outline (2-3 pages). For books, submit narrative outline (5-10 pages). Accepts e-mail and fax queries. Considers simultaneous queries. Responds in 3 days to queries. Responds in 4-6 weeks to screenplays and mss. Returns materials only with SASE.

Recent Sales This agency prefers not to share information on specific sales.

Terms Offers written contract, binding for 2 years. Agent receives 10% commission on screenplay sales; 15% commission on motion picture/TV rights sales for books and other non-screenplay literary properties.

Tips "Always include an SASE, e-mail address or fax number with query letters. Make it easy to respond."

◖ MONTEIRO ROSE DRAVIS AGENCY, INC.

17514 Ventura Blvd., Suite 205, Encino CA 91316. (818)501-1177. Fax: (818)501-1194. Web site: www.monte iro-rose.com. **Contact:** Candy Monteiro. Estab. 1987. Signatory of WGA. Represents 50 clients. Currently handles: 40% movie scripts; 20% TV scripts; 40% animation.

Member Agents Candace Monteiro; Fredda Rose; Jason Dravis.

Represents Feature film, TV movie of the week, episodic drama, animation. **Considers these script subject areas:** Action/adventure; cartoon/animation; comedy; contemporary issues; detective/police/crime; ethnic; family saga; historical; juvenile; mainstream; mystery/suspense; psychic/supernatural; romantic comedy; romantic drama; science fiction; teen; thriller.

　Oπ This agency specializes in scripts for animation, TV and film.

How to Contact Query with SASE. Accepts e-mail and fax queries. Responds in 1 week to queries; 2 months to mss. Returns materials only with SASE. Obtains most new clients through recommendations from others, solicitations.

Recent Sales This agency prefers not to share information on specific sales.

Terms Agent receives 10% commission on domestic sales. Offers written contract, binding for 2 years; 3-month notice must be given to terminate contract. Charges for photocopying.

Tips "We prefer to receive inquiries by e-mail, although snail mail is OK with a SASE. We do not return manuscripts. We suggest that all feature manuscripts be no longer than 120 pages."

◖ NIAD MANAGEMENT

15030 Ventura Blvd., Bldg. 19 #860, Sherman Oaks CA 91403. (818)505-1272. Fax: (818)505-1637. E-mail: queries@niadmanagement.com. Web site: www.niadmanagement.com. Estab. 1997. Represents 20 clients. Currently handles: 1% novels; 99% movie scripts.

Represents Movie scripts, feature film, TV movie of the week, miniseries, stage plays. **Considers these nonfiction areas:** Biography/autobiography. **Considers these fiction areas:** Action/adventure; detective/police/crime; family saga; literary; mainstream/contemporary; multicultural; mystery/suspense; psychic/supernatural; romance; thriller. **Considers these script subject areas:** Action/adventure; biography/autobiography; comedy; contemporary issues; detective/police/crime; ethnic; family saga; historical; horror; mainstream; multicultural; mystery/suspense; psychic/supernatural; romantic comedy; romantic drama; sports; teen; thriller.

How to Contact Query with SASE. Responds to queries only if interested. Accepts e-mail and fax queries. Considers simultaneous queries. Responds in 1 week to queries; 3 months to mss. Returns materials only with SASE. Obtains most new clients through recommendations from others.

Recent Sales *MacGyver* (the feature film), by Lee Zlotoff; *Moebius,* by Neil Cohen (Mandate); *Winter Woke Up,* by Aaron Garcia and Melissa Emery; *Under the Bed,* by Susan Sandler (Caldwell Theater).

Terms Offers written contract, binding for 1 year; 30-day notice must be given to terminate contract. Agent receives 15% commission on all gross monies received.

◉ DOROTHY PALMER

235 W. 56 St., New York NY 10019. (212)765-4280. Fax: (212)977-9801. Estab. 1968 (talent agency); 1990 (literary agency). Signatory of WGA. Represents 12 clients. Currently handles: 70% movie scripts; 30% TV scripts.

• In addition to being a literary agent, Ms. Palmer has worked as a talent agent for 36 years.

Represents Feature film, TV movie of the week, episodic drama, sitcom, miniseries, independent films. **Considers these script subject areas:** Action/adventure; comedy; contemporary issues; detective/police/crime; family saga; feminist; horror; mainstream; mystery/suspense; romantic comedy; romantic drama; thriller.

O➡ This agency specializes in screenplays and TV. Actively seeking successful, published writers (screenplays only). Does not want to receive work from new or unpublished writers.

How to Contact Query with SASE. Prefers to read materials exclusively. Returns materials only with SASE. Obtains most new clients through recommendations from others.

Recent Sales This agency prefers not to share information on specific sales.

Terms Agent receives 10% commission on domestic sales; 10% commission on foreign sales. Offers written contract, binding for 1 year. Charges clients for postage and photocopies.

Tips "Do not telephone. When I find a script that interests me, I call the writer."

◉ BARRY PERELMAN AGENCY

1155 N. La Cienega Blvd., Suite 412, W. Hollywood CA 90069. (310)659-1122. Fax: (310)659-1122. Estab. 1982; Signatory of WGA, DGA. Represents 40 clients. 15% of clients are new/unpublished writers. Currently handles: 100% movie scripts.

Member Agents Barry Perelman.

Represents Movie scripts, TV scripts, reality shows. **Considers these script subject areas:** Action/adventure; biography/autobiography; contemporary issues; detective/police/crime; historical; horror; mystery/suspense; romantic comedy; romantic drama; science fiction; thriller.

O➡ This agency specializes in motion pictures/packaging.

How to Contact Query with SASE, proposal package, outline. Responds in 1 month to queries. Obtains most new clients through recommendations from others, solicitations.

Recent Sales This agency prefers not to share information on specific sales.

Terms Agent receives 10% commission on domestic sales; 10% commission on foreign sales. Offers written contract, binding for 1-2 years. This agency charges clients for postage and photocopying.

◉ THE QUILLCO AGENCY

3104 W. Cumberland Court, Westlake Village CA 91362. (805)495-8436. Fax: (805)373-9868. E-mail: quillco2@aol.com. **Contact:** Sandy Mackey. Estab. 1993. Signatory of WGA. Represents 7 clients.

Represents Feature film, TV movie of the week, animation, documentary.

How to Contact Prefers to read materials exclusively. Not accepting query letters at this time.

Recent Sales This agency prefers not to share information on specific sales.

Terms Agent receives 10% commission on domestic sales; 10% commission on foreign sales.

◉ MICHAEL D. ROBINS & ASSOCIATES

23241 Ventura Blvd., #300, Woodland Hills CA 91364. (818)343-1755. Fax: (818)343-7355. E-mail: mdr2@msn.com. **Contact:** Michael D. Robins. Estab. 1991. Member of DGA; signatory of WGA.

• Prior to opening his agency, Mr. Robins was a literary agent at a mid-sized agency.

Represents Nonfiction books, novels, movie scripts, feature film, TV scripts, TV movie of the week, episodic drama, animation, miniseries, stage plays.

How to Contact Query with SASE. Accepts e-mail and fax queries. Considers simultaneous queries. Obtains most new clients through recommendations from others.

Recent Sales This agency prefers not to share information on specific sales.

Terms Agent receives 10% commission on domestic sales; 10% commission on foreign sales. Offers written contract.

N ⊞ ◉ SAYLE SCREEN, LTD

11 Jubilee Place, London England SW3 3TD, United Kingdom. (44)(207)823-3883. Fax: (44)(207)823-3363. E-mail: info@saylescreen.com. Web site: www.saylescreen.com. Estab. 1952. Represents 100+ clients. 5% of clients are new/unpublished writers. Currently handles: 50% movie scripts; 50% TV scripts.

Member Agents Toby Moorcroft; Jane Villiers; Matthew Bates.

Represents Movie scripts, TV scripts, episodic drama, sitcom. **Considers these script subject areas:** Action/adventure; comedy; contemporary issues; detective/police/crime; ethnic; experimental; fantasy; horror; mainstream; mystery/suspense; psychic/supernatural; romantic comedy; romantic drama; teen; thriller.

O→ Actively seeking writers and directors for film and TV.

How to Contact Query with synopsis, bio, SASE. No e-mail or fax queries. Responds in 2-3 months to queries; 2-3 months to mss. Returns materials only with SASE. Obtains most new clients through recommendations from others.

Recent Sales *Curious Incident of the Dog in the Nighttime*, by Mark Haddon (Warner Brothers); *Night Watch*, by Sarah Waters (BBC); *Dog Called Cork*, by Josie Doder (Xingu); *Dreamer*, by David Hilton (Rocket/Silver Creek).

Terms Agent receives 10% commission on domestic sales; 15% commission on foreign sales. Offers written contract; 1-month notice must be given to terminate contract.

◉ KEN SHERMAN & ASSOCIATES

9507 Santa Monica Blvd., Beverly Hills CA 90210. (310)273-8840. Fax: (310)271-2875. **Contact:** Ken Sherman. Estab. 1989. Member of BAFTA, PEN International; signatory of WGA, DGA. Represents approximately 35 clients. 10% of clients are new/unpublished writers.

● Prior to opening his agency, Mr. Sherman was with The William Morris Agency, The Lantz Office and Paul Kohner, Inc. He has taught "The Business of Writing For Film and Television and The Book Worlds" at UCLA and USC. He is currently a commissioner of arts and cultural affairs in the city of West Hollywood, and is on the international advisory board of the Christopher Isherwood Foundation.

Represents Nonfiction books, novels, movie scripts, TV scripts (not episodic), teleplays, life rights, film/TV rights to books. **Considers these nonfiction areas:** Agriculture/horticulture; americana; animals; anthropology/ archaeology; art/architecture/design; biography/autobiography; business/economics; child guidance/parenting; computers/electronic; cooking/foods/nutrition; crafts/hobbies; current affairs; education; ethnic/cultural interests; gardening; gay/lesbian issues; government/politics/law; health/medicine; history; how-to; humor/ satire; interior design/decorating; language/literature/criticism; memoirs; military/war; money/finance; multicultural; music/dance; nature/environment; New Age/metaphysics; philosophy; photography; popular culture; psychology; recreation; regional; religious/inspirational; science/technology; self-help/personal improvement; sex; sociology; software; spirituality; sports; theater/film; translation; travel; true crime/investigative; women's issues/studies; young adult; creative nonfiction. **Considers these fiction areas:** Action/adventure; comic books/ cartoon; confession; detective/police/crime; erotica; ethnic; experimental; family saga; fantasy; feminist; gay/ lesbian; glitz; gothic; hi-lo; historical; horror; humor/satire; literary; mainstream/contemporary; military/war; multicultural; multimedia; mystery/suspense; New Age; occult; picture books; plays; poetry; poetry in translation; psychic/supernatural; regional; religious/inspirational; romance; science fiction; short story collections; spiritual; sports; thriller; translation; westerns/frontier; young adult. **Considers these script subject areas:** Action/adventure; biography/autobiography; cartoon/animation; comedy; contemporary issues; detective/police/crime; erotica; ethnic; experimental; family saga; fantasy; feminist; gay/lesbian; glitz; historical; horror; mainstream; multicultural; multimedia; mystery/suspense; psychic/supernatural; regional; religious/inspirational; romantic comedy; romantic drama; science fiction; sports; teen; thriller; western/frontier.

How to Contact Contact by referral only. Reports in approximately 1 month to mss. Obtains most new clients through recommendations from others.

Recent Sales Sold more than 20 scripts in the last year. *Back Roads*, by Tawni O'Dell (Dreamworks); *Priscilla Salyers Story*, produced by Andrea Baynes (ABC); *Toys of Glass*, by Martin Booth (ABC/Saban Entertainment); *Brazil*, by John Updike (film rights to Glaucia Carmagos); *Fifth Sacred Thing*, by Starhawk (Bantam); *Questions From Dad*, by Dwight Twilly (Tuttle); *Snow Falling on Cedars*, by David Guterson (Universal Pictures); *The Witches of Eastwick—The Musical*, by John Updike (Cameron Macintosh, Ltd.).

Terms Agent receives 15% commission on domestic sales; 15% commission on foreign sales; 10-15% commission on dramatic rights sales. Offers written contract. Charges clients for reasonable office expenses (postage, photocopying, etc.).

Writers' Conferences Maui Writers' Conference; Squaw Valley Writers' Workshop; Santa Barbara Writers' Conference; Screenwriting Conference in Santa Fe; Aspen Summer Words Literary Festival.

◨ ◉ STONE MANNERS AGENCY

6500 Wilshire Blvd., Suite 550, Los Angeles CA 90048. (323)655-1313. E-mail: postmaster@stonemanners.com. Estab. 1982. Signatory of WGA.

Represents Movie scripts, TV scripts.

How to Contact Query with SASE. Accepts e-mail queries. No fax queries.

Recent Sales This agency prefers not to share information on specific sales.

Terms Agent receives 10% commission on domestic sales; 10% commission on foreign sales.

◉ SUITE A MANAGEMENT TALENT & LITERARY AGENCY

120 El Camino Drive, Suite 202, Beverly Hills CA 90212. (310)278-0801. Fax: (310)278-0807. E-mail: suite-a@juno.com. **Contact:** Lloyd Robinson. Estab. 1996; Signatory of WGA, DGA. Represents 76 clients. 10% of

clients are new/unpublished writers. Currently handles: 15% novels; 40% movie scripts; 40% TV scripts; 5% stage plays.

• Prior to becoming an agent, Mr. Robinson worked as a manager.

Member Agents Lloyd Robinson (adaptation of books and plays for development as features or TV MOW); Kevin Douglas (scripts for film and TV); Judy Jacobs (feature development).

Represents Feature film, TV movie of the week, episodic drama, documentary, miniseries, variety show, stage plays, CD-ROM. **Considers these script subject areas:** Action/adventure; cartoon/animation; comedy; contemporary issues; detective/police/crime; erotica; ethnic; experimental; family saga; fantasy; mainstream; mystery/suspense; psychic/supernatural; religious/inspirational; romantic comedy; romantic drama; science fiction; sports; teen; thriller; western/frontier.

O┅ "We represent screenwriters, playwrights, novelists, producers and directors."

How to Contact Submit synopsis, outline/proposal, logline. Obtains most new clients through recommendations from others.

Recent Sales This agency prefers not to share information on specific sales or client names.

Terms Agent receives 10% commission on domestic sales; 10% commission on foreign sales. Offers written contract, binding for minimum 1 year. Charges clients for photocopying, messenger, FedEx, postage.

Tips "We are a talent agency specializing in the copyright business. Fifty percent of our clients generate copyright (screenwriters, playwrights and novelists). Fifty percent of our clients service copyright (producers and directors). We represent produced, published, and/or WGA writers who are eligible for staff TV positions, as well as novelists and playwrights whose works may be adapted for film or TV."

☑ TALENT SOURCE

1711 Dean Forest Road, Suite H, Savannah GA 31408. E-mail: michael@talentsource.com. Web site: www.talent source.com. **Contact:** Michael L. Shortt. Estab. 1991. Signatory of WGA. 35% of clients are new/unpublished writers. Currently handles: 85% movie scripts; 15% TV scripts.

• Prior to becoming an agent, Mr. Shortt was a TV program producer/director.

Represents Feature film, TV movie of the week. **Considers these script subject areas:** Comedy; contemporary issues; detective/police/crime; erotica; family saga; juvenile; mainstream; romantic comedy; romantic drama; teen.

O┅ Actively seeking character-driven stories (e.g., *Sling Blade* or *Sex, Lies, and Videotape*). Does not want to receive science fiction or scripts with big budget special effects.

How to Contact Send a cover letter (query) with SASE, synopsis. Reports on queries in 10-12 weeks. No e-mail or fax queries. Obtains most new clients through recommendations from others.

Recent Sales This agency prefers not to share information on specific sales.

Terms Agent receives 10% commission on domestic sales; 15% commission on foreign sales. Offers written contract.

Tips "See the literary button on our Web site for complete submissions details. No exceptions."

☑ PEREGRINE WHITTLESEY AGENCY

279 Central Park W., New York NY 10024. (212)787-1802. Fax: (212)787-4985. E-mail: pwwagy@aol.com. **Contact:** Peregrine Whittlesey. Estab. 1986. Signatory of WGA. Represents 30 clients. 50% of clients are new/unpublished writers. Currently handles: 1% movie scripts; 99% stage plays.

O┅ This agency specializes in playwrights who also write for screen and TV.

How to Contact Query with SASE. Prefers to read materials exclusively. Accepts e-mail and fax queries. Responds in 1 week to queries; 1 month to mss. Obtains most new clients through recommendations from others.

Recent Sales Sold 20 scripts in the last year. Scripts sold to Actors Theatre of Louisville's Humana Festival, South Coast Repertory, Stratford Festival, Ontario Canada, Alabama Shakespeare Festival, ACT Seattle, Seattle Rep, Arena Stage, City Theatre Pittsburgh, Repertorio Espanol and producers in England, Germany and Spain.

Terms Agent receives 10% commission on domestic sales; 15% commission on foreign sales. Offers written contract, binding for 2 years.

Conferences

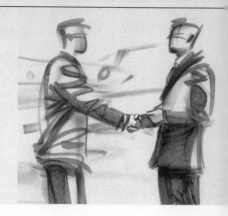

A ttending a writers' conference that includes agents gives you the opportunity to learn more about what agents do and to show an agent your work. Ideally, a conference should include a panel or two with a number of agents to give writers a sense of the variety of personalities and tastes of different agents.

Not all agents are alike: Some are more personable, and sometimes you simply click better with one agent versus another. When only one agent attends a conference, there is a tendency for every writer at that conference to think, "Ah, this is the agent I've been looking for!" When the number of agents attending is larger, you have a wider group from which to choose, and you may have less competition for the agent's time.

Besides including panels of agents discussing what representation means and how to go about securing it, many of these gatherings also include time—either scheduled or impromptu—to meet briefly with an agent to discuss your work.

If they're impressed with what they see and hear about your work, they will invite you to submit a query, a proposal, a few sample chapters, or possibly your entire manuscript. Some conferences even arrange for agents to review manuscripts in advance and schedule one-on-one sessions during which you can receive specific feedback or advice regarding your work. Such meetings often cost a small fee, but the input you receive is usually worth the price.

Ask writers who attend conferences and they'll tell you that, at the very least, you'll walk away with new knowledge about the industry. At the very best, you'll receive an invitation to send an agent your material!

Many writers try to make it to at least one conference a year, but cost and location can count as much as subject matter when determining which one to attend. There are conferences in almost every state and province that can provide answers to your questions about writing and the publishing industry. Conferences also connect you with a community of other writers. Such connections help you learn about the pros and cons of different agents, and they can also give you a renewed sense of purpose and direction in your own writing.

SUBHEADS

Each listing is divided into subheads to make locating specific information easier. In the first section, you'll find contact information for conference contacts. You'll also learn conference dates, specific focus, and the average number of attendees. Finally, names of agents who will be speaking or have spoken in the past are listed along with details about their availability during the conference. Calling or e-mailing a conference director to verify the names of agents in attendance is always a good idea.

Costs: Looking at the price of events, plus room and board, may help writers on a tight budget narrow their choices.

Accommodations: Here conferences list overnight accommodations and travel information. Often conferences held in hotels will reserve rooms at a discount rate and may provide a shuttle bus to and from the local airport.

Additional Information: This section includes information on conference-sponsored contests, individual meetings, the availability of brochures, and more.

REGIONS

To make it easier for you to find a conference close to home—or to find one in an exotic locale to fit into your vacation plans—listings are separated into the following geographical regions:

- **Northeast** (pages 255): Connecticut, Maine, Massachusetts, New Hampshire, New York, Rhode Island, Vermont.
- **Midatlantic** (pages 258): Washington D.C., Delaware, Maryland, New Jersey, Pennsylvania.
- **Midsouth** (pages 259): North Carolina, South Carolina, Tennessee, Virginia, West Virginia.
- **Southeast** (pages 261): Alabama, Arkansas, Florida, Georgia, Louisiana, Mississippi.
- **Midwest** (pages 263): Illinois, Indiana, Kentucky, Michigan, Ohio.
- **North Central** (pages 266): Iowa, Minnesota, Nebraska, North Dakota, South Dakota, Wisconsin.
- **South Central** (pages 267): Colorado, Kansas, Missouri, New Mexico, Oklahoma, Texas.
- **West** (pages 270): Arizona, California, Hawaii, Nevada, Utah.
- **Northwest** (pages 274): Alaska, Idaho, Montana, Oregon, Washington, Wyoming.
- **Canada** (pages 275).
- **International** (pages 276).

Quick Reference Icons

At the beginning of some listings, you will find one or more of the following symbols:

N: Conference new to this edition

Canadian conference

International conference

Find a pull-out bookmark with a key to symbols on the inside cover of this book.

NORTHEAST (CT, MA, ME, NH, NY, RI, VT)

ASJA WRITERS CONFERENCE

American Society of Journalists and Authors, 1501 Broadway, Suite 302, New York NY 10036. (212)997-0947. Fax: (212)768-7414. E-mail: staff@asja.org. Web site: www.asjaconference.org. **Contact:** Anne Peace, executive director. Estab. 1971. Annual conference held in April. Conference duration: 2 days. Average attendance: 600. Covers nonfiction and screenwriting. Held at the Grand Hyatt in New York. Speakers have included Dominick Dunne, James Brady, and Dana Sobel. Agents will be speaking at the event.
Costs $195-240, depending on when you sign up (includes lunch).
Accommodations "The hotel holding our conference always blocks out discounted rooms for attendees."
Additional Informations Brochures available in February. Registration form is on the Web site. Inquire by e-mail or fax.

BOOKEXPO AMERICA/WRITER'S DIGEST BOOKS WRITERS' CONFERENCE

4700 E. Galbraith Rd., Cincinnati OH 45236. (513)531-2690. Fax: (513)891-7185. E-mail: publicity@fwpubs.com. Web site: www.writersdigest.com/bea. **Contact:** Greg Hatfield, publicity manager. Estab. 2003. Annual conference held in May. Average attendance: 600. The conference offers instruction on the craft of writing, as well as advice for submitting work to publications, publishing houses, and agents. "We provide breakout sessions on these topics, including expert advice from industry professionals, and offer workshops on fiction and nonfiction. We also provide agents to whom attendees can pitch their work." The conference is part of the BookExpo America trade show. Registration for the conference does not allow you access to the trade show. Speakers have included Jodi Picoult, Jerry Jenkins, Steve Almond, John Warner, Donald Maass, Noah Lukeman and Jennifer Gilmore.

BREAD LOAF WRITERS' CONFERENCE

Middlebury College, Middlebury VT 05753. (802)443-5286. Fax: (802)443-2087. E-mail: ncargill@middlebury.edu. Web site: www.middlebury.edu/blwc. **Contact:** Noreen Cargill, administrative manager. Estab. 1926. Annual conference held in late August. Conference duration: 11 days. Average attendance: 230. Offers workshops for fiction, nonfiction, and poetry. Agents, editors, publicists, and grant specialists will be in attendance.
Costs $2,260 (includes tuition, housing).
Accommodations Bread Loaf Inn in Ripton, Vermont.

GOTHAM WRITERS' WORKSHOP

WritingClasses.com, 555 Eighth Ave., Suite 1402, New York NY 10018. (212)974-8377. Fax: (212)307-6325. E-mail: dana@write.org. Web site: www.writingclasses.com. **Contact:** Dana Miller, director of student affairs. Estab. 1993. Classes are held throughout the year. There are four terms, beginning in January, April, June/July, and September/October. Offers craft-oriented creative writing courses in general creative writing, fiction writing, screenwriting, nonfiction writing, article writing, stand-up comedy writing, humor writing, memoir writing, novel writing, children's book writing, playwriting, poetry, songwriting, mystery writing, science fiction writing, romance writing, television writing, article writing, travel writing, business writing and classes on freelancing, selling your screenplay and getting published. Also, Gotham Writers' Workshop offers a teen program, private instruction ,and classes on selling your work. Classes are held at various schools in New York City as well as online at www.writingclasses.com. Agents and editors participate in some workshops.
Costs $395/10-week workshops.

ⓝ GREEN MOUNTAIN WRITERS CONFERENCE

47 Hazel St., Rutland VT 05701. (802)236-6133. E-mail: ydaley@sbcglobal.net. Web site: www.vermontwriters.com. **Contact:** Yvonne Daley, director. Estab. 1999. Annual conference held in August. Covers fiction, creative nonfiction, poetry, journalism, nature writing, essay, memoir, personal narrative, and biography. Held at an old dance pavillion on on a remote pond in Tinmouth, Vermont. Speakers have included Joan Connor, Yvonne Daley, David Huddle, David Budbill, Jeffrey Lent, Verandah Porche, Tom Smith, and Chuck Clarino.
Costs $500 before June 15; $525 after June 15. Partial scholarships are available.
Accommodations "We have made arrangements with a major hotel in nearby Rutland and 2 area bed and breakfast inns for special accommodations and rates for conference participants. You must make your own reservations."

HIGHLIGHTS FOUNDATION WRITERS WORKSHOP AT CHAUTAUQUA

814 Court St., Honesdale PA 18431. (570)253-1192. Fax: (570)253-0179. E-mail: contact@highlightsfoundation.org. Web site: www.highlightsfoundation.org. **Contact:** Kent Brown, executive director. Estab. 1985. Annual conference held July 12-18, 2008. Average attendance: 100. Workshops are geared toward those who write for

children at the beginner, intermediate, and advanced levels. Offers seminars, small group workshops, and one-on-one sessions with authors, editors, illustrators, critics, and publishers. Workshop site is the picturesque community of Chautauqua, New York. Speakers have included Eve Bunting, James Cross Giblin, Linda Sue Park, Jane Yolen, Patricia Gauch, Jerry Spinelli, Eileen Spinelli, Joy Cowley and Pam Munoz Ryan.
Costs $2,200 (includes all meals, conference supplies, gate pass to Chautauqua Institution).
Accommodations "We coordinate ground transportation to and from airports, trains, and bus stations in the Erie, Pennsylvania and Jamestown/Buffalo, New York area. We also coordinate accommodations for conference attendees."
Additional Informations "We offer the opportunity for attendees to submit a manuscript for review at the conference." Workshop brochures/guidelines are available upon request.

HOFSTRA UNIVERSITY SUMMER WRITING WORKSHOPS

University College for Continuing Education, 250 Hofstra University, Hempstead NY 11549-2500. (516)463-5993. Fax: (516)463-4833. E-mail: uccelibarts@hofstra.edu. Web site: www.hofstra.edu/ucce/summerwriting.
Contact: Richard Pioreck, director of the summer writing workshops, or Judith Reed. Estab. 1972. Annual conference held in mid-July. Conference duration: 2 weeks. Average attendance: 65. Conference offers workshops in short fiction, nonfiction, poetry, and occasionally other genres such as screenplay writing or writing for children. Site is the university campus on Long Island, 25 miles from New York City. Speakers have inluded Oscar Hijuelos, Robert Olen Butler, Hilma and Meg Wolitzer, Budd Schulberg, Cynthia Ozick, and Rebecca Wolff.
Costs Check Web site for current fees. Credit is available for undergraduate and graduate students. Continental breakfast daily; tution also includes the cost of the banquet. All workshops include critiquing. Each participant is given one-on-one time for a half hour with a workshop leader. More details will be available in March. Accepts inquiries via fax and e-mail.
Accommodations Free bus operates between Hempstead Train Station and campus for those commuting from New York City on the Long Island Rail Road. Dormitory rooms are available.

IWWG MEET THE AGENTS AND EDITORS: THE BIG APPLE WORKSHOPS

c/o International Women's Writing Guild, P.O. Box 810, Gracie Station, New York NY 10028-0082. (212)737-7536. Fax: (212)737-9469. E-mail: iwwg@iwwg.org. Web site: www.iwwg.org. **Contact:** Hannelore Hahn, executive director. Estab. 1980. Workshops are held the second weekend in April and October. Average attendance: 200. Workshops promote creative writing and professional success. A 1-day writing workshop is offered on Saturday. Sunday morning includes a discussion with up to 10 recently published IWWG authors and a book fair during lunch. On Sunday afternoon, up to 10 literary agents introduce themselves, and then members of the audience speak to the agents they wish to meet. Many as-yet-unpublished works have found publication in this manner. Speakers have included Meredith Bernstein, Rita Rosenkranz, and Jeff Herman.
Costs $160/members for the weekend; $155/nonmembers for the weekend; $90/100 for Saturday; $80/105 for Sunday.
Additional Informations Information (including accommdations) is provided in a brochure. Inquire via fax or e-mail.

◪ MARYMOUNT MANHATTAN COLLEGE WRITERS' CONFERENCE

Marymount Manhattan College, 221 E. 71st St., New York NY 10021. (212)774-0780. E-mail: lfrumkes@mmm.edu. **Contact:** Lewis Frumkes. Estab. 1993. Annual conference held in June. 2007 keynote speakers: Cynthia Ozick and Sara Nelson, editor-in-chief of *Publisher's Weekly*. Conference duration: 1 day. Average attendance: 200. "We present workshops on several different writing genres and panels on fiction and nonfiction, literary agents, memoir and more." Over 60 distinguished authors, agents, and publicists attend. Keynote speakers have included Lewis Lapham and Joyce Carol Oates.
Costs $165 before June 1; $185 after June 1 (includes lunch, reception).

THE PERSPECTIVES IN CHILDREN'S LITERATURE CONFERENCE

226 Furcolo Hall, School of Education, U-Mass, Amherst MA 01003-3035. E-mail: childlit@educ.umass.edu. Web site: www.umass.edu/childlit. **Contact:** Katelyn McLaughlin, conference coordinator; or Masha Rudman, conference director. Estab. 1970. Annual conference held in late March/early April. The 2007 conference is on March 31. Conference duration: 1 day. Average attendance: 500. Conference focuses on various aspects of writing and illustrating children's books. Held at the University of Massachusetts Isenberg School of Management. Speakers have included Jane Yolen, Jerry and Gloria Jean Pinkey, Patricia and Emily MacLachlan, Jan Cherpiko, E.B. Lewis, Julius Lester, Eric Carle, and Leslea Newman.
Costs $70-75 (includes light breakfast, lunch, freebies, snacks). For an additional fee, attendees can earn academic credit.

Additional Informations During lunch, authors and illustrators are given the opportunity to converse and share experiences with editors. Books will be available for sale. Send inquiries via e-mail. See the Web site for list of this years speakers.

N ROBERT QUACKENBUSH'S CHILDREN'S BOOK WRITING & ILLUSTRATING WORKSHOP

460 E. 79th St., New York NY 10021-1443. (212)744-3822. Fax: (212)861-2761. E-mail: rqstudios@aol.com. Web site: www.rquackenbush.com. **Contact:** Robert Quackenbush, director. Estab. 1982. Annual workshop held during the second week in July. Conference duration: 4 days. Average attendance: limited to 10. Workshops promote writing and illustrating books for children and are geared toward beginners and professionals. Generally focuses on picture books, easy-to-read books, and early chapter books. Held at the Manhattan studio of Robert Quackenbush, author and illustrator of more than 200 books for children. All classes led by Robert Quackenbush.

Costs $650 tuition covers all the costs of the workshop, but does not include housing and meals. A $100 nonrefundable deposit is required with the $550 balance due two weeks prior to attendance.

Accommodations A list of recommended hotels and restaurants is sent upon receipt of deposit.

REMEMBER THE MAGIC

International Women's Writing Guild, P.O. Box 810, Gracie Station, New York NY 10028-0082. (212)737-7536. Fax: (212)737-9469. E-mail: iwwg@iwwg.org. Web site: www.iwwg.org. **Contact:** Hannelore Hahn, executive director. Estab. 1978. Annual conference held in June. Average attendance: 500. Conference to promote creative writing and personal growth, professional know-how and contacts, and networking. Site is the campus of Skidmore College in Saratoga Springs, New York (near Albany). Approximately 65 workshops are offered each day. Conferees have the freedom to make their own schedule.

Costs $1,004 single/$869 double for members; $1,034 single/$899 double for nonmembers. These fees include the 7-day program and room and board for the week. Rates for a 5-day stay and a weekend stay, as well as commuter rates, are also available.

Additional Informations Conference brochures/guidelines are available online or for a SASE. Inquire via e-mail or fax.

N ROMANTIC TIMES CONVENTION

55 Bergen St., Brooklyn NY 11201. (718)237-1097 or (800)989-8816, ext. 12. Fax: (718)624-2526. E-mail: jocarol @rtconvention.com. Web site: www.rtconvention.com. **Contact:** Jo Carol Jones. Annual conference held in April. Features 125 workshops, agent and editor appointments, a book fair, and more.

Costs $439/convention; $200/early bird registration; $125/preconvention program.

SEAK MEDICAL FICTION WRITING CONFERENCE

P.O. Box 729, Falmouth MA 02541. (508)548-7023. Fax: (508)540-8304. E-mail: mail@seak.com. Web site: www.seak.com. Annual conferences held on Cape Cod. The medical seminar is taught by *New York Times* bestselling authors Michael Palmer, MD and Tess Gerritsen, MD. Session topics include writing fiction that sells, screenwriting, writing riveting dialogue, creating memorable characters, getting your first novel published, and more. Agents will be speaking and available for one-on-one meetings.

SOCIETY OF CHILDREN'S BOOK WRITERS & ILLUSTRATORS CONFERENCE/HOFSTRA UNIVERSITY'S CHILDREN'S LITERATURE CONFERENCE

University College for Continuing Education, 250 Hofstra University, Hempstead NY 11549-2500. (516)463-5993. Fax: (516)463-4833. E-mail: uccelibarts@hofstra.edu. Web site: www.hofstra.edu/ucce/childlitconf. **Contact:** Judith Reed. Estab. 1985. Annual conference held in April. The conference brings together writers, illustrators, librarians, agents, publishers, teachers, and other professionals who are interested in writing for children. Each year the program is organized around a theme and includes 2 general sessions, 5 break-out groups, and a panel of children's book editors who critique randomly selected first-manuscript pages submitted by registrants. The conference takes place at the Student Center Building of Hofstra University, located in Long Island.

Costs 2007 rate: $82/members; $87/nonmembers (continental breakfast and full luncheon included).

WESLEYAN WRITERS CONFERENCE

Wesleyan University, 194 High St., Room 207, Middletown CT 06459. (860)685-3604. Fax: (860)685-2441. E-mail: agreene@wesleyan.edu. Web site: www.wesleyan.edu/writers. **Contact:** Anne Greene, director. Estab. 1956. Annual conference held the third week of June. Average attendance: 100. Focuses on the novel, fiction techniques, short stories, poetry, screenwriting, nonfiction, literary journalism, and memoir. The conference is held on the campus of Wesleyan University, in the hills overlooking the Connecticut River. Features a faculty of award-winning writers, seminars and readings of new fiction, poetry, nonfiction and mixed media forms—

as well as guest lectures on a range of topics including publishing. Both new and experienced writers are welcome. Participants may attend seminars in all genres. Speakers have included Esmond Harmsworth (Zachary Schuster Agency), Daniel Mandel (Sanford J. Greenburger Associates), Dorian Karchmar, Amy Williams (ICM and Collins McCormick), Mary Sue Rucci (Simon & Schuster), Denise Roy (Simon & Schuster), John Kulka (Yale University Press), and many others. Agents will be speaking and available for meetings with attendees. Participants are often successful in finding agents and publishers for their mss. Wesleyan participants are also frequently featured in the anthology *Best New American Voices*.

Costs Previous year day rate: Unspecified(includes meals); Student rate: $980 (includes meals and room for 5 nights); boarding student rate: $1,190 (includes meal and room for 5 nights).

Accommodations Meals are provided on campus. Lodging is available on campus or in town.

Additional Informations Ms critiques are available, but not required. Scholarships and teaching fellowships are available, including the Joan Jakobson Awards for fiction writers and poets; and the Jon Davidoff Scholarships for nonfiction writers and journalists. Inquire via e-mail, fax, or phone.

WRITERS' CONFERENCE AT OCEAN PARK

P.O. Box 7146, Ocean Park ME 04063-7146. E-mail: jbrosnan@jwu.edu. **Contact:** Jim Brosnan, Donna Brosnan. Estab. 1941. Annual conference held in mid-August. Conference duration: 4 days. Average attendance: 50. "We try to present a balanced and eclectic conference. In addition to time and attention given to poetry, we also have children's literature, mystery writing, travel, fiction, nonfiction, journalism, and other issues of interest to writers. Our speakers are editors, writers, and other professionals. Our concentration is, by intention, a general view of writing to publish with supportive encouragement. We are located in Ocean Park, a small seashore village 14 miles south of Portland. Ours is a summer assembly center with many buildings from the Victorian age. The conference meets in Porter Hall, one of the assembly buildings which is listed in the National Register of Historic Places." Speakers have included Michael C. White (novelist/short story writer), Betsy Shool (poet), Suzanne Strempek Shea (novelist), John Perrault (poet), Josh Williamson (newspaper editor), Dawn Potter (poet), Bruce Pratt (fiction writer), Amy McDonald (children's author), Anne Wescott Dodd (nonfiction writer), Kate Chadbourne (singer/songwriter), Wesley McNair (poet/Maine faculty member), and others. "We usually have about 8 guest presenters each year." Publishes writers/editors will be speaking, leading workshops, and available for meetings with attendees.

Costs $160 (includes conference, reception, Tuesday evening meal); $175 if registering after July 1. The fee does not include housing or meals, which must be arranged separately by conferees.

Accommodations An accommodations list is available. "We are in a summer resort area where motels, guest houses, and restaurants abound."

Additional Informations "We have 7 contests for various genres. An announcement is available in the spring. The prizes (all modest) are awarded at the end of the conference and only to those who are registered." Send SASE in June for the conference program.

MIDATLANTIC (DC, DE, MD, NJ, PA)

Ⓝ ALGONKIAN WRITER WORKSHOPS

2020 Pennsylvania Ave. NW, Suite 43, Washington DC 20006. (800)250-8290. E-mail: algonkian@webdelsol.com. Web site: www.webdelsol.com/algonkian. **Contact:** Michael Neff, director. Estab. 2001. Conference duration: 5 days. Average attendance: 15/craft workshops; 60/pitch sessions. Workshops on fiction, short fiction, and poetry are held 12 times/year in various locations. Speakers have included Paige Wheeler, Elise Capron, Deborah Grosvenor and Kathleen Anderson. Agents will be speaking and available for meetings with attendees.

Costs $495-1,295 (includes tuition, meals). Housing costs vary depending on the workshop's location.

Additional Informations "These workshops are challenging and are not for those looking for praise. Guidelines are available online or via e-mail."

BALTIMORE WRITERS' CONFERENCE

Citylit Project, 120 S. Curley St., Baltimore MD 21224. E-mail: info@citylitproject.org. Web site: www.towson.edu/writersconference. **Contact:** Greg Wilhelm, coordinator. Estab. 1994. Annual conference held in November. Conference duration: 1 day. Average attendance: 150-200. Covers all areas of writing and getting published. Held at Towson University. Topics have included: mystery, science fiction, poetry, children's writing, legal issues, grant funding, working with an agent, and book and magazine panels. Speakers have included Dana Gioia, Alice McDermott and Nina Graybill. Agents will be speaking at the event.

Costs $80-100 (includes all-day conference, lunch and reception).

Accommodations Hotels are close by, if required.

Additional Informations Writers may register through the BWA Web site. Send inquiries via e-mail.

N LIGONIER VALLEY WRITERS CONFERENCE

P.O. Box B, Ligonier PA 15658. (724)593-7294. E-mail: jgallagher@LHTC.net. Web site: www.ligoniervalleywriters.org. **Contact:** Sally Shirey, conference coordinator. Annual conference held last weekend in July. Conference duration: 2 days. Readings, seminars, and workshops cover nonfiction, fiction, children's, poetry, creative nonfiction, playwriting, screenwriting, memoir, travel, historical, fantasy, science fiction, romance, journaling, nature, horror, plot development, and editing. Speakers have included Julia Kasdorf, Paola Corso, Randall Silvis, David Walton, Hilary Masters, Amanda Lynch, and Kathleen George.
Costs $144-156/members; $168-184/nonmembers. Registration rates are also available for attending on Friday or Saturday only.
Accommodations A special rate is available at the Ramada Inn of Ligonier.
Additional Informations Attendees can submit up to 20 pages for a critique.

N MONTROSE CHRISTIAN WRITERS' CONFERENCE

5 Locust St., Montrose PA 18801. (570)278-1001 or (800)598-5030. Fax: (570)278-3061. E-mail: mbc@montrosebible.org. Web site: www.montrosebible.org. **Contact:** MBC Secretary/Registrar. Estab. 1990. Annual conference held in July. Offers workshops, editorial appointments, and professional critiques. "We try to meet a cross-section of writing needs, for beginners and advanced, covering fiction, poetry, and writing for children. It is small enough to allow personal interaction between conferences and faculty." Speakers have included William Petersen, Mona Hodgson, Jim Fletcher, and Terri Gibbs.
Costs $145/tuition; $35/critique.
Accommodations $245-290/week; $55-65/day for lodging and meals.

@ SANDY COVE CHRISTIAN WRITERS CONFERENCE

Sandy Cove Ministries, 60 Sandy Cove Rd., North East MD 21901. (410)287-5433. Fax: (410)287-3196. E-mail: info@sandycove.org. Web site: www.sandycove.org. Estab. 1991. Annual conference held the first week in October. Conference duration: 4 days. Average attendance: 200. There are major workshops in fiction, article writing, and nonfiction books for beginner and advanced writers. While Sandy Cove has a strong emphasis on available markets in Christian publishing, all writers are more than welcome. Speakers have included Francine Rivers, Lisa Bergen, Ken Petersen (Tyndale House), Linda Tomblin (*Guideposts*), and Karen Ball (Zondervan).
Costs Call for rates.
Accommodations Sandy Cove is a full-service conference center located on the Chesepeake Bay. All the facilities are first class, with suites, single rooms, and double rooms available.
Additional Informations Conference brochures/guidelines are available. Visit the Web site for exact conference dates.

WASHINGTON INDEPENDENT WRITERS (WIW) SPRING WRITERS CONFERENCE

1001 Connecticut Ave. NW, Suite 701, Washington DC 20036. (202)775-5150. Fax: (202)775-5810. E-mail: info@washwriter.org. Web site: www.washwriter.org. **Contact:** Jennifer Van Orman, membership manager. Estab. 1975. Annual conference held in June. Average attendance: 350. Focuses on fiction, nonfiction, screenwriting, poetry, children's writing, and technical writing. Gives participants the chance to hear from and talk with dozens of experts on book and magazine publishing, as well as on the craft, tools, and business of writing. Speakers have included Erica Jong, John Barth, Kitty Kelley, Vanessa Leggett, Diana McLellan, Brian Lamb, and Stephen Hunter. New York and local agents attend the conference.
Additional Informations See the Web site or send a SASE in mid-February for brochures/guidelines and fees information.

WINTER POETRY & PROSE GETAWAY IN CAPE MAY

(609)823-5076. E-mail: info@wintergetaway.com. Web site: www.wintergetaway.com. **Contact:** Peter Murphy, founder/director. Estab. 1994. Annual workshop held in January. Conference duration: 4 days. Offers workshops on short stories, memoirs, creative nonfiction, children's writing, novel, drama, poetry and photography. Classes are small, so each person receives individual attention for the new writing or work-in-progress that they are focusing on. Held at the Grand Hotel on the oceanfront in historic Cape May, New Jersey. Speakers have included Stephen Dunn (recipient of the 2001 Pulitzer Prize for poetry), Christian Bauman, Kurt Brown, Catherine Doty, Douglas Goetsch, James Richardson, Robbie Clipper Sethi and many more.

MIDSOUTH (NC, SC, TN, VA, WV)

N AEC CONFERENCE ON SOUTHERN LITERATURE

Arts & Education Council, 3069 S. Broad St., Suite 2, Chattanooga TN 37408. (423)267-1218. Fax: (423)267-1018. E-mail: info@artsedcouncil.org. Web site: www.artsedcouncil.org. **Contact:** Susan Frady Robinson, executive director. Estab. 1981. Biennial. Biennial conference held in March or April. Conference duration: 3 days. Average attendance: 1,000. Conference covers fiction, nonfiction, drama and poetry through panels and readings. Held at the Chattanooga Tivoli Theater. Speakers have included Reynolds Price, Wendell Berry, Ernest Gaines, Clyde Edgerton, Lee Smith, Alfred Uhry, Dorothy Allison, Sena Jeter Naslund and Edward Jones.

Costs $110 (includes admissions to all events and luncheon).

Accommodations Visit www.chattanoogafun.com for assistance with accommodations and airfare. A free shuttle service is provided between venues.

AMERICAN CHRISTIAN WRITERS CONFERENCES

P.O. Box 110390, Nashville TN 37222-0390. (800)219-7483. Fax: (615)834-7736. E-mail: acwriters@aol.com. Web site: www.acwriters.com. **Contact:** Reg Forder, director. Estab. 1981. Conference duration: 2 days. Average attendance: 60. Annual conferences promoting all forms of Christian writing (fiction, nonfiction, scriptwriting). Conferences are held throughout the year in 36 US cities.

Costs Approximately $189, plus meals and accommodations.

Accommodations Special rates are available at the host hotel (usually a major chain like Holiday Inn).

Additional Informations Send a SASE for conference brochures/guidelines.

CAPON SPRINGS WRITERS' WORKSHOP

P.O. Box 11116, Cincinnati OH 45211-0116. (513)481-9884. Fax: (513)481-2646. E-mail: beckcomm@fuse.net. **Contact:** Wendy Beckman, director. Estab. 2000. The next conference is set for sometime in 2008. Conference duration: 3 days. Covers fiction, creative nonfiction, and publishing basics. Conference is held at Farm Resort, a secluded 5,000-acre mountian resort in West Virginia.

Costs $500 (includes all seminars, meals, lodging).

Accommodations Facility has swimming, hiking, fishing, tennis, badminton, volleyball, basketball, ping pong, etc. A 9-hole golf course is available for an additional fee.

Additional Informations Brochures available for SASE. Inquire via e-mail or fax.

N CHATTANOOGA FESTIVAL OF WRITERS

Arts & Education Council, 3069 S. Broad St., Suite 2, Chattanooga TN 37408. (423)267-1218. Fax: (423)267-1018. E-mail: info@artsedcouncil.org. Web site: www.artsedcouncil.org. **Contact:** Susan Frady Robinson, executive director. Estab. 2006. biennial. Biennial conference held in late March. Conference duration: 2 days. Average attendance: 250. This conference covers fiction, nonfiction, drama and poetry through workshops and keynote. Held in downtown Chattanooga. Speakers have included Suzette Francis, Richard Bausch, David Magee, Philip Gerard, Elizabeth Kostova and Robert Morgan.

Costs $110 (includes admissions to all workshops, luncheon and dinner).

Additional Informations Visit www.chattanoogafun.com for assistance with accomodations and airfare.

N FALL WRITERS' SEMINAR

Council for the Written Word, P.O. Box 298, Franklin TN 37065. (615)790-5918. E-mail: nfblume@cs.com. Web site: www.asouthernjournal.com/cww. **Contact:** Nancy Fletcher-Blume, president. Annual conference held in September. An all-day event with local and area authors, agents, editors, publishers, and publicists teaching the art and business of writing.

HIGHLAND SUMMER CONFERENCE

Box 7014, Radford University, Radford VA 24142-7014. (540)831-5366. Fax: (540)831-5951. E-mail: jasbury@radford.edu. Web site: www.radford.edu/~arsc. **Contact:** JoAnn Asbury, assistant to the director. Estab. 1978. Annual conference held in June. Conference duration: 2 weeks. Average attendance: 25. Covers fiction, nonfiction, poetry, and screenwriting. Speakers have included Bill Brown, Robert Morgan, Sharyn McCrumb, Nikki Giovanni, Wilma Dykeman, Jim Wayne Miller, David Huddle, and Diane Fisher.

Costs The cost is based on current Radford tuition for 3 credit hours, plus an addidtional conference fee. On-campus meals and housing are available at additional cost. In 2007, conference tuition was $717/in-state undergraduates, $1,686/for out-of-state undergraduates, $780/in-state graduates, and $1,434/out-of-state graduates.

Accommodations "We do not have special rate arrangements with local hotels. We do offer accommodations on the Radford University campus in a recently refurbished residence hall. The 2005 cost was $26-36/night."

Additional Informations Conference leaders typically critique work done during the 2-week conference, but do not ask to have any writing sumbitted prior to the conference." Conference brochures/guidelines are available in March for a SASE. Inquire via e-mail or fax.

Ⓝ KILLER NASHVILLE

P.O. Box 680686, Franklin TN 37068-0686. (615)599-4032. E-mail: contact@killernashville.com. Web site: www.killernashville.com. **Contact:** Clay Stafford. Estab. 2006. Annual conference held in August. Conference duration: 3 days. Average attendance: 150+. Conference designed for writers and fans of mysteries and thrillers, including fiction and nonfiction authors, playwrights, and screenwriters. There are many opportunities for authors to sign books. Authors/panelists have included Carol Higgins Clark, P.J. Parrish, Reed Farrel Coleman, Gwen Hunter, Kathryn Wall, Richard Helms, Brad Strickland and Steven Womack.

NEW-CUE WRITERS' CONFERENCE & WORKSHOP IN HONOR OF RACHEL CARSON

New-Cue, Inc., Methodist College, Clark Hall, 5300 Ramsey St., Fayetteville NC 28311. (845)630-7047 or (910)630-7046. Fax: (910)630-7221. E-mail: info@new-cue.org. Web site: www.new-cue.org. **Contact:** Anne Way. Estab. 1999. Biannual conference held in June. Conference duration: 4 days. Average attendance: 100. This interdisciplinary event will be a blend of scholarly presentations, readings, informal discussions, and writing workshops. Held at The Spruce Point Inn in Boothbay Harbor, Maine. Speakers have included Lawrence Buell, Bill McKibben, Carl Safina and Linda Lear.

Costs Registration costs include sessions, meals and keynote reception.

Accommodations Special rates are available for participants at the Spruce Point Inn. Transportation and area information is available through the Boothbay Harbor Chamber of Commerce.

NORTH CAROLINA WRITERS' NETWORK FALL CONFERENCE

P.O. Box 954, Carrboro NC 27510-0954. (919)967-9540. Fax: (919)929-0535. E-mail: mail@ncwriters.org. Web site: www.ncwriters.org. **Contact:** Cynthia Barnett, executive director. Estab. 1985. Annual conference held in November in Research Traingle Park (Durham, North Carolina). Conference duration: 450. Average attendance: 450. The conference is a weekend full of workshops, panels, book signings, and readings (including open mic). There will be a keynote speaker, along with sessions on a variety of genres, including fiction, poetry, creative nonfiction, journalism, children's book writing, screenwriting, and playwriting. "We also offer craft, editing, and marketing classes. We hold the event at a conference center with hotel rooms available." Speakers have included Donald Maass, Noah Lukeman, Joe Regal, Jeff Kleinman, and Evan Marshall. Some agents will teach classes and some are available for meetings with attendees.

Costs Approximately $250 (includes 2 meals).

Accommodations Special rates are available at the Sheraton Hotel, but conferees must make their own reservations.

Additional Informations Brochures/guidelines are available online or by sending your street address to mail@ncwriters.org. You can also register online.

SEWANEE WRITERS' CONFERENCE

735 University Ave., Sewanee TN 37383-1000. (931)598-1141. E-mail: cpeters@sewanee.edu. Web site: www.sewaneewriters.org. **Contact:** Cheri B. Peters, creative writing programs manager. Estab. 1990. Annual conference held in July. Conference duration: 12 days. Average attendance: 120. "We offer genre-based workshops in fiction, poetry, and playwriting." The conference uses the facilities of Sewanee: the University of the South. The university is a collection of ivy-covered Gothic-style buildings located on the Cumberland Plateau in mid-Tennessee. Editors, publishers, and agents structure their own presentations, but there is always opportunity for questions from the audience." 2007 faculty members are fiction writers Richard Bausch, John Casey, Tony Earley, Diane Johnson, Randall Kenan, Alison Lurie, Jill, McCorkle, and Claire Messud; poets Brad Leithauser, Charles Martin, Mary Jo Salter, Alan Shapiro, Mark Strand, and Greg Williamson; and playwrights Lee Blessing and Melanie Marnich. Visiting agents include Gail Hochman and Georges Borchardt.

Costs $1,600 (includes tuition, board, basic room).

Accommodations Participants are housed in university dormitory rooms. Motel or bed & breakfast housing is available, but not abundantly so. Dormitory housing (shared occupancy) costs are included in the full conference fee. Single rooms are also available for a modest fee.

Additional Informations Complimentary chartered bus service is available from the Nashville Airport to Sewanee and back on the first and last days of the conference. "We offer each participant (excepting auditors) the opportunity for a private manuscript conference with a member of the faculty. These manuscripts are due 1 month before the conference begins." Brochures/guidelines are free. The conference provides a limited number of fellowships and scholarships; these are awarded on a competitive basis.

SOUTHEAST (AL, AR, FL, GA, LA, MS)

FLORIDA CHRISTIAN WRITERS CONFERENCE

2344 Armour Ct., Titusville FL 32780. (321)269-5831. Fax: (321)264-0037. E-mail: billiewilson@cfl.rr.com. Web site: www.flwriters.org. **Contact:** Billie Wilson. Estab. 1988. Annual conference held in March. Conference

duration: 4 days. Average attendance: 200. Covers fiction, nonfiction, magazine writing, marketing, Internet writing, greeting cards, and more. Conference is held at the Christian Retreat Center in Brandenton, Florida. **Costs** $485 (includes tuition, meals).
Accommodations "We provide a shuttle from the Sarasota airport." $625/double occupancy; $865/single occupancy.
Additional Informations "Each writer may submit 2 works for critique. We have specialists in every area of writing." Brochures/guidelines are available online or for a SASE.

FLORIDA FIRST COAST WRITERS' FESTIVAL

4501 Capper Road, C105, FCCJ, Jacksonville FL 32218. (904)766-6731. Fax: (904)713-4858. E-mail: dathomas@fccj.org. Web site: www.fccj.org/wf. **Contact:** Dana Thomas. Estab. 1985. Annual conference held in the spring. Average attendance: 300. Covers fiction, nonfiction, scriptwriting, poetry, freelancing, etc. Offers seminars on narrative structure and plotting character development. Speakers have included Andrei Codrescu, Gerald Hausman, Connie May Fowler, Leslie Schwartz, Larry Smith, Stella Suberman, Sophia Wadsworth, Amy Gash, David Hale Smith, Katharine Sands, Rita Rosenkranz, Jim McCarthy, David Poyer, Lenore Hart, Steve Berry and S.V. Date. "We offer one-on-one sessions at no additional cost for attendees to speak to selected writers, editors, and agents on a first-come, first-served basis."
Costs Visit the Web site for updated registration fees, including early bird specials.
Accommodations Crowne Plaza Jacksonville Riverfront has a special festival rate. Call 1-877-227-6963 and ask for a group booking code.
Additional Informations Brochures/guidelines are available for a SASE. Sponsors a contest for short fiction, poetry, novels and plays. Novel judges are David Poyer and Lenore Hart. Entry fees: $39/novels; $15/short fiction; $7/poetry. Deadline: varies. Visit the Web site often for festival updates and details.

GEORGIA WRITERS SPRING FESTIVAL OF WORKSHOPS

1071 Steeple Run, Lawrenceville GA 30043. (678)407-0703. Fax: (678)407-9917. E-mail: Festival@georgiawriters.org; President@georgiawriters.org. Web site: www.georgiawriters.org/Festival-2007.htm. **Contact:** Geri Taran, executive director. Estab. 1995. Annual conference held in May. Conference duration: 1 day. Conference covering all genres and business aspects of a writing career. Learn from the experts about editing, agents, contract negotiation, publishing, and the writing life. Held at the Smyrna Community Center in Smyrna, Georgia. Speakers have included Doug Crandell, Collin Kelley, Bobbie Christmas, Cec Murphey, Greg Johnson and Jackie Weldon White.
Costs $50-125, depending on membership status. Discounts for advance registration.

HARRIETTE AUSTIN WRITERS CONFERENCE

Georgia Center for Continuing Education, The University of Georgia, Athens GA 30602-3603. E-mail: adminhawc@gmail.com. Web site: www.coe.uga.edu/hawc. **Contact:** Diane Trap. Annual conference held in July. Sessions cover fiction, poetry, freelance writing, computers, how to get an agent, working with editors, and more. Editors and agents will be speaking. Ms critiques and one-on-one meetings with an evaluator are available for $50.
Costs $175-280, depending on the days registered (includes reception, sessions, lunch, book signings, cocktail party). Meals cost extra.
Accommodations Accomodations at the Georgia Center Hotel (georgiacenter.uga.edu).

Ⓝ NATCHEZ LITERARY AND CINEMA CELEBRATION

P.O. Box 1307, Natchez MS 39121-1307. (601)446-1208. Fax: (601)446-1214. E-mail: carolyn.smith@colin.edu. Web site: www.colin.edu/NLCC. **Contact:** Carolyn Vance Smith, co-chairman. Estab. 1990. Annual conference held in February. Conference duration: 5 days. Conference focuses on all literature, including film scripts. Each year's conference deals with some general aspect of Southern history. Speakers have included Eudora Welty, Margaret Walker Alexander, William Styron, Willie Morris, Ellen Douglas, Ernest Gaines, Elizabeth Spencer, Nikki Giovanni, Myrlie Evers-Williams, and Maya Angelou.

OXFORD CONFERENCE FOR THE BOOK

Center for the Study of Southern Culture, The University of Mississippi, P.O. Box 1848, University MS 38677-1848. (661)915-5993. Fax: (662)915-5814. E-mail: mheh@olemiss.edu. Web site: www.olemiss.edu/depts/south. **Contact:** Ann J. Abadie, associate director. Estab. 1993. Annual conference held in March or April. Average attendance: 300-400. Since its inauguration, the conference has celebrated books, writing, and reading, and has also dealt with practical concerns on which the literary arts and the humanities depend, including literacy, freedom of expression, and the book trade itself. Beginning in 1999, the conference has been open to the public without charge and broadcast on cable. Each conference presents 20-50 speakers, mostly writers (poets, literary fiction, popular fiction, nonfiction authors, academic authors, critics, reviewers), but also editors, agents, librarians, literacy volunteers/organizers, booksellers, and book technology experts. The conference is held in the university's new performing arts center—a campus facility with 1,000 seats. It is located near the town of Oxford. Speakers have included agents Julian Bach, Liz Darhansoff, Leigh Feldman, Sheldon Fogelman, David Gernert, Ronald Goldfarb, Wendy Weil and Amy Willams.

Accommodations "We provide a list of local hotels and arrange for a block of rooms for speakers and early conference registrants in the Downtown Inn—a motel near the town square. We also provide a shuttle service between Oxford and Memphis International Airport, about 60 miles away."

Additional Informations Brochures are available online or for a SASE. Inquire via e-mail or fax.

⊞ SANDHILLS WRITERS CONFERENCE

E-mail: akellman@aug.edu. Web site: www.sandhills.aug.edu. **Contact:** Anthony Kellman, director. Annual conference held the fourth weekend in March. Covers fiction, poetry, children's literature, nonfiction, plays, and songwriting. Located on the campus of Augusta State University in Georgia. Agents and editors will be speaking at the event.

Accommodations Several hotels are located near the university.

⊞ SOUTHEASTERN WRITERS WORKSHOP

P.O. Box 82115, Athens GA 30608. E-mail: purple@southeasternwriters.com. Web site: www.southeasternwriters.com. **Contact:** Tim Hudson. Estab. 1975. Held annually the third week in June at Epworth-by-the-Sea, St. Simons Island, Georgia. Conference duration: 4 days. Average attendance: Limited to 100 students. Classes are offered in all areas of writing, including fiction, poetry, nonfiction, inspirational, juvenile, specialty writing, and others. The faculty is comprised of some of the most successful authors from throughout the southeast and the country. Agent-in-Residence is available to meet with participants. Up to 3 free ms evaluations and critique sessions are also available to participants if mss are submitted by the deadline.

Costs 2007 tuition is $395.

Accommodations On-site accommodations (including meals) ranged from $420/double to $650/single in a variety of motel-style rooms. Meals are served cafeteria-style.

Additional Informations Multiple contests with cash prizes are open to participants. Registration brochure is available in March—e-mail or send a SASE. Full information, including registration material, is on the Web site.

◎ WRITING TODAY

Birmingham-Southern College, Box 549066, Birmingham AL 35254. (205)226-4922. Fax: (205)226-4931. E-mail: agreen@bsc.edu. Web site: www.writingtoday.org. **Contact:** Annie Green. Estab. 1978. Annual conference held during the second weekend in March. The 2008 dates are set for March 7-8. Conference duration: 2 days. Average attendance: 300-350. Conference hosts approximately 18 workshops, lectures, and readings. "We try to offer sessions in short fiction, novels, poetry, children's literature, magazine writing, songwriting, and general information of concern to aspiring writers, such as publishing, agents, markets, and research." The event is held on the Birmingham-Southern College campus in classrooms and lecture halls. Speakers have included Eudora Welty, Pat Conroy, Ernest Gaines, Ray Bradbury, Erskine Caldwell, John Barth, Galway Kinnell, Edward Albee, Horton Foote, and William Styron and other renowned writers.

Costs $150 for both days (includes lunches, reception, morning coffee/rolls).

Accommodations Attendees must arrange own transportation and accommodations.

Additional Informations For an additional charge, poetry and short story critiques are offered for interested writers who request and send mss by the deadline. The conference also sponsors the Hackney Literary Competition Awards for poetry, short stories, and novels.

MIDWEST (IL, IN, KY, MI, OH)

BACKSPACE AGENT-AUTHOR SEMINAR

P.O. Box 454, Washington MI 48094-0454. (732)267-6449. Fax: (586)532-9652. E-mail: karendionne@bksp.org. Web site: allagents.bksp.org/index.htm. **Contact:** Karen Dionne; Christopher Graham. Estab. 2006. Conference duration: 1 day. Average attendance: 100. Annual seminar held in November. Panels and workshops designed to educate and assist authors in search of a literary agent to represent their work. Only agents will be in program. Past speakers have included Scott Hoffman, Dan Lazar, Scott Miller, Michael Bourret, Katherine Fausset, Jennifer DeChiara, Sharlene Martin and Paul Cirone.

Costs $165.

Additional Informations "The Backspace Agent-Author Seminar offers plenty of gace time with attending agents.

This casual, no-pressure seminar is a terrific opportunity to network, ask questions, talk about your work informally and listen from the people who make their lives selling books.''

N BACKSPACE WRITERS CONFERENCE

P.O. Box 454, Washington MI 48094-0454. Phone/Fax: (586)532-9652. E-mail: karendionne@bksp.org. Web site: www.backspacewritersconference.com. **Contact:** Karen Dionne, Christopher Graham. Estab. 2005. Annual conference held in New York City in June or July. Conference duration: 2 days. Average attendance: 150. Conference focuses on all genres of fiction and nonfiction. Offers query letter workshop, writing workshop, and panels with agents, editors, marketing experts, and authors. Speakers have included Pulitzer-Prize-winning playwright Douglas Wright, Michael Cader, David Morrell, Lee Child, Gayle Lynds, Ron McLarty, C. Michael Curtis, Jeff Kleinman, Richard Curtis, Noah Lukeman, Jenny Bent, Dan Lazar and Kristin Nelson.
Costs $285 (includes 2-day, 2-track program and refreshments on both days). Banquet tickets cost $95.
Additional Informations This is a high-quality conference, with much of the program geared toward agented and published authors. Afternoon mixers each day afford plenty of networking opportunities. Go online for brochure, or request information via fax or e-mail.

COLUMBUS WRITERS CONFERENCE

P.O. Box 20548, Columbus OH 43220. (614)451-3075. Fax: (614)451-0174. E-mail: angelapl28@aol.com. Web site: www.creativevista.com. **Contact:** Angela Palazzolo, director. Estab. 1993. Annual conference held in August. Average attendance: 250+. In addition to literary agent and editor consultations, the conference offers a wide variety of fiction and nonfiction topics presented by writers, editors, and literary agents. Writing topics have included novel, short story, children's, young adult, science fiction, fantasy, humor, mystery, playwriting, finding and working with a literary agent, book proposals, query writing, screenwriting, magazine writing, travel, humor, cookbook, technical queries and freelance writing. The conference has included many writers, editors and literary agents, including Lee K. Abbott, Chuck Adams, Tracy Bernstein, Sheree Bykofsky, Oscar Collier, Lisa Cron, Jennifer DeChiara, Tracey E. Dils, Hallie Ephron, Karen Harper, Scott Hoffman, Jeff Kleinman, Simon Lipskar, Noah Lukeman, Donald Maass, Lee Martin, Erin McGraw, Kim Meisner, Doris S. Michaels, Rita Rosenkrantz, Ben Salmon and Nancy Zafris.
Additional Informations For registration fees or to receive a brochure (available in the summer), visit the Web site or contact the conference by e-mail, phone, fax, or postal mail.

FESTIVAL OF FAITH AND WRITING

Department of English, Fine Arts Center, Calvin College, 1795 Knollcrest Circle SE, Grand Rapids MI 49546. (616)526-6770. E-mail: ffw@calvin.edu. Web site: www.calvin.edu/academic/engl/festival.htm. **Contact:** Kristin Cocco or Shannon Hollemans, administrative assistants. Estab. 1990. Biennial festival held in April. Conference duration: 3 days. The festival brings together writers, editors, publishers, musicians, artists, and readers to discuss and celebrate insightful writing that explores issues of faith. Focuses on fiction, nonfiction, memoir, poetry, drama, children's, young adult, academic, film, and songwriting. Past speakers have included Joyce Carol Oates, Salman Rushdie, Patricia Hampl, Thomas Lynch, Leif Enger, Marilynne Robinson and Jacqueline Woodson. Agents and editors attend the festival.
Costs Estimated at $170; $85/students (includes all sessions, but does not include meals, lodging, or evening concerts).
Accommodations Shuttles are available to and from local hotels. Shuttles are also available for overflow parking lots. A list of hotels with special rates for conference attendees is available on the festival Web site. High school and college students can arrange on-campus lodging by e-mail.
Additional Informations Online registration opens in October. Accepts inquiries by e-mail, phone, and fax.

N KENYON REVIEW WRITERS WORKSHOP

The Kenyon Review, Kenyon College, Gambier OH 43022. (740)427-5207. Fax: (740)427-5417. E-mail: reacha@kenyon.edu. Web site: www.kenyonreview.org. **Contact:** Anna Duke Reach, Director of Summer Programs. Estab. 1990. Annual 8-day workshop held in June. Participants apply in poetry, fiction, or creative nonfiction, and then participate in intensive daily workshops which focus on the generation and revision of significant new work. Held on the campus of Kenyon College in the rural village of Gambier, Ohio. Workshop leaders have included David Baker, Ron Carlson, Rebecca McClanahan, Rosanna Warren and Nancy Zafris.
Costs $1,995 (includes tuition, housing, meals).
Accommodations Participants stay in Kenyon College student housing.

N Ⓒ MAGNA CUM MURDER

The Mid America Crime Writing Festival, The E.B. and Bertha C. Ball Center, Ball State University, Muncie IN 47306. (765)285-8975. Fax: (765)747-9566. E-mail: magnacummurder@yahoo.com. Web site: www.magnacum

murder.com. **Contact:** Kathryn Kennison. Estab. 1994. Annual conference held in October. Average attendance: 350. Festival for readers and writers of crime writing. Held in the Horizon Convention Center and Historic Hotel Roberts.

Costs $195 (includes breakfast, boxed lunches, opening reception, Saturday evening banquet).

MIDWEST WRITERS WORKSHOP

Department of Journalism, Ball State University, 2800 Bethel Ave., Muncie IN 47306. (765)282-1055. Fax: (765)285-5997. E-mail: info@midwestwriters.org. Web site: www.midwestwriters.org. **Contact:** Jama Bigger, registrar. Estab. 1974. Annual workshop held in July. Conference duration: 3 days. Covers fiction, nonfiction, poetry, writing for children, how to find an agent, memoirs, Internet marketing and more. Speakers have included Steve Brewer, Crescent Dragonwagon, Dennis Hensley, Nickole Brown, Nelson Price, Hanoch McCarty, Jane Friedman (Writer's Digest Books) and more.

Costs $90-275; $25/ms evaluation.

WALLOON WRITERS' RETREAT

Springfield Arts, P.O. Box 304, Royal Oak MI 48068-0304. (248)589-3913. Fax: (248)589-9981. E-mail: johndlamb@ameritech.net. Web site: www.springfed.org. **Contact:** John D. Lamb, director. Estab. 1999. Annual conference held in late September. Average attendance: 75. New and established writers and poets attend workshops, readings, and provocative panel discussions. Held at Michigania on Walloon Lake, Michigan. Michigania is owned and operated by the University of Michigan Alumni Association. Speakers have included Jane Hamilton, Jacquelyn Mitchard, Mary Jo Salter, Brad Leithauser, Doug Stanton, Craig Holden, Chuck Pfarrer, Gary Metras and M.L. Liebler.

Costs $535-600/single occupancy; $460-500/double occupancy; $360/no lodging (includes workshops, meals).

Accommodations Attendees stay in spruce-paneled cabins. Arranges shuttle rides to/from the Traverse City Airport.

Additional Informations Attendees may submit their work for craft discussion and/or conference tutorials; send 3 copies of 3 poems or 5 pages of prose.

N: WESTERN RESERVE WRITERS' CONFERENCE

Lakeland Community College, 7700 Clocktower Dr., Kirtland OH 44060-5198. (440)525-7116 or (800)589-8520. E-mail: deencr@aol.com. Web site: www.deannaadams.com. **Contact:** Deanna Adams, conference coordinator. Estab. 1983. Biannual. Biannual conference held in March and September. Average attendance: 120. Conference covers fiction, nonfiction, business of writing, children's writing, science fiction/fantasy, women's fiction, mysteries, poetry, short stories, etc. Classes take place on a community college campus. Editors and agents will be available for meetings with attendees.

Costs $65 for March mini-conference (half day); $79 for September all-day conference, including lunch. There is an additional fee for agent consultations.

Additional Informations Presenters are veterans in their particular genres. There will be a prestigious keynote speaker at the September conference. Check Web site 6 weeks prior to the event for guidelines and updates. Send inquiries via e-mail.

THE WOMEN WRITERS CONFERENCE

232 E. Maxwell St., Lexington KY 40506. (859)257-2874. E-mail: wwk.info@gmail.com. Web site: www.thewomenwritersconference.org. **Contact:** Julie Kuzneski Wrinn. Estab. 1979. Annual. The conference switches months and dates each year. Programming is presented in a festival atmosphere and includes small-group workshops, panel discussions, master classes, readings, film screenings, and performances. Presenters include Sara Vowell, Patricia Smith, Hayden Herrera, Diane Gilliam Fisher, Jawole Willa Jo Zollar and the Urban Bush Woman, Sonia Sanchez, Heather Raffo, Mabel Maney, Phoebe Gloeckner, Lauren Weinstein, Kim Ganter, Jane Vandenburgh, and Alex Beauchamp.

Additional Informations Visit the Web site to register and get more information.

WRITE-TO-PUBLISH CONFERENCE

WordPro Communications Services, 9118 W Elmwood Dr., #1G, Niles IL 60714-5820. (847)296-3964. Fax: (847)296-0754. E-mail: lin@writetopublish.com. Web site: www.writetopublish.com. **Contact:** Lin Johnson, director. Estab. 1971. Annual conference held June 4-7, 2008. Conference duration: 4 days. Average attendance: 250. Conference on writing fiction, nonfiction, devotions, and magazine articles for the Christian market. Held at Wheaton College in Wheaton, Illinois. Speakers have included Dr. Dennis E. Hensley, Ken Peterson (Tyndale House), Craig Bubeck (Cook), Joan Alexander, Allan Fisher (Crossway Books & Bibles), Joyce Hart (Hartline Literary Agency), Betsy Newenhuyse (Moody Publishers), and Ginger Kolbaba (Marriage Partnership).

Costs $450 (includes all sessions, Saturday night banquet, 1 ms evaluation); $95/meals.
Accommodations Campus residence halls: $220/double; $300/single. A list of area hotels is also on the Web site.

WRITERS RETREAT WORKSHOP

E-mail: wrw04@netscape.net. Web site: www.writersretreatworkshop.com. **Contact:** Gail Provost Stockwell, co-founder and creative director. Estab. 1987. Annual workshop held in May (through June). Conference duration: 10 days. Focuses on fiction and narrative nonfiction books in progress (all genres). This is an intensive learning experience for small groups of serious-minded writers. Founded by the late Gary Provost (one of the country's leading writing instructors) and his wife Gail (an award-winning author). The goal is for students to leave with a solid understanding of the marketplace, as well as the craft of writing a novel. Held at the Marydale Retreat Center in Erlanger, Kentucky (just south of Cincinnati, Ohio). Speakers have included Becky Motew, Donald Maass, Jennifer Crusie, Michael Palmer, Nancy Pickard, Elizabeth Lyon, Lauren Mosko (Writer's Digest Books), Adam Marsh (Reece Halsey North), and Peter H. McGuigan (Sanford J. Greenburger Literary Agency).
Costs $1,725 (includes meals, housing, consultations, materials). Scholarships are available.

NORTH CENTRAL (IA, MN, NE, ND, SD, WI)

GREAT LAKES WRITER'S WORKSHOP

Alverno College, 3400 S. 43rd St., P.O. Box 343922, Milwaukee WI 53234-3922. (414)382-6176. Fax: (414)382-6088. Web site: www.alverno.edu. **Contact:** Nancy Krase, nancy.krause@alverno.edu. Estab. 1985. Annual workshop held in June. Average attendance: 100. Workshop focuses on a variety of subjects, including fiction, writing for magazines, freelance writing, writing for children, poetry, marketing, etc. Participants may select individual workshops or opt to attend the entire weekend session. The workshop is held at Alverno College in Milwaukee, Wisconsin.
Costs In the past, the entire program cost $115 (includes breakfast and lunch with the keynote author).
Accommodations Attendees must make their own travel arrangements. Accommodations are available on campus; rooms are in residence halls. There are also hotels in the surrounding area.
Additional Informations View brochure online or send SASE after March. Send inquiries via fax.

GREEN LAKE WRITERS CONFERENCE

W2511 State Road 23, Green Lake WI 54941-9599. (920)294-3323. E-mail: program@glcc.org. Web site: www.glcc.org. **Contact:** Program coordinator. Estab. 1948. Annual conference held in August. Conference duration: 1 week. Faculty lead workshops on fiction, poetry, nonfiction, children's writing, and inspirational writing. Speakers have included Melanie Rigney, Ellen Kort, Barbara Smith, Joyce Ellis, Sharon Hart Addy, Mary Ann O'Roark, and Cecil Murphey.
Costs $942-1,082/single occupancy; $627-697 per person/double occupancy (includes program, housing, meals); $150/commuters. Scholarships are available.

IOWA SUMMER WRITING FESTIVAL

C215 Seashore Hall, University of Iowa, Iowa City IA 52242. (319)335-4160. Fax: (319)335-4039. E-mail: iswfestival@uiowa.edu. Web site: www.uiowa.edu/~iswfest. **Contact:** Amy Margolis, director. Estab. 1987. Annual festival held in June and July. Conference duration: Workshops are 1 week or a weekend. Average attendance: Limited to 12 people/class, with over 1,500 participants throughout the summer. "We offer courses across the genres: novel, short story, poetry, essay, memoir, humor, travel, playwriting, screenwriting, writing for children, and women's writing." Held at the University of Iown campus. Speakers have included Marvin Bell, Lan Samantha Chang, John Dalton, Hope Edelman, Katie Ford, Patricia Foster, Bret Anthony Johnston, Barbara Robinette Moss, among others.
Costs $500-525/week; $250/weekend workshop. Housing and meals are separate.
Accommodations Iowa House: $75/night; Sheraton: $88/night (rates subject to change).
Additional Informations Brochures are available in February. Inquire via e-mail or fax.

NEBRASKA SUMMER WRITERS' CONFERENCE

Department of English, University of Nebraska, Lincoln NE 68588-0333. (402)472-1834. E-mail: jagee@unl.edu; nswc@unl.edu. Web site: www.nswc.org. **Contact:** Jonis Agee, director. Annual conference held in June. Conference duration: 1 week. Faculty include Sara Gruen, Ron Hansen, Li-Young Lee, Sean Doolittle, Lee Martin, Dorianne Laux, Jim Shepard, Judith Kitchen, Joe Mackall, Hilda Raz, William Kloefkorn, agent Sonia Pabley, Timothy Schaffert, Brent Spencer, Stan Sanvel Rubin, agent Emma Sweeney, Jane Von Mehren (vice president, Random House).
Costs $250/weekend; $525/week; $700/combo; $800-1,300/master classes.

UNIVERSITY OF WISCONSIN AT MADISON WRITERS INSTITUTE

610 Langdon St., Madison WI 53703. (608)262-3447. Fax: (608)265-2475. Web site: www.dcs.wisc.edu/lsa. **Contact:** Christine DeSmet, director. Estab. 1990. Annual conference held in April. (The 2008 conference is set for April 18-20, 2008.). Average attendance: 200. Conference on fiction and nonfiction held at the university of Wisconsin at Madison. Guest speakers are published authors, editors, and agents.

Costs Approximately $225 for the weekend; $135 per day; critiques and pitch meetings extra.

Accommodations Information on accommodations is sent with registration confirmation.

Additional Informations Critiques are available. Go online for conference brochure.

SOUTH CENTRAL (CO, KS, MO, NM, OK, TX)

AGENTS AND EDITORS CONFERENCE

Writers' League of Texas, 1501 W. Fifth St., Suite E-2, Austin TX 78703. (512)499-8914. Fax: (512)499-0441. E-mail: wlt@writersleague.org. Web site: www.writersleague.org. **Contact:** Kristy Bordine, membership director. Estab. 1982. Annual conference held in the summer. Conference duration: 3 days. Average attendance: 300. Provides writers with the opportunity to meet top literary agents and editors from New York and the West Coast. Topic include: finding and working with agents and publishers, writing and marketing fiction and nonfiction, dialogue, characterization, voice, research, basic and advanced fiction writing, the business of writing, and workshops for genres. Speakers have included Malaika Adero, Stacey Barney, Sha-Shana Crichton, Jessica Faust, Dena Fischer, Mickey Freiberg, Jill Grosjean, Anne Hawkins, Jim Hornfischer, Jennifer Joel, David Hale Smith and Elisabeth Weed.

Costs $295-$345.

Additional Informations Contests and awards programs are offered separately. Brochures are available upon request.

ASPEN SUMMER WORDS LITERARY FESTIVAL & WRITING RETREAT

Aspen Writers' Foundation, 110 E. Hallam St., #116, Aspen CO 81611. (970)925-3122. Fax: (970)925-5700. E-mail: info@aspenwriters.org. Web site: www.aspenwriters.org. **Contact:** Jamie Kravitz, director of programs. Estab. 1976. Annual conference held the fourth week of June. Conference duration: 5 days. Average attendance: 150 at writing retreat; 300+ at literary festival. Retreat for fiction, creative nonfiction, poetry, magazine writing, food writing, and literature. Festival includes author readings, craft talks, panel discussions with publishing industry insiders, professional consultations with editors and agents, and social gatherings. Retreat faculty members include (in 2007: Andrea Barzi, Katherine Fausset, Anjali Singh, Lisa Grubka, Amber Qureshi, Joshua Kendall, Keith Flynn, Robert Bausch, Amy Bloom, Percival Everett, Danzy Senna, Bharti Kirchner, Gary Ferguson, Dorianne Laux. Festival presenters include (in 2007): Ngugi Wa Thiong,o, Wole Soyinka, Chimamanda Ngozi Adichie, Alaa Al Aswany, Henry Louis Gates, Jr., Leila Aboulela, and many more!.

Costs $475/retreat; $175-250/seminar; Tuition includes daily continental breakfast and lunch, plus one evening reception; a limited number of half-tuition scholarships are available; $200/festival; $35/professional consultation.

Accommodations Discount lodging at the conference site will be available. $170/one-bedroom condo; $255/ two-bedroom condo; $127.50/shared two-bedroom condo.

Additional Informations Workshops admission deadline is March 30, or until all workshops are filled. Juried admissions for some workshops; writing sampl required with application to juried workshops. Mss will be discussed during workshop. Literary festival and some retreat programs are open to the public on first-come, first-served basis; no mss required. Brochure, application and complete admissions information available on Web site, or request by phone, fax or e-mail. Include mailing address with all e-mail requests.

AUSTIN FILM FESTIVAL & CONFERENCE

1604 Nueces St., Austin TX 78701. (800)310-3378 or (512)478-4795. Fax: (512)478-6205. Web site: www.austinfilmfestival.com. **Contact:** Linnea Toney, conference director. Estab. 1994. Annual conference held in October. Conference duration: 4 days. Average attendance: 2,200. This festival is the first organization of its kind to focus on writers' unique creative contribution to the film and television industries. The conference takes place during the first four days of the festival. The event presents more than 75 panels, round tables and workshops that address various aspects of screenwriting and filmmaking. The Austin Film Festival is held in downtown Austin at the Driskill and Stephen F. Austin hotels. The AFF boasts a number of events and services for emerging and professional writers and filmmakers. Past participants include Robert Altman, Wes Anderson, James L. Brooks, Joel & Ethan Coen, Russell Crowe, Barry Levinson, Darren Star, Robert Duvall, Buck Henry, Dennis Hopper, Lawrence Kasdan, John Landis, Garry Shandling, Bryan Singer, Oliver Stone, Sandra Bullock, Harold Ramis and Owen Wilson.

Costs 2007 rate: $300 before May 16 (includes entrance to all panels, workshops, and roundtables during the 4-day conference, as well as all films during the 8-night film exhibitions and the opening and closing night parties). Go online for other offers.

Accommodations Discounted rates on hotel accommodations are availalbe to attendees if the reservations are made through the Austin Film Festival office.

Additional Informations The Austin Film Festival is considered one of the most accessible festivals, and Austin is the premier town for networking because when industry people are here, they are relaxed and friendly. The Austin Film Festival holds annual screenplay/teleplay and film competitions, as well as a Young Filmmakers Program. Check online for competition details and festival information. Inquire via e-mail or fax.

GLORIETA CHRISTIAN WRITERS CONFERENCE

CLASServices, Inc., 3311 Candelaria NE, Suite 1, Albuquerque NM 87107-1952. (800)433-6633. Fax: (505)899-9282. E-mail: info@classervices.com. Web site: www.glorietacwc.com. **Contact:** Linda Jewell, seminar manager. Estab. 1997. Annual conference held in October. Conference duration: Wednesday afternoon through Sunday lunch. Average attendance: 350. Includes programs for all types of writing. Agents, editors, and professional writers will be speaking and available for meetings with attendees.

Costs $450/early registration (1 month in advance); $495/program only. Critiques are available for an addition charge.

Accommodations Hotel rooms are available at the LifeWay Glorieta Conference Center. Santa Fe Shuttle offers service from the Albuquerque or Santa Fe airports to the conference center. Hotel rates vary. "We suggest you make airline and rental car reservations early due to other events in the area."

Additional Informations Brochures are available April 1. Inquire via e-mail, phone, or fax, or visit the Web site.

HEARTLAND WRITERS CONFERENCE

P.O. Box 652, Kennett MO 63857. (573)297-3325. Fax: (573)297-3352. E-mail: hwg@heartlandwriters.org. Web site: www.heartlandwriters.org. **Contact:** Harry Spiller, conference coordinator. Estab. 1990. Biennial (even years) conference held in June. Conference duration: 3 days. Average attendance: 160. Covers popular fiction (all genres), nonfiction, children's writing, screenwritin, and poetry. Held at the Best Western Coach House Inn in Sikeston, Missouri. Speakers have included Alice Orr, Jennifer Jackson, Ricia Mainhardt, Christy Fletcher, Sue Yuen, and Evan Marshall. Agents will be speaking and available for meetings with attendees.

Costs $215 for advance registrants; $250 for general registration (includes lunch on Friday and Saturday, awards banquet on Sunday, hospitality room, and get-acquainted mixer Thursday night).

Accommodations Blocks of rooms are available at a special rate ($55-85/night) at the conference venue and 2 nearby motels.

Additional Informations Brochures are available in late January. Inquire via e-mail or fax.

TONY HILLERMAN WRITERS CONFERENCE

304 Calle Oso, Santa Fe NM 87501. (505)471-1565. E-mail: wordharvest@wordharvest.com. Web site: www.hillermanconference.com. Estab. 2001. Annual conference held in November. Conference duration: 4 days. Average attendance: 150-200. Workshops on writing good dialogue, building your platform, writing series that sell, and adding humor to your writing are geared toward mystery writers. Held at the Hyatt Regency in Albuquerque, New Mexico. Speakers have included Tony Hillerman, Michael McGarrity, J.A. Jance, Margaret Coel, Sean Murphy, Virginia Swift, James D. Doss, Gail Larsen, Luther Wilson, and Craig Johnson.

Costs $395 before August 1; $435 after August 1; $200/Friday only; $250/Saturday only.

Accommodations $99/night at the Hyatt Regency.

PIKES PEAK WRITERS CONFERENCE

4164 Austin Bluffs Pkwy., #246, Colorado Springs CO 80918. (719)531-5723. E-mail: info@ppwc.net. Web site: www.ppwc.net. Estab. 1993. Annual conference held in April. Conference duration: 3 days. Average attendance: 400. Workshops, presentations, and panels focus on writing and publishing mainstream and genre fiction (romance, science fiction/fantasy, suspense/thrillers, action/adventure, mysteries, children's, young adult). Agents and editors are available for meetings with attendees on Saturday.

Costs 2007 costs: $295/PPW members; $350/nonmembers (includes all meals).

Accommodations Wyndham Colorado Springs holds a block of rooms at a special rate for attendees until late March.

Additional Informations Readings with critiques are available on Friday afternoon. Also offers a contest for unpublished writers; entrants need not attend the conference. Deadline: November 1. Registration and contest entry forms are online; brochures are available in January. Send inquiries via e-mail.

ⓃSANTA FE WRITERS CONFERENCE

Southwest Literary Center, 826 Camino de Monte Rey, A3, Santa Fe NM 87505. (505)577-1125. Fax: (505)982-7125. E-mail: litcenter@recursos.org. Web site: www.santafewritersconference.com. **Contact:** Jenice Gharib, director. Estab. 1985. Annual conference held in June. Conference duration: 5 days. Average attendance: 50. Conference offering intitmate workshops in fiction, poetry, and creative nonfiction. Speakers have included Lindsay Ahl, Elizabeth Benedict, Lisa D. Chavez, and Brian Kiteley.
Costs $575.
Accommodations A special rate is offered at the St. Francis Hotel.
Additional Informations Brochure are available online or by e-mail, fax, or phone.

ⓃSCENE OF THE CRIME CONFERENCE

Kansas Writers Association, P.O. Box 2236, Wichita KS 67201. (316)208-6961. E-mail: gordon@gordonkessler.com. Web site: www.kwawriters.org. **Contact:** Gordon Kessler. Annual. Annual conference held in April. Features agent/editor consultations, mixer, banquet and two days of speaker sessions with detectives, government agents, CSI professionals, editors, agents and authors.
Accommodations Wichita Airport Hilton.

THE SCREENWRITING CONFERENCE IN SANTA FE

P.O. Box 29762, Santa Fe NM 87592. (866)424-1501. Fax: (505)424-8207. E-mail: writeon@scsfe.com. Web site: www.scsfe.com. **Contact:** Larry N. Stouffer, founder. Estab. 1999. Annual conference held the week following Memorial Day. Average attendance: 175. The conference is divided into 2 componants: The Screenwriting Symposium, designed to teach the art and craft of screenwriting, and The Hollywood Connection, which speaks to the business aspects of screenwriting. Held at The Lodge in Santa Fe.
Costs $695 for The Screenwriting Symposium; $200 for The Hollywood Connection. Early discounts are available. Includes 9 hours of in-depth classroom instruction, over 2 dozen workshops, panel discussions, a screenplay competition, academy labs for advanced screenwriters, live scene readings, and social events.

SOUTHWEST WRITERS CONFERENCE MINI-CONFERENCE SERIES

3721 Morris St. NE, Suite A, Albuquerque NM 87111. (505)265-9485. Fax: (505)265-9483. E-mail: swwriters@juno.com. Web site: www.southwestwriters.org. Estab. 1983. Annual mini-conferences held throughout the year. Average attendance: 50. Speakers include writers, editors, agents, publicists, and producers. All areas of writing, including screenwriting and poetry, are represented.
Costs Fee includes conference sessions and lunch.
Accommodations Usually have official airline and hotel discount rates.
Additional Informations Sponsors a contest judged by authors, editors from major publishers, and agents from New York, Los Angeles, etc. There are 19 categories. Deadline: May 1. Entry fee is $29/members; $44/nonmembers. There are monthly contests with various themes—$5/member, $10/non-member. See Web site for details. Brochures/guidelines are available online or for a SASE. Inquire via e-mail or phone. A one-on-one appointment may be set up at the conference with the editor or agent of your choice on a first-registered, first-served basis.

STEAMBOAT SPRINGS WRITERS CONFERENCE

Steamboat Springs Arts Council, P.O. Box 774284, Steamboat Springs CO 80477. (970)879-8079. E-mail: sswriters@cs.com. Web site: www.steamboatwriters.com. **Contact:** Harriet Freiberger, director. Estab. 1982. Annual conference held in mid-July. Conference duration: 1 day. Average attendance: approximately 35. Attendance is limited. Featured areas of instruction change each year. Held at the restored train depot. Speakers have included Carl Brandt, Jim Fergus, Avi, Robert Greer, Renate Wood, Connie Willis, Margaret Coel and Kent Nelson.
Costs $45 prior to June 1; $55 after June 1 (includes seminars, catered lunch). A post-conference dinner is also available.
Additional Informations Brochures are available in April for a SASE. Send inquiries via e-mail.

TAOS SUMMER WRITERS' CONFERENCE

Department of English Language and Literature, MSC 03 217091, University of New Mexico, Albuquerque NM 87131-0001. (505)277-5572. Fax: (505)277-2950. E-mail: taosconf@unm.edu. Web site: www.unm.edu/~taosconf. **Contact:** Sharon Oard Warner, Barbara van Buskirk. Estab. 1999. Annual conference held in July. Conference duration: 1 week. Offers workshops in novel writing, short story writing, screenwriting, poetry, creative nonfiction, travel writing, historical fiction, memoir, and revision. Participants may also schedule a consultation with a visiting agent/editor.
Costs $300/weekend; $600/week; $825/both. Scholarships are available.
Accommodations $60-100/night at the Sagebrush Inn; $89/night at Comfort Suites.

◎ WRITERS WORKSHOP IN SCIENCE FICTION

English Department/University of Kansas, Lawrence KS 66045-2115. (785)864-3380. Fax: (785)864-1159. E-mail: jgunn@ku.edu. Web site: www.ku.edu/ ~ sfcenter. **Contact:** James Gunn, professor. Estab. 1985. Annual workshop held in late June or early July. Average attendance: 15. Conference for writing and marketing science fiction. Classes meet in university housing on the University of Kansas campus. Workshop sessions operate informally in a lounge. Speakers have included Frederik Pohl, Kij Johnson, and Chris McKitterick. Kij Johnson will offer a separate Novel Writers Workshop in 2007. Also, in 2007, writers may participate in the Campbell Conference, Science Fiction Research Association meeting, and Heinlein Centennial in nearby Kansas City during the second weekend in July.

Costs Tuition is $400. Housing and meals are not included.

Accommodations Housing information is available. Several airport shuttle services offer reasonable transportation from the Kansas City International Airport to Lawrence. During past conferences, students were housed in a student dormitory at $15.50/day (double); $33/day (single).

Additional Informations "Admission to the workshop is by submission of an acceptable story. Two additional stories should be submitted by the middle of June. These 3 stories are distributed to other participants for critquing and are the basis for the first week of the workshop. One story is rewritten for the second week. Send SASE for brochure/guidelines. This workshop is intended for writers who have just started to sell their work or need that extra bit of understanding or skill to become a published writer."

WEST (AZ, CA, HI, NV, UT)

◎ BYU WRITING AND ILLUSTRATING FOR YOUNG READERS WORKSHOP

348 HCEB, Brigham Young University, Provo UT 84602. (801)422-2568. E-mail: cw348@byu.edu. Web site: wfyr.byu.edu. Estab. 2000. Annual workshop held in June. Conference duration: 5 days. Average attendance: 100. Learn how to write/illustrate and publish in the children,s and young adult fiction and nonfiction markets. Beginning and advanced writers/illustrators are tutored in a small-group setting by published authors/artists and receive instruction from editors, a major publishing house representative and a literary agent. Held at Brigham Young University's Harmon Conference Center. Speakers have included Edward Necarsulmer, Tracy Gates, and Jill Davis.

Costs $439 (includes all workshops/sessions, Thursday banquet); $109/afternoon only.

Accommodations A block of rooms is reserved at the Super 8 Motel for $49/night. Airport shuttles are available.

Additional Informations Guidelines and registration are on the Web site.

◎ DESERT DREAMS

(866)267-2249. E-mail: desertdreams@desertroserwa.org. Web site: desertroserwa.org. **Contact:** Susan Lanier-Graham, conference coordinator. Estab. 1986. Conference held every other April. Conference duration: 3 days. Average attendance: 250. Covers marketing, fiction, screenwriting, and research. Upcoming speakers and agents will include Jessica Faust (BookEnds), Deirdre Knight (The Knight Agency), other agents, editors, Vicki Lewis Thompson, Lori Wilde, Mary Jo Putney, Sherrilyn Kenyon and more. Agents and editors will be speaking and available for meetings with attendees.

Costs $208-218 (includes meals, seminars, appointments with agents/editors).

Accommodations Discounted rates for attendees is negotiated at the Crowne Plaza San Marcos Resort in Chandler, Ariz.

Additional Informations Send inquiries via e-mail. Visit Web site for updates and complete details.

EAST OF EDEN WRITERS CONFERENCE

P.O. Box 3254, Santa Clara CA 95055. E-mail: vp@southbaywriters.com. Web site: www.southbaywriters.com. **Contact:** Vice President/Programs Chair of South Bay Writers. Estab. 2000. Biannual confereence held in September. Average attendance: 300. Writers of all levels are welcome. Pitch sessions to agents and publishers are available, as are meetings with authors and editors. Workshops address the craft and the business of writing. Location: Salinas, Calif.—Steinbeck Country.

Costs Costs vary. The full conference (Friday and Saturday) is approximately $250; Saturday only is approximately $175. The fee includes meals, workshops and pitch/meeting sessions. Optional events extra.

Accommodations Negotiated rates at local hotels—$85 per night, give or take.

Additional Informations The East of Eden conference is run by writers/volunteers from the California Writers Club, South Bay Branch. For details about our next conference(s), please visit our Web site or send an SASE.

LA JOLLA WRITERS CONFERENCE

P.O. Box 178122, San Diego CA 92177. (858)467-1978. Fax: (858)467-1971. E-mail: jkuritz@san.rr.com. Web site: www.lajollawritersconference.com. **Contact:** Jared Kuritz, co-director. Estab. 2001. Annual conference held in October. Conference duration: 3 days. Average attendance: 200. "In addition to covering nearly every genre, we also take particular pride in educating our attendees on the business aspect of the book industry by having agents, editors, publishers, publicists, and distributors teach classes. Our conference offers 2 types of classes: lecture sessions that run for 50 minutes, and workshops that run for 110 minutes. Each block period is dedicated to either workshop or lecture-style classes. During each block period, there will be 6-8 classes on various topics from which you can choose to attend. For most workshop classes, you are encouraged to bring written work for review." Literary agents from The Andrea Brown Literary Agency, The Dijkstra Agency, The McBride Agency and Full Circle Literary Group have participated in the past.

Costs $265 early bird; $325 regular (includes access to all classes, keynote addresses, Friday and Saturday evening receptions, author book signing).

Accommodations "We arrange a discounted rate with the hotel that hosts the conference. Please refer to the Web site."

Additional Informations "Our conference is completely non-commercial. Our goal is to foster a true learning environment. As such, our faculty is chosen based on their expertise and willingness to make themselves completely available to the attendees." Brochures are online; send inquiries via e-mail or fax.

LEAGUE OF UTAH WRITERS ANNUAL CONFERENCE AND ROUNDUP

P.O. Box 18430, Kearns UT 84118. Web site: www.luwrite.com. **Contact:** Dorothy Crofts. Estab. 1935. Annual conference held in September. Conference duration: 2 days. Offers up to 16 workshops, a keynote speaker, and an awards banquet. Speakers cover subjects from generating ideas, to writing a novel, to working with a publisher.

Additional Informations This conference is held in a different site in Utah each year. See the Web site for updated information.

MAUI WRITERS CONFERENCE

P.O. Box 1118, Kihei HI 96753. (808)879-0061. Fax: (808)879-6233. E-mail: writers@mauiwriters.com. Web site: www.mauiwriters.com. **Contact:** Shannon Tullius. Estab. 1993. Annual conference held at the end of August (Labor Day weekend). Conference duration: 4 days. Average attendance: 600. Covers fiction, nonfiction, poetry, screenwriting, children's/young adult writing, horror, mystery, romance, science fiction, and journalism. Held at the Wailea Marriot Resort. Speakers have included Kimberley Cameron (Reece Halsey North), Susan Crawford (Crawford Literary Agency), Jillian Manus (Manus & Associates), Jenny Bent (Trident Media Group), Catherine Fowler (Redwood Agency), James D. Hornfischer (Hornfischer Literary Management), and Debra Goldstein (The Creative Culture). Many of these agents will be at the 2007 conference, where they will be on panels discussing the business of publishing and will be available for one-on-one consultations with aspiring authors.

Additional Informations "We offer a comprehensive view of the business of publishing, with more than 1,500 consultation slots with industry agents, editors, and screenwriting professionals, as well as workshops and sessions covering writing instruction. Consider attending the MWC Writers Retreat immediately preceding the conference. Write, call, or visit our Web site for current updates and full details on all of our upcoming programs."

N NATJA ANNUAL CONFERENCE & MARKETPLACE

North American Travel Journalists Association, 531 Main St., #902, El Segundo CA 90245. (310)836-8712. Fax: (310)836-8769. E-mail: hillary@natja.org. Web site: www.natja.org/conference. **Contact:** Elizabeth H. Beshear, executive director. Estab. 2003. Annual conference held in May. Conference duration: 3 days. Average attendance: 250. Provides professional development for travel journalists and gives them the chance to market themselves to destinations and cultivate relationships to further their careers. Previous speakers have included Lisa Lenoir (*Chicago Sun-Times*), Steve Millburg (*Coastal Living*) and Peter Yesawich.

Costs $350 for media attendees (includes hotel accommodations, meals, in-conference transportation); $100 extra for round-trip airline tickets.

Accommodations Different destinations host the conference each year, all at hotels with conference centers.

Additional Informations E-mail, call, or go online for more information.

NO CRIME UNPUBLISHED™ MYSTERY WRITERS' CONFERENCE

Sisters in Crime—Los Angeles Chapter, 1772-J Avenida De Los Arboles, #233, Thousand Oaks CA 91362. E-mail: sistersincrimela@yahoo.com. Web site: www.sistersincrimela.com. Estab. 1995. Annual conference held in June. Conference duration: 1 day. Average attendance: 200. Conference on mystery and crime writing. Offers craft and forensic sessions, a keynote speaker, a luncheon speaker, author and agent panels, and book signings.

Additional Informations Conference information is available on the Web site or a brochure is available for SASE.

PIMA WRITERS' WORKSHOP

Pima College, 2202 W. Anklam Road, Tucson AZ 85709. (520)206-6084. Fax: (520)206-6020. E-mail: mfiles@pi ma.edu. Web site: www.pima.edu. **Contact:** Meg Files, director. Estab. 1988. Annual conference held in May. Conference duration: 3 days. Average attendance: 300. Covers fiction, nonfiction, poetry, and scriptwriting for beginner or experienced writers. The workshop offers sessions on writing short stories, novels, nonfiction articles and books, children's and juvenile stories, poetry, and screenplays. Sessions are held in the Center for the Arts on Pima Community College's West campus. Speakers have included Larry McMurtry, Barbara Kingsolver, Jerome Stern, Connie Willis, Jack Heffron, Jeff Hermon, and Robert Morgan. Agents will be speaking and available for meetings with attendees.

Costs $75 (can include ms critique). Participants may attend for college credit, in which case fees are $103 for Arizona residents and $164 for out-of-state residents. Meals and accommodations are not included.

Accommodations Information on local accommodations is made available. Special workshop rates are available at a specified motel close to the workshop site (about $65/night).

Additional Informations The workshop atmosphere is casual, friendly, and supportive, and guest authors are very accessible. Readings and panel discussions are offered, as well as talks and manuscript sessions. Participants may have up to 20 pages critiqued by the author of their choice. Mss must be submitted 3 weeks before the workshop. Conference brochure/guidelines available for SASE. Accepts inquiries by e-mail.

SAN DIEGO STATE UNIVERSITY WRITERS' CONFERENCE

SDSU College of Extended Studies, 5250 Campanile Dr., San Diego State University, San Diego CA 92182-1920. (619)594-2517. Fax: (619)594-8566. E-mail: jgreene@mail.sdsu.edu. Web site: www.ces.sdsu.edu/writers. **Contact:** Jim Greene, program coordinator. Estab. 1984. Annual conference held in January. Conference duration: 2 days. Average attendance: 375. Covers fiction, nonfiction, scriptwriting and e-books. Held at the Double-tree Hotel in Mission Valley. Each year the conference offers a variety of workshops for the beginner and advanced writers. This conference allows the individual writer to choose which workshop best suits his/her needs. In addition to the workshops, editor reading appointments and agent/editor consultation appointments are provided so attendees may meet with editors and agents one-on-one to discuss specific questions. A reception is offered Saturday immediately following the workshops, offering attendees the opportunity to socialize with the faculty in a relaxed atmosphere. Last year, approximately 60 faculty members attended.

Costs Approximately $365-485 (2008 costs will be published with a fall update of the Web site).

Accommodations Doubletree Hotel (800)222-TREE. Attendees must make their own travel arrangements.

SAN FRANCISCO WRITERS CONFERENCE

1029 Jones St., San Francisco CA 94109. (415)673-0939. Fax: (415)673-0367. E-mail: sfwriterscon@aol.com. Web site: www.sfwriters.org. **Contact:** Michael Larsen, director. Estab. 2003. Annual conference held President's Day weekend in February. Average attendance: 400. Top authors, respected literary agents, and major publishing houses are at the event so attendees can make face-to-face contact with all the right people. Writers of nonfiction, fiction, poetry, and specialty writing (children's books, cookbooks, travel, etc.) will all benefit from the event. There are important sessions on marketing, self-publishing, and trends in the publishing industry. Plus, there's an optional 3-hour session called Speed Dating for Agents where attendees can meet with 20+ agents. Speakers have included Gayle Lynds, Jennifer Crusie, ALan Jones, Lalita Tademy, Jamie Raab, Mary Roach, Bob Mayer, Firoozeh Dumas, Zilpha Keatley Snyder. More than 20 agents and editors participate each year, many of whom will be available for meetings with attendees.

Costs $595 with price breaks for early registration (includes all sessions/workshops/keynotes, Speed Dating with Editors, opening gala at the Top of the Mark, 2 continental breakfasts, 2 lunches). Optional Speed Dating for Agents is $45.

Accommodations The Intercontinental Mark Hopkins Hotel is a historic landmark at the top of Nob Hill in San Francisco. Elegant rooms and first-class service are offered to attendees at the rate of $152/night. The hotel is located so that everyone arriving at the Oakland or San Francisco airport can take BART to either the Embarcadero or Powell Street exits, then walk or take a cable car or taxi directly to the hotel.

Additional Informations Present yourself in a professional manner and the contact you will make will be invaluable to your writing career. Brochures and registration are online.

SANTA BARBARA WRITERS CONFERENCE

P.O. Box 6627, Santa Barbara CA 93160. (805)964-0367. E-mail: info@sbwritersconference.com. Web site: www.sbwritersconference.com. **Contact:** Marcia Meier, conference diretor. Estab. 1973. Annual conference held in June. Average attendance: 450. Covers poetry, fiction, nonfiction, journalism, playwriting, screenwriting, travel writing, young adult, children's literature, chick lit, humor, and marketing. Speakers have included Kenneth Atchity, Michael Larsen, Elizabeth Pomada, Bonnie Nadell, Stuart Miller, Angela Rinaldi, Katherine Sands, Don Congdon, Mike Hamilburg, Sandra Dijkstra, Paul Fedorko, Andrea Brown and Deborah Grosvenor.

Agents appear on a panel, plus there will be an agents and editors day when writers can pitch their projects in one-on-one meetings.

Accommodations Fess Parker's Doubletree Resort.

Additional Informations Individual critiques are also available. Submit 1 ms of no more than 3,000 words in advance (include SASE). Competitions with awards are sponsored as part of the conference. E-mail or call for brochure and registration forms.

◎ SOCIETY OF CHILDREN'S BOOK WRITERS & ILLUSTRATORS ANNUAL SUMMER CONFERENCE ON WRITING AND ILLUSTRATING FOR CHILDREN

8271 Beverly Blvd., Los Angeles CA 90048-4515. (323)782-1010. Fax: (323)782-1892. E-mail: scbwi@scbwi.org. Web site: www.scbwi.org. **Contact:** Stephen Mooser, president. Estab. 1972. Annual conference held in early August. Conference duration: 4 days. Average attendance: 1,000. Held at the Century Plaza Hotel in Los Angeles. Speakers have included Andrea Brown, Steven Malk , Scott Treimel, AShley Bryan, Bruce Coville, Karen Hesse, Harry Mazer, Lucia Monfried, and Russell Freedman. Agents willb e speaking and sometimes participate in ms critiques.

Costs Approximately $400 (does not include hotel room).

Accommodations Information on overnight accommodations is made available.

Additional Informations Ms and illustration critiques are available. Brochure/guidelines are available in June online or for SASE.

TMCC WRITERS' CONFERENCE

5270 Neil Road, #216, Reno NV 89502. (775)829-9010. Fax: (775)829-9032. E-mail: wdce@tmcc.edu. Web site: wdce.tmcc.edu. **Contact:** Michael Croft, director. Estab. 1991. Annual conference held in April. Average attendance: 125. Focuses on fiction, poetry, and memoir, plus an assortment of other forms of writing, such as screenwriting, thrillers, mysteries, and nonfiction. There is always an array of speakers and presenters with impressive literary credentials, including agents and editors. Speakers have included Dorothy Allison, Karen Joy Fowler, James D. Houston, James N. Frey, Gary Short, Jane Hirschfield, Dorrianne Laux, Kim Addonizio, Amy Rennert, and Laurie Fox.

Costs Track A ($399) includes 4 days of workshops in fiction, poetry, and memoir, plus afternoon lectures, readings, and talks on the craft of writing and the business of publishing. Track B ($139) includes 2 days of lectures and readings. All participants can attend the writers' reception and the roundtable luncheons, during which attendees can chat with agents.

Accommodations The Nugget offers a special rate and shuttle service to the Reno/Tahoe International Airport, which is less than 20 minutes away.

Additional Informations "We will be changing locations in 2008. We do not know the location yet." The conference is open to all writers, regardless of their level of experience. Individual workshops meet for 4 mornings and are conducted by the same workshop leader throughout. Every effort is made to see that writers are placed with the appropriate leader. Brochures are available online and mailed in the fall. Send inquiries via e-mail.

UCLA EXTENSION WRITERS' PROGRAM

10995 Le Conte Ave., #440, Los Angeles CA 90024. (310)825-9415 or (800)388-UCLA. Fax: (310)206-7382. E-mail: writers@uclaextension.edu. Web site: www.uclaextension.org/writers. **Contact:** Cindy Lieberman, program manager. Estab. 1891. Courses are held quarterly as 1-day or intensive weekend workshops, or as 12-week courses. A 4-day Writers Studio is held every February. "As the largest and most comprehensive continuing education writing program in the US, the UCLA Extension Writers' Program is committed to providing the highest quality writing courses possible, on site and online, to a broad-based and culturally diverse community. "We offer an extraordinary variety of individual courses (over 550 annually), as well as certificate programs to meet the needs of our students. We also offer a screenplay competition, master classes, and script and ms consulations. Adult learners study with professional screenwriters, fiction writers, playwrights, poets, nonfiction writers, and writers of children's literature who bring practical experience, theoretical knowledge, and a variety of teaching styles and philosophies to the classrooms. Our open admissions policy and supportive atmosphere ensure that all students, whether they seek to write only for themselves or as professsionals, are inspired and guided to achieve their best work."

Costs $95/1-day workshop; $495/full-length courses; $3,250/9-month master classes.

Accommodations Students make their own arrangements. Out-of-town students are encouraged to take online courses.

Additional Informations Some advanced-level classes have ms submittal requirements; instructions are detailed in the Writers' Program Quarterly or UCLA Extension course catalog. Inquire via e-mail or fax.

NORTHWEST (AK, ID, MT, OR, WA, WY)

FLATHEAD RIVER WRITERS CONFERENCE

P.O. Box 7711, Kalispell MT 59904-7711. E-mail: answers@authorsoftheflathead.org. Web site: www.authorsoftheflathead.org. **Contact:** Val Smith. Estab. 1990. Annual conference held in early mid-October. Conference duration: 3 days. Average attendance: 100. "We provide several small, intense 3-day workshops before the general weekend conference." Workshops, panel discussions, and speakers focus on novels, nonfiction, screenwriting, short stories, magazine articles, and the writing industry. Held at the Grouse Mountain Lodge in Whitefish, Montana. Past speakers have included Sam Pinkus, Randy Wayne White, Donald Maass, Ann Rule, Cricket Pechstein, Marcela Landres, Amy Rennert, Ben Mikaelsen, Esmond Harmsworth, Linda McFall, and Ron Carlson. Agents will be speaking and available for meetings with attendees.

Costs $150 (includes breakfast and lunch, but not lodging).

Accommodations Rooms are available at a discounted rate of $100/night. Whitefish is a resort town, so less expensive lodging can be arranged.

Additional Informations "By limiting attendance to 100 people, we assure a quality experience and informal, easy access to the presenters and other attendees." Brochures are available in June; send inquiries via e-mail.

ℕ THE GLEN WORKSHOP

Image, 3307 Third Avenue W., Seattle WA 98119. (206)281-2988. Fax: (206)281-2335. E-mail: glenworkshop@imagejournal.org. Web site: www.imagejournal.org/glen. Estab. 1991. Annual workshop held in August. Conference duration: 1 week. Workshop focuses on fiction, poetry, spiritual writing, playwriting, screenwriting, songwriting, and mixed media. Writing classes combine general instruction and discussion with the workshop experience, in which each individual's works are read and discussed critically. Held at St. John's College in Santa Fe, New Mexico. Faculty has included Scott Cairns, Jeanine Hathaway, Bret Lott, Paula Huston, Arlene Hutton, David Denny, Barry Moser, Barry Krammes, Ginger Geyer, and Pierce Pettis.

Costs $500-960 (includes tuition, lodging, meals); $395-475/commuters (includes tuition, lunch). A limited number of partial scholarships are available.

Accommodations Offers dorm rooms, dorm suites, and apartments.

Additional Informations "Like *Image*, the Glen is grounded in a Christian perspective, but its tone is informal and hospitable to all spiritual wayfarers." Depending on the teacher, participants may need to submit workshop material prior to arrival (usually 10-25 pages).

ℕ IDAHO WRITERS LEAGUE WRITERS' CONFERENCE

P.O. Box 492, Kootenai, ID 83840. (208)290-8749. E-mail: Lramsey@supersat2.net. Web site: www.idahowritersleague.com. **Contact:** Sherry Ramsey. Estab. 1940. Annual floating conference. Next conference: Sept. 28-29, 2007. Average attendance: 80+. We have such writers as magazine freelance and children's book author, Kelly Milner Halls; and author of the 2006 Christian Women's Fiction Book of the Year, Nikki Arana.

Costs Cost: $125.

Additional Informations Check out our Web site at ww.idahowritersleague.com. Conference will be held at the Coeur d'Alene Inn in Coeur d'Alene, Idaho.

PNWA SUMMER WRITERS CONFERENCE

PMB 2717, 1420 NW Gilman Blvd., Issaquah WA 98027. (425)673-2665. E-mail: pnwa@pnwa.org. Web site: www.pnwa.org. Estab. 1955. Annual. All conferences are held in July. Conference duration: 4 days. Average attendance: 400. Attendees have the chance to meet agents and editors, learn craft from authors and uncover marketing secrets. Speakers have included J.A. Jance, Sheree Bykofsky, Kimberley Cameron, Jennie Dunham, Donald Maass, and Jandy Nelson.

Costs For cost and additional information, please see the Web site.

Accommodations The conference is held at the Hilton Seattle Airport & Conference Center.

Additional Informations PNWA also holds an annual literary contest every February with more than $12,000 in prize money. Finalists' manuscripts are then available to agents and editors at our summer conference. Visit the Web site for further details.

SOUTH COAST WRITERS CONFERENCE

Southwestern Oregon Community College, P.O. Box 590, 29392 Ellensburg Avenue, Gold Beach OR 97444. (541)247-2741. Fax: (541)247-6247. E-mail: scwc@socc.edu. Web site: www.socc.edu/scwriters. **Contact:** Conference Coordinator. Estab. 1996. Annual conference held President's Day weekend in February. Conference duration: 2 days. Covers fiction, historical, poetry, children's, nature, and marketing. Larry Brooks is the next scheduled keynote speaker and presenters include Shinan Barclay, Jim Coffee, Linda Crew, Roger Dorband,

Jayel Gibson, Phil Hann, Rachel Ellen Koski, Bonnie Leon, John Noland, Joanna Rose and J.D. Tynan. **Costs** $55 before January 1; $65 after January 1; Friday night workshop is an addition $40.

WHIDBEY ISLAND WRITERS' CONFERENCE

P.O. Box 1289, Langley WA 98260. (360)331-6714. E-mail: writers@whidbey.com. Web site: www.writeonwhidbey.org. **Contact:** Elizabeth Guss, director. Annual conference held in March. Conference duration: 3 days. Average attendance: 250. Covers fiction, nonfiction, screenwriting, writing for children, poetry, travel, and nature writing. Class sessions include "Dialogue That Delivers" and "Putting the Character Back in Character." Held at a conference hall, with break-out fireside chats held in local homes near the sea. 2008 speakers include Elizabeth George, Maureen Murdock, Steve Berry, M.J. Rose, Katharine Sands, Doris Booth, Eva Shaw, Stephanie Elizondo Griest.
Costs $340 before December 5, 2007; $395 after December 1. Volunteer discounts are available; early registration is encouraged.
Additional Informations Brochures are available online or for a SASE. Send inquiries via e-mail.

WILLAMETTE WRITERS CONFERENCE

9045 SW Barbur, Suite 5-A, Portland OR 97219. (503)452-1592. Fax: (503)452-0372. E-mail: wilwrite@willamettewriters.com. Web site: www.willamettewriters.com. **Contact:** Bill Johnson. Estab. 1968. Annual conference held in August. Average attendance: 600. "Williamette Writers is open to all writers, and we plan our conference accordingly. We offer workshops on all aspects of fiction, nonfiction, marketing, the creative process, etc. Also, we invite top-notch inspirational speakers for keynote addresses. We always include at least 1 agent or editor panel and offer a variety of topics of interest to screenwriters and fiction and nonfiction writers. Speakers have included Laura Rennert, Kim Cameron, Paul Levine, Angela Rinaldi, Robert Tabian, Joshua Bilmes and Elise Capron. Agents will be speaking and available for meetings with attendees.
Costs Cost for full conference (including meals) is $395/members; $450/nonmembers.
Accommodations If necessary, arrangements can be made on an individual basis. Special rates may be available.
Additional Informations Brochure/guidelines are available for a catalog-sized SASE.

CANADA

ℕ 🔼 BLOODY WORDS

E-mail: info@bloodywords.com. Web site: www.bloodywords.com. **Contact:** Caro Soles. Estab. 1999. Annual conference held in June. Conference duration: 3 days. Average attendance: 250. Focuses on mystery fiction and aims to provide a showcase for Canadian mystery writers and readers, as well as provide writing information to aspiring writers. "We will present 3 tracks of programming: Just the Facts, where everyone from coroners to toxicologists to tactical police units present how things are done in the real works; and What's the Story—where panelists discuss subjects of interest to readers; and the Mystery Cafe, where 12 authors read and discuss their work."
Costs $125-175 (Canadian).
Accommodations A special rate will be available at The Downtown Marriott Hotel in Toronto, Ontario.
Additional Informations Registration is available online. Send inquiries via e-mail.

🔼 FESTIVAL OF WORDS

217 Main St. N., Moose Jaw SK S6J 0W1, Canada. (306)691-0557. Fax: (306)693-2994. E-mail: word.festival@sasktel.net. Web site: www.festivalofwords.com. **Contact:** Gary Hyland, Christie Saas. Estab. 1997. Annual festival held in July. 2008 dates: July 17-20. Conference duration: 4 days. Average attendance: 1,500. The festival celebrates the imaginative uses of language and features fiction and nonfiction writers, screenwriters, poets, children's authors, songwriters, dramatists, and filmmakers. Held at the Moose Jaw Public Library/Art Museum complex and in Crescent Park. Speakers have included Margaret Atwood, John Ralston Saul, Richard B. Wright, Alistair MacLeod, Roch Carrier, Jane Urquhart, Rohinton Mistry, Will Ferguson, Patrick Lane, Lorna Crozier, Ross King, Rex Murphy, Pamela Wallin and Sharon Butala.
Accommodations A list of motels, hotels, campgrounds, and bed and breakfasts is provided upon request.
Additional Informations "Our festival is an ideal place for people who love words to mingle, promote their books, and meet their fans." Brochures are available; send inquiries via e-mail or fax.

ℕ 🔼 THE SCHOOL FOR WRITERS SUMMER WORKSHOP

The Humber School for Writers, Humber Institute of Technology & Advanced Learning, 3199 Lake Shore Blvd. W., Toronto ON M8V 1K8, Canada. (416)675-6622. E-mail: antanas.sileika@humber.ca; hilary.higgins@humber.ca. Web site: www.humber.ca/creativeandperformingarts/writing. **Contact:** Antanas Sileika, Hilary Higgins.

Annual workshop held in July. Conference duration: 1 week. Average attendance: 100. New writers from around the world gather to study with faculty members to work on their novel, short stories, poetry, or creative nonfiction. Agents and editors participate in conference. Include a work-in-progress with your registration. Faculty has included Peter Carey, Roddy Doyle, Tim O'Brien, Andrea Levy, Barry Unsworth, Edward Albee, Ha Jin, Mavis Gallant, Bruce Jay Friedman, Isabel Huggan, Alistair MacLeod, Lisa Moore, Kim Moritsugu, Francine Prose, Paul Quarrington, Olive Senior, and D.M. Thomas.

Costs $949/Canadian residents before June 12; $1,469/non-Canadian residents before June 12; $999/Canadian residents after June 12; $1,519/non-Canadian residents after June 12 (includes panels, classes, lunch). Scholarships are available.

Accommodations $305/week for a modest college dorm room. Nearby hotels are also available.

Additional Informations Accepts inquiries by e-mail, phone, and fax.

INTERNATIONAL

▣ AUSTRALIAN PUBLISHERS AND AUTHORS BOOKSHOW

NSW Writers' Centre, P.O. Box 1056, Rozelle Hospital Grounds, Balmain Road, Rozelle NSW 2039, Australia. (61)(2)9555-9757. Fax: (61)(2)9818-1327. E-mail: nswwc@nswwriterscentre.org.au. Web site: www.nswwriter scentre.org.au. **Contact:** Irina Dunn, executive director. Annual event held the third week in November. Books and magazines from independent, Australian-owned publishing companies, distributors, small presses, niche publishers, self-publishers, and print-on-demand publishers will be showcased. Writers, librarians, booksellers, and members of the public and literary organizations are invited to attend to see what local publishers are doing. Books will also be available for purchase.

Additional Informations 2007 information: Saturday, March 31: CONTEMPORARY AUSTRALIAN FICTION. A festival celebrating and exploring contemporary Australian fiction in all its forms (novels, short stories, poetry, plays). June 30: WRITING FOR CHILDREN/YOUNG ADULTS. A day of readings, panel sessions, book launches and author talks from Australia's most popular writers of children,s and young adult books. Sept. 27: 2007 WRITING HISTORY. This exciting festival focuses on the nature of writing history in fiction and nonfiction. Nov. 24-25: AUSTRALIAN PUBLISHERS & AUTHORS BOOKSHOW. This weekend event showcases books and magazines from independent Australian-owned publishing companies, distributors, small presses, niche publishers, self-publishers, short-run and print-on-demand publishers. Writers, librarians, booksellers, members of the public and literary organisations are invited to attend to see what local publishers are doing and to purchase their books. The Bookshow will also feature talks from people in the writing and publishing industries, including booksellers, agents, distributors, editors, publicists, manuscript assessors, artists and illustrators, self-published writers and short-run publishers.

▣ DINGLE WRITING COURSES

Ballintlea, Ventry Co Kerry, Ireland. Phone/Fax: (353)(66)915-9815. E-mail: info@dinglewritingcourses.ie. Web site: http://www.dinglewritingcourses.ie. **Contact:** Nicholas McLachlan. Estab. 1996. Workshops held in September and October. Average attendance: 14. Creative writing weekends for fiction, poetry, memoir, novel, starting to write, etc. "Our courses take place over a weekend in a purpose-built residential centre at Inch on the Dingle peninsula. They are designed to meet the needs of everyone with an interest in writing, whether you have chosen this moment to begin your first literary effort, or whether you are a dedicated wordsmith seeking to develop and enhance your understanding of the craft. All our tutors are well-known writers, with experience tutoring at all levels." 2006 faculty include Paula Meehan, Colette Bryce, Niall Williams and Aubrey Flegg.

Costs 350 euros. Some bursaries are available from county arts officers.

Accommodations Provides overnight accommodations.

Additional Informations Some workshops require material to be submitted in advance. Accepts inquiries by e-mail, phone, and fax.

▣ NEW ZEALAND POST WRITERS AND READERS WEEK

New Zealand International Arts Festival, P.O. Box 10-113, Level 2, Anvil House, 138-140 Wakefield St., Wellington , New Zealand. (64)(4)473-0149. Fax: (64)(4)471-1164. E-mail: nzfestival@festival.co.nz. Web site: www.n zfestival.telecom.co.nz. **Contact:** David Inns. Biennial festival held in March. Conference duration: 5 days. Focuses on fiction, poetry, and serious nonfiction. Participants are selected by a committee of writers and other book professionals. Held at the Embassy Theatre.

Costs Tickets range from $13-50.

PARIS WRITERS WORKSHOP

WICE, 20, bd du Montparnasse, Paris 75015, France. (33)(14)566-7550. Fax: (33)(14)065-9653. E-mail: pww@wice-paris.org. Web site: www.wice-paris.org. **Contact:** Marcia Mead Lebre, director. Estab. 1987. Annual conference held in July. Conference duration: 1 week. Average attendance: 12/section. Each participant chooses one workshop section—creative nonfiction, novel, poetry, or short story—which meets for a total of 15 classroom hours. Writers in residence have included Vivian Gornick, Lynne Sharon Schwartz, Liam Rector, Ellen Sussman, and Katharine Weber. Located in the heart of Paris, the site consists of 4 classrooms, a resource center/library, and a private terrace.

Costs 500 Euros beofre May 24; 600 Euros after May 24. Scholarships are available.

Accommodations Hotel information is on the Web site.

N SYDNEY WRITERS' FESTIVAL

10 Hickson Rd., The Rocks NSW 2000, Australia. (61)(2)9252-7729. Fax: (61)(2)9252-7735. E-mail: info@swf.org.au. Web site: www.swf.org.au. **Contact:** Wendy Were. Estab. 1997. Annual festival held in May. The event celebrates books, reading, ideas, writers, and writing.

Costs Over 70% of events are free.

Glossary

#10 Envelope. A standard, business-size envelope.

Acquisitions Editor. The person responsible for originating and/or acquiring new publishing projects.

Adaptation. The process of rewriting a composition (novel, story, film, article, play) into a form suitable for some other medium, such as TV or the stage.

Advance. Money a publisher pays a writer prior to book publication, usually paid in installments, such as one-half upon signing the contract and one-half upon delivery of the complete, satisfactory manuscript. An advance is paid against the royalty money to be earned by the book. Agents take their percentage off the top of the advance as well as from the royalties earned.

Adventure. A genre of fiction in which action is the key element, overshadowing characters, theme and setting.

Auction. Publishers sometimes bid for the acquisition of a book manuscript with excellent sales prospects. The bids are for the amount of the author's advance, guaranteed dollar amounts, advertising and promotional expenses, royalty percentage, etc. Auctions are conducted by agents.

Author's Copies. An author usually receives about 10 free copies of his hardcover book from the publisher; more from a paperback firm. He can obtain additional copies at a price that has been reduced by an author's discount (usually 40 percent of the retail price).

Autobiography. A book-length account of a person's entire life written by the subject himself.

Backlist. A publisher's list of books that were not published during the current season, but that are still in print.

Backstory. The history of what has happened before the action in your script takes place, affecting a character's current behavior.

Bible. The collected background information on all characters and story lines of all existing episodes, as well as projections of future plots.

Bio. A sentence or brief paragraph about the writer; includes work and educational experience.

Blurb. The copy on paperback book covers or hardcover book dust jackets, either promoting the book and the author or featuring testimonials from book reviewers or well-known people in the book's field. Also called flap copy or jacket copy.

Boilerplate. A standardized publishing contract. Most authors and agents make many changes on the boilerplate before accepting the contract.

Book Doctor. A freelance editor hired by a writer, agent or book editor who analyzes problems that exist in a book manuscript or proposal and offers solutions to those problems.

Book Packager. Someone who draws elements of a book together—from the initial concept to writing and marketing strategies—and then sells the book package to a book publisher and/or movie producer. Also known as book producer or book developer.

Bound Galleys. A prepublication—often paperbound—edition of a book, usually prepared from photocopies of the final galley proofs. Designed for promotional purposes, bound galleys serve as the first set of review copies to be mailed out. Also called bound proofs.

Category Fiction. A term used to include all types of fiction. See *genre*.

Clips. Samples, usually from newspapers or magazines, of your published work. Also called tearsheets.

Commercial Fiction. Novels designed to appeal to a broad audience. These are often broken down into categories such as western, mystery and romance. See *genre*.

Concept. A statement that summarizes a screenplay or teleplay—before the outline or treatment is written.

Confession. A first-person story in which the narrator is involved in an emotional situation that encourages sympathetic reader identification, concluding with the affirmation of a morally acceptable theme.

Contributor's Copies. Copies of the book sent to the author. The number of contributor's copies is often negotiated in the publishing contract.

Co-Publishing. Arrangement where author and publisher share publication costs and profits of a book. Also called co-operative publishing.

Copyediting. Editing of a manuscript for writing style, grammar, punctuation and factual accuracy.

Copyright. A means to protect an author's work.

Cover Letter. A brief letter that accompanies the manuscript being sent to an agent or publisher.

Coverage. A brief synopsis and analysis of a script provided by a reader to a buyer considering purchasing the work.

Creative Nonfiction. Type of writing where true stories are told by employing the techniques usually reserved for novelists and poets, such as scenes, dialogue and detailed descriptions. Also called literary journalism.

Critiquing Service. An editing service offered by some agents in which writers pay a fee for comments on the salability or other qualities of their manuscript. Sometimes the critique includes suggestions on how to improve the work. Fees vary, as does the quality of the critique.

Curriculum Vitae (CV). Short account of one's career or qualifications.

D Person. Development person; includes readers, story editors and creative executives who work in development and acquisition of properties for TV and film.

Deal Memo. The memorandum of agreement between a publisher and author that precedes the actual contract and includes important issues such as royalty, advance, rights, distribution and option clauses.

Development. The process in which writers present ideas to producers who oversee the developing script through various stages to finished product.

Division. An unincorporated branch of a company.

Docudrama. A fictional film rendition of recent news-making events or people.

Electronic Rights. Secondary or subsidiary rights dealing with electronic/multimedia formats (the Internet, CD-ROMs, electronic magazines).

Elements. Actors, directors and producers attached to a project to make an attractive package.

El-Hi. Elementary to high school. A term used to indicate reading or interest level.

Episodic Drama. An hour-long, continuing TV show, often shown at 10 p.m.

Resources

Erotica. A form of literature or film dealing with the sexual aspects of love. Erotic content ranges from subtle sexual innuendo to explicit descriptions of sexual acts

Ethnic. Stories and novels whose central characters are African American, Native American, Italian American, Jewish, Appalachian or members of some other specific cultural group. Ethnic fiction usually deals with a protagonist caught between two conflicting ways of life: mainstream American culture and his ethnic heritage.

Evaluation Fees. Fees an agent may charge to evaluate material. The extent and quality of this evaluation varies, but comments usually concern the salability of the manuscript.

Exclusive. Offering a manuscript, usually for a set period of time, to just one agent and guaranteeing that agent is the only one looking at the manuscript.

Experimental. Type of fiction that focuses on style, structure, narrative technique, setting and strong characterization rather than plot. This form depends largely on the revelation of a character's inner being, which elicits an emotional response from the reader.

Family Saga. A story that chronicles the lives of a family or a number of related or interconnected families over a period of time.

Fantasy. Stories set in fanciful, invented worlds or in a legendary, mythic past that rely on outright invention or magic for conflict and setting.

Film Rights. May be sold or optioned by the agent/author to a person in the film industry, enabling the book to be made into a movie.

Floor Bid. If a publisher is very interested in a manuscript, he may offer to enter a floor bid when the book goes to auction. The publisher sits out of the auction, but agrees to take the book by topping the highest bid by an agreed-upon percentage (usually 10 percent).

Foreign Rights. Translation or reprint rights to be sold abroad.

Foreign Rights Agent. An agent who handles selling the rights to a country other than that of the first book agent. Usually an additional percentage (about 5 percent) will be added on to the first book agent's commission to cover the foreign rights agent.

Genre. Refers to either a general classification of writing, such as a novel, poem or short story, or to the categories within those classifications, such as problem novels or sonnets. Genre fiction is a term that covers various types of commercial novels, such as mystery, romance, Western, science fiction and horror.

Ghostwriting. A writer puts into literary form the words, ideas, or knowledge of another person under that person's name. Some agents offer this service; others pair ghostwriters with celebrities or experts.

Gothic. Novels characterized by historical settings and featuring young, beautiful women who win the favor of handsome, brooding heroes while simultaneously dealing with some life-threatening menace—either natural or supernatural.

Graphic Novel. Contains comic-like drawings and captions, but deals more with everyday events and issues than with superheroes.

High Concept. A story idea easily expressed in a quick, one-line description.

Hi-Lo. A type of fiction that offers a high level of interest for readers at a low reading level.

Historical. A story set in a recognizable period of history. In addition to telling the stories of ordinary people's lives, historical fiction may involve political or social events of the time.

Hook. Aspect of the work that sets it apart from others and draws in the reader/viewer.

Horror. A story that aims to evoke some combination of fear, fascination and revulsion in its readers—either through supernatural or psychological circumstances.

How-To. A book that offers the reader a description of how something can be accomplished. It includes both information and advice.

Imprint. The name applied to a publisher's specific line of books.

Independent Producers. Self-employed entrepreneurs who assemble scripts, actors, directors and financing for their film concepts.

IRC. International Reply Coupon. Buy at a post office to enclose with material sent outside the country to cover the cost of return postage. The recipient turns them in for stamps in their own country.

Joint Contract. A legal agreement between a publisher and two or more authors that establishes provisions for the division of royalties the book generates.

Juvenile. Category of children's writing that can be broken down into easy-to-read books (ages 7-9), which run 2,000-10,000 words, and middle-grade books (ages 8-12), which run 20,000-40,000 words.

Literary. A book where style and technique are often as important as subject matter. Also called serious fiction.

Logline. A one-line description of a plot as it might appear in *TV Guide*.

Mainstream Fiction. Fiction on subjects or trends that transcend popular novel categories like mystery or romance. Using conventional methods, this kind of fiction tells stories about people and their conflicts.

Marketing Fee. Fee charged by some agents to cover marketing expenses. It may be used to cover postage, telephone calls, faxes, photocopying or any other expense incurred in marketing a manuscript.

Mass Market Paperbacks. Softcover books, usually 4×7, on a popular subject directed at a general audience and sold in groceries, drugstores and bookstores.

Memoir. An author's commentary on the personalities and events that have significantly influenced one phase of his life.

MFTS. Made for TV series.

Midlist. Those titles on a publisher's list expected to have limited sales. Midlist books are mainstream, not literary, scholarly or genre, and are usually written by new or relatively unknown writers.

Miniseries. A limited dramatic series written for television, often based on a popular novel.

MOW. Movie of the week. A movie script written especially for television, usually seven acts with time for commercial breaks. Topics are often contemporary, sometimes controversial, fictional accounts. Also called a made-for-TV movie.

Multiple Contract. Book contract with an agreement for a future book(s).

Mystery. A form of narration in which one or more elements remain unknown or unexplained until the end of the story. Subgenres include: amateur sleuth, caper, cozy, heist, malice domestic, police procedural, etc.

Net Receipts. One method of royalty payment based on the amount of money a book publisher receives on the sale of the book after the booksellers' discounts, special sales discounts and returned copies.

Novelization. A novel created from the script of a popular movie and published in paperback. Also called a movie tie-in.

Novella. A short novel or long short story, usually 25,000-50,000 words. Also called a novelette.

Occult. Supernatural phenomena, including ghosts, ESP, astrology, demoniact possession and witchcraft.

One-Time Rights. This right allows a short story or portions of a fiction or nonfiction book to be published again without violating the contract.

Option. Instead of buying a movie script outright, a producer buys the right to a script for a short period of time (usually six months to one year) for a small down payment. If the movie has not begun production and the producer does not wish to purchase the script at the end of the agreed time period, the rights revert back to the scriptwriter. Also called a script option.

Option Clause. A contract clause giving a publisher the right to publish an author's next book.

Outline. A summary of a book's content (up to 15 double-spaced pages); often in the form of chapter headings with a descriptive sentence or two under each one to show the scope of the book. A script's outline is a scene-by-scene narrative description of the story (10-15 pages for a ½-hour teleplay; 15-25 pages for 1-hour; 25-40 pages for 90 minutes; 40-60 pages for a 2-hour feature film or teleplay).

Picture Book. A type of book aimed at ages 2-9 that tells the story partially or entierly with artwork, with up to 1,000 words. Agents interested in selling to publishers of these books often handle both artists and writers.

Pitch. The process where a writer meets with a producer and briefly outlines ideas that could be developed if the writer is hired to write a script for the project.

Platform. A writer's speaking experience, interview skills, Web site and other abilities which help form a following of potential buyers for his book.

Proofreading. Close reading and correction of a manuscript's typographical errors.

Property. Books or scripts forming the basis for a movie or TV project.

Proposal. An offer to an editor or publisher to write a specific work, usually a package consisting of an outline and sample chapters.

Prospectus. A preliminary written description of a book, usually one page in length.

Psychic/Supernatural. Fiction exploiting—or requiring as plot devices or themes—some contradictions of the commonplace natural world and materialist assumptions about it (including the traditional ghost story).

Query. A letter written to an agent or a potential market to elicit interest in a writer's work.

Reader. A person employed by an agent or buyer to go through the slush pile of manuscripts and scripts and select those worth considering.

Regional. A book faithful to a particular geographic region and its people, including behavior, customs, speech and history.

Release. A statement that your idea is original, has never been sold to anyone else, and that you are selling negotiated rights to the idea upon payment.

Remainders. Leftover copies of an out-of-print or slow-selling book purchased from the publisher at a reduced rate. Depending on the contract, a reduced royalty or no royalty is paid on remaindered books.

Reprint Rights. The right to republish a book after its initial printing.

Romance. A type of category fiction in which the love relationship between a man and a woman pervades the plot. The story is told from the viewpoint of the heroine, who meets a man (the hero), falls in love with him, encounters a conflict that hinders their relationship, and then resolves the conflict with a happy ending.

Royalties. A percentage of the retail price paid to the author for each copy of the book that is sold. Agents take their percentage from the royalties earned and from the advance.

SASE. Self-addressed, stamped envelope. It should be included with all correspondence.

Scholarly Books. Books written for an academic or research audience. These are usually heavily researched, technical, and often contain terms used only within a specific field.

Science Fiction. Literature involving elements of science and technology as a basis for conflict, or as the setting for a story.

Screenplay. Script for a film intended to be shown in theaters.

Script. Broad term covering teleplay, screenplay or stage play. Sometimes used as a shortened version of the word manuscript when referring to books.

Serial Rights. The right for a newspaper or magazine to publish sections of a manuscript.

Simultaneous Submission. Sending the same manuscript to several agents or publishers at the same time.

Sitcom. Situation comedy. Episodic comedy script for a television series. The term comes from the characters dealing with various situations with humorous results.

Slice of Life. A type of short story, novel, play or film that takes a strong thematic approach, depending less on plot than on vivid detail in describing the setting and/or environment, and the environment's effect on characters involved in it.

Slush Pile. A stack of unsolicited submissions in the office of an editor, agent or publisher.

Spec Script. A script written on speculation without confirmation of a sale.

Standard Commission. The commission an agent earns on the sales of a manuscript or script. For literary agents, the commission percentage (usually 10-20 percent) is taken from the advance and royalties paid to the writer. For script agents, the commission (usually 15-20 percent) is taken from script sales. If handling plays, agents take a percentage from the box office proceeds.

Subagent. An agent handling certain subsidiary rights, usually working in conjunction with the agent who handled the book rights. The percentage paid the book agent is increased to pay the subagent.

Subsidiary. An incorporated branch of a company or conglomerate (e.g., Knopf Publishing Group is a subsidiary of Random House, Inc.).

Subsidiary Rights. All rights other than book publishing rights included in a book publishing contract, such as paperback rights, book club rights and movie rights. Part of an agent's job is to negotiate those rights and advise you on which to sell and which to keep.

Syndication Rights. The right for a station to rerun a sitcom or drama, even if the show originally appeared on a different network.

Synopsis. A brief summary of a story, novel or play. As a part of a book proposal, it is a comprehensive summary condensed in a page or page and a half, single-spaced. See *outline.*

Teleplay. Script for television.

Terms. Financial provisions agreed upon in a contract.

Textbook. Book used in a classroom at the elementary, high school or college level.

Thriller. A story intended to arouse feelings of excitement or suspense. Works in this genre are highly sensational, usually focusing on illegal activites, international espionage, sex and violence.

TOC. Table of Contents. A listing at the beginning of a book indicating chapter titles and their corresponding page numbers. It can also include brief chapter descriptions.

Trade Book. Either a hardcover or softcover book sold mainly in bookstores. The subject matter frequently concerns a special interest for a general audience.

Trade Paperback. A soft-bound volume, usually 5×8, published and designed for the general public; available mainly in bookstores.

Translation Rights. Sold to a foreign agent or foreign publisher.

Treatment. Synopsis of a television or film script (40-60 pages for a two-hour feature film or teleplay).

Unsolicited Manuscript. An unrequested manuscript sent to an editor, agent or publisher.

Westerns/Frontier. Stories set in the American West, almost always in the 19th century, generally between the antebellum period and the turn of the century.

Young Adult (YA). The general classification of books written for ages 12-17. They run 50,000-60,000 words and include category novels—adventure, sports, career, mysteries, romance, etc.

Resources

Literary Agents Specialties Index

This index is divided into fiction and nonfiction subject categories. To find an agent interested in the type of manuscript you've written, see the appropriate sections under the subject headings that best describe your work.

FICTION

Action/Adventure

Acacia House Publishing Services, Ltd. 86
Ahearn Agency, Inc., The 87
Alive Communications, Inc. 88
Ambassador Literary Agency 90
Ampersand Agency, The 90
Amsterdam Agency, Marcia 91
August Agency, LLC, The 93
Authentic Creations Literary Agency 94
Barrett Books, Inc., Loretta 96
Bennett & West Literary Agency 98
Benrey Literary 98
Bial Agency, Daniel 99
Bova Literary Agency, The Barbara 102
Bradford Literary Agency 102
Brown, Ltd., Curtis 106
Browne, Ltd., Pema 107
Congdon Associates Inc., Don 113
D4EO Literary Agency 116
Dupree/Miller and Associates Inc. Literary 123
Dystel & Goderich Literary Management 123
Eady Associates, Toby 124
Fairbank Literary Representation 128
Farber Literary Agency, Inc. 129
Farris Literary Agency, Inc. 129
Fielding Agency, LLC, The 130
Finch Literary Agency, Diana 130

Goumen & Smirnova Literary Agency 140
Greenburger Associates, Inc., Sanford J. 142
Gregory Literary Agency, LLC 143
Halsey North, Reece 145
Hartline Literary Agency 146
Harwood Limited, Antony 147
Hawkins & Associates, Inc., John 147
Henshaw Group, Richard 148
Hidden Value Group 149
International Transactions, Inc. 153
Jabberwocky Literary Agency 154
JCA Literary Agency 154
JET Literary Associates 155
Klinger, Inc., Harvey 158
KT Public Relations & Literary Services 161
LA Literary Agency, The 161
Lampack Agency, Inc., Peter 162
Larsen/Elizabeth Pomada, Literary Agents, Michael 163
LaunchBooks Literary Agency 164
Lazear Agency, Inc. 165
Lecker Agency, Robert 166
Levine Literary Agency, Paul S. 167
Lindstrom Literary Management, LLC 169
Linn Prentis Literary 169
Lippincott Massie McQuilkin 170
Literary Group, The 171

Lord Literary Management, Julia 172
Lyons Literary, LLC 175
Mainhardt Agency, Ricia 177
Marshall Agency, The Evan 180
McBride Literary Agency, Margret 181
Mendel Media Group, LLC 181
Morrison, Inc., Henry 185
Mortimer Literary Agency 185
Mura Literary, Dee 185
Muse Literary Management 186
Naggar Literary Agency, Inc., Jean V. 187
Nappaland Literary Agency 187
Nashville Agency, The 188
Northern Lights Literary Services, LLC 190
Pavilion Literary Management 192
PMA Literary and Film Management, Inc. 195
Prospect Agency LLC 196
Quicksilver Books: Literary Agents 197
Raines & Raines 198
Redhammer Management, Ltd. 199
RLR Associates, Ltd. 203
Rotrosen Agency LLC, Jane 207
Russell & Volkening 208
Sanders & Associates, Victoria 210
Schulman Literary Agency, Susan 210
Scribe Agency, LLC 212
Serendipity Literary Agency, LLC 213

Horror

Humor/Satire

Occult

Picture Books

Specialties Index

Specialties Index

Young Adult

NONFICTION

Agriculture/ Horticulture

Americana

Animals

Biography/Autobiography

Business/Economics

Specialties Index

Child Guidance/ Parenting

Education

Ethnic/Cultural Interests

Gardening

Gay/Lesbian Issues

Government/Politics/Law

Health/Medicine

How-To

Humor/Satire

Interior Design/ Decorating

Juvenile Nonfiction

Nature/Environment

New Age/Metaphysics

Philosophy

Psychology

Self-Help/Personal Improvement

Sociology

Theater/Film

Translation

Women's Issues/ Studies

Young Adult

Script Agents Specialties Index

This index is divided into script subject categories. To find an agent interested in the type of screenplay you've written, see the appropriate sections under the subject headings that best describe your work.

Action/Adventure

Biography/ Autobiography

Cartoon/Animation

Comedy

Script Agents Format Index

This index organizes agents according to the script types they consider. To find an agent interested in your script, see the heading that best describes your work.

Agents Index

General Index